A year with your children
in the Bible

A year with your children
in the Bible

Jim Cromarty

 EVANGELICAL PRESS

EVANGELICAL PRESS
Faverdale North Industrial Estate, Darlington, DL3 0PH,
England

Evangelical Press USA
P. O. Box 825, Webster, New York, USA

e-mail: sales@evangelicalpress.org

web: http://www.evangelicalpress.org

First published 2004

British Library Cataloguing in Publication Data available

ISBN 0 85234 518 6

Printed and bound in the USA.

To Val

We are 'heirs together of the grace of life'.
1 Peter 3:7

Introduction

Several generations ago most families attended worship services on a regular basis. The Lord's Day was special and only works of necessity and mercy were carried out. Of course all were not Christians, but still most families respected the Lord's Day.

Forty or fifty years ago there was a change taking place as far as church attendance was concerned. In many cases, hardened soldiers returning from the Second World War pushed God out of their lives. Adults were having nothing to do with church but their children were sent to Sunday school – 'to get a bit of religion!' But parents gave very little encouragement to have their children attend the worship services.

Many pastors and elders were to blame because Sunday schools were held during the time devoted for worship. After the singing of several hymns and possibly a children's address, the children and Sunday school teachers left the service to conduct Sunday school. No wonder children regarded the time of worship as having no real value. Parents – even Christian parents – said they would not force religion upon their children – they could make up their own minds when they were old enough.

Today very few families attend worship and few children attend Sunday school. Go and talk to some young people and question them concerning their knowledge of the fundamental truths found in God's Word.

How many families are there who gather together for family worship? How many heads of Christian homes call the family together for a time of worship and edification – singing of Psalms, hymns and spiritual songs, the reading of the Scriptures, prayer and the learning of the catechism?

Today most parents are more concerned that their children excel in school examinations than seeing fine results in the things of God. Getting a well paid job has become more important than getting into heaven.

Parents, you are responsible for the spiritual well-being of your children. God will hold you accountable for your failure in this most important aspect of your child's life. There is a place called 'hell' and the Lord Jesus Christ has warned everyone that hell is their destiny unless they turn to him for salvation. The way to Paradise is through Jesus Christ who said, 'I am the way, the truth and the life. No one comes to the Father except through me' (John 14:6). You will not get to heaven because of all your good works! Faith in the Son of God is the only way.

I was motivated to write this book praying it may prove useful to those families where family worship is regularly held. It may also prove useful to those who live alone and need a structured way of conducting worship.

If you have never gathered your family together for the worship of God, then start now. You may find it hard to pray aloud in front of your family, but keep going with a sincere heart that loves God. Great blessings are poured out on those faithful families where there is a regular time set aside for family devotions.

May God bless all who make use of this devotional book – indeed who make use of any one of the God glorifying books that are readily available.

May it be that you see your sons and daughters grow up loving God and determined by the grace of God to serve him faithfully all their lives.

Many of the 'Sayings to Remember ' are taken, with kind permission, from *Gathered Gold* and *More Gathered Gold* by John Blanchard, published by Evangelical Press.

Jim Cromarty

January

The fear of
the LORD
is the begin-
ning of
knowledge

Proverbs 1:7

Isaiah
40:18-28.

'Now to the King eternal, immortal, invisible, to God who alone is wise, be honour and glory for ever and ever. Amen' (1 Timothy 1:17).

Today many people think of God as being someone who lives up in the heavens and who isn't really interested in what happens on earth. Some people say that God doesn't exist. They argue that matter has always existed. Other people suggest that it was reasonable to believe in God two thousand years ago, but today we live in the scientific age, and we are too intelligent to believe such tales.

The Scriptures tell us that there is only one God, who exists in three persons: Father, Son and Holy Spirit. Just by looking around us we can see evidence of what God has done. He has made everything there is to see; and he has also made everything we can't see. Nothing in the world around us has been placed there by accident; it has all come from the Lord. We are told in the Bible that 'In the beginning God created...' (Genesis 1:1). The creation shows us that God has almighty power.

We can't even compare ourselves to God. Isaiah wrote, 'Behold, the nations are as a drop in a bucket, and are counted as the small dust on the scales' (Isaiah 40:15). 'All the nations before him are as nothing, and they are counted by him less than nothing and worthless' (Isaiah 40:17). 'It is he who sits above the circle of the earth, and its inhabitants are like grass-hoppers' (Isaiah 40:22).

Our God is a God of grace, love and mercy. Even though we have all sinned, God's Son, the Lord Jesus Christ, willingly came into this world to live and die in order to redeem all of those people his Father has given him (John 6:37).

Our heavenly Father chose a people to be saved, even though they deserved eternal punishment. Not only were their sins forgiven because of Christ's death on the cross, but they have also been clothed in his perfect righteousness. Christ's salvation belongs to his people because of the work of the Holy Spirit, who makes them new people. They love God and have a saving faith in the Redeemer.

The Psalmist wrote, 'Oh come, let us worship and bow down; let us kneel before the LORD our Maker; for he is our God...' (Psalm 95:6-7).

May we, by the grace of God, be enabled to say in the words of the apostle Paul at the close of each day, 'Now to the King eternal, immortal, invisible, to God who alone is wise, be honour and glory forever and ever' (1 Timothy 1:17).

God is spirit; he can't be seen. But when the Messiah came into this world, he was visible. He had a human body but he was sinless. He had all the attributes (characteristics) of God, because he is God. As you read through this book, you will discover many more of God's attributes.

FIND OUT THE FACTS

1. Mention three things about God that you learnt from today's reading.

2. Why should we love God?

3. Which of God's attributes (characteristics) can you name?

Think about the animal and plant life which you see in the world around you. Thank God for the beauty of his creation which shows us his greatness and his power.

A saying to Remember

He who feeds his birds will not starve his babes. *Matthew Henry*

Psalm
102:25-28

'Your right hand, O Lᴏʀᴅ, has
become glorious in power; Your
right hand, O Lᴏʀᴅ, has dashed
the enemy in pieces' (Exodus
15:6).

Most people have no real interest in God. Some go to
church, read their Bibles and live what appears to be a
righteous life, but they are not united to the Lord Jesus by a
God-given faith.

A significant consequence of the new birth is that the
renewed soul has some understanding of the majesty and glory
of God. Once we are born again, we are no longer Satan's slaves,
but citizens of the kingdom of God. We begin to see something
of the glorious attributes of our heavenly Father. The glory of
God fills our minds, and with the eye of faith, we gaze upon
the unseen God, whose being is perfect in every way.

God's glory is described well in the answer to question 4 of
the *Westminster Shorter Catechism*. It states: 'God is Spirit,
infinite, eternal and unchangeable; in his being, wisdom,
power, holiness, justice, goodness and truth.'

As we think about the wonderful qualities which God has,
we can only cry out in awe, 'Who is like you, O Lᴏʀᴅ, among
the gods? Who is like you, glorious in holiness, fearful in
praises, doing wonders?' (Exodus 15:11). We can only bow
down humbly before the God of glory and praise his wonderful name.

Our God is a holy God, a 'God [who] is angry with the wicked
every day' (Psalm 7:11). And why is this so? All sin is an
offence to him. Habakkuk wrote, 'You are of purer eyes than to
behold evil, and cannot look on wickedness' (1:13). We are to
honour God and to worship him in the 'beauty of holiness'
(Psalm 96:9).

Our God is just in all his ways. His justice is seen in the salvation of sinners. God does not overlook sin. Sin must be punished. Above the head of every sinner there is the sword of God's anger. That sword will fall upon every person who does not repent of his sins. Each one will bear his own sin, guilt and shame for ever. But for all who are in Christ, the sword of anger has fallen upon the sin-bearer, the Lord Jesus. Frequently, the justice of God is seen in his dealings with sinners in this world.

Let us praise and honour God because he is immutable — that is, he does not and cannot change. He is always faithful to all of his promises and warnings. He is dependable. We have a wonderful God!

FIND OUT THE FACTS

1. 'God is spirit.' What does this mean?
2. Our God is holy. What does this mean?
3. What does God do to sinners to make them citizens of the kingdom of heaven?

Think about how great the God of the Bible is. Praise and worship him because he is a God of glory and majesty.

There is no higher mystery than God's eternity. *William S. Plumer*

Isaiah
40:9-17

'And there is no other God besides me, a just God and a Saviour; there is none besides me. Look to me, and be saved, all you ends of the earth! For I am God, and there is no other' (Isaiah 45:21-22).

We can't comprehend the majesty and glory of God. The God of the Bible is the great 'I AM' who has neither beginning nor end. He does not change. Our God is one, as today's scripture verse tells us.

In the eternal ages before this universe was created, there was God. There was no creation. God was alone. He was self-sufficient — that is, he was not dependent upon anyone else or any other being for his existence.

God did not have to create the universe, but he did so for reasons found within himself. Isaiah records his words, 'My counsel shall stand, and I will do all my pleasure' (46:10). God planned the creation for the display of his glory. The Scriptures indicate what we should all do: 'Stand up and bless the LORD your God for ever and for ever! Blessed be your glorious name, which is exalted above all blessing and praise!' (Nehemiah 9:5).

While God is one, within the Godhead there are three persons: Father, Son and Holy Spirit. Our God is Jehovah. The Father is Jehovah: 'But now, O LORD, you are our father; we are the clay, and you our potter; and all we are the work of your hand' (Isaiah 64:8).

We are taught that the Lord Jesus Christ is Jehovah God. The apostle John wrote of our Saviour: 'In the beginning was the Word, and the Word was with God, and the Word was God' (John 1:1). Isaiah had a vision of Jehovah seated upon the throne of his glory. The seraphim sang, 'Holy, holy, holy is the LORD of hosts; the whole earth is full of his glory' (6:3) and Isaiah said, 'For my eyes have seen the King, the LORD of hosts' (6:5).

What Isaiah saw that day, the apostle John tells us was a vision of Christ (John 12:41).

The Holy Spirit is God. Peter spoke to Ananias and Sapphira and said, 'Why has Satan filled your heart to lie to the Holy Spirit… You have not lied to men but to God' (Acts 5:3,4).

The Holy Spirit is eternal (Hebrews 9:14); he also knows everything (he is omniscient) (1 Corinthians 2:10,11); he is also everywhere (he is omnipresent) (Psalm 139:7); and was involved in the creation of this universe (Genesis 1:2).

That there are three persons in the Godhead is a real mystery. We can only believe what the Scriptures teach.

The *Westminster Shorter Catechism* defines the Godhead (Question 6) as follows: 'There are three persons in the Godhead; the Father, the Son, and the Holy Spirit; and these three are one God, the same in substance, equal in power and glory.'

This is our God!

FIND OUT THE FACTS

1. How many gods do Christians worship?
2. Find verses of Scripture that clearly teach that Jesus is God?
3. What are you taught in Isaiah 43:10-11?

Think about the fact that God has revealed himself to us in the Bible and thank him that we can know him through his Son, the Lord Jesus Christ.

The Trinity is (not 'are') God the Father, God the Son, and God the Holy Spirit.
Donald Grey Barnhouse

A saying to Remember

Romans
8:31-39

Hear O Israel: the LORD our God, the LORD is one! You shall love the LORD your God with all your heart, with all your soul and with all your strength' (Deuteronomy 6:4,5).

When a lawyer asked Jesus what the greatest commandment was his reply was the scripture verse quoted above.

God is love and when a sinner is 'born again', that person acknowledges the Lord Jesus as his Lord and Saviour. He falls in love with God the Father, God the Son and God the Holy Spirit.

The greatest way to display this love is by faithful obedience. Jesus said, 'You are my friends if you do whatever I command you' (John 15:14). Why then should Christians love God?

The reasons are similar to those that attracted me to my wife. First, before I had ever spoken to her, I looked and saw someone whose appearance appealed to me. Second, as the days went by, I found characteristics that she had that made me feel comfortable with her. Valerie was kind and helpful. Why then should Christians love God?

First, we love God because of what he has done for us in the Lord Jesus. God's love is a selfless love. He sent his Son into the world to save sinners. On the cross he suffered the penalty due to us because of our sin. He was abused by wicked men and died a horrible death on a Roman cross. He lived a life of perfect obedience to his Father and gave to his people his righteousness. Christ's righteousness is needed to enter into heaven. Christ's people love him because of what he has done for them. We love God because he has promised his people eternal life in heaven with Christ.

Second, we love God because of his character. This love grows as we get to know him more. We discover that God is a God of love, who showers that love upon a sinful world. He is a God of perfect wisdom. This we see in the work of salvation. Who would have thought of such a wonderful plan to save sinners? His wisdom is seen all about us in the detailed workings of creation.

Our God is a God of great power. He spoke the word and the universe came into being. In his death upon the cross, the Lord Jesus prepared a secure place in heaven for all who love and follow him.

God is holy. There is no sin in our God. He is light, and in him is no darkness.

God is just in all of his doings. Believers will not be punished for their sins because Christ has already paid the penalty. On the Day of Judgement, all that God does will be perfectly just. This is our God!

FIND OUT THE FACTS

1. What is love?

2. How do you show your love for God?

3. Why do Christians love God?

Think about the fact that God shows his love to sinful people. Thank God for his great love.

Don't throw God a bone of your love unless there's the meat of obedience on it. *John MacArthur*

Isaiah
14:12-15

'So the great dragon was cast out, that serpent of old, called the Devil and Satan, who deceives the whole world; he was cast to the earth, and his angels were cast out with him' (Revelation 12:9).

When we begin to read our Bibles, we are told that 'In the beginning God created the heavens and the earth' (Genesis 1:1). We are not told about the creation of angels. However, the apostle Paul refers to the creation of angels by God through Christ: 'For by him all things were created that are in heaven and that are on the earth, visible and invisible... All things were created through him and for him' (Colossians 1:16).

The invisible angels are quite unlike us because we have physical bodies and they don't. In the Scriptures we read of times when angels appeared on earth in human bodies (Genesis 18:1-8). We also learn that the number of angels was decided by God, because angels neither marry nor have children (Mark 12:25). In the beginning they were God's servants, obeying his commands and praising him.

The first time an angel is mentioned in the Scriptures is following Adam's fall into sin. He and Eve were expelled from the Garden of Eden. To make sure they didn't return, God placed a 'cherubim at the east of the Garden of Eden, and a flaming sword which turned every way, to guard the way to the tree of life' (Genesis 3:24).

One of God's glorious angels, Lucifer, rebelled against him in heaven. His sin was pride. He wanted to sit upon God's throne in the place of God. It seems probable that one third of the angels followed him in his rebellion (Revelation 12:4).

He successfully tempted Adam and Eve in the Garden of Eden. He appeared in heaven to accuse Job of serving God for the purpose of receiving many blessings (Job 1:9,10). Today's verse tells us that finally Satan and his demons were thrown out of heaven.

Before the death of the Lord Jesus on the cross, Satan appeared in heaven to accuse God of injustice because he allowed believers into heaven when no one had paid the price for sin. Following Christ's death, the saints have every right to enter heaven and Satan could no longer accuse God of being unjust.

The writer to the Hebrews said that the good angels are 'ministering spirits sent forth to minister for those who will inherit salvation' (Hebrews 1:14). In our meditations we shall read of the work of God's angels.

Today Satan goes 'about like a roaring lion, seeking whom he may devour' (1 Peter 5:8). We must always be on guard against the evil one.

FIND OUT THE FACTS

1. Why was Satan cast out of heaven? See Revelation 12:10-12.
2. How many 'I wills' are found in today's reading?
3. What was Satan's heavenly name?

Christ has defeated Satan. Thank the Lord Jesus that through his death he sets us free from the power of sin and Satan.

Satan promises the best, but pays with the worst; he promises honour and pays with disgrace; he promises pleasure and pays with pain; he promises profit and pays with loss; he promises life and pays with death.   *Thomas Brooks*

Genesis
1:1-3;
Proverbs
8:22-31

'In the beginning God created the heavens and the earth. The earth was without form, and void; and darkness was on the face of the deep.' (Genesis 1:1-2).

Michael, the boy next door, asked if I would give him some timber, nails, wire netting and a hammer as he wanted to build a cage for his guinea pigs. I doubted he would succeed as he was just four years old. But, when he had what he wanted, he began to work.

Some time later he stood up, and looking at his cage, he said, 'It's finished!' The 'building' was not a cage and when he touched one side, it collapsed. The guinea pigs would have escaped as soon as he put them through the 'door'. It was left to his father to complete the job.

Our verse tells us that way back in the beginning, God created the heavens and the earth. This was when there was nothing to use to make the universe. God displayed his almighty power by simply giving the command, and the heavens and the earth appeared. If I had said to Michael, 'Make your cage out of nothing', he would have thought that I had gone crazy.

God's powerful act of creation was performed through Christ. We read, 'All things were made through him [Christ], and without him nothing was made that was made' (John 1:3). The apostle Paul wrote, 'All things were created through him [that is, Christ] and for him' (Colossians 1:16).

Even though young Michael did his best to build his cage, using wood, nails and wire netting, the end result was a failure.

Of God's creation we read that 'the earth was without form, and void; and darkness was on the face of the deep' (Genesis 1:2). We are not to think that God made a mess of his creation. Never! God is perfect in all that he does. His plan for creation had started, and this was the first step.

In our reading from Genesis 1:1-2 we find that all was darkness. However, the Holy Spirit was 'hovering' over the water that covered the earth.

God knew what he was doing. It was now time to make a home suitable for Adam and Eve and every living thing. This home would display the glory, love, power and wisdom of the Creator.

FIND OUT THE FACTS

1. When did God create our universe?
2. What did God use to create the heavens and the earth?
3. God — Father, Son and Holy Spirit — were perfectly content without a universe. Why then do you think God created the heavens and the earth?
4. Some people say God does not exist. If this is true, do you think it possible for the heavens and earth to appear suddenly out of nothing?

God's wisdom is seen in everything he has created and in everything he does.
Thank the Lord that he is wise.

Of old you laid the foundation of the earth, and the heavens are the work of your hands.
The Psalmist — Psalm 102:25

Genesis
1:3-23

'The heavens declare the glory of God; and the firmament shows his handiwork' (Psalm 19:1)

Michael's father was amused to see his son's attempt at building a cage for his guinea pig. He looked at the 'building' and said, 'As soon as I change my clothes, I'll help you fix it up.'

Coming outside, dad carried a piece of paper and a pencil and told Michael they would first plan the cage. When this was done, Michael's 'cage' was pulled apart and soon the new cage began to appear.

First the floor was constructed, followed by four sides built perfectly upright, using a spirit level. When all the sides were covered in fine netting, a roof was carefully constructed. A small hutch was placed inside the cage to keep out the rain and sun. They used the material I had given them to build a sturdy cage which would keep the guinea pigs in and the dogs and cats out. Michael and his father were very pleased with the cage.

Today's reading tells us what happened on the first five days of creation.

On day one, God created light. On day two, God created space between the ocean and the clouds. On day three, God made the dry land to rise up through the oceans and seas. Plants were then caused to grow on the earth, and seaweed in the surrounding seas and oceans. On day four, God created the stars and planets we see in the sky. He also created our sun and moon to give us light and warmth. And on day five, God created the birds and the fish.

We should note that the Scripture text tells us that each day of creation had an evening and a morning and that it was God who did the creating.

When Michael and his dad had completed the cage, they stood back. Looking at their work, they said how pleased they were with their building. The home was now ready for the small pets.

As each day of creation came to an end, God too looked at his work and was satisfied because it was 'very good'.

There were no mistakes in God's creation. He was now ready to create the animals and also man to live on the earth.

God's plans are perfect.

FIND OUT THE FACTS

1. How does the creation show us God's power?
2. How does the world display God's wisdom?
3. Each day of creation has a morning and an evening. What does this teach us?

God is perfect and everything that he does is perfect. Praise God for his perfection.

The heavens declare the glory of God; And the firmament shows his handiwork. *King David – Psalm 19:1*

Genesis 1:24-31

'And the LORD God formed man of the dust of the ground, and breathed into his nostrils the breath of life; and man became a living being' (Genesis 2:7).

Michael's cage was ready for his pet guinea pigs. All he had to do now was to take them from the box in which they had lived for several days and put them in their well-built cage where they could eat the grass and playfully scamper around. When it rained, or a cat or dog appeared, the pigs hid in their hutch.

God's world was now prepared for the animals that would live on the earth. There was plenty of food and water. It was the sixth day and God first made the animals from the earth (Genesis 1:24). When he looked at his creation he said that it 'was good' (1:25). God was now to make the highest form of life: man, Adam.

In my school teaching days, my class often used clay to make models which were fired in the kiln. I well remember the time we all attempted to mould what was supposed to be a representation of our face. All I could say about our effort was that is was good fun.

God made man. We read, 'And the LORD God formed man of the dust of the ground, and breathed into his nostrils the breath of life; and man became a living being' (Genesis 2:7). When we die, our soul returns to God who gave it and our body returns to the earth from which it was made (Ecclesiastes 12:7).

Adam was to take care of God's creation. When sin entered the world and ruined our lives, it also ruined our earth. Looking about us, we can see that in many places we have done much damage. Rivers and land are polluted, and in some areas it is not safe for people to live and work.

However, when Adam was created, all was perfect. We read, 'Then God saw everything that he had made, and indeed it was very good. So the evening and the morning were the sixth day' (Genesis 1:31).

Of the seventh day we read, 'God blessed the seventh day and sanctified it, because in it he rested from all his work which God had created and made' (Genesis 2:3).

God's rest was that of an artist's, who, having completed his masterpiece, stands back and admires what he has done.

One day the saints will enter God's rest: the new heavens and earth in which dwells righteousness.

FIND OUT THE FACTS

1. God said, 'Let us make man in our image, according to our likeness' (Genesis 1:26). In what way was Adam like God?
2. The first Adam sinned. Who was the second Adam? Read 1 Corinthians 15:45.
3. What food was given to Adam to eat? What were the animals to eat?
4. What did God tell Adam to do in the new, perfect creation?

God has given human beings a position of privilege in his creation. Thank God for blessing the human race in this way.

You have made him [man] to have dominion over the works of your hands; you have put all things under his feet.
King David, – Psalm 8:6

Genesis 2:18-25
'And the LORD God said, "It is not good that man should be alone; I will make him a helper comparable to him"' (Genesis 2:18).

In Australia there is a saying: 'A dog is a man's best friend.' This was a common expression in the early days of settlement where, before their families arrived, the bushmen cleared the land, built homes and cared for their livestock. Out in the bush, a dog was 'a man's best friend'. He rounded up the livestock, caught rabbits for food, sounded the alarm when people were coming and proved to be a faithful mate.

God placed Adam in the Garden of Eden and instructed him to care for the plants and animals. God first brought the animals and birds to Adam so they could be named.

The Lord had created more than just one of each species; there were two: male and female. As a result, Adam understood that he needed a companion who would be his friend and helper, to carry out God's commands.

So it was that Eve was made from one of Adam's ribs. We read that he named her 'Woman' because she was 'taken out of man' (Genesis 2:23). An animal would no longer be Adam's best friend, but the woman, given to him by God. Later Adam named his 'wife' Eve, 'because she was the mother of all living' (Genesis 3:20).

Matthew Henry, who lived in the 18th century, wrote a commentary on the whole Bible. Of Eve he wrote that 'the woman was made of a rib out of the side of Adam; not out of his head to rule over him, nor out of his feet to be trampled upon by him, but out of his side to be equal with him, under his arm to be protected, and near his heart to be beloved.'[1]

The relationship was one of total joy as they helped each other to tend the Garden of Eden and to care for the animals. Together they worked in the paradise God had created for them.

There was no unhappiness, sorrow or death. All was perfect. They enjoyed an intimate relationship with God. We read, 'And they heard the sound of the LORD God walking in the garden in the cool of the day...' (Genesis 3:8). This was Christ who, before sin entered the world, took upon himself a human form and had loving fellowship with Adam and Eve in the Garden of Eden.

---

[1] Matthew Henry's Commentary on the Whole Bible, Vol. 1, Pickering & Inglis Ltd., London, p.20.

FIND OUT THE FACTS

1. What does the name Adam mean?
2. Why was Eve given her name?
3. What rivers flowed through the Garden of Eden? Read Genesis 2:10-14. Do we have any rivers in the world with these names?
4. Make a list of the things that would have made the Garden of Eden so wonderful.

God blesses us with friends and family. Thank him for these blessings.

A man and his wife are partners, like two oars in a boat.
Henry Smith

Genesis   'And I will put enmity between
3:1-17   you and the woman, and
               between your seed and her
               Seed; he shall bruise your
               head, and you shall bruise his
               heel' (Genesis 3:15).

During a university statistics examination, I knew one of my answers was incorrect. I checked my calculations four or five times, but couldn't see my mistake. On the bottom of my examination paper I wrote, 'I know there's an error, but I can't find it.'

Upon arriving home I told Val, and when I had sat down, I showed her my calculations. She looked at me and said, 'Three plus four is seven, not eight!' What a silly mistake!

Some mistakes in life have terrible consequences, even death.

God placed Adam and Eve in the Garden of Eden where they could eat whatever they liked, which was everything except the fruit of 'the tree of the knowledge of good and evil' (Genesis 2:17).

One day Satan appeared in the form of a serpent and suggested to Eve that God had lied, 'Has God indeed said, "You shall not eat of every tree of the garden?"' (Genesis 3:1).

In response Eve told him that they could eat from all the trees, except from the tree in the middle of the garden, the tree of the knowledge of good and evil. Satan then told Eve that God had indeed lied to them. He said, 'You will not surely die. For God knows that in the day you eat of it your eyes will be opened, and you will be like God, knowing good and evil' (Genesis 3:4-5).

Eve ate the forbidden fruit and gave some to Adam. They both deliberately disobeyed the commandment of their Creator. Instantly death entered the world and the ageing process began. Hell, the second death, opened its mouth to receive unrepentant sinners.

When God came to Adam and Eve in the cool of the evening, they hid from him because they had broken his law. When God asked them why they had sinned, Eve blamed the serpent, and Adam blamed Eve and God. He said, 'The woman whom *you* gave to be with me, she gave me of the tree, and I ate' (Genesis 3:12, italics mine).

As a result the ground was cursed. Thorns and thistles would grow and make gardening and any form of agriculture difficult. Eve was told that she would have pain in childbirth; and the serpent was told he would go about on his belly and 'eat dust' (Genesis 3:14).

Every baby born into the world would be born with a sinful nature. But God graciously promised them a Saviour: 'I will put enmity between you and the woman, and between your seed and her Seed; he shall bruise your head, and you shall bruise his heel' (Genesis 3:15). Then God expelled Adam and Eve from the Garden of Eden.

FIND OUT THE FACTS

1. Who tempted Eve to sin?
2. Why do you think Adam ate the forbidden fruit?
3. If a serpent spoke to me I would be very worried. Eve seemed unconcerned when the serpent spoke to her. Why?
4. What is sin?

Adam and Eve broke God's law, and so do we. Thank God that he sent his Son to be the Saviour of sinners.

The wicked have the seeds of hell in their own hearts. *John Calvin*

Genesis   'Am I my brother's keeper?'
4:1-15   (Genesis 4:9).

In our jails we find many men and women (and some children) who are guilty of murder. This is a terrible crime because it means that a person created in God's image has been deliberately killed.

Jesus explained that the commandment, 'You shall not murder' (Exodus 20:13), meant more than just killing someone. He said, 'Whoever is angry with his brother without a cause shall be in danger of the judgement… But whoever says, "You fool!" shall be in danger of hell fire' (Matthew 5:22).

Cain and Abel were brothers: Abel was a shepherd and Cain a farmer. No doubt their parents, Adam and Eve, taught them about God and the way that sin had entered the world. They were born with sinful natures and, sad to say, the brothers were not friends.

They both offered their sacrifices for sin to God but, in this, Cain failed. The Bible explains that without the shedding of blood there is no forgiveness (Hebrews 9:22).The only shed blood that saves is the blood of Jesus Christ. All Old Testament sacrifices pointed to that one perfect sacrifice of God's Son.

Cain offered God part of his crops, while Abel sacrificed one of his flock. Abel's sacrifice, which involved the shedding of blood, showed that he had a heart that was ashamed of disobeying God.

Having given Abel a repentant heart, God accepted his sacrifice for his sins. But Cain's was rejected. He had no real interest in serving God and made no effort to live a godly life. Cain was very angry that God had rejected his offering.

One day when they were out in the fields, Cain killed and buried his brother, hoping that he had not been seen. But the

Lord appeared and asked Cain, 'Where is Abel your brother?' Cain's answer was a lie: 'I do not know. Am I my brother's keeper?' (Genesis 4:9).

Of course, the Lord knew what had happened because nothing can be hidden from his sight. Jeremiah tells us this: 'For my eyes are on all their ways; they are not hidden from my face, nor is their iniquity hidden from my eyes' (16:17).

When the Lord punished Cain by commanding him to live as a fugitive and vagabond, Cain feared that someone might kill him. The Lord replied that if anyone killed him, that person would be punished sevenfold. God then put a mark on Cain to ensure that his life would be protected. From that time on, no one would kill him. God's anger would be upon them if they did.

All sin is offensive to our holy God. We should be praying that he would send his Spirit into our hearts so that we might love him and love his law.

Pray that God would keep you from sin.

FIND OUT THE FACTS

1. Why should people love one another?
2. What should be your relationship with the other members of your family?
3. What is a 'fugitive and a vagabond'?

Cain was angry with his brother Abel and murdered him. Think about what other things anger makes people do. Ask God to help you control your anger.

You shall love your neighbour as yourself. *The Lord Jesus Christ –* Matthew 19:19

1 Samuel   'His brother's name was Jubal.
16:14-23   He was the father of all those
            who play the harp and flute'
            (Genesis 4:21).

During my married life, Val and I have owned several dogs, all of which were good companions. The children loved to play with them and they also enjoyed the games. One particular dog hated music! One of our daughters was learning to play the violin which somehow grated on the dog's nerves. As soon as he heard the first note, he would lift his head and howl until the violin was put away.

In some books you will read that human beings evolved from some lower form of life. This is not true as the Bible tells us clearly that we are all descendants of the first male and female created by God: Adam and Eve. They were not hairy people who swung through the trees and who were unable to talk. Adam and Eve were perfectly human in every way, before sin entered the world. They and their descendants were intelligent. Before long, we find that they lived in tents and houses. Tubal-Cain made implements of bronze and iron (Genesis 4:22).

The first mention we have in the Scriptures of musical instruments is found in Genesis 4:21, which is our scripture verse. Musical instruments are mentioned frequently in the Scriptures. There is a great variety of them.

When I was in primary school, I was taught to play the flute. I was never very good at this, but I have always enjoyed listening to classical music. When we were young, my brother and I would turn on the radio each Saturday night and listen to 'World Famous Tenors'.

Music can have a calming effect upon people. From the scripture reading in 1 Samuel you will notice that King Saul asked his servants to find him someone who could play the harp. It was David, Israel's future king, who was nominated: 'Then one of the servants answered and said, "Look, I have seen a son of Jesse the Bethlehemite, who is skilful in playing, a mighty man of valour, a man of war, prudent in speech, and a handsome person; and the LORD is with him"' (1 Samuel 16:18). David was soon in King Saul's presence, playing soothing tunes which helped calm the king when he was upset.

Some of the music we hear today is terrible. The words are sinful and the beat intoxicating. We should be very careful to choose music that makes us calm in spirit and which has words that are God honouring.

FIND OUT THE FACTS

1. Make a list of the musical instruments that people today play.
2. Think of the songs that you sing during the time of worship; what do they mean to you? How do they affect you?
3. Why should we be careful in the choice of the music we hear?

Think about how music helps us to worship God. Thank God for the gift of music.

Among other things adapted for man's pleasure and for giving him pleasure, music is either the foremost, or one of the principal; and we must esteem it a gift from God designed for that purpose. *John Calvin*

Genesis
5:21-32

'By faith Enoch was taken away so that he did not see death "and was not found, because God had taken him"; for before he was taken he had this testimony, that he pleased God.' (Hebrews 11:5).

One of my daughters traced the Cromarty family tree back to Captain William Cromarty, who was the first of our ancestors to settle in Australia. Many years ago my father, whose name was Jim, read in the newspaper of another Jim Cromarty who was in town, taking part in an archery competition. We made it our business to go and meet him — three Jim Cromartys together!

About three years ago I began to subscribe to a magazine called 'Scots' and, to my surprise, the editor was Susan Cromarty. Later I discovered that she was the daughter of the Jim Cromarty I had met many years before. We have found out that our families had a common ancestor about 700 years ago!

My wife's brother has also put together his family tree. One day he rang with the news that one of his family's first ancestors arrived in Australia in chains: he was a convict.

The Jews kept careful family records because land belonged to families and tribes. The Levites, who worked in the temple, were descendants of Levi. The priests were descendants of Aaron. The family records were used to prove that Christ was descended from King David.

The scripture passage you have read lists families and descendants who lived very long lives compared to our seventy or eighty years.

With the exception of one person mentioned, they all had one thing in common: they died. Even Methuselah, who lived to the great age of 969 years, died.

The Bible tells us that death is the wages of sin. But one person mentioned here did not die. His name was Enoch. He lived 365 years and he 'walked with God' (Genesis 5:24).

He was a godly man, who loved, served and worshipped his Lord. We read that the day came when 'he was not, for God took him' (Genesis 5:24). Enoch passed into the presence of his God without facing death, the enemy of mankind. In the Scriptures there is only one other person who passed into heaven without death; that was Elijah. (2 Kings 2:9-12).

The only other people who will not die are those who are still living in this world when Christ returns. Christians who are still living on earth on that day will be changed in the twinkling of an eye and be given a glorious resurrection body, like that of our Saviour.

Our sinless Redeemer, Jesus Christ, 'the Lion of the tribe of Judah' (Revelation 5:5), took upon himself the sins of his chosen ones and died in their place.

Let us all prepare for the day of our death by turning in repentance to Christ. He lived and died for his people, and he is the only way into the presence of the heavenly Father.

FIND OUT THE FACTS

1. How old was Jared when he died?
2. Who was the oldest man who ever lived?
3. What is so unusual about the life of Enoch?
4. Discuss Hebrews 11:5 and Jude 14.

It is a great blessing to be born into a family of Christians. Thank God today for a dad and a mum, an uncle or an aunt, and for grandparents who love and serve the Lord.

Precious in the sight of the LORD is the death of his saints.
(The Psalmist – Psalm 116:15)

Genesis   '[God] did not spare the
7:1-16   ancient world, but saved Noah,
one of eight people, a preacher
of righteousness, bringing in
the flood on the world of the
ungodly' (2 Peter 2:5).

Floods are common in many parts of the world. They cause much heartache, because frequently lives and treasured possessions are lost for ever.

When I was young, I lived on the family farm which was flooded every couple of years. The water washed down the good soil from further up the valley, making our ground rich and fertile. My brother and I enjoyed it when the floods came, as it meant that we did not have to go to school!

Our scripture reading tells us that God saw the wickedness of mankind and 'was sorry that he had made man on the earth, and he was grieved in his heart' (Genesis 6:6).

The first punishment was to reduce the length of human life. God said, 'His days shall be one hundred and twenty years' (Genesis 6:3).

Noah was a 'preacher of righteousness' who 'found grace in the eyes of the LORD' (2 Peter 2:5; Genesis 6:8). The ark he built was to be big enough to save some of every kind of animal and bird on the earth.

We can well imagine what it must have been like when Noah set to work building that huge boat. The people would have mocked him for his apparent stupidity. It is likely that they had never experienced rain before, because we read that at that time 'a mist went up from the earth and watered the whole face of the ground' (Genesis 2:6). Noah preached, calling upon the people to repent and live righteous lives, but they only laughed.

At last the day came when Noah put all the animals, birds and his family in the ark. After the provisions necessary for life were carefully stacked away, 'the LORD shut him in'

(Genesis 7:16). No doubt the people laughed at Noah and his family. Then, suddenly, the rain began to fall and 'the fountains of the great deep were broken up' (Genesis 7:11).

The flood water rose and all life upon the earth perished, except for those in the ark. The ark is a picture of the salvation that is to be found only in the Lord Jesus. He invites sinners to repent of their sins and to come to him, where there is salvation freely available.

Jesus is the sinners' 'ark'. He saves his people from the lake of fire and brimstone. Christ, our 'ark', will bear us safely to the shores of paradise.

FIND OUT THE FACTS

1. Noah was a preacher of righteousness. What message would he have preached to those who listened?
2. Who was saved in the ark? Read Genesis 7:1.
3. Why was Noah's family saved?
4. How will God destroy the world when he returns? (Read 2 Peter 3:10-13).

Just as in Noah's day, many people today mock the Word of God. Pray that the Holy Spirit will convict people that they are sinners and that they need to repent.

Sin has dug every grave.
William Plumer

Genesis   'Then the dove came to him in
8:6-19   the evening, and behold, a
             freshly plucked olive leaf was
             in her mouth; and Noah knew
             that the waters had abated
             from the earth' (Genesis 8:11).

Imagine how Noah and his family felt when they heard the rain falling and the cries of people and animals drowning, while they were safe in the ark!

We all like to have our places of security. Many of us try to make our homes secure from intruders. Our house has security bars on every window, because twice a burglar has broken in and stolen some of our possessions. There are, however, no places of absolute security in our world.

The only place of safety during the Flood was in the ark. Those who saw their need to enter could have done so, but only Noah and his family believed what God had said about what was to take place.

God shut the door of the ark, before the waters lifted it up. After forty days Noah sent out a raven and a dove to see if the flood waters had gone down. The dove kept returning to the safety of the ark. Then, one day, it returned with an olive leaf in its mouth. Noah now knew that this meant that the flood waters had subsided and dry land was beginning to appear.

When the ark settled on Mount Ararat, God commanded Noah and his family to open the door and to go outside. The animals also were allowed to go free.

After making a sacrifice to God using some of the animals, God made a promise to Noah: 'Never again shall all flesh be cut off by the waters of the flood; never again shall there be a flood to destroy the earth' (Genesis 9:11).

God has faithfully kept that promise. The earth has had its floods and tidal waves, resulting in the deaths of thousands of people, but never has there been a flood to destroy all life on the earth.

God provided a place of safety for Noah when his judgement was poured out upon the world. The waters of the Flood covered the whole world and no high mountain peaks were to be seen. When Christ returns there will be only one place of security: the Lord Jesus. Of him we read, 'Nor is there salvation in any other, for there is no other name under heaven given among men by which we must be saved' (Acts 4:12).

Are you safe, trusting in the Lord Jesus Christ?

FIND OUT THE FACTS

1. Name Noah's three sons.
2. On which mountain did the ark come to rest?
3. How did the dove show Noah that the flood waters had dropped sufficiently for the ark's doors to be opened?
4. How does Jesus save his people?

God warned the people of Noah's day that he was going to send judgement. Thank God for the many warnings he gives us in the Bible of his anger and judgement against sin.

As Noah was safe in the ark so all God's people are safe in Christ. The worldwide flood is important because it is evidence of a final, universal judgement and as such must be taken seriously. *Peter Jeffery*

Genesis   'Thus I establish my covenant
9:8-17   with you: Never again shall all
            flesh be cut off by the waters
            of the flood; never again shall
            there be a flood to destroy the
            earth' (Genesis 9:11).

What is a 'covenant'? It is an agreement between two or more parties. During your life you may make many covenants. Probably the most important covenant I have ever made was the day Val and I were married. We both made vows in the presence of our friends and relatives and sealed the promises by signing the wedding certificate. We committed ourselves to each other until parted by death.

Sometimes people make agreements which are sealed with the shaking of hands. Maybe you have an arrangement with your parents: you are to keep your room tidy and do some odd jobs, and in return they will give you a certain sum of money as pocket money.

God is one who has made covenants with mankind. In every covenant he has made with human beings, it has been God who has come to men and laid down the conditions.

As we have read in earlier devotions, in the Garden of Eden, God commanded Adam and Eve not to eat the fruit from the tree of the 'knowledge of good and evil'. One part of the agreement was that if they disobeyed, the consequence would be death.

Following the Flood, God promised Noah and his descendants that never again would he send a flood to destroy both animals and human life. Noah was given a sign of this covenant — a rainbow — which would appear in the heavens when rain fell. The Lord said that this covenant would be an everlasting agreement. Today when the clouds are overhead and the rain begins to fall, we frequently see the rainbow in the sky. This is a covenant of grace to remind us of God's promise that he will never again destroy the earth by a flood.

Following the return of Christ, this world will be destroyed by fire and recreated as a dwelling place for all those who love and serve the Lord (2 Peter 3:10-13).

When the apostle John had a vision of God upon his throne in heaven he wrote, 'And he who sat there was like a jasper and a sardius stone in appearance; and there was a rainbow around the throne, in appearance like an emerald' (Revelation 4:3).

This rainbow is a symbol of God's grace, mercy and love which was won for mankind through the death of the Lord Jesus Christ on the cross.

FIND OUT THE FACTS

1. Name the colours of the rainbow.
2. What special significance did God place upon the rainbow?
3. Who made the covenant with Noah and his descendants?
4. What animals were sacrificed by Noah after the flood subsided?

When you next see a rainbow in the sky, remember to thank God for being faithful to his word.

Faith always sees the bow of covenant promise whenever sense sees the cloud of affliction. C. H. Spurgeon

Genesis   'You shall not murder' (Exodus
9:1-7   20:13).

I am always saddened when I read of someone's death because it reminds me that 'the wages of sin is death' (Romans
6:23). However, for God's people, death means passing into
the presence of the Lord where with all of the saints we will
wait for the uniting of our soul with our resurrected body. The
apostle Paul wrote, 'For to me, to live is Christ, and to die is
gain' (Philippians 1:21). Death means that we are parted from
our loved ones, and we leave behind our earthly possessions.

Murder is a terrible tragedy. When a criminal is caught, a
court case takes place. Those who are found guilty are
punished. Care must always be taken to make sure that the
one jailed is indeed the guilty party. In Australia there was the
well-known 'dingo' case, (a dingo is a native Australian dog, a
creamy ginger in colour) in which a woman was charged with
the murder of her daughter. She was found guilty, but later it
was proved that the dingo had killed the little child.

God made clear his law concerning life. Noah and his sons
— Shem, Ham and Japheth, with their wives — were to have
children in order to repopulate the earth. They were given
permission to kill animals and birds for food, but under no
circumstances were they to eat flesh containing blood. This
meant that animals killed for food were to have the blood
drained from the flesh before it was cooked.

If an animal or bird killed a person, it was to be put to death
as punishment. The Lord also outlined his law concerning
murderers: 'Whoever sheds man's blood, by man his blood shall
be shed' (Genesis 9:6). God explains why murder is so
abhorrent: we all bear God's image and so to kill a person is to
violate God's image in mankind.

God's law is totally fair (See Exodus 21:22-27). Jesus explained the full meaning of the Commandment in Exodus 20:13. We are not to be angry with a brother or sister without a just cause. If we are, then we stand in danger of judgement. To say, 'Raca' (meaning you blockhead or empty head) to a person, puts the speaker in danger of appearing before the Jewish council. To say, 'You fool' to another person puts the speaker in danger of hell fire (Matthew 5:22).

The apostle Paul did not oppose the death penalty. He said to Festus, 'For if I am an offender, or have committed anything worthy of death, I do not object to dying...' (Acts 25:11).

When our soul leaves our body, that is the first death, and we shall all die unless we are still living at the coming of the Saviour. The second death, which is hell, can only be avoided by having a saving faith in the Lord Jesus. 'Born once, die twice' is the destiny of all ungodly people. But I can say, 'Born twice and die once.' Can you?

FIND OUT THE FACTS

1. What reason did God give for forbidding humans to eat flesh containing blood?

2. Does this Commandment forbid blood transfusions? Why?

3. Why are animals usually afraid of humans?

The Bible tells us that the sin of murder needs to be dealt with in a drastic way. Thank God that he gives us such clear instructions on how to deal with sin.

Christian love is the distinguishing mark of Christian life. John Blanchard

Genesis   'Now the whole earth had one
11:1-9   language and one speech'
           (Genesis 11:1).

I am amazed at the number of languages we have in the world.
When I attended secondary school, I was in a class that stud-
ied French, which I found very difficult. My wife, Val, studied
French and German which she enjoyed.

In most cities of the world we hear a babble of voices
because migrants speak their own languages. With all the
different languages we find scattered throughout the world, it
is difficult to believe that there was a day, many centuries ago,
when just one language was spoken by the human family.

In our scripture passage we find a world populated by the
descendants of Noah and his wife. They were constructing a
tall building which they hoped would reach up into the heavens. This was associated with their corrupt worship and their
pride. Those people all lived in the land of Shinar, and had
not migrated to other parts of the world. This meant they were
not taking care of the creation, as God had commanded Adam
and Eve.

God would not tolerate their wickedness and, in order to
scatter them throughout the world, he performed the miracle
of changing their speech into many languages.

Try to imagine what happened when the carpenters asked
for wood and the labourers had no idea what was being said.
Children playing happily in the city streets suddenly couldn't
understand one another. I'm sure the games finished quickly,
or arguments and fights soon broke out.

The Lord had said, 'Come, let us go down and there
confuse their language, that they may not understand one
another's speech' (Genesis 11:7).

This verse is very interesting because we find that God, who is one, says, 'Come, let us go down...' This passage is fully explained in the Scriptures which, as we have seen, teach that there are three distinct persons in the Godhead: the Father, the Son and the Holy Spirit. This is a truth that is hard to understand, but it is taught in the Scriptures and therefore must be believed.

Whenever you hear someone speaking a different language, think back to the story of Babel. Also praise God for his revelation that in the godhead there are three distinct persons, one being the Redeemer who saved his people from God's anger because of their sins.

FIND OUT THE FACTS

1. Make a list of the languages you have heard spoken by other people.

2. In Jerusalem, on the Day of Pentecost, the followers of the Lord Jesus spoke to people from many countries in their own language. How many different nationalities are mentioned? Read Acts 2:5-13.

3. What does the word 'babel' mean?

To Think & to pray about

Think about how many languages the Bible has had to be translated into and pray for Bible translators.

A saying to Remember

Kind words are the music of the world.
Frederick W. Faber

Genesis
12:1-9

'I will bless those who bless you, and I will curse him who curses you; and in you all the families of the earth shall be blessed' (Genesis 12:3).

In 1834 my ancestors packed their belongings and sailed from Scotland to Australia to start a new life. I can only imagine what that move must have been like. They left Scotland where they had a home and employment to set off to a land that was known as a dumping ground for Britain's convicts.

When they reached Australia, Captain William Cromarty, who sailed his own ship, was given a grant of land, which in those days was little more than a tract of land covered in thick scrub, sand, water holes and where there were plenty of mosquitoes. It is land where, today, building blocks sell for many hundreds of thousands of Australian dollars, especially those that have a water frontage to the big inland bay.

Captain William and his family built their home and began farming the land. They transported cargo along the eastern coast of Australia in their sailing ship.

Captain William knew where he was going, as he had heard from others what to expect. However, in today's reading we find Abram (later called Abraham), his wife Sarai (later known as Sarah) and Lot, his nephew, setting out from Ur of the Chaldeans, with all their possessions, to go to the land of Canaan.

The reason for this important move was that God had commanded Abram to depart from his homeland and go to a land that one day would be settled by his descendants. When he reached Canaan, the Lord appeared to him and said, 'To your descendants I will give this land' (Genesis 12:7).

After building an altar to the Lord, Abram moved on to a place between Bethel and Ai where he made his home.

While he sinned many times and was foolish in some of his actions, he loved God and made every effort to be an obedient servant. He was called 'the friend of God' (James 2:23).

When he and Lot reached the plain of Jordan, Lot chose the land surrounding the city of Sodom as a place for his family and animals to live. We are told that the men of Sodom were very wicked.

Abram and Sarai, who had no children, settled in Canaan where once again the Lord appeared to Abram and said, 'Lift your eyes now and look from the place where you are — northward, southward, eastward, and westward; for all the land which you see I give to you and your descendants forever' (Genesis 13:14-15).

Abram and Sarai would have wondered how this could be, seeing they did not have children and they were in their old age.

FIND OUT THE FACTS

1. From what country did Abram and Sarai come?
2. Why did Abram build an altar to the Lord?
3. Who was Abram's father? Who was Sarai's father?
4. From your reading, list the promises that the LORD made to Abram and Sarai

You have read today of Abram building an altar and worshipping God. God was faithful to Abram. Thank God that he is faithful to all who call upon him and worship him.

A saying to Remember

You are my friends if you do whatever I command you.   John 15:14

Genesis
17:1-14

'And I will establish my covenant between me and you and your descendants after you in their generations, for an everlasting covenant, to be God to you and your descendants after you' (Genesis 17:7).

Most girls look forward to becoming mothers one day. Today there are many couples who have no children but sometimes medical science makes it possible for a baby to be born to a once childless couple. When Sarah and Abraham lived, childless couples usually remained childless. This was always distressing to them, because children were considered to be a blessing from God. They expected their adult children to care for them in their old age.

Abraham and Sarah had been promised by God that they would have a son and heir. God had established his covenant with Abraham and a son was part of that promise.

When Sarah overheard this promise, she began to laugh (Genesis 18:12). She couldn't believe they would have a child, as she was ninety years old and Abraham one hundred. While they were well past the age of childbearing, Abraham didn't doubt God's pledge. He believed what was said, and the Lord 'accounted it to him for righteousness' (Genesis 15:6). God's promise made him the father of all who believe.

God promised Abraham children, and also that he would become the father of many nations. In fact, he was promised descendants as numerous as the stars in the heavens (Genesis 15:5). This covenant was to be 'an everlasting covenant' (Genesis 17:7). The land of Canaan, which belonged to other nations, was promised to Abraham's descendants.

The seal and sign of God's covenant with Abraham and his descendants was the circumcision of all male babies — the covenant sign was cut into their flesh. God's wonderful assurance to Abraham and his descendants was: I will 'be God to

you and your descendants after you' (Genesis 17:7). This covenant was sealed by God with the shedding of blood. He 'cut' a
covenant with Abraham: animals were killed and blood shed
(Genesis 15:9,10).

After 'cutting' the covenant, Abraham fell asleep. We read,
'a deep sleep fell upon Abram; and behold, horror and great
darkness fell upon him' (Genesis 15:12). During this sleep God
revealed that his descendants would be slaves in another land
for four hundred years (see Genesis 15:12-16).

There would be hard times for Abraham and Sarah's
descendants, but God would never desert his people; his promises always come to pass!

FIND OUT THE FACTS

1. What is the 'covenant promise'?
2. When will God's people find this promise perfectly
   fulfilled? Read Revelation 21:1-4 and 22:1-5.
3. Why did Sarah laugh when she heard that she
   was to have a baby?
4. What did Abraham do when he heard the same
   promise?

Today you have read about God's
promises to Abraham. Find another
of God's promises in the Bible
and thank him for it.

A
saying
to
Remember

The whole covenant is a bundle of
promises. *Thomas Brooks*

Genesis   'Shall not the Judge of all the
18:16-33   earth do right?' (Genesis
             18:25).

Today there is so much sin in the world that many Christians believe it won't be long before the Lord Jesus Christ returns. Our Bibles tell us that the Lord will return in glory to judge the world in righteousness.

Many years ago I found our garden shed had been partly painted. Calling our daughters together, I asked who was responsible. Everyone claimed to be innocent, but one gave me the impression that she was guilty. I warned her of what would happen if she ever did such a foolish thing again. Now the girls laugh when they remind me of my mistake. I had blamed an innocent one!

The men of the city of Sodom and Gomorrah were wicked sinners (read Leviticus 20:13; Romans 1:26-27; 1 Corinthians 6:9-10). We know that 'the wages of sin is death' and in this incident, God carried out his sentence swiftly.

One day when Abraham saw three men walking towards him, he greeted them with an invitation to eat a meal. As a kind host, he had water brought to them to wash their dusty feet, while they rested under some trees near his tent.

One of the three men was called 'Lord' (Genesis 18:17). He was none other than Christ in human form, accompanied by two angels, also in human form. The Lord revealed to Abraham, 'the friend of God' (James 2:23), the reason for their visit: it was the destruction of Sodom because of its sin.

Abraham was concerned for the safety of Lot, who lived in Sodom. He didn't want him destroyed with the city, so, standing before the Lord, he pleaded for mercy: 'Would you also destroy the righteous with the wicked? Suppose there are fifty righteous within the city; would you also destroy the place and not spare it for the fifty righteous that were in it?' (Genesis 18:23-24). The Lord replied by saying that for the sake of fifty righteous people Sodom would be spared.

A discussion followed which ended with Abraham asking, "'Suppose ten should be found there?" And He [the LORD] said, "I will not destroy it for the sake of ten"' (Genesis 18:32).

When the two 'men' saw the wickedness of the city, they commanded righteous Lot, his wife and two unmarried daughters to escape from the city and not to look back. The husbands of Lot's other daughters didn't believe what they heard and they stayed behind.

Then the anger of God fell from heaven: fire and brimstone, which destroyed Sodom, the nearby wicked city of Gomorrah, and the area around the two cities. Lot's wife turned to look back at the city she loved and instantly became a pillar of salt.

FIND OUT THE FACTS

1. Why did Lot's wife look back over Sodom?
2. What did the husbands of Lot's daughters think when they were told to get out of the city? Do you think they loved the Lord?
3. What is meant by Abraham's words: 'Shall not the Judge of all the earth do right?'

Today's reading gives a serious warning about God's judgement on sin. Pray, asking the Lord to help you to hate sin and to run from it.

A saying to Remember

It is our duty to feel sin, to fear sin, and to flee sin as far as we can. *John Boys*

Genesis
21:1-7

'In your seed all the nations of the earth shall be blessed, because you have obeyed my voice' (Genesis 22:18).

In previous readings we have seen that the Lord had promised Abraham that his descendants would be as numerous as the stars in heaven, but Sarah thought she could never have a child, especially as she was well past the age of childbearing. She decided that Abraham should have a child and heir with Hagar, her Egyptian servant girl (Genesis 16:1-4). Sarah believed she could help God to bring his promise to pass.

Soon a son, Ishmael, was born, but he was not Sarah and Abraham's promised son.

During the visit of the three 'men' to Abraham, the Lord made a wonderful promise: 'Sarah your wife shall have a son' (Genesis 18:10). Sarah, who was listening behind the tent 'door', laughed. When she was asked why she laughed, she lied by saying, 'I did not laugh' (Genesis 18:15).

Perhaps there are times when you have told a lie to escape punishment. At school one day, a person stole a book belonging to a child in my class. I conducted the investigation and the thief said, 'It is my book! I didn't steal it!'

The owner replied, 'Sir, if you look inside the back cover, you will find my name and address.' I looked, and sure enough the child's name was there; the thief was caught.

God always keeps his promises because he has the power to do what he says he will do.

The time came when Sarah found that she was expecting a baby. Both she and Abraham were overjoyed. When a son was born, Abraham called him 'Isaac', which means 'laughter'.

On the eighth day, Abraham circumcised Isaac. From that day forward, he carried the mark of the covenant in his flesh. He was part of God's people.

All did not go well between Ishmael and Isaac, because Isaac was frequently mocked by his older 'brother'. Consequently, Sarah demanded that Abraham send Hagar and Ishmael away from their home. Abraham was upset, but God told him to do as Sarah had asked because 'in Isaac your seed shall be called' (Genesis 21:12).

It was through Isaac that God's promised Redeemer, the Lord Jesus Christ, would come, not Ishmael. The apostle Paul wrote of Christ that he was the true 'Seed' (Galatians 3:16), who would save his people from their sins.

But the Lord promised that Ishmael, like Isaac, would also be the father of a great nation (Genesis 21:18).

FIND OUT THE FACTS

1. Why was Sarah hiding behind the tent 'door'?
2. What do we mean when we say, 'Isaac was the child of promise'?
3. What nation was descended from Ishmael? Read Genesis 37:23-28.
4. Sarah thought she could help God bring his promises to pass. This was the wrong thing to do. Why?

God fulfilled his promise to Abraham by giving him a son, Isaac. Thank God that he fulfilled his promise to send his Son to be a Saviour.

There would be no Abraham, the father of believers, who has multitudes of spiritual sons, without this Seed.
R. *Lenski*

Genesis
22:1-18

'By faith Abraham, when he was tested, offered up Isaac, and he who had received the promises offered up his only begotten son, of whom it was said, "In Isaac your seed shall be called"' (Hebrews 11:17-18).

The death of a son or daughter is a tragedy. It is usually the aged who die first.

Many years ago I knew a young girl who was diagnosed with leukaemia. Her Christian parents were heartbroken, and for more than a year the child was in and out of hospital receiving severe treatment. At last there was nothing that could be done and the treatment was stopped. It was a very sad day when her little body was laid to rest.

Let us think of Abraham who was commanded to take Isaac, the child of promise, and sacrifice him to God. Abraham, the man of faith, the friend of God, was severely tested on that day: 'Take now your son, your only son Isaac, whom you love, and go to the land of Moriah, and offer him there as a burnt offering on one of the mountains of which I shall tell you' (Genesis 22:2).

With two servants and Isaac, Abraham set out to obey God. In the final stage of the journey, Abraham and Isaac walked to the place where Abraham was to sacrifice his son.

As they neared the spot, Isaac, who could see that they had everything needed for a sacrifice, except the animal to be sacrificed, asked, 'Where is the lamb for a burnt offering?' (Genesis 22:7). Abraham answered using words which were prophetic, 'My son, God will provide for himself the lamb for a burnt offering' (Genesis 22:8).

Isaac knew what was going to take place when his father bound him ready for the sacrifice. What a testing time for both of them! Both loved God and obeyed his command. Abraham believed that if Isaac was killed, God would raise him from the dead (Hebrews 11:19). Isaac had to live, because the promised Messiah would come through him.

As Abraham raised the knife, the Angel of the Lord spoke, saying, 'Do not lay your hand on the lad, or do anything to him; for now I know that you fear God, since you have not withheld your son, your only son, from me' (Genesis 22:12).

Having freed Isaac, Abraham saw a ram for the sacrifice caught in some bushes. The Lord repeated his promise to Abraham, 'In your seed all the nations of the earth shall be blessed, because you have obeyed my voice' (Genesis 22:18).

FIND OUT THE FACTS

1. What did God teach Abraham in this event?
2. Who is the true Lamb of God?
3. Today, where is the 'Lamb of God who takes away the sin of the world!' (John 1:29). Read Revelation 5:8 and 5:12.
4. What thoughts would Abraham and Isaac have had when Abraham raised his knife? Read Hebrews 11:17-19.

To Think & to pray about

Abraham was obedient to God's command even when God asked him to do something very difficult. Ask God to help you to obey his word even when it will cost you something.

•

A saying to Remember

When he saw Jesus passing by, he said, 'Behold the Lamb of God.' John 1:36

Genesis   'Then they called Rebekah and
24:42-60   said to her, "Will you go with
               this man?"' (Genesis 24:58).

Some time ago a man I knew well died when visiting England. He wanted to be buried beside his wife in Australia, the land he loved. His family went to great expense to take his body home and he is now buried beside his wife.

Abraham had grown rich because God had blessed him greatly. When Sarah died he had nowhere to bury her body so he bought the cave of Machpelah from Ephron, the Hittite as a burial ground for his people. However, he was very much concerned for his son Isaac who did not have a wife!

He called his eldest servant and made him swear by the Lord that he would not allow Isaac to marry one of the Canaanite women. He instructed this servant to return to his homeland and there, from his relatives, to find a wife for Isaac. In some parts of the world marriages are arranged, and couples do not meet until the day of their marriage. In the western world men and women usually choose their own husband or wife.

Abraham's servant obeyed promptly and reaching the homeland of Nahor, he waited beside a well where people drew water for household use and for their animals. There he met the beautiful Rebekah, who carried a pitcher of water. She gave him a drink and then said she would also give his camels a drink.

Abraham's servant had asked God to give him this very sign from a young woman, to indicate that she was the one God had selected to become Isaac's bride. Abraham's faithful servant gave Rebekah gifts of precious jewellery: nose rings and bracelets. He also gave more gifts of jewellery to her mother and Laban, her brother.

Abraham's servant then asked that Rebekah be allowed to return with him to marry Isaac. Calling Rebekah to them, the question was asked, 'Will you go with this man?' (Genesis 24:58).

Rebekah and her maids were soon on their way to Canaan. When they arrived, she modestly covered her face with a veil, and soon Abraham's servant was explaining to him what had occurred when he arrived at Nahor in Mesopotamia. Isaac was pleased to take Rebekah as his wife. We read, 'And he [Isaac] took Rebekah and she became his wife, and he loved her. So Isaac was comforted after his mother's death' (Genesis 24:67).

FIND OUT THE FACTS

1. How do men and women find a husband or wife in your society?
2. What should we look for in our life's partner?
3. Who should be the head of the family? Read Ephesians 5:22-24.

We need wisdom to choose our friends because they are the people who influence our thinking and our behaviour. Ask God to give you wisdom when you choose your friends.

Choose a wife rather by your ear than your eye. *Thomas Fuller*

Genesis
27:1-29

'Children, obey your parents in the Lord, for this is right. "Honour your father and mother," which is the first commandment with promise' (Ephesians 6:1-2).

For some time Rebekah and Isaac were childless. When Isaac prayed that God would give them a son, Rebekah soon announced that she was to have a baby. She was concerned as the baby in her womb seemed to be very active. She prayed that God would explain her unusual feelings.

This is what the Lord revealed to her: 'Two nations are in your womb, two peoples shall be separated from your body; one people shall be stronger than the other, and the older shall serve the younger' (Genesis 25:23).

Jacob was chosen by God to be an ancestor of Christ.

The first born was Esau, which means 'hairy'. He was covered with thick hair. Jacob was born with one hand gripping Esau's heel. As he grew older, Esau became a very capable hunter, but Jacob was quiet and helped his mother in the home. Isaac loved his son, Esau, because he provided him with the food he hunted. Finally, he upset his parents by marrying heathen women.

One day, on returning home and feeling very hungry, Esau gave his birthright (inheritance) to Jacob in exchange for some bread and a pot of stew. This meant that now Jacob would receive twice as much of Isaac's possessions when he died, as well as Isaac's blessing. This shows us that Esau was unconcerned about his birthright.

Rebekah, knowing that God had promised that the elder (Esau) would serve the younger (Jacob), decided to help God bring his prophecy to pass.

One day an aged Isaac asked Esau to gather some game for him, and have it cooked. Rebekah told Jacob to approach his father quickly, pretending to be Esau. Rebekah wrapped some hairy animal skin about his arms and gave him a meal, which she had cooked. Isaac was suspicious, but feeling what he thought were Esau's hairy arms, he blessed him.

When Esau returned and discovered what had happened, he hated his deceitful brother Jacob. The name Jacob means 'supplanter' or 'deceitful'. Esau was heard to say that after his father's death, he would kill his brother Jacob (Genesis 27:41).

Rebekah told Jacob to escape to her brother Laban, where he would obtain work and be protected from Esau. She and Isaac were also fearful that Jacob would marry a local pagan girl, as had Esau. No doubt they hoped that he would find a godly, young woman to marry in the land where Laban lived. Jacob had proved himself to be deceitful to his father and in so doing, he broke the Fifth Commandment.

Do you respect your parents? You should!

FIND OUT THE FACTS

1. Of the twins, who was the elder?
2. What do the names 'Jacob' and 'Esau' mean?
3. Why did Rebekah tell Jacob to lie to her husband, Isaac?
4. What is a lie? Can you think of any situation where it is right to lie?

To tell the truth is not always easy. Ask the Lord to give you the courage to be truthful at all times.

Falsehoods not only disagree with truths, but they usually quarrel among themselves. *Daniel Webster*

Genesis   "'I am the God of Abraham, the
28:10-22   God of Isaac, and the God of
              Jacob?" God is not the God of
              the dead, but of the living'
              (Matthew 22:32).

Many of you know what it is like to move from one home
to another. It is an exciting time preparing to move to a
new house. Because Jacob had wronged his brother, he knew
he had to escape quickly, so he departed for Haran. I don't
think he carried many of his possessions with him. He probably saddled his camel and sneaked away when Esau was
absent.

Each night he would have had to make camp, light a fire
and cook some food to eat. He would sleep on the ground
under some warm blankets. During the day the weather was
hot, but night-time in the desert was usually very cold.

One night, when Jacob settled down to rest, using a stone
for a pillow, the Lord gave him a special revelation in a dream.
I often dream but usually I can't remember what it was about.
Some people talk aloud in their dreams. Even our Maltese dog
Wags, dreams and makes 'doggy' noises.

In Old Testament times, God often revealed himself through
dreams. In Jacob's dream he saw a ladder (stairway) reaching
from earth into heaven, upon which God's angels were ascending and descending. But this was not all — the Lord spoke to
Jacob!

He promised him, just as he had promised Abraham and
Isaac, that the land of Canaan would one day belong to his
many descendants.

Then came the special promise: 'In your seed all the families of the earth shall be blessed' (Genesis 28:14; cf Galatians
3:8). Jacob would be an ancestor of the Lord Jesus Christ.

The Lord promised that he would watch over him wherever he went, and one day bring him safely back to the land
from which he had escaped.

When Jacob awoke, he knew that he had been in the presence of God. He said, 'How awesome is this place! This is none other than the house of God, and this is the gate of heaven!' (Genesis 28:17).

Taking the stone he had used as a pillow, he put it on a pillar and poured oil over it, naming the place 'Bethel', meaning 'house of God'.

Jacob vowed that the Lord would be his God if, one day, he safely returned to his father's house. He also promised to give to the Lord a tenth (tithe) of all he earned.

Jacob's ladder is fulfilled in the Lord Jesus Christ, the Son of God, the Son of Man, the only Mediator between God and man.

FIND OUT THE FACTS

1. Find out what a mediator is?
2. Who is the Mediator between God and man?
   Read 1 Timothy 2:5.
3. Compare Esau and Jacob's characters.

To Think & to pray about

God blessed Jacob! But God does bless sinners. Think of one of the blessings God has given you and thank him for it.

Jesus Christ, the condescension of divinity, and the exaltation of humanity. *Phillips Brooks*

A Saying to Remember

Genesis   'And Isaac begot Jacob, and
29:15-30   Jacob begot the twelve patri-
               archs' (Acts 7:8).

During my courting days, I frequently found myself help-ing Val's father do farm work. I sometimes thought I was another Jacob.

When Jacob arrived in Laban's homeland, he met his daugh-ter, Rachel, who was watering her father's sheep. Almost immediately he fell in love with her. When he was welcomed by Laban, he told him of his love for Rachel.

He agreed to work for Laban for seven years before he would receive Rachel as his wife. Now Rachel had a sister, Leah, who was not as attractive as Rachel.

After the seven years had passed, Laban invited his friends to a feast, to honour Jacob's marriage. At the end of the feast, when everyone had drunk well and night had fallen, Laban brought Jacob his new wife who was probably wearing her veil. When the sun rose the next morning, Jacob opened his eyes and was horrified to find that Leah was beside him in his bed! An angry Jacob wanted to know why he had been cheated of the woman he loved. But Laban replied, 'It must not be done so in our country, to give the younger before the firstborn' (Genesis 29:26).

Just as Jacob had deceived his father, so he had been deceived by Laban. But Jacob still wanted Rachel as his wife and agreed to live with Leah for a week as husband and wife. After this Laban agreed that he could also marry Rachel, pro-vided he worked for another seven years. To this Jacob agreed.

It was Leah who gave birth to many children, but Rachel found she was unable to have a child. In order to have a baby she could call her own, she behaved as Sarah, Jacob's grand-mother had done, and gave him her maid, Bilhah, who bore his children.

The day came when God answered Rachel's prayer and she gave birth to a baby boy who was named Joseph. Years later, following Jacob's return to his own homeland, Rachel gave birth to Benjamin.

Jacob continued to work for Laban in exchange for stock. Having been promised all the brown lambs and spotted and speckled goats, Jacob became a wealthy man (read Genesis 30:32-43).

The day arrived when Jacob, who had served Laban for twenty years, grew tired of his harsh treatment. When the Lord told him to return to Canaan, he was happy to obey. He gathered together his family and possessions and set out for his homeland, knowing that there he would meet his brother, Esau, who had sworn to kill him.

FIND OUT THE FACTS

1. What do you think of the wicked trick Laban played on Jacob? Did he deserve it?
2. Name as many of Jacob's children as you can.
3. Of Rachel and Leah, who did Jacob love the best?
4. Why was Jacob afraid to meet Esau?

There are many Jacobs and Labans living today: people who cheat and deceive one another. Ask God to help you to be honest and upright in the way you treat others.

Marry for love, and work for lucre. C. H. Spurgeon

Genesis
32:22-32

'And He [the Lᴏʀᴅ] said, "Your name shall no longer be called Jacob, but Israel; for you have struggled with God and with men, and have prevailed"' (Genesis 32:28).

I know a teacher who called her husband 'Orme'. When I asked why she gave him that nickname she replied, 'Every Saturday after football he complains about his injuries — "Orme leg! Orme back! Orme finger." Orme suits him perfectly!' There are others who legally change their name.

Jacob took all he possessed and commenced the long journey to Canaan, fearful of meeting with Esau whom he had cheated of their father's blessing. Along the way he was met by some angels who assured him of a warm welcome from Esau.

Dividing his possessions into three groups he sent them ahead, hoping that Esau would receive him as a brother. He prayed to the Lord: 'I am not worthy of the least of all the mercies ... which you have shown your servant... Deliver me, I pray, from the hand of my brother, from the hand of Esau... For you said, "I will surely treat you well, and make your descendants as the sand of the sea, which cannot be numbered for multitude"' (Genesis 32:10,11,12).

The night before meeting Esau, Jacob was alone beside the brook, Jabbok, where an unusual event occurred. Jacob was not alone! He spent the night wrestling with a 'Man'. He was face to face with God, the God of the Covenant, from whom Jacob wanted a blessing.

He struggled with this 'visitor' all through the night, both physically and in prayer. Hosea wrote, 'He [Jacob] took his brother by the heel in the womb, and in his strength he struggled with God. Yes, he struggled with the Angel and prevailed; he wept, and sought favour from him. He found him in Bethel, and there he spoke to us — that is, the LORD God of hosts' (Hosea 12:3-5).

During the encounter, the 'Man' touched Jacob's hip, putting it out of joint. Still Jacob refused to let the 'Man' go, saying, 'I will not let you go, unless you bless me!' (Genesis 32:26).

The reply came: 'Your name shall no longer be called Jacob, but Israel [Israel means 'Prince with God']; for you have struggled with God and with men, and have prevailed' (Genesis 32:28).

Jacob named that place Peniel, 'For I have seen God face to face, and my life is preserved.' (Genesis 32:30).

When Jacob met Esau, he bowed down before him seven times, but his brother, overcome with joy, threw his arms about him, kissed him and made him feel welcome.

FIND OUT THE FACTS

1. With whom did Jacob 'wrestle'?
2. What is meant by 'wrestle'?
3. What does the name 'Israel' mean?

Jacob spent time alone with God. Think about how and when you can spend time in prayer to God.

The divine person who is involved in this prayer experience of Jacob is, therefore, the very one who is at the centre of all true prayer, Christ the Mediator and Angel of God's saving covenant.
J. Douglas MacMillan

Genesis
37:1-11

'Now Israel loved Joseph more than all his children, because he was the son of his old age. Also he made him a tunic of many colours' (Genesis 37:3).

I was once appointed to a school because the person first appointed had relatives who lived in the area. He couldn't stand the thought of being close to them! Christ commands his people to love one another, even if that is hard to do.

Israel loved Joseph more than his other children because he was the child born in his old age. He showed his favouritism by making him a coat of many colours. This special attention caused Joseph's brothers to hate him and there were often cruel words spoken to Israel's favourite son. This hatred increased when Joseph told them of two dreams he had had.

In the first one, his brothers were in a field binding sheaves which bowed down to his sheaf. His brothers considered him to be a proud man because his dream meant that one day they would bow down to him and acknowledge him as their leader.

In his second dream, the sun, moon and eleven stars bowed down to Joseph. Even Israel (Jacob) asked if he really believed that his mother, father and brothers would one day bow down before him!

The day came when Israel (Jacob) asked Joseph to find his brothers who were caring for flocks of sheep and to make sure all was well. When they saw Joseph coming, the brothers made plans to kill him. But Reuben thought it better just to put him down into a pit. He planned to rescue Joseph when he had the opportunity.

Soon after, in the distance, they spied an Ishmaelite camel train carrying precious spices to be sold in Egypt. Judah suggested that Joseph be sold to the merchants which meant they would not be involved in the murder of their brother.

Later Reuben, who was absent when Joseph was sold for twenty shekels of silver, looked in the pit and discovered his brother was missing. He was greatly distressed by what had happened, knowing that his father would be heartbroken by Joseph's apparent death.

The brothers splashed the blood of a baby goat over Joseph's coat to give the impression that he had been killed by a wild animal. On their return home, they showed their father the coat and asked if he recognized it. Of course, Israel knew that it belonged to Joseph. At once, in mourning, he tore his clothes and threw ashes on his head, saying, 'For I shall go down into the grave to my son in mourning' (Genesis 37:35). In Egypt, Joseph was sold to Potiphar, a captain in Pharaoh's guards.

FIND OUT THE FACTS

1. Who was Pharaoh?
2. What is Christian love? Read 1 Corinthians 13.
3. How do you think Joseph felt when he was put down the pit?
4. Was Joseph acting wisely when he told his brothers about his dreams?

Envy or jealousy is a strong feeling which can make people do terrible things. Only the Holy Spirit can give us the strength to overcome these negative feelings. Ask the Lord to keep you from these destructive emotions.

Love seeks one thing only: the good of the one loved. *Thomas Merton*

Genesis
40:1-23

'How then can I do this great
wickedness, and sin against
God?' (Genesis 39:9).

D o you dream? Can you remember them when you wake
up? Do they have any special meaning to you? This is a
story about a butler and a baker who were in prison with Joseph.
They each had a dream which they couldn't understand.

God blessed all that Joseph did and soon Potiphar promoted
him to look after everything in his household, except the food
he ate. When Potiphar's wife wanted him to commit a wicked
sin with her, he refused and ran out of her room. However, the
woman grabbed his coat which she kept. When Potiphar
returned after work, she told him that Joseph had attacked
her.

Potiphar was furious and had Joseph locked up in prison.
Again the Lord blessed him. As a result the guard put him in
charge of the prisoners, and this is when he met Pharaoh's
chief butler and baker. Both men had dreams that upset them.
When Joseph heard about this he asked, 'Tell them to me,
please' (Genesis 40:8). He knew that God would give him their
meaning.

In his vision the butler saw a grape vine with three branches
laden with ripe grapes. He squeezed them into the cup and
handed it to his master. God gave Joseph the interpretation:
the branches represented three days, after which the butler
would be restored to his position and would again serve Pharaoh.

In the baker's dream he had three white baskets on his head.
In the top basket were all kinds of baked goods which the birds
ate. Joseph gave the interpretation: in three days Pharaoh will
have you beheaded and your body will hang on a tree where
the birds will eat your flesh.

All that Joseph had said came to pass. He asked the butler
to tell Pharaoh of his unjust jailing and to seek his release.

However, he forgot Joseph who remained in prison for two years.

One night Pharaoh also had a disturbing dream which he wanted interpreted. The chief butler remembered Joseph, and told Pharaoh of his God-given ability to interpret dreams. At once Pharaoh sent for him. In one dream he saw seven well-fed cows who were eaten by seven underfed cows.

The second was of seven full heads of corn being eaten by seven thin heads, after the hot winds had caused them to wither. Joseph, giving all the glory to God, told Pharaoh, 'The seven fat cows and heads of corn represent seven years of good seasons. The seven thin cows and thin heads of corn represent seven years of famine.'

When Pharaoh realized that Joseph's interpretation was correct he knew that his God had made him very wise. At once he appointed Joseph next to himself in importance and gave him authority to prepare for the time of drought.

FIND OUT THE FACTS

1. Why was Joseph successful in all he did in Egypt?
2. What is a 'butler' and a 'baker'?
3. Joseph was able to foresee the future. Is there any way we can accurately foretell the future?

How easy it is to forget the favours others do for us. Think of ways in which you can do good to others, especially those who have done good to you.

Patient waiting is often the highest way of doing God's will. *Jeremy Collier*

Genesis   'Pharaoh also said to Joseph,
41:33-49   "I am Pharaoh, and without
               your consent no man may lift
               his hand or foot in all the land
               of Egypt"' (Genesis 41:44).

When it was thought that the 'Millennium bug' would cause chaos and food shortages, my family laughed at the few extra supplies I purchased. I told them they would have to come to me to get something to eat when the shops ran out of food. Occasionally the subject comes up of 'dad's supplies' and everyone is amused!

Hearing Joseph's interpretation of his dream, and realizing that he was a very wise man, who was blessed by God, Pharaoh appointed him to rule the kingdom as governor. Joseph began building great storehouses and bought all the grain he could during the seven good years. So much grain was purchased that Joseph found it impossible to keep accurate records.

When the famine spread across the land, the people came looking for food. They asked Pharaoh for help, but he told them to approach Joseph, who was in charge of all grain sales. The famine was so widespread that when Israel (Jacob) and his family suffered, he decided to send his ten sons to Egypt for food. He would not allow Benjamin, his youngest son, to leave home.

As they were arriving in Egypt, Joseph saw his brothers approaching and decided to bring them to repentance for their treatment of him. When he accused them of being spies, they fearfully told him they were honest men. But Joseph had them all thrown into prison.

Upon their release he demanded that they return with Benjamin, their youngest brother, as proof of all they had said. The brothers spoke among themselves, believing that their trouble was the consequence of their mistreatment of Joseph. Joseph, knowing what they were saying, turned away because of the tears in his eyes. He issued instructions for Simeon to be locked in the prison and for his servants to fill the brothers' sacks with grain and to hide their purchase money in the bags.

On the way home when they opened one sack to get some grain for the camels, they discovered the money. Fearfully they asked, 'What is this that God has done to us?' (Genesis 42:28). When they arrived home, they explained Simeon's absence, much to Israel's distress. On tipping out the corn, they discovered the purchase money in each sack.

When the food supply ran low, the brothers knew they would have to return to Egypt. Israel (Jacob) didn't want Benjamin to accompany them, but knew it must be, or they would all die.

The day came when the brothers, including Benjamin, set out for Egypt, hoping that the governor would release Simeon and allow them all to return home. When Joseph saw his brothers approaching, he instructed his servants to escort them to his home where he would eat a meal with them.

FIND OUT THE FACTS

1. How was God disciplining Israel's sons?
2. Why was Benjamin Israel's dearest son?
3. Name Israel's (Jacob) sons.

Even though Joseph's brothers had done wrong, Joseph was gracious to them by giving them food. Thank God that he shows his grace and kindness to people who sin against him.

True repentance is to cease from sin.
Ambrose

February

Trust in the
LORD with all
your heart,
and lean not
on your own
understanding

Proverbs 3:5

Genesis 44:1-14   'God sent me before you to preserve life' (Genesis 45:5).

A ll of God's people repent of their sins and show their love to God by obedience to his commands. I was brought to repentance and faith in Christ while teaching at a one-teacher school named Repentance Creek Public School.

Joseph's brothers would soon realize how wickedly they had treated their brother. When Joseph met them they bowed down before him, just as had happened in his dreams. Meeting Benjamin, his full brother, he said, 'God be gracious to you, my son' (Genesis 43:29), and then with tears in his eyes, he left the room.

Upon returning he ordered his servants to serve the food, starting with the oldest and ending with Benjamin, the youngest, who was given five times more than the others. When the time came for his brothers to leave, Joseph commanded his steward to fill their sacks with corn and to put each brother's money in his bag. He had his silver cup put in the top of Benjamin's bag.

Shortly after his brothers departed, Joseph instructed his steward to overtake them and feign surprise when they found their money and Joseph's silver cup in their sacks. Before opening their bags, the brothers protested that they had stolen nothing, especially Joseph's cup. They said, 'With whomever of your servants it is found, let him die, and we also will be my lord's slaves' (Genesis 44:9).

The steward searched from the oldest to the youngest and found the goblet in Benjamin's sack. Immediately they returned to the city. Upon meeting Joseph, they bowed down and pleaded for mercy. Joseph responded by saying that all except Benjamin could return home.

Judah approached Joseph and told him what they had done to Joseph and how their old father was heartbroken. If Benjamin did not return, their grieving father would die. Judah asked Joseph, 'Now therefore, please let your servant remain instead of the lad as a slave to my lord, and let the lad go up with his brothers' (Genesis 44:33).

With tears streaming down his cheeks, Joseph instructed all his Egyptian servants to leave the room. When he was alone with his brothers, he said, 'I am Joseph; does my father still live?' (Genesis 45:3). Standing before Joseph, Pharaoh's commander, his brothers were terrified. Joseph attempted to put them at ease by saying, 'It was not you who sent me here, but God; and he has made me a father to Pharaoh, and lord of all his house, and a ruler throughout all the land of Egypt' (Genesis 45:8).

Joseph kissed his brothers and talked to them, finding out all that had happened since he had been sold into slavery. Joseph was the saviour of his family as Christ is of his people.

FIND OUT THE FACTS

1. Why didn't Joseph reveal himself to his brothers when he met them?
2. Why was Benjamin so precious to Israel (Jacob) and Joseph?
3. What is pride?

God's ways are higher than our ways. Thank God that his ways are perfect.

Pride goes before destruction, and a haughty spirit before a fall.
Proverbs 16:18

Genesis
47:1-10

'And he said, "I am God, the
God of your father; do not
fear to go down to Egypt, for
I will make of you a great
nation there"' (Genesis 46:3).

During my teaching career, Val and I moved seven times.
Then came a move to my congregation and finally to our
home in Wingham. Moving is always time consuming, but we
found that during the move we were able to dispose of many
useless things we had collected.

It was no different when Jacob and his family, with their
possessions, were invited to live in Egypt.

Joseph's brothers returned home carrying many gifts from
Joseph. But the best news of all was that their brother, Joseph,
was alive and was governor of Egypt.

Israel was an old man, almost one hundred and thirty years,
and his heart stood still when he heard that Joseph, the son he
believed to be dead, was, in fact, alive and well. Israel's sons
also carried the invitation from Pharaoh to come and live in
Egypt: 'Bring your father and your households and come to
me; I will give you the best of the land of Egypt, and you will
eat the fat of the land' (Genesis 45:18).

It was time to gather together all they possessed and set out
for Egypt, where they would be given land on which to dwell
and feed their stock. Old Jacob said, 'Joseph my son is still
alive. I will go and see him before I die' (Genesis 45:28).

When the pilgrims reached Beersheba, God spoke to Israel
in a dream, revealing to him that he should not worry about
going to Egypt, for there God would make of him a great nation
through his descendants. The Lord promised to be with these
descendants and assured Israel that Joseph would be with him
when he died.

God also promised him that his descendants would one day return to the land of Canaan: the land promised to Abraham many years before.

In Egypt, Joseph presented five of his brothers to Pharaoh. Then the day came when Pharaoh met his father Jacob. When he heard that Joseph's family were shepherds, he gave them the good land of Goshen.

Before leaving Pharaoh, Jacob blessed him and thanked him for the gift of land.

As the famine became more severe, Joseph was able to exchange the grain for all the land of Egypt (Genesis 47:19-20). And when the days of famine came to an end, the Egyptians paid Pharaoh a tax of one fifth of all their production in return for their land.

FIND OUT THE FACTS

1. What did the Egyptians think of shepherds? Read Genesis 46:34.
2. How old was Joseph when he died?
3. What promises did God make to Israel when he was at Beersheba? Read Genesis 46:2-4.

God made wonderful provision for Israel (Jacob) and his family. Thank God that he always provides for his children.

Kindness is a grace that all can understand. J. C. Ryle

Genesis
49:29-50:6

'Then Israel said to Joseph,
"Behold, I am dying, but God
will be with you and bring you
back to the land of your
fathers"' (Genesis 48:21).

I will never forget my grandfather's death. I was about eleven years old and, for the first time, I experienced what it was to have a close relative die.

My grandparents lived with us on the farm. I remember grandfather falling ill and being confined to bed where he was cared for at home by the members of the family.

One day my brother and I were called in to speak to him, but one at a time. He spoke his farewells to me, and taking my hand he told me to love God, and prayed that the Holy Spirit would give me a new heart that would love the Lord Jesus. We all wept when he died. He was buried in the family part of the graveyard.

When old Israel was dying, he called together his children and blessed each one of them, prophesying the future of their descendants.

Following his death, Joseph had his father's body embalmed. Then his sons, accompanied by Joseph's servants, and the elders of Israel and Egypt, took his body to the land of Canaan, where it was laid to rest in the cave that had been purchased many years before from Ephron the Hittite.

On their return to Egypt, Joseph's brothers were afraid that he might punish them for the manner in which they had treated him many years before. They again fulfilled the prophecy of Joseph's dreams by bowing down before him and saying, 'Behold, we are your servants' (Genesis 50:18).

Joseph replied, 'Do not be afraid, for am I in the place of God? But as for you, you meant evil against me; but God meant it for good, in order to bring it about as it is this day, to save many people alive' (Genesis 50:19-20).

The children of Israel lived peacefully in Egypt where Joseph made sure they had plenty of all they needed. Their numbers grew as did their possessions.

Joseph lived to the age of one hundred and ten years. When he realized that his death was at hand, he called together his brethren saying, 'I am dying; but God will surely visit you, and bring you out of this land to the land of which he swore to Abraham, to Isaac, and to Jacob' (Genesis 50:24).

He made his descendants and relatives promise that when God led them out of Egypt to the promised land, they would carry his bones and bury them with his forefathers.

Joseph believed in God's promise that the descendants of Abraham would one day live in the land of Canaan.

FIND OUT THE FACTS

1. 'The wages of sin is death' (Romans 6:23). What does this mean?
2. What is 'embalming'?
3. When the Lord Jesus returns, what will happen to all the bodies of the dead and the living? Read 1 Corinthians 15:51-52.

Israel said to Joseph that God would be with him. That was a great privilege and a blessing. What does it mean for God to be with you?

A saying to Remember

This world is the land of the dying, the next is the land of the living.
T. *Edwards*

Exodus	'By faith Moses, when he was
2:1-10	born, was hidden three months
	by his parents, because they
	saw he was a beautiful child;
	and they were not afraid of
	the king's command' (Hebrews
	11:23).

Following the death of Joseph and the Pharaoh who had made him governor, there arose in Egypt a Pharaoh who made slaves of the descendants of Israel. He didn't know the great stories of Joseph's help to the nation.

We should never forget those who have helped us. One day one of our daughters was standing on a jetty when she slipped and fell into the deep river. A young boy, who saw her fall, ran to the end of the jetty and reaching down grabbed her hair and saved her by lifting her head out of the water. I'm sure she will never forget the debt she owes to Henry.

The new Pharaoh forgot Joseph, and because he feared that the Israelites would become an enemy when they had increased in number, he decided to make them slaves. Wanting to keep their population growth under control, Pharaoh told the midwives to kill the baby boys and save the baby girls.

The midwives feared God. So they told Pharaoh that by the time they arrived to help the mother who was giving birth, the baby had already been born. How could they kill a baby who was alive? As the number of the Israelites grew, Pharaoh commanded the midwives to drown the baby boys in the River Nile.

When Moses was born, his parents hid him because there was something special about him. When he could be hidden no longer, his mother made a small boat out of bullrushes and coated it with tar to make it waterproof. She told her daughter to take little Moses down to the Nile, put him in the basket and watch to see what happened.

While she watched the small boat float down the river in the reeds, Moses' sister saw Pharaoh's daughter come to bathe.

The princess saw the small boat and asked her servants to bring it to her. Uncovering the top of the 'ark', she saw little Moses and said, 'This is one of the Hebrews' children' (Exodus 2:6).

At once Moses' sister approached Pharaoh's daughter and asked, 'Shall I go and call a nurse for you from the Hebrew women, that she may nurse the child for you?' (Exodus 2:7). The answer was, 'Yes'. Pharaoh's daughter called the baby 'Moses' because she had drawn him out of the water. The name Moses means 'drawn out'.

Now Moses' mother cared for him, teaching him about God and his commands. Soon the day arrived when Moses moved into the palace and learnt the ways of the Egyptians. He knew the day would come when he would sit upon Pharaoh's throne and from there could help his enslaved people.

FIND OUT THE FACTS

1. Why were the Egyptians afraid of the Israelites?
2. What work was given to the Israelite slaves? (Exodus 1:14).
3. Read God's words to Abraham in Genesis 15:12-16. How were they fulfilled?

Moses' mother taught him about God and his commands. Ask God to help you to learn about him today.

Train up a child in the way he should go, and when he is old he will not depart from it.
(King Solomon) Proverbs 22:6

Exodus	'Then he [the Lᴏʀᴅ] said, "Do
3:1-15	not draw near this place. Take

Exodus
3:1-15

'Then he [the Lᴏʀᴅ] said, "Do not draw near this place. Take your sandals off your feet, for the place where you stand is holy ground"' (Exodus 3:5).

Growing up in Pharaoh's palace meant that Moses would have inherited Egypt's throne, with all its treasures and pleasures. However, he knew he was a Hebrew, one of God's people. When he saw an Egyptian beating one of his people, he stopped the fight but the Egyptian was killed. The next day when two Israelites were fighting, he dragged them apart, saying, 'Why are you striking your companion?' (Exodus 2:13).

Moses then heard words that filled his heart with fear: 'Who made you a prince and a judge over us? Do you intend to kill me as you killed the Egyptian?' (Exodus 2:14). Before long Pharaoh heard what had happened and demanded that Moses be executed. To save his life Moses escaped to the land of Midian.

There Moses helped Zipporah, the daughter of Reuel, who was being bullied by some men at the sheep's watering troughs. When Reuel heard what had happened, he invited Moses to stay with him and eventually allowed him to marry Zipporah.

Moses became a shepherd, caring for Reuel's sheep. One day while watching over a flock, he saw something very strange. A bush was on fire, but it was not being burnt up. Deciding to look more closely at the mysterious sight, he approached the bush and there he heard God speak to him.

First, he was instructed to remove his sandals because he was standing on holy ground. Then God said, 'I am the God of your father — the God of Abraham, the God of Isaac, and the God of Jacob' (Exodus 3:6).

A fearful Moses was then told that God had seen his people being mistreated as slaves in Egypt. He instructed Moses to return and to lead them out of Egypt to the promised land of Canaan.

Moses said that the Israelites would not follow him, so he asked God, 'What is your name?' And God said to Moses, 'I AM WHO I AM... Thus you shall say to the children of Israel, 'I AM has sent me to you' (Exodus 3:14). This 'I AM' was none other than Christ, the only Mediator between God and man. On earth Jesus Christ often used the term 'I AM' revealing that he was God. (See John 6:35; 8:12; 8:58; 10:7; 10:11; 11:25; 14:6; 15:1).

When Moses objected by saying that he was not an eloquent speaker, God appointed his brother Aaron to be his spokesman. The Lord said that he would fulfil his promise by taking the Israelites out of Egypt, and settling them in the Promised Land.

FIND OUT THE FACTS

1. What did God mean by the name 'I AM WHO I AM'?
2. Name one of God's promises that you know?
3. In Exodus 3:1 we find 'Reuel' (Exodus 2:18), called 'Jethro'. Is there any reason for this?
4. What unusual feature caused Moses to go and look at the burning bush?

To Think & to pray about

God told Moses that he was standing on holy ground and should, therefore, take his sandals off. Think about how we should approach this holy God.

My own weaknesses make me shrink, but God's promises make me brave.
C. H. Spurgeon

A Saying to Remember

Exodus 7:1-13 · 'And Pharaoh said, "Who is the LORD, that I should obey his voice to let Israel go? I do not know the LORD, nor will I let Israel go"' (Exodus 5:2).

I have always enjoyed watching a 'magician' at work. A friend of mine is highly capable of making items disappear and then finding them somewhere else. I have tried to discover how he does his tricks, but he won't tell me!

Moses and Aaron returned to Egypt where they found that Pharaoh was forcing the Israelites to make bricks. The guards carried whips which they used to make the slaves work more quickly. Life was very difficult for God's people.

When Moses arrived in Egypt, he gathered together some of Israel's elders and told them that God was about to rescue his people from slavery. He told them that God had said, 'I will take you as my people, and I will be your God. Then you shall know that I am the LORD your God who brings you out from under the burdens of the Egyptians' (Exodus 6:7). God was soon to fulfil his covenant promises to Abraham, Isaac and Jacob, when his people made the land of Canaan their home.

The Lord told Moses to go to Pharaoh's palace and tell him to allow God's people to leave Egypt. This happened when Moses was eighty years old and Aaron eighty-three. God had instructed them what they were to do to convince Pharaoh that he must obey the Lord.

When Moses and Aaron presented themselves to Pharaoh, he asked, 'Who is the LORD, that I should obey his voice to let Israel go?' (Exodus 5:2).

Then he commanded the Israelites to continue making bricks, but without receiving the much needed straw. Now they would have to collect the straw for the bricks they made! When they failed to produce the same number of bricks, they were whipped.

Again Moses and Aaron approached Pharaoh, where Aaron threw his staff onto the floor and it became a serpent. Pharaoh's sorcerers threw down their rods which also became serpents. But, Aaron's snake swallowed the snakes of Egypt's sorcerers.

The next day Moses and Aaron visited Pharaoh beside the River Nile, where they again requested that the Israelites be allowed to go out into the wilderness and worship God. Again Pharaoh refused. Moses then told Aaron that he was to strike the water in the Nile with his rod. When he did, the water turned into blood. This was the first plague. Pharaoh's magicians did the same in some water they had.

For seven days the Egyptians had to dig wells to obtain water. The Lord then commanded Moses and Aaron to demand Pharaoh's permission for his people to leave and worship their LORD.

FIND OUT THE FACTS

1. What does this mean: 'I will harden Pharaoh's heart'? (Exodus 7:3).

2. What part of God's covenant with Abraham was about to happen?

3. What does God's name 'LORD' mean?

The Israelites were being tested in Egypt. Life was difficult. But God was going to do something marvellous. Think about what you can learn about God from this.

Absolutely nothing lies outside the scope of God's sovereignty.
Geoffrey B. Wilson

Exodus
9:1-7

'Thus says the Lord, "Let my people go, that they may serve me"' (Exodus 8:20).

The time came when the Lord would display his awesome power and humble Pharaoh.

Years ago when I was teaching, a student from the teachers' college came to spend a month at our school to observe classroom management in my lessons. On his first day when there were some discipline problems, I stepped in to restore order. The next day, after dressing in his judo clothing, he placed several bricks and roof tiles in position. With the class around him watching, he gave a loud yell and his hand smashed the bricks and tiles into pieces. The class looked on in awe. From that day, he was always obeyed.

Pharaoh was soon to face nine more plagues from almighty God which would destroy Egypt's power. Moses and Aaron approached Pharaoh requesting that the Israelites be allowed to leave Egypt and worship God in the wilderness. He was warned that if he didn't agree, the land would be filled with frogs. When Pharaoh refused Moses' request, Aaron held out his rod and a plague of frogs rose up out of the waters to fill the land. However, the land of Goshen was free of frogs.

In a small way, Pharaoh's magicians did the same. When the frogs were everywhere, Pharaoh asked Moses and Aaron to pray that God would remove them and in return he'd let the people go to worship in the wilderness. When the frogs died, a horrible stench filled the land.

But even though the frogs had gone, Pharaoh refused to allow the Israelites to leave. And this he did many times, when each of the plagues came to an end. He couldn't be trusted to honour his word!

After the plague of the frogs there came a plague of lice which infested both animals and human beings. All the time

Pharaoh's heart was filled with hatred for the Israelites and their God. After the lice, there came a plague of flies, then a disease of all livestock, followed by painful boils on both animals and human beings.

When Pharaoh again refused to let the Israelites go, God sent a storm of thunder, lightning, hail and fire balls. Never before was there such a storm in Egypt. Locusts were the eighth plague, which was followed by darkness covering the land, except for the land of Goshen.

Because of the plagues, Pharaoh's heart was hardened even more against the Israelites and their God. To Moses and Aaron he said, 'Get away from me! Take heed to yourself and see my face no more! For in the day you see my face you shall die!'.

To this Moses replied, 'You have spoken well. I will never see your face again' (Exodus 10:28-29).

FIND OUT THE FACTS

1. What did God command Pharaoh to do?
2. List, in order, the plagues mentioned already.
3. What was Pharaoh to learn about the God of Israel?

God takes it very seriously when people disobey his word; they are not left unpunished. Ask the Lord to give you the grace to fear him and to obey his commandments.

We should never tire of the thought of God's power. *Donald Barnhouse*

Exodus
12:1-14

'The blood shall be a sign for you on the houses where you are. And when I see the blood, I will pass over you' (Exodus 12:13).

When our children were young and away from home, Val usually prepared a special roast dinner for them when they returned. Often it would be a roast leg of lamb which everyone enjoyed. Even though that happened many years ago, the girls still remember those special meals.

The children of Israel experienced a wonderful day, because after eating the roasted lamb, they would leave Egypt and their life of slavery.

God told the Israelites to ask their Egyptian neighbours for articles of silver and gold when they left. God had so touched the hearts of the Egyptians that they willingly gave everything they could.

Moses told the people to select a lamb on the tenth day of the month of Abib, and by careful examination ensure that it had no blemishes, and to slaughter it at twilight on the fourteenth day .

The people used the blood to mark the doorposts and the lintel of their houses in such a way that it could be seen by anyone outside.

They were to pack their belongings, feast on the roasted lamb, some unleavened bread and bitter herbs, and dress themselves for a sudden departure from Egypt.

That night, when the Israelites were safe in their homes, the eldest in every family living in Egypt, including the animals, would die, except for those in houses where the blood had been placed according to God's command. The Lord told Moses and Aaron 'When I see the blood, I will pass over you; and the plague shall not be on you to destroy you when I strike the land of Egypt' (Exodus 12:13).

The Passover became one of Israel's annual feast days, when the covenant nation would commemorate their deliverance from slavery. Outsiders were forbidden to eat the Passover.

In 1 Corinthians 5:7 we read that 'Christ, our Passover, was sacrificed for us.' The lamb used in the Passover was to be male, in the prime of life and without blemish. This lamb pointed to the death of our sinless Saviour on the cross.

As the Israelites were saved from a life of slavery, so Christians are saved from slavery to sin, to become citizens of Christ's kingdom. True freedom is only found in Christ.

The blood on the doorway was a saving blood, because the Angel of Death would not enter those houses where it could be seen. This speaks of the saving work of the Lord Jesus, who is our Passover and Saviour. We read, 'Without [the] shedding of blood there is no remission' (Hebrews 9:22).

FIND OUT THE FACTS

1. Discuss these words: 'The blood of Jesus Christ his Son cleanses us from all sin' (1 John 1:7).

2. Why was the lamb's blood placed on the outside of the doorway?

3. Why is Jesus called 'the lamb of God'? (John 1:29,36).

The Passover feast pointed to the salvation of God's people from sin. Thank the Lord for this great salvation.

One drop of Christ's blood is worth more than heaven and earth. Martin Luther

Exodus   'Your right hand, O Lord, has
14:19-31   become glorious in power; your
             right hand, O Lord, has dashed
             the enemy in pieces' (Exodus
             15:6).

Occasionally the TV news contains reports about foolish people during a time of flooding. Once I saw some young people attempting to cross a low level bridge which was under water. Their car had stalled when they were half way across. When they saw a wall of flood water coming towards them, they set out for safety. Two were able to clamber up the river bank, but the other young man and the car were washed away. The young fellow drowned.

The Israelites walked out of Egypt, laden with their own possessions and all they had been given by the Egyptians. The second person of the Godhead, the 'Angel of God', went before them in a pillar of cloud during the day and a pillar of light during the night. In this way God continued to care for his people.

However, Pharaoh had a change of heart and decided that the Israelites should return to Egypt as slaves. Mustering his chariots, he chased the escaping Hebrews who were trapped between his forces and the Red Sea.

When the Israelites saw the Egyptian chariots getting closer, the frightened people began to pray to God for help. They complained to Moses, suggesting that it would have been better if they had remained in Egypt.

Moses replied, 'Do not be afraid. Stand still, and see the salvation of the Lord, which he will accomplish for you today. For the Egyptians whom you see today, you shall see again no more forever. The Lord will fight for you, and you shall hold your peace' (Exodus 14:13-14).

The Lord commanded Moses to lift his rod and stretch his hand towards the Red Sea. When he did this, a strong east wind blew, causing the sea to part. With a wall of water on each side and dry land under their feet, the Israelites passed over to safety on the other side.

The Angel of God in the pillar of cloud kept the Egyptian forces in total darkness, yet gave the Israelites the light to cross over.

When Israel was safe on the distant shore, the pillar of cloud lifted. The Egyptians followed their enemy on dry ground, between the walls of water, thinking that if the Israelites could cross over, so could they. However, Moses again stretched out his hand and the two walls of water rushed together, drowning all of Pharaoh's charioteers and horses.

Now the Israelites could move forward in safety. The Lord was certainly the all powerful God.

FIND OUT THE FACTS

1. Why were the Israelites afraid of the Egyptian chariots when they had seen God's awesome power in the plagues?

2. Who cared for Israel as they moved towards the land of Canaan?

3. Why were the Israelites going to the land of Canaan?

The Israelites had to trust the Lord to save them from the Egyptians. Think about what it means to trust the Lord in difficult situations.

I know not the way he leads me, but well do I know my Guide. What have I to fear? *Martin Luther*

Exodus 16:4-15

'If you diligently heed the voice of the LORD your God and do what is right in his sight, give ear to his commandments and keep all his statutes, I will put none of the diseases on you which I have brought on the Egyptians. For I am the LORD who heals you' (Exodus 15:26).

I often hear children, who are shopping with their parents, pointing and saying, 'Mum, I want that.' When refused they complain, 'Why can't I? Dad would let me have it.' They are grumbling, complaining children.

The Israelites grumbled and complained about so many things during their wilderness journey, yet rarely thanked God for taking them from the land of slavery. Moses heard their complaint, 'What shall we drink?' (Exodus 15:24).

God provided ample water, but the next complaint was: 'Oh, that we had died by the hand of the LORD in the land of Egypt, when we sat by the pots of meat and when we ate bread to the full! For you have brought us out into this wilderness to kill this whole assembly with hunger' (Exodus 16:3).

Now the Lord promised to give his complaining people, 'bread from heaven' each morning and meat at night. The Lord caused quails to cover the camp and the people caught what they needed for food. In the morning they discovered a 'small round substance, as fine as frost on the ground' (Exodus 16:14).

When the people asked Moses, 'What is it?', he told them it was the promised bread from heaven. The Israelites were to gather what manna (the word 'manna' means What is it?) they needed each morning and twice as much on Friday, in order to provide for the Sabbath. Those who didn't bother to collect the extra on Friday, went without on the Sabbath. On other days those who collected more than they needed and kept it overnight found that in the morning it was filled with maggots and had an odour.

The Lord provided his people with manna for forty years, until they were able to eat the produce of the land of Canaan. This 'bread from heaven' was food for the body, and pointed to Christ who said, 'I am the bread of life' (John 6:48). He alone is food for the soul!

Despite the Lord's care of his people, the complaining continued. They failed to rest in the almighty power of the Lord, even after they had seen God humble Pharaoh and over-throw Egypt's army.

FIND OUT THE FACTS

1. What did manna look like? Read Exodus 16:31.
2. Are you a complainer? Why is complaining wrong?
3. What should the Israelites have done when water and meat were in short supply?
4. Discuss this passage of Scripture: 'I am the bread of life. Your fathers ate the manna in the wilderness, and are dead. This is the bread which comes down from heaven, that one may eat of it and not die' (John 6:48-50).

God continued to provide for his people even when they complained so much. What does this show us about God's commitment to his people?

Those who complain most are most to be complained of.   *Matthew Henry*

Exodus
17:8-16

'So Moses cried out to the
Lord, saying, "What shall I do
with this people? They are
almost ready to stone me!"'
(Exodus 17:4)

Thirst is a terrible thing. We have all heard or read of people dying of thirst. Recently I read about two young men who worked on an outback cattle station in Queensland, Australia. They decided to take a trip to town, but when they didn't arrive, search parties set out to find them. Sadly they found the bodies of the two young men who had died of thirst.

When the Israelites camped at Rephidim they couldn't find a water supply. Instead of praying, they complained to Moses, who they said was leading them all to their death. Again the Lord commanded Moses to take the staff that he held out to part the Red Sea and strike a rock in Horeb. Moses did this and water flowed from the boulder. Consequently that place was named Massah (Testing) and Meribah (Quarrelling).

It was the Lord Jesus Christ who cared for his people, giving water, food and protection, as they wandered through the desert regions. The apostle Paul wrote, '...For they drank of that spiritual Rock that followed them, and that Rock was Christ' (1 Corinthians 10:4).

At Rephidim the children of Israel, led by Joshua, fought against the forces of Amalek. Moses, Aaron and Hur climbed a hill from which they could see the battle. When Moses held up his hand, the forces of Israel advanced, but when his hand was lowered because his arms ached, Amalek's soldiers moved forward.

Moses found difficulty holding up his arms, so Aaron and Hur helped him. They sat Moses on a rock, and with one on each side, they held his hands aloft until Amalek's army was completely overthrown. There Moses built an altar to the Lord, calling it 'The-Lord-Is-My-Banner' (Exodus 17:15).

God commanded Moses to keep a record of the day's events so later generations would be able to read of God fighting for his people. We have the words written by Moses in the first five books of the Old Testament, known as the Pentateuch. Today we can read of events that happened to God's people thousands of years ago.

We can take into our hands the Bible which is all the words that God has revealed to us. It should be read, studied and believed. The apostle Paul wrote: 'All Scripture is given by inspiration of God, and is profitable for doctrine, for reproof, for correction, for instruction in righteousness, that the man of God may be complete, thoroughly equipped for every good work' (2 Timothy 3:16-17).

FIND OUT THE FACTS

1. Who gave Joshua and his men the victory over Amalek?
2. What was the purpose of Moses holding his hands high in the air?
3. Who was it that gave the Israelites great blessings?

The Lord was with the Israelites even though they doubted this at times. Think about the fact that the Lord is always with his people. Thank him for this.

Christ himself was the author of all their blessings. *Geoffrey B. Wilson*

Exodus
20:1-17

'Now therefore, if you will indeed obey my voice and keep my covenant, then you shall be a special treasure to me above all people; for all the earth is mine. And you shall be to me a kingdom of priests and a holy nation' (Exodus 19:5-6).

Schools have rules as do the games we play. Our school had a rule making everyone responsible for keeping the playground tidy. One day when standing near a piece of paper, I was in trouble because I didn't pick it up!

Without rules we would have chaos. God gave his people ten rules, which were the foundation for all their laws.

The Lord led the people through the desert until they arrived at Mount Sinai where he revealed to Moses that Israel was his nation which was called to be holy.

Moses told the elders what God had said concerning his law (Exodus 19:5-6). Great blessings would be theirs if they obeyed. Hearing God's command the Israelites replied, 'All that the LORD has spoken we will do' (Exodus 19:8).

As a result God promised to speak to Moses on Mount Sinai. When the people saw what happened, they would fear God and obey their God-given leader Moses. The Lord told Moses to prepare everyone for that awesome day.

Mount Sinai was covered with a cloud of smoke which radiated from the Lord who descended in flames of fire. The mountain shuddered in the presence of the Lord. Then the Lord spoke to Moses, commanding him to bring Aaron with him. Together they climbed Mount Sinai where God delivered to Moses the Ten Commandments.

'And God spoke all these words, saying ...

"You shall have no other gods before Me.

You shall not make for yourself a carved image ...

You shall not take the name of the LORD your God in vain,

for the LORD will not hold him guiltless who takes his name in vain.

Remember the Sabbath day, to keep it holy. Six days you shall labour and do all your work, but the seventh day is the Sabbath of the LORD your God...

Honour your father and your mother, that your days may be long upon the land which the LORD your God is giving you.

You shall not murder.

You shall not commit adultery.

You shall not steal.

You shall not bear false witness against your neighbour.

You shall not covet your neighbour's house; you shall not covet your neighbour's wife..."(Exodus 20:3-17).

You and I are to obey the Lord's Ten Commandments because we love God (John 14:15).

FIND OUT THE FACTS

1. Who was the only person who kept God's Commandments perfectly?

2. What are the two great commandments? Read Mark 12:28-31.

3. Which is the first commandment with a promise?

At Mount Sinai the Israelites saw the greatness of God and they received his words. Think about how majestic God is.

The law is what we must do; the gospel is what God will give.
Martin Luther

Exodus	'Behold, I send an Angel
23:20-33	before you to keep you in the way and to bring you into the place which I have prepared. Beware of him and obey his voice; do not provoke him, for he will not pardon your transgressions; for my name is in him' (Exodus 23:20-21).

The Israelites were now near the Promised Land. The day approached when God's promise to Abraham concerning the land of Canaan was about to be fulfilled.

God always keeps his word, but very often we fail to do so. There were times when promises I made to my family couldn't be fulfilled. There was disappointment for the family, and I felt guilty for letting them down.

God's promises should encourage his people because he never fails to keep them. Christians eagerly look forward to the coming of Christ, and as the days pass we wonder when our Saviour will arrive.

Concerning the assurance of Christ's return we read, 'The Lord is not slack concerning his promise, as some count slackness, but is long suffering towards us, not willing that any should perish but that all should come to repentance' (2 Peter 3:9).

Today's reading concerns God's word to his covenant nation. He told them that obedience would mean success as they moved towards Canaan. Then came warnings that his people were to serve and worship him alone, and not to follow the gods of the pagan nations surrounding them.

The day was coming when Israel would fight to drive the seven nations out of the land of Canaan. They didn't have a trained army and would have faced defeat without the Lord's help. We read God's pledge that the nations would hear of the overthrow of Egypt and fear both God and Israel.

Many years later, Rahab, who lived in Jericho said to the two spies, 'I know that the LORD has given you the land, that the terror of you has fallen on us, and that all the inhabitants of the land are fainthearted because of you' (Joshua 2:9).

God would be the power behind the armies of Israel when they drove out the Canaanites. He promised to use the 'hornets' and other means to defeat the heathen armies.

God's promises gave the people courage to advance. They would be led by the 'Angel of the LORD,' the one in whom God's name was found. This was Jehovah Christ, the second person of the Godhead: our Lord and Saviour. In him alone is found forgiveness of sins. The Israelites did not have to trust in their own armies, but in their God.

Our salvation is the same. It is the result of the saving work of Christ upon the cross and of his life of perfect obedience to his heavenly Father.

FIND OUT THE FACTS

1. List as many of God's promises as you can think of. Discuss one of them.

2. Here we read of God's angel. Who is this 'Angel'? (Read Exodus 23:21).

3. Why is it that we can always depend upon God's promises?

The Israelites were given warnings about disobedience and strong encouragements to obey God. But God was patient with his people. Thank the Lord for his patience.

God never promises more than he is able to perform.   *Matthew Henry*

Exodus   'I will dwell among the children
30:1-10   of Israel and will be their God'
                (Exodus 29:45).

I'm sure that all of you will have seen some ministers dressed in colourful robes. Following Israel's arrival at Mount Sinai, Moses was told how the people should worship the Lord. The treasures of Egypt were freely put to use, making sure God's plans were carried out.

Exact instructions were given concerning the robes to be worn by the high priest and others involved in worship. Aaron, who was the high priest, wore a turban with the words 'HOLINESS TO THE LORD' engraved on a plate of pure gold.

The place of worship was the Tabernacle and God gave the exact measurements as to how it was to be constructed. He gave gifts to the people who would carry out the work. The citizens freely gave of their wealth to ensure everything was done as God commanded.

The Tabernacle was made of curtains and poles and other objects that could be packed up and carried when the nation moved.

God gave plans for everything that was to be placed in the Tabernacle. These were used in the worship of the Lord and pointed towards that great day when the Lord Jesus would come and save his people, in that one, perfect sacrifice for sin.

There was the bronze altar, the table holding the bread, the lampstand, the altar for incense and the basin to be used for washing.

Within the most Holy Place, 'The Holy of Holies,' was found the ark of the covenant which contained the Ten Commandments that came from the hand of God. The top of the ark was pure gold and had an angel with wings extended at each end. Between the angels God met with his people through the mediation of the high priest, who only once each year entered that sacred place, to sprinkle the mercy seat with blood.

The blood of animals could never remove sin's stain, but it pointed to Christ's sacrificial death on the cross which would wash away his people's transgressions. The Scriptures remind us that 'without [the] shedding of blood there is no remission' of sins (Hebrews 9:22). For ever the saints will sing the praises of their Lord Jesus, who shed his blood that they might live.

Now our Saviour reigns in heaven, seated at the right hand of his Father, giving blessings to his people and interceding on their behalf before God. We have a wonderful Redeemer!

FIND OUT THE FACTS

1. Describe the golden lampstand. Read Exodus 25:31-40.
2. What part of the Tabernacle was the Holy of Holies?
3. The Sabbath was a special day. Why? Read Exodus 20:8-11 and Deuteronomy 5:12-15.

When God gives instructions, he expects them to be obeyed exactly as he has given them. Think about what this means for people today.

A saying to Remember

From Christ's death flow all our hopes.
J. C. Ryle

Leviticus
10:1-11

'Then the glory of the Lᴏʀᴅ appeared to all the people, and fire came out from before the Lᴏʀᴅ and consumed the burnt offering and the fat on the altar. When all the people saw it, they shouted and fell on their faces' (Leviticus 9:23-24).

Today when Christians gather each Sunday for worship, the services are seen to be different. In the church I attend we only sing the psalms and that without any instrumental accompaniment. Most other Christians sing hymns with an organ accompaniment. I read from the New King James Version of the Bible while others use a different version; some people sit for prayer, while others stand for prayer.

We all are brothers and sisters in the Lord and we should tolerate these differences in our worship. We preach the same gospel of a Saviour who lived, died and rose again to save his people.

However, in the days of the Old Testament, worship was to be carried out just as the Lord commanded. Only the Levites could touch the holy vessels, and the priests, who carried out the sacrifices, were Aaron and his descendants. Aaron's sons, Nadab and Abihu would have seen the glory of the Lord at Mount Sinai, and his awful judgement upon Egypt.

The Tabernacle, where the Lord was worshipped and the sacrifices offered to the God of all grace, was constructed to the exact specifications given to Moses. God was to be worshipped according to his law, and not according to the ideas of sinful men and women.

Nadab and Abihu knew God's law and they had, no doubt, been told by their father of God's majestic glory. They would have known what was expected of them by the Lord, yet they dared to disobey. But why did they do this? Possibly the answer is found in the reading, where God gave the command:

'Do not drink wine or intoxicating drink, you, nor your sons with you, when you go into the tabernacle of meeting…' (Leviticus 10:9). Possibly they misused wine, the gift of God (Psalm 104:14-15); maybe they were drunk and did things they would not have done when they were sober. They were also doing the high priest's work. They took incense, which they set alight, not using the coals from the altar (Leviticus 16:11-13). They had violated God's strict law and their punishment was quick and deadly.

Later you will read of a Levite named Uzzah who was also struck down for disobeying the law of the Lord.

We too must worship God as he has prescribed: reading the Scriptures, praying, singing suitable 'psalms and hymns and spiritual songs,' (Ephesians 5:19) preaching, and practising the ordinances of baptism and the Lord's Supper.

FIND OUT THE FACTS

1. What did Jesus mean when he said that we are to worship God 'in spirit and in truth'? (John 4:24).
2. Why are there no animal sacrifices in the Christian church? Read Hebrews 7:24-27; 10:11-18.
3. Why did Aaron wear special garments? Should ministers today wear distinctive clothes? Why?

The judgement of Nadab and Abihu was severe. Think about what this means for people who think that God can be worshipped in any way.

Worship is the declaration by the creature of the greatness of his Creator. Herbert M. Carson

Leviticus
16:6-14

'For I delivered to you ... that which I also received: that Christ died for our sins according to the Scriptures, and that he was buried, and that he rose again the third day according to the Scriptures' (1 Corinthians 15:3-4).

In Israel it was not possible for a Levite to become king as the nation's rulers came from the tribe of Judah. The Lord Jesus holds three offices: Prophet, Priest and King. He is not only God's Priest, but also the Sacrifice to deal with the sins of his people.

In ancient Israel, God established a priesthood, whose various activities were a type of the saving work of our Lord.

God appointed one day in each year when the high priest was to enter the Holy of Holies to make a sacrifice for the sins of the nation. The 9th day of Tishri, the seventh month of the Jewish year, was to become known as 'The Day of Atonement' — Yom Kippur. It was one of the three feasts that all the adult males were to hold in Jerusalem and was followed by the Feast of Tabernacles.

God treats sin seriously and it is sin that has separated sinners from the holy God (Isaiah 59:2). We are told that without the shedding of blood there is no forgiveness (Hebrews 9:22).

The daily sacrifices for sin could not cleanse from sin, but pointed to the saving work of Christ. On the Day of Atonement, the priest dressed himself in his linen clothes and first sacrificed a bullock to cover his sins and that of the priesthood. Then with a censer of hot coals from the altar, he entered the holy place where he threw incense on the coals. The resulting cloud of smoke, covered the ark and the mercy seat.

The high priest sprinkled the bullock's blood both on the mercy seat and before the ark (Leviticus 16:11-15). Then the priest left the holy place.

Two goats were taken and one was sacrificed for the sins of the people. Again the high priest entered the Holy of Holies and sprinkled the goat's blood on the mercy seat.

Then the sacrificial bullock and goat were taken outside the city and burnt. This reminds us that Christ too was taken outside the city wall and crucified.

Then the priest placed his hands upon the living goat, the scapegoat, which was led into the wilderness and set loose, signifying that the nation's sins had been cast away.

All of this points to the Lord Jesus Christ who, by his one sacrifice for sins, has saved his people.

He ascended into heaven in his resurrected body and sits at God's right hand interceding for his people. We now have 'boldness to enter the Holiest by the blood of Jesus' (Hebrews 10:19).

FIND OUT THE FACTS

1. Why was it necessary to have an annual 'Day of Atonement'?
2. Why did the Lord die only once to save his people? Read Hebrews 10:14.
3. What is a 'scapegoat'?

Our meditation today has shown us that blood had to be shed because of sin. Think about what a serious thing it is to commit sin.

Christ's blood is heaven's key.
Thomas Brooks

Numbers   'But he [God] said, "You
12   cannot see my face; for no man
            shall see me, and live"'
            (Exodus 33:20).

I'm sure we can all remember being punished when we disobeyed our parents and our disobedience resulted in punishment! Many years ago, when I was attending primary school,
we were visited by our cousins. They lived hundreds of miles
away and it was always good to see them because it meant
there were more of us to play games.

Catriona enjoyed making mud pies and that led to a mud
pie fight. Dad warned us about throwing mud near the hay
stacks, but we thought we knew better. With two of us up on
the hay stack and two down below, we had a great time throwing mud at one another. But, all the time the hay was being
splattered with mud, making it unsuitable for the cows!

When Dad found out, we were punished for our disobedience and told, 'Keep away from the hay shed!' Sin always has
consequences!

Miriam, Aaron and Moses were brothers and sister. The day
came when Miriam was tired of Moses ruling the nation of
Israel. She criticized him for marrying an Egyptian woman
and claimed that she was just like Moses, a prophetess of God,
who wanted to be involved in making decisions. Moses was
'very humble, more than all men who were on the face of the
earth' (Numbers 12:3).

The Lord, who heard Miriam's complaints, commanded
Moses, Aaron and Miriam to come to the Tabernacle, where he
would speak to them. The Lord appeared in the 'pillar of cloud'
(Numbers 12:5) and commanded Aaron and Miriam to step
forward.

God then said that he spoke to Moses 'face to face' (Numbers 12:8). He also said that Moses was a faithful servant, with

whom he spoke plainly and not in riddles. Aaron and Miriam
should have shown Moses great respect because of his relationship with the Lord. God was angry with Miriam because
of her pride. When the Lord departed in the cloud from the
meeting place, Miriam stood there, a leper.

When Aaron saw what punishment God had inflicted upon
his sister, he begged Moses to pray for healing. However, the
Lord said she was to be put out of the camp for seven days
because of the leprosy. This was a just punishment for rebellion against God's faithful servant Moses. In future Miriam
would do as the Lord commanded! She would obey her brother
Moses. God always punishes sin.

Are you one of those people who loves the Lord Jesus
because he was punished for your 'leprosy', sin? All those he
has healed are welcomed into paradise.

FIND OUT THE FACTS

1. What is pride?
2. What is leprosy?
3. Miriam became a leper. Why?

Aaron and Miriam challenged the Lord.
Think of the many people today who
challenge God in their rebellion. Do
you think God will be patient
with them for ever?

Pride goes before, and shame comes
after. C. H. Spurgeon

Exodus
32:15-29

'And the LORD said to Moses, "Whoever has sinned against me, I will blot him out of my book"' (Exodus 32:33).

People make many excuses for neglecting the worship of God. I heard of a family who wanted to sell their home and prayed that the Lord would give them a quick sale. When there was not a quick sale, they blamed God and gave up attending worship. The house was eventually sold, but they did not return to worship. Of course, this suggests they were like the seed that fell among the thorns (Matthew 13:22).

Four times Moses climbed Mount Sinai where God gave him not only the Ten Commandments, but also the laws of worship and the civil law for Israel.

On the second occasion Joshua accompanied Moses part of the way up Mount Sinai, but Moses continued alone where he heard instructions concerning God's worship. He was again given a copy of the Ten Commandments written on stone.

Moses was with God for forty days, during which time many Israelites thought he had died. However, Joshua remained faithful and patiently waited for him to return.

During Moses' lengthy absence, the people demanded that Aaron make them a 'god' that they could see and worship. Their faith in Jehovah had again diminished!

Aaron sinfully asked the people for whatever gold they had, and moulded it into the shape of a calf. Calling the people together he said, 'This is your god, O Israel, that brought you out of the land of Egypt' (Exodus 32:4). The next day the people sacrificed to this 'god' and made a great feast. All this was a disgraceful sin. Aaron and some of the people knew better!

On the mountain, when the Lord handed Moses the Commandments on a slab of stone he gave the order: 'Go, get down! For your people whom you brought out of the land of Egypt have corrupted themselves' (Exodus 32:7).

Together Moses and Joshua returned to find the nation committing idolatry. In anger Moses threw down the commandments, breaking them in two (Exodus 32:19). Taking the golden calf, he ground it into fine powder, and threw it onto some water, which he made the people drink. How foolish this must have seemed to the Israelites — the people drinking their 'god'! Moses shouted, 'Whoever is on the LORD's side — come to me' (Exodus 32:26). Then, with the sons of Levi, 3,000 of the idolatrous people were killed.

Returning to Mount Sinai, Moses pleaded with God to forgive the people. But God blotted the names of those who had sinned out of his book and he plagued the people because they had made a golden calf.

God punishes all sinners, but to those who truly repent there is forgiveness through faith in the Lord Jesus Christ.

FIND OUT THE FACTS

1. Which Commandment was broken by the Israelites?

2. God always punishes sin? Who will be punished for your sins?

3. Where did Moses finally place the stone upon which the Commandments were written? Read Exodus 25:21.

To Think & to pray about

We see again today that God deals severely with sin. How thankful we should be that he has sent his only Son, the Lord Jesus Christ to bear the punishment for sin.

A saying to Remember

Sin kisses, but kills. C. H. Spurgeon

Numbers   'Your sons shall be shepherds
14:11-25   in the wilderness forty years,
             and bear the brunt of your
             infidelity, until your carcasses
             are consumed in the wilder-
             ness' (Numbers 14:33).

All wise generals send spies into the country they intend invading. In the Second World War the Allied Forces sent men and women into enemy territory to discover where the enemy soldiers were and what plans they had for attack. This was a very dangerous job, resulting in the death of many spies.

Moses was commanded by the Lord to send spies into the land of Canaan to discover what they could about the armies of the nations they were to attack. They were also told to bring back information about the fertility of the land. Twelve men, one from each tribe, were selected for what was a dangerous work.

After surveying the land the spies reported to Moses and Aaron. They said that Canaan was a land flowing 'with milk and honey' (Numbers 13:27). However, when speaking about what they saw there, ten of the spies claimed that the cities were well fortified and many giants, descended from Anak, lived in the region. They claimed that the Israelites were like grasshoppers compared to those men.

Joshua and Caleb gave a different report, recommending that the Israelites invade the land immediately. They urged the people to be faithful to God: 'Only do not rebel against the LORD, nor fear the people of the land, for they are our bread; their protection has departed from them, and the LORD is with us. Do not fear them' (Numbers 14:9).

But the Israelites listened to the ten cowards, even suggesting they should return to the land of slavery: Egypt! Now, in anger, the Lord met with Moses at the 'tabernacle of meeting' and told him he would make a great nation of his descendants in place of sinful Israel: the generation of complainers.

Moses pleaded with God, reminding him of his covenant with Abraham and his descendants. He argued that if the Israelites were disinherited, the heathen people would say, 'The God of Israel could not carry out his promises! He is not a great God at all!'

God replied that he would be faithful to his covenant promises, but all Israelites who had failed to believe in the Lord's power to conquer the enemy would not enter Canaan. They would die in the wilderness. Of that generation only two men were not punished: Joshua and Caleb, who had remained faithful to the Lord. One day, led by Joshua, Israel would enter the land of Canaan and see God's promises to Abraham fulfilled.

Christ has also promised the saints a place in paradise. He always keeps his promises and that should give all Christians courage to serve him faithfully.

FIND OUT THE FACTS

1. What made the difference between Joshua and Caleb and the other ten spies?
2. What is meant by the phrase 'milk and honey'?
3. Read Numbers 14:18. What are we taught in this passage of Scripture?

Unbelief has serious consequences. It will send people to hell. Ask the Lord to help you to trust him with all your heart.

A coward is one who in perilous emergency thinks with his legs.
Ambrose Bierce

Numbers   'I am the LORD your God, who
16:20-32   brought you out of the land of
             Egypt, to be your God: I am
             the LORD your God' (Numbers
             15:41).

About thirty years ago, I conducted a Bible study in our home. We had about a dozen people attending and all was going well until one member told me that he was not happy with the way I was leading the meetings. Foolishly I told him to take over, as I thought I would see how he got on. Within several weeks, the others in the group told me that if I didn't take the study they wouldn't come.

So I had to tell the misguided person in a gracious way that his time of leading the study had ended.

Moses faced a similar problem. His cousin, Korah, who was a descendant of Levi, with Dathan, Abiram, On, and supported by 250 men, came to him complaining that as everyone in the congregation was holy, others should be involved in the government of the nation! By this they meant themselves. (Numbers 16:3).

Korah and his supporters were not happy with their God appointed Levitical role; they wanted to be priests also!

Dathan, Abiram and their followers complained that they should have a priestly role in worship.

Moses challenged Korah and his supporters to meet him at the Tabernacle, where God would show his choice of leader. The 250, who were aspiring to be priests, were to come to the Tabernacle with censers burning incense.

Moses told the Israelites that God would prove who his appointed ruler was. If no judgement fell from heaven upon the rebels, then Moses was indeed a false leader.

At the appointed time the Lord acted: 'So they and all those with them went down alive into the pit; the earth closed over them, and they perished from among the assembly... And a fire came out from the LORD and consumed the two hundred and fifty men who were offering incense' (Numbers 16:33,35).

These men were not just proud people wanting a place of leadership in civil and religious matters, they were men who had rejected the Lord and his chosen leader for the nation.

God commanded Moses to have the censers hammered into plates for a covering of the altar of sacrifice.

It wasn't long before other Israelites accused Moses of killing their brethren. The Lord again appeared at the Tabernacle and in anger told Moses that the complaining Israelites would be destroyed by a plague.

Moses told Aaron to take his censer with incense and make 'atonement for the people' (Numbers 16:47). When he stood between the dead and the living, the plague stopped.

Over fourteen thousand people died, again proving that God does not tolerate sin in his people!

FIND OUT THE FACTS

1. What was Korah's sin?
2. Who should have offered incense to the Lord? Read Numbers 16:40.
3. What is God's attitude towards sinners?

People often think that they deserve more and should have a better deal in life. Think about how God responded to the discontent of Korah and his followers. Ask the Lord to keep you **from** a complaining spirit.

Discontent is the daughter of pride.
Augustus M. Toplady

Numbers 20:1-13

'Why have you brought up the assembly of the LORD into this wilderness, that we and our animals should die here?' (Numbers 20:4).

In the verse above, the children of Israel were complaining against Moses because they were without water in Kadesh. They forgot that the God who had overthrown the might of Egypt could easily provide his people with water. They complained that there was no variety of foods in the area. Where were the grain, figs, vines or pomegranates that Moses had spoken about?

The people didn't pray for water, but again blamed Moses for their situation.

Sometimes we are like the Israelites. We don't obey our parents. I remember a young boy who was told not to use the motor mower to cut the grass, unless his father was with him. He disobeyed and when the mower blade struck the concrete path, it broke off and cut his leg. A visit to the hospital followed where surgery removed the blade. It is always wise to obey those in authority.

Moses, who was very angry with the rebellious Israelites, spoke to them, saying, 'Hear now, you rebels! Must we bring water for you out of this rock?' (Numbers 20:10). In anger Moses struck the rock twice with his rod and water gushed out. So the Israelites and their stock had plenty of water to drink.

But Moses had disobeyed God, who had told him to *speak* to the rock. The consequence was that godly Moses was to be chastened by the Lord: he would not be permitted to enter the Promised Land.

Moses was a most humble man, but he did not show it here when he spoke to his people, calling them 'rebels'. His anger contained an arrogance which showed that he held the nation in contempt.

We are all to remember that God's laws are to be obeyed. We are not to add to them, nor take away from them as the Pharisees did in the time of Christ.

Moses' punishment was a warning to the citizens of Israel that they were to obey their covenant God. In the New Testament we read our Saviour's words: 'If you love me, keep my commandments' (John 14:15). Let us show our love for Christ by obeying his law.

Of course, we need to know God's law first before we can obey it! The law of the Lord is found in the pages of the Bible. We should all be conscientious students of the Word.

The righteousness we need to enter heaven comes from the Lord Jesus Christ, and is received by faith alone. Do you have this righteousness?

FIND OUT THE FACTS

1. Did Moses deserve to be punished? See Luke 12:48.
2. How do we show God that we love him?
3. Who are you to obey?
4. How do you think Moses felt when he heard God's punishment?

We can't obey God's law unless we know it. Ask the Lord to help you to read his Word every day.

Sin has the devil for his father, shame for its companion, and death for its wages.   Thomas Watson

Numbers 'And as Moses lifted up the
21:1-9   serpent in the wilderness,
         even so must the Son of Man
         be lifted up, that whoever
         believes in him should not
         perish but have eternal life'
         (John 3:14-15).

Our reading is about God sending the Israelites a plague of serpents. Most people find snakes somewhat frightening — not many children have a pet snake!

Many years ago when I was in hospital, a farmer was admitted as he had been bitten by a poisonous snake at about 6 p.m. The doctor gave him an anti-venom injection which made him violently ill until about 3.00 a.m. Then he hopped out of bed and said, 'I'm going home to milk the cows!'

The matron told him to go back to bed very quickly, took his cigarettes when he put one to his mouth and instructed him to be quiet. Snake bites can be very painful, even deadly!

The king of Arad fought against the Israelites, taking some of them prisoners. The children of Israel promised the Lord that if he fought for them, they would utterly destroy these Canaanite people.

While God gave them the victory, they continued their wilderness wandering. Complaints were made to Moses: 'Why have you brought us up out of Egypt to die in the wilderness? For there is no food and no water, and our soul loathes this worthless bread' (Numbers 21:5).

This complaint was not against Moses but against their covenant God, who punished them by sending 'fiery serpents' that bit the people. In repentance, they asked Moses to pray that the Lord would remove the snakes.

The Lord instructed Moses to make a model of the 'fiery serpent', and fix it to a pole where those bitten could see it. The Lord had promised his people: 'It shall be that everyone who is bitten, when he looks at it, shall live' (Numbers 21:8).

Salvation is ours if we gaze upon the Lord Jesus with saving faith and true repentance. In Isaiah 45:21-22 we read, 'And there is no other God besides me, a just God and a Saviour; there is none besides me. Look to me, and be saved, all you ends of the earth! For I am God, and there is no other.'

Salvation is found in the Lord Jesus Christ, who said, 'And as Moses lifted up the serpent in the wilderness, even so must the Son of Man be lifted up, that whoever believes in him should not perish but have eternal life' (John 3:14-15).

Sinners are to look 'unto Jesus, the author and finisher of [their] faith, who for the joy that was set before him endured the cross, despising the shame, and has sat down at the right hand of the throne of God' (Hebrews 12:2).

Readers, go to Jesus, who alone is the Saviour of sinners.

FIND OUT THE FACTS

1. Why are so many people afraid of snakes?
2. What does our verse teach us?
3. Look at Hebrews 12:2. What is the 'joy' spoken of here?

As we have seen, the Israelites questioned God's dealings with them again and again. Think about what this shows us about human nature.

We are not saved *for* believing, but *by* believing.   *Thomas Taylor*

Numbers   'This day I will begin to put the
21:21-35   dread and fear of you upon the
              nations under the whole
              heaven, who shall hear the
              report of you, and shall trem-
              ble and be in anguish because
              of you' (Deuteronomy 2:25).

Israel had seen the glory of God in his many miracles, and following their punishment they were repentant of their sinful behaviour. They had wandered in the desert for almost forty years, during which time almost every one of the rebellious population, who would not enter Canaan, had died. The nation was close to the River Jordan, the boundary between them and the Canaanite nations. Soon they would cross over and commence their conquest of the Promised Land.

Before my brother John and I went to secondary school, our mother read us *The Pilgrim's Progress*. Each night after our prayers, we went to bed and looked forward to hearing John Bunyan's wonderful story. It was at that early age that we understood that John Bunyan had pictured death as being like the River Jordan — the last obstacle to be crossed before God's people were in heaven: the 'Promised Land'.

The time had arrived for the Israelites to advance to the river boundary, but they first had to pass through the kingdoms of Bashan and the Amorites. Moses said they would travel by 'the King's Highway'. They promised to pay for any food or water used by the people, but Sihon, king of the Amorites said, 'No!'

He led his armies out to attack the Israelites, but God fought for his people and the land was captured. Now the children of Israel had gained the first section of the land that flowed with 'milk and honey'.

Og, the king of Bashan, and his forces attacked the Israelites, but again the Lord gave the victory to his covenant people, Israel. He had promised, 'Do not fear him, for I have delivered him into your hand, with all his people and his land; and you shall do to him as you did to Sihon king of the Amorites, who dwelt at Heshbon' (Numbers 21:34).

These people were the 'giants' that had struck fear into the hearts of the ten spies forty years before. King Og had an iron bed, nine cubits long and four cubits wide, because he was a very big man.

These victories encouraged the people. God could overthrow their enemies and soon they would cross the River Jordan to drive out the inhabitants of the Promised Land. Before long Israel would be living in Canaan, serving and praising the Lord for his goodness.

FIND OUT THE FACTS

1. What is a 'cubit?' Work out the size of King Og's bed.
2. At this time, who was Israel's leader?
3. Can any power frustrate God's plans? Why?
4. What is God's warning to those who hurt 'the apple of his eye'? See Zechariah 2:8-9.

What a wonderful God the God of the Bible is! He remained faithful to his covenant with Abraham and gave his people the Promised Land. Thank God for his faithfulness to his word.

The gates of hell could no more prevail against the Old Testament people of God than they ever will against the New Testament church. *Gordon J. Keddie*

Numbers   'And God said to Balaam, "You
22:22-35   shall not go with them; you
              shall not curse the people, for
              they are blessed"' (Numbers
              22:12).

Israel had reached the River Jordan and the Canaanite kings
knew that they would soon be fighting the army that had
overthrown Og and Sihon.

Because Balak, the king of the Moabites, realized that his
armies would soon be facing defeat, he called for Balaam to
curse his enemy. Maybe then Israel could be defeated! Balak
sent messengers to Balaam, a well-known 'prophet' from Mesopotamia.

After receiving his fee, Balaam was asked to return to Moab
and curse the Israelites. During the night the Lord said to
Balaam, 'You shall not go with them; you shall not curse the
people, for they are blessed' (Numbers 22:12).

After giving Balak the news, the messengers were told to
return and plead with Balaam to come and curse Israel. Balaam
told them, 'Though Balak were to give me his house full of
silver and gold, I could not go beyond the word of the LORD my
God, to do less or more' (Numbers 22:18).

During the night the Lord spoke to Balaam, giving him
permission to return to Moab with the Moabite nobles. This
was what Balaam wanted to do, but to do so was sin.

Along the track, the donkey became aware of something
strange and walked around what he saw. On the second occasion Balaam's foot was crushed against a wall as the donkey
tried to avoid the unseen angel.

The third time the donkey saw the vision he stopped; he
had nowhere to move. In anger Balaam struck the donkey with
his staff.

The Lord gave the donkey the ability to speak, 'What have I
done to you, that you have struck me these three times?'
(Numbers 22:28).

The Lord then opened Balaam's eyes to see the Angel of the Lord, with a drawn sword, standing on the roadway. In fear Balaam said that he would return home, but the Angel told him to continue, and only to say what the Lord commanded.

Upon meeting Balak the next day, seven altars for sacrifice were prepared as the Lord directed. When the time came for him to curse the Israelites, he spoke only blessings, foretelling the destruction of the people of Canaan. He also prophesied concerning the coming of Christ: 'A Star shall come out of Jacob; a Sceptre shall rise out of Israel' (Numbers 24:17).

After Balaam had blessed God's people, he returned home, leaving Balak to face the armies of Israel and their God.

Today God's people are surrounded by his unseen angels, the 'ministering spirits' who watch over them (Hebrews 1:14).

FIND OUT THE FACTS

1. Can you think of any other time when ungodly people have served God's purposes?
2. How is Romans 8:28 a source of comfort to Christians?
3. Read Proverbs 21:1. What are we taught in this verse?

The Lord truly rules all things, including men and women, boys and girls. Thank the Lord that he is in control of all events.

There is a war going on all the time against God and his people.
Gordon Keddie

Deuteronomy 34

'And the LORD said to Moses, "Take Joshua the son of Nun with you, a man in whom is the Spirit, and lay your hand on him; set him before Eleazar the priest and before all the congregation, and inaugurate him in their sight"' (Numbers 27:18).

As a school principal, I supervised the election of captains and prefects. Every child was given a voting paper listing the names of those senior pupils the teachers believed would be able to carry out the responsibilities of the office. The children usually voted for their friends. But, each year the most suitable person usually became school captain.

Israel was about to enter the Promised Land, but Moses had been told that because of his sin, he would not lead the nation into Canaan (Numbers 20:7-13). Joshua, who had been well trained, would replace him.

Moses had chosen him to lead the Israelite forces against Amalek. God gave the victory to his people, and Joshua had commenced his training for leadership.

Of the twelve spies, it was only Joshua and Caleb who encouraged the nation to advance and take Canaan by force.

Joshua loved the Tabernacle and frequently would have heard God speaking to Moses. He had accompanied Moses part of the way up Mount Sinai, and had patiently awaited his return. Joshua had objected when two of the seventy chosen elders who were not present with Moses at the Tabernacle, received the Spirit-given gift of prophecy. When he complained to Moses, believing it to be a slight upon his authority, Moses replied, 'Oh, that all the LORD's people were prophets and that the LORD would put his Spirit upon them!' (Numbers 11:29).

As Moses' death drew near he wanted to ensure a continuity of leadership, so he prayed, 'Let the LORD, the God of the spirits of all flesh, set a man over the congregation, who may go out before them and go in before them, who may lead them out and bring them in, that the congregation of the LORD may not be like sheep who have no shepherd' (Numbers 27:16-17).

The Lord told Moses, 'Take Joshua the son of Nun with you, a man in whom is the Spirit, and lay your hand on him; set him before Eleazar the priest and before all the congregation, and inaugurate him in their sight. And you shall give some of your authority to him, that all the congregation of the children of Israel may be obedient' (Numbers 27:18-20).

Now they had a leader upon whom the Spirit of God rested. The time for Moses' death was near.

FIND OUT THE FACTS

1. Who was Joshua's father?

2. What does the name 'Joshua' mean?

3. List the ways in which Joshua had been trained to lead Israel.

4. What happened to Moses' body after his death?

The Lord raises up leaders who will teach and lead his people. Thank the Lord for those in your congregation who teach you the Word of God and who lead you in his ways.

Precious in the sight of the LORD is the death of his saints.
Psalm 116:15

Deuteronomy 18:15-22

'And they asked him, "What then? Are you Elijah?" He said, "I am not." "Are you the Prophet?" And he answered, "No"' (John 1:21).

God's prophets called the people to repentance and faith, and frequently foretold events that would one day take place. But Israel was led astray by false prophets.

Things are no different today. Often when I turn on the TV, a 'prophet', using the name of Christ, tells me that I should not have to suffer pain or shortages of money. They usually ask for a gift of money to support their ministry and hint that the gift will result in prayers being answered.

We must beware of the Jehovah Witnesses who have not only proved their falsehood by their consistent failure to predict accurately the date of the Lord's return, but who also teach that the Lord Jesus Christ is not Jehovah, but a created 'god'; an exalted angel! They also deny the existence of hell, where lost sinners will be eternally punished for their sins. Their hell is annihilation, which means that when we die, we shall just cease to exist. Beware of people who peddle lies!

In Israel, before the coming of the Lord Jesus, a false prophet was put to death by stoning. If his prophecy did not come to pass, that prophet was to die.

The Israelites believed that Moses was their greatest prophet. But Jehovah revealed that one day a prophet would come who was greater than Moses: 'The LORD your God will raise up for you a Prophet like me from your midst, from your brethren. Him you shall hear' (Deuteronomy 18:15).

The citizens of Israel longed for the coming of that great prophet, the one who would be greater than Moses and who would speak God's words.

When Jesus, who was thirty years of age, suddenly appeared and preached the good news of the kingdom of God, people wanted to know who he was.

John, who had baptized Christ and had heard the voice of God speaking, knew that the long-awaited Christ had come. The leaders of the church asked John, 'Are you Elijah?' (John 1:21). They thought that he was the fulfilment of Malachi's prophecy: 'Behold, I will send you Elijah the prophet before the coming of the great and dreadful day of the Lord' (Malachi 4:5).

When he denied the charge they asked, 'Are you the Prophet?' Again John could honestly say, 'No, I am not.' He saw himself as the one who prepared the way of the Lord.

The prophet spoken of by Moses was the Lord Jesus Christ. John had baptized the 'Prophet' and declared that he was 'the Lamb of God who takes away the sin of the world!' (John 1:29).

The writer to the Hebrews said that God spoke in various ways to Israel of old, but 'has in these last days spoken to us by his Son' (Hebrews 1:2). The Lord Jesus was not just the Prophet, but also the Priest and King of his people.

FIND OUT THE FACTS

1. Why was the Lord Jesus called 'the Lion of the tribe of Judah'? (Revelation 5:5).
2. What is a prophet?
3. What was the difference between a false prophet and God's prophet?

God's prophets called the children of Israel to repentance and faith. Thank the Lord that today we have preachers who call us to repentance and faith.

Prophesying is a dangerous business for those who are not inspired. R. L. Dabney

 Deuteronomy
29:1-9

'We will not return to our homes until every one of the children of Israel has received his inheritance' (Numbers 32:18).

Many years ago we moved to a new home. Our belongings were packed in the removal truck and we set out. This reminded me of God's people who packed their belongings and set off for the Promised Land.

God provided everything they needed: food, water and, by a great miracle, prevented their clothing and shoes from wearing out. However, when they sinned by not invading Canaan immediately and continued complaining to Moses, God punished them by making them wander in the desert area for forty years. Forty years were wasted, and all those over twenty years of age at that time didn't set foot in the Promised Land.

When we were ready to leave for our new home, several hundred miles away, we caught the cat and put it in a box on the back seat of the car. Along the way we stopped for a picnic. The children wanted to take the cat out of the car. Despite my warning to hold the cord attached to his collar, Sox escaped. He saw his chance for freedom and ran for the nearest tree. As the girls called out to him, he climbed the tree and sat on a high branch, looking down at them. That was where he sat for over an hour. We wasted a lot of time because of that cat!

The consequence of Israel's disobedience was that they were forbidden to enter the land flowing with milk and honey. However, things were different now. Upon arriving at the River Jordan, they were given victory over the kingdoms of Sihon and Og. God was, as ever, with his people!

The tribes of Reuben, Gad and the half tribe of Manasseh asked to be allowed to occupy the land already captured from Sihon and Og, as it was ideal for the herds of cattle they owned. The armed forces of these tribes then promised to cross the

Jordan with their brothers and fight for the land of Canaan. Only when the other tribes were settled, would they return to their families: 'We will cross over armed before the LORD into the land of Canaan, but the possession of our inheritance shall remain with us on this side of the Jordan' (Numbers 32:32).

The time had come for God to use his people to overthrow the great sinners of Canaan. Now it was time to fulfil God's words to Abraham concerning his descendants: 'But in the fourth generation they shall return here, for the iniquity of the Amorites is not yet complete' (Genesis 15:16). The time for God's punishment of the inhabitants of Canaan had arrived.

Moses was dead and the people looked to Joshua for leadership. The time had come for Israel's wanderings to cease. Soon the nation would be home. Joshua was now to lead God's people into the land that flowed with milk and honey!

FIND OUT THE FACTS

1. What miraculous foods were provided for the Israelites while they were in the desert?

2. In what other way did God care for his people while they were in the wilderness?

3. How have you wasted time? List five good uses of time.

Moses died and Joshua was to assume the leadership of the children of Israel. Thank the Lord that he does not leave his people without a leader and a guide.

A saying to Remember

Time and words can never be recalled.

C. H. Spurgeon

| Joshua | 'The LORD spoke to Joshua the |
| 1:10-18 | son of Nun, Moses' assistant, |

Joshua 1:10-18   'The LORD spoke to Joshua the son of Nun, Moses' assistant, saying, "Moses my servant is dead. Now therefore, arise, go over this Jordan, you and all this people, to the land which I am giving to them — the children of Israel"' (Joshua 1:1-2).

Moses was 120 years old when he died. Before his death the Lord allowed him to view the Promised Land from Mount Nebo. We are also told that the Lord buried his body in the land of Moab (Deuteronomy 34:6).

It is always wise to examine land closely, if you are deciding whether or not you will live there. Once I received an appointment to a school in the western part of New South Wales, Australia. Val and I didn't really want to leave our coastal home or our faithful church, but we decided to visit the school.

It was summertime and after several hundred miles travelling, we came to a land swarming with grasshoppers. When we reached the school, the car was covered with insects and dust. We decided to remain at our coastal school!

Joshua was the leader of the nation of Israel! The time had come to cross the Jordan and enter the Promised Land which had been promised to Abraham and his descendants. Now they would take it by force!

Joshua issued the command, 'Prepare provisions for yourselves, for within three days you will cross over this Jordan, to go in to possess the land which the LORD your God is giving you to possess' (Joshua 1:11).

This was the first time the Israelites gathered food from the land they had taken from King Og and King Sihon. God's words are true: 'The wealth of the sinner is stored up for the righteous.' (Proverbs 13:22).

But between the Israelites and the inhabitants of Canaan was the flooded River Jordan. No one asked Joshua how they were to cross over. Maybe they remembered Moses parting the Red Sea, which allowed the people to pass through on dry land.

The leaders of the Reubenites, the Gadites and the half tribe of Manasseh made this promise to Joshua, 'All that you command us we will do, and wherever you send us we will go. Just as we heeded Moses in all things, so we will heed you' (Joshua 1:16-17). They even said that if anyone did not obey Joshua's commands, that person would be put to death.

We can only try to imagine what the people thought when Joshua gave his command. In the distance they could see the walled city of Jericho which they knew they would defeat because God had promised to fight for them. But how could they cross the River Jordan which was in flood?

These were exciting times for the Israelites.

FIND OUT THE FACTS

1. Why did the Israelites call Canaan 'The Promised Land'?
2. How do we show the Lord Jesus that we love him?
3. For how many years did the manna fall? Read Exodus 16:35.

In the Old Testament God gave to each of his leaders a specific task to perform. Thank the Lord that he gives his people the gifts and abilities they need to serve him. God still calls his people to serve him today.

The evidence of knowing God is obeying God. *Eric Alexander*

Joshua
2:8-21

'And they said to Joshua, "Truly the LORD has delivered all the land into our hands, for indeed all the inhabitants of the country are fainthearted because of us"' (Joshua 2:24).

When I was a member of the Sea Scouts, we played a game that I really enjoyed. We were divided into two groups: one to guard the Scout hall from the enemy, the other to find its way into the hall without being seen and blow out a lighted candle.

This game was played at night. No one was allowed to use a torch, and those guarding the hall had to be outside watching for the 'enemy'. In this situation, if you were caught, you were out of the game.

Joshua did what every good general should do: send out spies to gather valuable information about the enemy. Two men were sent to spy on the city of Jericho. It was the first city to be destroyed before Israel's armies advanced further into the land of Canaan.

Upon reaching the strongly walled city, they quickly entered through the gate, trusting that they had not been seen. Immediately they made their way to the home of Rahab, an immoral woman, who had many men calling to see her. The spies believed she would know a lot about the armies of Canaan.

When the king was told that two young men from Israel were in the city, he commanded that they be brought to him immediately. The soldiers soon made their way to Rahab's home, demanding that she bring them out. However, she hid them and told the soldiers, 'Yes, the men came to me, but I did not know where they were from' (Joshua 2:4). She then said that the men had escaped to the hills.

As soon as the soldiers left, Rahab told the spies that she had heard about their God: 'I know that the LORD has given you the land, that the terror of you has fallen on us, and that all the inhabitants of the land are fainthearted because of you ... for the LORD your God, he is God in heaven above and on earth beneath' (Joshua 2:9,11).

The spies gave her a crimson rope to hang in the window of her house, which was built on the city wall, and promised her the safety of everyone hiding in her home when the city was attacked. As there was safety in Rahab's house, so there is eternal security in Christ Jesus our Lord.

Rahab, the sinner, became an honourable citizen of Israel and an ancestor of our Saviour.

FIND OUT THE FACTS

1. What did Rahab believe about the God of the Israelites?
2. What message did the spies take back to Joshua?
3. What assurance did the spies give to Rahab?

Rahab seemed the most unlikely person to become a believer. This shows us that we should never consider anyone as being too sinful, too different or too bad for the gospel message. God saves all kinds of sinners. Pray for someone who needs the gospel today.

We fear men so much because we fear God so little. *William Gurnall*

March

Do not be
wise in your
own eyes; fear
the LORD and
depart from
evil

Proverbs 3:7

Joshua
3:9-17

'And the Lᴏʀᴅ said to Joshua,
"This day I will begin to exalt
you in the sight of all Israel,
that they may know that, as I
was with Moses, so I will be
with you"' (Joshua 3:7).

When I attended primary school, I crossed a river on a ferry. Together with my friends, we rode bikes and enjoyed playing marbles on the flat ferry floor. Frequently our marbles were thrown overboard. When the river flooded, we stayed at home as it was impossible to cross the river to reach the school. Many years later the council made it easy for people to cross the river: they built a bridge!

When Joshua gave the command to cross over the River Jordan, Israel faced the flood waters. I imagine that many people thought, 'Joshua is asking the impossible! How can we cross the Jordan while it is in flood?'

But the time had come for God to show his people that he was with Joshua, as he had been with Moses. He commanded the priests to carry the ark of the covenant to the edge of the water while the Israelites watched. The priests were accompanied by twelve men, one from each of the tribes, who had an important work to do.

When the feet of the priests carrying the ark touched the water, the Jordan stopped running upstream at a town called Adam, and the dry river bed appeared. Now the people could cross over. Some miles away, the citizens of Jericho must have been terrified by what they saw. The events of that day assured the Israelites that God was with Joshua, their leader.

When everyone had crossed the Jordan, the twelve men, who stood beside the priests, each took a large stone from the river bed and carried it to Gilgal, where an altar was erected, to remind the people of the great miracle that God had performed that day, the tenth day of the first month of the year! The *New King James Version* records that an altar was also erected in the middle of the River Jordan. But it would appear that the *New International Version* is more correct at this point. Just one altar was erected near Gilgal.

Joshua told the people that when their children saw the altar and asked what it meant, they were to tell them of the day when the nation crossed the River Jordan on dry land. In that way they would be taught that their God was the Lord of heaven and earth, and nothing was too great for him to do.

This miracle was similar to the one which God had performed when he parted the Red Sea, allowing the Israelites to escape from the Egyptian army.

As Joshua led the Israelites into the Promised Land, so also will Jesus lead his people into paradise.

FIND OUT THE FACTS

1. Of what event does the date of crossing the River Jordan remind you? Look at Exodus 12 if you don't remember.
2. What is a miracle?
3. Name five miracles performed by the Lord Jesus?

The stones were memorial stones to remind the children of Israel of God's dealings with them. Do you remember God's goodness to you in the past?

Man's faith may fail him some-times, but God's faithfulness never fails him. *William Greenhill*

Joshua
5:1-12

At that time the LORD said to Joshua, 'Make flint knives for yourself, and circumcise the sons of Israel again the second time' (Joshua 5:2).

A t one time or another, most of you have used secret signs that only a few select people have understood. Those signs were important to make you part of the group. Girl guides and boy scouts have a special salute and handshake.

The male members of Israel also had a secret sign cut into their flesh: circumcision. This was the covenant sign that the Lord had given to Abraham.

On the day when they crossed over the River Jordan, the people selected a lamb which was to be killed four days later, on the fourteenth day of Abib. This was the day the Passover would be celebrated. But this great feast could only be celebrated by those who were citizens of Israel. God had commanded Abraham and his descendants to ensure that all male members of the nation were circumcised.

The children born during Israel's forty years of wilderness wandering had not been circumcised, but now the Lord commanded Joshua to circumcise them at once. This does not mean that the males had to be circumcised a second time, but that all those who had been born in the wilderness and who had not been circumcised had to be circumcised.

This meant that for a time Israel's soldiers would be unable to fight. Had the soldiers from Jericho known about this and launched an attack, they may well have been victorious. They had seen the River Jordan stop running in flood time and they knew too what the God of Israel had done to Pharaoh, King Og and King Sihon. Their 'hearts melted' with fear!

Circumcision of the flesh spoke of the new birth, when God would 'circumcise the heart'. Outward circumcision made a person a citizen of the kingdom of Israel, but God's circumcision of the heart makes a person a citizen of the kingdom of heaven.

(Romans 2:28; Galatians 6:15; Colossians 2:10-14.) The apostle Paul wrote, 'He is a Jew who is one inwardly, and circumsision is that of the heart, in the Spirit...' (Romans 2:29). The Lord said to Joshua, 'This day I have rolled away the reproach of Egypt from you' (Joshua 5:9).

The Egyptians were laughing at the Israelites who, for forty years, had wandered about in the desert area. They mocked the Lord, believing him to be a weak 'god', who couldn't give his people a country in which to live.

But now, a nation of free people was in the land of Canaan, and all the mocking ceased! The Israelites could eat the produce of their new country, while the local Canaanites trembled in fear.

FIND OUT THE FACTS

1. Of whom does the Passover lamb speak? Explain your answer? Read 1 Corinthians 5:7.

2. Was Joshua wise to circumcise the males when the soldiers of Jericho were not far away? Why?

3. Who are citizens of heaven? How do you become a member of the kingdom of heaven?

To Think & to pray about

God is absolutely trustworthy. He takes care of every detail of the lives of his people. Think about what this means for your life.

A saying to Remember

The highway of holiness is the only path which leads to heaven. A. W. Pink

Joshua   'Then the Commander of the
5:13 - 6:5   Lord's army said to Joshua,
                "Take your sandal off your
                foot, for the place where you
                stand is holy"' (Joshua 5:15).

When the teacher asked her class, 'Who broke down the walls of Jericho?' one of the youngest boys, who thought the teacher was looking at him, replied with tears in his eyes, 'No, Miss Wood, it wasn't me!'

As Joshua was about to lead his troops to Jericho he met a 'Man' with a sword in his hand, who told him that he was the 'Commander of the Lord's army' (Joshua 5:15). This was the pre-incarnate Lord Jesus Christ, who had walked with Adam in the Garden of Eden. He spoke to Moses from the burning bush and Jacob had wrestled with him.

Now he appeared to Joshua, instructing him how to knock down the walls of the well fortified city. When Joshua told his people what they were to do, many would have been astounded!

'What! The soldiers march around Jericho's walls in silence, followed by the priests carrying the ark of the covenant. And then what?', some citizens would have asked.

Joshua would have replied, 'On the seventh day the seven priests will blow their rams' horns and when you hear the trumpets, you will shout out loudly. Then the city wall will fall down!'

Try to imagine what those standing on the wall of Jericho must have thought. 'This nation led by their great God can only march around the city!' Possibly, after watching the parade of Israelites around the city for several days, they would have shouted out insults at God's people.

On the seventh day, after marching seven times around Jericho, the priests blew their rams' horns and Joshua called out, 'Shout, for the Lord has given you the city!' (Joshua 6:16).

As soon as the people shouted, the walls of Jericho fell down, except where Rahab's home was located. As the fighting raged, the two spies went to her home and rescued all who were with her.

People and animals were all killed and the city was destroyed. The silver, gold and vessels of bronze and iron were removed and placed in the Lord's treasury, as was commanded.

Joshua warned the people that anyone who attempted to rebuild the city of Jericho would see his firstborn die. With the city destroyed, everyone knew that the victory belonged to Jehovah!

God's judgement on Jericho should remind you of a greater judgement when Jesus Christ returns in power and glory.

FIND OUT THE FACTS

1. Israel had commenced a 'jihad'. What is this?
2. Who was 'the Commander of the LORD'S army'?
3. How did the soldiers know where Rahab lived?
4. Who defied God by rebuilding Jericho? Read 1 Kings 16:33-34.

God's ways are always the best, even though they may not seem so to us. Think about the things that God has commanded you to do. Do you obey them?

The humiliating way he [Joshua] and his men walked around the city, only to destroy it with the sound of trumpets, was a lesson that this was God's battle. *Derek Thomas*

Joshua   'So the LORD said to Joshua,
7:16-21   "Get up! Why do you lie thus
              on your face?"' (Joshua 7:10).

Has your home been burgled? Twice so far, burglars have broken into our home, and it is an unpleasant experience. I have come to the conclusion that burying treasure in the ground would be the safest place for it. That is what the pirates did!

Today we read about Achan who sinned by hiding some bars of gold, some silver and some valuable clothes, in a hole in the ground inside his tent.

Having destroyed Jericho and its inhabitants, Joshua sent spies to report all they saw at Ai. When they returned, they said that only two or three thousand soldiers were necessary to destroy the city and its inhabitants. However, when they attacked Ai, the enemy soldiers defeated the Israelites, killing about thirty-six fighting men.

With the elders of Israel on their knees before the Lord, Joshua asked the question, 'Alas, Lord GOD, why have you brought this people over the Jordan at all — to deliver us into the hand of the Amorites, to destroy us?' (Joshua 7:7).

The Lord replied by telling Joshua to get up and find the person responsible — the one who had stolen the Lord's possessions. Joshua was instructed to have the people pass before him in tribes and the Lord would indicate the tribe in which the thief was to be found. This procession was followed by the families of the tribe responsible for the theft. Then the families would pass by in households. Finally the men from the accused household would pass before Joshua and then the guilty one would be identified.

The next day Joshua did as the Lord had commanded. It was Achan who had the Lord's finger pointed at him. He admitted his sin saying, 'When I saw among the spoils a beautiful Babylonian garment, two hundred shekels of silver, and a wedge of gold weighing fifty shekels, I coveted them and took them. And there they are, hidden in the earth in the midst of my tent, with the silver under it' (Joshua 7:21).

Joshua then took Achan, his family and all of his possessions, including the stolen property, and put his family and animals to death by stoning them. After burning all that remained, a great heap of stones was constructed over what was left. The place was called 'The Valley of Achor', which means trouble (Joshua 7:26).

FIND OUT THE FACTS

1. Why do you think Achan's family suffered the same punishment as he did? Find a clue in Joshua 7:21.
2. What reason had Achan for stealing the clothing, silver and gold?
3. Often when trouble strikes we are told to pray. If the boat is leaking and in danger of sinking, what should Christians do? Why?

Achan only confessed his sin when he was found out. God tells us to come to him willingly and confess our sins. He promises to forgive us. Do you do this?

A saying to Remember

Steal eels and they'll turn to snakes.

Anon

Joshua
8:1-8

'Then the LORD said to Joshua, "Stretch out the spear that is in your hand towards Ai, for I will give it into your hand"' (Joshua 8:18).

Our God always cares for his people, and our Saviour has all authority both in heaven and on the earth. Now that Israel had removed the sin from her midst, the Lord promised Joshua victory.

When I attended secondary school, I was a member of the school cadets and attended camps where we made secret plans to defeat the enemy forces in our war games. We were away for several weeks at a time, living in tents and eating the food soldiers ate. We had a lot of fun at those camps!

Often our plans came to nothing, and we suffered defeat. In today's scripture passage we read of the forces of Israel attacking Ai for the second time.

The Lord promised Israel victory over the enemy and told Joshua that everything taken from the city was to be shared among the citizens of the nation. The Lord also told Joshua of his plan to overthrow the city.

The people of Ai would have known about Israel's victory over Jericho. But since the troops had previously driven back the army of Israel, they believed they could do that a second time. This time the Lord told Joshua to tell some soldiers to hide behind the city. When the forces of Ai saw Joshua and those with him walking towards the city gates, they would come out and attack them as they did the first time.

Again the Israelites would turn and run with the enemy soldiers pursuing them, thinking the victory would be theirs a second time. The men hiding behind the city were then to cut off the forces of Ai and quickly run into the city and set it on fire. The signal for the ambush to start was Joshua holding out his spear. He was to do this until the victory had been completely won.

The city was overthrown and burnt to the ground, while all the inhabitants were put to death.

The king of the city was captured and hanged. This is clear teaching that God does not tolerate sin. Sin must be punished!

An altar of stones, not shaped by an iron tool, was built. Then followed the offering of sacrifices to the Lord, whole burnt offerings and peace offerings.

Joshua divided the nation into two groups, one standing in front of Mount Gerizim and the other in front of Mount Ebal as Moses had commanded. (Deuteronomy 11:29; 31:12). Joshua then read the law of God to the people, including the blessings and the curses (Joshua 8:34-35).

FIND OUT THE FACTS

1. Why would a God of love destroy the nations of Canaan? Read Genesis 15:16.

2. Who else had held out his arm in a time of battle?

3. What purpose was there in reading aloud the promises and curses of God?

After the victory at Ai, the children of Israel built an altar and worshipped the Lord. When the Lord gives you the strength to do something, do you praise and thank him?

The reality of God's wrath is as much a part of the biblical message as is God's grace. *Leighton Ford*

A saying to Remember

Joshua
9:3-15

'And that day Joshua made them [the Gibeonites] wood-cutters and water carriers for the congregation and for the altar of the LORD' (Joshua 9:27).

I'm sure that most people enjoy seeing 'magic' shows. Some people are able to perform sleight-of-hand tricks that amaze everyone.

Some time ago I took two of my grandsons, Scott and Joshua, fishing. Scott, the eldest, caught the only fish and young Joshua wished it had been him. To help him out, I took the fish and threw it gently to him. He caught it and went home to tell his mum that he had caught a fish. After receiving all the praise, he owned up.

Today's reading is about the Gibeonites who tricked Joshua into believing they didn't live in Canaan because they wanted to make a peace treaty with the nation of Israel.

The kings of Canaan had agreed to unite and drive the Israelites from their land, but the Gibeonites who had heard of Israel's victories, decided that war would end in their defeat. Their leaders decided that peace with Israel was the wisest move. They knew that following the great victories over Jericho and Ai, the remainder of Canaan would soon be overthrown by Israel's armies.

The decision was made to send some of their people as ambassadors to seek peace with Joshua. They put 'old sacks on their donkeys, old wineskins torn and mended, old and patched sandals on their feet, and old garments on themselves; and all the bread of their provision was dry and mouldy' (Joshua 9:4-5).

Arriving at Gilgal, they told Joshua they had come from a far distant country to make a peace treaty with Israel. They said that they had heard of the might and glory of the Lord, and the victories he had given his people over Egypt, Heshbon and Ashtaroth. Joshua believed what he heard and did not pray to God for guidance.

After making the treaty with the Gibeonites, the discovery was made that they lived in Canaan. In fact, the Israelites reached their cities after three days travel. The Gibeonites explained that they had heard the Lord's promises concerning Israel, and their action was the only way to escape destruction.

Now the decision had to be made by Joshua — what was to be done with the Gibeonites with whom they had sworn by the Lord God to leave in peace? Joshua and his elders could do nothing but remain faithful to their covenant. The decision was finally made that the Gibeonites would serve God's people by getting their wood and water. They would do the same for the priests and Levites as they conducted the altar services in the Tabernacle.

FIND OUT THE FACTS

1. What do you think of the Gibeonites' plan for peace with Israel?
2. God keeps his promises. Do you?
3. Why should we take our cares and hopes to the Lord in prayer?
4. In this story how did Joshua fail God?

The Gibeonites deceived Joshua. Think about the importance of seeking God's guidance when making important decisions.

A saying to Remember

Prayer is the mightiest agent to advance God's work. E. M. Bounds

Joshua
10:6-15

'And the LORD said to Joshua,
"Do not fear them, for I have
delivered them into your hand;
not a man of them shall stand
before you"'(Joshua 10:8).

Hailstones can be very dangerous! In one of my books I wrote about a hailstorm that occurred on our farm. The hailstones were large, and as the fowls ran for cover they were caught in the downpour.

The hailstones knocked some fowls unconscious and killed others. They looked a sorry sight after the storm. They tried to stand up, but many fell over, while others staggered back to their cage. Today we read that God fought for his people with large hailstones, which killed many soldiers.

The five kings of the Amorites met and agreed to fight side by side against Gibeon. They moved to the outskirts of Gibeon and made war against it. When the citizens of Gibeon appealed to Joshua for help, he prepared his forces for battle, the Lord having promised him the victory.

The Israelites marched all night and in the morning the Amorites found themselves about to be attacked. In the battle that followed, many Amorites were killed; the remainder turned and ran for their lives. While fleeing to Beth Horon, the Lord opened the heavens and caused great hailstones to fall, killing more men.

The day was almost over and it would soon be dark, but Joshua knew he needed more time to destroy the Amorites totally. The Lord showed his almighty power by answering Joshua's command, 'Sun, stand still over Gibeon; and Moon, in the Valley of Aijalon.' Instantly the sun and moon remained motionless until Israel had defeated their enemies (Joshua 10:12-13).

Joshua was given the five Amorite kings who had hidden themselves in a cave. Joshua had huge stones rolled against its mouth.

After the slaughter of the Amorites, their kings were brought out of the cave, and Israel's captains placed their feet on the kings' necks, signifying their victory.

The kings were killed and their bodies hanged upon a tree till evening when they were taken down and put inside their prison cave. Large stones were once again placed over the cave's mouth.

Further invasion of Canaan continued. Joshua knew that the Lord would fight for his people, and one by one the Canaanite kings and their people were killed, and their land captured by Israel.

Now Israel could say, 'If God is for us, who can be against us?' (Romans 8:31). This is our God!

FIND OUT THE FACTS

1. Which miracle would you say is God's greatest?

2. Name the five Amorite kings who joined together to fight Israel. Read some other verses following Joshua 10:3.

3. What was the significance of the captains of Israel placing their feet upon the necks of the defeated Amorite kings? Read Joshua 10:24.

People think that they can defy God and win. Thank the Lord that he always has victory over his enemies.

He was the God of Joshua and the victorious Israelites. Nothing is too great for him. *James Boice*

Joshua   'But the LORD said to Joshua,
11:16-20   "Do not be afraid because of
              them, for tomorrow about this
              time I will deliver all of them
              slain before Israel"' (Joshua
              11:6).

With the blessing of God, the Israelites advanced into enemy territory, overthrowing and destroying all that lay before them. With God fighting for his people, Israel had victory after victory.

Success is always good! I played 1st grade football at secondary school and our team did very well. We had many victories until a most important match was to be played against another secondary school.

All was going well until half time, when the girls from the opposition school arrived to clap and cheer their side. Suddenly their team started to play excellent football with the result that we lost the game.

I attended a secondary school for boys and had no understanding of the support that came from an audience of secondary school girls.

Joshua was now to invade other areas of Canaan. The children of Israel knew they fought with the power of God assisting them. According to Joshua 11:6, the Lord promised Joshua victory.

Just knowing that the Lord was supporting Israel gave the soldiers additional courage to fight. Not only had the Lord given him the promise of victory, but Moses had also told Joshua of the triumphs he would have: 'Be strong and of good courage, for you must go with this people to the land which the LORD has sworn to their fathers to give them, and you shall cause them to inherit it. And the LORD, he is the one who goes before you. He will be with you, he will not leave you nor forsake you; do not fear nor be dismayed' (Deuteronomy 31:7-8).

When the fighting ended, Israel's armies were victorious. They had totally destroyed and captured large areas of Canaan, as God had told them to do. All possessions of the defeated forces were taken by the soldiers to be distributed among the children of Israel.

Joshua was now an old man, but there was still much work for him to carry out. The children of Israel now had possession of very large portions of the land the Lord had given them, which meant that the time had arrived for the twelve tribes to settle on land they could call their own.

FIND OUT THE FACTS

1. To which patriarch was the first promise of God given concerning the land of Canaan?
2. Why is it important for God's people to know God's promises?
3. List three precious promises made by God.

God gave grace to the Israelites and strengthened them in times of difficulty. Thank God that he gives his people strength and grace in times of need.

God never promises us an easy time, only a safe arrival. *Anon*

Joshua	'Now therefore, divide this
14:6-15	land as an inheritance to the
	nine tribes and half the tribe
	of Manasseh' (Joshua 13:7).

Chapter 14 of Joshua concludes with the words: 'Then the land had rest from war.'

Our sinful world continues to have wars which result in many deaths and the destruction of property. However, the day always comes when there is peace, and rejoicing can be heard.

I can remember the end of the Second World War. I was nine years old and can still recall the huge bonfires being built in readiness for the celebrations. Early in the morning, just before we went into classes, the announcement came over the radio that Japan had surrendered. Someone rang the school bell until it fell off the bell post. The principal then announced that we could all go home and be ready for the bonfires, fireworks and a time of great rejoicing. Many of us were taken to worship where we gave thanks to God for the victory of the allied forces. That night we all had a great time!

The Lord had given Israel's armies many victories, and even though all the land had not been captured, peace settled over the occupied territory.

Joshua realized it was time to divide the land among the tribes. His friend, Caleb, approached him and made a request for the land of Hebron which Moses had promised him years before when he had returned with the spies. This would be his reward for wholly following the Lord and for standing firm with Joshua, when he argued for an immediate invasion of the Promised Land.

That promise was given forty-five years before (Deuteronomy 1:36); Caleb was eighty-five when he met and spoke to Joshua (Joshua 14:10). Caleb said that if the Lord were with him, his tribe would drive out all the people of Anakim and so have all the land they needed.

Now each tribe received a portion of the land of Canaan to call their own. The covenant promise made to Abraham and his chosen descendants concerning the land of Canaan had almost been fulfilled. All that was needed was for the tribes to occupy their land, and drive out every Canaanite still living in the region.

The land occupied was indeed a land flowing with milk and honey. The Israelites had taken possession of land that was producing crops and with houses ready for occupation. There must have been great celebrations when the tribes took possession of their land and realized that for a time there would be peace. God had now fulfilled some of his promises to the patriarchs!

FIND OUT THE FACTS

1. Where was the Tabernacle assembled? Read Joshua 18:1.

2. Peace between nations is good. How do we find peace with God?

3. Finish the passage: 'Blessed are the peacemakers, for they...' No clues this time!

God blessed the Israelites with an inheritance in the Promised Land. Think of the greater inheritance which Christians have through **the** Lord Jesus Christ.

You never pray with greater power than when you plead the promises of God. *William J. C. White*

Joshua
20:1-6;
21:1-8

'So the LORD gave to Israel all the land of which he had sworn to give to their fathers, and they took possession of it and dwelt in it' (Joshua 21:43).

Have you ever played a game of catchers where a certain spot gives you safety from being caught? I can't remember the name of the game, but one day at school my class was playing that game. I told the children I was to be an observer and was not to be tipped. However, one child ran towards me and suddenly put out his hand and touched me. Without thinking I put out my foot and he fell to the ground. Fortunately it was only a broken wrist!

Joshua had divided the land of Canaan among the tribes, but the Levites were to have special treatment. It was also necessary to have cities of refuge (Numbers 35:6).

The six cities of refuge were selected from the forty-eight Levite cities. These were set aside as places of safety for anyone responsible for the accidental death of another person(see Numbers 35:6-15). Frequently when a family member was killed, an 'avenger of blood' was appointed to find the person responsible and kill him.

In the city of refuge, the elders listened to the evidence and if they decided the killing was accidental, the one responsible was allowed to enter the city and live there until the death of the high priest. Then he could return to his family and property, assured of his safety.

Those cities of refuge remind us of sinners who can also run to a place of refuge: 'The name of the LORD is a strong tower; the righteous run to it and are safe' (Proverbs 18:10).

In Psalm 46:1 we read, 'God is our refuge and strength, a very present help in trouble.' We should know that the Lord Jesus is the one who is our refuge on the Day of Judgement. All who have placed their trust in him will 'not perish but have everlasting life' (John 3:16).

The Levites received special consideration. Their forty-eight cities, chosen by lot, were places in which they were to live. They owned no land, but were permitted to graze their herds upon designated pastureland outside the city precincts (Numbers 35:7). They had the high honour of serving the Lord and his people in the Tabernacle, and later in the Temple.

The Levites, descendants of Aaron, were the priestly family of Israel. Their work pointed to the priestly work of our Saviour, who was both the high priest and the sacrificial offering on the altar of the cross. In the cities where the priests and Levites lived, they instructed the people in matters concerning God. In their work at the Tabernacle, they pointed to Christ's work of redemption.

FIND OUT THE FACTS

1. Who is our refuge on the Day of Judgement? Why?
2. What was a city of refuge?
3. What was the work of the priest?

God provided a way of escape for those who had killed someone without evil intent. Thank God for his justice and his compassion in the way he deals with fallen men and women, boys and girls.

Our salvation is a pure gratuity from God. *Benjamin B. Warfield*

Joshua
22:1-13

'Far be it from us that we should rebel against the Lord, and turn from following the Lord this day, to build an altar for burnt offerings, for grain offerings, or for sacrifices, besides the altar of the Lord our God which is before his tabernacle' (Joshua 22:29).

With peace established, and the tribes given their inheritance, it was time for the tribes of Reuben, Gad and the half tribe of Manasseh to return to their inheritance on the eastern side of the River Jordan. The soldiers gathered up their possessions and spoils of war, and after bidding farewell to their brothers and Joshua, began the long walk home to their families and property.

They carried with them gold, silver, bronze, iron and an enormous amount of clothing. Joshua instructed them to share the spoils of war with those unable to fight in the Lord's army.

Having reached the River Jordan, the decision was made to erect a huge altar to remind everyone who saw it that the tribes of Reuben, Gad and Manasseh were one with their brothers who had settled on the other side of the River Jordan.

When the other tribes heard of this altar being built, they assumed that it would be used for worship and sacrifice, saving the people from making the long walk to Shiloh. The other tribes gathered at Shiloh and prepared for war. However, the decision was made to send Phinehas, the son of Eleazar the priest, and ten rulers to discover why the altar had been erected.

They could well remember how the nation suffered the anger of God because of the sin of a single person, Achan. Now they feared God's wrath if whole tribes rebelled against the Lord. When they reached the offending tribes, they demanded a reason for the building of the altar. These men wanted unity of faith between all the tribes, but not unity at the price of truth. They also made the offer of land from their own inheritance, if the tribes on the eastern side of the River Jordan believed their land was polluted.

The answer was given that the altar was not to be used for offering sacrifices, but to remind everyone who saw it of the unity of the tribes, and that all the tribes had fought as one, to take the land of Canaan.

When Phinehas and his comrades returned with a favourable report, the people rejoiced. There was no more talk about war with the Reubenites, Gadites and the half tribe of Manasseh. The builders of the monument called it 'Witness,' 'for it is a witness between us that the LORD is God' (Joshua 22:34).

The nation was united in their praise of the Lord who had guided them to the Land of Promise. Do you praise the Lord Jesus, and give him thanks for his work of salvation?

FIND OUT THE FACTS

1. What is an altar?
2. Why did the eastern tribes build an altar?
3. In what city was the tabernacle found?
4. Who were the Levities?

Phinehas found out the reason for the building of the altar before a war was started. This was a wise thing to do. Ask God to help you not to judge others before you know the reason for their actions.

A saying to Remember

Labour mightily for a healing spirit.
Thomas Brooks

Joshua 23:1-13

'Behold, this day I am going the way of all the earth. And you know ... that not one thing has failed of all the good things which the Lᴏʀᴅ your God spoke concerning you. All have come to pass for you; not one word of them has failed' (Joshua 23:14).

I'm sure that no one has kept every promise that he or she has made. We promise our children many things, but because of time, an extra work load, missing the train and a host of other reasons, we fail to keep our word.

Children also let us down. Promises are made, yet often they are not carried out. God's promises are so different. He has made many of them: some are very good and others are severe warnings. But, we cannot compare ourselves to God. When he makes a promise he never forgets, and he always has the power to carry it out.

To Abraham, God made a covenant to be his God, and promised his descendants the land of Canaan. He swore that Abraham and Sarah would have a son in their old age. He also promised that their 'seed' would be in number like the stars in the heavens. But a special pledge was made: from their descendants the Redeemer would come, and through him all the nations of the world would be blessed.

We know the one who was the promised 'Seed': The Lord Jesus Christ (Galatians 3:16-17).

Joshua knew that his death was fast approaching, and he wanted to remind the Israelites that God had kept his promises to them. He also wanted them to know that the nation would be punished if they turned away from worshipping their Lord and God.

He told the Israelites that God would drive out the remainder of the Canaanites, giving them all the land of Canaan. But there was a serious warning: 'Therefore be very courageous to keep and to do all that is written in the Book of the Law of Moses ...' (Joshua 23:6). They were not to intermarry with the ungodly nations, or even to mention the names of their gods, let alone bow down and worship them.

Joshua reminded the people that while they were faithful to the Lord, he had given them the victory, which would continue if they walked in the pathways of righteousness.

Our God is a covenant-keeping God who gave his Son to be the Saviour of his people. The apostle Paul spoke the truth when he said to the Philippian jailer, 'Believe on the Lord Jesus Christ, and you will be saved, you and your household' (Acts 16:31).

FIND OUT THE FACTS

1. What did Joshua mean when he said, 'Therefore take careful heed to yourselves, that you love the LORD your God' (Joshua 23:11).
2. How do children show that they love their parents?
3. Joshua told his people to keep away from ungodly people. Why? What does this mean to you?

God keeps his promises. His word never fails. Thank him again today that he is a faithful God.

Death is a mighty leveller.   J. C. Ryle

Joshua   'But as for me and my house,
24:14-28   we will serve the LORD' (Joshua
             24:15).

I don't know if you have ever attended a funeral. Unless the
Lord Jesus returns during your lifetime, you too will die one
day — we shall all die. We don't know when, but we shall one
day face death. The writer to the Hebrews said, And it is
appointed for men to die once, but after this the judgement'
(Hebrews 9:27).

One elderly woman in my congregation gave me letters to
give to her adult children after her death. Her letters told them
how much she loved them, and of her faith in the Lord Jesus.
They concluded with the hope that one day they would be
united in heaven to praise the Lord Jesus for his goodness to
them. Many of God's people have left final words of encouragement for those who remain behind.

There were about twenty years between Chapters 23 and
24. Now was the time of Joshua's death. He didn't spend time
talking about his aches and pains, or his feelings, but took the
opportunity to encourage and warn the leaders of the people.
He traced the promises God had made to Abraham and others
down to the time of his death. This was a call of recommit-
ment to God's covenant. It was his last official duty before he
died.

Again and again he praised God for overthrowing his
enemies, just as God had promised. He called upon the people
to 'fear the LORD, [and to] serve him in sincerity and in truth'
(Joshua 24:14). Then came his confession: 'But as for me and
my house, we will serve the LORD' (Joshua 24:15).

The elders of Israel replied, 'We also will serve the LORD, for
he is our God' (Joshua 24:18).

Then came Joshua's warning: 'If you forsake the LORD and serve foreign gods, then he will turn and do you harm and consume you, after he has done you good' (Joshua 24:20). To that warning they replied, 'No, but we will serve the LORD!' (Joshua 24:21).

Joshua recorded what they said in the 'Book of the Law of God'. A huge stone was set up under an oak tree as a witness to all the promises the Israelites had made.

Joshua, as Joseph did, lived one hundred and ten years. He was buried in his tribal land.

We are told that the Israelites remained faithful to the Lord during the lives of Joshua and the elders, who had promised to serve the Lord.

FIND OUT THE FACTS

1. What is the first death?
2. Why is there death in this world?
3. What oath did Joseph obtain from the children of Israel just before he died? See Genesis 50:24-26.

The children of Israel were being questioned by Joshua as to whether or not they would remain faithful to their God. We too are put in situations where our faithfulness to God is tested. Think about how you would respond in such a situation.

I am almost in eternity. I long to be there ... Lord, now let thy servant depart in peace.   David Brainerd

Judges
2:7-19

'Nevertheless, the LORD raised up judges who delivered them out of the hand of those who plundered them' (Judges 2:16).

It is so easy to forget! Some years ago I drove the car into town to purchase a bag of potatoes. Having bought them, I struggled home only to find the car was not in the garage. I called out to Val, 'Where's the car? Did you move it?' Val replied with a big smile, 'You drove it into town!'

So I began to think. I couldn't remember driving it anywhere and had no idea where I had parked it. Half an hour later the car was safely in our garage. Since then my family reminds me frequently of my memory — or lack of it!

During the days of Moses and Joshua, the children of Israel were given many ways to remind them of the Lord's goodness. The Passover was celebrated each year, and this feast reminded them of God's powerful hand in delivering them from the land of slavery, Egypt. Monuments were erected to remind the people of the miraculous crossing of the River Jordan.

The Israelites had the writings of Moses and Joshua to teach them about God and his works. As we read yesterday, before he died, Joshua told the people that he and his household would serve the Lord. The elders of Israel had also pledged their commitment to the Lord. And even when Joshua warned them of the consequences of turning away from God, they still insisted that they would only serve the Lord.

But a new generation had been born; a generation that forgot the goodness of the Lord. It wasn't long before they had turned their backs upon the God of Abraham, Isaac, Jacob and Joseph, and married people from the ungodly nations whom they were told to destroy. It is interesting to note that in Judges chapter 1 the words 'did not' frequently occur. The children of Israel failed to keep their promises to the Lord and to Joshua. Thus they suffered the anger of the Lord.

Soon the nations under their oversight grew in strength, until they were able to overthrow Israel and force them into slavery.

When they cried to God for help, he gave them a judge, a leader, who would regain their freedom.

We should always remember that each generation needs the gospel, as our God has no grandchildren. It is so important to instruct our children in the Word of God and to pray that they will turn to Christ in repentance and faith.

FIND OUT THE FACTS

1. List three sins of Israel at this time?
2. What was a 'judge'?
3. What is meant by 'God has no grandchildren'?

The problem with the children of Israel was that the next generation did not know their God. Think about the importance of teaching the next generation about God.

God pities weakness, but punishes wickedness. *C. H. Spurgeon*

| Exodus 34:13-17 | 'It came to pass, when Israel was strong, that they put the Canaanites under tribute, but did not completely drive them out' (Judges 1:28). |

What we now study is a very sad part of Israel's history. It is hard to believe the terrible sins committed by God's chosen people. He punished their ungodly behaviour, and when the people repented he sent judges to help them. The judges were really advisors, unlike our judges who are involved in court cases.

It is sad when children grow up and refuse to have anything to do with the God of their parents, the God who is the God and Father of the Lord Jesus. I know a man whose family regularly attended worship, but his wife gradually drifted away. It wasn't long before the children also were absent, playing sport on the Lord's day. Today that man is heartbroken and his children don't really care.

The children of Israel were like that man's family. They knew the law of God and promised to serve the Lord along with their families. They knew of the great miracles their God had performed for them and they also understood that disobedience would lead to punishment.

As we read yesterday a new generation of Israelites was born who had not seen God's miracles, even though they had been told of the way he had fought for them and brought the nation to the Promised Land. They also knew that they were to drive out and overthrow all the ungodly people still living in Canaan. God had promised, 'One man of you shall chase a thousand, for the LORD your God is he who fights for you, as he promised you' (Joshua 23:10).

The people enjoyed peace in the land and even became friendly with the Canaanites, marrying into their families, in spite of God's clear command: '"You shall make no covenant with the inhabitants of this land; you shall tear down their altars." But you have not obeyed my voice. Why have you done this?' (Judges 2:2). We read, 'And they took their daughters to be their wives, and gave their daughters to their sons; and they served their gods' (Judges 3:6).

Because of this disobedience God said, 'They shall be thorns in your side, and their gods shall be a snare to you' (Judges 2:3). Soon the Lord's people were worshipping Baal in all its wickedness.

Israel's problem was that they did not trust God to fulfil his promises to rid the land of the Canaanites. They made little effort to capture all of the good land of Canaan.

Sadly Israel's sin is found in the church today. Many young men and women from Christian families have deserted the God of their parents and are walking carelessly along that broad road leading to eternal death. Is this you?

FIND OUT THE FACTS

1. Who does God say a Christian man or woman should marry?
2. What had God commanded his people to do when they reached the Promised Land?
3. What is the church's responsibility in the world today?

The children of Israel did not fear the Lord as they should have. What does it mean to fear the Lord? Ask him to give you that fear.

Never be yoked to one who refuses the yoke of Christ. *Anon*

Judges   'In those days there was no
17   king in Israel; everyone did
            what was right in his own eyes'
            (Judges 17:6).

I know a man who decided to start his own church. He loved the Lord Jesus, but wanted to see miracles happening, especially the healing of the sick. As the months passed by and there were no miracles, he realized his mistake and became a member of an evangelical church. After studying God's Word, he became a minister of that church.

Today we read of a wicked man, Micah, who had stolen his mother's money: eleven hundred shekels of silver. When the mother cursed the person who had taken it, Micah admitted that he was to blame. His mother then told him that the money had been promised to the Lord, to make an idol. With two hundred shekels a silversmith moulded a fine looking idol which they set up in their home.

They forgot God's commandment: 'You shall have no other gods before me. You shall not make for yourself any carved image...' (Exodus 20:3-4).

Micah had one of his sons act as the family priest. This saved them travelling to Shiloh for the annual feast days. This family did whatever they wanted to do, and thought it pleased God. When a travelling Levite called into their home, Micah and his family were overjoyed. Now they could have a real priest for themselves — a descendant of Levi.

We know that the priests were not only descended from Levi, but were also descended from Aaron, who was a Levite. Micah offered good pay and conditions to the young Levite: ten shekels of silver each year in payment for his duties, a suit of clothes and all the food and comfort he needed.

Then Micah said, 'Now I know that the Lord will be good to me, since I have a Levite as a priest!' (Judges 17:13).

Micah, his mother and his family failed to understand the way of salvation which is faith in the living God. They believed they could please God by having their own way of approach to him. Abraham was a man of faith and he was saved, not by his works, but by faith in the living God.

The same applies to you and me. We are saved by faith in the Lord Jesus, the Son of God, who died on the accursed cross for his people. We read in Ephesians 2:8-9, 'For by grace you have been saved through faith, and that not of yourselves; it is the gift of God, not of works, lest anyone should boast.'

Are you trusting in the Lord Jesus for your salvation? Remember that there is nothing you can do to earn salvation. Salvation is all of God!

FIND OUT THE FACTS

1. What was the work of the Levites and the priests?
2. What happens in society when everyone does what he thinks is right? See Proverbs 16:25.
3. What is a shekel?

Micah committed a serious sin by worshipping an idol. Can you name some of the idols people worship today? Is this as serious a sin today?

An idol in the mind is as offensive to God as an idol of the hand. A. W. Tozer

Judges   'So they set up for themselves
18:14-26   Micah's carved image which he
                made, all the time that the
                house of God was in Shiloh'
                (Judges 18:31).

Today many church leaders have decided to conduct 'worship' in a way that is pleasing to themselves, but not to God. We see women with the title 'Reverend' leading worship. God has not appointed women to occupy the pulpit (1 Corinthians 14:34; 1 Timothy 2:11).

I am sure that some of you will have visited churches where strange things happen. I have seen people falling over and making strange noises. Their worship seemed chaotic! We are to worship God as he directs us.

Micah thought all was well with his Levite priest until he met members of the tribe of Dan, who had sent out five of their men to spy out the countryside and find a tract of good land upon which to settle.

When they arrived at Micah's house, they again met the priest. On their return to their tribe, they told their leaders about the young Levite in Micah's home and of the good land in the region.

Six hundred men of the tribe set out to take the land for a settlement, and they called in to speak to the young priest. When they arrived at Micah's house, the five spies went in and 'took the carved image, the ephod, the household idols, and the moulded image. The priest stood at the entrance of the gate with the six hundred men who were armed with weapons of war' (Judges 18:17).

So Micah gathered some men together and chased the six hundred Danites. When he complained about the theft of his idols and his Levite priest, he was told to be quiet because if the Danite soldiers heard his complaints they would kill him and all who were with him.

Micah then returned home while the Danites went to Laish where they killed the inhabitants and destroyed the city. After rebuilding the homes they called the city, 'Dan'.

They set up their stolen images and commenced a 'worship' completely different to that which God had commanded. Later they appointed their priests from the line of Jonathan, the son of Gershom, who was Moses' son.

It is very sad that men and women who have the Word of God ignore the Lord's commands and please themselves in what they do. We are to be like the Bereans who 'received the word with all readiness, and searched the Scriptures daily to find out whether these things were so' (Acts 17:11).

FIND OUT THE FACTS

1. Micah had no right to complain about the theft of his property. Why?
2. What does the New Testament have to say about worship? Read John 4:23-24.
3. Why should you obey the Word of God?

Our meditation raises the question of how we are to worship God. Think of the things God has told us to do when we worship him.

I am a Bible bigot. I follow it in all things, both great and small.
John Wesley

Judges
3:1-11

'When the children of Israel cried out to the LORD, the LORD raised up a deliverer for the children of Israel, who delivered them: Othniel the son of Kenaz, Caleb's younger brother' (Judges 3:9).

In today's world many nations have significant stores of the most destructive weapons. The world has rarely been at peace, so young men, and sometimes women, are obliged to spend some time being taught the art of warfare. It is almost impossible to calculate how much money is budgeted for buying or developing weapons of war.

The situation was no different from that which existed in the centuries following Israel's deliverance from slavery in Egypt. During the years when Moses and Joshua led Israel, their fighting men were most capable. We know that God gave them the victory, but still the men had to go out with their swords, bows and arrows and other weapons, to defeat the enemy.

During the life of Joshua the tribes of Israel were given their inheritance of land, and for a time lived in peace with their ungodly neighbours. We are told that God created this situation in order to know if the people would obey his commandment to destroy all the wicked people still living in the 'land of milk and honey'. The situation meant that fighting would be necessary to regain their freedom. In this way the Israelites would learn the art of war, which was needed to face their enemies.

However, the Israelites enjoyed living peacefully with the pagan nations. They married into their families and began to worship the Baals and Asherahs. Jehovah was forgotten!

In anger, the Lord allowed Cushan-Rishathaim, the king of Mesopotamia to enslave the Israelites for eight years, during which God's people suffered greatly. They began to cry out to the God of their fathers for help.

God heard the prayers of his people and raised up a 'judge' who would lead them to victory and freedom.

It was Othniel, the son of Kenaz, Caleb's younger brother, Israel's first judge, who organized an army to fight Cushan-Rishathaim. The Spirit of the Lord came upon him and gave him the victory. As a result the Israelites had peace with their neighbours for forty years.

This peace cost many lives! May we remember that our peace with God cost the life of the Lord Jesus, the Son of God.

FIND OUT THE FACTS

1. List three sins of the Israelites following the death of Joshua.

2. Find Mesoptamia in an atlas.

3. What must parents do to make sure their children don't forget the law and gospel of God?

4. In what way did Israel's judges prefigure the work of the Lord Jesus?

The Israelites began to live like the nations around them. It is very easy just to do something because others do it. Think about what it means to be willing to be different from those around you by following God's commands.

A saying to Remember

If there is anything in which earth, more than any other, resembles hell, it is its wars. *Albert Barnes*

Judges
3:15-30

'Then he [Ehud] said to them, "Follow me, for the LORD has delivered your enemies the Moabites into your hand"' (Judges 3:28).

Othniel's victory gave Israel peace for forty years, during which time they forgot their God and again fell into the ways of their ungodly neighbours.

It is strange how God's people frequently forget the Lord when things are going well. When trouble strikes, they turn to God for help. He does not ever desert his people, but often the difficult times are his way of making his people walk closer to him and repent of their sinful ways.

There was a new generation in Israel, who forgot their Lord and Othniel's saving work. Now King Eglon of the Moabites, supported by the Ammonites and Amalekites, captured some of Israel's land, making the people serve him.

Eglon established his headquarters at 'the city of palms' (Judges 3:13), where Jericho had once existed (Deuteronomy 34:3). (Joshua cursed the one who rebuilt Jericho. See Joshua 6:26.) Here Eglon, with ten thousand soldiers, felt very safe.

When Israel prayed to God for help to overthrow their cruel enemy, the Spirit of the Lord came upon Ehud, a left-handed Benjamite. He made himself a sharp doubled-edged dagger, hid it under his clothes, and set out to pay Eglon Israel's tribute money.

Having paid the tribute, he told Eglon that he had a message for him from God. At once Eglon sent his servants out of the room. Ehud walked towards Eglon, took the dagger out of his clothing and plunged it into the King's fat stomach. Leaving the dagger in Eglon's stomach, Ehud escaped, closing and locking the doors behind him. By the time Eglon's servants discovered their dead King, Ehud had made good his escape.

When he reached Seirah he blew the trumpet, which was a signal for Israel's warriors to come to the battle: 'Follow me, for the LORD has delivered your enemies the Moabites into your hand' (Judges 3:28).

In the fighting that followed, Israel slaughtered Eglon's ten thousand fighting men. This time Israel had peace for eighty years. God does not cast off his people for ever.

Jesus Christ, our Redeemer 'Judge', has won peace with God for all his people, a peace that never ends. If you are a stranger to that 'peace' then bow your head and ask God to send his Holy Spirit into your heart. With Christ as your Saviour, you will have perfect peace from the God of peace!

FIND OUT THE FACTS

1. Why did Israel continue to fall into sin?
2. What warning is there for us in this story?
3. Try and find out the meaning of the name 'Ehud'.
4. What did John Trapp mean when he wrote: 'War is the slaughter-house of mankind, and the hell of this present world'?

Disobeying God always brings sorrow of one kind or another. Think about how much sorrow was caused by the disobedience of the children of Israel.

To obey God is perfect liberty.
Seneca

Judges
4:1-10

'Thus let all your enemies perish, O Lord! But let those who love him be like the sun when it comes out in full strength' (Judges 5:31).

In the Western world the majority of people strive to have the best of everything, which is sin (1 John 2:15-17). A visitor from India was amazed with the luxury of our homes and that our cars had 'houses' in which to live. She said they were much more luxurious than most homes in Indian villages.

During Israel's eighty years of peace, her people once again fell into sin, worshipping foreign gods. The reason for peace was that the Canaanites feared an invasion from Egypt and had no time to enslave Israel. However, the Lord again brought hard times on Israel, to punish his people. We read, 'The Lord sold them into the hand of Jabin king of Canaan, who reigned in Hazor' (Judges 4:2). Led by Sisera, Jabin's fighting men with nine hundred iron chariots captured northern Israel.

When the Israelites cried to God for help, the Lord heard them and raised up Deborah. She was both a prophetess and judge in Israel at that critical time. She frequently sat under a palm tree in the mountain areas of Ephraim, giving advice and judgements to any Israelites who needed guidance.

Because of Sisera's cruel treatment of Israel, Deborah called upon Barak to take a force of fighting men and overthrow him. However, Barak refused to do so unless Deborah accompanied him. She agreed to this request and Israel's fighting men set out to the battle, with God's promise that he would give them the victory. Deborah even prophesied that Sisera would be killed by a woman.

When both armies faced each other, Deborah shouted to Barak, 'Up! For this is the day in which the Lord has delivered Sisera into your hand' (Judges 4:14). When Sisera saw that his forces were being defeated, he escaped, asking help from Jael, who was married to a Kenite. The Kenites lived at peace with Jabin, king of Hazor.

Jael covered Sisera with a rug, and after giving him a drink of milk, again covered him. Sisera asked Jael to lie if anyone asked if he was hiding in the area. When all was quiet, Jael took a tent peg and a hammer, and finding Sisera asleep, she hammered the peg through his temple and into the ground. When Barak arrived, he was presented with a dead Sisera.

After the victory, God gave Israel peace once again. Truly Deborah was 'a mother in Israel' (Judges 5:7). The song she and Barak composed would have been frequently sung.

FIND OUT THE FACTS

1. Why wouldn't Barak fight against the enemy? Why did he want Deborah to go with him?

2. Jael was called 'Most blessed among women ...' Name another woman of whom it was said, 'Blessed are you among women!' (Luke 1:28).

3. For what length of time was peace established after this victory? Read Judges 5:31.

When God's people live in comfort and ease, they can begin to forget to live depending on him. Why does God have to use something as drastic as suffering to cause his people to realize their dependence upon him?

Most blessed among women is Jael, the wife of Heber the Kenite. *Judges* 5:24

'And the Angel of the Lᴏʀᴅ appeared to him [Gideon], and said to him, "The Lᴏʀᴅ is with you, you mighty man of valour!"' (Judges 6:12).

It is hard to believe the ease with which the Israelites fell into sin. God had done so many great things for his people, which they quickly forgot.

But we are the same. We easily backslide, forgetting all that the Lord has done for us. We forget that the Lord has commanded his people to sit around the Lord's Table, and by partaking in the bread and wine to remember his sacrificial death for them. May we never forget what our Lord has done for us; the Israelites forgot, and they had seen the mighty works of God!

Gideon was one who was called by God to rescue his people from the Midianites, the Amalekites, and the people from the east. For seven years the Israelites had suffered the theft of their produce by invading armies. The Lord prepared his people for their rescue by sending them a prophet who told them of their disobedience to God's commands.

One day the 'Angel of the Lᴏʀᴅ' appeared to Gideon, commanding him to bring unleavened bread, meat and broth and lay them on a rock. The Angel touched the meat and unleavened bread and they were consumed by flames that came out from the rock.

When the vision disappeared Gideon cried out in fear, '"Alas, O Lord Gᴏᴅ! For I have seen the Angel of the Lᴏʀᴅ face to face." Then the Lᴏʀᴅ said to him, "Peace be with you; do not fear, you shall not die"' (Judges 6:22-23).

The Lord told Gideon to destroy his father's altar of Baal and cut down the wooden image that stood beside it. He was then to build an altar to the Lord on the rock from which the fire had come. The Lord instructed Gideon to sacrifice his father's two bulls, using the wood from the image as fuel for the fire.

Helped by ten friends during the night, Gideon did as the Angel had commanded. In the morning the people of Ophrah saw what had happened. They wanted Joash, Gideon's father, who admitted what his son had done, to kill him. Instead, his father told the assembled people that Baal could speak for himself if he was a 'god'.

Israel's enemy moved its troops forward and camped in the Valley of Jezreel. When the Spirit of the Lord came upon him, Gideon blew the trumpet announcing war. Israel's troops soon gathered ready for the battle. But before he led his men into combat, Gideon wanted God to give some visible proof that Israel's armies would be victorious.

FIND OUT THE FACTS

1. Who is pictured by the judges? Why do you give that answer?
2. Who is 'the Angel of the Lord'?
3. The 'Angel of the Lord' called Gideon a 'man of valour'. Was he?

God revealed himself in a special way to Gideon. Thank the Lord that he is still revealing himself to people today through his Word, the Scriptures.

A saying to Remember

An image lover is a God hater.
Thomas Watson

Judges
7:19-25

'When I blow the trumpet, I
and all who are with me, then
you also blow the trumpets on
every side of the whole camp,
and say, "The sword of the LORD
and of Gideon!"' (Judges 7:18).

Frequently we hear of people making bargains with God, especially when they are about to make important decisions. Think of the man who prays, 'Lord, I shall study for the ministry if someone pays all my expenses.' He fails to examine himself to see if he has the necessary qualifications for such a work. What would he do if someone were to give him the money for his studies?

The 'Angel of the LORD' told Gideon he would overthrow the Midianites, Amalekites and the people from the East. God had promised him victory, but Gideon wanted proof. He tested God by saying he would place a fleece of wool on the threshing floor. In the morning, if it was covered with dew while the ground about it was dry, he would believe God's promise.

In the morning the fleece alone was wet, but Gideon wanted more proof. Putting out another fleece, he asked that in the morning it would be dry and the surrounding area wet. For a second time the Lord did as Gideon asked.

Gideon was then ordered to reduce the size of his army, so that all the honour for the victory would go to God. When all the fearful soldiers departed, Gideon was left with ten thousand men.

The Lord again said that Gideon's army was too large. He commanded the soldiers to go down to a stream and drink. Those men who brought the water in their hand to their mouth, making it possible to keep a lookout for the enemy as they drank, were to remain in the army. This left him with three hundred men and the Lord to fight against the adversary!

As he came near to the enemy camp, Gideon heard two men discussing a dream: a falling loaf of bread had hit a tent which collapsed. The man interpreted this to mean that Gideon would be victorious.

Assured of victory, Gideon divided his soldiers into three groups, each man having a trumpet and a light in a pitcher, as the Lord commanded. When Gideon blew his trumpet, they were to blow their trumpets, smash their pitchers and shout 'The sword of the LORD and of Gideon'.

When the signal was given, the enemy awoke in fright, thinking they were under attack. During the fighting that followed in the confusion and the darkness, they killed their own men.

Then Israel's army became involved in the warfare. The Lord gave his people the victory. This was followed by forty years of peace. From this we learn that God's battles can be won with a few men, as easily as with many.

FIND OUT THE FACTS

1. Israel continually fell into sin. Why?
2. What causes Christians to backslide?
3. How is backsliding overcome?
4. Read Judges 6:11-18. What do we learn about the 'Angel of the LORD'?

Gideon felt timid and weak. But the Lord was with him and gave him the victory. Are there times when you feel timid and weak? Remember that the Lord gives grace to those who depend upon him for strength.

A saying to Remember

Never look back unless you want to go that way. *Anon*

Judges
9:1-15

'But Gideon said to them, "I will
not rule over you, nor shall my
son rule over you; the LORD shall
rule over you"' (Judges 8:23).

Some years ago the first referendum was held to determine
if Australia would become a Republic, with a governor as
head of state, instead of the English monarch. The answer was 'no'.

The people asked Gideon to become their king, but he
refused, saying that the Lord alone was King of Israel. Israel
looked at the surrounding nations who had kings and decided
that they also wanted a monarch. No longer were they content
with the Lord as King.

Gideon refused the position, yet lived like an oriental monarch. He had 688 ounces of gold, seventy sons by his many
wives and set up an ephod — a priestly garment, shoulder
cape or mantle — which was soon treated as an idol. Gideon
had asked for the gold earrings taken in the plunder (Judges
8:24). The gold was probably used to decorate the ephod, making it very valuable.

Gideon's illegitimate son, Abimelech, took advantage of the
situation, and with the help of the Canaanites made his plans.
Assisted by some local rogues, he killed all his half-brothers,
except Jotham, who went into hiding. Then he was crowned
king at Shechem by the Israelites and Canaanites living in that
area.

Jotham prepared a story which he spoke aloud from the top
of Mount Gerizim for everyone to hear. This fable was directed
at Abimelech and told the people they had picked the worst
person to become king of that part of Israel. Gideon had
refused to become king, as had other good men, but not
Abimelech. The fable prophesied that Abimelech would be
killed by his subjects: 'Fire [would] come from the men of
Shechem and from Beth Millo and devour Abimelech!' (Judges
9:20). Within three years, a disillusioned people rebelled
against Abimelech, who lived at Arumah and not at Shechem.

God determined that Abimelech's downfall would begin by a 'soldier of fortune', Gaal, who would win the people's support and cause them to rise up against Abimelech. In the fighting that followed, Abimelech overthrew his enemies, including the citizens of Shechem. Their city was destroyed and ploughed with salt. When many people sought refuge in a tower where Baal was worshipped, Abimelech set it on fire and many people were burnt to death that day.

Abimelech then attempted to kill the people of Thebez, who also took refuge in a tower. When he approached to set the tower on fire, a woman dropped a millstone, hitting him on the head. Mortally wounded he asked his armour-bearer to kill him, so no one could say he died at the hand of a woman.

Abimelech's followers, now leaderless, returned to their homes. Thus the Lord punished Abimelech for killing Gideon's sons, and the people of Shechem for making him their king.

FIND OUT THE FACTS

1. Describe Abimelech's character.
2. What is the character of godly people? Read Galations 5:22-23.
3. Describe Gideon's character.

In his pride Abimelech desired to become king. Why do you think that God hates pride?

Worthless men desire the honours which wise men decline.
Charles Simeon

A saying to Remember

Judges
11:29-40

'So the anger of the Lord was hot against Israel; and he sold them into the hands of the Philistines and into the hands of the people of Ammon' (Judges 10:7).

Following the death of Gideon, God sent two judges to rule the nation. However, following the death of Jair, the nation again worshipped the Baals and Ashtoreths of the Syrians. God then 'sold' Israel into the hands of the Philistines and the Ammonites.

This has happened to many in our age: people have loved the things of the world and God has given them over to their 'god' — greed!

When the Israelites cried to God for help, he advised them to cry out to their new 'gods'. The Israelites prayed for help and returned to the worship of the Lord. Consequently God decided to help his people: 'His soul could no longer endure the misery of Israel' (Judges 10:16).

The Ammonite forces gathered at Gilead, and Israel's troops camped at Mizpah. All Israel needed was a courageous man to lead its forces. Jephthah was such a man. But, because he was illegitimate, he was sent away from his relations and told he had no part in the family's inheritance. But Jephthah was a godly man with a saving faith in his Lord (Hebrews 11:32).

When war broke out between the Ammonites and the Israelites, word was sent to Jephthah: 'Come and be our commander, that we may fight against the people of Ammon' (Judges 11:6).

Before he returned, Jephthah remembered how he had been thrown out of his family and asked, 'If you take me back home to fight against the people of Ammon, and the Lord delivers them to me, shall I be your head?' (Judges 11:9).

As leader of Israel's forces, Jephthah warned the king and people of Ammon that it was the Lord who would decide the right of Israel's occupation of their land. However, Jephthah vowed that if his forces overthrew the Ammonites, he would make a burnt offering of the first thing to come out of his house (Judges 11:30-31).

After Israel's victory, Jephthah returned home to fulfil his vow to the Lord. As he approached his house, his only daughter joyfully ran out to meet him. What was Jephthah to do? He said, 'For I have given my word to the LORD, and I cannot go back on it' (Judges 11:35).

Jephthah's daughter agreed that he must fulfil his promise to the Lord, but she asked for two months to spend with her friends in the mountain regions. She was disappointed that she would die before she married and had children, but she knew a promise to the Lord had to be fulfilled.

We should be very careful of making vows, for they should all be kept!

FIND OUT THE FACTS

1. What does this story teach us about making promises?

2. Should Jephthah have kept his promise?

3. How did the Israelite girls remember Jephthah's daughter? Read Judges 11:39-40.

Jephthah was rejected by his family. But, when they needed him, they sought his help. Is it right only to accept another person when we need them to help us or to do us a favour?

Promises should be given with caution, and kept with care.
C. H. Spurgeon

Numbers
6:1-12

'He told her all his heart, and said to her, "No razor has ever come upon my head, for I have been a Nazirite to God from my mother's womb"' (Judges 16:17).

I can remember when it was fashionable for men to have long hair. I didn't think much of that fashion, especially as my hair was getting thin on top and I knew I'd never be fashionable.

Many people were offended by this fashion; they argued that the Lord said long hair was for women and short hair for men (1 Corinthians 11:14-15). When I opened a commentary which was written by Matthew Henry, I saw a picture of the author, wearing a white wig which had long, long hair. Most people imagine our Saviour to have had long hair. I don't know the reason why this is so!

Samson, a most godly man, is well known for his long hair. Have you ever wondered why he never cut his hair? The reason why he grew his hair and never cut it was because he was a Nazirite.

The Lord had laid down strict laws for those who wanted to separate themselves to serve the Lord, sometimes for a period of time, or for the remainder of their life. Samson was a Nazirite from his birth.

God's laws for those who took a Nazirite vow were:

1. They were not to eat or drink anything made from grapes. This included wine, vinegar, grape juice, grapes or raisins.

2. For the time that the Nazirite vow was to last, their hair was not to be cut.

3. They were not to touch or come near to the body of a dead person, even if it was the body of a very close relative. If the Nazirite accidentally touched a dead body, he was defiled and had to offer sacrifices to God and shave his head (Numbers 6:9-12).

When the time of the Nazirite vow ended, the person was to offer sacrifices to the Lord and shave his head. When the priest had completed the ceremony, the ex-Nazirite was allowed to eat and drink the fruit of the grape once again. When his hair was cut, Samson's Nazirite vow was broken and he became like any other person.

Amos warned of God's judgement upon those people who, by giving the Nazirites wine to drink, caused them to break their vow (Amos 2:11-12).

The Nazirites set themselves apart to serve the Lord in some special way. All who love the Lord Jesus are in some ways Nazirites. They are set apart by God's Holy Spirit to serve the Lord Jesus, all the days of their lives. Is this true of you?

FIND OUT THE FACTS

1. What does Acts 18:18 mean?
2. Why did a person take a Nazirite vow?
3. What laws were the Nazirites to obey?

The vows of the Nazirites show us how serious it is to keep our promises to God. Why does God take this so seriously?

A saying to Remember

Love is the root, obedience is the fruit. *Matthew Henry*

Judges	'So the woman bore a son and
13:15-25	called his name Samson; and
	the child grew, and the LORD
	blessed him' (Judges 13:24).

God has used a variety of ways to reveal his law and plans. In the days of the Old Testament, we often read of the 'Angel of the LORD' appearing and speaking. In today's reading we begin studying Samson, who is well known for his great strength and his love for Delilah.

The children of Israel again fell into sin. When they turned away from the worship of the Lord, the Philistines caused them great hardship. The nation was in need of some form of government which would bring about law and order. They were ready for a king from which the Lord Jesus would come, for he is the King of his people, the one to sit upon the throne of David.

Samson's parents had no child. One day the 'Angel of the LORD' appeared to his mother and announced that she would soon have a baby who would be a Nazirite all of his life. When she told Manoah, her husband, what had happened, he prayed that the 'Angel of the LORD' would appear again and tell them how they should raise this special child.

The 'Angel of the LORD' again appeared to Samson's mother, who quickly brought her husband to stand before the heavenly visitor. When Manoah asked him how they were to look after the promised son, the 'Angel of the LORD' replied by referring to his wife, 'She may not eat anything that comes from the vine, nor may she drink wine or similar drink, nor eat anything unclean. All that I commanded her let her observe' (Judges 13:14).

When Manoah invited the visitor to eat with them, he declined, but suggested that they offer a burnt offering to the Lord. Manoah then asked the 'Angel of the LORD', his name. To this the visitor replied, 'Why do you ask my name, seeing it is wonderful?' (Judges 13:18, compare Isaiah 9:6). This 'Angel of the LORD' was none other than a theophany, a visible manifestation to mankind, of Christ, the only mediator between God and man.

Manoah prepared a young goat and grain to offer to the Lord. When the offering was placed on a rock, a flame of fire shot up, consuming the offering. Then, in awe, they watched the 'Angel of the LORD' ascend in the flame of fire.

When they realized that they had been spoken to by the 'Angel of the LORD', Manoah said, 'We shall surely die, because we have seen God!' (Judges 13:22). But this did not happen and, in the appointed time, Manoah's wife gave birth to a son, whom they named Samson: 'The LORD blessed him. And the Spirit of the LORD began to move upon him at Mahaneh Dan between Zorah and Eshtaol' (Judges 13:24-25).

FIND OUT THE FACTS

1. In what way was Samson's birth unusual?
2. What is a Nazirite? Read several verses in Numbers 6, beginning at verse 1.
3. Where do we find God's Word to us today?

Samson was called from birth to serve the Lord. It is a great privilege to serve the Lord. Think of ways in which you can serve the Lord.

Angels are clothed with God's powers to accomplish his will in the realm of nature.   T. Hewitt

A Saying to Remember

To Think & to pray about

Judges
15:1-17

'And the Spirit of the LORD came mightily upon him, and he tore the lion apart as one would have torn apart a young goat, though he had nothing in his hand' (Judges 14:6).

Samson was a strong man, who faithfully served the Lord. He is mentioned among the 'heroes of the faith' (Hebrews 11:32). He became Israel's judge at a time when the nation was overrun by the Philistines. The Spirit of the Lord came upon him and prepared him for his great work. His parents objected to his marriage to a Philistine girl from Timnah, but Samson did this in order to have a reason for killing Israel's enemies. His marriage 'was of the LORD' (Judges 14:4).

On his way to Timnah, a lion attacked him, but the Spirit strengthened him to tear it apart. When he returned home, he found a hive of bees in the lion's carcass. He ate some of the honey and gave some to his parents without telling them where he had found it.

Later Samson gave a feast for thirty Philistines to whom he posed the riddle: 'Out of the eater came something to eat, and out of the strong came something sweet' (Judges 14:14). He gave the men seven days to explain the riddle, promising them thirty sets of clothing if they succeeded. If they failed, he was to receive thirty garments of linen from them.

His wife was asked by the Philistines to get the answer from her husband, and when he refused she wept, saying that he didn't love her. If he did, he would tell her the answer, she reasoned. Samson gave in and soon her countrymen knew the answer. They proudly told Samson, 'What is sweeter than honey? And what is stronger than a lion?' (Judges 14:18).

Samson was given great strength by the Spirit of the Lord and he killed thirty Philistines and gave their clothes to the men who answered the riddle. Later when he was with his parents, his wife was given to his best man.

When Samson found out, he caught three hundred foxes, tied their tails together around a burning torch, and hunted them into the Philistine crops. When the furious Philistines killed his wife and her father, Samson reacted by killing many Philistines.

Because of Samson, the Philistines prepared to attack Judah. Some representatives went and told Samson what was about to happen. He allowed himself to be bound with ropes and handed over to the enemy. On reaching the Philistine army, he broke free and grabbed a donkey's jawbone with which he killed a thousand of the enemy. Samson had now commenced his God-given task of beginning to destroy the power of the Philistines (Judges 13:5).

FIND OUT THE FACTS

1. Why did Samson marry a Philistine? Read Judges 14:4.
2. 'The Spirit of the LORD came mightily upon him.' (Judges 14:6). What does this mean?
3. What does 'A saying to remember' teach us? Read 2 Corinthians 6:14.

God gave Samson a special task. Today God still gives gifts to his people with which to serve him. Pray for someone you know who is in ministry or who is on the mission field.

Take not a wife from a wicked household. C. H. Spurgeon

A saying to Remember

Judges   'He had judged Israel twenty
16:21-31   years' (Judges 16:31).

O ften we read that Samson failed as a godly judge of Israel.
However, his name is in the list of heroes of the faith
(Hebrews 11:32). For twenty years he faithfully carried out his
God-given work. It was only during his last years that he gave
way to a sinful desire. We must always guard against Satan's
sinful suggestions. Many godly people have ruined their Christian witness because of sin.

The Israelites feared the Philistines, and it was Samson who
began to overthrow them. All the judges who delivered Israel
from their enemies pointed to the greatest deliverer of all: the
Lord Jesus.

For twenty years Samson judged the nation. He served the
Lord well, until he met a harlot living in Gaza and stayed overnight with her. When the Philistines knew of this, they planned
to capture him in the morning. But Samson escaped during
the night, carrying away the city gate and two gateposts.

When Samson fell in love with Delilah, who lived in the
Valley of Sorek, the Philistines instructed her to discover the
reason for his great strength. Delilah began to question him,
'Please tell me where your great strength lies, and with what
you may be bound to afflict you' (Judges 16:6). Samson gave
her many reasons for his strength. Each time Delilah tied his
hands and called out, 'The Philistines are upon you, Samson!'
(Judges 16:9), Samson responded by breaking his bonds.

When Delilah accused him of not really loving her, he told
her that his great strength was because of his Nazirite vow: his
hair had never been cut! If he were shaven, he would be like
other men. During his sleep Delilah had his hair cut off. When
she told him that the Philistines were upon him, he went out
but could not break the ropes that bound him. Samson was

taken prisoner and after he was blinded, was taken to Gaza. Later when the Philistine lords gathered to offer a sacrifice to their god Dagon, the people praised him for defeating Samson.

When the decision was made to bring Samson into the hall to be mocked, no one noticed that his hair had grown. He asked the boy who led him into the great hall to let him stand between the two pillars supporting the roof.

Samson prayed as he pushed the pillars, 'O Lord GOD, remember me, I pray! Strengthen me, I pray, just this once, O God, that I may with one blow take vengeance on the Philistines for my two eyes!' (Judges 16:28). His last words were: 'Let me die with the Philistines!' (Judges 16:30).

In the temple's collapse, Samson killed more Philistines than he had done during his life.

FIND OUT THE FACTS

1. What weakness did Satan find in Samson's character?
2. Where was Samson buried?
3. Samson fell into terrible sin. What do we learn from this?

Delilah pestered Samson until he told her the secret of his strength. This was his downfall. Ask the Lord to give you wisdom to know when to heed the requests of your friends and when not to.

A saying to Remember

Let us be watchful after the victory as before the battle. *Andrew Bonar*

| Ruth | 'But Ruth said, "Entreat me not to leave you ... for wherever you go, I will go ... your people shall be my people, and your God, my God ... The LORD do so to me, and more also, if anything but death parts you and me"' (Ruth 1:16-17). |
| 3:6-18 | |

Many years ago my ancestors left Scotland to travel to Australia, in the hope of finding a better life. Their hopes were fulfilled as were the hopes of thousands of other migrants.

During the time of the judges, Elimelech took his wife Naomi and two sons to Moab because of the famine in Israel. The boys grew up and married local girls. When Naomi's husband and two sons died, she decided to return to Bethlehem. The two daughters-in-law followed her, but Naomi urged them to stay and marry again among their own people.

Orpah took her advice, but Ruth refused. Her words are recorded for us in the verse quoted above.

Upon reaching Bethlehem at the time of the barley harvest, they were welcomed by old friends and relatives. Boaz, a close relative of Naomi's husband, lived there. He was very rich, owning large fields of barley, where the poor people gleaned seed. In Deuteronomy 24:21, God commanded farmers to leave some produce at the edges of the field for the poor to glean (gather). Ruth told Naomi to go to the fields of Boaz for grain. When Boaz saw her he asked, 'Whose young woman is this?' (Ruth 2:5).

When he discovered who Ruth was, he told her to glean in his field. He also told his workers to take care of her. When she asked why she was being treated so kindly, Boaz said that he had heard how she had cared for Naomi. Ruth was invited to eat a meal with the workers and told to glean her seed from among the barley sheaves. Naomi rejoiced when Ruth told her what had happened.

Boaz fell in love with Ruth, but Naomi had a closer living relative than Boaz who had the right to purchase Naomi's land and marry Ruth.

The near relative refused to purchase the land, giving Boaz the opportunity to do so. Having purchased the land, he married Ruth, a Moabitess. It wasn't long before Ruth and Boaz had a baby son. Naomi rejoiced to care for little Obed.

Isn't it wonderful that Ruth, the Moabitess, was an ancestor of our Saviour, the Lord Jesus, just as was Rahab the harlot? Obed was Jessie's father, who was David's father. The Lord Jesus was descended from King David and today rules the universe from his heavenly throne.

FIND OUT THE FACTS

1. What is the meaning of the scripture verse?
2. Was Elimelech right in taking his wife and sons to Moab? Why?
3. What does the quotation by Matthew Henry mean?

Ruth was brought into God's family. Thank the Lord that he is still bringing sinners into his family today.

In the conversion of Ruth the Moabitess, and the bringing of her into the pedigree of the Messiah, we have a type of the calling of the Gentiles in due time into the fellowship of Christ Jesus our Lord. *Matthew Henry*

1 Samuel
1:19-28

'Then she [Hannah] made a vow and said, "O Lᴏʀᴅ of hosts, if you will ... give your maidservant a male child, then I will give him to the Lᴏʀᴅ all the days of his life, and no razor shall come upon his head"' (1 Samuel 1:11).

A couple I know were unable to have children so they made a great effort to adopt a baby. When they eventually told him that he was adopted they said, 'You are so important to us. We love you. We chose you!'

Elkanah had two wives, Peninnah and Hannah, and they lived at Ramah. Peninnah had children, but Hannah was childless. This caused great sadness for Hannah.

Each year Elkanah travelled with his family to Shiloh to worship God and offer sacrifices. He gave his wives and children offerings to present to the Lord, but, it was noticeable that he loved Hannah best of all, because she received twice as much as everyone else.

Each visit to Shiloh saw Hannah going to the tabernacle only to be mocked and provoked by Peninnah because she was childless. Finally, on one of these visits, in great bitterness of soul Hannah prayed to the Lord and pleaded with him to give her a son. She made a vow that if God gave her a son, she would give him back to the Lord to serve him. Eli, the priest, saw her weeping as she prayed and thinking she was drunk said, 'How long will you be drunk? Put your wine away from you!' (1 Samuel 1:14).

When Hannah explained the reason for her tears, Eli said, 'Go in peace, and the God of Israel grant your petition which you have asked of him' (1 Samuel 1:17).

The Lord granted Hannah's prayer and she had a son whom she named 'Samuel' which means 'heard by God'.

The following year, Hannah and little Samuel didn't travel to Shiloh. She had decided to keep him at home until he was weaned. Then she would give him up to serve the Lord.

At last the time came when he was weaned and Hannah presented Samuel to Eli, to work in the tabernacle. That year Elkanah took three bulls to sacrifice to the Lord, as well as an ephah of flour and a skin of wine.

Hannah told Eli, 'For this child I prayed, and the LORD has granted me my petition which I asked of him. Therefore I also have lent him to the LORD; as long as he lives he shall be lent to the LORD' (1 Samuel 1:27-28).

When Elkanah and his family returned home, little Samuel remained behind at Shiloh with Eli.

FIND OUT THE FACTS

1. Name one other woman who had a baby because God performed a great miracle.

2. Read Psalm 127. What does the Psalmist say about children?

3. Discuss this statement: 'Prayer is the thermometer of grace.'

To Think & to pray about

Hannah was serious in her prayer for a son. God answered that prayer. Ask the Lord to help you to be sincere and serious when you pray.

A saying to Remember

If you are too busy to pray then you are too busy.   W. E. Sangster

1 Samuel
3:1-15

'Children, obey your parents in the Lord, for this is right. "Honour your father and mother," which is the first commandment with promise' (Ephesians 6:1-2).

Today most people have a Bible, but rarely if ever, do they open it and read what God has to say. Do you read your Bible? Our Bible is complete and we are not to expect more revelations from God.

Little Samuel served the Lord and was taught God's law by old Eli who had two wicked sons, Hophni and Phinehas. They used their position to steal the best meat from the sacrifices God's people offered. When the person offering the sacrifice objected, they threatened the use of force to get what they wanted.

These priests were only concerned about themselves and not about the worship of the Lord. Eli knew of their sinful ways and pleaded with them to obey God's law, but they took no notice of their father.

Hannah visited Samuel each year and brought him a little robe. Each time Eli thanked Hannah and Elkanah for Samuel, who 'grew in stature, and in favour both with the LORD and men' (1 Samuel 2:26).

Eli was also visited by a prophet who delivered a message from the Lord. He told him that because of his sin of not rebuking his sons but tolerating their wickedness, both would die on the same day, and so there would be no descendants of Eli to fulfil the role of a priest. God would raise up another priest who would serve him faithfully.

One night when everyone was asleep, God called Samuel, who thought it was Eli calling him. He ran to old Eli and said, 'Here I am!' (1 Samuel 3:4). Three times Samuel heard the voice calling him and each time he ran to Eli. Then Eli knew that the

Lord was calling Samuel and told him to answer the next call by saying, 'Speak, Lord, for your servant hears' (1 Samuel 3:9). When Samuel answered the Lord's next call, God told him that Eli's sons would be destroyed, and there was nothing that could be done to reverse God's punishment.

The next morning Eli demanded to be told all that God had said to Samuel. When he revealed what God intended to do, Eli said, 'It is the Lord. Let him do what seems good to him' (1 Samuel 3:18).

Samuel grew in his love for God and his desire to serve him. The Spirit of the Lord was upon him and he grew up to be a prophet and priest of the Lord.

FIND OUT THE FACTS

1. What does today's opening verse teach young people?
2. Why should people read their Bibles?
3. What was the work of the priest in the days of Eli?

Eli failed to discipline his sons and he had to face the consequences. Think about what may happen as a result of your behaviour before you act.

A saying to Remember

Do not do today what will grieve you tomorrow. C. H. Spurgeon

April

My son, keep my words and treasure my commands within you

Proverbs 7:1

1 Samuel   'Then she named the child
4:12-22   Ichabod, saying, "The glory
has departed from Israel!"
because the ark of God had
been captured' (1 Samuel 4:21).

War is terrible. It shows men and women at both their worst and their best. War does not cause more deaths than would ordinarily take place over time. However, they happen earlier and often in horrible circumstances.

The twentieth century saw two world wars and many smaller wars that caused much destruction and heartache.

In 1 Samuel 4, Israel goes out to attack the Philistines. But they were soundly defeated, and lost about four thousand men.

The elders decided they would take the ark of the Lord with them into battle, believing this was sure to give them the victory.

Israel was in such a state of spiritual decline that the ark of the covenant was now being used as a lucky charm. Today many people do just the same, taking their 'lucky' rabbit foot, or their St Christopher medal with them, believing that those items will bring good luck.

With their 'lucky charm' which Hophni and Phinehas took from the tabernacle in Shiloh, the ark of the covenant was taken to Israel's soldiers. When they saw the ark a great cheer went up. The Philistines heard the noise and wondered what was happening. Soon they discovered that Israel's soldiers had the ark of the covenant with them.

Now the Philistines were much afraid, thinking that Israel would defeat them. Their leaders urged the men to be strong and fight bravely, as defeat would mean becoming Israel's slaves.

In the battle, Israel was defeated, losing thirty thousand foot soldiers, including Eli's two sons, Hophni and Phinehas. The ark of the covenant fell into the hands of the Philistines.

A Benjamite soldier ran to Shiloh, where he gave the news of the defeat of Israel's army. He told Eli that his sons were dead and that the Philistines had captured the ark of the covenant. Eli, who had been sitting on a stool, fell over backwards in his distress and died, breaking his neck in the fall. He was ninety-eight years of age and overweight.

The news caused Phinehas' wife to give birth to a son whom she named Ichabod, because 'The glory [had] departed from Israel!' (1 Samuel 4:21).

The Philistines now believed that their god, Dagon, was more powerful than Israel's God. They took the ark of God into their temple and placed it by the idol Dagon.

FIND OUT THE FACTS

1. Why are there wars? Read James 4:1-2.
2. Exodus 15:3 reads, 'The LORD is a man of war; The LORD is his name.' What does this teach us?
3. What was the 'ark of God'?

The Israelites thought by taking the ark into the battle they would gain the victory. They did not ask the Lord if this was the right thing to do. What does this show us about how we should approach the Lord when we need his help?

God made man of the dust of the earth and man makes a god of the dust of the earth.
Thomas Watson

1 Samuel   'So the children of Israel said
5:6-12   to Samuel, "Do not cease to cry
             out to the Lᴏʀᴅ our God for us,
             that he may save us from the
             hand of the Philistines"'
             (1 Samuel 7:8).

Idols are of no value at all. In Singapore I bought a mask of
one of the old 'gods' of the people to use in my children's
talks. Idols are nothing, but Satan uses them to turn people
away from the living God.

When the Philistines placed the ark of God beside Dagon,
their fish god, they went home rejoicing in their victory. They
believed that Dagon had fought for them and proved, once
and for all, that he was more powerful than Jehovah.

In the morning when the people went to his temple, they
found that their 'god' had fallen on his face before the ark of
God. They stood their idol back in its place, and wondered
what had caused it to topple over.

The next day, once again Dagon was on his face before the
ark of God. This time his head and the palms of his hands
were broken off on the temple threshold. Later the Lord
punished the Philistines with a plague of rats which ate their
produce, and the people suffered with 'tumours'. We cannot
be sure what this disease was, but it caused the people much
discomfort and pain.

Instead of turning to the Lord in repentance, the decision
was made to get rid of Israel's ark of the covenant. With the ark
they sent an offering to the Lord of five golden rats and five
golden tumours; one for each of the lords of the Philistines.

The ark of the covenant was placed on a cart to which were
hitched two cows that had never pulled one. The Philistines
were pleased to see the ark disappear.

Reaching Beth Shemesh, the Israelites praised God for the
ark's return. The Levites carried it and put it with the golden
rats and tumours on a stone in Joshua's field.

The local men then made a fire with the wood from the cart, and after slaughtering the two cows, made an offering to the Lord. However, because the men of Beth Shemesh had looked into the ark the Lord killed fifty thousand and seventy of them.

The people of Beth Shemesh sent word to the people of Kirjath Jearim that they had the ark of God and urged them to come and remove it, which they did.

The ark was then placed in the house of Abinadab, and his son, Eleazar, was consecrated a priest, to care for it. The ark remained there for twenty years.

FIND OUT THE FACTS

1. Where should the ark of the covenant have been taken?

2. The people were punished for looking into the ark. What would they have seen in it?

3. What did the Philistines learn about the Lord while they had the ark of God in their possession?

It is clear from the events of this reading that God is not mocked. Think of ways in which people mock God today. Will they get away with it?

We should never tire of the thought of God's power.
Donald Grey Barnhouse

1 Samuel   'But his sons did not walk in his
8:10-19   ways; they turned aside after
            dishonest gain, took bribes,
            and perverted justice'
            (1 Samuel 8:3).

Too often the children of godly people grieve the Lord, the church and their parents. Eli's sons had been ungodly and now the sons of Samuel cared only for themselves.

Samuel was getting old, his sons were a disgrace, and the people wanted a king to rule over them like the surrounding nations. Through Samuel, God warned the people what would happen when the nation was ruled by a man. However, the cry went up, 'No, but we will have a king over us, that we also may be like all the nations, and that our king may judge us and go out before us and fight our battles' (1 Samuel 8:19-20). The people had rejected the Lord as their King and wanted a change.

A Benjamite, whose name was Kish had a son, Saul, who was a tall, good-looking young man. When his father's donkeys were lost, he and a servant were sent to find them. Arriving at the land of Zuph, they decided to visit Samuel, a 'man of God', who could tell them where to find the lost donkeys. But Saul had no gift to give Samuel. His servant suggested that Samuel be given a gift of the money which he carried: a quarter of a shekel of silver (1 Samuel 9:7). To this Saul agreed.

Before meeting Saul, the Lord revealed to Samuel that he was coming, and that he was to be anointed king of Israel, to lead the nation against the Philistines.

When they met, Samuel told Saul that his father's donkeys had been found. He then asked Saul to stay and eat with him that day.

The next day Samuel accompanied Saul to the outskirts of the city where Saul was told to send his servant on ahead. There he told Saul what the Lord had revealed to him and anointed him with oil (1 Samuel 10:1). Samuel also prophesied concerning many things that would happen before Saul reached his home. When he met some prophets, the Spirit of the Lord would come upon Saul and he would also prophesy.

Samuel called the tribes together and, probably by casting lots, chose a king. After choosing the tribe of Benjamin, Saul was chosen from the family of Matri. When Samuel announced that Saul was king, the people shouted, 'Long live the king!' (1 Samuel 10:24).

The Spirit of the Lord came upon Saul, giving him the abilities needed to rule the nation. The majority of the Israelites rejoiced with their king, but others despised him.

FIND OUT THE FACTS

1. Why did the people want an earthly king?

2. Why was the question asked of Saul, 'Is Saul also among the prophets?' (1 Samuel 10:11).

3. Who was Israel's last judge?

Saul was tall and good-looking. He seemed just the right sort of person to be king. But would his appearance necessarily make him a good king? Ask the Lord to help you not just to judge people by their appearance.

To Think & to pray about

God was the true King, while Saul was his earthly vicegerent.
Gordon Keddie

A saying to Remember

1 Samuel 13:1-15

'So Saul said, "Bring a burnt offering and peace offering here to me." And he offered the burnt offering' (1 Samuel 13:9).

There are many churches today who have admitted women to the office of elder and minister, which is contrary to the law of God. (See the qualifications for eldership in 1 Timothy 3:1-7 and Titus 1:7-9).

As we have said, God has appointed a way in which he is to be worshipped. Before Christ's sending of the Holy Spirit on the Day of Pentecost, worship was to be exactly according to God's law. Those involved in conducting worship were the Levites. From the descendants of Levi, it was the offspring of Aaron alone who could carry out priestly duties.

In these last days God has also prescribed what constitutes worship. Even so we find that churches have introduced into worship activities that are unacceptable to God.

As King Saul was of the tribe of Benjamin, he was not involved in the work of the Levites.

War broke out between Saul's army and the Philistines. When the Israelites saw the enemies' thirty thousand chariots, six thousand horsemen and a host of fighting men, they were filled with fear. The Philistines had prevented the Israelites from having any blacksmiths who could make swords or spears. When tools had to be sharpened they were obliged to use the Philistine blacksmiths (1 Samuel 13:19-24).

Saul had been instructed by Samuel to be courageous, to pray for the nation, to remain faithful to the covenant and refrain from war until he arrived seven days later.

When Samuel was late in coming, Saul took it upon himself to offer a burnt offering to the Lord. No sooner had he completed the sacrifice than Samuel arrived.

He asked Saul what he had done. At once Saul knew that he was guilty because he had done the work of a priest. So he began to explain why he had made the sacrifice to the Lord.

When Samuel heard Saul admitting his fear that the Philistines would attack before a sacrifice was offered to the Lord, he replied, 'You have done foolishly. You have not kept the commandment of the LORD your God, which he commanded you. For now the LORD would have established your kingdom over Israel forever. But now your kingdom shall not continue. The Lord has sought for himself a man after his own heart, and the LORD has commanded him to be commander over his people, because you have not kept what the LORD commanded you' (1 Samuel 13:13-14).

The kingdom of Saul would soon come to an end, and Jonathan, his son, would never sit upon Israel's throne because of his father's sin.

FIND OUT THE FACTS

1. From which tribe and family did the priests come?
2. How should we worship God now?
3. What is a church elder?

Saul's fear caused him to offer a burnt offering to the Lord when he should not have done so. Think about what it means to trust the Lord rather than being fearful.

A saying to Remember

Kings should have heads, as well as crowns. C. H. Spurgeon

1 Samuel   'Behold, to obey is better than
15:24-35   sacrifice' (1 Samuel 15:22).

One way Christians show their love to the Lord Jesus is by obedience to his commands. To disobey God's law is to invite his anger. God still punishes sinners but he also chastens his people because he wants them to be holy.

In yesterday's reading King Saul disobeyed God by offering a sacrifice to the Lord which was the task of the priests. The Lord punished Saul by refusing to have his son, Jonathan, sit upon Israel's throne. Jonathan and his armour bearer attacked a Philistine garrison knowing that God could give them the victory with a few men just as easily as with many. Jonathan and his armour bearer were triumphant.

Saul ordered his men into the battle, but said, 'Cursed is the man who eats any food until evening, before I have taken vengeance on my enemies' (1 Samuel 14:24). Jonathan didn't hear his father's command and when he saw some honey dripping, he stretched out his rod and dipped it in the honey. Then he ate it.

When the Philistines retreated, they left behind their valuable possessions, including the animals. The Israelites slaughtered some of the animals which they ate without first draining out the blood. This was sin! King Saul instructed the people to bring their animals to him where they would be slaughtered and drained of blood before being cooked and eaten. It was there in Aijalon that Saul built his first altar.

Saul wanted Jonathan to be put to death but the Israelites refused to obey Saul's command and Jonathan lived.

Saul fought against the Philistines, the people of Moab, Ammon, Edom and the kings of Zobah. In this way he established his kingdom. Samuel had told him to destroy the Amalekites and their possessions totally.

In the battle, the Amalekites were utterly overthrown. But, King Agag and the livestock were taken alive. This was sin as God's command was clear: 'Go, and utterly destroy the sinners, the Amalekites, and fight against them until they are consumed' (1 Samuel 15:18).

Samuel then announced the Lord's sentence on the king, 'Because you have rejected the word of the LORD, he also has rejected you from being king' (1 Samuel 15:23).

Saul, when pleading with Samuel to mediate with the Lord for forgiveness, grabbed his robe and tore it. Samuel replied, saying that just as his robe had been torn, so also the kingdom would be torn from Saul.

Taking a sword, Samuel then killed King Agag. From that day onwards Samuel and Saul did not meet.

FIND OUT THE FACTS

1. 'To obey is better than sacrifice' (1 Samuel 15:22). What does this mean?
2. Why was Saul attempting to destroy the ungodly nations living in Canaan?
3. In what ways did Saul sin against God?

The kingdom was taken away from Saul and his descendants because of disobedience to God's commands. Think again today of the seriousness of disobeying God's Word.

A saying to Remember

Obedience should be a child's first lesson. *C. H. Spurgeon*

1 Samuel
16:1-13

'Then Samuel took the horn of oil and anointed him in the midst of his brothers; and the Spirit of the LORD came upon David from that day forward' (1 Samuel 16:13).

It is always a time of celebration when a new monarch takes his or her place upon the throne. As I mentioned in a previous devotion, Queen Elizabeth II is Australia's head of state, but there is a movement to replace her with an Australian President. Our government is elected by the citizens, and before the new parliament sits the members swear upon the Bible, taking an oath of office.

In ancient Israel things were different. God gave his people Saul, who was a failure. This was to teach the people that having a king did not necessarily mean prosperity and peace.

Saul's kingship proved a dismal failure. It was David, the son of Jesse, of the tribe of Judah, whom God chose to be the king of Israel. This kingdom was to find its perfection in Christ's eternal kingdom.

David was an ancestor of the Lord Jesus Christ. Frequently we read of Christ being called 'Son of David' (Matthew 1:1; 9:27; 12:23; Luke 18:39).

Samuel was disappointed when God rejected King Saul. However, the Lord spoke to him, and commanded him to take a horn of oil and an heifer for a sacrifice, and go to Bethlehem, to visit Jesse where it would be revealed who was to be anointed the future king of Israel.

On arriving in Bethlehem, Samuel was met by the elders of the town who asked if he was coming in peace. He answered that he was indeed, and invited Jesse and his sons to be present at his sacrifice to the Lord.

When Samuel saw Jesse's sons he thought the best looking and strongest would surely be king. But, the Lord spoke to him saying, 'Do not look at his appearance or at his physical stature, because I have refused him. For the LORD does not see as man sees; for man looks at the outward appearance, but the LORD looks at the heart' (1 Samuel 16:7).

Jesse's seven sons were presented before Samuel, but the Lord said, 'No' to each one. When Samuel asked if there were any other sons, he was told about David, who was out watching over the sheep. Now David 'was ruddy, with bright eyes, and good looking' (1 Samuel 16:12).

He was called, and when Samuel saw him, the Lord said to him, 'Arise, anoint him; for this is the one!' (1 Samuel 16:12). We are told that the Spirit of the Lord came upon David. Saul's kingship ended in total failure because his heart was never a 'renewed' heart.

Now King Saul was confronted by David whom God had chosen to be Israel's next king.

FIND OUT THE FACTS

1. To what tribe did David belong?
2. What gifts did the Spirit give to David?
3. Why is a government so important? Read Romans 13:1-7.

To Think & to pray about

Samuel was told that God looks at the heart, not the outward appearance. Think about what it means to have a heart pleasing to God.

A saying to Remember

The Bible is the statute book of God's kingdom. *Ezekiel Hopkins*

1 Samuel 17:48-58 'Then David said to the Philistine, "You come to me with a sword, with a spear, and with a javelin. But I come to you in the name of the Lord of hosts, the God of the armies of Israel, whom you have defied"' (1 Samuel 17:45).

As David's three brothers were with Saul fighting against the Philistines, he was told to leave the sheep and take some food to them. When David arrived at the Valley of Elah, he found Israel's forces facing the Philistines. He soon found his brothers, having left the food with the supply keeper.

While talking to them, a giant Philistine stepped forward. Goliath was over three metres tall. His armour weighed about fifty-seven kilograms and the head of his spear weighed about seven kilograms. David asked, 'Who is this uncircumcised Philistine, that he should defy the armies of the living God?' (1 Samuel 17:26).

David was ashamed of his cowardly countrymen, and was told what the king had promised to the man who killed Goliath. King Saul's reward to the person who killed Goliath would be riches, his daughter as a wife and exemption from taxes to the person's father's household.

King Saul had David sent to him. When David volunteered to fight Goliath, he was reminded that he was a youth and couldn't hope to kill this giant of a man. David told Saul that he had killed a lion and a bear when these wild beasts had tried to kill his sheep. He continued, 'The Lord, who delivered me from the paw of the lion and from the paw of the bear, he will deliver me from the hand of this Philistine. And Saul said to David, "Go, and the Lord be with you!"' (1 Samuel 17:37).

David found the king's armour too heavy, so he took it off and set out to fight Goliath carrying his staff and a sling. He picked up five smooth stones from the brook which he put in his pouch.

When Goliath mocked Israel, and David in particular, he replied, 'I come to you in the name of the LORD of hosts, the God of the armies of Israel, whom you have defied' (1 Samuel 17:45).

David assured Goliath that the God of Israel would give him the victory. Taking a stone from his pouch, he put it in his sling and flung it in the direction of the giant. The stone struck Goliath on the forehead, killing him. David ran, stood over the Philistine and taking Goliath's sword, cut off his head.

The Philistine army, seeing their hero dead, turned and ran, only to be pursued by the Israelites, who killed many of them.

After the battle, David walked to Jerusalem, carrying Goliath's head. There he met King Saul. When Saul asked who he was, he replied, 'I am the son of your servant Jesse the Bethlehemite' (1 Samuel 17:58).

FIND OUT THE FACTS

1. What nationality was Goliath?
2. What had Saul promised to the one who killed Goliath?
3. Did David fight in his own strength?

God used a young shepherd boy to kill the great giant of a man, Goliath. God often uses the most unlikely people to do his work. He can use young people **and** children too.

A saying to Remember

Alas! Our heart is our greatest enemy.

C. H. Spurgeon

1 Samuel
18:17-30

'So the women sang as they danced, and said,
"Saul has slain his thousands,
And David his ten thousands"'
(1 Samuel 18:7).

In chapter 16 we are told that 'the Spirit of the LORD departed from Saul, and a distressing spirit from the LORD troubled him' (1 Samuel 16:14).

Because of Saul's deliberate sins against what he knew to be the truth, the Spirit of the Lord, who had given him great leadership abilities, was withdrawn. This made him easy prey for Satan and he behaved in a way that brought shame upon himself and the nation. Israel was to learn that the substitution of an earthly king for their heavenly King would bring much heartache.

The people began to praise David for his exploits and this earned him the jealousy and hatred of Saul who knew that God's Spirit was upon David. However, Saul's son, Jonathan and David became 'soul mates' — friends of the closest kind. Saul had David play the harp when he became depressed, and this helped cheer his heart. But several times Saul grabbed a spear and taking aim, threw it at David, narrowly missing him.

During the times when Saul tried to capture him, David always acted wisely. In anger Saul increased his efforts to catch and kill him.

Saul's daughter Michal loved David. When Saul agreed to their marriage, he set David a task that he hoped would result in his death at the hands of the Philistines (1 Samuel 18:25). David set out with his men to do as Saul had commanded and much to Saul's surprise returned in good health.

Saul commanded his servants and Jonathan to take every opportunity to kill David, but Jonathan spoke well of David, urging his father to have him play soothing music once again.

When war with the Philistines broke out again, Saul became distressed and once more tried to kill David with a spear, to pin him to the wall. David escaped and made his way to Michal who knew that spies had been sent to watch their home. Quietly she lowered her husband down through an open window.

David escaped. But when the soldiers entered Michal's room, they thought he was still in his bed. She had made the bed appear to have David under the covering, even putting goat's hair where his head would have been! When Saul found out that his daughter had tricked him, he was furious.

FIND OUT THE FACTS

1. Why did King Saul hate David?
2. Why was Saul disturbed about the song the women sang as they danced?
3. How should you treat other people?

Even though David served the Lord, his life was not easy. Think about the fact that those who serve the Lord often find themselves in difficulty. Why is this so?

And just as you want men to do to you, you also do to them likewise. *Luke 6:31*

1 Samuel
20:12-23

'But truly, as the LORD lives and as your soul lives, there is but a step between me and death' (1 Samuel 20:3).

I'm sure most of you have heard of someone who has escaped from the police and fled from place to place to avoid capture. After escaping from Saul, David made his way to Jonathan where they discussed Saul's fury towards him. Jonathan believed that his father would tell him of his plans to kill David. He would then tell David.

But, David knew that Saul would not tell Jonathan in case he revealed them to David. His words, 'There is but a step between me and death', were quite true (1 Samuel 20:3).

Together the friends devised a plan to let David know if Saul was planning to kill him. It was agreed that Jonathan would ask his father's intentions and then go to the field with his bow and arrows. If Saul was determined to kill David, Jonathan would shoot three arrows to the place where David had previously hidden from Saul. David was to listen to his command to the servant who was to collect the arrows. If he was told to search beside the spot, it would mean that Saul had no evil intention towards David. However, if the command was to go beyond the spot, it meant that David should escape as Saul was planning his death.

David was not present to eat at Saul's table and when Saul asked Jonathan why, he was told that David had asked permission to go to Bethlehem, where his family were to offer a sacrifice to God.

Saul was furious with Jonathan, calling him, '[the] son of a perverse, rebellious woman!' (1 Samuel 20:30). He told Jonathan that it was David who would prevent him from ever becoming king of Israel. Saul, in anger, threw his spear at Jonathan, who then knew that his father wanted David dead.

Jonathan went out into the field and, as agreed, gave David the sign to escape for his life.

Before David left, Jonathan gave his servant his bow and arrows and ordered him to take them away. When he was out of sight David and Jonathan met. They wept as they kissed each other farewell. Jonathan said, 'Go in peace, since we have both sworn in the name of the LORD, saying, "May the LORD be between you and me, and between your descendants and my descendants, for ever"' (1 Samuel 20:42).

Having said their farewells, they turned and went their separate ways.

FIND OUT THE FACTS

1. Saul hated David. What attitude are we to show to our enemies?
2. What is Christian love? Read 1 Corinthians 13:4-13.
3. What are the two great commandments? Read Matthew 22:36-40.

Jonathan's loyalty to David was proved by his willingness to help David in what was a dangerous situation. Think about what a good friend of sinners the Lord Jesus Christ is in that he has rescued sinners from a very dangerous situation: an eternity in hell.

In friendship there is one soul in two bodies. *Ralph Waldo Emerson*

1 Samuel   'Then Achish said to his serv-
22:9-19   ants, "Look, you see the man
            is insane. Why have you
            brought him to me?"' (1 Samuel
            21:14).

F ear is an emotion no one likes. At times David feared Saul. He spent a long time avoiding Saul and his men. There was indeed but a step between him and death!

When David reached Nob he approached Ahimelech, the priest, saying he was on the king's business and needed food. When Ahimelech said that the only food available was the consecrated bread, David replied that he and his men were 'holy'. The priest then gave them the holy bread to eat. Before leaving, David was given Goliath's sword. Doeg, an Edomite, saw what occurred and later reported it to Saul.

David, who had forgotten God's promise of protection, escaped to King Achish of Gath who was Israel's enemy. David feared the king when it was discovered that the king knew of his great victories. A backslidden, prayerless David failed to depend upon God, and made his own plans to save his life.

David, who pretended to be mad, scratched on the doors of the city gate and dribbled down his beard. He escaped to the cave of Adullam. There he made arrangements for his parents to stay in Moab where they'd find safety. He wrote Psalm 34 as a result of this incident.

When the prophet, Gad, told David to return to Judah, he made his way to the safety of Hereth forest where once again he was trained to occupy Israel's throne.

In the meantime, when Saul was told that the priests of Nob were traitors and had assisted David, he sent for Ahimelech and all his father's house. When he commanded his men to slaughter Ahimelech and all of his relations, he was met with a refusal. Turning to Doeg, the Edomite, he gave the command to kill the priest's family. Doeg killed eighty-five priests that day except for Abiathar, the son of Ahitub, who escaped.

Saul then turned his attention to the city of Nob and killed everyone. David wrote Psalm 52 in remembrance of this event. When Abiathar told David what had happened, David said, 'He who seeks my life seeks your life, but with me you shall be safe' (1 Samuel 22:23).

When news came of the Philistine invasion of Keilah, David was faced with the question: Should he act as king and attack the Philistine army or wait until he was crowned?

This time David prayed for God's guidance. The Lord responded by assuring him of victory, which was all David needed. In the battle that took place subsequently, Keilah was saved and David's men were rewarded with the capture of the Philistine's livestock.

FIND OUT THE FACTS

1. Why did David sin by escaping to Gath?
2. Why would David fear King Achish?
3. What was the 'showbread'? Read 1 Samuel 21:6.
4. What was Jesus' teaching in Luke 6:1-4?

David had to flee for his life. Think about God's people who live in countries today where the government is opposed to their Christian faith. Pray for them.

God will preserve you in your ways, not in your wanderings.
William Jenkyn

1 Samuel
24:1-15

And he said to his men, "The
LORD forbid that I should do
this thing to my master, the
LORD's anointed, to stretch out
my hand against him, seeing he
is the anointed of the LORD"'
(1 Samuel 24:6).

Today many people have no respect for their country's rulers. We are to honour our rulers. We are to 'honour the king' (1 Peter 2:17).

On this occasion David was in a situation where he could have killed King Saul. On his return from warfare against the Philistines, Saul was told that David was hiding in the Wilderness of En Gedi. With three thousand men he set out to find David.

It happened that David and his men were hiding in a cave when King Saul entered the cave to answer the call of nature. David arose and cut off a corner of Saul's robe.

He then felt ashamed that he had done this to Saul, whom God had appointed king of Israel. Once Saul had left the cave, David went outside the cave and shouted out to Saul, saying, I spared you, and I said, 'I will not stretch out my hand against my lord, for he is the LORD's anointed' (1 Samuel 24:10).

David protested against Saul's efforts to kill him, saying that he would not kill his king. When Saul recognized David's voice, he wept and called out, 'You are more righteous than I; for you have rewarded me with good, whereas I have rewarded you with evil' (1 Samuel 24:17). Saul's repentance didn't last. It was just worldly sorrow (2 Corinthians 7:10).

When Saul recognized that David would be the next king of Israel, he asked him to make a promise that he would allow Saul's descendants to live. To this request, David agreed.
Soon after this incident, Samuel died, and the nation mourned his death.

David and his men were in the area of the Wilderness of Paran where he asked a wealthy man, Nabal, for food. He insulted David, and when this was reported to David, he told his men to prepare for battle.

With two hundred men he set off to attack Nabal, but met Abigail, Nabal's wife, riding towards him. She had heard of David's need and her husband's rudeness and had come with food for David and his men. When they met, she bowed before him and pleaded for forgiveness.

David agreed, saying that had she not come, everything that Nabal owned would have been destroyed.

When Abigail told Nabal all that had happened, he was overcome with terror. Ten days later he died. Soon after Nabal's death, Abigail became David's wife.

FIND OUT THE FACTS

1. How should Christians behave towards their rulers?

2. Describe Nabal's character.

3. David made Abigail his wife. Was this a sin?

Think about Abigail. She was wise in the way she acted, by persuading David not to attack Nabal. Think about how you can influence others to choose the way of peace rather than anger and retaliation.

He who fears God has nothing else to fear. *C. H. Spurgeon*

A saying to Remember

1 Samuel   'Then Saul said, "I have sinned.
26:1-12   Return, my son David. For I will
            harm you no more, because my
            life was precious in your eyes
            this day. Indeed I have played
            the fool and erred exceed-
            ingly"' (1 Samuel 26:21).

David was always on the run, keeping away from King Saul and his men. Saul, however, was determined to kill him. He wanted the throne for his son, Jonathan, and David's popularity with the people to end.

This was a time of learning for David, who again and again found he had to rely completely upon God for his safety. He knew that God had assured him that he would sit on Israel's throne, and several times he acted as if he had forgotten God's promises. He did not always live by faith!

When Saul was told where David was hiding, he left for the Wilderness of Ziph with three thousand soldiers. Meanwhile David sent out spies to get an idea of Saul's movements. Soon David and his soldiers were watching Saul and his men. They observed Saul making sleeping arrangements in the middle of his troops, which presented another opportunity for David to kill him and seize the throne immediately.

Abishai agreed to accompany David when he made his way to where Saul lay asleep with his spear stuck in the ground near his head. They crept through the sleeping soldiers in complete safety, 'because a deep sleep from the LORD had fallen on them' (1 Samuel 26:12).

Standing beside the sleeping Saul, Abishai offered to kill him where he lay, but David instructed him not to do such a thing, 'for who can stretch out his hand against the LORD's anointed, and be guiltless?' (1 Samuel 26:9). David then said that Saul's death was in God's hands, but decided to take Saul's spear and the jug of water that were beside him.

David and Abishai made their escape, and when they stood on a hill out of Saul's reach, David called out to Abner, Saul's trusted guardian, 'This thing that you have done is not good. As the LORD lives, you deserve to die, because you have not guarded your master, the LORD's anointed. And now see where the king's spear is, and the jug of water that was by his head' (1 Samuel 26:16).

Saul knew it was David and shouted out that he had sinned against David. Then he asked David to return. Saul couldn't be trusted, but David invited him to send one of his men to collect both the jug and spear.

Both David and Saul went their separate ways.

FIND OUT THE FACTS

1. Why didn't David kill Saul when he had this second opportunity?
2. How was it that David and Abishai were able to take Saul's spear without being caught?
3. Find out something about Abner.

Once again, David did good to his enemy. Think of ways in which you can do good to those who may tease you, bully you or say unkind things about you.

Forgive and forget. When you bury a mad dog, don't leave his tail above the ground.
C. H. Spurgeon

1 Samuel   '...The Lᴏʀᴅ has torn the king-
28:1-19   dom out of your hand and given
             it to your neighbour, David'
             (1 Samuel 28:17).

Soldiers sometimes infiltrate the enemy lines. While pre-tending to be friends, they help destroy the enemy.

David escaped from Saul with six hundred men and found refuge with the Philistine, King Achish of Gath. He hoped that Saul would tire of looking for him and all would be well.

Again David sinned against the Lord by living with Israel's enemies. Frequently he and his men attacked the Canaanites, killing all the men and women and capturing their property for themselves. When King Achish asked where he had been, David lied by reporting that he was attacking Israel. As nobody lived to tell the story the Philistine king thought highly of David. When he asked for some land where he could dwell, he was given Ziklag by King Achish.

While David was living among the Philistines, they commanded their soldiers to attack the Israelites. Saul's men faced their enemy, but he was fearful of what would happen. Samuel was dead and Saul knew that the Spirit of God had left him. When he prayed for guidance from God, he received no answer. He was truly alone.

Because of Saul's fear of the Philistines, he decided to get an answer from a 'medium'. In disguise, he made his way to a 'witch' at En Dor, in spite of the fact that he had tried to expel the 'mediums' and 'spiritists' from Israel. When Saul reached the woman, he asked her to raise Samuel from the grave in order to obtain the information he needed.

What then happened resulted in the 'medium' exclaiming: 'I saw a spirit ascending out of the earth... An old man is coming up, and he is covered with a mantle.' We then read: 'And Saul perceived that it was Samuel, and he stooped with his face to the ground and bowed down. '...I am deeply distressed; for the Philistines make war against me, and God has departed from me and does not answer me anymore, neither by prophets nor by dreams. Therefore I have called you, that you may reveal to me what I should do' (1 Samuel 28:13-15).

To Saul it was revealed that his kingdom would be given to David and that Israel would be delivered into the hands of the Philistines. Finally Saul was told that he and his sons would die the following day.

Meanwhile David found his presence among the Philistines who were ready to attack Saul's forces most unwelcome. He was instructed to remove himself and his army, even though King Achish argued that he could be trusted.

FIND OUT THE FACTS

1. What is a 'medium'?
2. What should you do when someone asks you to take part in a 'seance'? Why?
3. Are fortune tellers able to predict the future? Why do you give your answer?

To Think & to pray about

The time finally came for Saul to die. What a disappointing king he had been! Think about what it means to get to the end of your life and to know that you have faithfully served the Lord. What a blessed way to die!

A saying to Remember

Liars should have good memories.
C. H. Spurgeon

1 Chronicles   'So David inquired of the LORD,
10   saying, "Shall I pursue this
               troop? Shall I overtake
               them?"' (1 Samuel 30:8).

It is not a pleasant thing to arrive home and find that some one has forced his way into your house and stolen some of your possessions. This has happened to my family twice. We were never able to recover what was stolen.

When David returned to Ziklag, having been told that his assistance was not required by the Philistines, he discovered that an Amalekite raiding party had ransacked the city and taken all the women and children away with them.

Before taking any action, David did what he should have done in other difficult times: he sought an answer from the Lord concerning the matter.

The Lord told David to pursue his enemy. Soon they met a lone Egyptian who was near to death, because he had neither eaten food nor drunk water for three days. His master had left him behind because he was ill. He agreed to take David and his men to the spot where the Amalekite raiders were to be found.

In the surprise attack the celebrating Amalekites were all killed, except for four hundred young men who escaped on camels. All the people's property was recovered by David and his soldiers.

David sent gifts to some of the Israelite people saying, 'Here is a present for you from the spoil of the enemies of the LORD' (1 Samuel 30:26).

Meanwhile in the battle being fought by Saul's men and the Philistines, the Israelites turned and ran. Saul's three sons — Jonathan, Abinadab and Malchishua — were killed. Saul, who was seventy years of age, was seriously wounded by an arrow shot by a Philistine archer. He didn't want the Philistines to find him alive and begged his armour bearer to thrust his sword into his body and kill him. When the man refused, Saul committed suicide by falling on his sword. His armour bearer also killed himself.

The Philistine army had a great victory over Israel that day. The following day, when searching for treasure from the fallen Israelites, they found Saul's body. After cutting off his head and taking his armour, they sent word to all their ungodly priests that Saul was dead. His body was exhibited for all to see and his armour placed before their gods.

That night, some brave men from Jabesh Gilead recovered Saul's body and those of his three sons, and cremated them in their city, before burying their bones under the tamarisk tree at Jabesh. This was a sad outcome for the nation who wanted its own way by asking for a king.

FIND OUT THE FACTS

1. Discuss the last two verses of your reading:
   1 Chronicles 10:13-14.
2. Why is suicide sinful?
3. Compare the death of Samson and Saul.

Saul brought destruction on his whole family. Think about the serious effects one person's sins can have on other people's lives.

Live so as to be missed.
Robert Murray M'Cheyne

2 Samuel   'So David said to him, "Your
2:1-11   blood is on your own head, for
            your own mouth has testified
            against you, saying, 'I have
            killed the Lord's anointed'"'
            (2 Samuel 1:16).

S ome people are greedy and will do almost anything to obtain rewards.

Saul was dead, and David was told the news by an Amalekite
who had come from the battlefield. He appeared to have an
intimate knowledge of Saul's end. However, what he told David,
was untrue (see 2 Samuel 1).

He claimed that Saul and Jonathan were dead. The
Amalekite said he had heard Saul calling. When he approached
Saul, the king asked him to kill him so he would not fall into
the hands of the Philistines. The young man then showed David
a crown and bracelet that he had taken from Saul's body.

David and his men mourned the death of Saul and Jonathan,
and all the Israelites who had been killed. David again questioned the young man and commanded that he be immediately put to death for killing the Lord's anointed.

David was unsure what he should do next and took the
matter to the Lord in prayer, asking, 'Shall I go up to any of the
cities of Judah?' The Lord then commanded him to go up to
Hebron (2 Samuel 2:1).

David was welcomed by the inhabitants of Hebron, who
anointed him king of Judah. When he found out that the men
of Jabesh Gilead had buried Saul and his sons, he gave thanks
for their kindness and promised to repay them.

However, David was king of Judah while Saul's son,
Ishbosheth, had been crowned king of Israel. When Abner with
Ishbosheth's servants met Joab and David's servants at the pool
of Gibeon they organized a fight. Twelve from each side fought
and when the fighting had ended all were dead. Thus the name
'Field of Sharp Swords' was given to that spot.

In an ensuing battle between David's men and the Israelites under the rule of Saul's son, Ishbosheth, David was victorious.

David failed the Lord in many ways. Very notable was his marriage to many wives which was contrary to the law of God: 'Neither shall he [the king] multiply wives for himself, lest his heart turn away' (Deuteronomy 17:17).

Many citizens of Israel lost their lives during the next seven years and six months while David consolidated his rule, making Jerusalem his capital. It was from (Jeru) Salem that Melchizedek had come (Genesis 14:18). Finally the elders of Israel acknowledged David as God's anointed king. He then ruled the nation for thirty-three years.

FIND OUT THE FACTS

1. David had many wives. In doing this he broke the law of God. Which law? (Deuteronomy 17:17).

2. What happened to Saul's son, Ishbosheth? Read 2 Samuel 4:5-7.

3. What relationship was David to Ruth and Boaz?

David never failed to acknowledge the good deeds done to him by others. Think about how you can follow his example.

How the mighty have fallen, and the weapons of war perished.
2 Samuel 1:27

2 Samuel   'Then David danced before the
6:12-23   LORD with all his might; and
            David was wearing a linen
            ephod' (2 Samuel 6:14).

David had victories over the Philistines, just as the Lord had said. However, he knew that one important part of worship was missing: the ark of the covenant, which was the Lord's meeting place with Israel.

With a great crowd he went to the house of Abinadab, and placed the ark on a new cart, driven by Uzzah. Many people were singing and playing musical instruments but David had failed to approach the Lord concerning the ark's movement. Maybe he just decided to move the ark as did the Philistines. This was a very exciting time for David and the people of Israel, but all did not go as planned.

When the cart reached Nachon's threshing floor, the oxen pulling it, stumbled. Uzzah didn't want the ark falling from the cart and reached out his hand to steady it. His intention was good, but he disobeyed God's command. Instantly the Lord struck him down. David looked at the scene and was both angry with and fearful of God. He named the place 'Perez Uzzah', which means outburst against Uzzah. We learn that God's commands cannot be taken lightly. The movement of the ark, which was God's appointed meeting place with Israel's high priest, was to be moved as God commanded.

David, fearful of God's punishment, left the ark in the house of Obed-Edom for three months. When he was told that God had greatly blessed Obed-Edom, he made arrangements for the ark to be carried to Jerusalem. This time it was transported correctly: not on a cart, but carried by priests descended from Kohathite, using poles through the appropriate rings.

We read that before the ark had moved six paces David sacrificed oxen and sheep. When the people surrounding the ark reached Jerusalem, the excitement increased: 'Then David danced before the LORD with all his might; ... wearing a linen ephod' (2 Samuel 6:14). Michal, who was Saul's daughter and David's wife, saw him dancing and said to him, 'How glorious was the king of Israel today, uncovering himself today in the eyes of the maids of his servants, as one of the base fellows shamelessly uncovers himself!' (2 Samuel 6:20).

David's reply was that he danced before the Lord, the God who removed her father from Israel's throne and gave it to him. David then warned her that there would be times in the future when he would do so again. God punished Michal by making her childless — another affliction on the house of Saul.

FIND OUT THE FACTS

1. Why was David angry that God had struck Uzzah down?

2. Where did David place the ark in Jerusalem? See 2 Samuel 6:17.

3. In 2 Samuel 6:9 we read that David was 'afraid' of the Lord. Why?

To Think & to pray about

The return of the ark to Jerusalem was a time of great rejoicing for the children of Israel. Think about occasions when you have had reason to rejoice in the Lord. Thank him for them.

A saying to Remember

There is terror in the Bible as well as comfort. *Donald Grey Barnhouse*

1 Chronicles 'But my mercy shall not depart
17:3-17   from him [David], as I took it
           from Saul, whom I removed
           from before you. And your
           house and your kingdom shall
           be established forever before
           you. Your throne shall be
           established forever' (2 Samuel
           7:15-16)

For a time, David rested from war in his palace in Jerusalem. He was concerned that the house of God was still the tabernacle. He believed that because he had a royal palace in which to live, so also the house of God should be a permanent building.

God revealed to Nathan the prophet that he had moved about in a tent, and up to this time, he had never commanded that a 'house of cedar' be built for the Lord (2 Samuel 7:7). Nathan was commanded to tell David that all his victories had come from the Lord and his greatness was because of God's care.

The Lord promised that he would make David's descendants sit on the throne, and one of his children would build a place of worship. God then promised David, saying, 'I will establish the throne of [your] kingdom for ever' (2 Samuel 7:13).

David bowed before the majesty of God: 'Therefore you are great, O Lord GOD. For there is none like you, nor is there any God besides you, according to all that we have heard with our ears' (2 Samuel 7:22).

In this conversation, God established his covenant with David, promising that his throne would last for ever. David later died as did his son, Solomon, and all his descendants. Finally there was not a descendant of David on the throne of Israel. However, David's greatest Son was yet to be born and claim his throne. The Lord Jesus was descended from David and is the eternal King who would sit upon David's throne. In Psalm 2:6 God says, 'Yet I have set my King on my holy hill of

Zion.' It is the Lord Jesus who is 'Lord of lords and King of kings' (Revelation 17:14).

All who have trusted their eternal salvation to Christ are members of the kingdom of God. We can praise God and the Lamb of God for his goodness to us.

David praised God for his covenant promises and then asked if there were any of Saul's descendants still living. When he was told of Mephibosheth, who was lame, he invited him to Jerusalem where he looked after him. This act of kindness was so unlike that of the kings of the surrounding nations who usually killed any living relatives of the defeated king.

David's soldiers continued to fight against the surrounding Canaanite nations, which should have been destroyed in Joshua's day.

FIND OUT THE FACTS

1. Why did David want to build a more permanent house for worship?
2. Who is David's greatest Son?
3. Who are citizens of the kingdom of heaven?

God did not give David the task of building a house for the Lord. This was to be done by Solomon. Think about the fact that the Lord has different tasks for each of his people.

The whole covenant is a bundle of promises. *Thomas Brooks*

Psalm   'Yea, though I walk through
23   the valley of the shadow of
             death, I will fear no evil' (Psalm
             23:4).

King David composed many psalms, the best known of which is Psalm 23. Even people who have no interest in spiritual matters have a knowledge of this psalm. Many good books have been written about this psalm; one of these is *The Lord our Shepherd* written by the late J. Douglas MacMillan. Frequently when I have sat with a dying Christian, I have been asked to read this comforting passage of scripture.

In the New Testament we read the words of our Saviour: 'I am the good shepherd. The good shepherd gives his life for the sheep' (John 10:11). We must look upon our Saviour as a God who cares for his people, as a caring shepherd for his sheep. In the days of Israel's kings, they were to act like shepherds to the people. This is the role of the Redeemer. He cares for his people and ensures that they finally reach heaven.

Our Lord is a mighty God who rules the world. Isaiah contrasted the might of the Lord God with his gentleness. This is a passage of Scripture which should gladden your heart. We read: 'Behold, the Lord GOD shall come with a strong hand, and his arm shall rule for him; behold, his reward is with him, and his work before him.'

This is followed by comforting words: 'He will feed his flock like a shepherd; he will gather the lambs with his arm, and carry them in his bosom, and gently lead those who are with young' (Isaiah 40:10-11).

Can you say, 'The LORD is my shepherd; I shall not want'? (Psalm 23:1). God takes care of his people and leads them along the pathways of righteousness. He cares for his people all the days of their life, and especially at the time of their death. And just as David knew that he would dwell in paradise for all eternity with his Lord, so also will all of God's sheep.

Do you know the story of the two men involved in an elocution competition which involved saying Psalm 23? The trained man said the psalm, showing clearly his well-trained voice, while the other, who was an aged pastor, said the words from the heart. He showed that he loved his Lord. Of course, the trained man won the prize. But he was heard to say to the judge, 'My rendition showed I knew the psalm, but that pastor obviously knows the Shepherd.' Which applies to you? Do you know the psalm? Do you know the Shepherd?

The best of all is to know both the psalm and the Shepherd. I know we don't brand sheep, but someone once said that if Christ's people were branded, the brand would have on it an ear and two feet: 'My sheep hear my voice, and I know them, and they follow me. And I give them eternal life, and they shall never perish' (John 10:27-28).

We have a wonderful Shepherd!

FIND OUT THE FACTS

1. Who is the Good Shepherd of Psalm 23?

2. Why would a brand of an ear and feet be suitable for Christ's people?

3. Who wrote Psalm 23? How do you know?

Thank the Lord that he is with his people throughout their lives, and particularly as they pass through death.

Sheep may fall into the mire; swine wallow in it. *C. H. Spurgeon*

A saying to Remember

2 Samuel   'Your servant Uriah the
11:14-27   Hittite is dead also' (2 Samuel
           11:24).

It was spring, the time when the kings went out to war. But, instead of fighting beside his men, David remained at home in the comfort of his palace. Joab was the commander of the army. One day David saw a beautiful woman bathing on her rooftop. Immediately he asked one of his servants who the woman was. He was told that it was Bathsheba, the wife of Uriah the Hittite who was fighting for David on the battlefield.

Foolishly David gave way to his lust and asked for her to be brought to the palace. As a loyal subject and not knowing why she was being summoned to the king's palace, Bathsheba obeyed her sovereign. When David's intentions became clear, Bathsheba should have done all she could to prevent his advances. In the account of the incident in 2 Samuel 11, Bathsheba remains a passive participant. Before long David was in love with Bathsheba and she was expecting his child. As he didn't want the people to know of his terrible sin, he commanded Bathsheba's husband, Uriah, to be sent home.

When he arrived for the night, David told him he could go to his home. In this way he hoped that everyone would think that Uriah was the father of Bathsheba's baby. However, Uriah remained at the palace. He felt guilty living in comfort while his friends were risking their lives, fighting for the king. David then gave Uriah alcohol and made him drunk. Again he refused to go to his own bed.

At last David sent him back to the battlefield, with a letter to Commander Joab, instructing him to place Uriah in the fiercest part of the battle. Joab was to make sure that Uriah was killed in battle. Then David knew that he could legally marry Bathsheba.

It wasn't long before Joab sent word to David that Uriah was dead. When he received the news, David called his death a misfortune of war and urged Joab to get on with the battle.

Bathsheba mourned for Uriah. When that time was over, she went to live with David in the palace. David now had another wife. He was both a murderer and an adulterer. God was most displeased with him because of his sinful ways. For many months he refused to acknowledge his sin before God or man — it was a very low point in his reign. What he needed to do was to go to the Lord with a repentant heart, confess his sin and ask the Lord for forgiveness. That was yet to happen.

FIND OUT THE FACTS

1. Name the two Commandments that David broke in the story.
2. Explain the meaning of today's 'Saying to remember'.
3. What position in David's army did Joab hold?
4. In what way does Proverbs 6:29 apply to this story?

First David lusted after Bathsheda, then he committed adultery and had Uriah killed in battle. One sin so easily leads to another. God's Word warns us to flee from every appearance of sin.

Remember the shame of sin when tempted by the sweetness of sin.
C. H. Spurgeon

2 Samuel
12:1-15

'The sacrifices of God are a broken spirit, a broken and a contrite heart — these, O God, you will not despise' (Psalm 51:17).

David had committed two great sins: adultery and murder. He didn't kill Uriah himself, but arranged for him to be placed in that part of the battle where he was sure to be killed. He felt safe now that Bathsheba's husband was dead. He took Bathsheba for his wife and kept silent about his sin. In some ways he was like the stubborn mule and horse (Psalm 32:3,9).

As David was God's chosen king of Israel and the one in whose line of descendants Christ would come, he had to be brought to repentance.

About nine months later God commanded the prophet Nathan to visit David and tell him a short story which would convict him of his sin. When Nathan spoke, David felt sure that he was speaking of some true injustice that had happened in his kingdom. David was furious that the rich man had stolen a poor man's lamb, cooked it and made a meal of it for himself and his visitor.

An angry David responded, 'As the LORD lives, the man who has done this shall surely die! And he shall restore fourfold for the lamb, because he did this thing and because he had no pity' (2 Samuel 12:5-6). David was shocked by Nathan's reply, 'You are the man!' (2 Samuel 12:7).

The Lord then pronounced judgement on David. His own son would hurt his family and the child who was born to Bathsheba would die. David accepted the Lord's discipline in a humble manner. Psalms 32 and 51 were his psalms of repentance. David feared that God would remove his Spirit from him as had happened to Saul (Psalm 51:11).

When God calls a person to citizenship in his kingdom, repentance and faith are essential. Like David, we are all sinners who need forgiveness. The way of forgiveness is through the Lord Jesus Christ, who in his own body upon the cross, carried the sins of his people. All the punishment due to his people from an offended God fell upon Christ. If you and I want forgiveness, we must acknowledge our sins as did the tax collector in Christ's parable. That man had gone to the temple to pray. All he could say was 'God, be merciful to me a sinner!' (Luke 18:13). That man returned home justified: forgiven and clothed in Christ's righteousness.

True repentance means turning from our sins to a life of righteousness: obedience to Christ's commands. It is to the Lord Jesus Christ sinners must go. For in him alone there is forgiveness and salvation.

FIND OUT THE FACTS

1. Why did David ask God not to remove his Spirit from him? (Psalm 51:11).
2. What were David's sins in this story?
3. What did David mean when he wrote, 'In sin my mother conceived me'? (Psalm 51:5).

As God's child, David was brought to the point of repentance and God forgave him. But the effects of his sin would be felt in his family. Even though God forgives sin, he does not **always** remove its consequences.

A saying to Remember

Sin is like seed — to cover it is to cultivate it. *Anon*

2 Samuel 'Moreover Absalom would say,
15:1-12 "Oh, that I were made judge
         in the land, and everyone who
         has any suit or cause would
         come to me; then I would give
         him justice"' (2 Samuel 15:4).

There are many unhappy families in the world today. Marriages fall apart, children leave their parents and family life is ruined because of the destructive influence of things such as the use of illegal drugs. King David's family was no different. By committing adultery with Bathsheba, he had set a very bad example for his offspring.

David failed to discipline his children and they caused him and the nation much heartache. When Amnon, his eldest son, molested his half-sister, David, who was very angry, should have disciplined him, but did nothing. What could David really do, since he was guilty of sexual sin? Absalom hated Amnon because of his wicked deed. He waited his time and two years later had Amnon murdered. Then he escaped from Israel and remained with the king of Geshur for three years.

David loved Absalom and was distressed that he had run away. When Absalom returned, David instructed him to go to his own home, saying that he didn't want to see his face. Later Absalom had Joab organize a meeting with his father. When they met, he bowed down to the ground before his father. King David then kissed his wayward son.

Absalom, however, was determined to rebel against his father and capture the throne of Israel for himself. He organized horses and chariots and fifty men to run before him. He also stood at the gate saying that if he were king, he would give favourable rulings to the complainants.

This created the opinion that Absalom was indeed an important and wise man, a person who would make a good king. We read that by his behaviour he 'stole the hearts of the men of Israel' (2 Samuel 15:6). He then instigated an insurrection,

which caused David to flee from Jerusalem with his six
hundred faithful men.

When David heard that Ahithophel was one of Absalom's
supporters, and would be surely asked for advice, he prayed,
'O Lord, I pray, turn the counsel of Ahithophel into foolishness' (2 Samuel 15:31)! This was a terrible time for David. His
much-loved son, Absalom, was causing him so much heartache. All David could do was keep moving and then consolidate
his forces. As he made his way from Jerusalem, he was abused
by Shimei, a relative of Saul. David accepted his words as coming from God. As he passed, Shimei threw stones and dust
over him.

FIND OUT THE FACTS

1. How should children behave towards their parents?
   Read Exodus 20:12.

2. Why does God discipline his people? Read
   Hebrews 12:5-11 and 1 Corinthians 11:20-22 and
   30-34.

3. How should brothers and sisters treat one another?

Like Absalom many children today show
no respect for their parents. Think
about all that your parents do for you
because they love you and care for
you. What should your attitude
be to them?

Children may make a rich man
poor, but they make a poor man
rich.   C. H. Spurgeon

2 Samuel 'And as he [David] went, he
18:6-15 said thus, "O my son Absalom
— my son, my son Absalom —
if only I had died in your place!
O Absalom my son, my son!"'
(2 Samuel 18:33).

W hen we ask for guidance, we should make sure it is wise
advice. Too many people have been led astray by
accepting the suggestions of fools.

Absalom was now the most powerful man in Jerusalem. By
receiving guidance from Ahithophel, he was led to take his
father's wives and concubines for himself. By so doing, he
openly displayed his contempt for his father (see 2 Samuel
12:11-12). As a result David and Absalom were enemies for
ever.

Ahithophel also advised Absalom to send out his soldiers
to catch and kill his father. He believed David's men would be
hungry and weary, and with David dead they would return to
their homes and cause no more trouble. Only then could they
say, 'The king is dead! God save King Absalom!'

Hushai, David's friend, told Absalom that Ahithophel's
advice was wrong. He urged him to assemble a vast army from
all of Israel's tribes and then attack his father's few men.
Absalom agreed and made no immediate effort to capture and
kill David. Hushai then sent word to David that he should cross
the Jordan in case Absalom changed his mind and immediately send soldiers after him. The Lord had answered David's
prayer and Ahithophel, realizing that Absalom's rebellion
would fail, committed suicide. Meanwhile David organized
his soldiers, and when the command was given to move out,
they told him it would be best if he remained in the city.
Before Joab, Abishai and Ittai departed David said, 'Deal gently for my sake with the young man Absalom' (2 Samuel 18:5).

The forces of David and Absalom met in the timbered area
of Ephraim, where David's men were victorious. Absalom tried

to escape on his mule and rode under a tree with low branches where his long hair became entangled. The mule trotted on, leaving him hanging from the tree.

When Joab instructed some soldiers to kill Absalom, they refused. They didn't want to be guilty of killing the king's son, but Joab knew that Absalom had to die. If he returned to David, he would continue to be a cause of distress to his father.

The three spears that Joab had were soon through Absalom's heart. After cutting down his dead body, it was thrown into a deep pit, which was covered with stones. When David heard that Absalom was dead, he lamented his death, saying, 'O my son Absalom — my son, my son Absalom — if only I had died in your place! O Absalom my son, my son!' (2 Samuel 18:33).

These were the words of an emotional grieving father. However his grief was no excuse for the neglect of his faithful army for whom he had a responsibility.

FIND OUT THE FACTS

1. Why did Joab kill Absalom?
2. How are you to know if the advice you receive is wise or foolish?
3. Describe Absalom's character.

Absalom's rebellion against his father resulted in his death. Think about the seriousness of the sin of rebellion.

The wages of sin is death.
The Apostle Paul, Romans 6:23

1 Chronicles   'He [The LORD] is the tower of
21:1-8   salvation to his king, and shows
                mercy to his anointed, to David
                and his descendants for ever-
                more' (2 Samuel 22:51).

In history there have been many kings who were killed by those who wanted to seize their throne. The Roman Empire is marked by many such assassinations.

David's throne was returned to him by the Lord who had made an eternal covenant with him. This covenant was fulfilled by the Lord Jesus Christ who took his seat upon David's throne (Psalm 2:6-7; Revelation 5:7).

David spent much of his life at war. When he asked the Lord for permission to build a permanent temple, the Lord answered, 'You shall not build a house for my name, because you have been a man of war and have shed blood' (1 Chronicles 28:3). The Lord revealed that his son, Solomon, would be the one to build the Temple. David began collecting material that Solomon could use to build a temple, worthy of the Lord.

David arranged for a census of all Israel and Judah to be taken. It took nine months and twenty-one days for this census to be completed. However, David sinned in his heart after he had the census taken.

When David realized he had sinned, he prayed that God would forgive him. But, the Lord gave him the choice of one of three punishments: first, seven years of famine; second, David would spend three months eluding men who wanted him dead; or third, three days of plague.

David chose the plague because he preferred to fall into the hand of God rather than the hand of man. The plague resulted in the death of seventy thousand men. Seeing the distress he had caused, David repented and offered a burnt offering and a peace offering to the Lord. God took notice of David's prayers and the plague ended.

In his latter days, when death was drawing near, the old king felt the cold. A young woman cared for him, making sure his bed was warm.

David looked back over his life. He had written many psalms for use in worship. These were inspired by the Spirit of God. His best known is Psalm 23. Before he died, Adonijah claimed David's throne, but David was able to say that Solomon would sit upon his throne. David advised Solomon how he should rule. After that he 'rested with his fathers, and was buried in the City of David' (1 Kings 2:10).

David had ruled Israel for forty years. Despite his sin, he was one who loved God and attempted to please him. He is described as 'a man after [God's] own heart' (1 Samuel 13:14) A thousand years later David's greater son, Jesus Christ, established his kingdom and rules from David's throne for ever.

FIND OUT THE FACTS

1. Learn Psalm 23.
2. Why did God refuse David's request to build the Temple?
3. What did David do to help Solomon construct a temple for the Lord?

To Think & to pray about

David's life was not perfect, but it was a life of confession and repentance. This is a life that pleases God. What does it mean to confess your sins and to live a life of repentance?

A saying to Remember

Death is the funeral of all our sorrows. *Thomas Watson*

1 Kings   'And Solomon loved the Lord,
3:1-9   walking in the statutes of his
            father David, except that he
            sacrificed and burned incense
            at the high places' (1 Kings 3:3).

In Great Britain the law states who will occupy the throne when the ruling monarch dies. In days gone by it was frequently the most powerful and popular child who claimed the throne, after killing those who stood in their way.

Before David died, his son, Adonijah, who was rarely disciplined by his father, was encouraged by Joab, the commander of David's army, and Abiathar, the priest, to claim the throne. The prophet Nathan protected Solomon while Bathsheba asked David to announce that Solomon was to succeed him as king.

Solomon was to be seated on his throne while Zadok, the priest, and Nathan blew the horn and shouted, 'Long live King Solomon!' (1 Kings 1:34). Zadok was to anoint Solomon with the oil from the tabernacle while the people shouted, 'Long live King Solomon!' (1 Kings 1:39).

Adonijah's plans came to nothing and his supporters deserted him. He went quickly to the tabernacle where he took hold of the horns of the altar, which was a place of refuge, until Solomon assured him that he would not be put to death for his rebellion.

When Adonijah sent Bathsheba to petition Solomon to give him permission to marry Abishag, Solomon saw this as an attempt to undermine his kingship and had Adonijah executed. Abiathar, the priest, was told to return to his home where he could live in safety, only because he had served David. Joab knew that he was about to die because he had helped Adonijah, so he made his way to the altar where he thought he would be safe, holding onto its horns. After a short exchange of words, Joab was put to death. Solomon appointed Zadok as priest and Benaiah as commander of the army.

Shimei, who had abused David and thrown stones and dirt over him, was told to remain on his property where he would be safe. But when two slaves escaped, he left his home in search of them. When Solomon heard of this, Shimei was put to death. Solomon went to Gibeon and on a tall mountain sacrificed a thousand burnt offerings to the Lord.

While he was there the Lord appeared to him and said, 'Ask! What shall I give you?' (1 Kings 3:5).

Solomon's reply showed he loved the Lord: 'Therefore give to your servant an understanding heart to judge your people, that I may discern between good and evil. For who is able to judge this great people of yours?' (1 Kings 3:9).

Solomon's request showed great humility and wisdom.

FIND OUT THE FACTS

1. What sort of a king was Solomon in his early years?

2. How do we get wisdom? See Proverbs 1:7; 2:6; James 1:5-6.

3. What request did Adonijah make from David? Read 1 Kings 2:17.

Solomon began his reign by taking some firm decisions. Think about why it is important for leaders in the church and of a country to take firm decisions. Pray for them that they may rule well.

Wise men give good counsel, but wiser men take it. *Anon*

1 Kings
3:16-28

'And all Israel heard of the judgement which the king had rendered; and they feared the king, for they saw that the wisdom of God was in him to administer justice' (1 Kings 3:28).

Despite his sins, David was a good and popular ruler. It appeared that Solomon, who loved the Lord, would follow in his footsteps.

He showed kindness to some of his enemies and removed others who created difficulties. However, one of his first errors of judgement was to take a pagan wife who was the daughter of the Pharaoh of Egypt. This marriage sealed a treaty with Egypt which was sinful. He should have trusted in the Lord who had set him upon the throne.

When offering sacrifices at Gibeon, the Lord appeared to him in a dream, offering him whatever he wanted. When Solomon asked for wisdom, the Lord said that he would be given not only wisdom, but riches and honour. Obedience to the law of God would result in a long life.

One of the first judgements which Solomon was asked to make involved two women who claimed to be the mother of the baby who had been brought to him. Having heard the evidence from the two women, he set a trap to discern who really was the mother of the baby. He asked for a sword and said that he would cut the baby in half and give each of the women a half of the baby.

One woman was happy to see this done, but the mother was willing to sacrifice her desire to have her baby for the child's welfare. Having seen the compassion of the baby's mother, Solomon knew that she was indeed the mother. As news of this incident circulated throughout the nation, the people feared such a wise king, who was able to make just judgements.

We are told that 'Solomon's wisdom excelled the wisdom of all the men of the East and all the wisdom of Egypt' (1 Kings 4:30). He also wrote three thousand proverbs and one thousand and five songs.

Following this event, Solomon set about the task of organizing his kingdom. He built up a strong army of forty thousand horses for chariots and twelve thousand horsemen. The Israelites paid their taxes which increased Solomon's wealth.

So great was Solomon's kingdom that many overseas rulers visited his palace to hear his wisdom and see his nation. Israel was a picture of contentment for we read in 1 Kings 4:25: 'Judah and Israel dwelt safely, each man under his vine and his fig tree ... all the days of Solomon.'

FIND OUT THE FACTS

1. Who gave Solomon such great wisdom?

2. What mistake did Solomon make in marrying Pharaoh's daughter? See Deuteronomy 17:16-17 and Exodus 34:13-16.

3. God spoke to Solomon in a dream. In what other ways did God speak to people?

Solomon asked God for wisdom to rule his people. Pray for your national leaders today that they would turn to God and seek his wisdom in the way they rule your country.

Knowledge is the fountain of wisdom.
Stephen Charnock

2 Chronicles   'Then Solomon spoke, "The
7:1-7   Lord said he would dwell in the
               dark cloud. I have surely built
               you an exalted house, and a
               place for you to dwell in for-
               ever"' (2 Chronicles 6:1-2).

David was not permitted to build a permanent place of worship but he collected much for it that could be used by Solomon.

With the nation at peace, Solomon commenced assembling all the building material that was needed. He obtained cedar and cypress logs from Lebanon, and stone was quarried nearby.

The building commenced four hundred and eighty years after Moses had led the Israelites out of Egypt. This was in the month of Ziv, in the fourth year of Solomon's reign. He selected thousands of employees who began the God-honouring work of constructing the temple. The stone used in the building was made to size at the quarry so that no noise was made on the temple site.

David's gold and silver and other gifts were used to magnify the glory of the temple, which was the place where the Lord met with his people. The moving of the ark of the covenant to its resting place in the holy of holies was done according to God's law.

When the temple was completed, and the ark of the covenant was in its place, 'the cloud filled the house of the Lord, so that the priests could not continue ministering because of the cloud; for the glory of the Lord filled the house of the Lord' (1 Kings 8:10-11). Solomon prayed to the Lord before the assembled people, glorifying, and giving thanks for his goodness to Israel. He recalled God's covenant promise to have a descendant of David always sitting upon the throne.

Many sacrifices were offered to the Lord during the celebrations. Later the Lord appeared to Solomon in a dream, making this promise: 'When I shut up heaven and there is no rain, or command the locusts to devour the land, or send pestilence among my people, if my people who are called by my name will humble themselves, and pray and seek my face, and turn from their wicked ways, then I will hear from heaven, and will forgive their sin and heal their land' (2 Chronicles 7:13-14).

Today the Lord is building his temple using the saints as the building bricks — a temple in which God dwells by his Spirit (Ephesians 2:19-22). Each believer is also the temple of the Holy Spirit (1 Corinthians 6:19).

Our God is gracious and holy. He must be approached with holy awe through the Mediator, the Lord Jesus Christ. But we are invited to 'come boldly to the throne of grace, that we may obtain mercy and find grace to help in time of need' (Hebrews 4:16).

FIND OUT THE FACTS

1. What had happened on the temple building site?
   Read 2 Chronicles 3:1.
2. Describe the mercy seat. See Exodus 25:17-22.
3. Who is the 'stone which the builders rejected'?
   (Psalm 118:22; Matthew 21:42).

To Think & to pray about

When Solomon dedicated the temple, he prayed that God would hear the prayers of his servants which were prayed in that place. Thank God that he hears and answers the prayers of his people.

A Saying to Remember

God's glory is that which makes him glorious. A. H. Strong

2 Chronicles
9:1-12

'However I [the Queen of Sheba] did not believe the words until I came and saw with my own eyes; and indeed the half was not told me. Your wisdom and prosperity exceed the fame of which I heard' (1 Kings 10:7).

When our retirement home was finished, we were visited by friends who wanted to see what we had built. The light switches were easy to turn on and off, and some we could reach while lying in bed. Now that we are living in it, we have found some things we should have done differently.

Solomon's kingdom was glorious and the Lord granted him great blessings. His fame as one who could solve difficult problems became known outside of Israel. It was the wealthy Queen of Sheba who decided to visit Solomon and see for herself if his kingdom was as good as she had heard it to be.

When she arrived at Solomon's court, she discovered that Solomon was indeed very wise. She saw the peace and tranquillity in Israel and the glory of the king's possessions.

Before she returned to her own kingdom, she presented Solomon with 'one hundred and twenty talents of gold, spices in great abundance, and precious stones; there never were any spices such as those the queen of Sheba gave to King Solomon' (2 Chronicles 9:9). In return Solomon gave her anything she wanted, which was much more than she had given to him.

After seeing his kingdom, she said that what she had heard was only partly true. Now that she had seen everything with her own eyes, she knew it to be more glorious than she had imagined: 'indeed the half was not told me' (1 Kings 10:7).

Solomon's kingdom was marvellous to see, but the kingdom of the Lord Jesus Christ is of far greater wonder. The Bible tells us something about the kingdom the saints will inhabit, but really only a fraction of its glory has been revealed.

The apostle John caught a glimpse of what awaits God's people: 'And God will wipe away every tear from their eyes; there shall be no more death, nor sorrow, nor crying. There shall be no more pain, for the former things have passed away' (Revelation 21:4). 'There shall be no more curse, but the throne of God and of the Lamb shall be in it, and his servants shall serve him. They shall see his face, and his name shall be on their foreheads. There shall be no night there: they need no lamp nor light of the sun, for the Lord God gives them light. And they shall reign forever and ever' (Revelation 22:3-5).

How true it is: the best is yet to be!

Is there a home reserved for you in heaven?

FIND OUT THE FACTS

1. What do you think will be best in heaven?
2. Read Philippians 1:21-23. What is Paul teaching there?
3. Why was Solomon's kingdom so glorious?

Solomon's glory and his fame soon spread beyond the borders of Israel. Thank the Lord Jesus Christ that one day his glory and his greatness as a king will be seen and acknowledged by all the nations of the world.

The earth has no sorrow that heaven cannot heal. *Thomas Moore*

1 Kings
11:1-8

'For it was so, when Solomon was old, that his wives turned his heart after other gods; and his heart was not loyal to the LORD his God, as was the heart of his father David' (1 Kings 11:4).

The day will come when many of you will marry. Our Lord has given us instructions on what Christians should do: Christians must marry Christians. We have no right to say, 'I'll marry who I like!' Obedience is a mark of Christ's people.

Solomon started his reign so well. The nation was at peace and was rich; he'd built the great temple for the Lord; and he had that great God-given gift of wisdom. However, Solomon's obedience didn't last. He knew that God's law clearly stated that intermarriage with the ungodly was forbidden (Exodus 34:13-16). But he had seven hundred wives and kept three hundred concubines. Most of them came from the surrounding pagan nations and they demanded the right to worship their own gods. Consequently, Solomon began to participate with them in their ungodly worship and he 'was not loyal to the LORD his God, as was the heart of his father David' (1 Kings 11:4).

Solomon was soon to learn that sin does not go unpunished; the Lord was angry with him. We know that chastisement comes from God, who wants his people to be holy.

The Lord said to Solomon, 'Because you have done this, and have not kept my covenant and my statutes, which I have commanded you, I will surely tear the kingdom away from you and give it to your servant' (1 Kings 11:11).

For the sake of David, his father, this would not happen during his reign, but Solomon's son would suffer the loss of ten tribes — only Judah and Benjamin would remain.

Before his death Solomon faced many difficulties. His servant, Jeroboam, attempted to overthrow him and when that proved unsuccessful, Jeroboam escaped to Egypt.

He was aware that he would rule the ten tribes because the prophet Ahijah had met him and torn his new garment into twelve pieces. He had told Jeroboam to take ten pieces saying, 'Thus says the LORD, the God of Israel: "Behold, I will tear the kingdom out of the hand of Solomon and will give ten tribes to you"' (1 Kings 11:31).

Solomon reigned over Israel for forty years and upon his death the throne passed to his son, Rehoboam. Solomon's life was spoilt by his disobedience. May you never end up like Solomon but, by the grace of God, may you remain a faithful citizen of the kingdom of heaven.

FIND OUT THE FACTS

1. What is your guide in seeking a life's partner?
2. What were Solomon's great sins?
3. Why didn't the Lord destroy Solomon's kingdom when he sinned?
4. What does 1 Corinthians 6:19 teach us about the Holy Spirit?

Solomon had tests and temptations. But he failed one important test: he turned and worshipped other gods. Why did Solomon, who had been blessed by God so easily turn to other gods. What is the warning to us?

A happy marriage is the union of two good forgivers. *Robert Quillen*

1 Kings
12:6-20

'My father [Solomon] made your yoke heavy, but I [Rehoboam] will add to your yoke; my father chastised you with whips, but I will chastise you with scourges!' (1 Kings 12:14).

King Rehoboam travelled to Shechem, where he was crowned king of Israel. He asked his father's wise elders for advice on how he should govern the nation. They replied, 'If you will be a servant to these people today, and serve them, and answer them, and speak good words to them, then they will be your servants for ever' (1 Kings 12:7).

Rehoboam, Solomon's son, was politically foolish because he ignored wise advice and listened to his young friends who suggested that he make life more difficult for the people, tax them heavily and keep them in subjection. Three days later the young king told his people of his intention.

Now the Lord's prophecy to Solomon, that the nation would be divided, was to be fulfilled. (1 Kings 11:29-39). When the people heard Rehoboam's words, they departed. The result was that soon he found himself king of only Judah and Benjamin. When Adoram was commanded to collect some revenue, stones were hurled at him and he was killed. Consequently, the king quickly returned to the safety of Jerusalem, where he assembled one hundred and eighty thousand soldiers to fight against Israel and reunite the nation.

The ten tribes of Israel, hearing that Jeroboam had returned from Egypt, made him their king. Now there appeared to be the possibility of civil war in the nation, but the Lord directed Shemaiah to speak to Rehoboam: 'You shall not go up nor fight against your brethren the children of Israel. Let every man return to his house ...' (1 Kings 12:24).

Rehoboam ruled for seventeen years, during which Judah became more sinful. In an effort to prevent any possibility of Israel uniting with Judah, Jeroboam took action to provide a place of worship for the people which would save them the long, tiring journey to Jerusalem.

After setting up two golden calves— one in Bethel (the capital of the nation) and the other in Dan — Jeroboam announced, 'Here are your gods, O Israel, which brought you up from the land of Egypt' (1 Kings 12:28). The priests were not of the tribe of Levi and the feast days were not those of the Lord. Soon shrines appeared on the high places as the nation slipped further into sinful ways.

Rehoboam suffered defeat by Egypt, who removed the treasures from the temple and the palace. Warfare also erupted continually between Israel and Judah. Sin brought terrible consequences, including Jeroboam's death.

FIND OUT THE FACTS

1. Why did Rehoboam lose part of his kingdom?
2. What was Jeroboam's sin?
3. Why did God preserve the nation of Judah? See Revelation 5:5.

To Think & to pray about

Rehoboam thought he knew better than to take the elder's advice. That is the attitude of many young people today. Thank the Lord for the experience of older people to help you understand the circumstances of life.

A saying to Remember

What or whom we worship determines our behaviour. *John Murray*

| 1 Kings 17:8-16 | 'And Ahab made a wooden image. Ahab did more to provoke the LORD God of Israel to anger than all the kings of Israel who were before him' (1 Kings 16:33). |

Frequently, it happens that young people who profess to love the Lord Jesus marry non-Christians, and it is not long before they have returned to the world. We should always be on guard that others do not take us down that pathway which leads to hell.

Israel had a new king, Ahab, the son of Omri. He married an ungodly woman, Jezebel, the daughter of the king of the Sidonians. She brought her pagan gods to Israel and it wasn't long before most people became involved in worshipping them.

The Lord raised up Elijah, the prophet, to confront Ahab and Jezebel, and to warn them of their impending doom: 'As the LORD God of Israel lives, before whom I stand, there shall not be dew nor rain these years, except at my word' (1 Kings 17:1). The Lord then warned Elijah to hide beside the Brook Cherith. There he would have a supply of water and the Lord promised that the ravens would bring him food.

What seemed impossible took place: the ravens carried bread and meat to him. Our God is the God of the impossible! When the River Jordan and the Brook Cherith ran dry because of the drought, the Lord told Elijah, 'Arise, go to Zarephath, which belongs to Sidon, and dwell there. See, I have commanded a widow there to provide for you' (1 Kings 17:9).

When he arrived in Zarephath, Elijah met a widow gathering some wood to cook her last meal. Upon asking for a drink of water and some bread, the woman told Elijah of her desperate situation. She had only enough flour and oil to make a last meal. After that they would starve to death.

Elijah asked her to make the bread and give him the first piece. He said, 'The bin of flour shall not be used up, nor shall the jar of oil run dry, until the day the LORD sends rain on the earth' (1 Kings 17:14). Elijah stayed with the widow and her son, and they all ate well.

One day when the widow's son died, Elijah prayed that God would restore him to his mother. He then 'stretched himself out on the child three times, and cried out to the LORD and said, "O LORD my God, I pray, let this child's soul come back to him"' (1 Kings 17:21).

The child recovered. When Elijah brought him to his mother, she thanked him saying, 'Now by this I know that you are a man of God, and that the word of the LORD in your mouth is the truth' (1 Kings 17:24).

FIND OUT THE FACTS

1. Why do people so quickly turn away from Christ?

2. Who in the New Testament was compared to Elijah? Compare Malachi 4:5 and Matthew 11:13-14.

3. Read James 5:13-18. What are you taught in that passage of Scripture?

God sent the ravens to feed Elijah. He never leaves those who trust him and serve him. At times, he provides in the most unexpected ways, but he provides!

It is impossible on reasonable grounds to disbelieve miracles.
Blaise Pascal

May

The fear of
the LORD
is to hate evil

Proverbs 8:13

1 Kings
18:30-40

'Lord God of Abraham, Isaac, and Israel, let it be known this day that you are God in Israel ... Hear me, O Lᴏʀᴅ ... that this people may know that you are the Lᴏʀᴅ God ... you have turned their hearts back to you again' (1 Kings 18:36-37).

The Lord commanded Elijah to return and face Ahab. Then it would rain. During the drought, Ahab had sent Obadiah in search of water for the animals.

The ungodly Jezebel had killed many of the Lord's prophets, but Obadiah had saved one hundred of them and had hidden them in caves.

While looking for water, Obadiah met Elijah who was returning to confront Ahab. Elijah told him to tell Ahab that he would soon see his face, but Obadiah feared that if he told Ahab this, Elijah would again hide himself and he, Obadiah, would be executed. After Elijah promised to meet Ahab, Obadiah returned with the message. When they met, Ahab said, 'Is that you, O troubler of Israel?' (1 Kings 18:17).

Elijah's response was that Ahab had brought trouble to Israel because he and Jezebel worshipped Baal, the storm god. Then he offered a challenge: 'Now therefore, send and gather all Israel to me on Mount Carmel, the four hundred and fifty prophets of Baal, and the four hundred prophets of Asherah, who eat at Jezebel's table' (1 Kings 18:19).

A great crowd of Israelites gathered on Mount Carmel, where Elijah challenged them, 'How long will you falter between two opinions? If the Lᴏʀᴅ is God, follow him; but if Baal, follow him' (1 Kings 18:21).

Elijah explained the challenge. Both were to prepare a sacrifice. The proof of who was the true and living God would be seen in fire coming down from heaven and consuming the sacrifice.

Baal's prophets prepared their altar and sacrifice, and called upon their god to send fire from heaven to consume the offering. Elijah mocked them suggesting they call louder as Baal might be absent on a journey or asleep. They shouted out louder, cutting themselves, but nothing happened.

Elijah's turn came. After preparing the altar and the sacrifice, he poured so much water over it that the trench around the altar was filled.

Elijah prayed the words which are recorded in 1 Kings 18:36-37, and fire fell from heaven burning the sacrifice, altar and water. The people bowed to the ground, crying out, 'The Lord, he is God! The Lord, he is God!' (1 Kings 18:39). When Elijah gave the command the people killed all of the prophets of Baal.

FIND OUT THE FACTS

1. List some of Ahab's sins.
2. What are we taught in Proverbs 14:34?
3. What was Elijah's challenge going to prove?

Ahab was a very wicked man who reigned in Israel for a time. Thank the Lord that even when the wicked rule, the people of God remain spiritually safe and secure.

I had rather stand against the cannons of the wicked than against the prayers of the righteous.
Thomas Lye

1 Kings
18:41 - 19:8

'Hear me, O LORD, hear me, that this people may know that you are the LORD God, and that you have turned their hearts back to you again' (1 Kings 18:37).

Elijah was downcast. He'd been God's spokesman to the wicked Ahab and Jezebel, which was a dangerous task. God had overthrown the prophets of Baal on Mount Carmel, and while King Ahab went to eat, Elijah had walked further up Mount Carmel and had sat down exhausted. He told his servant to report what he could see on the horizon. Six times the servant returned to say there was nothing unusual on the horizon.

After the seventh look, he returned to say, 'There is a cloud, as small as a man's hand, rising out of the sea!' (1 Kings 18:44). Elijah knew that the drought was about to end, so he sent word to Ahab to return to his palace because torrential rain was soon to fall.

Ahab left, while Elijah, given extra strength by the Lord, ran ahead of Ahab's chariot.

When Jezebel was told of the day's events and the death of her prophets, she was furious and sent a messenger to Elijah, saying, 'So let the gods do to me, and more also, if I do not make your life as the life of one of them by tomorrow about this time' (1 Kings 19:2).

To save his life Elijah escaped from Israel. He crossed the border and went far into Judah where he would be safe. There, under a broom tree, he prayed that God would take his life. But God didn't answer that prayer, as he had more work for Elijah to do. He still intended to bless him.

Suddenly an angel appeared and told Elijah to stand up and eat what had been prepared for him: a cake baked on coals and some water. So Elijah arose, ate and drank and lay down again. The angel told him a second time to arise and eat. So he arose and ate and drank a second time. He then set out for Horeb, a journey of forty days, during which time he had nothing else to eat. It was the Lord who gave him the strength.

At last he found a cave in which to rest, and there the Lord appeared to him and asked, 'What are you doing here, Elijah?'

To this he replied, 'I have been very zealous for the LORD God of hosts; for the children of Israel have forsaken your covenant, torn down your altars, and killed your prophets with the sword. I alone am left; and they seek to take my life' (1 Kings 19:9,10).

God would soon act to cheer Elijah!

FIND OUT THE FACTS

1. What causes Christians to become downcast?

2. What reasons do Christians have to be joyful always?

3. Elijah was downcast. He should have been rejoicing. Why?

Elijah was depressed and exhausted. Think about the fact that the Lord showed his care for him even when he was feeling these emotions.

He who feeds his birds will not starve his babes. *Matthew Henry*

1 Kings
19:19-21

'Yet I have reserved seven thousand in Israel, all whose knees have not bowed to Baal, and every mouth that has not kissed him' (1 Kings 19:18).

Sometimes, in many parts of the Western world, when we attend worship and see many empty seats, we wonder what the Lord is doing and if God has forgotten us?'

We are to keep praying, witnessing to others about the goodness of God and spending time studying the Scriptures, because that is how God speaks to his people now, not in dreams and visible appearances.

At Horeb Elijah said, 'I alone am left ...' (1 Kings 19:10). The Lord told him to go out and stand on the mountain. A strong wind blew about him, breaking rocks, but God was not in that wind. This was followed by an earthquake, but the Lord did not appear in the earthquake, nor was the Lord in the fire that followed. This demonstration of God's strength must have encouraged Elijah!

Following the fire, Elijah heard a soft, whispering voice. He quickly moved to the mouth of the cave and heard God speak in a quiet voice, asking what he was doing there. Elijah once again complained, 'I alone am left' (1 Kings 19:14).

The Lord told him to return to the Wilderness of Damascus and anoint Hazael as king of Syria, Jehu as king of Israel, and also to call Elisha to follow him.

Then the Lord surprised the downcast Elijah with the news that in Israel seven thousand people had remained faithful to the Lord. This would have been wonderful news for him.

Before long he met Elisha, who was ploughing his father's field with twelve yoke of oxen. As he passed, Elijah threw his cloak over him which was his call to Elisha to follow him.

When Elisha asked permission to go and say farewell to his mother and father, Elijah granted his request. Before leaving his parents, he did something that showed he had made a total break with his old ways. He killed a yoke of oxen and boiled their flesh, stoking the fire with his ploughing equipment. After a pleasant meal together, farewells were spoken and Elisha stood up and followed Elijah in the work of the Lord.

We are to be like Elisha. When God calls us to do his work, we must obey, always remembering the words of the Lord Jesus: 'If you love me, keep my commandments' (John 14:15).

Remember that delayed obedience is disobedience.

Let us show the world the love we have for the Saviour.

FIND OUT THE FACTS

1. Elisha was permitted to say farewell to his parents. Read and explain Christ's words in Luke 9:59-62.

2. How do we know today what God would have us do?

3. How do you show your school friends or work mates that you love God?

4. Mums and dads can help their children grow spiritually. How?

To Think & to pray about

God spoke to Elijah in a still, small voice. Thank the Lord for his Word in which he speaks to us, telling us of his covenant and his promises. We have everything in his Word to enable us to live the Christian life.

A saying to Remember

God is a totalitarian Ruler who demands full allegiance from his subjects.   R. B. Kuiper

1 Kings
21:17-24

'And concerning Jezebel the
LORD also spoke, saying, "The
dogs shall eat Jezebel by the
wall of Jezreel"' (1 Kings
21:23).

God's people are called to obedience. This means that we
need to understand God's Word, so that we know what
we are to obey. That is why in many Christian homes, families
gather for the reading of God's Word, a time of prayer, discussion, and possibly the singing of a hymn or psalm.

When Ben-Hadad, the king of Syria, gathered his forces
together to overthrow Samaria, he was supported by thirty-
two kings. When he confronted Ahab, he demanded Ahab's
gold, silver, his wives and children (1 Kings 20:3). When Ahab
refused, a prophet of God prophesied that the foreign armies
would suffer a serious defeat. God fights for his people
because of his covenant promises, and also to remind the
Syrians that Jehovah was almighty wherever his people fought.
The Syrians worshipped the god of the valleys, but Jehovah
was God of the hills and the valleys! (1 Kings 20:28).

During the battle, Israel was victorious. Ahab, who had been
commanded by God to kill the Syrian king, allowed him to
return to Syria, after signing a treaty with him.

God was angry with Ahab's disobedience, and said he and
many in Israel would pay for this sin with their lives. Meanwhile Ahab wanted to purchase Naboth's vineyard in Jezreel.
Naboth refused saying, 'The LORD forbid that I should give the
inheritance of my fathers to you!' (1 Kings 21:3).

King Ahab went away displeased. He sulked and refused to
eat his food. When Jezebel asked him what was wrong, he told
her of Naboth's refusal to sell his vineyard.

Jezebel devised a scheme to get rid of Naboth. She organized a feast to which he was invited. He was to be given a
place of honour beside several men who, during the feast,
would accuse him of having blasphemed both God and the king.

This happened just as Jezebel planned it. No sooner had the men told their lies than Naboth was taken outside the city and stoned to death. When that wicked deed had been carried out, Jezebel sent word to Ahab, 'Arise, take possession of the vineyard of Naboth ... for Naboth is not alive, but dead' (1 Kings 21:15).

The Lord commanded Elijah to face Ahab and to say, 'In the place where dogs licked the blood of Naboth, dogs shall lick your blood, even yours' (1 Kings 21:19). When he found King Ahab, Elijah spoke all he had been told to say, including these words: 'And concerning Jezebel the LORD also spoke, saying, "The dogs shall eat Jezebel by the wall of Jezreel"' (1 Kings 21:23).

When Ahab humbled himself before God, he was told that the prophecy concerning his throne would take place in the time of his son.

FIND OUT THE FACTS

1. Why was Ahab led into terrible sin?
2. Why was Ben-Hadad allowed to live? See 1 Kings 20:32-34.
3. Why should God be obeyed?

Ahab had again behaved most wickedly. But when he humbled himself, put on sackcloth and tore his clothes, the Lord said that the punishment would not come about during his reign, but in the days of his son. What does this tell us about the Lord?

A saying to Remember

The way to rise is to fall.
Thomas Manton

'But Micaiah said, "If you [Ahab] ever return in peace, the LORD has not spoken by me"' (1 Kings 22:28).

When I read the Bible I know that I can trust its teachings, because what is written is inspired by the Holy Spirit. God's prophets always spoke the truth, and frequently their words pointed to the saving work of the Lord Jesus Christ.

Ahab and Jezebel were wicked people. They turned the Israelites away from the worship of the Lord. When Ahab wanted to hear a favourable prophecy, he asked the false prophets to outline the future. He had made a pact with Jehoshaphat, the king of Judah, to attack Syria and recapture Ramoth Gilead which was a portion of Israel's territory.

When he called about four hundred prophets together to seek their advice, they said, 'Go up, for the LORD will deliver it into the hand of the king' (1 Kings 22:6).

There was only one prophet who had not been called. He asked for the Lord's prophet, Micaiah. Ahab told Jehoshaphat that he hated Micaiah, because he prophesied truth, which was often not what Ahab wanted to hear. When the king's messenger spoke to Micaiah, he encouraged him to give the king a favourable prophecy. But Micaiah replied, 'As the LORD lives, whatever the LORD says to me, that I will speak' (1 Kings 22:14).

So, Micaiah sarcastically told Ahab that he should go and fight against Syria and the victory would be his. But Ahab demanded to know the truth. Micaiah then told him that Israel would be defeated and left without a 'shepherd'. At once Ahab rejected his prophecy. Micaiah went on to tell Ahab that the Lord had sent a lying spirit into the mouth of his prophets to prophesy falsely concerning the battle. Ahab had him sent to the city governor, with the instruction that he was to be put in prison and fed only bread and water. Often God's people suffer for being truthful!

As the armies took their place for battle, Ahab disguised himself. The king of Syria instructed his soldiers to find Ahab. One soldier shot an arrow into the air and it hit Ahab through a join in his armour. Blood flowed, and with their king dying, the Israelites turned and fled.

Ahab's body was returned to Samaria to be buried. There, in a spring that flowed through Naboth's field, his chariot was washed and the dogs lapped up his blood as had been prophesied (1 Kings 21:19).

All that God promises will surely come to pass!

FIND OUT THE FACTS

1. In the days of the Old Testament how did God's people know if a prophet spoke God's words?
2. Try and find out something about the character of Jehoshaphat. Read 2 Chronicles 17:7-9; 19:1-9; 20.
3. How should our rulers today act towards their people, and towards God? Read Romans 13:1-7.

People with evil intentions, like Ahab, do not like to hear the truth. The Lord calls his people to be people of truth. What are the consequences of being truthful in a world which loves to hear lies?

Lies hunt in packs. *C. H. Spurgeon*

2 Kings
2:12-18

'...As they continued on and talked, that suddenly a chariot of fire appeared with horses of fire, and separated the two of them; and Elijah went up by a whirlwind into heaven' (2 Kings 2:11).

I don't like heights. To be above the ground, fills me with fear. Why? I remember climbing a ladder when I was young; one of the rungs of the ladder broke and I fell and hurt myself.

When Ahaziah, king of Israel, had a serious fall from a palace window, he sent his servants to ask Baal-Zebub, the god of Ekron, if he would recover. The angel of the Lord met Elijah and told him to intercept Ahaziah's servants and tell them that the king would die.

When they returned to their king, he demanded to know who had told them. They reported to Ahab that it was a hairy man who wore a leather belt around his clothing. At once the king knew it was Elijah to whom they had spoken.

Ahaziah sent fifty men to Elijah, commanding 'the man of God' to come to him. Elijah's reply was that if he was a 'man of God', fire would fall from heaven and destroy them. The fire fell and they were destroyed. So Ahaziah sent another fifty men, but Elijah responded in the same way. On the third occasion, the king's fifty men pleaded with Elijah to save them by visiting the king. This time the angel of the Lord told Elijah to follow them and prophesy that the king would die.

The time had now come for Elisha to take up Elijah's task. Elijah knew that God would soon remove him from the earth. Many sons of the prophets followed to observe what occurred, but they remained at a distance and watched. When Elijah and Elisha reached the Jordan, Elijah rolled up his cloak and hit the water which parted. Both men crossed over on dry land. When Elijah asked Elisha what he could do for him before he was taken away, Elisha replied, 'Please let a double portion of your spirit be upon me' (2 Kings 2:9). Elijah told him that if he saw his departure then he could take that as a sign that God had granted his request.

As they walked and talked, 'suddenly a chariot of fire appeared with horses of fire, and separated the two of them; and Elijah went up by a whirlwind into heaven' (2 Kings 2:11). In Psalm 68:17 God tells us about his chariots.

Elisha cried out and tore his clothes. Picking up Elijah's cloak, he struck the Jordan, the water separated and he walked over on dry ground. When the sons of the prophets met him they bowed to the ground acknowledging him as Elijah's successor: 'The spirit of Elijah rests on Elisha' (2 Kings 2:15).

FIND OUT THE FACTS

1. What other prophet was similar to Elijah? Read Matthew 11:14.
2. Who, by God's power, divided water to allow his people to safely cross?
3. Who are in heaven in their glorified bodies? Think carefully!

Elijah's work was complete; it was time for him to leave this world. Before he was taken up into heaven, he passed his mantle on to Elisha. Thank the Lord that he has never left this fallen world without a messenger, a witness.

A saying to Remember

Train a child in the way you should have gone. C. H. Spurgeon

2 Kings   '...and as he was going up the
2:19-25   road, some youths came from
             the city and mocked him, and
             said to him, "Go up, you
             baldhead! Go up, you
             baldhead!"'(2 Kings 2:23).

Some years ago several boys rudely shouted out to their school principal, 'Old baldhead!' That wasn't because they knew the story of Elisha and the young men, but because the principal was bald.

Elisha had seen Elijah taken into heaven in a whirlwind and soon the news spread. The prophets from Jericho knew that the spirit of Elijah rested upon Elisha. Some others wanted a search party sent out to find Elijah, as they thought that God had simply moved him to another place. Elisha did not agree with this suggestion. But the men pleaded with him to agree to them going to look for Elijah. He said that fifty men could search for three days. After that time, they had to accept the truth that God had removed Elijah from the earth.

There followed a series of miracles that established Elisha as the Lord's prophet. The first miracle was to make Jericho's drinking water sweet to drink and the land fertile. He asked for a new bowl into which he put some salt. Then he went to the source of the river and threw the salt in there. The water was made pure.

While Elisha was walking from Jericho to Bethel some young men met him. They had heard of Elijah being taken into heaven so invited Elisha to do the same: 'Go up, you baldhead! Go up, you baldhead!' (2 Kings 2:23). When Elisha cursed them in the name of the Lord, two ferocious female bears appeared from the forest and mauled forty-two of the boys.

A poor woman, the wife of one of the sons of the prophets who had died, was desperately in need of money. The creditors were coming to take her two sons. Elisha told her to get as many empty 'vessels' as she could find and then pour the oil from her last jar into the containers. Soon she had a huge supply of oil which was sold to pay her debt. It was God who paid her debt, just as Jesus paid the debt of his people for their sin.

Some time later Elisha met a well-to-do woman at Shunem, who invited him in for a meal. She had seen him pass by before, and knowing him to be a prophet, asked her husband to build a small room where Elisha could rest. In the room was placed a bed, a table, a chair and a lampstand. This act of kindness would be repaid by Elisha.

J. C. Ryle wrote, 'A life of self-denying kindness to others is the true secret of greatness in God's kingdom.'

FIND OUT THE FACTS

1. Name three periods in history when there were many miracles.
2. What did the young men mean when they told Elisha to go up?
3. Have you ever opened your home to someone in need? Why?

The woman at Shunem showed Elisha great kindness. Ask the Lord to help you to see opportunities when you can show kindness to others.

Kind words bring no blisters on the tongue that speaks them, nor on the ear which hears them. C. H. Spurgeon

2 Kings   'For thus says the LORD, "They
4:18-38   shall eat and have some left
               over"' (2 Kings 4:43).

We are sometimes told that God does not perform miracles today. But every time a sinner is converted, a great miracle has taken place. Instead of having no interest in God, the Holy Spirit gives the sinner a new, repentant heart, which loves God and has a saving faith in the Lord Jesus. Great miracles were performed in the days of Elijah and Elisha.

As the woman had had a room built for Elisha, he wanted to show great kindness to her. He asked his servant, Gehazi, to find out what he could do for the Shunammite woman and her husband. Gehazi returned with the news that her husband was old and they didn't have a son.

Elisha called for the woman and told her that in a year's time she would be holding her baby boy in her arms. The woman didn't believe what Elisha told her, but at the appointed time she gave birth to a son.

One day, years later, the boy complained to his father of a severe headache. He was taken from the field to his mother where he died upon her knee.

The woman took his body up to Elisha's room and closed the door so no one would know of his death. Then, accompanied by a servant, she set out to find the prophet.

Gehazi, Elisha's servant, saw them coming and told Elisha, who ordered his servant to run and meet the woman and find out what was wrong. But the woman kept running, and falling at the prophet's feet, asked for help. Immediately Elisha sent Gehazi ahead, with his staff, which was to be placed on the boy's face. When Elisha and the woman arrived they were told, 'The child has not awakened' (2 Kings 4:31).

On entering the room where the body lay, Elisha closed the door and lay on the body, putting 'his mouth on his mouth, his eyes on his eyes, and his hands on his hands' (2 Kings 4:34). Gradually the boy's body became warm. After walking around the house, he performed this action again. The child sneezed seven times and then opened his eyes.

Elisha asked the woman to come and take her son who was alive. The woman entered the room and, with thanksgiving, bowed down before Elisha. We can only try to imagine the joy in the mother's heart — her son who was dead was now alive.

Let us all give thanks to God who gave his only begotten Son to die, bearing his people's sins on the cross. He died and rose again that we might live.

FIND OUT THE FACTS

1. What kindnesses can we show to our pastors?
2. When was the last time in history that many miracles were performed?
3. What do you think was the greatest miracle ever performed? Why?

Think about the fact that the woman's kindness to Elisha was rewarded by the gift of a baby son and then the raising of that son to life again. Should we expect our acts of kindness to be rewarded?

Death will cut us down, but he shall not eternally keep us down.
William Secker

2 Kings   'If you confess with your
5:8-14   mouth the Lord Jesus and
             believe in your heart that God
             has raised him from the dead,
             you will be saved' (Romans 10:9).

It is always good when God uses you to tell a person about the Lord Jesus. It is a sad thing if you have never told anyone about him. Christians are called to be courageous and to tell others about the Lord they love and serve.

Naaman was the commander of Syria's armed forces. God had given him many victories. The king of Syria thought he was a great man. During a raid into Israel, his men captured a young girl, who became a servant of Naaman's wife. Naaman had all he could want, except his health: he was a leper!

The little girl told her mistress that there was a prophet in Israel who could cure her husband. When Naaman heard this, he asked the king for permission to visit the prophet. The king gave him a letter to the king of Israel, seeking his assistance. Naaman also took ten talents of silver, six thousand shekels of gold and ten changes of clothing. When the letter was presented to the king, he was horrified. He tore his clothes in anguish, saying that he could not heal anyone of leprosy.

Elisha sent word to the king, telling him to send Naaman to him. When Naaman arrived and asked to see Elisha, he was told by Gehazi, the prophet's servant, to wash seven times in the River Jordan and he would be cured. Naaman was very angry because he expected Elisha to come out and perform some healing ritual. He also believed that the rivers in Syria were much better for washing than all the rivers of Israel. As he was about to leave his servant pleaded with him to do as the prophet had told him. After dipping himself seven times in the River Jordan, he saw his flesh was as healthy as ever.

He returned and on meeting Elisha he said, 'Indeed, now I know that there is no God in all the earth, except in Israel;

now therefore, please take a gift from your servant' (2 Kings 5:15). But Elisha refused to accept any gift.

Shortly after Naaman departed, greedy Gehazi ran after him, saying that Elisha would accept two changes of clothes and a talent of silver. Naaman gave him more than he asked for and soon Gehazi had the treasure hidden in his home. When Elisha asked him where he had been, he lied.

Elisha, knowing what Gehazi had done, pronounced a punishment on him, 'Therefore the leprosy of Naaman shall cling to you and your descendants forever' (2 Kings 5:27). The witness of a little girl resulted in a Gentile army general being healed of leprosy and believing in her God. We have a wonderful story of salvation in Christ. Let us start telling our friends and neighbours about the Lord Jesus.

FIND OUT THE FACTS

1. What do we learn from that little girl who was the servant of Naaman's wife ?
2. What does today's verse mean?
3. Make a list of the ways your church could witness about Christ.

In his pride Naaman expected Elisha to come out to him and to perform some great ritual. Ask the Lord to give you a humble spirit which is willing to obey whatever he commands.

A saying to Remember

Sin is learned without going to school.
C. H. Spurgeon

2 Kings
6:13-23

'And Elisha prayed, and said,
"Lord, I pray, open his eyes
that he may see." Then the
LORD opened the eyes ... and he
saw...the mountain was full of
horses and chariots of fire all
around Elisha' (2 Kings 6:17).

When I was young, an axe was an important implement. As it was needed to cut the fire wood, it was always kept very sharp. Cutting the kindling and wood was one of the jobs my brother and I had to do.

When the sons of the prophets found their living quarters too small, it was suggested they go to the River Jordan and cut down some trees to be used for building. One man was very upset when the axe head he had borrowed fell into the river. When Elisha was told where the axe had fallen he took a stick, threw it into the water and the heavy axe head floated.

When the king of Syria attacked Israel, Elisha told the king of Israel where his enemy was hiding. The Syrian king believed he had a traitor in the camp, but was told that the prophet Elisha, who was in Dothan, told the king where the enemy troops were.

In the morning, when Elisha and his servant went to look from the city walls, they saw the Syrian army had surrounded the city. The servant cried out in fear, 'Alas, my master! What shall we do?' (2 Kings 6:15).

Elisha told him that he should not fear because the enemy was outnumbered by those who would fight to protect them. When Elisha prayed that God would open the young man's eyes and show him the angels in chariots of fire between them and the Syrians, the Lord answered his prayer (See Psalm 91:11).

Elisha then prayed that God would strike the Syrian army with blindness. When his prayer was answered, he went out to the Syrians and led them to Samaria.

He again prayed that the Syrian's eyes would be opened. When this happened, the troops were surprised to see that they were inside the city walls. Israel's king wanted to kill them all, but a kind Elisha ordered food to be brought to the captives before they returned to Syria.

There is a battle taking place in the unseen world about us! Satan and the demons are real. The apostle Peter warns us: 'Be sober, be vigilant; because your adversary the devil walks about like a roaring lion, seeking whom he may devour' (1 Peter 5:8). God protects his people from demons and wicked people, sometimes through death, when God's people are taken to be with Christ.

Satan can never capture one of Christ's people. It is our Lord Jesus who has all power in heaven and on this earth (Matthew 28:18).

FIND OUT THE FACTS

1. What is the purpose of miracles?
2. Where in the Bible are we told that Christ has all power in heaven and on earth?
3. Explain Hebrews 1:14.

God acts in amazing ways to protect his people. Thank the Lord that he never leaves his people to fight the powers of evil unaided.

Angels will never be kings. They will always be servants. *Andrew Bonar*

2 Kings   'You shall see it with your eyes,
7:1-8   but you shall not eat of it'
              (2 Kings 7:19).

In the western world food is plentiful and few people go to bed hungry. Maybe the day will come when God will punish our nations with bad seasons because of sin. We should always be praying that God would send revival.

Israel was again under attack by the Syrian army which surrounded Samaria. The surrounding nations were suffering a widespread drought, and food was very scarce. As the king of Israel passed two women who were squabbling, one asked for help. He was told of an agreement they had made. They had killed one of their sons for food and now it was time for the other child to be killed, but his mother had hidden him. This was a fulfilment of Deuteronomy 28:53.

Upon hearing this, the king of Israel tore his clothes in distress, and blaming Elisha for the famine, decided to kill him.

When the king came to Elisha, he accused him of being responsible for the troubled times, but Elisha prophesied: 'Tomorrow about this time a seah of fine flour shall be sold for a shekel, and two seahs of barley for a shekel, at the gate of Samaria' (2 Kings 7:1).

The king's servant asked, 'Look, if the LORD would make windows in heaven, could this thing be?' (2 Kings 7:2). Elisha replied that his prophecy would come to pass; the doubting servant would see it, but not eat the food.

Four starving lepers, who were outside the city walls, decided to surrender to the Syrian army, regardless of what might happen to them. They walked to the camp of the Syrians in the twilight and were surprised to find that all was very quiet.

Some time beforehand the Lord had made the noise of a huge army, which caused the Syrians to flee. The cry went up,

'Look, the king of Israel has hired against us the kings of the Hittites and the kings of the Egyptians to attack us!' (2 Kings 7:6). The Syrians had left behind weapons, food and treasures. The surprised lepers had food to eat, clothes to wear, and treasures which they hid.

Realizing that the king and people in the city were desperate for food, they told the gatekeepers, who advised the king. He was suspicious and thought it was a trick to make the people leave the city and then be attacked. However, the lepers' report proved to be true.

The citizens were soon taking whatever they wanted from the Syrian camp, and a seah of flour could be bought for a shekel and two seahs of barley for a shekel, just as Elisha had prophesied.

In the crush of people at the city gate, the king's doubting servant was trampled and he died, just as Elisha had said he would.

FIND OUT THE FACTS

1. Is there any limit to what God can do? See Titus 1:2.
2. Why would the king tear his clothes?
3. How do we see God's care of his people here?

The doubting officer did not believe Elisha's words. This cost him his life. Think about the seriousness of not believing what God says.

Fear is the beginning of defeat. *Anon*

2 Kings   'The dogs shall eat Jezebel on
9:27-37   the plot of ground at Jezreel,
              and there shall be none to bury
              her' (2 Kings 9:10).

Have you ever heard someone call a woman 'Jezebel'? The name Jezebel seems to be used by some people to describe women who wear too much make-up and jewellery. I trust that you are not a 'name caller'.

Elisha gave a bottle of oil to one of the prophet's sons and instructed him to visit Ramoth Gilead and anoint Jehu, the son of Jehoshaphat, who would replace Joram as king of Israel.

The servant did just as Elisha had instructed. He anointed Jehu and told him he was to kill Ahab's descendants. This was to avenge the death of God's prophets by wicked Ahab and Jezebel. Of Jezebel he said, 'The dogs shall eat Jezebel on the plot of ground at Jezreel, and there shall be none to bury her' (2 Kings 9:10).

When Jehu told his friends what had happened, they placed some of their clothes on the stairs where he would walk. They blew their trumpets, announcing that he was king of Israel.

Jehu and his followers set off for Jezreel to carry out Elisha's instructions. Upon approaching the city, King Joram sent a servant to find out if Jehu came in peace or not. When this failed to bring a response, King Joram and Ahaziah, king of Judah, went out to meet him. When Jehu said he had come to destroy Jezebel and her witchcraft, Joram turned and fled. Jehu quickly fired an arrow, which fatally wounded him.

Jehu told Bidkar, his captain, to throw Joram's body onto Naboth's field, while he chased Ahaziah. Upon catching up with Ahaziah, he had him killed.

Jezebel and all of Ahab's seventy sons in Samaria were to be put to death. When Jehu reached Jezreel, Jezebel, realizing her life was soon to end, prepared for her death by making up her face.

Jehu gave the command to throw her down from her upper room. Some of her blood splattered on the ground, the wall, and on the nearby horses. Jehu decided to have his meal before disposing of Jezebel's body. Later when he ordered some men to remove the body for burial, little was left. The dogs had eaten her flesh and the horses had trampled her body underfoot. Only her skull, feet and the palms of her hands were found.

Who was buried at Jezreel? The prophecy of Elisha had been fulfilled: 'On the plot of ground at Jezreel dogs shall eat the flesh of Jezebel; and the corpse of Jezebel shall be as refuse on the surface of the field, in the plot at Jezreel, so that they shall not say, "Here lies Jezebel"' (2 Kings 9:36-37).

FIND OUT THE FACTS

1. Why do you think Jezebel went to all the trouble of painting her face and wearing something special on her head? (See 2 Kings 9:30).
2. How could Elisha know the future?
3. Ahab made a big mistake by marrying Jezebel. What do we learn from his mistake?

The events which are described in today's devotion clearly show that God is the one who gives the verdict on people's lives. How should this influence the way we live?

A successful marriage is always a triangle: a man, a woman and God.
Anon

2 Chronicles   'Behold, the king's son shall
22:10-12   reign, as the Lᴏʀᴅ has said of
                the sons of David' (2 Chroni-
                cles 23:3).

God made a great promise to David, that one of his descend-ants would rule his people. His greatest Son is Christ our Saviour. In order for this promise to be fulfilled, David was to have a line of descendants down to the Lord Jesus.

King Jehu cleansed Israel of Baal worship, but the people continued to worship the Lord, represented by two golden calves. King Hazael of Syria captured some of the land.

Meanwhile in Judah, Ahaziah died. His mother, Athaliah, took action to kill all the royal heirs which meant that David's line would come to an end. But the Lord was in control!

Jehoshabeath, King Joram's daughter, hid little Joash (often called Jehoash) in the temple for six years during the reign of Athaliah. During the seventh year of her reign, Jehoiada, the high priest, won over the Levites and elders of the people. In the temple they made a covenant to protect Joash from Athaliah's soldiers. Soon the people of Judah were armed and ready to take action against her.

Joash was taken to the temple and crowned while all the people called out, 'Long live the king!' (2 Chronicles 23:11). When Athaliah came to discover the reason for the rejoicing, she was met by crowds of people singing and playing instru-ments. She tore her clothes, crying out, 'Treason! Treason!' (2 Chronicles 23:13).

Jehoiada gave the command that Athaliah was to be taken from the temple and killed. How true it is that we reap what we sow! Jehoiada, the high priest, King Joash and the people made a covenant stating that the nation would serve only the Lord. The temples of Baal were destroyed and his priests were put to death.

Joash, who was just seven years old, was escorted to the royal palace and the nation rested. He grew to be a king who was faithful to the Lord for a time. He repaired the neglected temple. Money was needed for this work, so a box was placed at the entrance to receive the people's contributions.

After much work the temple was restored. However, when the high priest, Jehoiada, died, the king and the nation slipped back into idolatry. The Lord's prophet, Zechariah, the son of Jehoiada, was stoned at the command of King Joash, because he preached righteousness to the Lord. His dying words were 'The LORD look on it, and repay!' (2 Chronicles 24:22). God's people often suffer when they stand on the Lord's side.

As punishment, the Syrians captured the land and seriously wounded Joash. His servants then killed the king, and Amaziah, his son, ruled.

FIND OUT THE FACTS

1. Why did God save the life of Joash?
2. What was promised David, in God's covenant with him?
3. Discuss: 'You are accountable to God for everything you do and say.'

While Jehoiada, the high priest, was alive, Joash was faithful to the Lord. When Jehoiada was removed, Joash fell into idolatry. Our faith in the Lord should not be supported by the influence of others.

We cannot rely on God's promises without obeying his commandments. *John Calvin*

2 Kings
13:14-21

'And as it is appointed for men
to die once, but after this the
judgement' (Hebrews 9:27).

Recently I attended the funeral of a member of our congregation. I had visited him in hospital several days before he died and he spoke to me and to everyone who could hear him of his love for Christ and his joy in going home to be with God, his Saviour.

Elisha had a different character than Elijah, but they both loved and served their God. While Elijah came from the wilderness to denounce Ahab and Jezebel for their wickedness, his life was continually in danger and his passing from this earth was extraordinary.

Elisha, however, was a gentle man whose life consisted of teaching God's will and mercy. His life was also marked by many miracles.

As with all people, the time came for him to die. Joash, the king of Israel, came to visit the sick Elisha, at a time when the nation had suffered serious defeats at the hands of the king of Syria.

On meeting the prophet, he wept and said, 'O my father, my father, the chariots of Israel and their horsemen!' (2 Kings 13:14). He knew that Elisha's good influence would be a loss to the nation.

Elisha directed the king to get a bow and arrows and prepare to fire one arrow out of the east window which faced Syria. Elisha put his hands over the king's hands as the arrow was fired. Elisha then prophesied, 'The arrow of the LORD's deliverance and the arrow of deliverance from Syria; for you must strike the Syrians at Aphek till you have destroyed them' (2 Kings 13:17).

Elisha told the king to take an arrow and hit the ground with it. After the king had struck it only three times, Elisha said, 'You should have struck five or six times; then you would have struck Syria till you had destroyed it. But now you will strike Syria only three times' (2 Kings 13:19). Soon after this Elisha died and was buried.

Some time later, when a man was being buried near Elisha's tomb, a raiding party from Moab appeared. The burial party quickly dropped the dead man into Elisha's tomb. No sooner had the dead body touched Elisha's bones than it was revived. The man stood up and walked out of the tomb.

This miracle reminds us that death does not have the final victory. The day will come when Christ returns, the graves will be opened and the resurrection will take place. In our glorified bodies we shall have perfect joy in Christ's presence for ever.

In the years that followed, King Jehoash recaptured his land from the king of Syria. But, as Elisha had told him, he defeated the Syrians only three times.

FIND OUT THE FACTS

1. What is a prophet?
2. What is meant by the scripture verse?
3. Who is the Judge of mankind? Read Acts 17:30-31.

Elisha's ministry and death was different from Elijah's. Think about the fact that the Lord deals with us as individuals.

At a funeral we bury something not someone; it is the house not the tenant that is lowered into the grave.
Verna Wright

2 Kings
19:32-37

'Now therefore, O Lᴏʀᴅ our God, I pray, save us from his hand, that all the kingdoms of the earth may know that you are the Lᴏʀᴅ God, you alone' (2 Kings 19:19).

I don't know of any country in this world where Christians control the government and have introduced the laws of God. However, there have been privileged nations in the past, such as Great Britain and the USA, where Christians have had a great influence upon the government. In the new heavens and earth, God will be all in all, and we shall praise him for his grace and enjoy his eternal kingdom.

In Judah, Hezekiah became king. He was one of the most godly kings that Judah ever had. He destroyed the places where idols were worshipped, including Moses' bronze serpent.

Hezekiah was faithful to God's laws. Temple worship was reintroduced, as were the feast days. He rebelled against the king of Assyria and overcame many of the Philistine kings.

When Israel was defeated by the forces of Sennacherib, king of Assyria, he turned his army towards Judah, capturing some cities. Hezekiah offered tribute to prevent Sennacherib from attacking him again, but even though the tribute was paid, Sennacherib's army advanced towards Judah's capital.

When the Assyrians set up their camp outside the city walls, the commander of the Assyrian army, known as the 'Rabshakeh', demanded a surrender. He reminded the people watching from the city wall that no god had saved other nations from his forces and so the Lord could not save Judah.

Hezekiah dressed himself in sackcloth as a sign of sorrow and went to the temple to seek the Lord's help. He sent his servants to Isaiah who told them to stand firm because God would cause the Assyrian commander to return home, thinking he was needed by Sennacherib. When told to go home, he warned Hezekiah, that it was foolishness to trust in the Lord.

In the temple, Hezekiah prayed that the Lord would preserve his people and overthrow the Assyrians: 'Now therefore, O LORD our God, I pray, save us from his hand, that all the kingdoms of the earth may know that you are the LORD God, you alone' (2 Kings 19:19).

Isaiah sent word to Hezekiah that God had heard his prayer and would protect the city. Begin at Isaiah 37:21 and read a few verses. Hezekiah now felt secure, even though the Assyrian commander had returned to his post.

That night the angel of the Lord killed one hundred and eighty-five thousand Assyrian soldiers, and a humbled Sennacherib returned to Nineveh. There, while he was worshipping his god, his sons killed him.

Later when death was near, Hezekiah prayed for extra days of life and the Lord gave him another fifteen years.

FIND OUT THE FACTS

1. What should we do when trouble strikes? Read Psalm 50:15.

2. What was the title given to the commander of the Assyrian army? See 2 Kings 19:8.

3. Who saved Jerusalem from King Sennacherib?

God answered Hezekiah's prayers. Thank the Lord that he hears the prayers and the cries of his people whenever and wherever they pray.

God is a law unto himself, and ... he is under no obligation to give an account of his matters to any.
A. W. Pink

2 Chronicles   'Moreover Manasseh shed very
33:10-20   much innocent blood, till he
                had filled Jerusalem from one
                end to another, besides his sin
                by which he made Judah sin,
                in doing evil in the sight of the
                LORD' (2 Kings 21:16).

The Lord Jesus told the parable of the prodigal son where a young man took his inheritance and wasted it in sinful living. However, he repented and was welcomed home by his father. The story of Manasseh reminds me of that parable.

Manasseh was just twelve years old when he became king of Judah. His reign lasted fifty-five years and commenced with a period of great wickedness. He rebuilt the 'high places' and the altars where Baal could be worshipped.

He encouraged the people to worship the moon, stars and the sun, and even built altars in the Lord's temple. His subjects were instructed to worship his gods, and those who refused were put to death. The blood of innocent people stained the streets of Jerusalem from one end to another. Manasseh was so wicked that he even sacrificed a son to the false god Moloch.

The Lord punished this wicked king by allowing the Assyrian army to invade Judah and take him to Babylon as a prisoner in the twenty-third year of his reign. He was tied up with bronze chains and led with a hook to Babylon. This was a very humbling experience for Manasseh.

In Babylon he was a prisoner for twelve years, during which time the Lord convicted him of his sinful ways. A humbled Manasseh turned to God in repentance. We are told that Manasseh prayed to God who 'heard him'.

The Lord enabled Manasseh to return to Jerusalem. During the final twenty years of his kingship, he tried to undo all the evil he had encouraged during his early years as king. The foreign idols were destroyed and the idols in the temple were removed. The temple altar was repaired and again worship was rendered to God as he had commanded.

Not everyone returned to the purity of worship demanded by the Lord. Some still went to make sacrifices in the high places.

When Manasseh died, he was buried with his ancestors and was followed by his son, Amon, who encouraged the worship of idols. How sad it is that frequently children follow in the sinful footsteps of their parents. Parents must set a godly example for their children. We must teach them the law of God and show them that Christ is the only way of salvation. If we act like Amon, we have no right to expect that God will turn our offspring to the Lord Jesus in repentance and faith. May God bless each one of us.

FIND OUT THE FACTS

1. In what way was Manasseh like the prodigal son?
2. Where was the 'pig pen' of Manasseh's repentance?
3. What is repentance?
4. The vilest sinner has hope. Discuss.

God showed mercy to wicked king Manasseh. What does this show us about God's character?

A saying to Remember

The sinner's heart is the devil's mansion house. *Thomas Watson*

2 Chronicles   'Thus it happened, when the
34:14-21   king heard the words of the
                   Law, that he tore his clothes'
                   (2 Chronicles 34:19).

Have you ever read about the great revivals that took place in various parts of the world in centuries gone by? There have been times when God has given life to his dying church and many people have been won into the kingdom of heaven. We should be praying for revival today.

Josiah was eight years old when he became king, following the death of wicked Amon, his father. This young boy began to serve the Lord in his early years. At twenty years of age he had the idols removed and worship of the Baals brought to an end.

At thirty years of age he had the temple repaired. Money was contributed for the work and before long it had regained some of its original splendour. This was a satisfying time for Josiah and the people of Judah.

One day Hilkiah, the priest, found a dusty manuscript while at work in the temple. When he opened it he said, 'I have found the Book of the Law in the house of the LORD' (2 Chronicles 34:15). Immediately the Scriptures were taken to Josiah, who had them read to him.

What he heard caused him great distress. He saw clearly the sins of the nation, and also what God expected of his people. He tore his clothes which showed great humility before the Lord because he now knew why Judah was suffering so much: God was punishing the nation because of its sin!

Josiah's servants were sent to Huldah, the prophetess, to hear what she had to say about God's promise of punishment upon the nation.

The servants were told to return to the king and tell him that the nation would suffer all the curses written in the Scriptures. However, they were to tell Josiah, 'Because your heart was tender, and you humbled yourself before God when you heard his words against this place and against its inhabitants, and you humbled yourself before me, and you tore your clothes and wept before me, I also have heard you... Surely I will gather you to your fathers, and you shall be gathered to your grave in peace; and your eyes shall not see all the calamity which I will bring on this place and its inhabitants' (2 Chronicles 34:27-28).

King Josiah was greatly disturbed by all that he was told.

FIND OUT THE FACTS

1. God blessed the repentant King Josiah. What blessing do we receive if we truly repent of our sins?

2. What is the end of those people who refuse to repent of their wickedness?

3. We read that Shaphan was a 'scribe'. (2 Chronicles 34:18). What's a scribe?

4. What does Proverbs 29:18 mean: 'Where there is no revelation, the people cast off restraint; but happy is he who keeps the law'?

To Think & to pray about

God told Josiah that he would not bring judgement upon the nation during his lifetime. Thank God for his patience and mercy to sinners.

A saying to Remember

Repentance is never too soon.

C. H. Spurgeon

2 Chronicles
34:22-33

'Then the king stood in his place and made a covenant before the LORD, to follow the LORD, and to keep his command-ments ... with all his heart and all his soul, to perform the words of the covenant that were written in this book' (2 Chronicles 34:31).

It is a time of joy when sinners are convicted of their rebel-lion against God and turn to Christ with a repentant heart. Have you ever heard a sinner confess his love for Christ and his hatred of his sins?

Josiah truly loved the Lord and wanted his people to turn from their sinful ways and serve the living God. He gathered together the priests, Levites, and as many people as possible in the temple. There he read the words of the scroll which had been found in the temple. Josiah made a covenant with the Lord to obey all the commandments written in the Scriptures. He then made a greater effort to rid the land of idols and all false worship.

From the book of the law he read about the Passover, and had this feast introduced, providing lambs for those who could not afford them. The priests and Levites carried out their duties during that important feast, which was held in the eight-eenth year of Josiah's reign.

There must have been great rejoicing during the Passover because the people would have remembered the majesty of their God, who overthrew the power of Pharaoh and led his people into the land of Canaan. The sons of Asaph sang the psalms; and burnt offerings were made to the Lord, just as Moses had recorded in the Scriptures.

When war broke out between Egypt and Carchemish, Josiah marched with his troops to fight against the Egyptians. They sent word to King Josiah that he was not to be involved in these battles, as Egypt had not come to attack Judah. However, Josiah decided to play a part in the battle, and was wounded by an arrow while still in his chariot. His men quickly transferred him to a second chariot which took him back to Jerusalem where he died. Josiah was buried with his ancestors, while the citizens of Judah mourned the loss of their godly king.

God had promised that his people would be punished following the death of King Josiah. This soon came about.

We should remember that God will punish all sin! Every judgement of God in our age is a reminder of that great judgement when the Lord Jesus calls sinners to give an account of themselves. Are you ready for that day?

FIND OUT THE FACTS

1. Why is our Bible such an important book?

2. Josiah was a godly king who took action to establish righteousness in the nation. What is righteousness?

3. 'Righteousness exalts a nation, but sin is a reproach to any people' (Proverbs 14:34). What does this mean?

When God's laws were obeyed and he was worshipped in the right way, there was a time of great rejoicing. Think about the joy which comes as a result of obeying God and worshipping only him.

It may be hard going forward, but it is worse going back. C. H. Spurgeon

Isaiah   'Holy, holy, holy is the Lord of
6:1-10   hosts; the whole earth is full
             of his glory!' (Isaiah 6:3).

The Bible reveals that God created the angels before he created the universe in which we live. Some people think
that Jesus was an angel, but this is not so! The Lord Jesus Christ
is God's only uncreated, eternal Son!

God's people in Judah were sinning wilfully. They took very
little notice of his law, and consequently they were punished
with seventy years of captivity in Babylon. God wants his people to repent of their sins. The prophet Isaiah spoke of the
Lord as a saving God: '"Come now, and let us reason together,"
says the Lord, "though your sins are like scarlet, they shall be
as white as snow; though they are red like crimson, they shall
be as wool"' (Isaiah 1:18).

Before Isaiah commenced his work as God's prophet, he
saw Jehovah upon his heavenly throne. He saw the Lord 'high
and lifted up, and the train of his robe filled the temple' (Isaiah
6:1). About the throne were seraphim; each had six wings,
'with two he covered his face, with two he covered his feet,
and with two he flew' (Isaiah 6:2). They cried out, 'Holy, holy,
holy is the Lord of hosts; the whole earth is full of his glory!'
(Isaiah 6:3).

The throne room was filled with what appeared to be smoke.
When Isaiah saw that vision of the majesty and glory of God,
he was filled with awe. He realized that he was nothing but a
sinner, standing before the holy God. He then cried out, 'Woe
is me, for I am undone! Because I am a man of unclean lips,
and I dwell in the midst of a people of unclean lips; for my
eyes have seen the King, the Lord of hosts' (Isaiah 6:5).

When Isaiah was told that his sins were forgiven, he agreed
to go to the nation and warn the people of God's coming judgement. He was told that the Israelites had ears, but they would

not hear, eyes that would not see, and a heart that would not understand what he would say.

Isaiah had a difficult work to do, but he could always look back to that amazing vision of Jehovah sitting upon his heavenly throne.

Our reading reveals that the one sitting upon God's throne was 'Jehovah'. The apostle John said that it was the Lord Jesus Christ who was seen by Isaiah. We read, 'These things Isaiah said when he saw his glory and spoke of him' (John 12:41).

Paul said of Christ, 'He is the image of the invisible God, the first born over all creation' (Colossians 1:15).

Our Saviour is Jehovah!

FIND OUT THE FACTS

1. How can it be said of God, 'The whole earth is full of his glory' (Isaiah 6:3). Read Psalm 19:1-6.

2. How did Isaiah react when he had the vision of God?

3. How can sinful people gain entry into heaven? See Acts 3:19.

When Isaiah had his vision of the Lord, he was made deeply aware of his own sinfulness. Think about the fact that, in the New Testament age, the Holy Spirit brings sinners to an awareness of their sin and turns them to Christ.

A saying to Remember

They lose nothing who gain Christ.
Samuel Rutherford

Isaiah
42:1-9

'And there is no other God besides me ... Look to me, and be saved, all you ends of the earth! For I am God, and there is no other' (Isaiah 45:21-22).

One of my university essays was returned with the comment 'Fail! Do not attempt religious essays!' I later discovered that the examiner was the president of the St Thomas More Society (Thomas More was beatified by Pope Leo XIII in 1886). For a time I avoided anything that irritated that history lecturer. I am not ashamed of my Saviour and of being called a 'Christian'. I trust that you love God and stand firm for his truth and salvation.

Isaiah had much to say about God's 'Servant' who would save his people. Isaiah was not ashamed to preach God's word, even though he was treated with contempt by many who heard him.

On one occasion he wrote, 'For unto us a Child is born, unto us a Son is given; and the government will be upon his shoulder. And his name will be called Wonderful, Counsellor, Mighty God, Everlasting Father, Prince of Peace. Of the increase of his government and peace there will be no end, upon the throne of David and over his kingdom...' (Isaiah 9:6-7). All of these names could not apply to an earthly ruler, but they are fulfilled in the Lord Jesus Christ.

Isaiah also said of the coming Messiah, 'And in that day there shall be a Root of Jesse, who shall stand as a banner to the people; for the Gentiles shall seek him...' (Isaiah 11:10).

Christ would be a descendant of Jesse, David's father, and we know that people from every nation have acknowledged him as their Saviour. Do you?

Isaiah had prophesied concerning the coming captivity, when God's people would be removed from their homeland and taken to Babylon. However, the promise of God was that he would never forget them. He would bring back a faithful remnant, who would serve and worship him. God referred to Israel as his servant when he made the promise: 'You are my servant, I have chosen you and have not cast you away...' (Isaiah 41:9).

God has chosen a people to be saved through faith in Christ. The Lord Jesus is 'a light to the Gentiles', He is the one who will 'open blind eyes,... bring out prisoners from the prison, [and] those who sit in darkness from the prison house' (Isaiah 42:6-7).

Have you trusted your eternal well-being to him? We are all spiritually blind until that day when the Holy Spirit gives us a new heart that loves God and enables us to repent of our sins and to live a life of faith in Christ. Is Jesus your Saviour?

FIND OUT THE FACTS

1. What did our eternal life cost Jesus? See Isaiah 53:4-10, Ephesians 2:8-9 and Philippians 2:5-8.

2. Name two of God's great servants mentioned in the Old Testament.

3. Discuss the names given to Christ in Isaiah 9:6-7.

Thank the Lord that the Messiah came to save not only the Jews, but also the Gentiles.

For God so loved the world that he gave his only begotten Son, that whoever believes in him should not perish but have everlasting life. *The Lord Jesus Christ* - *John 3:16*

Isaiah
53

'All we like sheep have gone astray; we have turned, every one, to his own way; and the LORD has laid on him the iniquity of us all' (Isaiah 53:6).

We all sin because we are born with a sinful nature. We continue to sin which means we must face God, the Judge, who has been offended. How often in your life has somebody been punished instead of you, when you have done something wrong? No! We usually suffer for all our mistakes.

Isaiah, who lived some six hundred years before Christ, prophesied many things about our Saviour. In our last devotional passage we read some wonderful prophecies written by that prophet.

Isaiah tells us that God's Servant was going to be exalted. When we read Isaiah 53, we have a description of our suffering Saviour. There was nothing about the Lord Jesus that attracted people to him. Very few wanted to follow him; in fact we read, 'He [was] despised, and rejected by men, a Man of sorrows and acquainted with grief. And we hid, as it were, our faces from him. He was despised and we did not esteem him' (Isaiah 53:3).

We have here a picture of our Lord being rejected by his people. He was whipped, crowned with a crown of thorns, mocked, abused and finally nailed to a Roman cross. He carried the sins of his people to that cross and there was punished by God in their place.

Isaiah recorded that 'he was cut off from the land of the living' (Isaiah 53:8). Our Saviour died! And before he died, while hanging on that cross and bearing the weight of his people's sins, he cried out, 'My God, my God, why have you forsaken me?' (Mark 15:34). These are the opening words of Psalm 22 which was written by David. The Bible has many prophecies concerning the Lord's saving work.

Isaiah indicated that the Lord Jesus would die with the wicked and be buried with the rich (Isaiah 53:9). We know that Christ was nailed to a cross between two criminals. He must have looked like any other criminal who was deserving of death.

When Christ was pronounced 'dead', it was the very rich Joseph of Arimathea who came with Nicodemus to claim Jesus' body. Joseph placed it in his own tomb which he had prepared for the day of his death.

Chapter 53 of Isaiah is a perfect prophecy of the life and death of the Saviour. It is good to be able to read these words. But do you believe them? Have you trusted your eternal well-being to the Lord Jesus?

FIND OUT THE FACTS

1. Why is Christ called a 'Servant'? (Isaiah 52:13-15).
2. How could Isaiah know so much about the death of the Lord Jesus?
3. In what way did the Lord Jesus fulfil Isaiah 53:5-6?

Thank the Lord Jesus that on the cross he endured the wrath of God against sin.

Christ is a great Saviour for great sinners. *C. H. Spurgeon*

Isaiah
55:1-11

'Ho! Everyone who thirsts, come to the waters; and you who have no money, come, buy and eat. Yes, come, buy wine and milk without money and without price' (Isaiah 55:1).

Rarely has anyone offered me something worthwhile at no cost but Isaiah 55 commences with words that offer something which is worth more than all the treasure in the world for no cost at all. It is freely offered to anyone who would like it! It is salvation in the Lord Jesus. We cannot save ourselves. We are sinners and there is nothing we can do for God or give to God in order to be saved. God's only Son came to this earth, lived a sinless life and died in the place of his people!

That salvation which is free to us cost God the death of his Son. It cost the Lord Jesus a life of humility and a death upon a Roman cross. God has invited people from all parts of the world to reach out and receive that salvation for themselves. He has revealed that he 'is longsuffering towards us, not willing that any should perish but that all should come to repentance' (2 Peter 3:9).

Isaiah records God's call to sinners, 'Ho! Everyone who thirsts, come to the waters; and you who have no money, come, buy and eat. Yes, come, buy wine and milk without money and without price... Hear, and your soul shall live' (Isaiah 55:1,3). We are invited to look to Christ for salvation.

When should you look to Christ? Isaiah tells us: 'Seek the LORD while he may be found, call upon him while he is near' (Isaiah 55:6). And what better time is it to seek Christ than today? All who seek the Saviour and repent of their sins can rejoice in Isaiah's words: 'Let him return to the LORD, and he will have mercy on him, and to our God, for he will abundantly pardon' (Isaiah 55:7).

Our Saviour, the Lord Jesus, said, 'And as Moses lifted up the serpent in the wilderness, even so must the Son of Man be lifted up, that whoever believes in him should not perish but have eternal life' (John 3:14-15).

The writer of the epistle to the Hebrews records that Christians are to look 'unto Jesus, the author and finisher of [their] faith' (Hebrews 12:2).

When Jesus walked upon the water and approached the boat in which his disciples were crossing the sea, Peter said, 'Lord, if it is you, command me to come to you on the water.' Christ replied, 'Come' (Matthew 14:28). When Peter took his eyes off the Lord Jesus and looked at the waves, he began to sink.

You are to look to Jesus and pray that he will send the Holy Spirit into your heart. If you are sincere, the Holy Spirit will make you a new person and give you a saving faith in God's Son, a hatred of sin and a love of righteousness.

FIND OUT THE FACTS

1. What is meant by 'Look unto Jesus'?
2. Read Isaiah 55:8-11. What does this passage mean?
3. What response does God require of sinners in order for them to be saved?

Thank the Lord that his message of salvation is preached to all nations and that he saves people from all nations.

God is looking for some wicks to burn. The oil and the fire are free.
J. Hudson Taylor

Habakkuk   'How lonely sits the city that
1:1-2:4   was full of people! How like a
             widow is she, who was great
             among the nations!' (Lamenta-
             tions 1:1).

Jeremiah had warned the people of the coming judgement,
but no one took any notice. The result was that Israel and
Judah were taken into captivity by the Babylonians. And why?
Because God's people had rebelled against Jehovah, their God.
Israel was taken into captivity by the armies of Nebuchadnezzar
because of their sins. War was used by God to punish his covenant people. 'The LORD is a man of war' (Exodus 15:3).

In Habakkuk 1 we read the words that Habakkuk used in
his prayer to God. His cry was 'Violence!' because he saw the
wickedness of Judah (Habakkuk 1:2-4). He prayed that God
would revive the church. He longed to see Judah faithfully
serving and worshipping the Lord God.

He was very surprised when the Lord revealed that instead
of an immediate, gracious work of the Holy Spirit, the church
would suffer terribly at the hands of the cruel Chaldeans
(Habakkuk 1:6). He couldn't understand the reason for God
doing this. Why should God's people suffer? Why should God
raise up such a nation to chasten his people?

Habakkuk wrote of the wickedness of Nebuchadnezzar's
armies. They captured countries and took the people away like
fish. This was done by the cruel Babylonians — people were
chained together with hooks through their lips.

Despite the tragedy facing Judah, Habakkuk wrote, 'We shall
not die' (Habakkuk 1:12). He knew that God, who cannot lie,
would not destroy the nation. God had promised Abraham that
the world would be blessed through his Descendant (Seed)
(Galatians 3:16-19).

God had promised King David that one of his descendants
would sit upon Israel's throne as King of his eternal kingdom
(1 Chronicles 17:12-15). Christ was to belong to the tribe of

Judah, so it was impossible for the nation to be completely destroyed.

Habakkuk knew that God always kept his promises. So the nation would survive all that the Babylonians did to them. With such hard times coming upon Judah, how were the people to live? Again Habakkuk wrote, 'The just shall live by his faith' (Habakkuk 2:4).

This is how all of God's people should live. In Hebrews 11 we have a list of God's people who 'lived by faith'. They were able to look beyond this world's troubles to their God who controls the affairs of this sin-sick world.

This is how we should live in troubled times. God rules this world to his own glory and for the good of the church. All of the saints are promised eternal life despite the difficulties of this world. Are you living the life of faith?

FIND OUT THE FACTS

1. What is 'faith'? Read Hebrews 11:1.

2. What did Habakkuk mean by 'the just shall live by his faith'? (Habakkuk 2:4).

3. Are there ways in which the society of Habakkuk's day is similar to our day? In what way is this so?

Habakkuk found God's dealings with his people hard to understand. Thank the Lord that, even when we don't understand, he is fully in control and knows exactly what he is doing.

Faith's eye sees in the dark.

C. H. Spurgeon

2 Chronicles 36:15-21

'Blessed are those who are persecuted for righteousness' sake, for theirs is the kingdom of heaven ... Rejoice ... for great is your reward in heaven, for so they persecuted the prophets who were before you' (Matthew 5:10-12).

I live in an Australian state where corporal punishment in schools is forbidden. The Lord said, 'Do not withhold correction from a child...' (Proverbs 23:13). The day will come when parents are forbidden to smack their naughty children. God punishes sinners because of disobedience.

King Nebuchadnezzar sent his armies to Jerusalem during the reign of Manasseh and took him to Babylon in chains. Later, however, Manasseh returned to Jerusalem where he encouraged his people to serve the living God. After his death, his son, Amon, worshipped the idols of the pagan nations. Josiah saw revival, but during the reign of Jehoiakim, the Babylonian army again invaded Judah.

This time the soldiers removed some of the important articles used in worship. Nebuchadnezzar had them placed in the temple of his god, which was a sign to the Babylonians that their gods were far superior to the God of Judah.

Later, Nebuchadnezar appointed Zedekiah, king of Judah and Jerusalem. Soon the priests and Levites led the people even further into vile sin, serving the gods of the surrounding people. Zedekiah had sworn an oath by God to remain faithful to the king of Babylon. However, when the opportunity arose he rebelled.

God sent many prophets to his people, but their warnings were ignored, just like people today who ignore the warnings found in the Scriptures. They do not care that sin has its wages: death! How true it is; the natural human heart has not changed. People sin because they are sinners by nature.

God's time had arrived for the king of the Chaldeans and his immense army to invade Judah again and to strip the land bare, taking most of its citizens captive to Babylon where they would live for many years.

The soldiers destroyed Jerusalem's city wall, burnt the houses to the ground, and demolished the king's palace and Solomon's temple. Everything of value was taken back to Babylon and placed in their god's treasury.

What a tragedy was suffered by the people who made up God's chosen nation! Because they mocked God's messengers, despised his words and scoffed at his prophets, they faced seventy years of captivity. They had ignored the Sabbath, worshipped foreign gods and failed to allow the land to have its rest every seven years (Leviticus 25:3-5). The covenant people failed to obey the law of their Lord.

FIND OUT THE FACTS

1. Discuss Leviticus 25:1-7.

2. For how many years had the people ignored this law? Read 2 Chronicles 36:21.

3. What is God's attitude towards sin and the sinner?

To Think & to pray about

The fall of Jerusalem and the captivity in Babylon caused great humiliation to the people of Judah. What do we learn about God, who punished them severely even though they were humiliated by this defeat?

A saying to Remember

At every door where sin sets its foot, there the wrath of God meets us. *William Gurnall*

Daniel   'And in all matters of wisdom
1:11-21   and understanding about which
              the king examined them, he
              found them ten times better
              than all the magicians and
              astrologers who were in all his
              realm' (Daniel 1:20).

I am sure that everyone who reads this book has faced testing of one sort or another. I failed three subjects in my first year at teachers' college which meant I had to spend my Christmas holiday preparing for another set of examinations which I passed. I made sure that I didn't fail again.

Daniel, Hananiah, Mishael and Azariah, with thousands of Israelites, were taken captive to Babylon. Daniel was about fourteen years old. On their arrival there, King Nebuchadnezzar gave instructions for them to be trained in the ways of Babylon because they were intelligent young Israelites. They were placed in a training school and given new Babylonian names. Daniel became known as Belteshazzar, Hananiah was named Shadrach, Mishael was called Meshach and Azariah became Abed-Nego. The plan was to get them to forget their homeland and become loyal servants of King Nebuchadnezzar.

Daniel and his friends knew that the law of God stated that certain foods were unclean, and to eat them was sinful. Daniel spoke to the steward who was responsible for their training, asking permission to eat only vegetables and drink water.

The steward was concerned that they would not appear to be in good health and then King Nebuchadnezzar would punish him. However, he agreed to give Daniel and his three friends ten days to eat just vegetables and to drink just water. At the end of the time the steward found them all looking very healthy and in better physical condition than those young men who had eaten the food from the king's table and drunk his wine.

Daniel, Hananiah, Mishael and Azariah set an example of godliness to all who knew them. They would not disobey God's commands! God rewarded their faithfulness with knowledge, skill and wisdom. Before long they all had a sound understanding of Babylonian literature and to Daniel the Lord gave an additional gift of understanding dreams.

Remember that Christians serve God and obey his commandments. There are now no laws telling us what we may or may not eat. But we are to love God — Father, Son and Holy Spirit — and to care for our fellow-man, even our enemies.

We should always show the people about us that we love the Lord. This will take courage. Just as God gave courage to the four young men in Babylon, so he will give it to you.

FIND OUT THE FACTS

1. What difficulties did Daniel face in Babylon?

2. How do we show our love of the Lord Jesus? Read John 14:15.

3. What is the 'great commandment'? Read Matthew 22:37-40.

4. Why were the four young men given Babylonian names?

To Think & to pray about

Four young Israelites were in a foreign country but they did not forget their God. Why is it so easy to forget to obey God's commands when we are in the company of people who do not love and follow the Lord?

A saying to Remember

Religion is not a matter of fits, starts and stops, but an everyday affair.
David Livingstone

Daniel
2:36-45

'The king answered Daniel, and said, "Truly your God is the God of gods, the Lord of kings, and a revealer of secrets, since you could reveal this secret"' (Daniel 2:47).

King Nebuchadnezzar had a dream and he awoke very troubled. He wanted to know what his dream meant. He sent for his magicians, the astrologers, the sorcerers, and the Chaldeans demanding to know not only the meaning of his dream but also the dream itself. Of course, this was impossible and those responsible for the interpretation of dreams began to feel the king's anger.

When they argued that the king was asking the impossible, he replied that they were impostors and would all be executed. This meant that Daniel, Hananiah, Mishael, and Azariah would also be killed. Daniel knew God could make known the interpretation of the dream, so he asked for time so he and his companions could pray.

In Daniel's prayer he praised God, who raised up rulers and removed them when he saw fit. He also acknowledged that the interpretation of dreams came from God and thanked God that he had been given both Nebuchadnezzar's dream and its interpretation.

He then went in to tell Nebuchadnezzar his dream. He had dreamt of a huge image with a golden head, a silver chest and arms, a bronze belly and thighs, legs of iron and feet of both iron and clay. Daniel told the king that he was the head of gold, and the other parts of the image represented kingdoms of the future.

However, there was something unusual about the image: 'A stone was cut out without hands, which struck the image on its feet of iron and clay, and broke them in pieces' (Daniel 2:34). Daniel told Nebuchadnezzar that this stone represented the kingdom of God. The Lord would establish an eternal kingdom which would be far greater than all these other kingdoms. If you're a Christian, then you're a citizen of this kingdom.

What joy it is to be a member of Christ's kingdom! God is the one who sends the Holy Spirit into the hearts of his people and changes them so they love both God and his righteousness. God gives his people faith in Christ and a hatred of sin.

Nebuchadnezzar said in response, 'God is the God of gods, the Lord of kings' (Daniel 2:47). This reminds me of the words of the apostle Paul who wrote that the Lord Jesus is 'King of kings and Lord of lords' (1 Timothy 6:15).

FIND OUT THE FACTS

1. In the days of the Old Testament God often spoke through dreams. How does God speak to us today?
2. Name one other person who could interpret dreams.
3. Why was Daniel able to interpret the king's dreams?
4. What attributes (characteristics) of God are seen in Daniel's prayer?

No circumstance or situation is too great for God to deal with. Think about what a comfort this is for Christians.

When God is about to do something great, he starts with a difficultly. When he is about to do something truly magnificent, he starts with an impossibility. *Armin Gesswein*

Daniel
3:16-30

'And do not fear those who kill the body but cannot kill the soul. But rather fear him who is able to destroy both soul and body in hell' (Matthew 10:28).

Over the years thousands of Christians have died as martyrs rather than deny their God and Saviour. Today there are many people in other countries who are persecuted simply because they love the Lord Jesus.

The story of Shadrach, Meshach and Abed-Nego is one of courage and obedience to the living God, in spite of the cost. They were always faithful to God in the hostile environment of Babylon.

King Nebuchadnezzar was a proud man who expected obedience and could easily dispose of anyone who did not obey him. He had his artisans construct a golden image about thirty metres tall and commanded the important citizens to come to the dedication of the image and bow down when the music sounded. Those who disobeyed would be thrown into a fiery furnace. When the music sounded Shadrach, Meshach, and Abed-Nego remained standing upright. They would not disobey God's commandment! (Exodus 20:1-6).

When the king was told that the men had remained standing, he demanded that they appear before him. They were told to bow down when the music played, but they answered the king, saying, 'O Nebuchadnezzar, we have no need to answer you in this matter ...our God whom we serve is able to deliver us from the burning fiery furnace, and he will deliver us from your hand, O king' (Daniel 3:16-17).

In anger the king, who had forgotten the lesson he had learnt, decreed that the furnace be made seven times hotter and that the three young men be thrown into its flames. Quickly they were tied up and thrown into the furnace by the cruellest soldiers. Those soldiers died carrying out the king's order, so hot were the flames.

Instead of seeing the three men die, Nebuchadnezzar was astonished to see four people walking in the furnace, one 'like the Son of God' (Daniel 3:25). God's people were saved *in* the fire not *from* it! Nebuchadnezzar approached the mouth of the furnace and commanded them to come out. When they did, he was amazed to see that the flames had not even burnt a hair on their heads.

He then issued the decree that no one was to speak a word against the living God, who saved his faithful servants. We too should never fear man, but entrust our eternal security to the Lord Jesus, who alone can save sinners.

Take heart from the words: 'If God is for us, who can be against us?' (Romans 8:31).

FIND OUT THE FACTS

1. The king promoted Shadrach, Meshach, and Abed-Nego. Why?
2. How does God reward faithfulness?
3. What does the verse teach you?
4. What are we taught in Isaiah 43:2?

Shadrach, Meshach and Abed-Nego were willing to be thrown into the fiery furnace rather than disobey God. Could you do the same?

The title deed to this world does not belong to dictators, to Communism, nor to the devil, but to God.
Vance Havner

Daniel
4:28-37

'All the inhabitants of the earth are reputed as nothing; he does according to his will ... No one can restrain his hand or say to him, "What have you done?"' (Daniel 4:35).

God gave Daniel a remarkable gift to interpret dreams. King Nebuchadnezzar had a strange dream and when the astrologers and others failed to give him an interpretation, he called for Daniel. The king told Daniel that in his dream he saw a tree growing to such a height that it could be seen world wide. The birds nested in the branches and the animals found shade under them.

An angel appeared and gave the order to cut down the tree, and to strip off the leaves and branches, making it of no use to the birds and animals. However, the stump and roots were left with an iron band about the stump.

Then God said, 'Let his heart be changed from that of a man, let him be given the heart of a beast, and let seven times [years] pass over him' (Daniel 4:16). This was followed by words acknowledging that the Lord, the 'Most High' ruled the earth and controlled the affairs of rulers and kingdoms.

Daniel told King Nebuchadnezzar that the tree represented him. He also said that he would have a great kingdom which would result in him becoming very proud. The king was told that in the course of time he would lose his mind and wander the fields like an animal. This would continue for seven years, after which he would acknowledge that Jehovah ruled. Then he would regain his sanity and be restored to his throne.

One day, while King Nebuchadnezzar was boasting about his great kingdom, the Lord struck him down. He wandered about with the animals and ate grass for seven years. After that time, the king's sanity was restored and he praised the Lord who ruled the universe. He regained his throne and said, 'Now I, Nebuchadnezzar, praise and extol and honour the King of heaven, all of whose works are truth, and his ways justice. And those who walk in pride he is able to put down' (Daniel 4:37).

In his book *Dare to stand alone*, Stuart Olyott writes, 'The most merciful thing that God can do to a sinner is to knock him down. In that position a man or a woman is always safe. The only way he can turn his eyes is upwards. The only place to which he can appeal is heaven.'[1]

Are you a proud person? Remember this one thing: the Lord hates 'a proud look'! (Proverbs 6:16-17).

---

[1] Stuart Olyott, *Dare to Stand Alone*, Evangelical Press, England, 1995, p. 61.

FIND OUT THE FACTS

1. Why are people proud?
2. Is it possible for some people to be proud of their humility? Why is this?
3. Have you any reason to be proud? Read 1 Corinthians 15:10.

To Think & to pray about

King Nebuchadnezzar was foolish to think that he alone was responsible for his greatness as a king. Many people today see themselves as being fully responsible for their success. How should we see our achievements?

A saying to Remember

The sun should not set upon our anger, neither should it rise upon our confidence. *C. C. Colton*

Daniel
5:22-31

'Then the king's countenance changed, and his thoughts troubled him, so that the joints of his hips were loosened and his knees knocked against each other' (Daniel 5:6).

King Belshazzar, a descendant of Nebuchadnezzar, had organized a great feast for a thousand lords who served him. While everyone was enjoying the wine he provided, he decided to mock the Lord, the God of the Jews. He knew that Nebuchadnezzar had taken the precious gold and silver goblets from Solomon's temple and stored them in the treasury of the temple of Babylon's gods.

The king should have been well aware of the great deeds of the almighty God of the Jews. A proud, drunken Belshazzar instructed his servants to bring the goblets to the feast, so his guests could drink wine from them.

The lords, their wives and concubines mocked the Lord of heaven and earth by drinking and praising their gods of gold, silver, bronze, iron, wood and stone. By doing this they were saying that the God of the Israelites was just like any other god. They drank toasts to their gods and enjoyed themselves immensely until something terrifying happened.

God's patience had come to an end. Suddenly the fingers of a man's hand appeared. They were large enough to be seen in the light of the lamps in the hall. Everyone present saw what was written on the wall: 'Mene, Mene, Tekel, Upharsin' (Daniel 5:25). In his book *Dare to stand alone*, Stuart Olyott describes the wall as resembling a gravestone.

When the drunken king saw the four words, he stood up with trembling knees. At once he called for someone to interpret the words and the queen, possibly Nebuchadnezzar's wife, told Belshazzar that Daniel could do so. After Daniel was called, the king asked him to interpret the words, promising him the position and robes of a ruler.

Daniel told Belshazzar that in his pride he had mocked Jehovah, the living God, by using the vessels from his temple in Jerusalem. He then gave the interpretation of the words:

MENE — 'God has numbered your kingdom and finished it';

TEKEL — 'You have been weighed in the balances, and found wanting';

PERES — 'Your kingdom has been divided, and given to the Medes and Persians' (Daniel 5:25-28).

For this Daniel was rewarded and made the third ruler of the kingdom. That very night the forces of Darius, the king of the Medes and Persians, entered Babylon, killed Belshazzar and established a new empire.

FIND OUT THE FACTS

1. Who controls the affairs of this earth?

2. Name King Belshazzar's great sin that night.

3. When people worship idols, who is really being worshipped? Read 1 Corinthians 8:4 and 1 Corinthians 10:19-22.

To Think & to pray about

Even today people think that they can provoke God's anger and nothing will happen to them. Think about what this story teaches us about such an attitude.

If we are proud of our talents we betray our lack of gratitude to God. *John Calvin*

A saying to Remember

Daniel
6:1-9

'For he [Daniel's God] is the living God ... He delivers and rescues, and he works signs and wonders in heaven and on earth, who has delivered Daniel from the power of the lions' (Daniel 6:26-27).

Jealousy is an emotion that can cause much heartache. Think of families where one child has something the other one wants. The complaint is; 'It's not fair! I want one also!'

Daniel was a faithful servant to Darius, the Persian king, and was being considered for a promotion that would give him more power.

Some other officials, who were jealous of his success, wanted to get rid of him. But they couldn't find anything that they could use to get the king to change his mind concerning Daniel's promotion. The only way they could attack Daniel was through his faith in God. They approached King Darius and asked him to make a law which would require everyone to pray to him only for thirty days. Proud king Darius agreed with the proposal because it meant that the people would look upon him as a god.

The law was signed. The laws of the Medes and Persians were fixed and could not be changed (see Esther 1:19; 8:8 and Daniel 6:15). Anyone who disobeyed the king's command would be thrown into a den of lions. Daniel continued to pray openly to the Lord, three times each day. He was not concerned about the king's law but prayed at his open window where anyone could see him. Daniel knew that it was better to obey God rather than man.

At once he was reported to the king, who realized that he had been tricked into signing a law that would result in Daniel's death. As the law had to be obeyed, Daniel was placed in the lion's den and the opening sealed. The king found he could not sleep because of his respect for Daniel. However,

Daniel, who trusted in God, had the Angel of the Lord watching over him. This was none other than an Old Testament manifestation of the Lord Jesus Christ who shut the mouth of the lions.

Early in the morning Darius went to the den, had the stone removed, and called, 'Daniel, servant of the living God, has your God, whom you serve continually, been able to deliver you from the lions?' (Daniel 6:20).

Daniel replied that the Lord had saved him by closing the lions' mouths. Immediately he was taken from the den and replaced by the men and their families, who had plotted his death.

Darius glorified Daniel's God, commanding the people to tremble and fear Jehovah.

Daniel's God is our God!

FIND OUT THE FACTS

1. Name one character in the Bible who was martyred because of his faith in God.
2. Why didn't the lions kill Daniel?
3. What are you taught in Daniel 6:25-27?

To Think & to pray about

God's people will always be opposed in this sinful world. When we face opposition, is it time to stop what we are doing, to change our course of action or to continue just as we **were** before? What do you think?

A saying to Remember

Forget a frowning world, and serve a smiling God. C. H. Spurgeon

Daniel
7:1-10

'I watched till thrones were put in place, and the Ancient of Days was seated; his garment was white as snow, and the hair of his head was like pure wool' (Daniel 7:9).

Parts of the Bible are hard to understand. Many Christians don't read the book of Revelation because the images are difficult to interpret. This chapter deals with events that occurred during the reign of King Belshazzar, king of Babylon.

Daniel dreamt about four strange animals that came up out of the sea. The first was like a lion which had the wings of an eagle and represented the Babylonian kingdom; the second was like a bear, representing the kingdom of the Medes and Persians, and the third was like a leopard, representing the Greek empire of Alexander the Great.

The last animal was 'dreadful and terrible, exceedingly strong. It had huge iron teeth; it was devouring, breaking in pieces, and trampling the residue with its feet. It was different from all the beasts that were before it, and it had ten horns' (Daniel 7:7). The horn was a symbol of power. This was the kingdom of Rome.

Daniel could see the last animal and its horns, when suddenly a little horn appeared, which had 'eyes like the eyes of a man, and a mouth speaking pompous words' (Daniel 7:8). This little horn is none other than the 'man of sin' of 2 Thessalonians 2:3. The 'man of sin' is the antichrist who is the one who attempts to occupy the place of the Lord Jesus Christ. He hates Christianity and does what he can to destroy Christ's kingdom.

Do you remember the great statue that Nebuchadnezzar had seen in his dream? Remember the small stone that fell from the statue and destroyed it? That was the kingdom of Christ, and in Daniel 7:13-14 we see the same event happening again.

We have a picture of God, surrounded by a multitude of angels, sitting upon his heavenly throne and ruling the world.

The antichrist is defeated. God rules history; it is 'his-story', and Christ's kingdom extends to all nations of the earth and will never be destroyed.

We read that 'the books were opened' — the books recording the activities of the kingdoms of the world. They stand before God, the Judge. In Revelation 20:12 we read of that same day when the books are opened.

Are you prepared for that day? If you have entrusted your life to the Lord Jesus you will be safe on the Day of Judgement and you will take your place in God's new heavens and earth.

No one is able to escape the Day of Judgement. Every person who has ever lived will appear before Christ, the Judge.

As the Boy Scouts say, 'Be prepared!'

FIND OUT THE FACTS

1. What beast represented the kingdom of Alexander the Great?
2. Where do we find the kingdom of God? See Luke 17:21.
3. How do sinners gain entry into God's kingdom?
4. Read Daniel 7:8. Who is the person described there?

Daniel was given the interpretation of his dream. Thank the Lord that he gives believers the understanding of his Word and his ways by his Holy Spirit.

A saying to Remember

As death leaves us, so judgement will find us. *Thomas Brooks*

June

He who keeps
instruction is
in the way of
life, but he
who refuses
correction
goes astray

Proverbs 10:17

Daniel
7:13-14,
26-27

'I was watching in the night visions, and behold, one like the Son of Man, coming with the clouds of heaven!' (Daniel 7:13).

Occasionally we see a TV programme which shows the pomp and ceremony of Queen Elizabeth II seated upon her throne.

In our reading we have a description of the Son of Man, approaching the 'Ancient of Days'. This is Christ approaching God the Father (John 20:17) and taking his seat upon God's throne. This momentous event took place when, following his resurrection, Christ ascended into heaven from where he rules the heavens and earth (Matthew 28:18).

In Psalm 2:6-8 we read these words: 'Yet I have set my king on my holy hill of Zion. I will declare the decree: the LORD has said to me, "You are my Son, today I have begotten you. Ask of me, and I will give you the nations for your inheritance, and the ends of the earth for your possession."'

Here we read of the heavenly Father seating his Son, the God-man upon heaven's throne, from where he rules the world for the glory of God and the good of the church. Think of what a day it was when the angels stood and watched the coronation of King Jesus (Psalm 24:7-10)!

In Revelation 5 we have the same picture. God is seated upon the throne with a scroll in his hand. Someone who is worthy must open it, for it contains the outline of history between the first and second comings of the Lord Jesus, and also into eternity.

The one who stepped forward to take the scroll from the hand of God was none other than 'the Lion of the tribe of Judah,' who looked like 'a Lamb as though it had been slain' (Revelation 5:5,6).

This is our Lord Jesus, the King of the church, our Saviour, the Lamb of God, the 'KING OF KINGS AND LORD OF LORDS' (Revelation 19:16).

Today, so many people mock Christians and only use the name of the Saviour when they swear. But we are told that the day will come when 'at the name of Jesus every knee should bow, of those in heaven, and of those on earth, and of those under the earth, and that every tongue should confess that Jesus Christ is Lord, to the glory of God the Father' (Philippians 2:10-11).

All the kingdoms of the earth will come to nothing, just as they have in times gone past. The kingdom of the antichrist will be destroyed and the kingdom of Christ will dwell in the new heavens and new earth.

FIND OUT THE FACTS

1. Why is Christ called 'the Lion of the tribe of Judah'?
2. Who will be the judge when Christ returns? Read Acts 17:31.
3. Christ has all power in heaven and earth. How does this knowledge encourage persecuted Christians?

Thank the Lord again today that he is seated on his throne in heaven and that he rules the universe from that position of power.

No man ever errs on the side of giving too much honour to God the Son. J. C. Ryle

Daniel
9:1-9

'And I prayed to the LORD my God ... and said, "O Lord, great and awesome God, who keeps his covenant ... with those who keep his commandments, we have sinned and committed iniquity"' (Daniel 9:4-5).

Do you really pray to God, thanking him for his goodness, praising his name, asking for blessings and the forgiveness of your sins? I don't mean do you say some prayers you have memorized. Children need to be taught how to pray. Parents should establish the habit of prayer, of attendance at worship and daily Bible reading.

Please take the time to read all of Daniel's prayer, as it is one of the great prayers in the Bible. It contains all we need to remember when we pray: adoration, confession, thanksgiving and supplication.

Daniel knew that it was the time to ask God for the forgiveness of the nation's sins. Judah had been taken into captivity by Nebuchadnezzar because of its rebellion against the Lord. The length of the captivity was known to Daniel because he had read the Scriptures where several prophets had prophesied concerning the length of the exile.

Jeremiah had written, 'For thus says the LORD: "After seventy years are completed at Babylon, I will visit you and perform my good word toward you, and cause you to return to this place"' (Jeremiah 29:10).

Daniel knew when he had been taken to Babylon and simply added seventy years to that date. He knew the time when the Lord would cause King Cyrus to release God's people (Isaiah 44:28; 45:1). Daniel was confident that his prayer would be answered because God's promises could be trusted. He prayed that God would forgive the nation and cause King Cyrus to permit the covenant people to return home.

He was concerned for the good name of his Lord. For many years the surrounding nations had laughed at the people of Judah and their God, saying that their God was unable to protect his people. The pagan nations believed their gods to be more powerful than Jehovah, the living God.

He prayed, 'O Lord, hear! O Lord, forgive! O Lord, listen and act! Do not delay for your own sake, my God, for your city and your people are called by your name' (Daniel 9:19).

We should all read our Bibles because it is there that we discover God's will. Then we can pray according to his will and always in the name of our Mediator, the Lord Jesus (1 Timothy 2:5). Of course, you can pray for those special blessings you need. But when you pray, mean it with all your heart!

FIND OUT THE FACTS

1. Why was Daniel's prayer sure to be answered?

2. Who is the Mediator between God and man? Read 1 Timothy 2:5.

3. Why should you pray to God?

4. What two activities were Daniel's secret to godly living? Read Daniel 9:2-3.

Daniel was concerned for God's glory. He prayed that God's name would be honoured. Think about how you can be concerned that God's name will be honoured in the community where you live?

The effective, fervent prayer of a righteous man avails much. James 5:16

Daniel
9:24-27

'Know therefore and understand, that from the going
forth of the command to
restore and build Jerusalem
until Messiah the Prince, there
shall be seven weeks and
sixty-two weeks... And after
the sixty-two weeks Messiah
shall be cut off, but not for
himself...' (Daniel 9:25-26).

God has made many promises and he can be trusted to keep
them. Throughout the Bible we have prophecies concerning the coming of the Lord Jesus Christ. The first promise is
found in Genesis 3:15 where we read, 'I will put emnity
between you and the woman, and between your seed and her
Seed; he shall bruise your head, and you shall bruise his heel.'

I wonder if Adam and Eve really knew what that promise
meant? Did they think that one day someone would come to
overthrow Satan? Later God promised Abraham that his 'Seed'
would bless the nations. (Genesis 22:18; Galatians 3:16).

In Micah we are told that the promised one would be born
in Bethlehem: 'But you, Bethlehem Ephrathah, though you are
little among the thousands of Judah, yet out of you shall come
forth to me the one to be ruler in Israel, whose goings forth are
... from everlasting' (Micah 5:2).

We are told that the coming one would be known as
'Wonderful, Counsellor, Mighty God, Everlasting Father, Prince
of Peace' (Isaiah 9:6). He would sit upon David's throne, and
rule his eternal kingdom. In him the Gentiles would find peace
(Isaiah 11:10). If we turn to Isaiah 53 we have the whole chapter speaking about God's servant, whose death and resurrection
would save his people.

There are many prophecies found in the Old Testament
concerning the Messiah (Christ), some of which are yet to be
fulfilled. During Christ's life on earth many Israelites expected

the Messiah to come. The reason for that expectation is found in Daniel 9:24-26.

One of your questions asks you to find some other Old Testament prophecies concerning the coming of Christ. There is no doubt that the Israelites were expecting Messiah to come when he did. But the Christ they expected was so different from the Saviour who was born in Bethlehem.

But Christ did come and he lived, died and rose again, to save his people from their sins. The resurrection is an essential part of the Christian's faith because without it, our faith is useless (1 Corinthians 15:13-19).

Are you one of his people?

FIND OUT THE FACTS

1. Find several prophecies concerning Christ's coming in the Old Testament.
2. What does the name 'Christ' mean?
3. About whom is Psalm 110:1 speaking? See also Acts 2:34-36.

God revealed to his people that he would send a Messiah, a Saviour. Thank the Lord that he has revealed in his Word all that we need to know. He has not kept any essential teaching or truth from us.

In Christ Jesus heaven meets earth and earth ascends to heaven. *Henry Law*

Jonah
1:10-17

'So he said to them, "I am a Hebrew; and I fear the LORD, the God of heaven, who made the sea and the dry land"' (Jonah 1:9).

My brother John and I spent many enjoyable days on the ocean in my small twelve foot boat. Several times sharks were so close that we moved, as neither of us wanted to end up as a juicy steak for the shark!

Many people don't believe that Jonah existed, but our Lord, when asked for a sign that he was the Messiah spoke of him, saying, 'For as Jonah was three days and three nights in the belly of the great fish, so will the Son of Man be three days and three nights in the heart of the earth' (Matthew 12:40).

The prophet Jonah is mentioned in 2 Kings 14:25 and it is believed that he lived during and following the days of Elisha. The Lord instructed Jonah to go to Nineveh, the capital of the Assyrian empire, and warn them of the coming judgement. Jonah should have obeyed, but he decided he would go in the opposite direction.

We don't know why he disobeyed God. Perhaps he was afraid of the people. Perhaps he decided that the cruel citizens of Nineveh didn't deserve God's mercy, or that Jehovah was the God of the Israelites and should not be preached to the cruel Ninevites. Possibly he thought that God's power and authority ended at Israel's border or that God would show mercy to the people of Nineveh to make him look foolish.

Upon reaching Joppa he found a ship ready to sail to Tarshish, paid his fare and was soon on board and asleep. But God sent a 'great wind', and when the ship was in danger of sinking, the crew threw the cargo overboard. The huge waves became so dangerous that the captain called upon Jonah to pray to his God.

Then the sailors cast lots, believing that someone had offended their god. When the lot fell upon Jonah, he was asked what he had done that had so greatly upset his God.

His reply is given in the words of our scripture verse. He suggested that if they threw him overboard, the sea would become calm.

In spite of more efforts to save the ship, Jonah was thrown into the ocean and a calmness settled over the sea.

No doubt Jonah thought he was about to drown, but God had prepared a huge fish to swallow him — Jonah would be made to obey his command! In the belly of that fish Jonah was convicted of his sins and prayed to God for forgiveness and salvation. We read, 'So the Lord spoke to the fish, and it vomited Jonah onto dry land' (Jonah 2:10).

FIND OUT THE FACTS

1. What event in Jonah's life points to the great saving act of Christ?
2. Why do you think Jonah ran away from God?
3. Can anyone really escape from God's presence?

Jonah resisted God's word to him. How does this incident show that God's will will ultimately be done in our lives?

If you are not as close to God as you used to be, you do not have to guess who moved. *Anon*

Jonah
4

'Then God saw their works, that they turned from their evil way; and God relented from the disaster that he had said he would bring upon them, and he did not do it' (Jonah 3:10).

I didn't want to mow the lawn, but I knew it needed doing, so I went outside into the cool air and started work. Can you think of the times when you didn't do what someone asked you to do, or you obeyed but complained all the time?

Jonah didn't want to visit Nineveh, but three days in the belly of that fish changed his mind. He repented and asked for forgiveness. Three days later Jonah found himself on a beach, and at once set out for Nineveh.

When he arrived, he began warning the people of God's coming judgement: 'Yet forty days, and Nineveh shall be overthrown!' (Jonah 3:4). I'm sure Jonah said more than these few words.

There is something wonderful about the prophet being sent to Nineveh. And it is this: the good news of a God of love and righteousness was to be preached to Gentiles. This was a foretaste of the age in which you and I live — today the gospel is preached across the globe to both Jews and Gentiles! How we should thank God for the good news of the Lord Jesus Christ, who died to save sinners.

As Jonah preached, the people took serious notice of what he said. All the Ninevites, from the king down to the ordinary citizens began to fast and wear sackcloth, which was a sign of repentance. Even the animals were to be involved in the fasting. Everyone hoped that God would accept the people's genuine repentance and not bring disaster upon the city.

God forgave the people their sins, which made Jonah very angry. He spoke to God saying, 'Ah, LORD, was not this what I said when I was still in my country? ... I know that you are a gracious and merciful God, slow to anger and abundant in lovingkindness... Therefore now, O LORD, please take my life from me, for it is better for me to die than to live!' (Jonah 4:2,3). How disappointing to hear Jonah complaining when God had saved sinners in Nineveh!

Jonah went outside the city, made a shelter, and waited to see what God would do. The Lord caused a plant to grow, giving Jonah shade. The next day the plant withered, and, sitting in the sun, Jonah wanted to die.

The Lord rebuked the hard-hearted, sulking prophet who thought more of the plant than he did of the salvation of the citizens of Nineveh. This city had more than one hundred and twenty thousand people and much cattle. One day, in heaven, we shall meet some of those citizens of Nineveh.

FIND OUT THE FACTS

1. What sort of people does God save? Read 1 Corinthians 1:26-29.

2. What is 'the sign of Jonah the prophet? Read Matthew 12:38-41.

3. Why did Jonah complain when God saved the citizens of Nineveh?

God sent Jonah to preach to the people of Nineveh. Think of ways in which you can spread the message of salvation where you live.

Repentance looks upon the past with a weeping eye, and upon the future with a watchful eye. C. H. Spurgeon

Job
1:20-22

'Naked I came from my mother's womb, and naked shall I return there. The Lᴏʀᴅ gave, and the Lᴏʀᴅ has taken away; blessed be the name of the Lᴏʀᴅ' (Job 1:21).

I was once invited to visit the home of an old Christian who told me I could have some of his books. I enjoy reading and was soon there to see what books he had. He told me they were in the shed where he milked his cows. And true enough, there we found the books which had been feasted on by rats and silverfish. I was very disappointed!

Many Bible commentators believe the book of Job to be the oldest book of the Bible. It could well have been written before Moses wrote the first five books of the Scriptures. From this book of Job we learn some very important truths.

Job was a wealthy man, who had been greatly blessed by God. He had seven sons and three daughters, 'seven thousand sheep, three thousand camels, five hundred yoke of oxen, five hundred female donkeys, and a very large household, so that this man was the greatest of all the people of the East' (Job 1:3).

One day Satan appeared before God, claiming that Job held God in awe only because God had richly blessed him. The challenge was made: 'But now, stretch out your hand and touch all that he has, and he will surely curse you to your face!' (Job 1:11). Satan is always looking for believers whom he can tempt, hoping they will blame God for the evil that happens to them. But God always gives the grace his people need to remain faithful. The Lord gave Satan permission to do as he pleased with Job's possessions, but he was not to touch Job.

In a short time Job lost most of his worldly goods; his sons and daughters died when a strong wind destroyed the home in which they were feasting, causing it to fall upon them; the oxen and donkeys were taken by a raiding party that also killed all but one of his servants; the sheep were destroyed in a fire storm and his camels were taken by Chaldean raiding parties. Job was utterly distressed by all the news he heard. As a sign of his mourning, he shaved his head, tore his clothes and bowed down before God, worshipping him.

Job knew that he had brought nothing into this world and while here would only enjoy what God gave him. He would not curse God, who gave him treasures to enjoy and then took them away. God was the sovereign Ruler of the universe who did as he pleased in human affairs.

We should remember that all we have comes from God. Remember to thank him for his goodness to you.

FIND OUT THE FACTS

1. Does Satan appear before God now, complaining about what God does? Read Revelation 12:7-9.
2. Why do you think Satan was cast out of heaven?
3. Has Satan any power today? Read 1 Peter 5:8.

Job lost his family and his possessions in one day. Yet he didn't get angry with God or demand to know why this had happened to him. Think about Job's response recorded in Job 1:20-**22**.

Patient waiting is often the highest way of doing God's will.
Jeremy Collier

Job
2:11-13

'"Shall we indeed accept good from God, and shall we not accept adversity?" In all this Job did not sin with his lips' (Job 2:10).

There are times when things don't turn out as we have planned, but they are exactly as God has planned. God is teaching us to depend upon him in every situation. The joys and trials in our lives are for God's own glory and our benefit.

When he lost his possessions and his family, Job did not respond as Satan had said he would. So Satan asked for God's permission to harm Job, because he believed Job would surely curse God if he suffered in his own body. Satan was given permission, but with one restriction: don't take Job's life!

When Satan covered Job's body with boils, he sat in a heap of ashes, a sign of distress, and scraped the sores with a broken piece of a clay pot. He was so ill that he wished he had never been born. At this time Job's wife came to him saying, 'Curse God and die!' (Job 2:9). She should have been patient and trusted God, just as Job did.

Before long, Job's three friends, Eliphaz, Bildad and Zophar, who had heard of his troubles, called to see their friend. When they saw him, they sat down beside him, tearing their clothing and throwing ashes into the air and all over themselves. They remained beside Job for seven days, without saying a word. What could they say to their friend in his deep suffering?

Job had no idea why he was suffering. God had not told him about Satan's defiant challenge. Job's friends didn't know all the facts, but they believed they knew why their friend was suffering, and they also thought that they knew exactly what he should do.

These men judged by appearances. They knew that God punished sinners and they incorrectly concluded that Job had sinned greatly. They urged him to confess his sin and repent.

The Lord Jesus warns us to be careful when passing judgement on others: 'Judge not, that you be not judged. For with what judgement you judge, you will be judged; and with the same measure you use, it will be measured back to you' (Matthew 7:1-2). Job's friends were sincere in what they did and said, but they were sincerely wrong.

Before you and I make any judgements about another person, we should make every effort to find out all the facts and to deal with our own prejudices. Even then we can make mistakes because we don't know God's plan. Each one of us ought to be a true comforter to those who suffer, and this means that sometimes we shall simply sit without speaking and hold the hand of a suffering friend.

FIND OUT THE FACTS

1. God's judgement is carried out through the Lord Jesus and will be perfect. Why?

2. We read in Job 14:1 'Man who is born of woman is of few days and full of trouble.' What does this mean?

3. What can you do to help someone who is suffering?

Job's friends suggested to Job that the reason for his suffering was sin. Our words can sometimes be most unhelpful to those who are in need. Ask the Lord to help you to speak **wisely** and sensitively to others.

Be kind. Remember that every one you meet is fighting a hard battle. *Henry Thompson*

Job
19:21-27

'For I know that my Redeemer lives, and he shall stand at last on the earth' (Job 19:25).

There are times when I wonder how much both Old Testament saints and today's Christians know about Christ and his salvation.

When reading the Old Testament, we find many insights that help to give us an idea of what our Saviour is like. We are not given a complete picture, but there is enough for us to recognize those prophecies that were fulfilled in the Lord Jesus.

In our Bible reading we discover that Job, who lived several thousand years before the birth of Christ, spoke with confidence of the coming Redeemer.

Job was suffering the loss of his health, possessions and the sympathy of his friends, but his faith in the Lord was strong. He knew that God would never cast him aside. He wanted his words of sadness written in a book for everyone to read. He even wanted them inscribed on a rock (like today's billboards), for all to see.

These words of confidence form the climax of his message: 'For I know...' Job knew some important and comforting truths. Job's Redeemer lived and would one day stand on the earth. Two thousand years later the Lord Jesus was born of the virgin Mary and, as a man, bore his people's sins upon the cross. Job's Redeemer would live a perfect life of obedience to his Father in Job's place. Are you able to say, 'Job's Redeemer is my Redeemer'?

Job also knew that after he died and his body returned to the dust from which it came, he would see God: the Lord Jesus, our Saviour.

When writing to Titus, Paul said he was 'looking for the blessed hope and glorious appearing of our great God and

Saviour Jesus Christ, who gave himself for us, that he might redeem us from every lawless deed...' (Titus 2:13-14). This was Job's hope. Within his heart he longed for that day, just as we should.

We are born to know trouble because of sin! Believers long for the day when Christ will return in glory and power to gather his people to himself.

In our resurrected body we shall see the Lord Jesus. Do you long for that day? If you belong to Christ, that day will be the one when your salvation will be complete, your resurrected body will be reunited to your soul and you will take your place in the new heavens and earth, where righteousness dwells.

FIND OUT THE FACTS

1. What is the resurrection?
2. Why was Job suffering so much?
3. Why did Job ask for pity from his friends?
4. Why could Satan appear in the court of heaven?

To Think & to pray about

Job was confident about his future. He knew where he would go when he died. Are you sure about where you will go?

A saying to Remember

God never saves a spectator.
Robert Brown

Job
42:1-6

'After this Job lived one hundred and forty years, and saw his children and grandchildren for four generations. So Job died, old and full of days'(Job 42:16-17).

Have you ever had a question which you can't answer but which you can't get out of you mind? Sometimes, as you are drifting off to sleep, the answer comes to you.

Job's friends, including a young man Elihu, accused Job of being responsible for all the things he was suffering. They were proud men who pointed to Job and said, 'You're to blame for all that has happened. Confess your sin; repent; seek forgiveness and when God forgives you, all will be well.'

Job maintained his cause by declaring his innocence. He believed that he had not given God any cause to afflict him. But he was unable to see the hand of Satan in his trials.

Some time later the Lord would teach Job by asking him searching questions which would reveal to him God's character: 'Where were you when I laid the foundations of the earth? Tell me, if you have understanding' (Job 38:4). Job was being led to see the majesty and power of God. Again and again, God asked Job questions that would make him realize that he was nothing of importance when compared to the all powerful, almighty God.

When the Lord had completed his questioning (Job chapters 38 - 41), Job replied in the words of the scripture passage. His final statement summed up his feelings: 'I have heard of you by the hearing of the ear, but now my eye sees you. Therefore I abhor myself, and repent in dust and ashes' (Job 42:5-6). He realized that God was testing him, not punishing him.

When Isaiah had a vision of Jehovah Christ, seated upon the throne of his glory, he was humbled and cried out, 'Woe is me, for I am undone! Because I am a man of unclean lips, and

I dwell in the midst of a people of unclean lips; for my eyes have seen the King, the LORD of Hosts' (Isaiah 6:5). The majesty and purity of God should awaken in us a sense of horror about our sins.

In an incident Peter, the apostle, was brought to see his great sinfulness. He had fished all night without a catch, but when the Lord appeared he was told to lower the net again. This time the catch was so heavy that Peter had to be helped by other men. He saw the power and glory of the Lord Jesus and, falling down before him, he cried out, 'Depart from me, for I am a sinful man, O Lord!' (Luke 5:8).

Have you caught a glimpse of the purity of your God and seen your sins? Go to Jesus if you have and seek forgiveness.

Our story concludes with God greatly blessing Job.

FIND OUT THE FACTS

1. What were the new blessings God gave to Job? Read Job 42:10-17.
2. From his trials what was Job taught about God?
3. List and discuss three attributes of God found in today's study.

Job learnt a great deal from his suffering. Ask the Lord to help you to learn from any difficulties or trials that he may bring into your life.

If you lay yourself at Christ's feet he will take you into his arms.
William Bridge

Ezra
1:1-5

'Thus says Cyrus king of Persia: "All the kingdoms of the earth the LORD God of heaven has given me. And he has commanded me to build him a house at Jerusalem which is in Judah"' (Ezra 1:2).

I always enjoy going home where Val, my wife, waits for me and where Wags is wagging his tail. Home is where my study is full of books and an empty chair is waiting for me. At home I feel at ease and my heart is at rest.

When God's people die, they will go home to be with the Saviour who loved them and gave himself for them.

The Israelites had been taken captive in Babylon by King Nebuchadnezzar. But, now a Persian king ruled the empire, King Cyrus. He discovered that his name had been made mention of in the holy book of the Jews years before he was born.

Isaiah, the prophet, had prophesied concerning an edict which would be issued by a Persian king named Cyrus. This edict would allow the Jews to return to Jerusalem to build the temple (Isaiah 44:28; 45:1,13). The prophet Jeremiah had indicated that the duration of the captivity would be seventy years (Jeremiah 25:11-12; 29:10). In the year 458 B.C., King Cyrus gave permission for the Jews to return to their homeland.

In captivity the Jews had sung the words: 'By the rivers of Babylon, there we sat down, yea, we wept when we remembered Zion' (Psalm 137:1). But now it was time to return to the Promised Land, the land that flowed with milk and honey, the covenant land that God had given his people. The hearts of many of the people were filled with joy; they could go home to the land they loved!

Not everyone would return to Israel at that time, but Ezra gives us the list of the families who were moved, by God's Spirit, to pack their belongings and accompany Zerubbabel to

Judah. We also have a list of 'the articles of the house of the LORD, which Nebuchadnezzar had taken from Jerusalem and put in the temple of his gods' (Ezra 1:7).

Try and imagine the excitement these families must have felt as they packed their belongings for the long journey home. The old people would have remembered the land and would have been speaking, not just about the homeland, but also about Jehovah, the God against whom they had sinned.

They knew that Jerusalem was in ruins and that nothing much remained of Solomon's great temple. There was work to be done when they arrived home: a city, the wall and the temple had to be built. Yes, there was much work to be done.

FIND OUT THE FACTS

1. Of what Empire was Cyrus the king?
2. What part of King Nebuchadnezzar's dream concerning the great image, depicted the Persian Empire? See Daniel 2.
3. What had Jeremiah and Isaiah prophesied concerning King Cyrus and the Jews?

It is amazing that King Cyrus should have had the interests of God's people at heart. Yet that is the work of God. God is able to cause even umbelievers to further the interests of his kingdom. **How should you pray for your rulers?**

Home is home, be it ever so homely.
C. H. Spurgeon

Ezra
4:1-5

'And they sang ... to the LORD:
"For ... his mercy endures forever towards Israel." Then all
the people ... praised the LORD,
because the foundation of the
house of the LORD was laid'
(Ezra 3:11).

O ur second home was built by a friend during the early
days of his retirement. We told him there was no need to
hurry, as we thought it would be some years before it was
needed. It took three years or more for the building to be completed, but it was ready for occupation when it was needed.

In Jerusalem the sacrifices to God were commenced according to the law given to Moses as soon as possible.

The Israelites worked hard, and out of the ashes and the
rubble, the foundation of the temple could be seen. The priests
and Levites, with instruments praised God.

The people then shouted in praise to God, while others wept,
because they remembered the first temple which was more
spectacular than the new building.

The leaders of the surrounding nations feared the Jews and
urged King Darius to stop further building. They complained
that the Jews would soon have the city walls constructed and
then they would revolt against the king.

King Artaxerxes gave the order for the work to be discon-
tinued. After some time the Israelites recommenced their
building, only to face opposition. A letter was sent to King
Darius, asking him to search out the command of Cyrus that
gave them the permission to do what they were doing. A letter
came from the king declaring that Cyrus had indeed given the
Jews permission to return to their homeland and to rebuild
the city of Jerusalem, with its wall and temple: 'I Darius issue
the decree; let it be done diligently' (Ezra 6:12).

God also sent prophets to urge the people to complete the
rebuilding of the city. God spoke through Haggai: 'Is it time for

you yourselves to dwell in your panelled houses, and this temple to lie in ruins?' (Haggai 1:4). The people had suffered poor seasons and were accustomed to worshipping among the ruins. But now the citizens were commanded to get on with the building.

Zerubbabel and the people were promised that the glory of this temple would be greater than that of Solomon's majestic structure (Haggai 2:9). This was because Messiah would enter the temple, and through him both Jews and Gentiles would find salvation.

Today, the temple is the body of Christ, the church (1 Corinthians 12:12-27, especially verse 27 and Ephesians 2:19-22), which will reach its perfection in the new heavens and new earth, where the redeemed will dwell with Christ for ever.

FIND OUT THE FACTS

1. Why did the people stop building the temple?

2. How did God punish his people? Read Haggai 1:6.

3. Why did the older people weep over the new temple?

In every age, Satan tries to frustrate or stop the Lord's work in some way. How did the people of Judah respond in such circumstances? What attitude should we have in such circumstances?

Unity is the essence of the body of Christ. R. B. Kuiper

Ezra
9:1-4

'Blessed be the LORD God of our fathers, who has put such a thing as this in the king's heart, to beautify the house of the LORD which is in Jerusalem, and has extended mercy to me before the king and his counsellors ...' (Ezra 7:27-28).

Today we find many professing Christians marrying people who do not love God. What usually happens is that both people end up with an unhappy marriage, or return to the world, having no further interest in the Lord Jesus. The Bible tells us that Christians are to marry Christians!

About eighty years had passed since the time of our previous Bible reading. Ezra obtained permission from King Artaxerxes to return to Jerusalem, where he taught the people God's law, appointed magistrates and beautified the temple. The king gave him a vast sum of gold and silver for the adornment of the house of worship, in return for prayers being made to the God of Israel for his well-being.

Ezra made several trips to Israel to bring back more of the people who had made Babylon their home. He served the Lord faithfully, even refusing an escort of soldiers and proclaiming that Jehovah would protect him along the way.

Ezra was a priest and he had spent many hours praying and studying the Scriptures which he put into practice. He was also a scribe, who helped preserve the Word of God. He proved himself to be a good administrator.

When the leaders of the nation complained that many Levites, priests and ordinary people were still living with their pagan wives, he tore his clothing and pulled out some of the hair of his head and beard. He went aside to fall upon his knees and pray on behalf of the sinful people. He confessed the sins of the nation and pleaded with the Lord for mercy.

While he prayed in the temple, the people gathered about him and confessed their sins. They made a covenant with God to put away their pagan wives.

The decree was issued for all the descendants of the people taken into captivity to meet at Jerusalem. There Ezra issued the command: 'You have transgressed and have taken pagan wives, adding to the guilt of Israel. Now therefore, make confession to the LORD God of your fathers, and do his will; separate yourselves from the peoples of the land, and from the pagan wives' (Ezra 10:10-11).

God does not tolerate sin, and this meant such sinful marriages had to be put to an end, even when there were children born to the families.

Let us all beware of falling into this sin! God hates sin!

FIND OUT THE FACTS

1. Why should Christians only marry Christians? Read Deuteronomy 7:1-5; 2 Corinthians 6:14 and Malachi 2:15.

2. What responsibilities do married partners have to each other?

God's blessing had been upon the people by enabling them to return to Jerusalem and to build the temple. Yet they still sinned by marrying pagan women. Think about what this teaches us about sin.

A successful marriage requires falling in love many times — always with the same person. *Mignon McLaughlin*

Nehemiah   'And I said, "I pray, Lord God
4:13-18   of heaven, O great and awe-
                some God, you who keep your
                covenant and mercy with those
                who love you and observe your
                commandments"' (Nehemiah
                1:5).

Nehemiah, who was King Artaxerxes' cupbearer, was saddened when Hanani, possibly his brother, returned from
Jerusalem with the disappointing news that the city was in a
state of disrepair. This included the city walls. He knew that
he could help the people and after much prayer decided to ask
for the king's permission to return home for a time.

It was always risky to request something of King Artaxerxes,
as he was the absolute ruler of the Persian Empire and, as such,
he did as he pleased. But Nehemiah knew that Jehovah ruled
the world. Had not Nebuchadnezzar said of Daniel's God: 'He
does according to his will in the army of heaven and among
the inhabitants of the earth. No one can restrain his hand or
say to him, "What have you done?"' (Daniel 4:35). Nehemiah
took his concern to God, in prayer (see Nehemiah 1:5-11).

One day when Nehemiah brought wine to the king,
Artaxerxes saw that he was downcast and asked the reason
why. Nehemiah told him about the situation in Jerusalem and
the king responded by giving him permission to return home.

He was also given letters from the king to the governors of
the surrounding countries, requesting that he be given safe
passage. There was a letter to Asaph, the man who cared for
the king's forest, instructing him to provide Nehemiah with
the timber he would need. Upon reaching Jerusalem, he took
time one moonlit night to look over the broken walls and the
burnt gates. After assessing the condition of the wall, Nehemiah
called together the leaders of the people and told them of his
concern to see the walls rebuilt. He encouraged them to get on
with the work and said that he too would be involved.

The leaders of the surrounding countries mocked Nehemiah and the builders. But when they heard that the walls were up to nearly half their height, they planned to invade and create confusion. As a result Nehemiah placed armed guards about the city wall and had all the builders carry their weapons as the work went on. Jerusalem was an armed camp, ready to repulse any enemy.

But above all, Nehemiah could say to the people, 'Our God will fight for us' (Nehemiah 4:20). The city walls gave protection for all inside, just as Christ protects his people from God's anger on the Day of Judgement.

FIND OUT THE FACTS

1. Who conspired to attack Jerusalem because the city walls were being rebuilt? See Nehemiah 4:7-8.
2. What use were city walls?
3. Why did the builders carry arms as they worked?

When he heard news of the state of Jerusalem, Nehemiah didn't leave immediately for the city. He spent time in prayer first. What does this tell us about how we should approach difficult situations?

God is a totalitarian Ruler who demands full allegiance from his subjects. *Anon*

A saying to Remember

Nehemiah
13:23-31

'And Ezra blessed the LORD...Then all the people answered, "Amen, Amen!" while lifting up their hands. And they bowed their heads and worshipped the LORD with their faces to the ground' (Nehemiah 8:6).

There are many times when Christians realize they are sinning. They are breaking the law of God and need to confess their sin and ask for forgiveness. This has always been the situation for God's people in all ages.

Nehemiah and the citizens of Judah rejoiced when Jerusalem's walls were rebuilt and they could put down their weapons. It was the year 444 B.C. and now the people thought they could settle down to peaceful living. However, there were sins that needed to be rooted out of the nation.

A sad situation had developed among the people. Those who were wealthy had made loans to their brethren and charged them interest. This was breaking God's law: 'If you lend money to any of my people who are poor among you, you shall not be like a moneylender to him; you shall not charge him interest' (Exodus 22:25). Nehemiah spoke to the money lenders and reminded them of God's law. 'And all the assembly said, "Amen!" and praised the LORD' (Nehemiah 5:13).

He also took the register of those who had returned earlier with Ezra and Zerubbabel, to determine who were laymen, priests, Levites, singers, gatekeepers and temple servants. It was also used to determine where family property was located.

Ezra was asked to read 'the Book of the Law of Moses' (Nehemiah 8:1). Standing on a platform constructed for the occasion, the people listened attentively to all that he read. The Israelites were being revived by the Holy Spirit to obey God's law. As Ezra preached, the people were convicted of their sins and asked the Lord for forgiveness.

From the reading of the law, the people realized that it was the time for celebrating the Feast of Tabernacles. This joyful feast was a time of thanksgiving for all that the Lord had done for them in bringing them out of Egypt, the land of captivity.

A covenant was made with the Lord, where the people promised to obey his law. No more would they allow their children to intermarry with the surrounding pagan nations; no more would they desecrate the Sabbath day. Now worship would be conducted according to the law of the Lord. Jehovah would once again be all in all to his covenant people!

Oh, how we can praise our Saviour for rescuing us from slavery to Satan. Now we have freedom to worship and praise God!

FIND OUT THE FACTS

1. Solomon's rule was ruined by his marriage to pagan women. How? Read Nehemiah 13:26.
2. Of what was the Feast of Tabernacles a reminder? Read Leviticus 23:41-43 and Deuteronomy 16:16-17.
3. Why was it important to list the people according to their tribe?

It is always a sad state of affairs when God blesses his people but they continue to sin. Think about how this can be prevented.

Revival is God rending the heavens and coming down upon his people. *Vance Havner*

Leviticus   'You shall observe the Feast of
23:39-43   Tabernacles seven days, when
                 you have gathered from your
                 threshing floor and from your
                 winepress' (Deuteronomy
                 16:13).

Today we are going to consider the Feast of Tabernacles, one of Israel's feast days that must have been a lot of fun, especially for the children. This feast day was frequently named the 'Feast of Ingathering,' (Exodus 34:22) and the festival of 'Booths' (Leviticus 23:43). It was kept from the fifteenth to the twenty-first of Tishri, the seventh month.

The Lord had commanded that all adult male Israelites were to visit Jerusalem to celebrate this feast. They brought with them their tithes and offerings.

On the first day of the feast there was to be a sacrificial burnt offering of 'thirteen young bulls, two rams, and fourteen lambs' (Numbers 29:13). The number of bulls sacrificed each day was to be one less than the previous day. On the seventh day, the burnt offering consisted of 'seven bulls, two rams, and fourteen lambs' (Numbers 29:32). These sacrifices pointed to the redemptive work of Christ, the Lamb of God.

Following this feast, a sacred assembly was held, which involved the offering to the Lord of one bullock, one ram, and seven lambs. Water was then carried to the altar and used to cleanse it. This was the day which ended the annual cycle of feast days.

It is this eighth day that is spoken of in the New Testament. Jesus had quietly made his way to Jerusalem, and on this last day he stood and spoke loudly, saying, 'If anyone thirsts, let him come to me and drink. He who believes in me, as the Scripture has said, out of his heart will flow rivers of living water' (John 7:37-38).

The apostle John, inspired by the Holy Spirit, interpreted Christ's words as making reference to the Holy Spirit's work in the sinner. He invited those who thirsted for righteousness to come to him and drink. This speaks of the day when God dwells with the saints in the eternal, heavenly kingdom.

The feast was a joyful celebration which remembered the years when the nation had lived in 'booths' during their wilderness wandering. Often the 'booths'were made from animal skins and palm fronds. During this festival the temple was brightly lit, which added to the joy of this feast.

The Feast of Tabernacles was held when the nation had settled in Canaan, and was a time of thanksgiving to God for the rain that fell and the crops that grew to feed the nation.

All the crops were stored away, and the people looked forward to the rain and the planting of seed for the next harvest. The Feast of Tabernacles was truly a time of national joy.

FIND OUT THE FACTS

1. Why was this feast called the Feast of Booths?

2. Why were animals sacrificed?

3. In what way was the Feast of Tabernacles exciting for children?

The Feast of Tabernacles was a time of joyful celebration. How is the Lord's Day a day of celebration for Christians?

A saying to Remember

We are saved, not by merit, but by mercy. *Anon*

Joel
2:28-32

'Count fifty days to the day after the seventh Sabbath; then you shall offer a new grain offering to the LORD' (Leviticus 23:16).

I sometimes ask people, 'How many birthdays have you had?' Most people reply by telling me their age. We have just one birthday, the day of our birth. We then have a celebration each year on that day.

Today's Scripture passage is fulfilled in Acts 2:16-21, the birthday of the extension of the church to include the Gentiles. Great things happened on the first Day of Pentecost, following the ascension of our Saviour: the Holy Spirit was poured out upon the church.

Why then is this 'Day of Pentecost' often called 'firstfruits'? (Leviticus 23:10). This day of rejoicing was held fifty days after the Passover Sabbath, which meant that Pentecost was held on Sunday, the first day of the week. It was the second of the great annual feasts of the Lord, when every male was expected to go up to Jerusalem and there give thanks to God for the coming successful harvest.

Sacrifices, involving the shedding of blood, were offered to the Lord, as well as two baked loaves of bread containing leaven. These loaves were the same as the bread for everyday use.

The priest also brought a sheaf of barley into the temple. It was to be from the same field as the wheat that was used to produce the flour to make the two loaves of bread. This sheaf of barley was looked upon as the first of many that would come from the land to feed the nation.

The offering of the 'firstfruits' to the Lord, in anticipation of the harvest to follow, should remind us of words written about our Saviour. The apostle Paul, speaking of the resurrection of the saints, says, 'For as in Adam all die, even so in Christ all shall be made alive. But each one in his own order:

Christ the firstfruits, afterward those who are Christ's at his coming' (1 Corinthians 15:22-23).

Here the saints are given a promise: as surely as the Lord Jesus rose from the dead, so will all of his people on that wondrous day when the Lord of glory comes with his holy angels to judge the world in righteousness. As the sheaf of barley was the first of the assured harvest to follow, so also is Christ the first of the many who will rise from their graves when the Head of the church returns in power and glory. Christ is 'the firstfruits of those who have fallen asleep' (1 Corinthians 15:20).

Joel spoke of the events that would occur on a future Day of Pentecost. This was the day when the Holy Spirit would be poured out in great power. The gospel would be taken to all the world by Christians filled with the Holy Spirit.

We live in a wonderful age!

FIND OUT THE FACTS

1. Name the three feasts where the men were to go up to Jerusalem? Read Deuteronomy 16:16

2. What does Pentecost mean?

3. In what way can Christ be found in the feast of Pentecost?

This festival was celebrated in anticipation of the coming harvest. How are we to show gratitude to God for the way in which he provides for our needs?

Understanding can wait. Obedience cannot.   *Geoffrey Grogan*

Esther
2:1-11

'For the queen's behaviour will become known to all women, so that they will despise their husbands ... when they report, "King Ahasuerus commanded Queen Vashti to be brought in before him, but she did not come"' (Esther 1:17).

The Persian king, Ahasuerus, had invited his nobles and princes to a great feast where he was to show them the glory of his kingdom. He was a proud man. Wine flowed and during the feast he requested that Queen Vashti come to his feast so he could show his guests her beauty.

Queen Vashti was also holding a feast for the important women of the empire. When the command was received to appear before her husband, she refused to do so as she knew that her husband, King Ahasuerus, had drunk too much wine.

The king was furious when he heard her refusal and asked his wise men how he should handle the situation. The law of the land demanded instant obedience to the king's command. His wise men advised him to divorce Queen Vashti in order to make sure that other wives did not refuse to obey the commands of their husbands.

After King Ahasuerus divorced Queen Vashti, a royal 'decree' was circulated to all parts of the empire instructing wives to honour their husbands, no matter what social position their husbands held. The king's servants suggested they find another wife for him; so the search began.

Christianity teaches that women are to be treated with dignity and respect. No longer are they to be downtrodden by men. Also from this story we should note that bad decisions are often made when a person is under the influence of alcohol. Let us beware!

An Israelite, Mordecai, who had not returned to Israel, cared for Esther, his uncle's daughter. God would use her to prevent his covenant people who remained in Ahasuerus' kingdom from being killed.

Esther was taken to the king's harem. She was a beautiful, young woman, and after preparations to become the king's wife, Ahasuerus took her to his royal palace. We read that 'the king loved Esther more than all the other women, and she obtained grace and favour in his sight more than all the virgins; so he set the royal crown upon her head and made her queen instead of Vashti' (Esther 2:17). But King Ahasuerus did not know that Esther was an Israelite.

FIND OUT THE FACTS

1. How many times is the word 'God' found in the book of Esther? Does this mean that God has no part in this historical story?

2. Why did King Ahasuerus instruct Queen Vashti to appear before him? Why did she refuse to obey?

3. King Ahasuerus had many wives. How many wives does God say a man may have? See Genesis 2:24; Matthew 19:5.

God controls all events. He had brought Esther into the king's palace because he had a task for her to perform. Ask the Lord to help you to see his ruling hand in all the situations in which you find yourself.

A saying to Remember

Pride is a weed that will grow on any dunghill.   C. H. Spurgeon

Esther
2:21-23

'When Haman saw that Mordecai did not bow or pay him homage, Haman was filled with wrath' (Esther 3:5).

If you discover the plans of evil people, you should do what you can to prevent them from being carried out. When Esther's cousin, Mordecai, overheard plans to kill King Ahasuerus, he told Esther, who, in turn, told the king. After the men were caught and hanged, the whole story was recorded in the king's 'chronicles' (diary).

The king had promoted his servant Haman, an Amalekite, who expected everyone within the king's gate to bow down to him as the king had instructed. When Mordecai, who feared God more than man, refused to do so, a furious Haman planned to have him killed.

Upon discovering that Mordecai was a Jew, he persuaded the king to set a time when all his citizens would have permission to kill the Jewish people. Haman told the king that the Israelites had their own laws and therefore refused to obey the laws of the Medes and Persians. The king willingly signed the legislation that Haman presented to him, and it was circulated throughout the empire. It was agreed that all the wealth taken from the Jews was to be paid into the king's treasury.

When Mordecai heard about the new law, he tore his clothes, put on sackcloth and walked about the city weeping loudly. Mordecai sent a message to his cousin, Esther, asking her to speak to the king on behalf of the Israelites. He warned her that she would also die if the king's word was carried out. She had to act! Mordecai saw the hand of God in having Esther as the king's wife. He said, 'Yet who knows whether you have come to the kingdom for such a time as this?' (Esther 4:14).

Esther asked Mordecai to get the people to fast (and no doubt pray) for three days, after which she would approach the king.

This was a dangerous business as no one was permitted freely to enter the king's presence.

When Esther entered the king's room, he held out his royal sceptre towards her, which was his invitation for her to step forward and speak. Her only request was to invite the king and Haman to her rooms for a banquet.

At the banquet, when the king asked what was her request, she again invited the two to another banquet. At that banquet she renewed her invitation to attend a third banquet.

Haman was overjoyed with these invitations, as he thought this was a sign of his popularity with the king and queen. As he passed through the king's gate he became furious as Mordecai continued to refuse to show him honour and respect by bowing down to him.

FIND OUT THE FACTS

1. In what way are Esther and Moses alike?
2. Is pride a sin? Read Proverbs 8:13; 14:3; 16:18.
3. Why are many rulers proud people?

It made Haman feel good to have people bow down to him. Think about how easily people are filled with pride when they gain wealth or status. Ask the Lord to give you a humble spirit.

When anger was in Cain's heart, murder was not far off.
Matthew Henry

A saying to Remember

Esther
5:6-14

'That night the king could not
sleep. So one was commanded
to bring the book of the
records of the chronicles; and
they were read before the
king' (Esther 6:1).

It is almost always a happy time when someone gives a party.
There is usually much laughter and plenty of good food.
Haman was enjoying himself at the queen's feasts and went
home to tell his family the good news.

He gathered his friends and relatives together and told them
of his promotion and of the fact that he alone of the king's
servants had been invited to the queen's feasts. He had already
attended one of Esther's banquets and there was another to
come.

The night before Queen Esther's second feast, King
Ahasuerus could not sleep. He commanded one of his servants to bring his chronicles to him and to read from them.
When the name of Mordecai came up, the king asked what
had been done to reward him for his part in saving the king's
life. When the answer was, 'Nothing,' he asked who was available in the court. Haman had just arrived at the palace.

Haman had been hard at work, having some high gallows
constructed. He intended to have Mordecai hanged from them
on the day when the people were to kill the Israelites. No longer
would Mordecai treat him with contempt!

When he appeared before King Ahasuerus, he was asked,
'What shall be done for the man whom the king delights to
honour?' (Esther 6:6). Immediately Haman thought to himself,
'The king is going to honour me.'

He then gave a list to the king of all the things he wanted
for himself: clothe the man in a robe the king had worn and
parade him through the streets of the city on a horse the king
had ridden. Others should shout out, 'Thus shall it be done to
the man whom the king delights to honour!' (Esther 6:9).

The king told Haman to do this immediately for Mordecai, and not to fail in doing any of the things he had suggested.

Following the parade organized by Haman, the king's servants arrived at his home to escort him to the queen's banquet. There the king asked Esther what her request was, telling her she could ask for anything, even up to half the kingdom.

Try and imagine how Haman must have felt. He had just been forced to bestow a great honour on Mordecai, the man he hated and wanted to hang on his newly constructed gallows. His wise men and his wife had warned him with these words: 'If Mordecai, before whom you have begun to fall, is of Jewish descent, you will not prevail against him but will surely fall before him' (Esther 6:13).

Frequently God uses the weakest people to accomplish his purposes.

FIND OUT THE FACTS

1. What well-known proverb fits Haman's situation here?
2. Our God rules the world. In our story how do we see this truth?
3. Why couldn't the king sleep?

Quite unexpectedly Haman's situation changed. Thank the Lord that he changes events to protect his people.

It ought to be as habitual for us to thank as it is to ask. *C. H. Spurgeon*

Esther
7:5-10

'Then King Ahasuerus said to Queen Esther and Mordecai the Jew, "Indeed, I have given Esther the house of Haman, and they have hanged him on the gallows because he tried to lay his hand on the Jews"' (Esther 8:7).

Haman was now with the king and queen, and again the king asked Esther what her request was. When she began telling him that her people were about to be destroyed, including herself, the king became very angry and demanded to know who was responsible. I think that at that moment in the discussion, Haman's knees would have begun to knock, his teeth chatter and he would have been covered in perspiration.

Of course, Queen Esther answered, 'The adversary and enemy is this wicked Haman!' (Esther 7:6). The king, filled with anger, left Esther's banquet and walked in the garden while deciding what he should do to Haman. When he returned he saw his queen sitting upon her royal couch and Haman, who had fallen across the couch, pleading for his life. King Ahasuerus thought that Haman was about to assault his queen. When he was told of Haman's high gallows, he pointed to Haman and said to his servants, 'Hang him on it!' (Esther 7:9).

Then the king told Esther, whom he loved, to write a decree for the Jews which he would seal with his royal signet ring. This decree commanded the Jews to gather together on the day they were to be killed and to fight against those who wanted them dead. Many were killed that day, including Haman's ten sons who were hung on the gallows which their father had built.

Mordecai was given a position of great importance in the palace; he was to be involved in the government of the empire. He was highly respected, and Queen Esther was firmly established as King Ahasuerus' queen.

The date for the killing of the Israelites was the thirteenth day of the month of Adar. When the Jews were at peace, the fourteenth and fifteenth day became feast days for Israel, days to remember the great deliverance which God had brought about for his people. We read 'that they [the Jews] should make them days of feasting and joy, of sending presents to one another and gifts to the poor' (Esther 9:22).

In the story of Esther the Lord cared for his people. All who have a saving faith in the Lord Jesus are daily being prepared for heaven. Even the Lord's chastening out of love produces holiness.

May each person who reads this book live the life of holiness, commanded by our Lord.

FIND OUT THE FACTS

1. The Jews had several feast days. Name two of them.
2. How do Christians remember the death of the Lord Jesus? Read 1 Corinthians 11:23-26.
3. When do Christians remember the resurrection of the Saviour?

To Think & to pray about

Thank the Lord for the book of Esther which so clearly teaches us about God working all things for the good of his people.

A saying to Remember

Prosperity is good campaigning weather for the devil. C. S. Lewis

Malachi
1:6-14

'Behold, I will send you Elijah the prophet before the coming of the great and dreadful day of the LORD. And he will turn the hearts of the fathers to the children, and the hearts of the children to their fathers, lest I come and strike the earth with a curse' (Malachi 4:5-6).

The book of Malachi is the last book in the Old Testament, which concludes with the words: 'Lest I come and strike the earth with a curse'. The Septuagint, however, concludes with our verse 4: 'Remember the law of Moses...' The Jews didn't want their Scriptures to conclude with 'a curse'. The Septuagint is a translation of the Hebrew Old Testament into Greek in the third century B.C. by some seventy scholars.

Malachi lived at the time of Ezra and Nehemiah, and wrote about the sins of the people at that time. His opening words must have been confusing: '"I have loved you," says the LORD. "Yet you say, 'In what way have you loved us?'"' (Malachi 1:2).

Some of the Israelites who had returned after the Babylonian captivity, asked the question, 'Why is God not blessing us?' Malachi lists the sins of the nation. First, their sacrificial offerings were not the best of their flock. The Lord said, 'You offer defiled food on my altar' (Malachi 1:7-9).

The priests and Levites considered the work in the temple to be boring. The Lord asked, 'Who is there even among you who would shut the [temple] doors?' (Malachi 1:10). The Lord would rather have no worship than hypocritical, dreary worship!

Family life was destroyed by men divorcing their wives for trivial reasons. Many had married foreigners who worshipped idols, with the result that their children also worshipped idols. Many citizens failed to give tithes to the Lord's work. They were stealing what rightfully belonged to God. The Lord challenged the people to give to the work of the priests and Levites, and in return he would greatly bless them.

Finally, we read of the promised coming of Christ, preceded by 'Elijah' the prophet (Malachi 4:5). This was not the Elijah of the Old Testament, but John the Baptist who did a similar work to Elijah.

In spite of Israel's sins, good things were in store for repentant sinners: the Lord Jesus would come to save his people from all nations.

FIND OUT THE FACTS

1. Who was the 'Elijah' of the New Testament? Read Matthew 17:10-13.
2. Find out all you can about John the Baptist.
3. In what way was John the Baptist similar to Elijah?
4. Learn the final verse of the Old Testament.

In the days of Malachi, the priests were careless in the way they approached the work of the temple. What should our attitude be to the worship of God? Ask God to help you to have that attitude.

The cost of repentance is expensive. *Anon*

Isaiah
6:1-5;
John
12:37-41

'Jesus said to them, "Most assuredly, I say to you, before Abraham was, I AM"' (John 8:58).

W e all have birthdays which we usually celebrate each year. Sometimes there is a party and gifts are received. This was not so for the Lord Jesus Christ who is both God and man in one person. As God, he is eternal; as man, his human life commenced when he was born to Mary.

Our scripture verse comes from a time when the Jews were laughing at Christ. He said that Abraham longed to see his day. This was his claim that he existed before Abraham. Christ is the great 'I AM'.

It was the name that Moses heard when God spoke to him from the burning bush (Exodus 3:14). Isaiah had a vision of Jehovah sitting upon the heavenly throne. The apostle John said that this vision was of the Lord Jesus Christ (John 12:41). Christ, God's only Son, had no beginning. In the book of Proverbs our Saviour is referred to as 'Wisdom', and we read, 'I have been established from everlasting, from the beginning, before there was ever an earth' (Proverbs 8:23).

In the beginning Christ was there, just as the apostle John wrote, 'In the beginning was the Word, and the Word was with God, and the Word was God. He was in the beginning with God' (John 1:1-2). Before the worlds were created, God existed. Our one God is triune: Father, Son and Holy Spirit. God did not need a world to fill any emptiness in his being or existence, because there was perfect harmony in the Godhead. This world came into being so that God could display his glory, wisdom, power, justice, grace and mercy.

Because of sin, our Redeemer became man and lived a life of perfect obedience to his heavenly Father. He died on a Roman cross, bearing the anger of God against sin — and all of this in the place of his people.

Our Saviour is both perfect man and God in one person. If we desire to know anything about God, we have only to read what the Scriptures say about Christ, 'for in Him dwells all the fulness of the Godhead bodily' (Colossians 2:9). The universe was created through the Lord Jesus. It was God — Father, Son and Holy Spirit — who planned the salvation of sinners.

Before the world existed, the heavenly Father chose a people whom he gave to his Son (Ephesians 1:3-14; John 6:37); the Lord Jesus agreed to die for these people; and the Holy Spirit applied Christ's saving work to their sinful hearts.

Our uncreated Lord Jesus Christ is eternally God.

FIND OUT THE FACTS

1. It is difficult to comprehend the notion of 'eternity' or to be 'eternal'. State two or three things about eternity and where you find them in scripture.
2. Find other verses of scripture that prove Christ had no beginning.
3. Who created this universe? Read John 1:3.

Think about the fact that each person of the Trinity — Father, Son and Holy Spirit — is actively involved in the work of the salvation. Thank the Lord for his great salvation.

The Saviour of sinners knows what it is to be poor. J. C. Ryle

Matthew   'The book of the genealogy of
1:1-17   Jesus Christ, the Son of
           David, the Son of Abraham...'
           (Matthew 1:1).

My brother-in-law has spent many long hours researching his family tree. He has discovered that one ancestor came to Australia, as a convict on the Second Fleet. He served fourteen years imprisonment for theft. Another family line included Mr Pitt, a prime minister of England. I'm sure that if we each traced our family tree, we would find a mixture of people there, some having a fine character and others we wouldn't like to mention.

The Lord Jesus, as perfect man, had a family tree. In Matthew 1 we read a list of Christ's ancestors, from Abraham to Joseph, the husband of Mary, the mother of the Lord Jesus. Matthew was writing his Gospel mainly for Jewish people and so he was concerned to show that the Saviour had indeed been in the line of descendants of David and Joseph, the supposed father of the Lord Jesus. According to Jewish law, Jesus truly was the Son of David.

It is believed that Luke wrote his Gospel for the Romans and the Greeks. He also showed that Joseph, whose father was Heli, was a descendant of Israel's great King David, just as God had promised (1 Chronicles 17:14). The ancestry of our Lord from Joseph went right back to Adam, 'the son of God' (Luke 3:38). Jesus Christ thus was descended from both Gentiles and Jews. Some commentators, however, do argue that Luke's genealogy is really that of Mary, whose father was Heli.

From the Saviour's 'family tree' there is no doubt that he was descended from David, king of Israel. He is the King of God's kingdom, which has citizens from every age and in every part of the world.

As we look at the records in the genealogies, we find the names of great sinners as well as of godly men and women.

Both Matthew and Luke (Luke 3:32) record the name of Salmon who married Rahab, the repentant harlot (Matthew 1:5). Matthew also includes the name of the wicked King Manasseh who sacrificed his children to Moloch (Matthew 1:10).

Luke traced Christ's ancestry to Adam, showing that he is related to all of mankind. If we are to be sons or daughters of the living God, we need to be born again, and to live the life of faith in the Lord Jesus. Can you say this of yourself?

Christ rightfully claimed to be descended from King David, and we know this to be true from the carefully preserved family records.

Our Saviour is the King of kings, the Son of God!

FIND OUT THE FACTS

1. How far back can you trace your 'family tree'?

2. Why were 'family trees' so important to the Jewish people?

3. Who is truly the one and only Son of God? Read John 3:16. Why then did Luke say that Adam was 'the son of God'? (Luke 3:38).

Christ's ancestors included ordinary sinful people. Thank the Lord that he has identified himself so closely with sinful men and women, boys and girls.

The only kingdom that will prevail in this world is the kingdom that is not of this world. *Anon*

Luke
1:5-17

'[John the Baptist] will also go before him in the spirit and power of Elijah, "to turn the hearts of the fathers to the children," and the disobedient to the wisdom of the just, to make ready a people prepared for the Lord' (Luke 1:17).

Have you ever met an angel? I am not sure that I have ever seen one. Perhaps an angel has come to my assistance in the form of a person. After all we read in Hebrews 1:14 that the angels are 'ministering spirits sent forth to minister for those who will inherit salvation'. Angels are mentioned in many places in the Scriptures. In fact the word 'angel' is found two hundred and one times in the Bible and the word 'angels' appears ninety-three times.

God's angels take care of believers in the battles that are fought against Satan and his demons. Some angels surround God's throne, praising him day and night, while others stand ready to carry out his commands immediately. Before the crucifixion, Jesus went to the Garden of Gethsemane to pray. He was soon to bear the anger of God as the sin bearer of his people. This weighed heavily upon him, but we read, 'Then an angel appeared to him from heaven, strengthening him' (Luke 22:43).

In the book of Revelation we read of warfare, when the great angel Michael and his angel warriors threw Satan and his demons out of heaven (Revelation 12:7-9).

Our scripture reading is about Zacharias who was married to Elizabeth. They were an aged couple who had no children. They loved God and were overjoyed to serve him. Zacharias was a priest who spent many months working in the temple, where he was responsible for the offering of incense to the Lord. While he was carrying out his duties, the angel Gabriel appeared and revealed to him that God had heard his prayers for a child. He was assured that his wife, Elizabeth, would have a son who would 'be filled with the Holy Spirit' (Luke 1:15) and would have a character like Elijah. Because Zacharias doubted God's promise, he was struck dumb.

Soon he was on his way home unable to speak. It wasn't long before his wife discovered that she was expecting a baby. I'm sure there would have been much rejoicing when Zacharias and Elizabeth knew that they would soon be parents. Children were seen as a gift from God, and many people believed that childless couples were being punished by God for their sins.

Zacharias and Elizabeth were indeed a joyful couple, as they were not just expecting any baby, but the one who would prepare the people for the coming of Messiah.

FIND OUT THE FACTS

1. What are we taught in Psalm 127:3-5?
2. Who created the angels?
3. What is the work of an angel?
4. Zacharias was struck dumb. Why?

To Think & to pray about

Zacharias and Elizabeth were people who feared the Lord. Think of people you know who love and serve the Lord. Thank the Lord for their godly example.

The most important thing a father can do for his children is to love their mother. *Theodore M. Hesburgh*

A saying to Remember

Matthew 1:18-25   'Then the angel said to her, "Do not be afraid, Mary, for you have found favour with God. And behold, you will conceive in your womb and bring forth a Son, and shall call his name JESUS"' (Luke 1:30-31).

There is usually much rejoicing when a married couple find out that they are expecting a baby. Val and I were very happy when we knew we were going to be parents. When a mother-to-be is pregnant she usually visits a doctor who confirms her pregnancy.

Mary, the mother of the Lord Jesus, was visited by the angel Gabriel and was told, 'Rejoice, highly favoured one, the Lord is with you; blessed are you among women!' (Luke 1:28). Mary was a godly young woman, chosen by God to be the mother of Jesus.

When she was told this by Gabriel, Mary was very surprised because she and Joseph were not yet married. They were engaged as both had made promises of marriage to each other. But now Mary discovered she was expecting a baby. Her Son would sit on the throne of King David and rule an eternal kingdom.

The child in Mary's womb was the result of a great miracle. It was by the power of the Holy Spirit that she had fallen pregnant.

Joseph was alarmed about the situation and began to doubt what Mary had told him. He decided to cancel the plans for the forthcoming marriage, but one night an angel appeared to him in a dream and said, 'Joseph, son of David, do not be afraid to take to you Mary your wife, for that which is conceived in her is of the Holy Spirit' (Matthew 1:20).

The angel then revealed to Joseph that the Son who was to be born, would be given the name 'JESUS, for he will save his people from their sins' (Matthew 1:21).

Matthew tells us that this miracle was the fulfilment of the Old Testament prophecy: "Behold, the virgin shall be with child, and bear a Son, and they shall call his name Immanuel, which is translated, "God with us"' (Matthew 1:23 and Isaiah 7:14).

When Joseph awoke he knew that Mary's baby was conceived by the almighty power of the Holy Spirit. Joseph took Mary as his wife, but did not live with her as such until after Jesus was born.

The Son to be born was the Saviour promised by God. He would live a life of perfect obedience to his God and heavenly Father, including his death on a Roman cross in the place of his people. In so doing he would gain for them salvation.

Is the Lord Jesus Christ your Saviour? If so, eternal life is yours, which means you have a great reason to serve and praise God.

FIND OUT THE FACTS

1. What does the name 'Jesus' mean?

2. Of whom was Jesus the 'Son'?

3. Explain the meaning of Genesis 3:15.

Think about the fact that the Son of God came into this world as a baby, born into a human family. Thank him for becoming a perfectly sinless human being.

Jesus was not the first Christian; he was and is the Christ. *Herman Bavinick*

Luke
1:39-45

'For with God nothing will be impossible' (Luke 1:37).

There are times when many wonderful things happen in our lives: holidays, examination results, getting the car licence, Christmas presents and so the list could go on.

At this particular time in history many great events were taking place. The 'impossible' was happening in Jerusalem: an old couple was to have a baby; a young woman was to have a Son, who was to be called Jesus; the land of Israel was ruled by the Romans and many people were anticipating the arrival of the Messiah. Things that seemed 'impossible' to human beings were happening because 'with God nothing will be impossible' (Luke 1:37).

Mary was told by the angel that her relative, Elizabeth, who lived in a city of Judah, was six months pregnant. She decided to visit her. When Mary arrived at her home and greeted her, the babe in Elizabeth's womb jumped for joy. Then, Elizabeth, filled with the Holy Spirit, spoke these wonderful words of greeting: 'Blessed are you among women, and blessed is the fruit of your womb!' (Luke 1:42).

This was a moment of great joy because both of them realized that their babies were to play momentous roles in God's plan of salvation. Elizabeth's child, John, would prepare the way for the coming Lord Jesus Christ, the Saviour of the world.

Mary, also filled with the Holy Spirit, spoke words that brought glory to God. She said that many of God's promises would be fulfilled in her baby: 'My soul magnifies the Lord, and my spirit has rejoiced in God my Saviour' (Luke 1:46-47). She knew that her Son would be great, and she would be called 'Blessed' by the generations to come. She explained that God was showing his almighty power in what had been done. Her

God was the one who 'put down the mighty from their thrones, and exalted the lowly' (Luke 1:52).

She said that her God was 'holy' and would destroy the proud. He was the one who would show mercy to his people just as he had promised Abraham and his descendants. Mary's God was indeed the 'God of the impossible'.

She stayed with Elizabeth for three months. When Elizabeth gave birth to a son, her neighbours and relatives rejoiced with her, because of God's great miracle that made possible the birth of a baby in old age.

FIND OUT THE FACTS

1. It seems that Elizabeth didn't tell people she was pregnant. Why?

2. List five miracles which occurred about the time of the birth of the Lord Jesus?

3. John the Baptist fulfilled a prophecy in the book of Malachi. How? Read Malachi 3:1 and 4:4-5 and Matthew 11:12-15; 17:10-13.

When they met during their pregnancies, both Mary and Elizabeth responded by praising God. Thank the Lord for godly mothers.

The voice of one crying in the wilderness: 'Prepare the way of the LORD; Make straight in the desert a highway for our God.' Isaiah 40:3

Luke
1:57-66

'And you, child, will be called the prophet of the Highest; for you will go before the face of the Lord to prepare his ways...' (Luke 1:76).

Usually it takes some years before we make a decision concerning the work we would like to do. Young boys often say they would like to be firemen, policemen or fishermen, but frequently these plans change as the years pass. None of us has a message from God telling us what we should do.

This was not the case with the son who was born to Zacharias and Elizabeth. Zacharias had been dumb since the day he had disbelieved the angel's message which was that he and Elizabeth would soon have a child.

The promised son was born, and there was much rejoicing with their relatives and friends. On the eighth day, in accordance with the law of God, the baby son was to be circumcised. This was usually the day when the parents named their child. Everyone expected the son to bear his father's name, but Elizabeth said, 'No; he shall be called John' (Luke 1:60).

This surprised their friends as none of their relatives was called John. When Zacharias was asked what name should be given to his son, he asked for a writing slate and on it he wrote, 'His name is John' (Luke 1:63).

At once he began to speak again, and he praised God for all that he had done. People who knew them questioned God's purpose in giving Elizabeth and Zacharias a son in their old age. They also wondered what God had in store for John.

Zacharias, filled with the Holy Spirit, prophesied that God had 'visited' his people with salvation. He also prophesied that his son, John, would be 'the prophet of the Highest; for [he] will go before the face of the Lord to prepare his ways' (Luke 1:76).

John was to prepare Israel for the coming of the long-awaited Messiah, who had been promised by God through his prophets. John was to call the people to repentance and holiness as a way of life. Christ would 'give light to those who sit in darkness and the shadow of death, to guide [their] feet into the way of peace' (Luke 1:79).

John was the 'Elijah' prophesied by Malachi (Malachi 4:5, compare Matthew 11:13-14). He lived in the desert region and crowds of people went out to hear him preach repentance. Those who did repent were baptized in the River Jordan. John wore clothes made from camel hair. He had a leather belt about his waist, and for food he ate locusts and wild honey.

John was to be a great servant of God.

FIND OUT THE FACTS

1. Why were baby Jewish boys circumcised? See Genesis 17:9-14.
2. What was to be John's work?
3. In what way was John the Baptist like Elijah?

John the Baptist had a distinctive role to play in preparing the way for the Messiah. Thank the Lord for the ministry of John the Baptist.

Ministry that costs nothing accomplishes nothing. J. H. Jowett

Luke
2:1-7

'But when the fulness of the time had come, God sent forth his Son, born of a woman, born under the law' (Galatians 4:4).

Whenever a baby is born there is usually great excitement. A very special baby was to be born in the city of Bethlehem, who would ensure, through his life, death and resurrection, the salvation of a great multitude of people that no one can count. This person was the Lord Jesus Christ, the son of Mary and the only Son of God. So great was he that human history uses his birthday as the division between two eras. Today I live in the year A.D. 2004. The A.D. stands for 'Anno Domini' — 'the year of the Lord'. Years before the birth of Christ are counted B.C. — 'Before Christ'.

Mary was expecting a baby who would have the name 'Jesus', which means 'Saviour'. The citizens of Israel were expecting the promised 'Christ' to arrive soon, because of the writings of the ancient prophets. Daniel had given the greatest clue to the time of Christ's appearance (Daniel 9:23-27).

Joseph and Mary knew that Jesus would soon be born. The prophet Micah had prophesied: 'But you Bethlehem Ephrathah, though you are little among the thousands of Judah, yet out of you shall come forth to me the one to be Ruler in Israel, whose goings forth are from of old, from everlasting' (Micah 5:2).

Mary and Joseph didn't live in Bethlehem, they lived in Nazareth. But God had arranged history so that the Roman Emperor, Caesar Augustus, would issue a decree that a census of the Empire should be taken. This meant that Mary and Joseph had to return to the city of their tribe which was Bethlehem.

The city was crowded with families returning for the census, and Joseph found the only accommodation available which was in a stable, where animals were kept and fed. It was there that Mary gave birth to Jesus. She wrapped him in swaddling cloths and laid him in a manger.

The baby Jesus was both God and man in the one person. This meant that Christ, the second person of the Godhead, humbled himself by coming into the world as a baby, born to Mary, his human mother. The Lord Jesus had now commenced his work on earth that would result in the salvation of his people.Many of the prophecies in the Old Testament would be fulfilled, proving that this growing child was truly the Son of God, the Saviour of the world.

FIND OUT THE FACTS

1. In what way did Christ humble himself by becoming man?
2. Learn a scripture verse that tells us that Christ was God's only Son. Try John 3:16.
3. Christ called himself 'the Son of man' (Daniel 7:13). What did he mean by this?

The Lord Jesus was not born in a place of comfort and luxury. Thank him for his willingness to stoop so low as to be born in a stable.

Jesus Christ is God in the form of man; as completely God as if he were not a man; and completely man as if he were not God.   A. J. F. Behrends

Luke
2:8-20

'And suddenly there was with the angel a multitude of the heavenly host praising God and saying, "Glory to God in the highest, and on earth peace, goodwill towards men!"' (Luke 2:13-14).

Christ was born during the warm summer months because we are told that the shepherds watched over their flocks during the night. We can imagine those men keeping watch while it was dark. Sometimes they would become sleepy, but the noise of a sheep or lamb would wake them up.

I'm sure, though, that everyone would have been wide awake when an angel appeared to give them the unexpected news that 'in the city of David a Saviour, who is Christ the Lord' had been born (Luke 2:11).

Every eye would have been staring in awe at the wonderful angel who stood before them. Suddenly the angel was surrounded by a multitude of his heavenly companions who praised God with the words:

Glory to God in the highest,
And on earth peace,
Goodwill towards men
(Luke 2:14).

No doubt those shepherds had heard their religious leaders speaking about the coming Christ. Now they had word from God himself that Christ, the Saviour, had been born 'in the city of David', which was Bethlehem.

At once the shepherds set off for Bethlehem as they wanted to see proof of the angel's message. Upon arriving at the stable where animals had been feeding, they entered and found the baby Jesus lying in a clean feeding trough.

As soon as they left the stable, they spread the news of what they had heard and seen. Many of the people who heard them speaking found it difficult to believe them. Mary knew, however, the truth about the baby she held in her arms.

The baby Jesus was similar to any other baby. When he was hungry he cried for milk, and drank from his mother's breast. The Lord Jesus was truly man. He crawled across the floor before he learnt to walk; he cried when he hurt himself and laughed when he was happy.

Christ, our Saviour, is as truly human as is any other person, except that he was born without sin; and during his entire life, he kept God's law perfectly.

FIND OUT THE FACTS

1. What is a stable?
2. What was the difference between the baby Jesus and any other human baby?
3. Why was it important for Jesus to be a human being? Read Hebrews 2:14-18.

To Think & to pray about

The angel appeared and spoke to the shepherds. Thank the Lord that he sends his word to people of all walks of life.

A Saying to Remember

In Christ Jesus heaven meets earth and earth ascends to heaven.   *Henry Law*

Genesis
17:9-14

'And when eight days were completed for the circumcision of the child, his name was called JESUS, the name given by the angel before he was conceived in the womb' (Luke 2:21).

Today, many little boys are circumcised because their parents believe that circumcision should be performed for health reasons. As far as Jewish boys were concerned, circumcision was a requirement. If we go back to the time of Abraham, who was chosen by God to be his friend (James 2:23), we discover the reason for circumcision.

God called Abraham to move from Haran to the land of the Canaanites, where God made a covenant with him: 'To your descendants I will give this land' (Genesis 12:7). Even though Abraham lived in that land for many years, he only ever owned a small plot which was used as a burial ground for his wife, Sarah, and their descendants.

God made many promises to Abraham. Even though he and Sarah were too old to have a child, God promised that Abraham would be the father of a great nation (Genesis 12:2) and that through Abraham and Sarah the people of the earth would receive great blessings. These blessings came to mankind because of the life and death of the Lord Jesus Christ who was in the line of their descendants. His life and death opened the way for sinners to become citizens of God's kingdom.

God also promised Abraham that he would be 'God to [him] and [his] descendants after [him]' (Genesis 17:7). This promise will be complete on the day we enter the new heavens and new earth to live for ever with our Saviour.

In our readings in the Old Testament we found that God always had people from his chosen nation, Israel, to serve him faithfully. Abraham's son, Isaac, served the Lord. Right down through the ages there were Jewish men and women who loved

God and longed for the coming of the promised Messiah, the Christ. This was God's covenant with his people: to be their God and the God of their descendants. In return, the people of Israel were to love him and show that love by obeying his laws. The Lord commanded Abraham to cut into his flesh, the flesh of his male children and all the male members of his household, the covenant sign; they were to be circumcised.

Today the covenant sign is not circumcision but baptism (Colossians 2:11-12; Matthew 28:19; Galatians 3:27; Romans 2:28-29).

Jesus was truly a boy, descended from Abraham, and as a male he was circumcised on the eighth day. Our Saviour obeyed God's law perfectly.

FIND OUT THE FACTS

1. What is a 'covenant'? Name some of those mentioned in the Bible.
2. What was the Old Testament sign that a person was a covenant member of Israel?
3. What is the New Testament sign that a person is a covenant member of the kingdom of God?

The New Testament tells us about the covenant of grace. Thank the Lord for his covenant with his people.

Obedience should be a child's first lesson. *Anon*

July

The way of
the LORD is
strength for
the upright

Proverbs 10:29

Matthew
2:1-12

'And when they had come into the house, they saw the young child with Mary his mother, and fell down and worshipped him ... they presented gifts to him: gold, frankincense, and myrrh' (Matthew 2:11).

When a baby is born, gifts usually arrive. This is one way of celebrating the arrival of a newborn child. The Lord Jesus was also to receive valuable gifts.

His birth was similar to that of other babies, except that his was the birth of a king, who would rule on the throne of his 'father' David, and a birth which had been prophesied many centuries before it took place.

It was during the reign of King Herod that some 'wise men from the East came to Jerusalem' seeking the newly born 'King of the Jews' (Matthew 2:1-2). These men either came from the region inhabited by the Persians, or were from Babylon. Still living in these areas were some of the descendants of the people of Israel and Judah, who had been taken captive by King Nebuchadnezzar centuries before. They had not returned to their homeland, but had the writings of Daniel and knew when the Christ was to be born.

Matthew tells us that they followed the star which finally led them to Jerusalem. There they met the chief priests and scribes whom they asked where the King could be found. These Jewish leaders knew the Old Testament scriptures and told the wise men that the Christ would be born in Bethlehem (Micah 5:2).

King Herod was very interested in what he heard and said that he wanted to know where the child could be found, so that he too could go and worship the 'King of the Jews'. But he was really an angry man who wanted to kill the infant Jesus. He didn't want anyone to lay claim to his throne, in spite of the fact that he was an old man. The citizens of Jerusalem were also disturbed by the arrival of the wise men because it meant that Herod was likely to cause them heartache.

The wise men followed the star which led them to the house where Mary, Joseph and the Lord Jesus were. These visitors worshipped the Baby — by prostrating themselves before him, they acknowledged him to be God — and presented him with gifts of gold, frankincense and myrrh. Their presents were an indication of the status of the Lord Jesus. They gave him gold because he was a King, frankincense because that indicated that he was God, and myrrh because as a man he would die.

Then they returned to their homes without passing through Jerusalem and reporting to King Herod. God had warned them in a dream to return home in secret.

FIND OUT THE FACTS

1. The wise men were warned in a 'dream'. Why doesn't God reveal his plans in dreams today?
2. Why didn't the wise men tell Herod where the baby Jesus could be found?
3. Who prophesied the time of Christ's birth?

The wise men undertook a journey to find the King and to worship him. They must have considered it to be something of great importance. Do you consider it important to worship the King?

In the baby the wise men saw the King of kings and Lord of lords. *Anon*

Matthew 2:12-23

'An angel of the Lord appeared to Joseph in a dream, saying, "Arise, take the young child and his mother, flee to Egypt, and stay there until I bring you word; for Herod will seek the young child to destroy him"' (Matthew 2:13).

Australia has allowed many migrants into the country over the years. Many of these people were forced to leave their homelands which they loved and begin a new life in 'The Land Down Under'.

The infant Jesus, his mother and Joseph were living in a house when the wise men made their visit. However, when it was time to return to their home in Judea, an angel visited Joseph in a dream and warned him of impending danger from King Herod: 'Arise, take the young child and his mother, flee to Egypt, and stay there until I bring you word; for Herod will seek the young child to destroy him' (Matthew 2:13).

King Herod knew that a baby had been born who would one day sit upon the throne of King David. He was furious that the wise men had returned to their homeland without paying the respect he thought he deserved: they had failed to reveal to him the place where Joseph and his family were living.

Immediately, upon receiving God's warning, Joseph and his family escaped to the safety of Egypt, where they remained until they received word that King Herod was dead.

Meanwhile cruel King Herod gave orders to his soldiers to visit Bethlehem and the surrounding districts and to put to death every male baby under the age of two years.

This vile command fulfilled the words spoken by the prophet Jeremiah centuries before: 'A voice was heard in Ramah, lamentation, weeping, and great mourning, Rachel weeping for her children, refusing to be comforted, because they were no more.' (Matthew 2:18, compare Jeremiah 31:15).

We can only imagine the heartache for parents who had their baby sons snatched from them and killed before their eyes. Jeremiah's prophecy was certainly fulfilled, but God cared for his Son. Herod would never find him now that Joseph had moved his family to the safety of Egypt, just as the angel had told him.

When King Herod died, an angel appeared to Joseph in a dream and told him to take his family back to Israel.

Before reaching his home, Joseph was again visited by an angel who warned him not to go to Judea. Thus it was that he made his home in Nazareth. This also fulfilled the prophecy of Isaiah: 'He shall be called a Nazarene' (Matthew 2:23).

Now Christ could grow up in safety.

FIND OUT THE FACTS

1. Describe the character of King Herod.

2. Who is a Nazarene?

3. Why didn't Joseph settle in Judea? Read Matthew 2:22.

Right from earliest years, there were those who desired to kill the Lord Jesus. Think about the hatred that was shown by Herod. Thank the Lord Jesus that he came to live in a world that would hate him and eventually kill him.

To Think & to pray about

The Son of God ... came to seek us where we are in order that he might bring us to be with him where he is. J. I. Packer

A saying to Remember

Luke
2:40-52

'And Jesus increased in wisdom and stature, and in favour with God and men' (Luke 2:52).

Growing up should be a happy time for young people. It is a time when our bodies grow and develop, knowledge increases and we make plans for the future.

We are not told much about the Lord when he was young other than that '[he] grew and became strong in spirit, filled with wisdom; and the grace of God was upon him' (Luke 2:40). Jesus did not break any of the commandments of God, his heavenly Father.

Jesus would have done those things that young people do, but always without sinning. He would have played games with his brothers and sisters and the other children living in Nazareth. When he was happy, he would have laughed; he would have cried when he was hurt.

We are told that Joseph, who was known to be his father, was a carpenter and no doubt Jesus learnt the trade. As he worked under Joseph's guidance, he would have learnt how to use a saw and a hammer. The things he constructed would have been made to a very high standard.

The Holy Spirit guided his ways and he 'grew ... in spirit' (Luke 2:40). In his human nature Jesus grew physically and mentally. He did not know everything and continued to grow in knowledge as the years passed (Hebrews 5:8).

Jesus lived in perfect harmony with his heavenly Father. There was always a perfect love between the persons of the Godhead. The closeness that existed between Father and Son is shown in the story we read here.

His godly parents visited Jerusalem each year for the Passover. When Jesus turned twelve, he was taken to Jerusalem at the time of the feast. This was probably his first visit to Jerusalem.

After the Passover celebrations, Joseph and Mary began the journey back home. After a day's travelling, they discovered that Jesus was missing. This meant that they would need to return to Jerusalem to look for him. Back in Jerusalem they found him in the temple asking questions and listening to the teachers of God's law. This was the usual method of teaching, but Jesus was asking questions that showed great spiritual insight.

Mary was upset with Jesus' behaviour and told him so. His reply to her was: 'Why did you seek me? Did you not know that I must be about my Father's business?' (Luke 2:49).

Jesus was indeed the Son of God, and he was becoming more aware of his life's work.

FIND OUT THE FACTS

1. What did Jesus mean when he answered Mary's rebuke?
2. What is the Passover?
3. Was Jesus truly man? How do you know?

Jesus would have been a perfect child. Think about what it means never to want to be disobedient, cheeky or to tell a lie. Ask the Lord to help you to be more like the Lord Jesus.

If you want to know what God has to say to you, see what Christ was and is. C. H. Spurgeon

Matthew
3:1-12

The voice of one crying in the wilderness, "Prepare the way of the LORD; Make straight in the desert a highway for our God"' (Isaiah 40:3).

John the Baptist was a prophet who lived in the wilderness area of Judea, where he ate 'locusts and wild honey' and was clothed in camel's hair, with a leather belt around his waist' (Matthew 3:4). He must have looked like a wild man, but what he said attracted people to him. He went about preaching this message: 'Repent, for the kingdom of heaven is at hand!' (Matthew 3:2).

John had a special God-given task. He had been chosen by God to prepare Israel for the coming of the Lord Jesus Christ. The words of Isaiah in the scripture verse were being fulfilled, and there was an expectation in the land that the coming of the Messiah was soon to be. Some even thought that John was the long-awaited Son of God (John 1:21). He denied this and on one occasion said, 'I indeed baptize you with water; but one mightier than I is coming, whose sandal strap I am not worthy to loose. He will baptize you with the Holy Spirit and fire' (Luke 3:16).

There was an expectation that the Christ would come baptizing (John 1:25). Christ's baptism would not be with water, but with the Holy Spirit (John 1:33). (Some suggest that baptism was the sign of a Gentile becoming a member of the covenant people. This was not so. Circumcision of the male was the covenant sign.)

Not only did John call his listeners to repentance, but he baptized those who openly confessed their sins and repented. He urged his repentant listeners to do the works of righteousness; they were to live godly lives.

He warned those who continued in their sinful ways that they would be like useless trees which are cut down and thrown into the fire. When the people asked him what they should do, he told them to share their possessions with those who were in need. He told the tax collectors to take only the correct amount of money which was due to the authorities. Many Roman soldiers used their power to steal from the people. John told them that they were to be content with their wages.

When some of the proud Pharisees and Sadducees came to hear John preaching, he said to them, 'Brood of vipers! Who has warned you to flee from the wrath to come? Therefore bear fruits worthy of repentance' (Matthew 3:7-8).

John's work was to prepare the people for the coming of Christ.

FIND OUT THE FACTS

1. Why did people expect Christ to come baptizing?
   Read Isaiah 52:15; Ezekiel 36:25.
2. Explain the meaning of John 1:23.
3. What was the subject of John's preaching?
4. Today what is the purpose of faithful preaching?

To Think & to pray about

John told the people to repent of their sins. To repent of sin is something God calls sinful men and women, boys and girls to do. Do you understand what it means to repent of your sins?

A saying to Remember

Sin and hell are married unless repentance proclaims the divorce. C. H. Spurgeon

John
1:29-34

'And immediately, coming up from the water, he saw the heavens parting and the Spirit descending upon him like a dove. Then a voice came from heaven, "You are my beloved Son, in whom I am well pleased"' (Mark 1:10-11).

For some reason many people believe their children must be baptized or they will never enter heaven. This is not so! The people who enter heaven are those who have a saving faith in the Lord Jesus Christ. When I have been asked by people who don't normally attend church to baptize their baby, my answer has always been to explain what baptism means and then to invite them to attend worship for at least three months before raising the subject again. Usually that is the last I see of the parents.

John the Baptist was faithfully preaching a gospel of repentance from sin and a turning to righteous living. He knew the Lord Jesus; they were cousins and he had been told, 'He who sent me to baptize with water said to me, "Upon whom you see the Spirit descending, and remaining on him, this is he who baptizes with the Holy Spirit"' (John 1:33).

John saw Jesus coming and said, 'Behold! The Lamb of God who takes away the sin of the world!' (John 1:29). God had revealed to him that Jesus was the Messiah.

Often the question is asked, 'Why did the sinless Jesus need John's baptism of repentance from sin?' Some will say that this was the first way Christ publicly identified himself with sinners. He would bear the sins of his people on the cross.

Others say that the baptism of Christ was his public acceptance of his role as our great High Priest. Those who were descendants of Levi and Aaron commenced their duties in the temple at thirty years of age (Numbers 4:3,47; 8:6-7). Just as the priest was baptized and began his work at thirty years, so did Christ.[1] Christian baptism was introduced after Christ's resurrection (Matthew 28:19).

John's baptism of Jesus was the beginning of his public ministry. In a voice that could be heard, the Father spoke from heaven, acknowledging Jesus Christ to be his one and only Son. At the same time the Holy Spirit descended upon Christ in the form of a dove.

In this moment of time, God the Father, Son and Holy Spirit were present. The eternal covenant of God was about to be played out on earth in order that sinners might be saved.

Those sinners given to the Son have their names written in the Book of Life. The Holy Spirit was always with Christ, and he would soon commence his work of applying Christ's redemption to those whose names were written in the heavenly records.

[1.] For a full discussion of this matter read Jay E. Adams: *Meaning and Mode of Baptism*, P&R, USA, 1976, pp 16-20

FIND OUT THE FACTS

1. What is baptism?
2. With what are people baptized?
3. What is 'baptism by the Holy Spirit'?

To Think & to pray about

John the Baptist was a humble man. Even though he baptized the Lord Jesus, he later said that Christ must increase and he must decrease. Ask the Lord to give you a humble **spirit**.

A saying to Remember

Without the Spirit of God we can do nothing but add sin to sin.
John Wesley

Matthew
4:1-11

'Then Jesus said to him, "Away
with you, Satan! For it is written, 'You shall worship the Lᴏʀᴅ
your God, and him only you
shall serve'"' (Matthew 4:10).

I have never seen the devil or any of his demons, but I have
seen the damage he does. We are told that sin pays wages —
death! Satan tempted Adam and Eve in the Garden of Eden
and because of their disobedience sin entered the world. Since
then every person born into the world has a sinful nature, and
the consequence of this is that we sin!

But there was one exception to this. One perfectly righteous person was born. He did not have a sinful nature and
never committed a sin. That person is our Saviour, the Lord
Jesus Christ.

Following his baptism, he was led into the wilderness to be
tempted by Satan. This was to be the first earthly battle
between the Son of God and the evil one. Before this battle
commenced, Christ fasted for forty days, and no doubt spent
time in prayer to his heavenly Father. The Holy Spirit would
have strengthened him spiritually in preparation for the battle
that was soon to commence.

First, the devil commanded Christ to turn stones into bread
in order to satisfy his hunger. But the Lord answered, 'It is
written, "Man shall not live by bread alone, but by every word
that proceeds from the mouth of God"' (Matthew 4:4).

For the second temptation Satan took Jesus to the top of the
temple and then suggested that he jump off because God had
promised that his angels would catch him and prevent him
from being hurt. But Jesus again replied, quoting the Scriptures, 'It is written again, "You shall not tempt the Lᴏʀᴅ your
God"' (Matthew 4:7, also Psalm 91:11-12).

Satan's final temptation was to ask Jesus to fall down
before him and worship him. In return he would give him all
the kingdoms of the world. Christ knew that this was not the

way that sinners would be saved. Salvation could only be achieved by his sacrificial death on the cross. How could he bow down to the one who had caused so much harm in the world? This time the Lord Jesus said, 'Away with you, Satan! For it is written, "You shall worship the LORD your God, and him only you shall serve"' (Matthew 4:10).

After this rebuke, a defeated Satan turned away and departed. At that moment Satan was a defeated foe. It was just a foretaste of the future.

The angels came and cared for Christ, no doubt bringing food and drink, and encouraging words from his heavenly Father. When you are tempted, you too can have victory over the tempter (1 Corinthians 10:13).

FIND OUT THE FACTS

1 What is one work of God's angels? Read Hebrews 1:14.

2. Name two angels?

3. What is Satan's end? Read Revelation 20:10.

4. How can you have victory over temptations? Read Ephesians 6:10-18.

To Think & to pray about

If Christ, who is sinless, was tempted by Satan, we, who are sinful, should expect him to tempt us. Ask the Lord to help you to recognize Satan's temptations and to resist them.

A saying to Remember

We must not get so busy counting demons that we forget the holy angels. *Billy Graham*

John   'Then [Jesus] said to his
1:35-51   disciples, "The harvest truly is
            plentiful, but the labourers
            are few"' (Matthew 9:37).

We don't have many people today who call themselves disciples, but every Christian is a disciple of the Lord Jesus Christ. He is our teacher from whom we learn the truth concerning God and ourselves.

The Bible speaks about those people who were the disciples, followers of John the Baptist and the Pharisees (Mark 2:18).

The Lord Jesus Christ was a teacher and was called Rabbi (Mark 9:5). He came into the world to save sinners through his life of perfect obedience to his heavenly Father and by carrying their sins to the cross, where he died in their place. But that was not all, Christ revealed God the Father to his disciples (John 17:6-8).

As we have seen, after he was baptized, Jesus faced Satan's temptations in the wilderness. The next step was to gather men to listen to his teachings. They would be made willing to preach the good news of Christ's death and resurrection.

On one occasion we are told that Jesus had seventy disciples (Luke 10:1) whom he sent out in twos. These men depended upon the kindness of others to provide their food and clothing.

Jesus' call was to people who would sacrifice everything for him, even their lives, if necessary. There were some men who desired to become his disciples, but made excuses for not following him immediately. One wanted time to bury his father, another wanted time to say farewell to his relatives, while others couldn't bear the idea of having nowhere to sleep (Luke 9:57-62). There were some who were offended by his teachings (John 6:60-66). Eventually Jesus had just twelve disciples.

They were Peter, James and John (the sons of Zebedee), Andrew, Philip, Bartholomew, Matthew, Thomas, James (the son of Alphaeus), Thaddaeus, Simon the Canaanite and Judas Iscariot (Mark 3:14-19). These men followed Jesus during his three and a half years of preaching and performing miracles. They had left their daily work to follow the person they believed was the long-awaited Messiah.

There were three disciples who were very special to Christ: Peter, James and John. Among the twelve there was Judas Iscariot who betrayed him. The twelve heard the Lord's teaching, saw his miracles and were all taught the great truths about God.

The faithful disciples, chosen by Christ, were sent to preach the gospel to all the world.

FIND OUT THE FACTS

1. Why do you think Jesus chose twelve disciples and not ten?
2. Make a list of the twelve disciples and, if possible, write their occupations before they became disciples.
3. How should Christ's followers live today?

To be Christ's disciple involves sacrifice but it is the only way to live. Think about what becoming a disciple of Christ really means.

A disciple is a person who learns to live the life his teacher lives.
Juan Carlos Ortiz

A saying to Remember

John
2:1-12

'This beginning of signs Jesus did in Cana of Galilee, and manifested his glory; and his disciples believed in him' (John 2:11).

Weddings are very happy occasions, when a man and a woman pledge themselves to each other for as long as they live. After the wedding ceremony there is a reception at which the family and friends of the newly weds join them in celebrating the joyous event. I can remember my wedding over forty years ago. It was a very happy day!

The Lord Jesus, his mother and his disciples were invited to a wedding at Cana in Galilee. This was at a time where wedding receptions could last several days. In this story the host ran out of wine, which would have been very embarrassing. When Mary heard about this she turned to her son, Jesus, and said, 'They have no wine' (John 2:3).

The angel had told her and Joseph many years before that her baby was special. He was the Son of God who would save his people from their sins. They would have known that their son was the Messiah, who would be greater than Moses. Mary knew he could perform great miracles.

Jesus replied by telling Mary that he would do the will of his heavenly Father. It was time for Mary to release her son to do the work to which he had been called. He replied, 'Woman, what does your concern have to do with me? My hour has not yet come' (John 2:4).

We might think that it was rude of Jesus to call his mother, 'Woman'. In those days, it was like addressing her as 'dear woman'.

Jesus instructed the servants to fill the six big waterpots with water. He then told them to take a drink to the master of the feast. The man was amazed. It was excellent wine, and he was surprised that the best had been kept till last. Usually guests were given the best wine first, and so when they were merry, they wouldn't mind what they drank. The inferior wine was served when the guests had had too much to drink.

This was Christ's first public miracle. Soon the nation would know that Jesus, the teacher and miracle worker, was claiming to be the 'Son of Man', the Messiah. However, he wanted his identity to become known at the right time.

The disciples who were with him must have been amazed at what they saw. The apostle John said that this miracle revealed the glory of the Son of God (John 2:11).

FIND OUT THE FACTS

1. How much water did each pot hold?
2. Read Psalm 104:14-15. What are we taught about wine? See also Proverbs 20:1; 23:29-32; 31:6-7.
3. Why did most people in Jesus' day drink wine?

To Think & to pray about

The life of Jesus Christ was a blessing to many. Thank him for the many blessings he showered on people who came to him in their need.

Those who need miracles are men of little faith.   John Huss

A saying to Remember

John   'Zeal for your house has eaten
2:13-22   me up.' (Psalm 69:9).

Every year many people celebrate Christmas Day, wrongly believing it to be Christ's birthday. God does not require Christians to celebrate the Lord's birthday. Others call Easter a religious festival which remembers the death of the Lord Jesus. Again people are misled, because we are to remember our Saviour's sacrificial death in the Lord's Supper.

Nowhere in Scripture are Christians instructed to celebrate festivals. However, in the Old Testament the people celebrated many ceremonies. The Passover was a reminder of the time when the Lord brought Israel out of Egypt, the land of slavery (Deuteronomy 16:1-6).

Each family, that is, the men of the family, were expected to travel to Jerusalem for the Passover and have the priest kill the sacrificial lamb. The Passover meal would then be eaten with much joy and praise to God, who had saved his people from Egypt. The Passover pointed to the day when Christ, 'the Lamb of God' would die for his people.

Jesus and his disciples went up to Jerusalem to celebrate the Passover feast. They reached the temple, entered the court-yard, and found it was filled with men who sold animals for sacrifice. Sitting at tables were money changers, who exchanged foreign currency for the local coin. This was needed to pay the annual temple tax and for freewill offerings.

Solomon's temple was a majestic structure, but the temple of Christ's day was more glorious because Christ, the God-man, had entered its precincts. What Jesus saw caused him to show a righteous anger. The temple was God's house and therefore a place of worship.

The Lord made a whip and drove out the money changers, the sheep and oxen, and those involved in trading, saying, 'Take these things away! Do not make my Father's house a house of merchandise!' (John 2:16). The local Jews asked on whose authority he did this. They also asked for a sign to prove he had the right to take such action.

The Lord's answer was, 'Destroy this temple, and in three days I will raise it up' (John 2:19). Here he spoke of his body and his resurrection which would follow his crucifixion. Those who heard him speak thought he was speaking of Herod's temple.

FIND OUT THE FACTS

1. For what was the temple used?
2. Read Haggai 2:9. What does it mean?
3. Can you remember how the first Passover was celebrated? Refer to Exodus 12:1-13 if you need to refresh your memory.
4. What is righteous anger? See Ephesians 4:26.

To Think & to pray about

There is nothing wrong with doing business and making money. Think about why the Lord Jesus was so angry with these people for conducting business in the temple.

Regeneration is a universal change of the whole man ... it is as large in renewing as sin was in defacing.
Stephen Charnock

A saying to Remember

John
3:1-8

'Jesus answered and said to him, "Most assuredly, I say to you, unless one is born again, he cannot see the kingdom of God"' (John 3:3).

Nicodemus is one person in the Bible I shall never forget. His name is mentioned three times in the Scriptures and each time it is evident that he is moving closer to the Lord Jesus.

Nicodemus, who was a Pharisee, saw Jesus at night as he didn't want anyone to see what he was doing. The Pharisees hated Jesus, but Nicodemus wanted to talk to him and find out if he was the Messiah. Nicodemus loved God and wanted a heavenly home, but he didn't know how it could be obtained!

When he came face to face with Jesus, he acknowledged him as a Rabbi, a teacher, who did many good deeds. Jesus told him that he had to be 'born again' if he wanted to be a citizen of the kingdom of God. Even though Nicodemus had studied the Old Testament, he didn't know what being 'born again' meant. He even thought that it could mean that he had to return to his mother's womb and be born a second time. But Jesus explained that being 'born again' was the work of God's Holy Spirit in changing the sinner's heart, so that he loved God and obeyed his commandments.

Nicodemus should have known the teaching of Ezekiel: 'I will give you a new heart and put a new spirit within you; I will take the heart of stone out of your flesh and give you a heart of flesh. I will put my Spirit within you and cause you to walk in my statutes, and you will keep my judgements and do them' (Ezekiel 36:26-27).

Jesus told Nicodemus that the work of the Holy Spirit was like the wind which blew and produced an observable presence: the leaves in the trees could be seen to move. That was how the Holy Spirit acted: the result of his work could be seen.

Later Nicodemus was the only Pharisee to defend Jesus at the Feast of Tabernacles. The Pharisees wanted to see Christ killed, but Nicodemus wanted him to be heard before anyone condemned him.

Following the death of Christ, it was Joseph of Arimathea and Nicodemus who asked Pilate if they could take the Saviour's body in order to lay it to rest in a tomb.

Do you notice that the fearful Nicodemus, who visited Jesus during the night, asked for his body and wasn't worried who heard about it? I'm sure that one day we shall see Nicodemus in paradise. Do you love and obey the Lord Jesus?

If so, you have been 'born again'.

FIND OUT THE FACTS

1. Why do you think Nicodemus visited Jesus at night-time?
2. What is a Pharisee?
3. In the salvation of sinners, what is the work of the Lord Jesus Christ?
4. What are you taught in John 14:15?

Nicodemus was not turned away when he asked Jesus questions. Jesus is our great teacher who shows us the way of salvation. Thank him that he teaches sinners the truth of God.

All that is here is condemned to die — to pass away like a snowball before a summer sun.
Samuel Rutherford

A saying to Remember

Numbers   'For God so loved the world
21:4-9   that he gave his only begotten
              Son, that whoever believes in
              him should not perish but have
              everlasting life' (John 3:16).

Many years ago I knew a little boy named John, who was learning John 3:16. For a while when anyone asked him his name he would reply, 'John 3:16'. Our scripture verse is probably the best known verse in the Bible and one which everyone should know.

Christ's conversation with Nicodemus ends at verse 21 of John chapter 3, and in it are recorded some of the most precious words spoken by the Saviour.

Nicodemus would have known the story of the fiery serpents who attacked the disobedient Israelites as they made their way through the desert. The Lord told Moses to mould a bronze serpent and put it on a pole. When a person was bitten by a snake, all he had to do was look at the serpent on the pole and he would live.

The Israelites were expecting the Messiah to come and judge the world and establish the throne of King David, upon which he would sit as King. Nicodemus needed to be told the truth. The Lord told him that he had come from heaven to save sinners. He would be lifted up and anyone who believed in him would live for ever.

It is important that we know that Christ's first coming into this lost world of ours was to save sinners. He came to live in perfect obedience to his heavenly Father and to die on a Roman cross, carrying the sins of all his people. He did what Adam failed to do.

John 3:16 tells us that any sinner who looks in faith to the crucified and risen Saviour will be saved. Nicodemus must have gone away and thought about Christ's words. So should you and I!

Our salvation is found in God. The Father sent his willing Son to save all those people given to him. Christ convicts his people of their sins by the Holy Spirit who works in their hearts and changes them. Christ is the 'light' that comes into the repentant sinner's heart, driving out the darkness of sin (John 8:12). Nicodemus was told that all who did not believe in the Lord Jesus were already condemned.

Our salvation cost the Son of God a time of great humiliation, ending in death. Even though the cost of this salvation is incomprehensible, it is made freely available to sinners. Isaiah wrote of this redemption, 'Ho! Everyone who thirsts, come to the waters; and you who have no money, come, buy and eat. Yes, come, buy wine and milk without money and without price' (Isaiah 55:1).

FIND OUT THE FACTS

1. Repeat the verse John 3:16 and state what it means.
2. How did Jesus save sinners?
3. Nicodemus is mentioned in two other places in the Bible ¯ John 7:50 and John 19:39. What does this tell us about him?

Thank the Lord for the work of the Holy Spirit who convicts people of sin and changes their heart. Has he changed your heart?

We are not saved by our giving; we are saved by God's giving.
A.W. Pink

John
4:21-26

'God is Spirit, and those who worship him must worship in spirit and truth' (John 4:24).

The highlight of the week for every Christian should be worship on the Lord's Day. Believers gather together to offer the Lord 'the sacrifice of praise' which is 'the fruit of [their] lips' (Hebrews 13:15). It should be a time of joy to hear the pastor teach the whole counsel of God. We all need to be reminded that we are sinners, saved by grace alone. We need to be constantly reminded of the saving work of Christ. It is wonderful to be told of the attributes (characteristics) of God, who is Spirit.

The Lord Jesus and his disciples were on their way to Galilee; they were resting not far from a Samaritan city named Sychar. Jesus' disciples had gone into the city to buy some food while he waited near Jacob's well. While he was resting, a woman from Sychar came to get water for her home. She was surprised when Jesus asked her for a drink. The Samaritans were hated by the Jews, and to have a Jew asking for water was something she had probably never heard nor seen before. The Jews usually refused to touch anything that belonged to the Samaritans. To do so made them ceremonially unclean.

The Saviour spoke to the woman, saying that he could give her 'living water'. Pointing to the water in Jacob's well, he continued, 'Whoever drinks of this water will thirst again, but whoever drinks of the water that I shall give him will never thirst' (John 4:13-14).

The woman wanted the water of which he spoke because she thought Jesus was speaking of the water from the well, which, if taken home, would last for ever. She would never again have to spend her time carrying water.

Jesus told her things about herself that made her think, 'How can he know this about me?' Jesus said that she had had five husbands and the man she was living with at that time was not her husband. The Saviour went on to say that the day was coming when God could be worshipped anywhere. And how could this be?

Jesus' answer was: 'God is Spirit, and those who worship him must worship in spirit and truth' (John 4:24). This means that God can be worshipped everywhere: in a special building, in the car, at home, on holiday. God is spirit and we worship him with our heart and mind.

We also worship him in 'truth', which is through the one and only Mediator between God and men: the Lord Jesus (1 Timothy 2:5).

FIND OUT THE FACTS

1. What is worship?
2. Discuss what is meant by the words of 1 Timothy 2:5.
3. Discuss the answer to Question 4 of *The Westminster Shorter Catechism*.

Jesus was not ashamed to associate with people who were despised by others. Do you know people who others look down upon? Would you be willing to take the gospel message to them?

Worship is the highest function of the human soul. *Geoffrey R. King*

A saying to Remember

John
4:46-54

'Then Jesus said to him, "Unless you people see signs and wonders, you will by no means believe"' (John 4:48).

There are many people today who claim to have the ability to perform great miracles in the name of the Lord Jesus. I have never seen anyone perform a miracle as Jesus did, especially raising the dead. Christ said that being able to perform miracles was not necessarily a sign that the person was a Christian.

Jesus warned the people who heard him preach that great 'Sermon on the Mount': 'Not everyone who says to me, "Lord, Lord" shall enter the kingdom of heaven, but he who does the will of my Father in heaven. Many will say to me in that day, "Lord, Lord, have we not prophesied in your name, cast out demons in your name, and done many wonders in your name?" And then I will declare to them, "I never knew you; depart from me, you who practise lawlessness!"' (Matthew 7:21-23).

Jesus had already performed a miracle in Cana. We have read of how he turned water into wine. But now he faced a distressed father, whose son was dying. He was an important man; one who worked for King Herod and had heard that Jesus was able to perform amazing miracles. It is possible that he attended the wedding at Cana.

The nobleman set out to meet Jesus, as he knew the doctors couldn't help his son. It was the Lord Jesus alone who could perform such a healing miracle. But Jesus was concerned that people would only believe he was the Messiah if they saw him performing great miracles as our verse tells us. As soon as the man asked him for help, Jesus replied, 'Go your way; your son lives' (John 4:50).

As the man was travelling home, he was met by his servants who told him that the boy was well. Later they found out that he had recovered at precisely the moment that Jesus had said, 'Your son lives.' There and then the nobleman believed that Jesus was who he claimed to be: the Messiah.

This man and his family were very thankful for what the Lord had done for their seriously ill son. We are told that all the nobleman's family believed in the Lord Jesus Christ.

Our Saviour can heal people today, just as he did when walking the roads of Israel. If we need the healing hand of Christ then we should pray, in the same way that Christ prayed to his Father: 'Not my will, but yours, be done' (Luke 22:42).

FIND OUT THE FACTS

1. What is a miracle?

2. Why could Jesus perform miracles?

3. What great miracle does the Holy Spirit perform in the hearts of God's people?

The Saviour showed great compassion for people in their need. Think about the people to whom you can show compassion. Ask the Lord to help you to do this.

The miraculous is absolutely basic to Christianity.   E. H. Andrews

Luke
4:20-30

'The Spirit of the Lord is upon me, because he has anointed me to preach the gospel to the poor ... to proclaim the acceptable year of the Lord' (Luke 4:18,19).

When I became the pastor of a congregation which had many old friends and relatives in its membership, I wondered how they would treat me. Even though I had not had contact with many of them for years, most remembered me. They knew what I was like at school. Val and I were welcomed by them and made to feel at home. They treated me like the long-lost son, who had returned home. My years with those people were some of the most wonderful of my life.

Jesus preached the good news to people who gathered in the synagogues, on the hillsides, in a boat, or in any place where people were willing to listen.

When he came to Nazareth, he went into the synagogue on the Sabbath day, where he took the scroll of the book of Isaiah and read words about himself: 'The Spirit of the Lord is upon me, because he has anointed me to preach the gospel to the poor; he has sent me to heal the brokenhearted, to proclaim liberty to the captives and recovery of sight to the blind, to set at liberty those who are oppressed; to proclaim the acceptable year of the Lord' (Luke 4:18-19; compare Isaiah 61:1-2).

When he had finished reading, he announced that the prophecy was being fulfilled that very day. The congregation looked at Jesus and asked one another, 'Is this not Joseph's son?' (Luke 4:22). Jesus had grown up in their midst. He hadn't gone to the universities of the day, yet he spoke with great authority, teaching what his Father would have him say.

He always spoke the truth! He spoke of death, eternity, heaven, hell and the need to repent and live a righteous life. His words irritated the Pharisees and Scribes because they knew that some of his preaching was critical of them. Jesus had healed on the Sabbath and this was against their man-made law.

Christ spoke of God's love for sinners, calling them to repentance. Many loved to hear his interesting parables. But they thought to themselves, 'Why doesn't he say and do the things he did in Capernaum here?' Those people knew that Christ had performed miracles; but he knew they didn't honour him. He said, 'No prophet is accepted in his own country' (Luke 4:24).

When he spoke of God's love for the Gentiles — Elijah had been cared for by a Gentile widow and Elisha had healed Naaman, a leper from Syria — the congregation was filled with rage. They took Christ to a cliff to throw him off it, but he turned and walked through the crowd and left the city.

FIND OUT THE FACTS

1. Why did the people hate Christ and want to see him dead?

2. Jesus didn't perform many miracles in Nazareth. Why? Read Matthew 13:58.

3. What is the meaning of the 'Saying to remember'?

To the people of Nazareth Christ was just an ordinary man. But he is not. Think of some of the things that make him who he is, the **Son of** God, and praise him for them.

A saying to Remember

Familiarity breeds contempt.
Anon

Matthew
4:18-22

John
1:35-49

'Then he said to them, "Follow me, and I will make you fishers of men"' (Matthew 4:19).

Having spent time in prayer, the Lord gathered his disciples together and chose the twelve. They were to be prepared for a special work of teaching others of God's great salvation. Judas Iscariot was chosen, even though Jesus knew he would betray him, as had been prophesied (Matthew 10:4). He was one of the tares among the wheat.

Simon and Andrew, the sons of Jonah, were brothers in a fishing business. It seems that they were partners with John and James, the sons of Zebedee.

Andrew and Simon were followers of John the Baptist, and it was Andrew, with John (the apostle), who heard John (the Baptist) say of Jesus, 'Behold the Lamb of God!' (John 1:36). Andrew and John had spent some hours with Jesus and knew they had found the long-awaited Messiah. Immediately Andrew found his brother Simon (Peter) and told him, 'We have found the Messiah' (John 1:41). John, no doubt, set out to find James, his brother, and tell him the good news.

The following day when Jesus was leaving Bethsaida (House of fish) for Galilee, he met Philip and said to him, 'Follow me' (John 1:43). Immediately Philip, who knew the Old Testament teaching, set out to find his friend, Nathanael, and told him he had found Christ. He invited him to come to Jesus, who, when he met him, said, 'Behold, an Israelite indeed, in whom is no deceit! ... Before Philip called you, when you were under the fig tree, I saw you' (John 1:47,48).

Nathanael knew that this was indeed the Messiah, because he spoke of things he had not seen with his physical eyes. All he could say was, 'Rabbi, You are the Son of God! You are the King of Israel!' (John 1:49).

Soon Christ had disciples who spent time following him, but who also carried out their daily work whenever possible. One day Jesus came to the spot where Simon, now called Peter, and Andrew were fishing. The Lord called them to full-time discipleship. 'Follow me, and I will make you fishers of men,' he said (Matthew 4:19).

A short distance further, the Saviour met John and James who were with their father, Zebedee, mending their fishing nets. When Jesus called them to follow him, they dropped what they were doing and joined Peter and Andrew.

FIND OUT THE FACTS

1. What is meant by the 'Saying to remember'?

2. What did the Lord mean when he told Peter, Andrew, James and John that they would become 'fishers of men'?

3. Did Christ make a mistake in calling Judas Iscariot to be a disciple? Read John 6:70-71 and Psalm 41:9.

4. Explain the meaning of this statement: 'Delayed obedience is disobedience.'

Jesus called these men to follow him and to be his disciples. Jesus is still calling people to follow him. Think seriously about what that means for you.

A Christian is the world's Bible — and some of them need revising.
D. L. Moody

 | Mark | 'But Jesus rebuked him, say-
| 1:21-28 | ing, "Be quiet, and come out of
| | him!"' (Mark 1:25).

There are some countries in the world where missionaries do meet people who are demon possessed. During the days of the Lord Jesus, Satan and his army of demons were very active. A great war was under way in the spiritual world. Christ, the Son of God, was attacking Satan's kingdom. Christ's death, resurrection and ascension overthrew Satan's power and assured the Lord's people of their salvation.

Jesus and some of his disciples travelled down to Capernaum. This town was situated on the shore of the Sea of Galilee. Every one who travelled to the town went down, as the Sea of Galilee was some 200 metres below sea level.

On the Sabbath Day, Jesus worshipped in the local syna-gogue. Being well known for his teaching, Jesus was invited by the synagogue rulers to read the Scriptures and preach a sermon. Those who heard him speak were surprised at his words and the manner in which he spoke. They found it hard to believe that a carpenter's son could teach with such authority.

Christ always spoke the truth in a straightforward manner. He spoke of the issues of life and death in such a way that people thronged to hear his words.

There, in the synagogue, he was confronted by a man who was possessed by a devil. The devil called out to Christ, 'Let us alone! What have we to do with you, Jesus of Nazareth? Did you come to destroy us? I know who you are — the Holy One of God!' (Luke 4:34). In this verse the demon said that he knew Christ's intention. We should remember this truth. Satan can quote the Scriptures better than most of us can. He is a power-ful being who has done and will yet do great harm to the church and the saints.

The demon was asking why the Lord had come from heaven? Had he come to destroy their power? This demon knew that Christ was God's Holy One, who had come to fulfil the prophecy of Genesis 3:15: 'And I will put enmity between you and the woman, and between your seed and her Seed; he shall bruise your head, and you shall bruise his heel.' Christ had defeated Satan in the wilderness and shown the demonic host that their cause was a lost one. Christ now simply looked at the demon-possessed man and said, 'Be quiet, and come out of him!' (Mark 1:25).

The demon resisted Christ's command, but had to obey. The people in the synagogue were amazed at what they saw and spread the news of the healing far and wide. It was the Sabbath day!

FIND OUT THE FACTS

1. What is a synagogue?
2. How can we fight against Satan? Read Ephesians 6:10-18.
3. Who are Satan and his demons? Read Revelation 12:7-12.

Satan tries to deceive Christians into believing that he has greater power than he has. This incident clearly shows that Christ is indeed the all-powerful one. Thank him for his great **power** over Satan and his demons.

Let us learn not to fondle Satan.
Augustus H. Strong

Mark
1:29-34

'And demons also came out of many, crying out and saying, "You are the Christ, the Son of God!" And he, rebuking them, did not allow them to speak, for they knew that he was the Christ' (Luke 4:41).

When a doctor who has great skills becomes known, many people start making appointments to take advantage of his expertise.

The same applied to the Lord Jesus. Soon his reputation for miraculously healing the sick spread throughout the region. Everyone who was sick and could make their way to where he was, was made well. Our Saviour was a man of great compassion. He was one who wept at the tomb of his friend, Lazarus. He was well aware of the wages of sin which are sickness and death.

Having left the synagogue where he had healed the demon-possessed man, he went to Andrew and Peter's house, where Peter's mother-in-law lay ill. Jesus simply took her by the hand and lifted her up. She was made well again. At once she began preparing a meal for the group of men.

The Roman Catholic church requires of her priests that they remain unmarried. It is evident from the passage which you have read that Peter was a married man. Where his wife was when Christ visited his home, we are not told.

Many years later, the apostle Paul had reason to claim his rights as an apostle. He had the right to be supported by the churches. He also claimed the right, as he moved about, 'to take along a believing wife, as [did] also the other apostles, the brothers of the Lord, and Cephas [Peter]' (1 Corinthians 9:5).

That afternoon Jesus found himself the centre of attention. The news about his healing the man in the synagogue had quickly spread and all who were sick or demon possessed came to be healed. Mark records that 'the whole city was gathered together at the door' (Mark 1:33). Jesus told the demons, who knew who he was, not to speak. He knew it was not his Father's time for him to be taken before the authorities and put to death. He also didn't want crowds of people following him in order to be healed. Christ was yet to preach the gospel of the kingdom and invite people to turn to him and be saved.

This healing ministry of our Lord was the fulfilment of Isaiah's prophecy which Matthew records as: 'He himself took our infirmities and bore our sicknesses' (Matthew 8:17, compare Isaiah 53:4). Christ was to suffer distress, death and hell for his people, all of which are the consequences of sin. In dealing with our sins, Jesus dealt with our infirmities and sicknesses.

On earth, by healing the sick and casting out demons, we know that he triumphed over Satan.

FIND OUT THE FACTS

1. Why do humans die?
2. How was it that our Lord could heal those who were sick?
3. Should people be forbidden to marry? See 1 Timothy 4:1-3 and 1 Corinthians 9:5.

While living on earth, Jesus went about doing good. Think of ways in which you can do good to others.

Jesus takes to heart the sufferings of his friends. *William Hendriksen*

Mark
2:1-12

'When Jesus saw their faith, he said to the paralytic, "Son, your sins are forgiven you"' (Mark 2:5).

Sometimes we visit people who are very good friends. Recently on TV there was a report on two men who had fought in the Vietnam war many years ago. They were good mates, but didn't see each other very often.

One day the wife of one told her husband's friend that her husband was dying; his kidneys had failed and he needed a kidney transplant in order to live. When his friend was told this news, he made arrangements for his mate to have one of his kidneys. Medical tests showed they were compatible, and within a short time the surgery was done and both men were well and getting on with their lives. What made the story so appealing was that one man was white and the other black.

Matthew records the story of four good friends who went to extreme measures to help their sick friend. In no way were these men 'fair weather friends'. The paralysed man, lying on his bed, was carried by his companions to the place where Jesus was.

There was no possibility of forcing their way into the room because of the crowd that had gathered there. Fully aware that the only hope for their paralysed friend was a healing from the Lord, the men did some quick thinking and made their way onto the flat roof of the house where they began removing some of its covering. When they had made a hole big enough, they lowered their friend, still on his stretcher, down from the roof into the room. They wanted to see what Jesus would say and do.

Looking at the sick man and his friends, the Lord, who knew that his condition was the result of sin, said, 'Son, your sins are forgiven you' (Mark 2:5).

These words angered the scribes who were present, and they asked one another, 'Why does this man speak blasphemies like this? Who can forgive sins but God alone?' (Mark 2:7).

Jesus knew their thoughts and asked them, 'Which is easier, to say to the paralytic, "Your sins are forgiven you," or to say, "Arise, take up your bed and walk"? But that you may know that the Son of Man has power on earth to forgive sins ... I say to you, "Arise, take up your bed, and go to your house"'(Mark 2:9-11).

In this healing we see the tenderness of the Saviour, the Shepherd of his sheep. We also see the Lord's divinity, for the scribes spoke the truth when they said, 'God alone can forgive sins.' The crowd who witnessed the miracle praised God, saying, 'We never saw anything like this!' (Mark 2:12).

Jesus is my Saviour. Is he yours?

FIND OUT THE FACTS

1. Who alone can forgive sins?
2. What do we learn about the sick man's four friends?
3. How can your sins be forgiven?

When people are convinced that they need something, they will do anything to obtain that thing. If you are convinced that Jesus is the only one who can save you from your sins, nothing will hinder you from turning to him.

No man ever thought too much of Christ.   J. C. Ryle

Matthew   'And when the Pharisees saw
9:9-13   it they said to his disciples,
              "Why does your teacher eat
              with tax collectors and sin-
              ners?" When Jesus heard
              that, he said to them, "Those
              who are well have no need of a
              physician, but those who are
              sick"' (Matthew 9:11-12).

In our part of the world very few parents give their children names that have a special meaning. Mums and dads give their sons and daughters names that appeal to them. My wife and I agreed not to use some names because they reminded us of unruly children we had taught.

Matthew, who was to become a disciple of Christ, worked as a tax collector! He worked for the Roman Emperor. People despised tax collectors because they usually demanded more tax than was required and kept the extra for themselves.

The name 'publican' or 'tax collector' was usually associated with the word 'sinner' (Luke 15:1). At that time the word 'publican' was used to refer only to a person who collected taxes. The word did not refer to an inn keeper or to anything associated with the sale of alcohol. Just as in those days, the Taxation Department is not very popular today.

Originally Matthew had the name 'Levi', which means 'joined'. As a descendant of Levi, at times he would have served in the temple. He was probably well known to Jesus. The Lord had marked Levi out for a very special work: he would become a disciple and later an apostle.

One day as he was sitting at his tax collector's table at Capernaum, Jesus walked up to him and said, 'Follow me' (Luke 5:27). Levi did not waste any time. Immediately he left the tax booth and escorted Christ to his home where he gave a feast to celebrate what had happened. No longer was he Levi, but Matthew, meaning 'the gift of God'.

He invited many friends and relatives to his feast; some were tax collectors; because he was saying farewell to them all. When the Pharisees and scribes saw this, they began to complain about the Lord Jesus and his disciples, saying, 'Why do you eat and drink with tax collectors and sinners?' (Luke 5:30). Matthew 9:12 gives Christ's answer to that question.

Matthew would have been overjoyed that he was now a disciple of Christ. Later he would write the Gospel that bears his name. He was able to write what he saw and heard of the Lord Jesus, being guided in his words by the Holy Spirit.

Today Christ calls sinners to come and follow him. Ask God to give you repentance and faith in Christ, the Saviour.

FIND OUT THE FACTS

1. Why would the people have hated the tax collectors?

2. Matthew was from the tribe of 'Levi'. Who were the Levites?

3. Matthew once served the Roman Emperor. Which King did he now serve? How did he serve this King?

Christ called Matthew into his kingdom to perform a specific task. When Christ saves a person, he has good works which he calls that person to do. Thank the Lord that he turns lives of sin into lives of service to God.

The alternative to obedience is disaster. *Anon*

Luke
5:33-39

'But the days will come when
the bridegroom will be taken
away from them; then they will
fast in those days' (Luke 5:35).

Today many people deprive themselves of food for a time
or even go on a fast. The Lord had just come from a feast
with Levi (Matthew) and his friends. Matthew had been called
by Jesus to follow him as one of his disciples. The followers of
John the Baptist and the Pharisees raised the question, 'Why
do we fast while Christ and his disciples do not fast. They
enjoy feasting; why can't we?'

It appears that it was only on the Day of Atonement that the
Israelites were expected to fast, but, over the years, additional
fasting laws had been introduced. And, in the days of our Lord,
the Pharisees boasted that they fasted twice each week (Luke
18:12). In the 'Sermon on the Mount', the Lord rebuked those
who fasted in order to make a show of their 'holiness'
(Matthew 6:16).

Jesus replied to the Pharisees' question by saying that his
disciples were with the bridegroom. This was a time of joy
and feasting, certainly not a time to fast. The bridegroom's
attendants were the ones to provide the feast for the happy
occasion. A wedding was not the time for fasting, but for feasting.
The Lord instructed his disciples that fasting was not something to be carried out according to the calendar, but according
to the situation.

The disciples were warned of a coming time of sadness,
when the bridegroom (Christ) would be put to death — he
would be taken away from them. Then there would be a
reason for fasting and prayer.

In the short parable of patching an old garment with a piece
of new cloth, or putting new wine into old wineskins, he taught
his disciples that the old religious ways of Israel were finished.

The teachings of the Pharisees were replaced by the teachings of Christ. There was no point in trying to patch up the old ways with the new. The change had to be complete, just as new wineskins were needed for new wine. The time had come to throw away the old and to live in the light of the new. It was time to take up the life of grace and faith in the Son of God (John 1:16-17).

Jesus concluded his remarks by pointing especially to the Pharisees who loved their old ways, and who claimed that 'the old is better' (Luke 5:39). This was not true. The time had come to set aside the old ways, and rejoice in the newness that came through Christ, the Saviour.

FIND OUT THE FACTS

1. What use had the Pharisees made of the law?

2. Christ said his people could pray and fast. When and why?

3. Read Luke 5:36. What was Christ teaching in this verse?

Ecclesiates 3:1-8 says there is a time and a purpose for every activity. Christ was teaching that to the Pharisees in our devotion today. Thank him that he has a purpose for everything that will take place in your life today.

A blind man will not thank you for a looking glass. *Thomas Fuller*

John
5:1-15

'Jesus said to him, "Rise, take up your bed and walk"' (John 5:8).

Frequently in the Scriptures we read about angels. I'm not sure if I have ever met an angel, but I know they exist. God uses them as his servants 'to minister for those who will inherit salvation' (Hebrews 1:14). There is a warfare taking place in the invisible world between God's holy angels and Satan and his demons. One day I'm sure believers will thank God for the way in which he has cared for them.

Angels were active in the days when the Lord was on earth. They announced his forthcoming birth to Mary and Joseph; they announced to the shepherds that the Messiah had been born; and an angel appeared to the Lord Jesus in the Garden of Gethsemane, strengthening him for what lay ahead.

Today's reading tells us of a healing that took place beside a pool named 'Bethesda' — 'House of Mercy,' by the Sheep Gate, in Jerusalem. Many sick people were there because an angel went down and stirred the water at a certain time, and the first sick person to get into the water was then healed.

A thirty-eight year old man who was incapacitated was unable to get into the pool before others, when the angel stirred the water. When Christ saw him lying there, he asked, 'Do you want to be made well?' (John 5:6). The sick man said he was unable to get into the water first, but Jesus replied, 'Rise, take up your bed and walk' (John 5:8).

This healing filled the onlooking Jews with anger. They claimed that taking up a bed and carrying it home constituted work and it broke God's law recorded by Jeremiah: 'Thus says the LORD: "Take heed to yourselves, and bear no burden on the Sabbath day, nor bring it in by the gates of Jerusalem; nor carry a burden out of your houses on the Sabbath day, nor do any work, but hallow the Sabbath day, as I commanded your fathers"' (Jeremiah 17:21-22).

This commandment was dealing with working on the Sabbath by carrying of goods for sale. This was strictly forbidden! The Sabbath day was not a day to be used for trading or for one's normal work. But God's commandments didn't prevent acts of necessity and mercy, which Jesus had performed when he healed the sick man. Carrying home his mattress did not constitute work. The Pharisees made their own laws that prevented people from doing what was lawful on the Sabbath.

Later Jesus met the man in the temple and warned him against sinning further, as God could inflict a worse punishment on him. Now the Jews wanted Christ put to death because they believed he had broken God's law, which was worthy of the death penalty.

FIND OUT THE FACTS

1. What were the Israelites taught in Exodus 31:14-17? Does this law apply today?
2. What does the word 'Sabbath' mean?
3. Does the Lord heal the sick today? How?

Christ noticed this one man who had been lying at the pool of Bethesda for many years. Thank the Lord that he takes note of individuals and does a work in their lives.

A saying to Remember

The chief care of a sick man should be for his soul. *Thomas Manton*

Matthew   'For the Son of Man is Lord
12:1-8   even of the Sabbath' (Mat-
              thew 12:8).

Christians throughout the world are persecuted because they love and serve a risen Saviour. Jesus, who faced many enemies, told his disciples that this would happen to them when they took up their cross to follow him (John 17:14).

The Pharisees, who were fanatics when it came to the matter of Sabbath observance, expected the Jews to obey God's law, plus the multitude of laws they had invented.

The disciples were hungry and the seed in the field was ripe so they plucked some heads of grain, crushed them to get rid of any husk and then ate the seed. The Pharisees, who watched closely, were enraged at what they saw. They considered the disciples were guilty of working on the Sabbath as they had harvested, husked, winnowed and crushed the seed before eating it. The Pharisees had almost forty regulations concerning farming on the Sabbath, the breaking of which they said deserved the death penalty. They now believed the disciples had broken the Fourth Commandment.

When they accused Jesus of allowing his disciples to break God's law, Jesus replied that David had eaten the 'showbread', which was contrary to God's law (1 Samuel 21:1-6). As we saw in a previous devotion, David and his men were not starving, but they were hungry. They were given the 'holy bread' which they ate without breaking God's law. Jesus pointed to the Sabbath work of the priests which was not considered sinful. They had to slaughter the animals for sacrifice and circumcise male babies who were eight days old.

Christ then declared that he was greater than the temple saying, 'Yet I say to you that in this place there is one greater than the temple' (Matthew 12:6). He then declared that he was

'Lord even of the Sabbath' (Matthew 12:8). Because of his sacrificial work, the temple, all its ceremonies and the Sabbath which was observed on the seventh day would disappear.

He protected his disciples against the charges of those who did not fully understand the teaching of the Old Testament. They failed to take to heart the words of God in Hosea 6:6: 'For I desire mercy and not sacrifice, and the knowledge of God more than burnt offerings.' The sacrifices of the Old Testament were acceptable to God only if the heart was right.

The disciples had not broken the Sabbath law, only the regulations laid down by the Pharisees. Christ, as Lord of the Sabbath, would not tolerate this perversion of the day that he had instituted.

FIND OUT THE FACTS

1. What day of the week do Christians keep holy? Why?

2. Why could Christ say he was Lord of the Sabbath?

3. How would you answer Christ's question, 'Is it lawful on the Sabbath to do good or to do evil, to save life or to kill?' (Mark 3:4).

The Pharisees were guilty of judging Christ and his disciples unfairly. How easy it is to judge others. Ask the Lord to keep you from this sin.

Perfect obedience is God's right as God. *Graham Heaps*

Mark
3:1-6

'He said to them, "Is it lawful on the Sabbath to do good or to do evil, to save life or to kill?" But they kept silent' (Mark 3:4).

The Lord's Day has always been a very special day in my life. Sometimes it has been called the Christian Sabbath, but the Sabbath, which means rest, was the day that the Israelites kept holy; it was the seventh day of the week. In the Ten Commandments the Fourth Commandment reads, 'Remember the Sabbath day, to keep it holy. Six days you shall labour and do all your work…' (Exodus 20:8-9).

The Lord Jesus kept this holy day because he obeyed all of God's laws perfectly. The Pharisees had made a lot of extra rules for the Sabbath. One such law prevented people from carrying a handkerchief in their pocket, because to carry something was to work. If the handkerchief was worn around one's neck like a necktie then it was all right because it formed part of one's Sabbath clothing.

We have already seen that Jesus and his disciples did good on the Sabbath. King David and his men ate the 'showbread' because they were hungry, even though it was for the priests. Jesus reminded the Pharisees that the Sabbath was made for man — a day to rest from his weekly work and to worship God. It was to be a joyful day, a day on which to do good. Then he told the Pharisees that he, 'the Son of Man', was the 'Lord of the Sabbath' (Mark 2:28). He had given the Commandments and knew what they meant.

Then Christ asked the question in Mark 3:4. Those proud Pharisees couldn't reply; they knew it was permissible to do good on the Sabbath, but they wouldn't admit it! Jesus then asked the man with the withered hand to stretch it out. As he did, it was made well. So the Pharisees and King Herod's servants started to make plans as to how they could get rid of the Lord Jesus Christ.

The world has been given the Lord's Day, a day of rest and worship. It is a happy day because Christians remember that their Lord and Saviour rose from the dead on that day many years ago. The Lord's Day gives us a day when Christians can gather together for worship and fellowship. It is a day in which we have time for good works. We can visit the sick and lonely, write letters to missionaries, teach in the Sunday Schools and do all those acts of necessity and mercy that we don't usually have time for during the working week.

May we all make a special effort to show our neighbours that we keep the Lord's Day in a special way because we are followers of Christ.

FIND OUT THE FACTS

1. Why do Christians keep Sunday holy?
2. How should Christians spend the Lord's Day?
3. Make a list of the works of necessity and mercy.
4. Should sport be played on Sunday? Why?

The Lord's Day is given to us as a day of rest from the activities that take up our time during the week. Thank the Lord that he has built into our weekly routine a time for rest.

If you want to kill Christianity, you must abolish Sunday.
François Voltaire

Psalm
109:1-8

'Jesus answered them, "Did I not choose you, the twelve, and one of you is a devil?"' (John 6:70).

Most of us have a group of people we call friends, yet we have very few 'soul mates'. My 'soul mate' is my wife. I can tell her everything about myself, 'warts and all', and she still loves me! During my life, I have also had three men I call 'soul mates', people I can trust with knowing the real Jim. I certainly don't have friends, people who ridicule and hurt me in many ways.

Of the Lord's twelve disciples, three — Peter, John and James — were good friends, but John was 'the disciple whom Jesus loved' (John 21:20).

Then there was Judas, the one who would betray his Master. Jesus deliberately chose him that the Scriptures might be fulfilled (John 13:18).

Today's scripture verse records the words of Jesus concerning Judas, whom he said was 'a devil'. Jesus Christ, the God-man, was betrayed by Judas, the devil-man.

We don't really know anything about Judas before the Lord called him to become one of the twelve, but there are passages in the Old Testament which prophesy concerning Judas. Psalm 109, particularly verse 8, tells of the awful work of Judas, even including the detail of his replacement by another man. Acts 1:26 describes the election of Matthias to replace Judas, who had committed suicide.

Zechariah prophesied that someone would sell his Master: 'Then I said to them, "If it is agreeable to you, give me my wages… " So they weighed out for my wages thirty pieces of silver. And the LORD said to me, "Throw it to the potter" — that princely price they set on me. So I took the thirty pieces of silver and threw them into the house of the LORD for the potter' (Zechariah 11:12-13).

In our Saviour's high priestly prayer he called Judas 'the son of perdition' (John 17:12). This title was given by the apostle Paul to 'the man of sin' (2 Thessalonians 2:3). Judas walked with the disciples, heard Christ's teaching, witnessed the miracles he performed, and may even have performed miracles himself. Yet he betrayed the Lord.

We know that he couldn't be trusted. He was the disciple who cared for the finances. When Mary used her costly ointment to anoint Christ's feet, he complained, saying, '"Why was this fragrant oil not sold for three hundred denarii and given to the poor?" This he said, not that he cared for the poor, but because he was a thief, and had the money box; and he used to take what was put in it' (John 12:5-6).

This thief betrayed his Master!

FIND OUT THE FACTS

1. How did Judas betray Christ? See Luke 22:48.
2. Why did Christ call Judas to become a disciple?
3. What is taught by our 'Saying to remember'?
4. What is taught in Psalm 41:9?

Even though Christ knew that Judas would betray him, he was never bitter against him. Think about how you would respond if you knew that someone who was close to you was going to betray you.

A Saying to Remember

The devil's boots don't creak.
Anon

Matthew   'Blessed are the poor in spirit,
5:1-5   for theirs is the kingdom of
            heaven' (Matthew 5:3).

Almost every person born into this world is a citizen of
Satan's kingdom. The Lord Jesus wasn't, John the Baptist
wasn't (Luke 1:15) and Jeremiah wasn't (Jeremiah 1:5). Most
people, grow up loving the world and do all they can to enjoy
life. They fall in love, marry, have families, build their houses,
work hard, save their money, enjoy holidays, retire and die,
never giving a thought to God's rightful claim on their lives.

But there is an alternative society called the kingdom of
heaven where all members live a different lifestyle. In the
'Sermon on the Mount' the Lord Jesus explains the character
of the citizens of heaven. This is found particularly in the
Beatitudes (Matthew 5:3-12).

First we read, 'Blessed are the poor in spirit, for theirs is the
kingdom of heaven' (Matthew 5:3). The 'poor in spirit' are
people who have a genuine God-given humility. They, like the
humbled prodigal son, cry to God for mercy. With a repentant
heart and a God-given faith in Christ, they become citizens of
the 'kingdom of heaven'.

We also read, 'Blessed are those who mourn, for they shall
be comforted' (Matthew 5:4). What is spoken of here is the
mourning over sins which offend a holy God. A true knowledge of sin brings repentance and, like the tax collector, those
convicted cry out, 'God, be merciful to me a sinner!' (Luke 18:13).

These sinners find comfort from our Lord who forgives all
their iniquities because he loves them. He has paid the penalty for their sins and has provided them with the covering of
his own perfect righteousness.

Words from the Old Testament show us that the almighty
God we worship is so gentle with his people: 'He will feed his

flock like a shepherd; he will gather the lambs with his arm, and carry them in his bosom, and gently lead those who are with young' (Isaiah 40:11).

We also read, 'Blessed are the meek, for they shall inherit the earth' (Matthew 5:5). Meekness is one of the fruits of the Spirit, and means we have a gentle, courteous and considerate nature. The meek person acknowledges God's wisdom in all that happens. When things go wrong he isn't angry, but quietly accepts that God only does what is best.

Today it is the rich and powerful who have great possessions. But it is the meek lovers of Christ who will inherit the new heavens and earth.

The three characteristics mentioned so far are: 'the poor in spirit', 'those who mourn' and 'the meek'. These are the marks of those who are to be found among the citizens of the kingdom of God. Are these characteristics found in you?

FIND OUT THE FACTS

1. List the 'fruit of the Spirit'. See Galatians 5:22-23.

2. Name one person who perfectly exhibited all the fruit of the Spirit.

3. Who are members of the kingdom of heaven?

It is difficult to be meek in a world which admires force and strength. Ask the Lord to help you to be meek even if others consider it to be a weakness.

No man is living at his best who is not living at his best spiritually.
W. Marshall Craig

Luke
10:30-37

'Blessed are those who hunger and thirst for righteousness, for they shall be filled' (Matthew 5:6).

When a person becomes a member of the kingdom of heaven there is great rejoicing in heaven and in the church on earth. The King is none other than our Lord and Saviour, Jesus Christ. All the citizens of his kingdom love righteousness. The Holy Spirit brings about the new birth, and commences the work of moulding the new Christian into the likeness of the Lord Jesus. The characteristics listed in the Beatitudes become a lifelong part of the Christian's distinctiveness. So we read, 'Blessed are those who hunger and thirst for righteousness, for they shall be filled' (Matthew 5:6).

Our world hungers for riches, power and the promotion of self. Many families struggle to 'keep up with the Joneses', which often leads to broken marriages and ill health. In these families the children are never satisfied with what they have and are always asking for more. Jesus' question forms a stark contrast to this attitude. He asks, 'For what will it profit a man if he gains the whole world, and loses his own soul?' (Mark 8:36).

Christians who hunger for righteousness will be filled. The Holy Spirit who gives his people that hunger and then directs them to that place where God's word is found: the Bible! Your Pastor, church elders and other Christians will give you a feast of godly instruction. As your hunger is satisfied, your desire will grow stronger for a deeper knowledge of God! The righteousness of Christ is put to the believer's account. What joy this is to the citizen of the kingdom of heaven!

This Beatitude is followed by: 'Blessed are the merciful, for they shall obtain mercy' (Matthew 5:7). Citizens of God's kingdom should always be looking out for those situations where they can show a godly concern for others. This means Christians are to show compassion to *anyone* in need, not just friends and relatives.

The parable of the Good Samaritan teaches us that everyone has a claim upon our mercy, even our enemies! The prophet Hosea says: 'For I desire mercy and not sacrifice…' (6:6) Those kind acts should not be done grudgingly. Paul wrote, 'He who shows mercy, [must do so] with cheerfulness' (Romans 12:8).

Our God does not overlook the acts of kindness done by his people: 'He who has pity on the poor lends to the LORD, and he will pay back what he has given' (Proverbs 19:17).

It is God who has given his people a merciful heart. Our kind acts will be remembered on the Day of Judgement.

FIND OUT THE FACTS

1. How can people show mercy to others?
2. Where can people find their thirst for righteousness satisfied?
3. How can family members show kindness to one another?

Jesus placed great value on being merciful and on desiring to be righteous. Do you consider these things as important as he did? Ask God to help you to focus attention on those things that are really important.

If God should have no more mercy on us than we have charity one to another, what would become of us?
Thomas Fuller

Psalm   'Blessed are the pure in heart,
24:1-6   for they shall see God'
             (Matthew 5:8).

Today, very few people want to be 'pure in heart'. Most Christians can remember the time when they enjoyed living in the kingdom of Satan. Their sinful way of life they found delightful, and they had no wish to become Christlike.

Christ preached the 'Sermon on the Mount' to Jews who were concerned about external appearances. By contrast Jesus drew their attention to the state of the heart. A pure heart was needed by everyone who was to be a citizen of the kingdom of heaven. The psalmist asks the question, 'Who may ascend into the hill of the Lord?' The answer is: 'He who has clean hands and a pure heart' (Psalm 24:3,4). But how do sinners acquire a new heart? No doctor can give them a pure heart transplant — only God can!

God said through Ezekiel, 'I will give you a new heart and put a new spirit within you; I will take the heart of stone out of your flesh and give you a heart of flesh. I will put my Spirit within you and cause you to walk in my statutes, and you will keep my judgements and do them' (Ezekiel 36:26-27).

There is a true joy in the hearts of the citizens of God's kingdom, because they know that they will see God in the person of Christ. We will see the God-man in all his glory.

Our next Beatitude is: 'Blessed are the peacemakers, for they shall be called sons of God' (Matthew 5:9). Every Christian is expected to be a peacemaker in the church, in society, and between himself or herself and God. Our Saviour is the author of peace between God and man. Paul wrote, 'For it pleased the Father that in him all the fulness should dwell, and by him to reconcile all things to himself, by him, whether things on earth or things in heaven, having made peace through the blood of his cross' (Colossians 1:19-20).

When the Holy Spirit changes sinners' hearts, they 'become children of God' (John 1:12) and call God 'Abba, Father' (Romans 8:15), a name which indicates that there is a close relationship with the heavenly Father. A good equivalent in modern English would be 'Dearest father'.

When we have peace with God we are called to be ambassadors of peace. Christians pray and work for peace in the church, with their Christian brothers and sisters, and in society at large. Are you a child of God working to establish peace in society? I pray that God will bless all who read this book.

FIND OUT THE FACTS

1. What does it mean 'to see God'?
2. Think of the name of someone whom you believe to be a peacemaker? Why do you think so?
3. How does a sinner become a child of God?

People are more inclined to assert their rights than to be willing to yield to others in the interests of keeping the peace. Ask the Lord to help you to be a peacemaker, even when it will cost you something to do so.

Peace if possible, but truth at any rate. *Martin Luther*

1 Peter
4:12-16

'Blessed are those who are persecuted for righteousness' sake, for theirs is the kingdom of heaven' (Matthew 5:10).

Often we hear of Christians being persecuted and martyred because they love God. In the 'Sermon on the Mount', our Saviour teaches us that Christians who are persecuted have every reason to 'rejoice and be exceedingly glad' because of their great reward in the kingdom of God (Matthew 5:12).

In our scripture passage Peter warned the believers to expect persecution. As they stood firm in the day of their trial, they would bring glory to God. They were not to be ashamed of their faith in Christ, knowing that their Lord would distribute great rewards to his people upon the Day of Judgement.

Christ told his disciples of the persecution that would come from the Jews and others who rejected his claim to be the Messiah. The Lord prayed for his disciples, saying, 'The world has hated them because they are not of the world, just as I am not of the world. I do not pray that you should take them out of the world, but that you should keep them from the evil one' (John 17:14-15).

Christ prayed for all Christians, asking his Father to keep them faithful in their darkest hour. The Scriptures have encouraging words for believers — no believer will be lost: 'My sheep hear my voice, and I know them, and they follow me. And I give them eternal life, and they shall never perish; neither shall anyone snatch them out of my hand. My Father, who has given them to me, is greater than all; and no one is able to snatch them out of my Father's hand' (John 10:27-29).

These words are of great comfort to Christians, whether they suffer persecution or not. Christians are secure; they have their passports to heaven and Christ will guide them home.

Our experience can be likened to walking across a trawler's deck in rough seas. We shall frequently stumble, but not fall overboard, because there is a safety rail to prevent such an accident. In our spiritual life we may fall, but God will pick us up and help us along that narrow way that leads to heaven.

Millions of Christians have been martyred in horrible ways. Once when I was asked how a Christian could cope with such a painful death, I replied that God would give him the necessary grace to die bravely. The death of Stephen in Acts 7:54-60 is an example of God sustaining one of his children through this kind of death (2 Corinthians 12:9 and Psalm 23:4). Today we don't need the grace to die, but the grace to cope with the activities of today. At the time of our death, God will give us the grace to die.

Always remember that persecution will result in a great heavenly reward.

FIND OUT THE FACTS

1. What are we taught in Philippians 1:6?
2. What should Christians do to those who persecute them? Read Luke 6:27.
3. Name one Christian who died a martyr's death.

To Think & to pray about

Being mocked and laughed at because you follow Christ's commands and not the world's ways is a form of persecution. Thank the Lord that he will greatly reward those who remain faithful to him when they are persecuted.

The wind of persecution often fans the torch of truth.
David Thomas

A saying to Remember

Matthew
5:13-16

'Then Jesus spoke to them again, saying, "I am the light of the world. He who follows me shall not walk in darkness, but have the light of life"' (John 8:12).

Our scripture passage tells Christians that they are both salt and light. Frequently I am told not to put too much salt on my food because it can do physical harm. Doesn't it seem strange then to be told that I am the salt of the earth?

Today most people preserve their food using refrigeration, and salt is mainly used to flavour food. Before refrigeration, salt was a very important preservative for food, as well as a means of giving it flavour. It was also used as an antiseptic for the treatment of sores.

Christians should use their influence in the world in such a way that the law of God will make an impact on society. The law of love binds God's people together and as they live according to God's commands, others are attracted to the Saviour.

Today the influence of believers and the church as an institution in society mean very little, with the result that society is falling apart. Greed, self, immorality and the love of money are destroying our societies. We should exert our influence for good, otherwise we shall end up like the impure salt of Christ's day; we shall be useless and be thrown out.

Christians are the light of the world and should be visible to the world around them. Light is something to be used in the darkness, but it is of no value to anyone if it is hidden. Light is meant to shine and expel the darkness!

Christ, the sinless Son of God, is himself the 'light of the world'. He is pure light in whom no darkness is found. Christians are not pure light, but are like the moon that reflects the light of the sun. When the world looks at us, they ought to see our Christian character shining brightly and reflecting the 'Light of life'.

When Moses came down from the mountain after seeing the Lord, we are told that 'the skin of his face shone' (Exodus 34:30). The people looked at him and were afraid to approach him. Christians should have a character that not only reflects the glory of Christ, but also attracts sinners to the Saviour.

Let the members of Satan's kingdom see the works of love done by Christians and be attracted to the kingdom of heaven. Let Christ's people so act that other Christians are encouraged to do good works that glorify their heavenly Father.

Look at your life and ask yourself, 'Am I acting like salt and light in the community and so bringing glory to God?'

FIND OUT THE FACTS

1. What is meant by 'witnessing for Christ'?
2. How can you be a witness for your Saviour in your part of the world?
3. In what way are Christians like salt?

Think of ways in which you can be salt and light in your community. Ask the Lord to help you to see the opportunities around you.

Every believer is a witness whether he wants to be or not.
Donald Grey Barnhouse

Matthew   'For I say to you, that unless
5:17-20   your righteousness exceeds
           the righteousness of the
           scribes and Pharisees, you will
           by no means enter the kingdom
           of heaven' (Matthew 5:20).

Sometimes when we arrive home from worship we can't even remember the text. We should make every effort to listen carefully and to put into practice in our daily life what we have been taught.

I feel sure that the disciples who heard Christ preach what is known as the 'Sermon on the Mount', would have remembered it well. It was so different from what was being taught by the Pharisees.

Members of the kingdom of heaven were to exhibit the characteristics of the Beatitudes in their lives. They were to be ready to suffer persecution, act as salt and light in the community and live a godly life where their righteousness exceeded that of the Pharisees.

The Pharisees were looked upon as models of godly behaviour. But now the people were told that a new era had dawned. The Scribes and Pharisees used the Scriptures as their source of spiritual knowledge, but now they were dealing with a man who spoke on his own authority: 'For I say to you…' Jesus said, 'Do not think that I came to destroy the Law or the Prophets. I did not come to destroy but to fulfil…' (Matthew 5:17). At another time he said, 'My food is to do the will of him who sent me, and to finish his work' (John 4:34).

Christ was the fulfilment of the Old Testament ceremonial system. Jesus Christ fulfilled the prophecies which had been given about the Messiah, and he perfectly obeyed God's law. He did not observe the laws added by the Pharisees. Some aspects of the law and the prophets are yet to be fulfilled by our Lord.

Members of the kingdom of heaven walk in the footsteps of their Lord and follow his law which is one of love to God and man. Christians can say with the apostle Paul, 'I delight in the law of God...' (Romans 7:22). But the law cannot save us

Obedience to God's Word is the evidence of a changed heart and of peace with God. Christ overthrew the laws made by the Pharisees. They were hypocrites, 'whitewashed tombs' (Matthew 23:27), 'they say, and do not' (23:3).

The righteousness of the Lord's people exceeds that of the Pharisees because it comes from a changed heart. The Pharisees looked on the outward appearance, but the Lord looks on the heart. The righteousness of Christians exceeds that of the Pharisees because they have the imputed righteousness of the Lord Jesus. It is the saints who can say, 'Praise the Lord!'

FIND OUT THE FACTS

1. Read John 14:15. What does it teach?
2. What is one mark of a saving faith? Read James 2:26.
3. What is taught in Matthew 15:8?

The Pharisees taught their own kind of righteousness but it was not true righteousness. Ask the Lord to help you to know when the teaching you are being given is truly from his Word.

Jesus has spoken; his is the Word, ours is the obedience.
Dietrich Bonhoeffer

Matthew 5:21-26   'But I say to you that whoever is angry with his brother without a cause shall be in danger of the judgement. And whoever says to his brother, "Raca!" shall be in danger of the council. But whoever says, "You fool!" shall be in danger of hell fire' (Matthew 5:22).

We live in an unhappy world. Families are torn apart; strikes are common in the workplace; and angry nations often brandish their weapons of war. Frequently anger between Christians divides churches.

One of the Beatitudes which we have already discussed says, 'Blessed are the peacemakers, for they shall be called sons of God' (Matthew 5:9). This is one characteristic of God's people that should always be visible, but sadly we often fail.

The Sixth Commandment is: 'You shall not murder' (Exodus 20:13). The Pharisees had always taught this law, and could hold their heads high because they had not taken a weapon and killed someone. They had taught that murder was an offence deserving the death penalty.

Jesus said that he had not come to render the law of God null and void, but rather to teach the full implications of it. This applied equally to the Sixth Commandment. His teaching was not something brand new.

The Lord explained that sinful anger can lead to murder. This anger has its root in the heart, and it was this teaching that 'those of old' and the Pharisees had neglected. They had preached that only the sin of the outward act of murder was wrong and had neglected the clear teaching of the Old Testament: 'You shall not hate your brother in your heart... You shall not take vengeance, nor bear any grudge against the children of your people, but you shall love your neighbour as yourself: I am the LORD' (Leviticus 19:17,18).

The Lord corrected the teaching of 'those of old' and the Pharisees, by reminding them that the law dealt not only with the external act of murder, but the sinful anger of the heart. Those men knew the words of the Lord describing Cain's feelings when his offering was rejected: 'And Cain was very angry, and his countenance fell. So the Lord said to Cain, "Why are you angry?"' (Genesis 4:5-6). Cain's jealous anger towards Abel, which ended in his murdering Abel, commenced with an attitude of mind.

Any offering to God gains its value from the state of the giver's heart. Thus if any person went to the temple to present his gift to the Lord and there remembered that he had offended someone, he was to make peace with the offended person immediately and then present his gift. The failure to do this would result in the matter being sorted out on the Day of Judgement, where hell would be the sentence for the guilty party.

FIND OUT THE FACTS

1. What is Christ teaching in Matthew 5:22?

2. Think of one word that summarizes the law of God? Read Luke 10:27.

3. What sort of 'heart' is acceptable to God?

Anger is a dangerous emotion. Ask the Lord to help you to guard your heart against sinful anger.

Give from the bottom of your heart, not from the top of your purse. *Anon*

August

Whoever
loves instruc-
tion loves
knowledge,
but he who
hates correc-
tion is stupid

Proverbs 12:1

Matthew 5:27-30   'If your right eye causes you to sin, pluck it out and cast it from you; for it is more profitable for you that one of your members perish, than for your whole body to be cast into hell' (Matthew 5:29).

I once read of a man who took today's scripture verse at face value and attempted to cut off his hand because it had been used in a sinful activity. He was quickly taken to hospital with his hand almost severed from his arm. When he came round after the surgery, he discovered that his hand was back where it should have been. He had been very foolish.

Today we read of Jesus explaining the full meaning of the Seventh Commandment: 'You shall not commit adultery' (Exodus 20:14).

'Those of old' and the Pharisees explained the Commandment in the literal way. To them only the external act of adultery was sinful. Once again, the state of the heart was ignored.

Jesus was talking about a heart full of lust that could so easily lead one into the sin of adultery. The Old Testament did not only condemn the physical act of adultery, but the impurity of a heart which lusted after sexual gratification. We read in Proverbs 6:23-25: 'Reproofs of instruction are the way of life, to keep you from the evil woman, from the flattering tongue of a seductress. Do not lust after her beauty in your heart, nor let her allure you with her eyelids.' Here the Lord pointed to the sin of lust which is in the heart.

We should remember that marriage is a lifelong contract between a man and a woman. Husbands are to 'rejoice with the wife of [their] youth ... and always be enraptured with her love' (Proverbs 5:18,19).

The passage of Scripture you have read warns people not only against the physical act of adultery, but also the temptations of the heart which often lead to unfaithfulness.

However, some would argue, 'I can't help the lusting. My eyes are to blame.' To this the answer is: 'Be disciplined about where you go and about what you look at!' We must deal drastically with sin!

We are all to have the same attitude as Job: 'I have made a covenant with my eyes; why then should I look upon a young woman?' (Job 31:1).

When Origen of Alexandria attempted to overcome the lust in his heart by making himself a eunuch, the Council of Nicea in A.D. 325 outlawed the practice.

God's answer to lust in the heart is not to make oneself a eunuch or to live alone, but to get married! (1 Corinthians 7:9). While waiting for that day, one should pray for God's grace to avoid sin, read the Scriptures and find one's company among Christians. The victory can be yours!

FIND OUT THE FACTS

1. Name some of the sins of the eye.

2. How do people overcome the sin of lust?

3. What should we do about TV programmes which portray immorality?

We live in a world which indulges in sexual immorality. Ask the Lord to give you the grace to keep yourself free from this sin.

The law may express sin but it cannot suppress sin.
Thomas Adams

 1 Corinthians 7:10-16 'But I say to you that whoever divorces his wife for any reason except sexual immorality causes her to commit adultery; and whoever marries a woman who is divorced commits adultery' (Matthew 5:32).

Today, in the Western World statistics show that almost half the number of marriages ends in divorce. In the days of the Old Testament divorce was tolerated 'because of the hardness of [men's] hearts' (Matthew 19:8). Moses instructed men who were divorcing their wives to give them a divorce certificate (Deuteronomy 24:1-2), making it possible for women to remarry.

Human beings are social beings who long for companionship. The Lord said to Adam, 'It is not good that man should be alone' (Genesis 2:18). He then created a perfect companion for him. Adam and Eve lived in perfect happiness before sin entered the world.

In a perfect world, divorce would have no place. But in a fallen world, the Lord has granted grounds for divorce — that is, where there has been sexual immorality. However, God considers divorce for any trivial reason as sinful.

When divorce occurred, even the innocent man or woman carried the stigma of guilt. If the innocent party remarried, the new partner carried the stigma of the one divorced. Neither had committed a sin, but many societies reacted by calling such marriages adulterous.

In the days of the prophet Malachi, the Lord condemned his covenant people because of divorce for trivial reasons. Many had turned away from the wife of their youth to marry a woman who worshipped a foreign god. The Jews frequently served the gods of their heathen wives. Rarely did a heathen marriage partner turn to serve Jehovah, the living God.

Christians are commanded to marry Christians because they are not to be unequally yoked with unbelievers (2 Corinthians 6:14). People of the kingdom of heaven have nothing in common with citizens of Satan's kingdom. Christian families are exhorted to bring up their children to fear God. As they care for the spiritual well-being of their offspring, they, by the grace of God, are producing a 'godly offspring'.

Today's reading states that when one member of a marriage becomes a servant of the Lord, he or she is to remain faithful to his or her marriage partner. However, if the unbelieving partner leaves, Paul tells us that the Christian may remarry, and there is no sin attached to such an action on the believer's part (1 Corinthians 7:15).

FIND OUT THE FACTS

1. Why do people marry?
2. What restriction is placed upon Christians when they look for a marriage partner?
3. What responsibilities do the marriage partners have to each other? Read Ephesians 5:22-33.

In a world which presents being unfaithful to one's marriage partner as being progressive and modern, pray that Christian people will be kept from falling into this sin.

God is the witness to every marriage ceremony and will be the witness to every violation of its vows.
Thomas V. Moore

A saying to Remember

Matthew   'If a man makes a vow to the
5:33-37   LORD, or swears an oath to bind
               himself to some agreement, he
               shall not break his word; he
               shall do according to all that
               proceeds out of his mouth'
               (Numbers 30:2).

When people make lawful promises, they should fulfil them. I'm sure that most of you have had promises made to you that were never carried out. God expects us all to do as we have promised. He always keeps his word!

The Lord again speaks of 'those of old' and the Pharisees who rightly demanded that people fulfil the oaths they had made. They were to do as promised or be guilty of sin.

But 'those of old' had changed the emphasis. They said that only oaths made in the Lord's name had to be kept. Where once they had stressed truthfulness when making any oath — 'You shall not swear by my name *falsely*' (Leviticus 19:12) — now the emphasis was: 'You shall not swear *by my name* falsely' (italics mine).

So every promise made in the name of the Lord was to be faithfully kept, but what about oaths made 'by heaven', 'by earth', 'by Jerusalem' or 'by one's head'? The teaching of 'those of old' and the Pharisees was that such oaths did not have the same significance as oaths made in the Lord's name.

The result was that the Pharisees added to their normal speech vows that they had no intention of keeping. But the Lord taught them what the Scriptures had always taught: all oaths are binding and had to be fulfilled. Those who swore an oath in ordinary speech — 'By heavens…'— were to fulfil that oath because it was an oath sworn by God's heavenly throne! God's law said, 'That which has gone from your lips you shall keep and perform, for you voluntarily vowed to the LORD your God what you have promised with your mouth' (Deuteronomy

23:23). Oaths came from the heart and were to be kept, and this included all those oaths made in ordinary speech.

As far as speech was concerned a simple 'Yes' or 'No' by a Christian was sufficient and binding. If an oath also had to be added it meant that the person's 'Yes' or 'No' could not be trusted.

Jesus docs not forbid the use of oaths in civil affairs, but they have no place in the church and between Christian believers. Our word is our bond!

Today the language of so many is interlaced with vile oaths that people have no intention of keeping. Let this not be so of you and me.

FIND OUT THE FACTS

1. What sort of promises do you make? Do you keep them?
2. Name one of God's promises?
3. List three situations where people today are required to swear an oath.

So much trouble is caused in the world by broken promises and false words. Think of one or two international conflicts where failed expectations and dishonesty have stirred up strife. Pray for these nations.

Promises may get friends, but only performances can keep them.
C. H. Spurgeon

Matthew 5:38-42   'If a man causes disfigurement of his neighbour, as he has done, so shall it be done to him — fracture for fracture, eye for eye, tooth for tooth...' (Leviticus 24:19-20).

'Under Saudi Arabia's Islamic code, the death sentence is mandatory for murderers, rapists and drug smugglers; flogging for theft, and amputation of a hand for repeated theft.' So stated a report in the *Sydney Morning Herald* on the 15 June 1991. At present the laws of many Western nations are so lenient that frequently the criminal is out of jail before the victim is out of hospital!

The law of God given to Israel provided a just system of punishment for those who broke it. The law did not allow a punishment that was more harsh than the crime committed. God's law was 'fracture for fracture, eye for eye, tooth for tooth... But whoever kills a man shall be put to death' (Leviticus 24:20,21).

In Israel justice was to be carried out by the civil magistrate and not by the offended party. The same teaching is found in the New Testament, where we are taught that the civil magistrate is ordained by God: 'He is God's minister to you for good. But if you do evil, be afraid; for he does not bear the sword in vain; for he is God's minister, an avenger to execute wrath on him who practises evil. Therefore you must be subject, not only because of wrath but also for conscience' sake' (Romans 13:4-5).

We obey our government because God has commanded us to obey it. If the magistrate fails us, we leave the matter in the hands of God who said, 'Vengeance is mine, I will repay' (Romans 12:19).

The Lord teaches us that if a wicked man slaps us on the cheek, we are to respond, not by violent retaliation, but by turning the other cheek because we love the Lord.

Christ's word is that if legal action is pending against us over some minor matter, we should sort it out before the court case commences. Give the person more than your coat and go the extra mile with the person who demands your company. When someone wants to borrow something, we should lend it willingly and not turn him away empty handed.

Paul wrote, 'Repay no one evil for evil... If your enemy is hungry, feed him; if he is thirsty, give him a drink... Do not be overcome by evil, but overcome evil with good' (Romans 12:17,20,21). But remember that we have every right to ask the civil magistrate to act on our behalf. Paul did so (Acts 25:11).

FIND OUT THE FACTS

1. What does the 'Saying to remember' mean? See 2 Thessalonians 3:10.

2. How do people know that our citizenship is in the kingdom of heaven?

3. What can Christians do to encourage governments to make laws in accordance with God's law?

In some countries the government is opposed to the gospel and believers can find themselves convicted of some imagined crime by the authorities and imprisoned for their faith. Pray for Christians who are being persecuted in this way.

A saying to Remember

If anyone will not work, neither shall he eat.   2 Thessalonians 3:10

1 Corinthians 'But I say to you, love your
13:1-13   enemies, bless those who
               curse you, do good to those
               who hate you, and pray for
               those who spitefully use you
               and persecute you' (Matthew
               5:44).

Our Saviour refers to the comment made by some: 'You shall love your neighbour and hate your enemy' (Matthew 5:43). Today this rule is often taught to the young: 'Fight your enemies. Hit those who hit you.'

The Pharisees taught something that could not be found in the Scriptures. We read in Leviticus 19:18, 'You shall not take vengeance, nor bear any grudge against the children of your people, but you shall love your neighbour as yourself: I am the LORD.' Perhaps they thought, 'If one is to love one's neighbours, then the opposite must be true — hate your enemies!'

This was not the teaching of the Old Testament or that of the Lord Jesus. The words of Proverbs 25:21 were ignored: 'If your enemy is hungry, give him bread to eat; and if he is thirsty, give him water to drink; for so you will heap coals of fire on his head, and the LORD will reward you.'

God's people are to love everyone, including their enemies. This love means doing good to others and genuinely desiring the best for them. God has established this pattern of love. He causes the sun to shine on everyone, and gives rain to all.

Taking up this theme, Christ said that there is no reward for showing love only to those who love us. He pointed to the hated tax collectors, saying that they showed this self-centred love by greeting only those people who greeted them.

When Christ was asked the question: 'Who is my neighbour?', he answered by telling the parable of the Good Samaritan (Luke 10:30-37). In this story the one whom Christ commends is a hated Samaritan, not the priest and the Levite, thereby signifying that genuine Christian love knows no boundaries.

Every person has a claim upon our love. Jesus said, 'But I say to you, love your enemies, bless those who curse you, do good to those who hate you, and pray for those who spitefully use you...' (Matthew 5:44).

Jesus himself is our greatest example of what it means to love one's enemies. He died upon the cross, bearing the sins of his people. Christ loved them while they were sinners and hated him.

We are to walk in the footsteps of our Saviour, who set us the example of godly love. The love we are to demonstrate should not depend upon the person concerned. It is a love that does what is best for others, and expects nothing in return. It is a love that does not display itself in order to gain the praise of men and women.

Frequently Christian love conquers an enemy, and he becomes a friend!

FIND OUT THE FACTS

1. Discuss the teaching of the parable of the Good Samaritan. See Luke 10:30-37.

2. What is Christian love? See 1 Corinthians 13.

3. How did Jesus show his love to sinners?

Our scripture verse encourages us to pray for those who spitefully use us and persecute us. In short, to pray for our enemies. Pray for one such person today.

A saying to Remember

Love is the very essence and life of the Christian religion.
Matthew Henry

Matthew   'But when you do a charitable
6:1-8; 16-18   deed, do not let you left hand
               know what your right hand is
               doing' (Matthew 6:3).

Many people do everything they can to win the praise of others. They are filled with pride when others recognize their activities. They bask in the glory which should be given to God.

The Pharisees used their good works and their prayers to win the admiration of the people. The Lord Jesus had something to say about this. Again, it was the state of the heart that concerned him. Those who had the means to help others were required to do so, but in such a way that God's name was exalted and he was given the glory. But the Pharisees wanted to take the glory for themselves when doing some good work. It was as if they wanted a bugler walking before them to attract attention to themselves. This was sinful. Generosity was important, but the state of the heart and the reason for the good works were what counted before God. The apostle John wrote of the Pharisees that 'they loved the praise of men more than the praise of God' (John 12:43).

God expects his people to do their good works in secret. On the Day of Judgement they will be revealed for everyone to see.

The Pharisees also enjoyed being known as men of prayer. They made sure that at times of prayer they were on the street corners where they would be seen by the citizens of the city.

In one of the Lord's parables he spoke of a Pharisee at prayer. 'The Pharisee stood and prayed thus with himself, "God, I thank you that I am not like other men — extortioners, unjust, adulterers, or even as this tax collector. I fast twice a week; I give tithes of all that I possess"' (Luke 18:11-12). As people looked on, the Pharisee received praise from them. In no way did this prayer glorify the God of all grace.

The Lord is not saying that we are not to pray in public. We do so at our prayer meetings, where the Lord is honoured. Our Saviour is urging his people to go to a room and in private to pray to God, who hears in private. We are promised that the day will come when he will reward our secret prayers in such a way that all the world will see and praise him.

When the Pharisees fasted they made sure they wore a solemn face and told others of their fasting. Again all the praise went to themselves and not to God.

In all we do we should make sure that the glory and honour goes to God who alone is worthy.

FIND OUT THE FACTS

1. Why should our good deeds be done in private?
2. What is wrong with praying on the street corner?
3. Should you give thanks for your food wherever you eat?

There are many Christians who give sacrificially, but anonymously, to support the Lord's work. Pray that the Lord will honour their gifts by bringing success to the gospel as it is preached in all parts of the world.

A penny in one hand and a trumpet in the other is the posture of hypocrisy.   *C. H. Spurgeon*

Matthew 'But now, O LORD, you are our
6:9-15 Father; we are the clay, and
you our potter; and all we are
the work of your hand' (Isaiah
64:8).

You have just read what is known as 'The Lord's Prayer'. It would be better called 'The Disciples Prayer' because it was the prayer that Christ used to teach them how to pray. In Luke 11:1-4 we find the Lord answering the disciples' question: 'Lord, teach us to pray, as John also taught his disciples.' Jesus' answer, recorded in Matthew 6, was:

'Our Father in heaven, hallowed be your name.'

First, we acknowledge God who has been revealed to his people as a 'Father'. He becomes our 'Father' through the work of the Holy Spirit, who gives us a new heart and makes us members of God's family. God is one to be approached with awe and reverence. His name is to be hallowed and not used in common speech.

'Your kingdom come. Your will be done on earth as it is in heaven.'

This part of the prayer is for missionary endeavour which seeks to win the world for the Lord of glory. Yes, we are to be his witnesses to the uttermost parts of the earth. The words look forward to that eternal day when the kingdom of heaven will finally come.

'Give us this day our daily bread.'

Here our Lord is concerned with humanity. This request asks God to supply the food we need for each day. It is an acknowledgement that God controls the weather and the seasons which are so important for the production of food.

'And forgive us our debts, as we forgive our debtors.'

This petition (request) is linked to the words in Matthew 6:14-15. We are to forgive all who seek our forgiveness, just as we expect the Lord to forgive our sins when we repent.

'And do not lead us into temptation, but deliver us from the evil one.'

Forgiven people long for righteousness and protection from sin. God does not tempt us to sin. It is the world, the flesh and the devil that tempt us to disobey God. Jesus prayed for his disciples that they should be kept from 'the evil one' (John 17:15).

This prayer concludes with words of praise:

'For yours is the kingdom and the power and the glory for ever. Amen.'

God will not share his glory with another. All who are citizens of his kingdom willingly give him honour and praise. God's kingdom is here today, but when Christ returns we shall see the glory of God in the Lord Jesus in a far greater way. You can use the 'Disciples' Prayer' as a model for your prayers.

FIND OUT THE FACTS

1. How do the kingdoms of this world differ from the 'kingdom of heaven'?

2. Why should you forgive those who have hurt you?

3. What does the word 'hallow' mean?

Select one request from the Lord's Prayer; think about what it means and make it part of your prayer today.

I never pray for more than ten minutes, and never go ten minutes without prayer. *C. H. Spurgeon*

'For what will it profit a man if he gains the whole world, and loses his own soul?' (Mark 8:36).

Our Lord is concerned about our attitude of heart towards the things of the world. The majority of this world's citizens live for themselves. They are concerned with the size of their bank balances and their personal comfort. We need to note the words of Job, who wrote, 'Naked I came from my mother's womb, and naked shall I return there' (Job 1:21).

There is no real security in this world for our possessions. In Christ's day moths ate clothing and rust destroyed many precious items. Today thieves have put the safety of our property at risk. We try to make our homes secure, but nothing can keep out the determined rogue.

Then there is our greatest enemy, death, which separates us from all of our earthly possessions. We never see a removal van following a hearse.

The apostle John wrote, 'Do not love the world or the things in the world. If anyone loves the world, the love of the Father is not in him. For all that is in the world — the lust of the flesh, the lust of the eyes, and the pride of life — is not of the Father, but is of the world. And the world is passing away, and the lust of it; but he who does the will of God abides for ever' (1 John 2:15-17).

Our earthly treasures come and go, but all that really matters is our heavenly treasure. We are called to use our possessions for the well-being of those in need. As we do these good works, we build up treasure in heaven.

Christ said, 'But love your enemies, do good, and lend, hoping for nothing in return; and your reward will be great, and you will be sons of the most High. For he is kind to the unthankful and evil. Therefore be merciful, just as your Father also is merciful' (Luke 6:35-36).

We must ask ourselves and answer with complete honesty: 'What do I prize most of all — my possessions or my relationship with God?'

This earth is passing away, and the Day of Judgement will most certainly dawn. Are you living for heaven or earth? Always remember that heaven is eternal and Christ is the way into God's kingdom.

A saving faith in the Lord Jesus will be seen in our love for God and in acts of love towards our fellow-man. James wrote, 'For as the body without the spirit is dead, so faith without works is dead also' (James 2:26).

You can't serve God and possessions!

FIND OUT THE FACTS

1. What are we taught in Matthew 6:19-21?

2. What is meant by 'heavenly treasure'?

3. Why can't you serve God and possessions?

The challenge of the reading today is this: whom or what do we really love and serve? Pray that God will help you to love him and serve him as you grow up.

Whenever the gospel is taught and people seek to live according to it, there are two terrible plagues that always arise: false preachers who corrupt the teaching and then Sir Greed, who obstructs right living. *Martin Luther*

 Matthew   'But seek first the kingdom of
6:22-34   God and his righteousness, and
                all these things shall be added
                to you' (Matthew 6:33).

The first part of today's reading refers to the 'eye'. So much
depends upon having healthy eyesight. Without specta-
cles I cannot read or drive the car safely. Christ tells us that
'the lamp of the body is the eye. If therefore your eye is good,
your whole body will be full of light' (Matthew 6:22). What
does this mean?

Our eye is the lamp of the body, which sees what the world
has to offer us. The Christian sees the world as a gift from God.
He prays, 'Open my eyes, that I may see wondrous things from
your law' (Psalm 119:18).

When the saint has been spiritually illuminated (born again),
he finds spiritual treasures in the Scriptures. The glory and
wonder of salvation burst upon his soul and he knows that he
is just a pilgrim upon this earth. Heaven is his destiny. How
we must thank God for his gift of that 'good' eye.

Unlike the 'good' eye, which is not governed by greed or
worldliness, the 'bad' eye opens up a world of objects that are
desirable to own. The 'bad' eye is governed by the 'bad' heart
which longs for more and more of the world.

The second section of our passage commences: 'Therefore I
say to you, do not worry about your life, what you will eat or
what you will drink; nor about your body, what you will put
on. Is not life more than food and the body more than clothing?' (Matthew 6:25).

Our Lord is dealing with anxiety. The ungodly often spend
time worrying about reaching their goals of comfort, wealth,
possessions, status and power. Their concerns all relate to
being able to live comfortably and to enjoy life. They do not
trust God to provide all that they need.

Christians, however, know they have a wise, good God, who provides for the needs of all his creation. They know that if that is so, he will also provide for the needs of his people.

Anxiety is not cured by obtaining more of this world. Possessions create more anxiety! The Lord told his listeners to 'seek first the kingdom of God and his righteousness, and all these things [the necessities of life] shall be added to you' (Matthew 6:33).

Our Lord's words to us are: carry out today's work and let tomorrow worry about itself. Let us rest in God's promise of daily food and clothing. Of course, some of today's work will be preparation for tomorrow. God does not encourage us to be lazy. On the contrary, we are to work well each day, believing that as we work God will make provision for us. The birds keep busy; they don't worry; and God always provides for them.

Let us trust our God to provide all we need.

FIND OUT THE FACTS

1. Describe the clothes God gives the plants?
2. Is this statement true or false? 'Worry is like heathen unbelief.'
3. Read Psalm 39:4-6. What do these verses teach you?

God makes provision even for the birds of the air and the tiny insects which are found beneath the rocks. Thank God for his love and care for all of his creation.

To Think & to pray about

A saying to Remember

The Christian must live in the world, but he must not let the world live in him. *Anon*

Luke   'Judge not, that you be not
6:37-42   judged' (Matthew 7:1).

Every day people make many judgements. When they get out of bed, they choose what clothes to wear. Decisions are made about what to eat at breakfast, which books to read, and so the list could go on. When we make judgements about other people, the Lord gives a very clear warning. He says, 'Be fair how you judge others!'

We are not told that judgements cannot be made, but we are warned to find out all the facts before we reach our conclusions. One reason for making fair judgements is that we are inviting God to use the standard we measure the conduct of others by when he judges us. I'm sure we would be concerned for him to know all the facts before he makes his evaluation of us. He knows our sins. But before his assessment is made, we would want him to be aware of all the facts. The most important consideration is that Christ is our Saviour. In the light of all the information, God always makes right decisions.

If you willingly forgive people who ask for forgiveness, you set a standard for God's judgement of you — that is, forgiveness!

In this parable, Jesus warns his disciples that they are expected to be fair in their dealings with others. Just as a trader, who gives good measure when he sells grain, can expect that others will do the same to him. This again points to the justice of God on the Day of Judgement.

The scribes and Pharisees were the spiritually blind leaders of the church. They taught a doctrine that kept the people in ignorance. The result of the blind leading the blind was that they both ended up in the wrong place: hell. The scribes and Pharisees were likened to a self-righteous person who had a big log in his eye, a piece of wood that could be used as a rafter in a house. Try and imagine such a foolish man attempting to remove a small piece of straw from another person's eye. It is an impossible situation!

To make fair judgements and guide the spiritually lost to the Lord Jesus require an act of sovereign grace. With a changed heart the log will disappear from the eye and the new person will have the ability to help the spiritually blind.

By the grace of God, fair judgements will be made. Instead of condemnation there will be love and mercy, and a hand to lift up the downtrodden. Every word of unjust condemnation comes from a heart filled with pride. God calls this sin!

May we all understand that there is a day of justice coming and our only preparation for that day is a saving faith in Christ, the Saviour.

FIND OUT THE FACTS

1. What is 'justice'?

2. Why should you make fair judgements?

3. Why do sinners need their heart changed by the Holy Spirit?

It is so easy to criticize others and attribute wrong motives to their actions. Ask God to help you to be fair in the way you think and speak about others.

Indeed, I tremble for my country when I reflect that God is just. *Thomas Jefferson*

Matthew   'Do not give what is holy to the
10:5-15   dogs; nor cast your pearls
           before swine, lest they tram-
           ple them under their feet, and
           turn and tear you in pieces'
           (Matthew 7:6).

Pigs love playing in the mud. If you wash them and put
them back in their sty, it won't be long before they are roll-
ing in the filth again.

Hudson Taylor, a missionary to China, and a companion of
his had nowhere to sleep one night. They saw a pigsty which
they thought might do for a bed for the night. After pushing
the pig out, they lay down on some wooden planks they found.
They propped other planks against the doorway, and made
sure the roof was covered, as it had started to rain. Inside the
sty it was very smelly, but dry. It wasn't long before the pig
decided he wasn't going to sleep outside in the rain, and pushed
the door down. That night the pig and two men slept well, but
pigs are not always so friendly.

Our verse tells us that some people act like pigs or dogs.
The dogs mentioned here are the ferocious ones that roam the
streets in packs, eating any rubbish or refuse they find. Both
animals are to be avoided as they are unclean. Their pattern of
behaviour was to return to the mud and filth. Frequently these
dirty animals would even attack any person who fed them.

Here Christ is teaching that some people are like unclean
pigs or dogs. They will blaspheme the truth, pour scorn on our
beloved Saviour and want nothing to do with the gospel. When
this happens, it is time to move on to more receptive people.
This happened to Paul and Barnabas when they were thrown
out of Antioch — 'they shook off the dust from their feet against
them' (Acts 13:51).

On one occasion Jesus sent his disciples out to visit towns
and cities in Israel, with the command, 'And as you go, preach,
saying, "The kingdom of heaven is at hand"' (Matthew 10:7).

They were commissioned to perform miracles, healing those who were ill, even raising the dead (Matthew 10:8). Christ told them not to take much with them, not even money, but to stay where they were welcomed.

Then came the harsh words which express the same idea as that of our verse: 'And whoever will not receive you nor hear your words, when you depart from that house or city, shake off the dust from your feet. Assuredly, I say to you, it will be more tolerable for the land of Sodom and Gomorrah in the Day of Judgement than for that city!' (Matthew 10:14-15).

When the Jews crucified Christ, they were no longer the covenant nation. The gospel was to be taken to all nations of the world (Romans 10 – 11). May none of you be included among those who reject the Lord Jesus.

FIND OUT THE FACTS

1. What is the 'gospel'?
2. Why was the gospel taken from the Jews and preached to the Gentiles?
3. Discuss the meaning of today's 'Saying to remember'.

It is a serious thing to reject Christ. Pray for your family and friends that they may be receptive to the gospel message.

The gospel is neither a discussion nor a debate. It is an announcement. *Paul Rees*

Matthew   'Therefore, whatever you want
7:7-12   men to do to you, do also to
             them, for this is the Law and
             the Prophets' (Matthew 7:12).

It is always good to have friends you can depend upon at all times. During your life you will meet many people, but only have a couple of very good friends.

Jesus continued addressing the people, telling them of a way to live that pleased God. When people were in need, they usually approached a friend and asked for help. The words 'ask,' 'seek' and 'knock' indicate an action which continues until the person obtains what is needed.

Jesus went on to say that when a human father is asked by his son for bread, he doesn't give him a stone, but bread. If the son asks for some fish, the father doesn't hand him a snake. Jesus' next words are very well known. He mentioned what is commonly called 'The Golden Rule'. 'Therefore, whatever you want men to do to you, do also to them, for this is the Law and the Prophets' (Matthew 7:12).

Elsewhere Jesus said, 'But love your enemies, do good, and lend, hoping for nothing in return; and your reward will be great, and you will be sons of the most High' (Luke 6:35). This 'Golden Rule' is not just to be practised among Christians but between all people.

Jesus then stated that if a human father gave good gifts to his children, how much more would the heavenly Father give good gifts to those who asked him.

In Luke 11:13 Jesus repeated this teaching, but concluded, 'If you then, being evil, know how to give good gifts to your children, how much more will your heavenly Father give the Holy Spirit to those who ask him!' We have to do the asking! Here we find a wonderful promise given by God, a God who does not break his word.

How often have you prayed for some spiritual blessing, and given up quickly when God didn't give an instant reply? God's delay may well mean that you are not spiritually mature enough to cope with the gift. The delay may be to give you time to strengthen your faith, thereby preparing you to receive the gift for which you have prayed. God could also be testing you to see how strongly you believe his promises.

The Lord Jesus is inviting his people to knock continuously at the door of heaven, praying for good gifts from their heavenly Father. He listens and frequently answers the prayers of his people in ways far beyond anything they had ever expected.

Rejoice, because we have a good God who answers prayers! He will never let us down!

FIND OUT THE FACTS

1. What is the Golden Rule and how do you put it into practice?
2. God answers some prayers with a 'No'. Why does he do this?
3. Discuss some prayers God has answered for you.

God shows his generosity by giving good gifts to those who ask them of him. Pray that God will help you to be generous in your dealings with others.

Our good deeds are to be scattered upon all men, Christian and non-Christian. *Jerry Bridges*

John
14:1-6

'Enter by the narrow gate; for wide is the gate and broad is the way that leads to destruction, and there are many who go in by it. Because narrow is the gate and difficult is the way which leads to life, and there are few who find it' (Matthew 7:13-14).

Jesus now commences a new section of the 'Sermon on the Mount'. Our verse mentions the two roadways men and women travel. The narrow entrance leads to paradise and the broad way ends in hell. When you meditate upon these two verses you might be reminded of a book, *The Pilgrim's Progress*, by John Bunyan which I have read several times. This is the story of a man called 'Christian' who commences his walk to heaven. If you have not read this book, go to your library and borrow a copy!

It is easy to pass through the wide gate and walk on the broad road. Most people are walking along this road, laughing and enjoying their worldly pleasures, without a moment's thought about death and judgement. There is no difficulty entering the broad way. It is the happy way of 'eat, drink and be merry' (Ecclesiastes 8:15).

The narrow gate, which represents the sinner's conversion, is difficult to pass through. Everything that was once held to be precious must be left behind. Good works cannot be taken along because the narrow way is the pathway of faith. Travelling this way means suffering the insults and mocking of an ungodly world.

It is the way of obedience to the commands of the Captain of the faith. This means taking up one's God-given cross daily. Self-denial is very much part of taking up one's cross, and the devil will not fail to place temptations in the way.

But the narrow way is the way of peace: peace with God and peace with your spiritual brothers and sisters. The broad way is certainly not the way of peace. Isaiah wrote, '"There is no peace," says the Lord, "for the wicked"' (Isaiah 48:22).

The apostle Paul wrote of the difficulties faced by those who travelled the narrow way. He concluded that 'having nothing', [they possessed] 'all things' (2 Corinthians 6:10).

When you come to the crossroads at which the two pathways meet, don't be led astray by the crowds who happily pass onto the broad way. The pleasures of sin do not last for ever, but hell does.

Enter through Christ, the narrow gate, leaving your good deeds and sinful ways behind you. Live the life of faith in the Saviour, Jesus Christ. The number walking this way may be small, but as Christians they make wonderful companions.

FIND OUT THE FACTS

1. Who wrote *The Pilgrim's Progress*?
2. Through which entrance do most people pass?
3. What 'baggage' is left behind at the entrance to the narrow gate?

To Think & to pray about

The broad way offers a great many things to tempt and attract us. Ask the Lord to give you a clear view of the value of taking the narrow way.

A saying to Remember

Pleasure, profit, preferment are the worldling's trinity. *John Trapp*

Matthew	'Beware of false prophets, who
7:15-20	come to you in sheep's cloth-
	ing, but inwardly they are
	ravenous wolves' (Matthew
	7:15).

Today the church has many false prophets leading people astray. They appear on TV, encouraging viewers to send in gifts of money for which they promise, in return, good health and wealth. They say that all that is needed is the prayer of faith. And, if good health and money are not the result, then the person is accused of having insufficient faith.

False prophets are found in every generation. Christ warned his disciples about them, as did the apostle Paul who told the Ephesian elders, 'Take heed to yourselves and to all the flock, among which the Holy Spirit has made you overseers, to shepherd the church of God which he purchased with his own blood. For I know this, that after my departure savage wolves will come in among you, not sparing the flock' (Acts 20:28-29). These 'wolves' attack and scatter the flock and then move on.

Jesus told Christians that these wicked 'wolves' would be known by their 'fruit'. Just as an unhealthy tree produces bad fruit, and a good tree produces delicious fruit, so we can judge preachers and professing Christians by their words and deeds. The unhealthy tree is good for nothing other than to be cut down and burnt.

Every Christian should know what the Scriptures teach in order to make sound judgements about leaders in the church. How do you know that what I have written is true? You might like to ask your minister if it is correct. But how do you know if his reply is right? You need to know the teachings of Christ so that a sound decision can be made. Study your Bible!

The apostle Paul mentions the Bereans who, once they had heard him speak, checked his teachings against the teachings of the Old Testament (Acts 17:10-11). You should do the same using both the Old and New Testaments.

Christ uttered some of the most fearful words recorded in the Scriptures: 'Not everyone who says to me, "Lord, Lord," shall enter the kingdom of heaven, but he who does the will of my Father in heaven' (Matthew 7:21).

The Scriptures clearly teach that we are saved by faith alone (Romans 5:1; Ephesians 2:8-9). Saving faith never exists alone; it is always accompanied by works of righteousness (James 2:26). The apostle Paul said plainly that good works are the fruit of saving faith: 'For we are his workmanship, created in Christ Jesus for good works, which God prepared beforehand that we should walk in them' (Ephesians 2:10).

Christ spoke terrifying words to those who claimed to have done great works in his name, but were, in fact, strangers to grace: 'And then I will declare to them, "I never knew you; depart from me, you who practise lawlessness!"' (Matthew 7:23). Will this be said to you?

FIND OUT THE FACTS

1. How can you tell if a person is a Christian?
2. How can you tell if you're a Christian?
3. Who are today's 'ravenous wolves'?

It is easy to follow a person because he or she looks good, speaks well or seems in some way attractive. Ask the Lord to give you the ability to assess people according to his **Word** so that you are not deceived.

The hypocrite has much angel without, more devil within.
Thomas Adams

A *saying* to Remember

Luke
6:46-49

'Now, therefore, you are no longer strangers and foreigners, ... having been built on the foundation of the apostles and prophets, Jesus Christ himself being the chief cornerstone ...' (Ephesians 2:19-20).

The reading in Luke describes a scene that must have been witnessed many times by the Israelites. If houses are to stand firm against floods and wind they need firm foundations. To build a house in the sand of a creek bed is to invite disaster when floods come. The house will be washed away.

Those houses fixed firmly to a rock would remain standing when the floods came. To destroy this house, the rock foundation would also have to be destroyed. The foolish builder built his house on shifting sand, while the wise builder built his home on the 'Rock'.

This parable followed Christ's teaching on the Christian being known by its fruit. Good works came from the godly man who gives all the glory to Christ, while the ungodly seek the praise of the people around them.

Christ rebuked those people who called him 'Lord' yet failed to obey his teaching. Obedience to the Saviour's commands marked a person out as a wise builder; his life was built on the Lord Jesus Christ.

The church consists largely of people who confess their love for God and who have faith in the Lord Jesus Christ. Those who come under the title of 'wise' are those who are born again and don't just profess to be Christians, but live the Christian life. They should be humble people, 'rich in good works, ready to give, willing to share, storing up for themselves a good foundation for the time to come, that they may lay hold on eternal life' (1 Timothy 6:18-19).

The apostle Peter states, 'Behold, I lay in Zion a chief cornerstone, elect, precious, and he who believes on him will by no means be put to shame' (1 Peter 2:6, compare Isaiah 28:16). These people will stand firm because they do not stand alone; they stand with the protective arms of Christ about them.

The foolish builder represents professing Christians, who are strangers to the new birth. They know the Bible's teaching about repentance, faith and love, yet have little or nothing to do with the truth of salvation.

The greatest flood of all will be the day of our death or the day of Christ's return. The saints will stand firm because their spirituality is established in Christ. The foolish people are those who will be condemned because they stand alone.

Who are you in this parable?

FIND OUT THE FACTS

1. Who is the foundation spoken of in 1 Corinthians 3:10?
2. What is a 'moral life' built upon?
3. How can you be sure that you have a saving faith in Christ? Read James 1:27; 2:26; 1 John 4:20; 5:2.

To Think & to pray about

Today's devotion has focused on the subject of foundations. Think about the foundation of your life. Is it a good or a bad one?

Only if we walk in the beauty of God's law do we become sure of our adoption as children of the Father. *John Calvin*

A saying to Remember

Luke
7:1-17

'Then fear came upon all, and they glorified God, saying, "A great prophet has risen up among us"; and, "God has visited his people"' (Luke 7:16).

The Lord still performs miracles. Every time a sinner enters the kingdom of heaven a miracle has taken place in the person's heart. While on earth Jesus performed many miracles. He entered Capernaum where some elders brought him a request from a centurion to come and heal his servant. This man loved God and had built a synagogue for the Jews.

Before Jesus reached the sick man, some of the centurion's friends brought word that he did not expect Christ to come to him. As a soldier, he knew that someone in authority could simply give a command and it would be done. The soldier had said, 'Therefore I did not even think myself worthy to come to you. But say the word, and my servant will be healed' (Luke 7:7). Jesus marvelled at the centurion's faith. When his friends returned to him, they found the servant well.

Jesus then moved on to the city of Nain, where he found a funeral in progress. A widow's only adult son was being carried to his grave for burial. Jesus knew that without anyone to support her, she would find life extremely difficult. Looking at the weeping woman he said, 'Do not weep' (Luke 7:13). Then touching the open coffin, the Lord said, 'Young man, I say to you, arise' (v. 14).

The news of such wonderful miracles was spread around the country, even to the disciples of John the Baptist. John, who had been put in jail by Herod, sent two of his followers to Christ to ask him the question: 'Are you the coming one, or do we look for another?' (Luke 7:20).

Christ replied by performing more miracles and by telling John's disciples to go back and report all they had seen him do: lepers were healed, the blind received their sight, the lame could walk, deaf people regained their hearing, the dead were being raised to life and the gospel of salvation was being preached.

Jesus then praised John, declaring that he was the fulfilment of the words in Malachi 3:1. 'Behold, I send my messenger before your face, who will prepare your way before you' (Luke 7:27). Christ also said that John was the greatest prophet of all times, 'but [that] he who is least in the kingdom of God is greater than he' (Luke 7:28).

Jesus rebuked those who were listening, by reminding them that they had said that John was demon possessed because he didn't eat bread or drink wine, and that Christ, the Son of Man, was an alcoholic, a glutton and a friend of sinners because he enjoyed good food, wine and companionship. Both carried out their appointed task and sinners were converted.

FIND OUT THE FACTS

1. What was a synagogue?
2. What is a centurion?
3. What was John the Baptist's work?

To Think & to pray about

God has performed many miracles in the lives of people by bringing them from the darkness of sin into the light of his gospel. Pray for greater faith to trust a great and powerful God who is at work in this world.

A saying to Remember

Doubt breeds distress, but trust means joy in the long run.   C. H. Spurgeon

Matthew
11:1-19

So she, having been prompted by her mother, said, "Give me John the Baptist's head here on a platter" (Matthew 14:8).

Today's reading tells you more about the brave man, John the Baptist. He was a man who feared no one but God. John's outspoken condemnation of Herod's sin of marrying his brother's wife meant that Herod wanted him executed. But, as he was afraid of the people, he left John in prison.

Soon an opportunity arose for Herod to have him put to death. John was the greatest prophet of all. He fulfilled the prophecies made about him in the Old Testament, and he prepared the way for the King of kings, the Lord Jesus.

Our scripture verse tells us that the kingdom of heaven was experiencing opposition, but the good news was still being preached. Repentant sinners were entering the kingdom. We know that no one enters the kingdom of God apart from the work of the Holy Spirit. When a sinner is born again, a disciplined life is required. There is prayer, worship, reading the Scriptures, turning away from ungodly behaviour and keeping oneself from the love of the world.

In prison John was allowed to receive visitors. Yesterday we read that he sent a messenger to Jesus, asking if he truly was the Christ, the Anointed One.

On Herod's birthday, Herodias' daughter danced at his feast, after which he promised her that she could have anything she wanted. The young girl's mother told her what to request, 'Give me John the Baptist's head here on a platter' (Matthew 14:8).

What a foolish oath Herod had made. Those at his party had heard him speak and now he had to keep his word. At once he sent soldiers to John's prison. There John was executed and his head was presented on a platter to the girl, who gave it to her mother. John's disciples came to the prison and lovingly removed his body for burial.

But Herod's troubles with John the Baptist did not end there. When he heard of the miracles, authority and preaching of the Lord Jesus, he believed that John had risen from the dead.

John the Baptist was a courageous man who loved God and went about preaching repentance. He baptized those who claimed they had turned away from their sins. His preaching had prepared the nation for the coming of Christ. John was the Elijah who was to precede the coming of Christ. Jesus said, 'Indeed Elijah is coming first and will restore all things. But I say to you that Elijah has come already, and they did not know him but did to him whatever they wished' (Matthew 17:11-12, compare Malachi 4:5-6).

One day Christians will meet this great prophet. Will you?

FIND OUT THE FACTS

1. Why was John murdered?

2. Why didn't Herod want to have John killed? (See Matthew 14:5)

3. Find out all you can about John the Baptist.

John the Baptist was faithful to his witness for Christ even though it cost him his life. All Christians are tested at some time for their faith. Pray that they will remain faithful, just as John the Baptist did.

One cannot sleep his way into the kingdom. *William Hendriksen*

Matthew   'And that servant who knew his
11:20-30   master's will, and did not pre-
             pare himself ... shall be beaten
             with many stripes. But he who
             did not know, yet committed
             things deserving of stripes,
             shall be beaten with few. For
             everyone to whom much is
             given, from him much will be
             required' (Luke 12:47-48).

It is good to *know* what is expected of us, but it is better when we *know* and *obey*. Our verse states that God's Day of Judgement will take into consideration the privileges we have had. Most people in the Western world have Bibles which are easily accessible and churches in their communities where the truth is preached for all to hear. If this is your situation, then remember that God expects great things from you. He expects you to repent of your sins and come to Christ in faith.

In our reading some cities had seen great miracles and heard the gospel preached, yet very few repented in those cities and trusted in Christ for their salvation. Jesus said that the Day of Judgement would be less frightening for the citizens of Tyre, Sidon and Sodom. He even suggested that if the citizens of those cities had seen his works, they would have repented and been saved.

Jesus gave thanks to God that the gospel was being revealed to the humble people of the land and that he had been able to reveal his heavenly Father to his people. The apostle John tells us that God cannot be seen. He is spirit, but the Son of God who is one with his Father 'has declared him' (John 1:18).

Jesus had preached the word given him by his Father. The world cannot know God except through the one and only Mediator, the Lord Jesus Christ, who is both God and man in one person. In his high-priestly prayer, Jesus prayed, 'O right-eous Father! The world has not known you, but I have known you... And I have declared to them your name, and will declare it, that the love with which you loved me may be in them, and I in them' (John 17:25,26).

Jesus invited sinners to come to him, because his way of salvation was not a burden compared with that preached by the Pharisees. Salvation was not to be found in keeping the law, but by a simple, saving faith in Christ. Jesus said, 'For my yoke is easy and my burden is light' (Matthew 11:30).

The keeping of the law as a means to earn salvation was impossible; the yoke was too heavy.

Which is the way of salvation: by the keeping of the law or by faith in Christ alone? It is by faith alone!

FIND OUT THE FACTS

1. How many Bibles are there in your home?

2. Do you have a Bible-reading plan to help you read through your Bible?

3. Do all people receive the same reward or punishment on the Day of Judgement? See Romans 2:12-16.

How many times you have heard the gospel message. Have you obeyed God's command to repent and to turn to Christ in response to this message?

God and his truth cannot be changed; the gospel is not negotiable. *John Marshall*

Luke
7:36-50

'Then [Christ] said to the woman, "Your faith has saved you. Go in peace"' (Luke 7:50).

The passage of Scripture for today tells us of God's love for his people. We can't be sure who the woman was, but we do know that she dearly loved Christ her Saviour because he had forgiven her many sins.

Jesus had been invited to eat in the house of Simon, a Pharisee. Frequently people came as spectators to these meals so that they could listen to the conversation. Those who sat down to eat would have been sitting on cushions.

As they were eating, a woman who was known to be a great 'sinner' entered the room and approached Jesus. There were tears running down her cheeks because she knew what a great sinner she was and had the desire to repent. She must have wondered, 'Will God ever forgive me?'

She knew that by going to Jesus there was hope. In her hand she carried a costly 'alabaster flask of fragrant oil' (Luke 7:37). It is quite possible that she had purchased this precious oil with money earned from her immoral life. The Pharisees, knowing her character, would have considered its use on Christ as sinful (Deuteronomy 23:18).

Kneeling behind Jesus and with tears running from her cheeks onto his feet, she used her long hair as a towel to wipe them away. After kissing the Lord's feet she anointed them with the costly oil.

Simon, who had invited Christ to the meal, thought to himself, 'Why doesn't this man, who says he's a prophet, know the character of the woman who has touched him?' He failed to understand that Jesus mixed with sinners in order to bring them to himself! Knowing his thoughts the Lord told the short parable you have read. Then he asked, 'Tell me, therefore, which of them will love him more?' To this Simon answered, 'I suppose the one whom he forgave more' (Luke 7:42,43).

Jesus rebuked Simon for the poor welcome he had received. No one had washed his feet or kissed him. Simon hadn't anointed him with oil.

Turning to the woman Christ said, 'Therefore I say to you, her sins, which are many, are forgiven, for she loved much. But to whom little is forgiven, the same loves little. Then he said to her, "Your sins are forgiven"' (Luke 7:47-48). Everyone at the table asked one another, 'Who is this who even forgives sins?' (Luke 7:49). That repentant sinner loved the Lord Jesus greatly. Do you love him?

The Holy Spirit had given her new life and forgiveness. She was justified by God's grace alone. She left Christ rejoicing because God was at peace with her and that peace flowed into her heart.

FIND OUT THE FACTS

1. Why did the woman love Christ?
2. Was Simon a good host? Why?
3. How did God show his love towards sinners?

It is very easy to condemn those who may be caught in some sin and not see the opportunity to share the gospel with them. Pray that the Lord would enable you to share the gospel rather than condemn others.

A saying to Remember

Forgiveness forms the church.
R. C. Lucas

Mark   'If a kingdom is divided against
3:20-27   itself, that kingdom cannot
            stand' (Mark 3:24).

In a home where all members respect and love one another, there will be peace. This is the type of home we should all be aiming to have. It requires effort to control tempers and to be helpful whenever possible. It is of great benefit for such a family to come together each day for worship: to read the Scriptures, pray, discuss a passage of Scripture, and possibly to sing a hymn or a psalm. Homes built on these foundations usually stand firm when Satan comes calling.

On one occasion the Scribes said that Jesus was mad: 'He has Beelzebub,' and 'By the ruler of the demons he casts out demons' (Mark 3:22).

Jesus knew their argument to be false. The demons were under the control of Satan and were working together to overthrow the kingdom of God. It just didn't make sense for a demon to do the opposite because he would be working to overthrow his master, Satan, and his kingdom.

Christ was not a demon because he taught the gospel which was destroying Satan and his kingdom. Then Christ told his listeners a great truth concerning himself: 'No one can enter a strong man's house and plunder his goods, unless he first binds the strong man. And then he will plunder his house' (Mark 3:27). Jesus was in the process of stripping Satan of all power. He had been defeated in the wilderness when he tempted the Lord. Daily, sinners were being snatched from his kingdom and transferred to the Lord's kingdom. Those who called Jesus a member of Satan's kingdom had committed a terrible sin.

The Lord went on to say that forgiveness is freely available to all who repent and turn to God for pardon. But he added that the sin against the Holy Spirit could not be forgiven and would result in eternal death (Mark 3:28-29). This is the sin of attributing to Christ the works of Satan. It is the sin of a heart that is hardened against the gospel. It is the sin of refusing to turn to Christ in faith and to walk the narrow way that leads to paradise.

Many people in every age have committed this sin by rejecting the free offer of the gospel. May this not be you! Remember that Christ will not turn away those who come to him with true repentance in their heart. He said, 'All that the Father gives me will come to me, and the one who comes to me I will by no means cast out' (John 6:37).

When his mother and brothers came to see him, he looked at the people about him and said, 'For whoever does the will of God is my brother and my sister and mother' (Mark 3:35).

To be one with Christ is the best place of all!

FIND OUT THE FACTS

1. Who is Beelzebub?
2. What is the unforgivable sin?
3. Describe a happy home.

There is no neutral ground. Think seriously today about whether you are in bondage to the ways of sin and Satan or whether you are under the control of the Holy Spirit.

The devil is most devilish when respectable.
Elizabeth Barrett Browning

Matthew	'For as Jonah was three days
12:38-42	and three nights in the belly

Matthew
12:38-42

'For as Jonah was three days and three nights in the belly of the great fish, so will the Son of Man be three days and three nights in the heart of the earth' (Matthew 12:40).

Have you ever been asked to prove the truth of what you have said? Sometimes it is difficult to do this to the satisfaction of the person who is asking the question.

Jesus made great claims about himself. He accepted the names, 'The Son of Man', 'The Son of God', 'I AM' and other names applicable to God and the Messiah alone. The Israelites longed for Messiah's coming. They believed he would restore David's throne and drive out the Romans.

The church leaders couldn't believe that the humble Jesus was their long-awaited Messiah. They didn't want the people following such a humble person. So, they asked Jesus a pointed question. They wanted him to do something — perform a miracle — that would prove to everyone that he was the Messiah. Jesus replied that he would give them just one sign, that would prove who he was.

After rebuking the Pharisees and the people generally, Jesus said, 'An evil and adulterous generation seeks after a sign, and no sign will be given to it except the sign of the prophet Jonah' (Matthew 12:39). Then followed the words of our verse. The resurrection of Jesus was the proof that he was who he claimed to be — Jehovah's Messiah!

The Old Testament clearly recorded the events of Jonah's life, and the people knew that he had been in the belly of the big fish for three days. Now Jesus was saying he would spend three days and three nights in the grave. This would not be a literal seventy-two hours, but a portion of three days as the Jews counted time.

Jesus knew the church leaders were trying to trap him in what he said, but he rebuked them, saying that people from the Gentile nations would believe his claims, while Israel rejected him. He pointed to the repentance of Nineveh when Jonah preached, and he was greater than Jonah.

Jesus gave his generation a severe warning. Individuals needed to repent of their sins and live a godly life, controlled by the Holy Spirit. To claim to have repented, but not to show its fruit, left the heart empty and ready for the demon who once lived there to return with his companions. Christ cannot cohabit with demons. It is one or the other!

Look at your own life and see if there is evidence of 'the fruit of the Spirit' (Galatians 5:22-23) and the works of righteousness (Ephesians 2:10) shining brightly.

FIND OUT THE FACTS

1. In what way is Christ greater than Jonah?

2. List the fruit of the Spirit. Learn Galatians 5:22,23.

3. Name a situation where a man was inhabited by many demons. See Mark 5:9.

In Jesus' day people looked for a sign before they would believe. Is it still the same today? Why, do you think, God wants us to believe that his word is true and reliable?

No sooner is a temple built to God, but the devil builds a chapel nearby.

Matthew   'Because it has been given to
13:10-17   you to know the mysteries of
             the kingdom of heaven, but to
             them it has not been given'
             (Matthew 13:11).

Most people enjoy reading the parables of the Lord Jesus. I'm sure those people who heard him telling them listened closely, because he spoke about things with which they were familiar. The stories were good, but very few hearers were able to understand the truth being taught.

When Christ was asked the reason why he spoke in parables, he replied by saying that this was the fulfilment of a prophecy found in Isaiah 6:9 where the words of God to the prophet are recorded: 'And he said, "Go, and tell this people: 'Keep on hearing, but do not understand; keep on seeing, but do not perceive.'"' John 12:41 shows that it was Jehovah Christ who sat upon the throne of glory (Isaiah 6:3).

Isaiah was told that his preaching to the Jewish people would not result in repentance for their sins. The people would hear and see, but would not understand the truth of his words.

The spiritual leaders of Israel didn't teach the truth concerning sin and the way of salvation. The Pharisees believed that salvation could be earned by doing good works. They thought that God would be obligated to reward them with eternal life because of what they had done. This meant they believed that sin was not a serious matter.

The Pharisees made life so difficult for the people because they added to the law of God and then demanded that the people obey both. Those proud Pharisees were soon to be humbled. Because the people found the spiritual burdens placed on them by the Pharisees very heavy, our Saviour said, 'Come to me, all you who labour and are heavy laden, and I will give you rest. Take my yoke upon you and learn from me, for I am gentle and lowly in heart, and you will find rest for your souls. For my yoke is easy and my burden is light' (Matthew 11:28-30).

The salvation of Christians was won for them by the works of the Lord Jesus. The 'burden' he places on his people is saving faith in himself, which is the free gift of God.

Soon the Jewish people would crucify the Lord. He was not the Messiah they expected and wanted. So it was that Jesus spoke in parables. The people would enjoy the stories, but fail to find the truth.

When you read a parable, look for the truth being taught, and when you have found it, obey it!

FIND OUT THE FACTS

1. What is a parable?

2. Name three parables that you know?

3. Why couldn't the Jewish people find the truth in Christ's parables?

In Psalm 119 the psalmist ask God to open his eyes that he may see wondrous things in God's Word. Make this request your prayer today.

A saying to Remember

Truth famine is the ultimate and worst of all famines. *Carl F. H. Henry*

Matthew   'He who has ears to hear, let
13:1-9   him hear!' (Matthew 13:9).

When I was young I often saw my dad and grandfather 'broadcasting' the seed in the ploughed ground. They had a bag of seed hanging around their necks, and as they walked along in a straight line they threw the seed about. Later they used a 'fiddle' which cast the seed about more evenly.

Jesus spoke some parables which are called 'Kingdom Parables'. There must have been a big crowd of people listening because he spoke from a boat. What truth does this first parable teach? I trust that you have ears to hear what Jesus is teaching and a mind that will understand the truth.

I'm sure that all who listened to Christ would have been able to picture the scene he described. They would all have seen a man sowing seed in a field at some time. As the man threw the seed, some would have fallen on each place mentioned in the parable. The great truth that Christ taught here concerns membership of the kingdom of heaven.

The seed, thrown by the wayside, would have been quickly eaten by the birds. This grain would just lie on the top of the soil which would have been trampled solid by the people who had walked on it. The seed represents the gospel, and the hard ground is the hard heart that refuses to turn to Christ for salvation.

These people are described in Romans 1:18: 'For the wrath of God is revealed from heaven against all ungodliness and unrighteousness of men, who suppress the truth in unrighteousness.'

The seed on stony places represents those people who hear the gospel with joy, and follow Christ for a short time; but like a plant that grows in stony places, they do not persevere (Matthew 13:20-21). When troubles and persecution come because of the gospel, they return to the world and go back to their ungodly lives.

The third type of soil was full of weeds and thorns that strangled the plants. This represents people who rejoice for a short time when they hear the gospel, but soon find the attraction of the world too great and return to the life they love (Matthew 13:22).

However, some seed falls on good ground and grows. This represents those whose hearts have been prepared by the Holy Spirit to receive the gospel with joy. They live a righteous life, loving both God and man. And just as this seed can produce heads with a multitude of grains, so Christians can be faithful as they serve and bear witness to their Saviour, the Lord Jesus Christ.

FIND OUT THE FACTS

1. Which ground is represented by the rich man in Mark 10:17-22.

2. What is the fruit that Christians bear? (Matthew 13:23, compare Galatians 5:22-23).

3. What does the seed represent?

Think about which type of ground best describes you. Do you need to change?

Whoever marries the spirit of this age will find himself a widower in the next. *Ralph Inge*

Matthew   'Be sober, be vigilant; because
13:24-30   your adversary the devil walks
               about like a roaring lion, seek-
               ing whom he may devour'
               (1 Peter 5:8).

This is a parable about a farmer's crop but this time we are told that two types of plants are growing. I know from gardening that sometimes it is difficult to tell the difference between the good plants and the weeds. I have occasionally dug out the wrong plants when doing some weeding.

The man in the parable had planted good seed that would grow into wheat, but no sooner had he done this than a wicked person came along one night and tossed in some bad seeds, some weeds which when they sprouted would look just like the stalks of wheat.

The owner of the field had servants who wanted to dig out what they thought were the weeds, but they were prevented from doing this. The farmer knew that it was best to let both weeds and wheat grow together until they matured. Then it would be easy to harvest the wheat, because the weeds would be easily recognized at that stage. At the time of harvest the weeds would be gathered, bundled up and used as fuel for the fire.

The Lord Jesus again gave the interpretation of this parable. The field represented the assembly of professing Christians. The Lord Jesus is the sower of the good seeds which represent people who are citizens of his kingdom. They are people, born again by the Holy Spirit. The tares represent those people who profess faith in Christ, but are hypocrites. Their names are found on church membership rolls, but not in the Lamb's Book of Life. They mix with believers and often for years are indistinguishable from the saints. Some will only be identified on the Day of Judgement as being tares rather than wheat (Matthew 7:21-23; 25:1-3).

Luke wrote about these people when he quoted the words of the apostle Paul to the Ephesian elders: 'Therefore take heed to yourselves and to all the flock, among which the Holy Spirit has made you overseers, to shepherd the church of God which he purchased with his own blood. For I know this, that after my departure savage wolves will come in among you, not sparing the flock' (Acts 20:28-29).

At the end of the age the holy angels will gather Christ's enemies and throw them into hell, just as Malachi has said, 'Behold, the day is coming, burning like an oven, and all the proud, yes, all who do wickedly will be stubble. And the day which is coming shall burn them up' (Malachi 4:1). Christians then, dressed in their perfect resurrection bodies, will 'shine forth as the sun' in the kingdom of heaven (Matthew 13:43).

We need to be very careful when making judgements about people who claim to be Christians. Let us make sure that we are numbered among the 'wheat'.

FIND OUT THE FACTS

1. What is a hypocrite?
2. How do you tell a Christian from a hypocrite?
3. What will happen to hypocrites on the Day of Judgement?

We should be more concerned about making sure that we are part of the wheat than trying to hunt for the tares.

No hypocrite can carry the cross.
Henry Smith

Matthew   'On the mountain height of
13:31-35   Israel I will plant it; and it will
             bring forth boughs, and bear
             fruit, and be a majestic cedar.
             Under it will dwell birds of
             every sort; in the shadow of
             its branches they will dwell'
             (Ezekiel 17:23).

Frequently when our children were young we made our own
bread. They enjoyed mixing the dough, adding yeast and
watching the dough rise on a sunny window-sill. When cooked,
they always appreciated eating the fresh bread with butter and
golden syrup.

In Matthew 13:33 we read, 'The kingdom of heaven is like
leaven, which a woman took and hid in three measures of meal
till it was all leavened.' This woman was ready to bake quite a
large number of loaves and used her ingredients to mix all she
needed. Then she waited for the leaven to permeate the dough.

Christ was using a common, everyday activity as an illustration of the kingdom of God. The church consists of people
who are born again by the Holy Spirit. This gracious work of
the Holy Spirit has an effect upon every part of the church.

Each member lets his light shine in the world, so that glory
and praise are given to God (Matthew 5:16). The fruit of the
Spirit is seen and Christian morality affects every aspect of
life: at home, at work, at play and at worship. A Christian's life
should demonstrate the love of Christ, and obedience to the
Saviour's commands. The Holy Spirit who changes the whole
person strengthens the church also.

The short parable found in Matthew 13:31-32 speaks of the
growth of the church throughout the world. Before the Day of
Pentecost one hundred and twenty disciples met in the upper
room for prayer. Within a short time on the Day of Pentecost
three thousand people were brought into the kingdom, as a
result of the Holy Spirit applying Peter's sermon to their hearts.

Before that day the Christian church was just a small group of believers who had little influence in the world. But the church was to experience miraculous growth. Just as a mustard seed could not grow into a huge tree without God's intervention, so the church grew as God added to it. Within several decades the gospel had spread throughout the known world (Colossians 1:6). It was like that huge tree with its inviting branches. Men and women were attracted to the gospel and rested in the church, as did the birds in the tree. The growth of the church across the known world was indeed a miracle.

The church will continue to grow until the last sinner has been called into its membership and then the King of the church will come in all his splendour to receive his spotless bride.

FIND OUT THE FACTS

1. What is the new birth?
2. What effect does the new birth have upon a person?
3. What is the church? Where is the church found?

The gospel is God's power to salvation. This was clearly demonstrated on the Day of Pentecost. Pray for your community today that power of God's gospel will be clearly seen in the lives of friends and neighbours.

We don't go to church; we are the church! *Ernest Southcott*

Matthew   'But what things were gain to
13:44-46   me, these I have counted loss
               for Christ' (Philippians 3:7).

My brother was told that a gold sovereign had been buried in a time capsule in an old building on the church property. There was no record of it having been found and as the property was to be sold, he started searching with his gold detector. He detected every inch but the metal capsule could not be found.

The property has been sold with the caveat (which means with the condition) that if the capsule is ever found it must be returned to the congregation. In the container are some gold sovereigns and if one particular one is found, it is worth many tens of thousands of Australian dollars.

Our two short parables tell of great treasure. One was buried in a field and was accidentally found, while the other required a lengthy search to find the valuable pearl.

The first parable (Matthew 13:44) is about a person who stumbled across some treasure that was hidden in the earth. Before the days when banks existed people frequently hid their treasures in the ground, thinking that they would be safe there. If the person died without telling anyone what he had done, the treasure would lie hidden until someone discovered it accidentally.

This is an illustration of the work of the Holy Spirit. Suddenly he awakens a person to the reality of heaven and hell. A friend of mine was walking along the street when suddenly he thought, 'What will happen to me when I die?' At once he found a Bible and was led by the Holy Spirit to repentance and faith in Christ. His treasure was Christ and salvation. He turned his back on the pleasures of the world and commenced a life of service to the Lord in the ministry.

The second parable (Matthew 13:45,46) concerns a person who knew what he was looking for. He had seen his sins and began a search to find peace with God. He tried living according to God's law, but failed. He began going to church, reading his Bible and praying, but in spite of the value of those things he had no peace in his heart. Like the man who knew what he wanted, he sold everything to buy that precious pearl.

This is the person who wants to be saved from his sin and searches until he finds Christ. The Holy Spirit reveals to him that salvation can not be earned, but is only to be had through faith in the Redeemer. The way to God is through Christ who said, 'I am the way, the truth, and the life. No one comes to the Father except through me' (John 14:6).

The people in the two parables knew their treasure was of immense value and did not rest until they had it in their grasp. The call to sinners is this: give up everything for Jesus and gain eternal life!

FIND OUT THE FACTS

1. What do the treasures in both parables represent?
2. Why is salvation so important?
3. Why were treasures hidden in the earth?

What value do you place on salvation? Would you be willing to give up everything for it?

We are not saved for believing, but by believing.   *Thomas Taylor*

Matthew 13:47-52	'These you may eat ... whatever in the water has fins and scales, whether in the seas or in the rivers — that you may eat... Whatever in the water does not have fins or scales — that shall be an abomination to you' (Leviticus 11:9,12).

God's law restricted what the Israelites could eat. I'm so pleased that I live in the New Testament era, as I have a real liking for oysters, prawns and lobsters. Christians have no such restrictions on their diet!

This 'Kingdom Parable' commences with the words: 'Again, the kingdom of heaven is like a dragnet...' (Matthew 13:47). Some of the disciples had been fishermen and would have had a good understanding of the story in this parable. In fact, all the people would have understood what Christ was speaking about.

A dragnet is a long net, possibly one hundred metres long and two metres deep, with corks on the top and weights at the bottom. Two men work the net. One stands on the shore while the other rows out and around in his boat, allowing the net to slide into the water. When the second man returns to the shore with his end of the net, the fish are caught. The men slowly pull the net onto the beach where they separate the fish that can be sold and eaten from the sea creatures that are 'unclean'.

This parable taught the disciples that one day, at the end of the age, there would be a judgement when Christ's people would be separated from the ungodly. This separation is the work of the holy angels who accompany Christ upon his return to earth from heaven.

The gospel of salvation was to be preached to all the world. Christ's servants were to go everywhere — into the highways and byways — preaching the good news concerning the risen Lord Jesus (Matthew 22:10).

Many people believe the gospel, but many are hypocrites (Acts 5:1-11). The fish of no value are those people who live for themselves and the pleasures of this world. They are 'in' the church, but not 'of' the church. The angels will throw these people into hell, 'the furnace of fire, [where there will] be wailing and gnashing of teeth' (Matthew 13:50).

The saints are those who love God, serve the Lord Jesus Christ and live by grace according to the Scriptures. They long for the time when this sin-sick world will come to an end, and they will find their home in the new heavens and new earth, in which righteousness will dwell.

On that day all tears will be gone because sin will be no more, but God will be all in all.

Are you longing and praying for that day? I trust you are.

FIND OUT THE FACTS

1. List four sea creatures the Israelites were not to eat.
2. When is the Day of Judgement?
3. What is meant by the 'Kingdom Parables'?

Think about the seriousness of claiming to be a Christian when, in fact, one is not. Pray for someone today who thinks that he or she is a Christian but whose life does not show that to be so.

Too many church members are starched and ironed but not washed. *Vance Havner*

Mark
4:35-41

'And they feared exceedingly, and said to one another, "Who can this be, that even the wind and the sea obey him!"' (Mark 4:41).

I have been out on the ocean in a small boat when a strong wind suddenly blew up. Within a few minutes a calm sea was turned into breaking waves and I thought my boat would be filled with water. I started the outboard motor and, pointing the boat's bow in the direction of the shore, I set out very slowly.

Some of the waves came into the boat and soon I was holding the steering wheel in one hand and a bailer (a bucket used to scoop the water out of the boat) in the other. I can understand how the disciples felt when they were caught out on the sea in strong winds.

Jesus had finished his work at Capernaum and wanted to cross over to 'the country of the Gadarenes' (Mark 5:1). There he had a work to perform and he told the disciples what to do. Some of them were fishermen who knew the sea, and obeyed their teacher's command immediately. Jesus was not only God, but also truly man and he felt weary after a full day's work.

He lay down in the stern of the boat, and with his head on a headrest, fell asleep. Jesus rested in the boat, trusting his heavenly Father to watch over him.

The Sea of Galilee, which is more than 200 metres below sea level, was known for sudden strong winds. Cool air which was formed on Mount Hermon, frequently swept down the slopes and across the sea, causing very rough waves to arise.

Try and imagine what it was like for the disciples when the waves began to smash into the sides of the boat, and then fill the boat with water. They could see the possibility of drowning if something was not done. And there in the stern of the boat lay their Master, asleep.

The disciples had seen Christ perform amazing miracles on land, and no doubt they believed he could help them in this situation. These fearful men shouted to Jesus, 'Teacher, do you not care that we are perishing?' (Mark 4:38).

Jesus rebuked them for having 'no faith'. He wasn't afraid of the wind and waves. Standing up the Lord 'rebuked the wind, and said to the sea, "Peace, be still!"' (Mark 4:39). At once the wind stopped blowing and the sea was calm. The wind and the waves created by God through Christ, obeyed his voice immediately.

The reaction of the disciples was fear and awe. They asked one another, 'Who can this be, that even the wind and the sea obey him!' (Mark 4:41). He is our Saviour!

FIND OUT THE FACTS

1. Why could Jesus control the wind and waves?
2. When we see the holiness of God, what do we learn about ourselves?
3. On a map, find the Sea of Galilee.

The disciples had to turn from fear to trusting Christ. Think about how you would have reacted in such a situation. Would you have found it easy to trust Christ?

The fear of the LORD is the beginning of wisdom. *Proverbs 1:7*

Mark
5:1-17

'And behold, the whole city came out to meet Jesus. And when they saw him, they begged him to depart from their region' (Matthew 8:34).

What would you do if you opened your front door and found the Lord Jesus standing there? Would you invite him in, or tell him to go away? What a terrible thing if you were to say, 'Depart!'

The disciples had already seen their Master perform many great miracles. He controlled the demons, the wind and waves, and healed the sick. Having crossed the Sea of Galilee, he came to the country of the Gergesenes, because he had a miracle to perform there.

No sooner had Christ stepped off the boat than he was confronted by a demon-possessed, naked man, who had come out of a tomb which he used as his shelter. The local people were much afraid of him. They frequently tried to tie him up, but the demon gave him such great strength that he broke whatever they used, even the chains!

Running towards Jesus, the man stopped and 'worshipped him' (Mark 5:6). The demons, realizing they were in the presence of the Son of God, their great enemy, asked the Lord, 'What have we to do with you, Jesus, you Son of God? Have you come here to torment us before the time?' (Matthew 8:29).

Jesus commanded the demons, called 'Legion' to come out of the man. They were afraid that he would immediately send them to hell. They knew that in the final judgement they would all be confined to the lake of fire and brimstone. No more would they freely roam about hurting people!

The demons wanted freedom to remain in that area, and seeing the herd of pigs nearby begged the Lord to allowed them to enter the swine. Christ gave them permission to do as they had asked.

At Christ's command the demon-possessed man was sane again, but the herd of pigs, now the home of the demons, raced down the hillside and into the sea where they drowned. In this miracle we see the love of God in the Person of the Lord Jesus. We also see the majesty and power of the Son of God, the one who is the Redeemer of God's people.

The man wanted to follow Christ, but was told to return home and tell his friends of the Lord's compassion. When the citizens of that region arrived to see the demonic healed, they were filled with fear. Instead of rejoicing to see the man in his right mind, they begged Jesus to leave their part of the world. They valued pigs more than they did a friend!

FIND OUT THE FACTS

1. What work did Christ give the healed man?
2. Why were the people afraid of Christ?
3. Why do you think the citizens wanted Christ to leave their region?

Christ had compassion on all kinds of people. Do you?

One ray of mercy is better than a sun of pleasure. *William Secker*

Mark	'And he said to her, "Daugh-
5:21-34	ter, your faith has made you
	well. Go in peace, and be healed
	of your affliction"' (Mark
	5:34).

While on earth Jesus performed great miracles proving that he was the Christ, of whom the prophets of old prophesied. The Lord is now in heaven seated at the right hand of God and from there he still performs glorious miracles. Every person who is 'born anew' has experienced that saving work of the Holy Spirit. Now instead of loving sin the saint hates sins and loves righteousness. We are now going to consider more glorious miracles Christ performed while on earth.

He was once met by Jairus, a ruler of a synagogue, whose daughter of twelve was almost dead. Jarius knew that Jesus could heal her and asked him to accompany him to his home. Many people followed Christ, hoping to witness a miracle.

As he walked with Jairus, a woman who had been ill for twelve years, reached out and touched his clothes, believing that this would make her well. The woman had spent a fortune on doctors, but was no better. No sooner had she touched Christ's clothes than she was healed; and Jesus knew that someone had been made well. He asked, 'Who touched my clothes?' (Mark 5:30).

The disciples told him that there were many people about him, and it was therefore impossible to know who had touched his clothes. But Jesus looked around and saw the woman who had been healed. Then the woman came to the Lord and fell down before him. She told him her story, and Christ answered in the words of our verse. The sick woman had great faith. She believed with all her heart that just a touch of the Master's clothes would make her well.

No doubt Jairus was anxious for Christ to hurry along to his home and heal his daughter. He would have been concerned that Jesus was wasting precious time. As the Lord was speaking to the woman, a person came to Jairus and said that his daughter had died. He thought that it was now pointless for Jesus to come to his home. Jesus, however, spoke words of comfort: 'Do not be afraid; only believe' (Mark 5:36).

He then asked for Peter, James and John to accompany him to Jairus' home. Upon arriving there he heard a loud crying coming from the mourners. Turning to them he said, 'Why make this commotion and weep? The child is not dead, but sleeping' (Mark 5:39).

With his three disciples, and Jairus and his wife, Jesus entered the child's bedroom. Taking her by the hand he said, 'Little girl, I say to you, arise' (Mark 5:41). The little girl stood up and a kind Jesus asked her parents to give her something to eat, and not to tell anyone about the great miracle which had been performed.

FIND OUT THE FACTS

1. Why could Jesus perform such great miracles?
2. Name someone else who was raised from the dead by our Lord?
3. Where did the Jews worship God?

Jesus was a blessing to many who met him. How can your life be a source of blessing to those around you?

The miracles of Jesus are signs of what lies ahead ... for the people of God.   *James Dennison*

John
6:1-14

'Then those men, when they had seen the sign that Jesus did, said, "This is truly the Prophet who is to come into the world"' (John 6:14).

Many people enjoy picnics. You need plates, cups, knives and forks, a rug to sit on and food to eat! Val and I remember one picnic we had. We sat under a tree and were about to start eating when a kookaburra dived down from a branch and grabbed a sausage from my plate. I guess he had done this many times. I say this because I held out another sausage on my fork and this time Val photographed the thieving bird as he grabbed the second sausage.

Jesus and the disciples were followed by about five thousand people anxious to see the miracles he performed and to hear him speak. The Passover was soon to be celebrated and many in the crowd would have come from far away.

Jesus asked Philip how they could possibly feed so many people. His replied by saying that there wasn't much that could be done as they only had a little bread. He pointed to a boy who had five barley loaves and two small fish, and said to Jesus, 'But what are they among so many?' (John 6:9).

Jesus knew what he would do, so he told the disciples to get the people to sit down. Then, having given thanks, he handed the pieces of fish and the bread to the disciples to distribute to the people. Everyone had food to eat and when the leftovers were collected, there were twelve baskets of fish and bread pieces.

The people who witnessed the miracle said, 'This is truly the Prophet who is to come into the world' (John 6:14). The people then wanted to make Christ their king, because they thought that they would never go hungry again if that were so. But Jesus moved away to a mountain where he could be alone, while the disciples set out across the sea to Capernaum. Darkness had fallen and the wind began to blow strongly. Without warning, having rowed three or four miles, they saw Jesus walking across the water towards their boat,

The disciples were very afraid, but Jesus set their hearts at rest by calling out, 'It is I; do not be afraid' (John 6:20). The disciples helped Jesus into their boat and immediately another miracle was performed; their boat was at its destination.

Many people had seen the disciples leave in their boat, but believed Jesus still to be with them. They set out to catch up with the disciples, but when they saw Jesus they asked in surprise, 'Rabbi, when did you come here?' (John 6:25).

FIND OUT THE FACTS

1. Why did Jesus ask Philip: 'Where shall we buy bread, that these may eat?
2. Why did the people want to make Jesus their king?
3. We often read of Christ going somewhere to be alone. Why was this? (See Matthew 14:23; Mark 6:46 and Luke 6:12).

Thank the Lord for his compassion towards us. He even provides for all our physical needs.

A religion without wonder is false. *William Plumer*

September

He who des
pises the
word will be
destroyed,
but he who
fears the
commandment
will be
rewarded

Proverbs 13:13

<table>
<tr><td>John
6:27-40</td><td>'Do not labour for the food which perishes, but for the food which endures to ever-lasting life, which the Son of Man will give you, because God the Father has set his seal on him' (John 6:27).</td></tr>
</table>

People need food to keep their bodies alive and active. We work to earn wages which can be used to provide homes and food.

According to Jesus, this is not what life is all about. He urged people to think about the food that produces eternal life. He was that food: 'For the bread of God is he who comes down from heaven and gives life to the world' (John 6:33).

Jesus invited sinners to come to him. In coming to him, he knew they would never hunger or thirst. Because they still hunger for food and thirst for drink, Christians know that Jesus was not talking about physical food when he said this, but spiritual food.

Jesus knew the ones who would come to him: 'All that the Father gives me will come to me, and the one who comes to me I will by no means cast out' (John 6:37). To believe in the Lord Jesus is to have eternal life (John 6:47).

Jesus is the true spiritual bread that comes down from heaven. He gave his life to redeem his people. The Lord repre-sented his people when he came to earth. He obeyed God perfectly in their place, and on the cross he carried their sins and suffered the punishment of God for them.

All of those people, given by God the Father to his Son, are the ones who come and trust their eternal security to the Lord Jesus. The Holy Spirit draws them to Christ where they feast upon him spiritually — he is the food of the soul. Just as our body needs food to exist, so the soul needs Christ to persevere in the Christian life.

Jesus was saying that his flesh and blood would be sacrificed for those who would come to him by faith and receive his spirit. He said, 'The words that I speak to you are spirit, and they are life' (John 6:63).

Christ made the claim that he is divine with the result that many turned away. The people thought he was the son of Joseph and Mary and was just a man. They also objected to eating his flesh and drinking his blood because they thought this was cannibalism and against God's law. They did not understand that Christ was meaning this in the spiritual sense.

Jesus looked at the twelve remaining disciples and asked if they were going to leave him too. Peter replied, 'Lord, to whom shall we go? You have the words of eternal life. Also we have come to believe and know that you are the Christ, the Son of the living God' (John 6:68-69).

FIND OUT THE FACTS

1. Who is the bread of life?
2. How do we 'eat' Christ's flesh and 'drink' his blood?
3. Why did so many turn away from following Jesus?

Thank the Lord Jesus that he is the 'bread of God': the one who nourishes all spiritual life.

Faultfinding is one talent that ought to be buried. *Anon*

Matthew   'Not what goes into the mouth
15:1-20   defiles a man; but what comes
           out of the mouth, this defiles
           a man' (Matthew 15:11).

I'm sure most of us wash our hands before we eat. To eat with dirty hands is a risk to our health. In our scripture reading we find the scribes and Pharisees complaining to Jesus that his disciples didn't wash their hands before they ate.

These religious leaders weren't concerned about some physical disease, but a spiritual sickness. If some dust from a Gentile were to land on them or on their food, they would be worried that they might eat it unknowingly. The Pharisees taught that this made a person spiritually unclean. In order to avoid spiritual contamination, the Pharisees and scribes expected sensible Jews to wash their hands before eating.

Christ replied in the same way as we might have done. In essence he said, 'You are fine ones to talk! You break God's law with your traditions!' He rebuked them because when their own parents asked to borrow something from them, they frequently responded by saying that the item had been dedicated to the temple and so was not available to be loaned. This Jesus said was not the way to show honour and respect to one's parents. Then Jesus called the church leaders, 'Hypocrites!' (Matthew 15:7).

Hypocrites were actors who wore a mask so that they could take on a new character in a play. The Pharisees were great hypocrites – they pretended to be righteous people, but were wicked sinners. Christ said of the church leaders that they were 'blind leaders of the blind' (Matthew 15:14). They were plants not watered by Christ's heavenly Father. Instead, they were citizens of Satan's kingdom and were watered by the evil one.

Jesus taught them that it wasn't what went into the mouth that defiled a person, but what came from a stony heart and passed through the mouth. It is from the unregenerate heart that come 'evil thoughts, murders, adulteries, fornications, thefts, false witness [and] blasphemies' (Matthew 15:19). These sins defile men and women in God's sight.

When the stony heart is replaced with a heart of flesh (Ezekiel 11:19), the fruit of the Spirit comes forth: 'love, joy, peace, longsuffering, kindness, goodness, faithfulness, gentleness [and] self-control' (Galatians 5:22-23).

All who have been born again are brought into the kingdom of heaven by the heavenly Father. They are clean in the sight of God because they wear the righteous robes of their Lord Jesus.

How is it with you today? Do you have a heart of flesh doing works of righteousness?

FIND OUT THE FACTS

1. What does it mean to be 'born again'?

2. Discuss the fruit of the Spirit. How does this fit in with the 'Saying to remember' for today?

3. Why did Jesus call the scribes and Pharisees 'hypocrites'?

Jesus said that it is what comes out of a person's mouth that defiles him. Think carefully about the words you speak today.

Regeneration is the fountain; sanctification is the river.
J. Sidlow Baxter

Matthew   'Then Jesus answered and said
15:21-28   to her, "O woman, great is your
           faith! Let it be to you as you
           desire." And her daughter was
           healed from that very hour'
           (Matthew 15:28).

A minister whom I know well told me in confidence the story of a man who came to his door one day. He wore old, tattered clothes, was unwashed and looked starved. When my friend opened the door, the poor man said, 'Sir, can you help me?' He was taken inside, allowed to have a shower, given some clean clothes, a meal and told the gospel before he went on his way.

This was the kind of story my friend could have told many people. In fact, most people like to boast about what they do — the more who hear about it the better! This is a sign of pride.

Jesus left Israel and made his way to an area near Tyre and Sidon. There he was mixing with Gentiles because he had a miracle to perform. A house was found where he could spend some time in quietness, but before long he was surrounded by the citizens of the region.

A Gentile woman who had a demon-possessed daughter came to him, fell down before him, and began pleading with him to heal her daughter. She knew the one to whom she was speaking, 'Have mercy on me, O Lord, Son of David! My daughter is severely demon-possessed' (Matthew 15:22).

The disciples came to Jesus urging him to send her away. He knew the woman's heart but responded with words that would have given her no hope of help: 'I was not sent except to the lost sheep of the house of Israel' (Matthew 15:24). The woman persisted. She fell down before the Lord and 'worshipped him' saying, 'Lord, help me!' (Matthew 15:25).

Jesus replied, 'It is not good to take the children's bread and throw it to the little dogs' (Matthew 15:26). Jesus was saying that his blessings belonged to the 'children' of Israel, not outsiders.

The woman knew that the Lord was not calling her a mongrel that roamed the streets, but the lovable pet dog that ate the scraps of food that fell from the table. She was content to be called a 'dog' — anything to have the daughter she loved healed. She replied, 'Yes, Lord, yet even the little dogs eat the crumbs which fall from their master's table' (Matthew 15:27).

The Lord had compassion upon both the woman and her daughter saying, 'O woman, great is your faith! Let it be to you as you desire' (Matthew 15:28).

That very moment the child was healed.

FIND OUT THE FACTS

1. Who are the Gentiles?
2. What is demon possession?
3. We read of the activity of demons when Christ was on earth. Why?

Jesus spoke about those who would believe that he was able to meet their needs. Ask the Lord to help you to believe this of him today.

Divine love is so infinite and marvellous that it even praises a human being for exercising a gift — in this case faith — with which this divine love has endowed her.   William Hendriksen

Mark
7:31-37

'Immediately his ears were opened, and the impediment of his tongue loosed, and he spoke plainly' (Mark 7:35).

Jesus' reputation was spreading throughout the land, which caused the religious leaders great concern. They refused to recognize him as the Messiah, and were making plans to get rid of him. Jesus came to the Sea of Galilee, where he was asked to heal a man who was deaf and unable to speak clearly.

The people asked him just to put his hand upon the man and heal him. But Jesus was to do things his own way. He took the man aside, away from those who had brought him, and first placed his fingers in the man's ears. This he did to indicate that his hearing was to be healed. He spat upon his finger and placed it upon the man's tongue, this time indicating that the man's speech required attention.

Having done this, Jesus looked up to heaven, which showed that the healing came from God. Then he sighed. This was no doubt a sigh of sympathy for the man and for humanity who suffered the terrible effects of sin. With that Jesus said in Aramaic, 'Be opened' (Mark 7:34). At once the man could both hear and speak. Jesus told those who saw the miracle to keep the matter quiet, but the story spread far and wide.

Later Jesus found a great crowd of people following him (Mark 8:1-10). They wanted to hear his teaching and see any miracles he performed. The people apparently had carried some food with them, but not sufficient for three days.

Again we see a compassionate Saviour, concerned for the physical well-being of those four thousand people who were with him. He didn't want to send them on their way hungry in case some fainted and collapsed before they reached their home.

When he asked the disciples what food they had, they replied that they had just seven loaves of bread, (these were flat bread, cakes, just like a big pancake) and a few undersized fish.

As he had done when he fed the five thousand, he thanked God for the food they had and broke off pieces of bread and fish which were distributed by the disciples.

Everyone present ate as much as was needed, and when the leftovers were collected there were seven large baskets full. Again Jesus had performed a majestic miracle, just as he had when the five thousand were fed.

After the people were sent to their homes, Jesus and the disciples boarded a boat and set out for Dalmanutha.

FIND OUT THE FACTS

1. Jesus was compassionate. What does this mean?
2. Who gave Jesus power to heal the sick?
3. Jesus did things his own way as is seen in the healing of the man in this devotion. Why?

Jesus showed concern for the needs of others wherever he went. Think of how you can show concern for those who may be in need today?

Miracles are not to be expected when ordinary means are to be used. *Matthew Henry*

A saying to Remember

'As long as I am in the world, I am the light of the world' (John 9:5).

Jesus was God's Servant who could 'open blind eyes' (Isaiah 42:7). In the New Testament we find many situations where Christ opened the eyes of both the physically and the spiritually blind.

In Matthew 9:27-31 two blind men called out to Jesus, saying, 'Son of David, have mercy on us!' (9:27). The men believed that Jesus could give them their sight, which he did. The Lord told them to keep quiet about the miracle, but soon everyone knew.

When Christ visited Bethsaida, he met a blind man whose friends begged the Lord to heal him with a touch. Jesus took the blind man's hand and led him out of the town. He spat on the man's eyes indicating that the miracle would involve sight. Jesus touched the man, his sight returned, and he said, 'I see men like trees, walking' (Mark 8:24). Jesus touched him again and he saw everything clearly. Again the man was told to keep the miracle quiet, but soon everyone in the district knew.

In today's scripture reading the apostle John records another healing of the blind. The disciples asked the Lord why the man was born without sight. Was it the result of some sin? But Jesus said that the man's blindness created an opportunity for God's works to be seen in his life.

This time Jesus healed the man in a different way: he made a mixture of clay and saliva, and put this over the man's eyes. Jesus then told him to go the pool of Siloam and wash. When he did this, his sight was perfect.

The local people knew the man had been born blind and demanded to know how he had been healed. The man didn't know as he was blind when Jesus first spoke to him. When the

Pharisees heard of the miracle, they were furious because the healing had been carried out on the Sabbath.

First they questioned the man's parents and then the man himself. The religious leaders demanded that the healed man praise God for the healing, not Jesus who they claimed was a sinner. To this the man replied, 'Whether he is a sinner or not I do not know. One thing I know: that though I was blind, now I see' (John 9:25).

When the Pharisees asked more questions the man asked them, 'Do you also want to become his disciples?' (John 9:27). He continued praising Jesus and concluded with these words: 'If this man were not from God, he could do nothing' (John 9:33). Upon hearing those words the Pharisees put him out of the place where they were, which was most likely the temple.

FIND OUT THE FACTS

1. What was it about the miracle that upset the Pharisees?

2. Why did the Pharisees demand that the man praise God and not Jesus?

3. Why was the man thrown out of the temple?

To think & to pray about

The Lord Jesus blessed the man in our devotion with sight. He has blessed you with many things. Think of some of these things and thank the Lord for them.

A saying to Remember

Every blessing God has for man is in and through Jesus Christ.
A. Lindsay Glegg

Matthew	'You are the Christ, the Son
16:13-23	of the living God' (Matthew
	16:16).

The disciples had been with Christ for some time and had heard his teaching concerning himself. They had also heard the abuse that was directed at their teacher, and at times they must have wondered who Jesus really was.

When the Lord and the twelve reached the district of Caesarea Philippi, he gathered them together and asked, 'Who do men say that I, the Son of Man, am?' (Matthew 16:13). The disciples answered by mentioning many names, but Christ rephrased his question, asking them who they thought he was. Peter spoke on behalf of the twelve and said, 'You are the Christ, the Son of the living God' (Matthew 16:16). Christ replied that his heavenly Father had revealed this great truth to Peter.

Jesus' reply has been a source of discussion for many centuries: 'And I also say to you that you are Peter, and on this rock I will build my church.' (Matthew 16:18). The church of the Lord Jesus is built upon Christ and the confession Peter made was that Christ was the promised Messiah. The Roman Catholic Church wrongly claims that Peter's words make him the first among equals and the first Pope.

The Lord promised that his bride, the church, would never be destroyed by Satan. The keys to the kingdom were first placed in the hands of the disciples. This means they admitted or rejected people who sought admission to the church, and exercised discipline to keep the church as pure as possible. As the Scripture teaches, sins can be said to be forgiven or not forgiven in the courts of heaven.

Jesus went on to tell the disciples clearly that he would go to Jerusalem where the religious leaders would take action to have him killed. He also said that on the third day he would rise from the tomb. When Peter heard this, he privately rebuked Christ, saying, 'Far be it from you, Lord; this shall not happen to you!' (Matthew 16:22).

Peter, who had just acknowledged that Christ was the Messiah, now heard Christ's words, 'Get behind me, Satan! You are an offence to me, for you are not mindful of the things of God, but the things of men' (Matthew 16:23).

Jesus taught his disciples that they had to take up their cross daily, a cross that would bring persecution with it, and follow him, and be ready, if necessary, to lay down their lives in his service. Salvation is of more value than the possession of all that the world can offer. You and I must believe that these words are of the greatest importance. Christ must have the place of supremacy in your heart. Any other place means you are not one of God's people.

FIND OUT THE FACTS

1. Who is Christ, according to this reading?

2. Who did Peter say that Christ was?

3. How do Christians take up their cross and follow Jesus? See Matthew 16:24.

In Christ's day there was much dispute about who he really was. It is still the same today. Pray for someone who does not really know who Jesus is.

Sins are remitted as if they had never been committed.
Thomas Adams

Matthew
16:27 - 17:9

'While he was still speaking, behold, a bright cloud over-shadowed them; and suddenly a voice came out of the cloud, saying, "This is my beloved Son, in whom I am well pleased. Hear him!"' (Matthew 17:5).

To hear a voice speaking from heaven would be awesome. God spoke from heaven several times, acknowledging that Jesus was his Son.

Jesus told his disciples that the day would come, following his death and resurrection, when he would return to this earth in majestic glory and reward his people. These gracious rewards would be far superior to owning the whole world for a few short years.

He went on to say that some who stood there would not die before they saw 'the Son of Man coming in his royal dignity.'[1] These words refer to events that would take place during the lifetime of some who were standing before him that day.

God's anger fell upon Israel in A.D. 70, when the Roman armies destroyed Jerusalem and scattered the covenant people across the known world. The Lord spoke of his 'coming in his kingdom' (Matthew 16:28). When the Holy Spirit was poured out on the Day of Pentecost, Christ's kingdom began to spread far and wide. He takes up residence in the hearts of his people through the indwelling Spirit.

Judas didn't live to see these events and James, the brother of the Lord, only saw a few years of growth in the church. The disciples saw the glorified Lord following his resurrection. To them he was the King of kings and the Ruler of the world. In fact most of the disciples saw Christ coming in his kingdom.

Six days after speaking to the disciples, the Lord invited Peter, James and John to accompany him to a high mountain, where they would witness a small part of the majestic glory of Christ, the Son of God.

As Jesus was praying on the mountain, 'the appearance of his face was altered, and his robe became white and glistening' (Luke 9:29). The three disciples were filled with fear as they saw their Master speaking to Moses and Elijah about his forthcoming death at Jerusalem.

They didn't really know what to say, but they did hear a voice from heaven which said, 'This is my beloved Son, in whom I am well pleased. Hear him!' (Matthew 17:5).

Filled with fear the disciples fell on their faces. Jesus told them to stand up and not to be afraid. He then told them not to mention the transfiguration until after his resurrection.

---

[1] This translation comes from Hendriksen, W., *Matthew*, Banner of Truth, Great Britain, 1976, p.659.

FIND OUT THE FACTS

1. What did the three disciples see when Jesus was transfigured?
2. Why were the disciples afraid?
3. How did Peter want to mark the transfiguration?

When Jesus was on earth, God spoke twice directly from heaven. Today he speaks to us through his Word. Think about how seriously you read and study God's Word.

In Christ Jesus heaven meets earth and earth ascends to heaven. *Henry Law*

A saying to Remember

Mark
9:14-29

'If you have faith as a mustard seed, you will say to this mountain, "Move from here to there," and it will move; and nothing will be impossible for you. However, this kind does not go out except by prayer and fasting' (Matthew 17:20-21).

How often it is when you have experienced something thrilling, that it is followed by a disappointment. Peter, James and John had just witnessed the majestic transfiguration of their Lord and Master, Jesus Christ.

When they came down the mountain, they were met by the other disciples who could not heal a boy who was possessed by a demon. They were being ridiculed by the scribes because of their failure. People had gathered around to hear the heated words. But when the disciples saw Jesus approaching, they ran to welcome him. No doubt they heaved a sigh of relief as they could now escape from the mocking of the scribes.

Jesus asked the disciples what the issue was which was being discussed, but he was interrupted by a distraught father who had his deaf and mute son with him. The boy was demon possessed and frequently suffered from fits. As Jesus was absent, the man had asked the disciples to free him from the demon. But they had failed, even though on other occasions they had been able to do so (Mark 6:13).

Jesus asked the man to bring his son forward. He rebuked his disciples for their lack of faith and then said, 'This kind [of demon] does not go out except by prayer and fasting' (Matthew 17:21). They needed a faith that would not give up when they failed.

Jesus asked the man if he had faith sufficient to believe that Jesus could cast out the demon. The loving father replied, 'Lord, I believe; help my unbelief!' Christ then rebuked the demon,

'Deaf and dumb spirit, I command you, come out of him and enter him no more!' (Mark 9:24,25). Jesus took the boy's hand and lifted him to his feet.

From this miracle we see the love of a father for his ill son. He did all he could to ensure his son was made well. We also observe the loving compassion of the Lord for a father and his son who had suffered from the onslaughts of the evil one. Our Saviour loved his people with a love that took him to the accursed cross. Do you love him?

We also recognize that little faith does not achieve great things for God. May we pray for that faith which believes the impossible and do everything to the glory of God.

FIND OUT THE FACTS

1. Why couldn't the disciples heal the boy?

2. What names did the boy's father call Jesus?

3. How can a person increase his faith in God?

Jesus told his disciples that they needed to be more dependent on God if they were to cast out demons of this kind. How easily do you depend on God to help you in difficult situations?

The more godly any man is, the more merciful that man will be.
Thomas Brooks

Matthew   'Jesus said to him, "...Then the
17:24-27   sons are free"' (Matthew
             17:26).

Everyone who earns wages is expected to pay tax which, in many countries in the Western world, is used for the common good: building schools, roads, hospitals, caring for the aged and other necessities.

Jesus had again taught the disciples that the day was coming when he would be put to death. He revealed that he would rise on the third day. They heard the truth and were saddened. Yet when it came to pass just as Jesus had said, they became afraid and tried to disappear into the crowds.

Jesus and his disciples set out for Capernaum, where they had accommodation. Peter was walking to the house when he was met by a person who was responsible for the collection of the temple tax. He was asked, 'Does your teacher not pay the temple tax?' (Matthew 17:24). This tax was used for the upkeep of the temple and was to be paid by every Jew twenty years of age and over. It was sometimes called 'Redemption money'. This was a serious, searching question. As Jesus had the reputation for challenging the Pharisees, the questioner wanted to find out if this was going to be another disputed issue.

After Peter replied that Christ paid these taxes, he set out for home where he intended to discuss the matter with the Lord. It was the Lord who asked him first, 'What do you think, Simon? From whom do the kings of the earth take customs or taxes, from their own sons or from strangers?' (Matthew 17:25). Peter knew that royalty didn't pay taxes, but were supported by the taxes paid by the citizens of the nation.

Christ, the Son of God, wasn't required to pay the tax, because the temple was a place where God, his heavenly

Father, was worshipped. Because the disciples were friends of the Son of God, they could be excused from this tax. Christ paid the tax in order to prevent any misunderstanding with the Jews. Not to pay might have been interpreted to mean that Christ objected to the temple, and then, in turn, he and the gospel would be ignored.

Jesus sent Peter fishing, telling him that in the mouth of his first catch he would find a 'stater', the equivalent of four drachmas. This was the pay for two days' work. He was told to use the money to pay the temple tax for both of them. The other disciples were left to pay the tax themselves. This unusual miracle is another indication that Christ is God!

This tax was to be paid until A.D. 70 when the Romans utterly destroyed the temple.

FIND OUT THE FACTS

1. Why could Jesus have said, 'No' to paying the temple tax?
2. Why did others pay the tax?
3. Why is the tax not paid today by citizens of Israel?

Being a law-abiding citizen is part of the witness of a Christian. How can you live in a way that respects the laws of your country?

We rob Christianity of all excitement when we evacuate the miraculous. *Stephen Olford*

| Mark 9:33-48 | 'If your hand or foot causes you to sin, cut it off and cast if from you. It is better for you to enter into life lame or maimed, rather than having two hands or two feet, to be cast into the everlasting fire' (Matthew 18:8). |

The disciples were arguing about who was the greatest in the kingdom of God. Jesus replied, 'If anyone desires to be first, he shall be last of all and servant of all' (Mark 9:35).

Lovingly, Jesus took a little child in his arms and said, 'Assuredly, I say to you, unless you are converted and become as little children, you will by no means enter the kingdom of heaven' (Matthew 18:3). Small children are humble and trust others. This is to be the character of Christians: humble, trusting, loving and not self-seeking.

The disciples were warned against harming these little children. Jesus said to hurt a little child was sin and would invite God's anger: 'It would be better for him if a millstone were hung around his neck, and he were thrown into the sea' (Mark 9:42). Those who showed kindness to such a child would be rewarded by Christ in the world to come.

The disciples then complained that a person who was not numbered among the twelve was casting out demons in the Lord's name. This they believed was sinful and was undermining their position.

Jesus replied that the person should be left to do his work, and that he was not to be numbered among those who opposed him. The man would not be speaking evil of the Lord in whom he trusted.

Jesus told the disciples that righteousness was one of the marks of a Christian. Sin was to be hated and avoided. By using such an extreme measure to avoid sin — the cutting off of a hand or a foot — Christ was saying that drastic action was needed to overcome sin. To avoid lustful thoughts the believer was to avoid going to those places that caused the sinful thoughts. Paul had fought this fight: 'But I discipline my body and bring it into subjection, lest, when I have preached to others, I myself should become disqualified' (1 Corinthians 9:27).

Paul knew that it was the Holy Spirit who gave the strength to live a holy life, but Christians had to make an effort also. Ungodly living was a sign of being unconverted, and would result in condemnation to eternal hell. This place is called 'Gehenna', the refuse tip to the south of Jerusalem which burned continuously. It was here that Ahaz and Manasseh sacrificed their children to Moloch (2 Kings 16:3; 2 Kings 21:6).

This place symbolized eternal hell, the place for unrepentant sinners. Where will you spend eternity?

FIND OUT THE FACTS

1. Describe the Christian's character?
2. Why is sin so evil?
3. What was Gehenna?
4. What is a millstone?

Ask the Lord to help you to understand how evil sin is when you are next tempted to do something wrong.

I preach and think that it is more bitter to sin against Christ than to suffer the torments of hell.
Chrysostom

Matthew 18:15-20   'Dare any of you, having a matter against another, go to law before the unrighteous, and not before the saints?' (1 Corinthians 6:1).

Members of the church in Corinth were rebuked by the apostle Paul for resorting to the civil authorities to sort out disputes. He told them that they should be ashamed of what they were doing (1 Corinthians 6:5). Wise men in the church could listen to both sides of the argument and then make a decision on the matter. He asked the question, 'Do you not know that the saints will judge the world?' (1 Corinthians 6:2). 'Do you not know that we shall judge angels?' (v. 3).

In the Sermon on the Mount, Jesus warned Christians to be reconciled to an offended party before the matter reached the court (Matthew 5:23-26).

However, disputes do occur between members of congregations. Once there were six churches in our district, but today we have seventeen. Many groups have broken away because of unresolved disputes. Knowing the human heart, Jesus set out rules to be followed by those involved in disputes. This is found in today's Scripture reading.

First, the offended person is to visit the one responsible for the hurt and talk the matter over. Hopefully, it can be resolved in that way.

If that fails, the offended person is to take along one or two witnesses to the discussion. This follows the law of the Old Testament (Deuteronomy 17:6; 19:15). Witnesses are able to offer wise advice and bring the matter to a satisfactory conclusion. If this proves a failure, the matter is handed over to the church for a hearing and decision.

In many churches this means that the elders hear the evidence and give a decision which is to be binding on both parties. If one person refuses to accept the decision, he is to be excommunicated and treated as a heathen or tax collector (Matthew 18:17).

Paul gave advice to the Corinthian congregation to excommunicate a man involved in sexual sin (1 Corinthians 5:1-5). The object of discipline is to restore the sinner to the church, and this happened in Corinth (2 Corinthians 2:5-8).

Jesus went on to say that the final court of appeal, the church leaders (elders), was to use the Lord's teaching to reach a decision. The church is commanded to pray for guidance which will be given.

It was Luther who said that combined prayer is precious and effective. All our prayers should conclude with the words: 'Not my will, but yours be done.' Jesus assures those praying for guidance that he will be in their midst. This he is through the Holy Spirit.

FIND OUT THE FACTS

1. What are the steps which should be taken to solve arguments between Christians?
2. In what way is Christ with his people?
3. What is the aim of church discipline?

Pray that the Lord will help you to resolve disagreements with others in a way that honours him.

I live in the spirit of prayer. I pray as I walk about, when I lie down and when I rise up. And the answers are always coming.
George Müller

Matthew   'If you, LORD, should mark
18:21-35   iniquities, O Lord, who could
           stand? But there is forgive-
           ness with you, that you may be
           feared' (Psalm 130:3-4).

Christians must always forgive anyone who asks for forgiveness, because we know that God also forgives us our
many sins. His promise is that 'if we confess our sins, he is
faithful and just to forgive us our sins and to cleanse us from
all unrighteousness' (1 John 1:9).

Peter asked how many times he should forgive a 'brother'
who had sinned against him. He suggested seven times, which
he believed to be very generous.

Christ told a parable about the kingdom of heaven and the
forgiveness of sins. The king had forgiven a man who owed
him a vast sum of money. That man had a man who owed him
a small amount of money thrown into jail, where he would
stay until the last denarii was paid.

The poor man's friends told the king about the wicked
behaviour of the man who had been forgiven so much. The
king had the man brought before him and he said to him, 'You
wicked servant! I forgave you all that debt because you begged
me. Should you not also have had compassion on your fellow
servant, just as I had pity on you?' (Matthew 18:32-33).

The master gave instructions for the wicked servant to be
handed over to the torturers (prison) where he would remain
until the last coin had been paid. This meant for ever! Peter
was then told he should forgive others as many times as they
asked his forgiveness — 'seventy times seven' (Matthew 18:22).

We learn from this parable that God will forgive his people
whenever they sin and ask for forgiveness. God's people should
always forgive others who hurt them and ask them for forgiveness. We see God's grace in the forgiveness of sins. Compare
this to what we do! God's love and mercy cannot be measured.

We frequently fall into sin, yet when we confess our sins, God is faithful and just to forgive us because of Christ's sacrificial life and death for his people.

Justice and mercy are linked together. In Psalm 101:1 we read, 'I will sing of mercy and justice; to you, O LORD, I will sing praises.'

The Lord Jesus paid the debt we owed God because of our sins, and in turn we receive undeserved mercy, God's grace! Mercy does not do away with justice. Christ died as the substitute for his people. Because of that sacrifice, forgiveness is extended towards sinners who ask for pardon.

If you do not forgive those who ask for forgiveness, the judgement day will be awful for you!

FIND OUT THE FACTS

1. What is justice?
2. What is mercy?
3. What is forgiveness?
4. Why will God forgive your sins?
5. Read James 2:13. What does it teach?

We do not find it easy to forgive those who have wronged us. Ask the Lord to help you to have a forgiving spirit.

Sin forsaken is the best evidence of sin forgiven. *Anon*

John
7:32-52

'On the last day, that great day of the feast, Jesus stood and cried out, saying, "If anyone thirsts, let him come to me and drink"' (John 7:37).

The Feast of Tabernacles was a joyful feast. The people lived outside in buildings made of tree and palm branches, in memory of the nation's wandering in the wilderness for forty years after leaving Egypt.

Jesus gave no indication that he was going to Jerusalem for this festival, despite being urged to do so by his relatives. They believed that he would win popular support there. But Jesus said it was not the right time for such an open display of his Messiahship. The disciples went to Jerusalem, but Jesus going quietly by himself. Many people expected him, some saying he was a good person and others that he was a hypocrite.

During the festival Jesus went to the temple where he debated issues, including work on the Sabbath. He argued that if the priests could circumcise on the Sabbath without sinning, he could heal a person on the Sabbath. There was much discussion concerning his claim to be the Messiah, but Jesus told them that he came from God, a God the people did not know (John 7:28-29).

The officers, who were sent by the temple officials, heard Christ say that soon he would no longer be with them, but would return to the one who sent him. Later they reported to the priests, 'No man ever spoke like this man!' (John 7:46).

On the last day of the feast, Jesus stood up and said, 'If anyone thirsts, let him come to me and drink. He who believes in me, as the Scripture has said, out of his heart will flow rivers of living water' (John 7:37-38).

Here Jesus spoke about spiritual thirst. Isaiah had said to the people, 'Therefore with joy you will draw water from the wells of salvation' (Isaiah 12:3). He pointed to someone else, but now Christ pointed to himself as the well from which spiritually thirsty sinners could drink (Isaiah 58:11; Zechariah 14:8).

It was through the work of the Holy Spirit that those who hungered and thirsted after righteousness would be satisfied. Just one drink would secure salvation. This then would be like a spring of spiritual water bubbling up within the redeemed person and which would influence others.

When the priests' officers returned without Christ, it was Nicodemus who spoke out on his behalf, 'Does our law judge a man before it hears him and knows what he is doing?' (John 7:51). Don't make a judgement concerning Christ until you have considered all the evidence found in the Scriptures.

FIND OUT THE FACTS

1. Nicodemus appears three times in the gospel of John. Name the chapters?
2. What is the work of the Holy Spirit in salvation?
3. If Jesus is now in heaven, how can he be with his people on earth? Read John 15:26 and Acts 2:5-21 to help you with the answer.

Thank the Lord for the Holy Spirit who has been sent to convict needy sinners of their need of Christ.

There is not a better evangelist in the world than the Holy Spirit. D. L. Moody

John
10:11-29

'I am the good shepherd. The good shepherd gives his life for the sheep' (John 10:11).

In the tenth chapter of the Gospel of John, Jesus first says that he is the 'door' to the sheepfold. Those who desire to shepherd God's flock must enter through the 'door' to gather the sheep together and care for them.

Every pastor in the Christian church should have his eyes upon the Lord and lead believers in 'green pastures'. Sad to say, there are some in the church who are there for other reasons. Perhaps it presents a pleasant and secure occupation for them. Others enjoy being respected by the congregation. This feeds their pride. These people are like the Pharisees, the 'blind who lead the blind'.

Christ's words apply to every person concerned about his salvation: 'I am the door. If anyone enters by me, he will be saved, and will go in and out and find pasture' (John 10:9). The same advice was given to the Philippian jailer by Paul and Silas: 'Believe on the Lord Jesus Christ, and you will be saved, you and your household' (Acts 16:31).

Jesus then went on to say that he was the Saviour of his sheep: 'I am the good Shepherd. The good Shepherd gives his life for the sheep' (John 10:11).

As the Shepherd, Jesus was to unite two groups of sheep: the Jews and the Gentiles. Ever since the day Adam fell into sin there has been just one church, and that is how it will always be. As the gospel is preached in all parts of the world, believers from every nation became part of that one great assembly of believers.

Speaking of the Gentile believers, Paul wrote, 'For [Christ] himself is our peace, who has made both one, and has broken down the middle wall of separation... Now, therefore, you [that is, the Gentile believers] are no longer strangers and foreigners, but fellow citizens with the saints and members of the household of God' (Ephesians 2:14,19).

Someone once said that if Christ's sheep were to be branded, their brand should be of a foot and an ear. And why? Jesus said, 'My sheep *hear* my voice, and I know them, and they *follow* me' (John 10:27, italics mine).

Everyone belonging to Jesus is assured of salvation. Our Shepherd said of his sheep, 'And I give them eternal life, and they shall never perish; neither shall anyone snatch them out of my hand. My Father, who has given them to me, is greater than all; and no one is able to snatch them out of my Father's hand' (John 10:28-29).

When you read Psalm 23, remember you are reading about the 'Good Shepherd', who will one day welcome each one of his sheep home. Will you be there?

FIND OUT THE FACTS

1. What did Christ mean when he said he was the 'door'?
2. Sing Psalm 23.
3. What does this mean: 'the blind lead the blind'?

Thank the Lord that he is the faithful shepherd who never abandons his sheep.

Security is not the absence of danger, but the presence of God, no matter what the danger. *Anon*

Luke
10:25-37

'Then Jesus said to him, "Go and do likewise"' (Luke 10:37). 'But be doers of the word, and not hearers only, deceiving yourselves' (James 1:22).

It makes a person feel good when he or she is able to help someone else. The question should always be asked: 'Why am I helping this person?'

Christ was confronted by an expert in the law who asked what he had to do to inherit eternal life. When the Lord asked him what the law said, he replied correctly that it required love to God and, flowing from that, love to one's fellow man. This meant that the lawyer already knew the answer to his question and was just trying to trap Jesus. Rather than facing the issue of salvation, he tried to take the conversation in another direction and asked the question: 'And who is my neighbour?' (Luke 10:29).

Jesus then told the parable of 'The Good Samaritan' which pointedly rebuked the Jews who failed to obey God's law. They knew the teaching of the Old Testament which said, 'But you shall love your neighbour as yourself: I am the LORD' (Leviticus 19:18). In the parable Jesus did not reveal the nationality of the victim, but the nationality of the priest and the Levite was made plain: they were Israelites. We are told that the one who gave practical help was a Samaritan, a member of a much-hated nation.

A pastime of many Jewish leaders was the discussion of minor points of the law. No doubt they had tried many times to define the word 'neighbour'. This had become more important than the act of helping one's 'neighbour'. When the lawyer said that the true neighbour was the one who showed mercy, Christ commanded him, 'Go and do likewise' (Luke 10:37).

We have a special obligation towards our families: 'But if anyone does not provide for his own, and especially for those of his household, he has denied the faith and is worse than an unbeliever' (1 Timothy 5:8). We are to have a special love for our Christian brothers and sisters and then all people: 'Therefore, as we have opportunity, let us do good to all, *especially* to those who are of the household of faith' (Galatians 6:10, italics mine).

Christian love extends beyond our neighbour to encompass even the enemy. Christian love is clearly taught in 1 Corinthians 13. We are to show that love because God has commanded it. We should love our neighbours because all human beings are made in the likeness of God which is to be respected.

Are you willing to give your money, time and energy to help those in need? I pray so.

FIND OUT THE FACTS

1. Who is your neighbour?
2. Of faith, hope and love which is the 'greatest'? Why? Read 1 Corinthians 13:13.
3. What is the greatest act of love the world has ever seen? Why?

Think of lessons which you can learn from today's devotion.

Obedience to God is the most infallible evidence of sincere and supreme love to him.
Nathanael Emmons

Luke
11:5-13

'If you then, being evil, know how to give good gifts to your children, how much more will your heavenly Father give the Holy Spirit to those who ask him!' (Luke 11:13).

Do you pray? Prayer is always difficult, probably because it takes time and effort. A friend of mine has made himself a prayer room under his house. He has a light there and a map of the world on which he has marked the places where missionaries he knows are working. Each morning, before leaving for work, he gets out of bed so he can spend an hour or more with his Lord.

The apostle Paul wrote of the prayer life of Christians: 'Pray without ceasing' (1 Thessalonians 5:17). This doesn't mean that every moment is to be spent on our knees in prayer, but that we are to be constantly offering up prayers to the Lord at any time of the day.

Many homes in Israel consisted of one room used as a sitting room, dining room, and at night a bedroom. Sleeping mats were placed in a row on the floor after the door had been locked by using a solid wooden rod, resting through two rings. When everyone was in bed, the light was extinguished. No one was expected to disturb the night's rest by getting up and walking about.

In this parable, the father was awakened soon after midnight by a neighbour who needed food to feed a friend who had just arrived tired and hungry. It was the custom of the people to offer hospitality to all travellers, especially friends. At first the man made an excuse for not getting up. He'd wake his children who were lying asleep beside him. But his neighbour kept asking and finally the man rose, opened the door and gave him the bread he wanted.

Our Lord gave the reason for the man getting out of bed. It was not because he was a neighbour, but because his friend kept asking. Persistence paid off!

The Lord Jesus continued to say that Christians are to 'ask, and it will be given to [them]; seek, and [they] will find; knock, and it will be opened to [them]' (Luke 11:9). He then went on to say that sincere, persistent asking, seeking, and knocking would result in God hearing the prayer and answering it in such a way that his name is glorified and the prayerful person edified.

Christ gave a special promise to those wanting to possess saving faith. It is our scripture verse for today. If you are seeking salvation in Christ, keep praying, and don't give up. God will answer your sincere, persistent prayer.

May God bless all who read these encouraging promises.

FIND OUT THE FACTS

1. Why does God answer prayers?
2. In what way does prayer glorify God?
3. What are you taught in Hebrews 4:16?

Prayer is an essential part of a Christian's life. Ask the Lord to enable you to develop the habit of praying regularly.

Prayer is the key of the morning and the lock of the night.
C. H. Spurgeon

| Luke 11:37-54 | 'And [Jesus] said, "Woe to you also, lawyers! For you load men with burdens hard to bear, and you yourselves do not touch the burdens with one of your fingers"' (Luke 11:46). |

O ur scripture verse reminds me of the book *The Pilgrim's Progress* by John Bunyan. The man, Christian, carried a great burden of sins on his back. He found that the only sure way to get rid of this burden was by going to the foot of the cross.

Jesus had accepted an invitation from a Pharisee to eat at his home. The Pharisee had also invited some of his friends to be present.

The host was surprised that Jesus did not wash his hands before eating. He was afraid that he might consume some dust from a Gentile and so be ceremonially unclean. Jesus rebuked him saying that the Pharisees were more concerned with outward appearances than with the state of the heart. One of their sins was pride and Jesus said that much of what they did — tithing and occupying the best seats in the synagogue — was done to attract the attention of others, not because they had a heart that loved God.

He accused the Pharisees of being like unmarked graves over which people walked. Without knowing it, these people became ceremonially unclean because of this. Likewise to follow the teaching of the Pharisees made a person spiritually unclean (Luke 11:44).

When another guest, a lawyer, said that Christ was reproaching those present at the meal, the Lord accused the lawyers and Pharisees of devising plans to avoid the rules and regulations themselves while placing the heavy burden of rule-keeping upon others.

The washing of hands was expected of every person before eating a meal; healings could not be done on the Sabbath, unless the person's life was in danger; and stooks of wheat could not be brought under shelter, even if rain was approaching. But the religious rulers had a law that made it permissible to carry a spoon on the Sabbath. So if a storm approached, they could place a spoon on a stook of wheat and carry it into a place of shelter. After all it was another way to carry a spoon!

Christ also said that the ancestors of those present were guilty of killing the prophets God had sent them. The religious leaders had removed the knowledge of salvation so they themselves were lost. They made no effort to help others.

Elsewhere Jesus said, 'Come to me, all you who labour and are heavy laden, and I will give you rest. Take my yoke upon you and learn from me, for I am gentle and lowly in heart, and you will find rest for your souls. For my yoke is easy and my burden is light' (Matthew 11:28-30).

FIND OUT THE FACTS

1. How are people saved?
2. What place do works have in salvation?
3. Find a copy of *The Pilgrim's Progress* and read it.

It is so easy to become self-righteous like the Pharisees did. Ask the Lord to keep you from this sin.

Salvation is not deliverance from hell alone, it is deliverance from sin.   C. H. *Spurgeon*

A *saying* to Remember

Luke
12:1-12

'Also I say to you, whoever confesses me before men, him the Son of Man also will confess before the angels of God' (Luke 12:8).

We are told that 'the fear of the LORD is the beginning of wisdom' (Proverbs 9:10). There are two types of fear. One is the dread people have of God because he has the power to throw sinners into hell. The other fear is the 'reverence' a person has for God, because he came into the world to save sinners. This is not a 'dread' of God but is accompanied by love for God.

Jesus warned his disciples against the hypocrisy of the Pharisees, which was deception! He went on to say that a day was coming when their hypocrisy would be unveiled for all to see.

On the Day of Judgement the books will be opened, 'and the dead [will be] judged according to their works, by the things which [are] written in the books' (Revelation 20:12). On that day 'the secrets of men' will be revealed for all to hear (Romans 2:16). Those matters discussed in secret will be exposed.

All who belong to the Lord Jesus should not fear those who would want to kill them because of their faith in Christ. These people have no control over eternity. The one to fear is God, who has power over both physical death and eternal death. Only God can sentence a sinner to hell, and he alone has the power to carry out his sentence.

God is aware of all that is happening in this world. He is mindful of what befalls the little sparrows, and even knows the number of hairs on your head. So follow these words of comfort and love for the believers: 'Do not fear therefore; you are of more value than many sparrows' (Luke 12:7). Never will the Saviour desert his people, not in life nor in death (Romans 8:38-39).

The saints, because they fear God and don't fear men, will openly confess Christ as their Lord and Saviour. Because of this the Lord has promised to confess them before the angels of God, in the courts of heaven. To deny Christ in this world is to invite condemnation in the world to come.

All sin can be forgiven by God, except the sin against the Holy Spirit. Those who ascribe to Jesus the work of Satan invite everlasting doom upon themselves. When Christians sin, they grieve the Holy Spirit and frequently God chastens them.

The disciples need not fear the anger of others because they serve Christ. The Holy Spirit will encourage them too. They will be given the words to speak in their defence, and so bring glory to the Lord Jesus.

FIND OUT THE FACTS

1. Do you 'fear' God? Why?
2. Discuss the Day of Judgement.
3. What is the sin against the Holy Spirit?

Think about the fact that on the Day of Judgement every word and every deed will be made public. How should this make us live life today?

Proper understanding of the Scriptures comes only through the Holy Spirit. *Martin Luther*

Luke
12:13-21

'The fool has said in his heart,
"There is no God." They are
corrupt, and have done abominable iniquity' (Psalm 53:1).

We have here a parable about a man who had ignored God and lived for himself. There are many people like that in the world. They despise the God who created them and use their money to buy, buy, buy! Such people are spiritual fools, who will face the heavenly Judge all alone.

I knew a worldly man who, after retiring, went on a world trip, stopping first in London, where he had a fatal heart attack. His life came to a sudden end.

The man in our parable believed that he had earned his wealth through his own efforts, in spite of the warning in the Old Testament. Deuteronomy 8:17-18 states: 'Then you say in your heart, "My power and the might of my hand have gained me this wealth." And you shall remember the LORD your God, for it is he who gives you power to get wealth.'

The Lord had given this foolish man good ground, rain at the right time and good health to work his farm. He had a big bank balance and had decided to enjoy the rest of his life. It is sad, but riches can be a trap for people. Jesus said, 'It is easier for a camel to go through the eye of a needle than for a rich man to enter the kingdom of God' (Matthew 19:24). He warned the person who spoke to him that his life shouldn't consist only of his possessions.

Sin is not found in money, but in the *love* of money (1 Timothy 6:10), as Achan (Joshua 7:21), and Ananias and Sapphira discovered (Acts 5).

I once read a tract that had the title: 'A removal truck does not follow a hearse.' It warned people like the 'rich fool' that when they died they couldn't take their wealth and posses-sions with them. Everything is left behind for others to enjoy.

In Proverbs we read good advice: 'Better is a little with the fear of the LORD, than great treasure with trouble' (Proverbs 15:16).

From this parable we learn that we should be 'rich towards God' (Luke 12:21). Faith in the Lord Jesus is a great treasure, as are works of righteousness done humbly in order to glorify God.

Let us all remember the words of James 4:13-14: 'Come now, you who say, "Today or tomorrow we will go to such and such a city, spend a year there, buy and sell, and make a profit"; whereas you do not know what will happen tomorrow. For what is your life? It is even a vapour that appears for a little time and then vanishes away.'

Use your time wisely!

FIND OUT THE FACTS

1. Why is this parable called 'The Rich Fool'?
2. What is meant by the 'Saying to remember?
3. Make a list of the ways money can be used wisely.

The world admires people who earn lots of money and own valuable possessions. Think about the Bible's teaching on money and pray that you will be enabled to view wealth in the right way.

We are immortal until our work is done.   *George Whitefield*

 Luke
13:6-9

'Repent therefore and be converted, that your sins may be blotted out' (Acts 3:19).

The disciples believed that those Galileans who had been murdered by Pilate's soldiers while offering their sacrifices and others who were killed by the falling tower of Siloam must have been terrible sinners (Luke 13:1-5). But Jesus corrected them by saying that this was not correct. He went on to say that unless they repented and were converted, they, too, would perish. Christ's teaching was not just repentance, but repentance *at once*!

Jesus then told the parable of the barren fig tree. The law of Moses had something to say about trees which produced fruit. For three years after planting a tree, any fruit was unclean. In the fourth year the fruit was holy and was an offering to the Lord. Afterwards the fruit was freely available for anyone to eat (Leviticus 19:23-25).

A man had planted a fig tree and after a time came to pick some fruit, but found that there was none. He did this for three years, and after finding no fruit, told the workman to cut it down. The barren tree took up ground that could well be used for planting some other tree.

The keeper of the vineyard asked the owner for more time, 'Sir, let it alone this year also, until I dig around it and fertilize it. And if it bears fruit, well. But if not, after that you can cut it down' (Luke 13:8-9).

Israel was like that tree (Jeremiah 8:13; Hosea 9:10). The nation was not producing spiritual fruit. Again and again God had tended his covenant nation by sending his prophets to them, calling them to repentance. Soon they were to crucify the Lord Jesus, God's only Son.

In the parable, the fig tree was given another year's grace. If there were no figs at the end of that year, it was to be cut down.

Our God is longsuffering, but the day will come when justice replaces grace. The day is coming when history will come to an end. The last believer to be saved will have come to Christ, the bride of Christ will be complete, and the Lord will appear in majesty and glory to carry out judgement.

In your prayers, do you ask for time in which to take the gospel to others? The apostle Paul pleaded with God for the salvation of Israel: 'Brethren, my heart's desire and prayer to God for Israel is that they may be saved' (Romans 10:1).

With the death of God's only Son, Israel was cast aside and the gospel taken to the nations of the world.

In the parable, we are not told what happened to the fig tree, but you and I know.

FIND OUT THE FACTS

1. What happened to the fig tree in the parable?
2. God is 'longsuffering'. What does this mean?
3. What is repentance?

The gospel message is a serious call to repentance. Pray for someone whom you know who has heard the gospel many times but is still living in sin and unbelief.

A saying to Remember

Wherever God designs to give life he gives repentance. *Matthew Henry*

Luke	'Remember the Sabbath day,
13:10-17	to keep it holy' (Exodus 20:8).

S ome years ago I preached on the Christian's responsibility to keep the Lord's Day. When I raised the subject of the donkey being pulled out of the pit, I substituted a cow to make the parable more relevant. I said, 'If your cow falls into a pit on the Lord's Day, pull it out! If it falls in a second, third and fourth time, pull it out.' Then I added, 'If it falls in a fifth time, take out the gun and shoot the silly animal!' Most people smiled, but one elderly woman was most upset. I had to visit her and explain my unwise words.

In our reading, we again find the Lord doing good on the Sabbath Day. Jesus was attending worship in a synagogue, where he met a woman who for eighteen years had been most unwell. She was bent over and unable to stand upright. In today's world she would have been given back surgery, but she stood before the greatest surgeon of body and soul that there ever was: the Lord Jesus Christ.

Upon seeing her condition he immediately decided to heal her. Here we again see the compassion of our Lord, who used this situation to bring glory to God. He called the woman over to him and laid his hands on her, saying, 'Woman, you are loosed from your infirmity' (Luke 13:12). At once she stood upright and glorified God.

It is hard to comprehend what followed. The synagogue ruler was incensed by the Lord's healing. He was the one who selected men to pray, read the Scriptures and to preach. He would have been the chairman of the board of local elders.

Possibly he objected to Jesus doing something in the syna-gogue without his permission. However, his words clearly show that he objected to a healing being done on the Sabbath. He disapproved of what he considered to be a 'work', which, in his view, broke the Sabbath day. His attitude was that there were six other days in the week for healing people. He considered that man was made for the Sabbath, not the Sabbath for man (Mark 2:27-28).

Jesus reminded the synagogue ruler that works of mercy and necessity could be carried out on the Sabbath. Animals were fed and given water, even pulled out of a pit if necessary. Why not then heal a poor woman who had been in bondage for eighteen years? What better day than the Sabbath to overthrow Satan's works!

The people present rejoiced when they saw the things done by Christ. Remember that the Lord's Day speaks of the resurrection of our Lord. Hallelujah!

FIND OUT THE FACTS

1. Read Micah 6:8. What does this teach?
2. Jesus called the ruler a 'hypocrite'. Why?
3. What can be done on the Lord's Day?

The Lord often does the great works of spiritual healing on Sunday as the gospel is preached in church services. People are converted under the sound of God's Word. Pray that your church will be blessed with conversions.

Sunday is a divine and priceless institution.
Winston Churchill

Luke
14:7-14

'For whoever exalts himself will be humbled, and he who humbles himself will be exalted' (Luke 14:11).

Pride is the curse of every Christian. Even the most humble people occasionally are tempted by Satan to believe that they are the most humble of all! They are proud of their humility!

When Jesus was invited to a meal in a Pharisee's home, he noticed how some people made sure that they sat in the most important seats. The Lord used this as an opportunity to tell the parable you have just read.

Before the meal he was met by a man with 'dropsy'. Jesus asked those present if it was wrong to heal on the Sabbath. No one replied, so Jesus healed the man immediately. Following this he commenced his parable of the wedding feast.

At the feast the host sat at the head of the table with the most important person beside him. The least important person sat furthest away. This happened when people took their seats at the meal where Jesus was present. When left to themselves to select a seat, selfishness, conceit and pride could well be their guide. Jesus said that the wise move was to sit in a place of little importance. When the host's servants saw this, they would come and move the person to a seat of greater importance.

Our Lord was really expounding what Proverbs 25:6-7 taught: 'Do not exalt yourself in the presence of the king, and do not stand in the place of the great; for it is better that he say to you, "Come up here," than that you should be put lower in the presence of the prince.'

Jesus not only taught table manners to those present, but he also laid down some rules concerning the ones invited to a meal.

Usually invitations to a meal in Christ's day were sent to people of the same social status. This would result in a return invitation in the future. Jesus described the ones who should also be invited to a meal. He said, 'But when you give a feast, invite the poor, the maimed, the lame, the blind' (Luke 14:13). These people could never repay the one who gave them the invitation, but God would not overlook those acts of kindness.

Today this law of Christ should be followed. There are many professing Christians who have so much, and keep it all to themselves and their friends. We are to share our abundance with those who have little, especially those who are Christian brothers and sisters. Jesus said, 'Inasmuch as you did it to one of the least of these my brethren, you did it to me' (Matthew 25:40). Do you?

FIND OUT THE FACTS

1. Why is pride sinful?
2. How should you help the less fortunate?
3. How could the church help those less fortunate people?

An effective way to demonstrate God's character in this world of greed is by being generous. God is so generous that he even gave his one and only Son. Think about how you can be generous with the many things God has blessed you with.

A saying to Remember

The worms of pride breed soonest in rotten wood.   *George Swinnock*

Luke
14:15-24

'Then the master said to the servant, "Go out into the highways and hedges, and compel them to come in, that my house may be filled"' (Luke 14:23).

Because Jesus attended many feasts he was accused of being a glutton. Because he drank wine he was accused of being a drunkard. The Lord told a parable about a wealthy man who had invited many people to a banquet. The date had been set and invitations had been sent out. The guests were ready to come!

The custom then was to invite people to the feast, giving the date. As the day approached a reminder was sent to those who had accepted the first invitation. It was then in this story that excuses began to arrive. One person wanted to inspect some land he had purchased. This was a 'lame' excuse. Most sensible people inspected land before they bought it. Another man wanted to test the oxen he had purchased, while another man had recently been married. Of course, he couldn't be away from his wife!

The master was furious when his servants reported this to him. As he was determined to have every seat occupied at his feast, he sent his servants out to bring in the poor, the lame and the blind.

When there were still more empty seats, the servants were sent out to compel others, by loving persuasion, to come in to the feast and be seated. Soon no seats were available for those who had made excuses. Social obligations were taken very seriously, and someone has suggested that to refuse the second invitation was tantamount to a declaration of war.

No doubt the Lord was ridiculing some in society who made such excuses in an effort to avoid their spiritual obligation. Never must we allow earthly concerns to replace our love for God and the service we must render to him.

These people would have read in the Old Testament that a newly married man was excused from war service for the first year of marriage; and those who had just built a new house, planted a vineyard or become engaged were to be sent home from the battlefield so they might enjoy their possessions for a while.

The Jews failed to come to the great feast, so the gospel was taken to the Gentiles. When the well-to-do Gentiles refused to come to Christ, the gospel was taken to the lowly outcasts. In the eyes of the Saviour such people are precious and we read that 'he is not ashamed to call them brethren' (Hebrews 2:11).

When you are presented with the gospel, don't linger or turn away or your day of opportunity may be lost for ever.

FIND OUT THE FACTS

1. What must be done in order to obtain your seat at the great supper? Read Acts 3:19.
2. Why was the gospel taken to the Gentiles?
3. What is taught in 1 Corinthians 1:26-29?

It is important not to miss the opportunity to turn to Christ in repentance. Have you repented of your sins and found salvation in Christ? Think about this today.

There are no incurable cases under the gospel. Any sinner may be healed if he will only come to Christ. J. C. Ryle

Luke
14: 25-33

'And whoever does not bear his cross and come after me cannot be my disciple' (Luke 14:27).

Every now and again we read of someone going bankrupt because he spent all his money before the project was completed. Before they commence an undertaking, sensible people sit down and count the cost involved.

In Luke 14:26 Jesus uses the word 'hate' which means to love less. Refer to Genesis 29:30 for another example of this. Jacob loved Rachel more than Leah. Verse 31 tells us that Leah was 'unloved' or 'hated'.

Jesus was followed by a large crowd of people, many of whom wanted to follow him and be part of the kingdom they expected him to restore. They mistakenly believed that Christ would restore the throne of David.

Jesus was demanding the total devotion of those who followed him, in spite of the difficulties which would be experienced along the way. Jesus had once said, 'No one, having put his hand to the plough, and looking back, is fit for the kingdom of God' (Luke 9:62).

Now it was time to explain more fully what discipleship entailed. Jesus did this in the two short parables you have read. When Val and I built our house we had to work out the amount of money we would have to pay the builder.

Jesus' first parable was about a farmer who saw the need for a tower in which he could store farm produce and tools. To run out of money while having it built would result in his being mocked by the neighbours for his foolishness.

The second parable was about a king who was considering going to war. A wise king would compare his forces with those of the enemy and then decide what should be done. The parable suggests that if his army was small, the wise move would be to make peace.

Both parables emphasize the same wisdom. Count the cost before anything is undertaken. The same should be done before anyone becomes a Christian.

Jesus told the parable of the sower which is about people who don't count the cost. They are like the seed that falls on rocky places. When they hear the gospel they rejoice, but when faced with persecution they return to the world (Matthew 13:20-21).

If you are considering becoming a Christian, you must count the cost. You will have to be willing to sacrifice everything you hold dear, even your life. When this is done, you have another assurance that your faith in Christ is a saving faith.

Remember that God is a mighty King and you must make peace with him before you die or before Christ returns.

FIND OUT THE FACTS

1. What does the first parable teach us?

2. Can you name one thing you have that is more precious than Christ?

3. What does the second parable teach us?

Counting the cost is a valuable principle to apply in life. Pray that you will be given the wisdom to know which choices to make when you are faced with big decisions.

Look before you leap, but be sure you do so in the right direction.
William Hendriksen

Luke
15:1-10

'Likewise, I say to you, there is joy in the presence of the angels of God over one sinner who repents' (Luke 15:10).

We have all lost something precious, and rejoiced when it has been found. I know a woman who lost her engagement ring in the garden and looked for it for many years. A few years before her death she saw a magpie pecking at something bright in the grass and, upon closer inspection, found her long, lost treasure.

We are now to consider two parables which tell us about something that was lost and found.

A wealthy man, who had one hundred sheep, discovered that one was missing. Sheep usually graze in flocks, but one of the flock had wandered off. After telling his friends what had happened, he set out to find it. At last he found his sheep, and carried it home to the fold. When his friends saw him coming, there was great rejoicing.

The lost sheep represents those who were considered by the religious people of the day to be outcasts of the kingdom of heaven. They were the tax collectors and the prostitutes, who were hated by the self-righteous Jews.

They were lost and unable to save themselves, but the loving, good Shepherd sent the Holy Spirit to seek and find them. They were his sheep and when they became members of the kingdom of God, there was rejoicing in heaven.

The second parable concerned a woman who lost a precious coin. Often a groom gave his bride a selection of coins linked together by a chain, which she wore on her forehead. When she lost one coin she had really lost part of her husband's wedding gift to her. It meant that her husband would be rather upset when he returned from work and discovered the coin missing. It was not possible for the wife to hide the fact from her husband.

So she began looking for the lost coin. She would have looked everywhere for it, and maybe asked her female neighbours to help her search. Much to her joy, and that of her friends, the coin was found. There was great rejoicing. The precious coin had been lost, but now was back where it could be seen by everyone.

So also in heaven there is great rejoicing when a sinner repents, is converted and is translated from the kingdom of Satan into the kingdom of heaven.

Isaiah wrote of lost sheep, 'All we like sheep have gone astray; we have turned, every one, to his own way' (53:6). The good Shepherd, 'the Son of Man [came] to seek and to save that which was lost' (Luke 19:10). And this he has done! Praise God!

FIND OUT THE FACTS

1. How do we know that believers are precious to God?

2. Why is there joy in heaven when a sinner is saved?

3. Who does the work of the 'new birth'?

The greatness of God's love is shown in the fact that he came to seek and to save lost sinners. Thank him for his great love for sinful human beings.

God did not save us to make us happy but to make us holy. *Vance Havner*

Luke
15:11-24

'And bring the fatted calf here and kill it, and let us eat and be merry; for this my son was dead and is alive again' (Luke 15:23-24).

Many young people today want to leave home as soon as possible and do as they please. This parable serves as a warning to everyone who thinks like that.

Jesus was surrounded by tax collectors, sinners, scribes and Pharisees when he heard some complaining, 'This man receives sinners and eats with them' (Luke 15:2). Knowing their thoughts Jesus told them this parable.

The parable is about a boy who asked his father for his share of the inheritance and then left for a far off land where he intended to 'live it up'. The young son serves as an illustration of all sinners, Gentiles and Jews.

When a famine swept across the country, his money ran out, leaving him without food. He obtained work caring for pigs and was ready to eat their food, so hungry was he. Pigs were 'unclean' animals and no true Israelite would have done this work.

There in the pigsty 'he came to himself' (Luke 15:17). He repented of his sins and prepared to return home because of the Holy Spirit's work of grace in his heart.

These two aspects of salvation are seen in Christ's words: 'All that the Father gives me will come to me, and the one who comes to me I will by no means cast out' (John 6:37).

The repentant young man stepped out of the pigsty saying, 'I will arise and go to my father, and will say to him, "Father, I have sinned against heaven and before you, and I am no longer worthy to be called your son. Make me like one of your hired servants"' (Luke 15:18-19).

The man's father was waiting, looking daily down the road, hoping to see his son returning. When he saw his son's familiar figure, he ran to him and, with compassion, hugged him and kissed him.

When the son humbly said how sorry he was, his father welcomed him with the words: 'Bring out the best robe and put it on him, and put a ring on his hand and sandals on his feet. And bring the fatted calf here and kill it, and let us eat and be merry; for this my son was dead and is alive again; he was lost and is found' (Luke 15:22-24). Before entering the house the prodigal was dressed in the clothes of a son.

If we wish to be saved, we must repent of our sins and be converted. Before we enter heaven, we must have the clothing of a believer — that is, the righteousness of our Lord! This is freely available to all who have seen their sins and have turned to God in repentance.

Is this you?

FIND OUT THE FACTS

1. What was the work of the Holy Spirit in the young man's life?

2. Can you think of anyone like the lost son? Describe him.

3. What causes a person to be converted?

To Think & to pray about

This parable demonstrates God's forgiveness of sins. Thank the Lord that he does not treat us as our sins deserve.

A Saying to Remember

Repentance is the tear in the eye of faith.   D. L. Moody

Luke
15:25-32

'It was right that we should make merry and be glad, for your brother was dead and is alive again, and was lost and is found' (Luke 15:32).

I'm sure that you have often read the story of the 'Prodigal Son' which we read yesterday, but we don't' usually take time to consider his self-righteous brother.

The older brother was a worker on his father's farm. He hoped he would inherit everything. He believed that his brother would get nothing, as he was such a wasteful man. But we find that the older brother's character was just like that of the Pharisees.

First, he was more interested in the farm he would inherit than in his brother.

Second, he would not acknowledge his young brother as a brother. He simply said to his father, 'This son of yours...' (Luke 15:30). To this his father replied, 'Your brother was dead and is alive again.' (Luke 15:32).

Third, the older brother kept a detailed record of all he had done for his father. He had worked on the farm while his brother had wasted his inheritance. Because of what he had done, the older brother expected to be rewarded. He claimed, 'Lo, these many years I have been serving you.' (Luke 15:29). This was the religion of the Pharisees. They obeyed God's law, thinking that God owed them eternal life because of it. The older son could not understand that God's gifts were given purely on the basis of grace and love.

A repentant sinner did not approach God to claim a blessing. No! He saw that his sin made him only deserving of eternal death. If he received a blessing, it would be the result of grace alone. This truth the older brother could not understand. Sinners must go to God, pleading nothing but the merit of the Lord Jesus Christ. They should be able to say, 'Oh, give thanks to the Lord, for he is good! For his mercy endures for ever' (Psalm 107:1).

The words of Christ concerning the tax collector and the publican illustrate the spiritual state of the Pharisees: 'The Pharisee stood and prayed thus with himself, "God, I thank you that I am not like other men — extortioners, unjust, adulterers, or even as this tax collector. I fast twice a week; I give tithes of all that I possess..."' (Luke 18:11-12).

We should rejoice because God is good. He is the one who saves people by pure grace, and the grace of God is not determined by works.

We should all rejoice when we read the words: 'For the law was given through Moses, but grace and truth came through Jesus Christ' (John 1:17).

May we serve the Lord because we love him!

FIND OUT THE FACTS

1. What is meant by 'grace'?
2. What is the way of salvation?
3. What was wrong with the Pharisee's doctrine of salvation?

It is very easy to be blind to our own sins and faults. Ask God to help you to see your own faults before you criticize and condemn others.

Nothing that comes from God will minister to my pride or self-congratulation.   A. W. Tozer

Luke
16:1-13

'And the King will answer and say to them, "Assuredly, I say to you, inasmuch as you did it to one of the least of these my brethren, you did it to me"' (Matthew 25:40).

Many people find this parable the most difficult to understand. But Jesus uses the ways of a worldly person to teach a spiritual truth.

A farm manager was asked by his employer to explain why he had wasted farm produce. The man knew that he was guilty and would be fired. He was not up to working for a living and was too proud to beg for food.

Before he reported to his employer he called together all his employer's debtors and had them reduce the amount owing on their accounts.

God's law stated that usury — interest — was not to be charged on any debt owed by a fellow Israelite. What usually happened was that the manager added interest to the debt and told the debtor that the total including the interest was just the debt. Perhaps, in this situation, the manager reduced the debt to the legal amount. When he was out of work, these debtors would be under an obligation to take care of him. Appearing before the farm owner, who knew what he had done, he was told that he was shrewd.

There are several clear teachings in this parable, but never think that the 'shrewd' manager was a good and righteous man. He was a thief and knew he'd soon appear before his employer to explain what he'd been doing.

So is it for you and me. When we realize that we'll soon appear before the Lord Jesus to explain our use of God's good gifts, we need to take action to be at peace with God. We must go humbly to the Lord, confessing our sins and trusting our eternal well-being to his saving work. The man in the parable was worldly wise.

We must be spiritually wise in the use of God's good gifts to us. Our wealth should be used to extend the kingdom of God. Today's verse says that what we do for people on earth, especially God's people, is the same as doing it for Christ. If we don't use our gifts in God's service, we invite the anger of God.

Those who heard Christ speak were the religious leaders, great sinners and the disciples. They all knew that wealth could be either misused or used wisely.

King David said that all we have comes from God, and, in fact, we only give to God what he has given us. (1 Chronicles 29:14). Use God's gifts wisely because soon 'the dust will return to the earth as it was, and the spirit will return to God who gave it' (Ecclesiastes 12:7).

You and I will cross that black and stormy river called death and appear before the heavenly Judge. Have you made preparations for that day? I trust you have!

FIND OUT THE FACTS

1. Who was the rogue in this parable?
2. What does this parable teach you?
3. What is heavenly treasure?

We can misuse and abuse things the Lord has given us. Pray that you will have the wisdom to use these blessings in a way that honours him.

A saying to Remember

Money burns many.
C. H. Spurgeon

Luke
16:19-31

'But he said to him, "If they do not hear Moses and the prophets, neither will they be persuaded though one rise from the dead"' (Luke 16:31).

This parable is frightening because what it teaches is so real. We are not given the rich man's name, but we see him suffering in hell fire!

Lazarus had nothing except ulcers and sores which the dogs licked. He begged at the rich man's gate, hoping to be fed with the crumbs that fell from the wealthy man's table.

The rich man always dressed in his best clothes. He often wore purple which was the sign of royalty and great wealth. He frequently enjoyed feasts with his friends and brothers and had everything he could possibly want. Every time he returned to and went out from his home, he would see a fellow Israelite begging for help. Yet he did nothing!

Death for Lazarus was wonderful. The angels carried him into heaven, and there, like a child on his mother's breast, he had peace. The rich man died and was instantly in hell fire. No doubt there was a big funeral where people sang his praise and believed him to be in paradise.

The rich man was in the place of torment because he had no faith in God. There he suffered God's eternal punishment because of his sins.

We are told that both men could see each other. From the place of no hope, the now 'poor' man asked for help. He expected Lazarus to come with water to cool his tongue.

There is a great truth to be seen here: there is no mercy in hell! No one came with a cup of cold water to cool his burning tongue. That would be his lot for ever!

In Revelation 14:10-11 we read of sinners: 'He shall be tormented with fire and brimstone in the presence of the holy angels and in the presence of the Lamb. And the smoke of their torment ascends for ever and ever; and they have no rest day or night, who worship the beast and his image, and whoever receives the mark of his name.'

Now Lazarus had his heart's desire. He was in the presence of the God he loved. The rich man had his heaven on earth, and now he was in hell because he had no interest in the God who had given him so many blessings while he lived in this world.

When the man in Hades asked if Lazarus would go to his brothers and warn them about hell, Abraham told him that if they didn't believe Moses' words, they wouldn't believe even if someone rose from the dead.

The Lord Jesus did just that! He was crucified, died and was buried. He rose on the third day. Many people saw and spoke to him, but very few people believed in him. Do you?

FIND OUT THE FACTS

1. Why was the rich man in hell?
2. Why was Lazarus in heaven?
3. What should Christians do to help the poor?

This parable is a solemn reminder that worldly wealth and status do not guarantee anything in the kingdom of heaven. May you be given the grace and wisdom to live for God's kingdom and not for this world.

Hell is truth seen too late.

H. G. Adams

John
11:17-44

'Jesus said to her, "I am the resurrection and the life. He who believes in me, though he may die, he shall live. And who-ever lives and believes in me shall never die"' (John 11:25-26).

At a home in Bethany there was great sadness; death had caused a separation. Christ's friend, Lazarus, had died. The Lord had planned a great miracle, and to prove that Lazarus was truly dead he arrived four days after his death.

Lazarus was very ill, so his sisters sent a message, 'Lord, behold, he whom you love is sick' (John 11:3). Jesus had often stayed at their home, enjoying their friendship.

He knew that Lazarus would die, but told his disciples they would not return to Mary and Martha's home for several days. When Christ and the twelve arrived, Lazarus had been in the tomb for four days. Some Jews believed that a dead person's soul hovered near the body for a few days after death. Christ didn't want anyone claiming that Lazarus was not really dead or that the miracle he was about to perform only needed the command for the nearby soul to return to its body.

When Jesus and the disciples reached Bethany, he was met by Martha. She had come to meet Jesus. She said that if he had only come earlier, he could have saved her brother. 'Jesus said to her, "Your brother will rise again"' (John 11:23). Jesus went on to say the words which are recorded in our scripture verse, when Martha said she knew her brother would rise on the last day. She also said she believed that Jesus was 'the Christ, the Son of God, who is to come into the world' (John 11:27).

Surrounded by weeping women including Mary and Martha, Jesus asked where Lazarus' body had been placed. When he arrived at the tomb, he requested that the stone covering the entrance be removed. Martha was concerned that, as Lazarus had been dead for four days, there would be an odour; but the tomb was opened.

Jesus told Mary and Martha that they would see the glory of God. Looking heavenward and giving thanks to his heavenly Father, Christ gave the command, 'Lazarus, come forth!' (John 11:43).

As Lazarus came out of the tomb, Jesus told the women to remove the death shawl from his body. Lazarus was alive! What an amazing miracle!

And just as Christ raised Lazarus from the tomb, so too will he raise every body from its resting place, when he comes the second time.

Mary and Martha rejoiced in having their brother returned to them, but the chief priests and Pharisees made plans to have Jesus put to death. The chief priests plotted to have Lazarus put to death, thereby getting rid of the evidence of this miracle (John 12:10-11).

FIND OUT THE FACTS

1. Discuss the meaning of John 11:49-53.

2. What does 'resurrection' mean?

3. When will the resurrection take place?

To Think & to pray about

The raising of Lazarus showed the Lord's power over death. Thank him that he has conquered death.

The victim of Calvary is now ... loose and at large.
J. I. Packer

A saying to Remember

October

> He who walks
> with wise men
> will be wise,
> but the com-
> panion of
> fools will be
> destroyed
>
> *Proverbs 13:20*

Luke
17:11-19

'And he said to him, "Arise, go your way. Your faith has made you well"' (Luke 17:19).

Leprosy is a terrible disease. It kills the nerves so the sufferer doesn't feel any pain in the fingers and toes. Lepers are not aware when they hurt those parts of the body. Gradually the fingers and toes become diseased and waste away. A person diagnosed by the priest as having leprosy was isolated from other people. He was declared 'unclean' and would not be allowed to live in the towns (Leviticus 13:46). Life was very hard for people in this situation.

Jesus met ten lepers who probably lived together to help one another. It happened that one of the ten was a Samaritan. When the lepers saw Jesus, they called out, 'Jesus, Master, have mercy on us!' (Luke 17:13). No doubt they had heard of Christ's great miracles, and knew that this was their chance to be made well. Jesus simply said to the ten, 'Go, show yourselves to the priests' (Luke 17:14).

As they walked along, their skin became as new. They were healed! Those ten men should have rushed back to thank Jesus for making them well. Only one turned around, and praising God, returned to the Lord. When he came to Jesus, he fell down on his face and thanked him for what he had done.

The one who returned was a Samaritan! The nine Jews who had been healed made their way to the priests where they would be declared cleansed. Jesus kindly lifted the man to his feet and said, 'Arise, go your way. Your faith has made you well' (Luke 17:19).

This man did what was right. He took the time to thank Jesus Christ for his healing. No doubt he saw the other nine quickly making their way to the priests to be declared cleansed. Because the majority did not thank Jesus, it did not make it right. From this we should understand that the majority of people are not always correct. R. C. Lenski rightly wrote, 'It is still true that God and one make a majority.'[1]

The religious leaders failed to recognize Christ as the long-awaited Messiah: 'He came to his own, and his own did not receive him' (John 1:11).

Are you a thankful person? Too often we forget to thank God for our homes, our warm beds, the food on our tables, our salvation in Christ, our good health, and many other things. We should be like that Samaritan and always thank God for his kindness.

Do you thank people who help you: your mum and dad, your teacher and your pastor?

---

[1] Lenski, R. *The interpretation of St Luke's Gospel*, Augsburg Publishing House, USA, 1946, p. 878.

FIND OUT THE FACTS

1. Why did one leper return to Christ?
2. Make a list of things for which you should thank God.
3. When did you last thank a member of your family for some kindness?

There are many verses in the Bible which tell us to be thankful. Ask God to help you to be thankful for everything he has given you.

A thankful man is worth his weight in gold. *Thomas Brooks*

| Luke
18:1-8 | 'Then [Jesus] spoke a parable to them, that men always ought to pray and not lose heart.' (Luke 18:1). |

Prayer is an important part of the Christian's life. God does listen to the prayers of his people, and even when it appears that he is not answering us, we should pray on. George Müller prayed every day for sixty years that two of his friends would be saved. One was converted a year before his death and the other during the last sermon he heard Müller preach, several days before Müller's death!

God has always cared for the widow. The Psalmist says he is 'a defender of widows' (Psalm 68:5). Moses, speaking the words of God, said, 'Cursed is the one who perverts the justice due the ... widow' (Deuteronomy 27:19).

The widow in the parable had a right to demand justice before the courts, but she failed to gain a hearing until her persistence irritated the heartless judge who didn't fear God or man. This was nothing new in Israel, for Isaiah wrote centuries before of Judah's princes: 'Everyone loves bribes, and follows after rewards. They do not defend the fatherless, nor does the cause of the widow come before them' (Isaiah 1:23).

At last the widow received a satisfactory hearing from the judge. Christ then spoke encouraging words to his people: 'And shall God not avenge his own elect who cry out day and night to him, though he bears long with them?' (Luke 18:7).

The parable clearly teaches that God hears the cries of his people. He knows what we need before we ask, and will answer as he sees fit, for our well-being and for his glory. We should also know that when we go to God in prayer, it is through the only Mediator, 'the man Christ Jesus' (1 Timothy 2:5).

This parable is not intended to teach us that we shall receive anything for which we ask. Never! Let us pray according to God's revealed will, and our prayers are sure to be answered. God has promised justice for his people who pray to him day and night.

It may seem that God does not hear our prayers, but at the appropriate time we shall see him working out his purposes in our lives. We should not grow weary in praying, but continue in faith, with the assurance that our heavenly Father does hear our cries for help.

The parable ends with words that seem out of place: 'Nevertheless, when the Son of Man comes, will he really find faith on the earth?' (Luke 18:8). Christ had been talking about his Second Coming when true justice will be handed out. He asked if there would be a praying people when he returned. I know it will be so!

FIND OUT THE FACTS

1. Read James 5:16. What are you there taught about prayer?
2. How do you discover God's will?
3. Make a list of the things for which you are praying. Use that list when you pray.

To Think & to pray about

When Christians pray, they are speaking to the all-powerful God. Be encouraged, therefore, to pray without ceasing.

I am daily waiting for the coming of the Son of God.   *George Whitefield*

A saying to Remember

Luke
18:9-14

'...This man went down to his house justified rather than the other; for everyone who exalts himself will be humbled, and he who humbles himself will be exalted' (Luke 18:14).

Prayer is a solemn activity because when we pray we, who are sinners, approach a holy God. The more we know about God, the more we see the wickedness of our sins.

Our Saviour told the parable you have just read. It was a scene the citizens of Israel would have been familiar with. The Pharisees made it their business to be noticed at prayer in the temple or on the street corners. Passers-by would say, 'Look at that holy man at prayer. If anyone gets into heaven, he will.'

Christ told the story of two men who went to the temple to pray — a respected Pharisee and a hated tax collector who worked for the Roman Emperor. First, he described the self-righteous Pharisee who trusted in himself for salvation. The Pharisee looked at his works and said, 'I'm a holy person who deserves to be saved because of all I have done.' He then listed all the things he had done.

He fasted twice a week, whereas fasting was only required on the Day of Atonement. He tithed of everything he possessed, which was not necessary. He thanked God that he was not like other men, certainly not like the tax collector who forced or threatened people into giving him money. He also told God that he had never committed adultery and was not unjust in his activities. This was the prayer of an arrogant man, who was pleased with himself. He could not see his sins!

On the contrary, the tax collector saw his sinfulness. He couldn't look up to God whose law he had broken so frequently. He knew there was nothing he did or could do that commended him to God. But he knew that God was a God of grace, mercy and love. He beat himself on his chest and prayed in sincerity, 'God be merciful to me a sinner!' (Luke 18:13).

This man had seen, with the eye of faith, the holiness of God, and had become aware of his sinfulness. He was totally sincere in his prayer. He knew there was nothing about him to be proud of. Unlike the Pharisee, he was not proud of himself and knew he was not righteous. His salvation was all of grace. God accepted his confession and he went home justified.

This means that in the court of heaven, God had forgiven him all his sins and clothed him in Christ's perfect righteousness. In God's sight he was holy, and his citizenship was in the kingdom of heaven. All of this was made possible because of the sacrificial work of Christ, our Saviour. He went home a saved man!

FIND OUT THE FACTS

1. When is a sinner 'justified'? In the *Westminster Shorter Catechism*, the answer to question 33 reads: 'Justification is an act of God's free grace, wherein he pardons all our sins, and accepts us as righteous in his sight, only for the righteousness of Christ imputed to us and received by faith alone.'

2. Why was the tax collector justified?

3. Why do some people despise others?

To Think & to pray about

People are impressed by a good image, but God is not. He values a humble, repentant spirit. Does that describe you?

A saying to Remember

Justification does not make the sinner any different: it *declares* him just in the eyes of the law. *Ernest Kevan*

1 Peter
1:10-21

'You [are] not redeemed with
corruptible things, like silver
or gold ... but with the precious
blood of Christ, as of a lamb
without blemish and without
spot' (1 Peter 1:18,19).

Recently I read of a dog who was to get a bravery award for
saving the family whose pet he was. A fire had broken out
and smoke was beginning to fill the house. The dog ran into
each bedroom, barking loudly to awaken the family. The house
was burnt to the ground, but the dog was the hero.

The greatest act of redemption ever to be performed was
that of the Lord Jesus Christ for his unworthy people. Without
Christ, sinners would be doomed to eternal punishment. The
inspired prophets of the Old Testament were given a hazy
vision of the redemption that would come through the death
of the Messiah, God's one and only Son. The Old Testament is
full of Christ, the suffering Servant of God. Isaiah 53 is a chapter which describes the sacrificial work of Christ in detail.

The apostle Peter had walked with Christ and listened to
his teaching. He had seen Christ being crucified, as well as his
dead body. But he could also bear witness to the risen Saviour,
whom he had seen with his own eyes.

Oh, readers, do you see that there would have been no hope
for sinful men and women, boys and girls, if Christ had not
died in their place as a sacrifice for sin. Peter knew that slaves
could be redeemed with gold and silver. But gold and silver
could not pay the penalty for sin! The salvation of Christ's
people would cost the life and death of the one who was God
and man in one person. It was of the Lord Jesus Christ that the
prophets of the Old Testament wrote. In these last days we see
more clearly Christ's salvation.

The Passover lamb was to be a male without blemish. Its
blood had to be shed to save everyone in the house. John the
Baptist saw Christ approaching him and confessed, 'Behold!

The Lamb of God who takes away the sin of the world!' (John 1:29).

He carried the sins of his people from every age and nation to the cross, and there suffered their hell. He was deserted by God and man, so that his people might never be deserted. He fully paid our debt for sin. God was satisfied with this sacrifice for sin and three days later raised Christ from the dead!

Christ's life of perfect obedience to God purchased the righteousness we need to enter heaven. When the salvation of his people had been accomplished, he cried out, 'It is finished!' Nothing more was needed.

Sinners are invited to turn to God and seek the indwelling Holy Spirit who gives a new repentant heart and a saving faith in the Lord Jesus Christ. Have you?

FIND OUT THE FACTS

1. What is there about the blood of Christ that makes it so precious?
2. In what way did the Passover lamb point to Christ's sacrificial death?
3. What gives sinners the hope of eternal life?

If you have not yet turned to Christ in repentance and faith, turn to him today. If you are a Christian, thank him for his great salvation.

Christianity is a religion of the cross. *Leon Morris*

Luke
18:18-30

'For it is easier for a camel to go through the eye of a needle than for a rich man to enter the kingdom of God' (Luke 18:25).

Most people love the world and what it has to offer. A fortune is spent pampering their bodies and purchasing things which will increase their comforts. How many times have you heard someone say, 'I'd be a millionaire if I didn't have to buy food.' For the body we have a nice bed, lovely clothes, a car to make it easy to move about, makeup to improve facial looks and so many other things to make ourselves presentable to the world.

Most people in the West want the best the world has to offer and care very little about their standing before God. In the day of our Lord it was just the same.

A rich, young man was concerned about his soul and wanted to be saved. He came to Jesus, knelt down and humbly asked, 'Good teacher, what shall I do to inherit eternal life?' (Luke 18:18). This young fellow was a 'ruler,' probably a manager of the local synagogue. He was very respectful when speaking to Jesus. From his question we can see that he really wanted to be saved. He had done many good works, but he still didn't have peace in his heart. No doubt he hoped that by keeping the Commandments, he would win God's approval and be saved.

Jesus, the God-man, knew the young man's heart. He knew that there was something he loved even more than God; he loved his money, and he was very wealthy.

Jesus answered his question by saying, 'You still lack one thing. Sell all that you have and distribute to the poor, and you will have treasure in heaven; and come, follow me' (Luke 18:22). These words were like an arrow that hit him exactly where it hurt — in his money bag! The young man loved his wealth more than he desired to be saved, and so he turned away from the Saviour. As he left the Lord, he would have heard Christ's words, 'How hard it is for those who have riches to enter the kingdom of God!' (Luke 18:24).

When Jesus added the words in our verse, someone asked, 'Who then can be saved?' To this he replied, 'The things which are impossible with men are possible with God' (Luke 18:26,27). Jesus promised that anyone who had turned away from riches, family and a life of ease to follow him, would receive great blessings and eternal life.

Are you willing to make sacrifices for the Lord Jesus? Remember it is the same for the rich and the poor — both can love wealth!

Elsewhere Christ warned his hearers: 'For what will it profit a man if he gains the whole world, and loses his own soul?' (Mark 8:36). What is your great love?

FIND OUT THE FACTS

1. What is taught in 1 Timothy 6:10?

2. What was the young man's sin?

3. What must take place before anyone can follow Christ?

It may not be money which prevents you from following Christ. It could be anything which you love too much and are not willing to give up. Think about your own life in the light of today's devotion.

Money is a good servant, but a bad master.   C. H. *Spurgeon*

Matthew   'So the last will be first, and
20:1-16   the first last' (Matthew
               20:16).

This parable is about salvation by grace alone. No one deserves to be saved, but because God is a God of grace, mercy
and love, sinners are saved. We have no say in the matter
because it is God who chooses those sinners who are given to
his Son (Ephesians 1:4). Christ died to save these people, and
the Holy Spirit applies that redemption to the elect alone.
Salvation is all of God!

A rich landowner, who was ready to harvest his grapes,
was in need of workers to work in his vineyards. Usually
labourers waited in the market place until an employer made
an offer of work and pay. The working day in the vineyard was
6:00 a.m. to 6:00 p.m. Workers usually earned enough money
to buy a day's supplies. We read, 'The wages of him who is
hired shall not remain with you all night until morning'
(Leviticus 19:13). Those who didn't get work depended upon
charity for food.

The kingdom of heaven is likened to the landowner who
wanted to hire workers. The foreman went to the market place
and hired men to commence work at 6:00 a.m. Their pay for
the day was a denarius. The foreman then visited the town
market every three hours and gave work to men who were
unemployed. No mention was made of a rate of pay other than
'whatever is right I will give you' (Matthew 20:4).

At the end of the day the men were paid, with the last to be
employed first in the line. All those employed later in the day
received a denarius, which gave the men who had worked the
longest the idea that they would and should receive more than
the agreed denarius. When they were handed one denarius,
they complained, arguing that they had worked longer than
the others, in the heat of the day, and so deserved more. They

were just like people who believe that salvation can be obtained by works. The longer they try and the more work they do, the greater the blessing they should receive, so they think.

But salvation is all of grace. Just as the landowner paid the same to everyone, so God's blessing of eternal life is the outworking of his marvellous grace, won for sinners by the Lord Jesus Christ. All who have a God-given faith in Christ will receive the same 'payment' — eternal life!

Heavenly rewards are based upon our works. Some who commence their Christian walk late in life will receive greater rewards than those who have followed the Lord from an early age. Many who have held places of importance in the church will find their heavenly seating at the end of the row. And why? Because God rewards his people according to their works (Revelation 20:12 Luke 19:11ff).

Our greatest reward is to possess citizenship in the kingdom of heaven and to see Jesus face to face.

FIND OUT THE FACTS

1. Was it fair to give every worker the same pay? Why?
2. What is salvation?
3. What does the text mean?

Thank the Lord that salvation is by grace alone.

Our salvation is a pure gratuity from God. *Benjamin Warfield*

Luke
18:31-43

'And the third day he will rise again' (Luke 18:33).

S ometimes knowing the future can be disheartening. I was once told that my medical problem could only be solved by throat surgery. I went into hospital knowing what would happen. I'd have my throat cut! I now have a scar across my throat where the doctor did his work and saved my life.

Jesus set his face towards Jerusalem, knowing that very soon he would die on a Roman cross, after some humiliating, cruel torture at the hands of the Roman soldiers.

All that had been prophesied concerning his death was soon to take place. Christ, the Son of God, would be handed over by the leaders of the temple to Pilate, who in turn, would allow brutal soldiers to abuse the Saviour. The disciples were told plainly that their teacher would die, and on the third day be raised again (Luke 18:31-33).

The words of Psalm 22 and Isaiah 53 would be fulfilled. Even the sign of Jonah the prophet would come to pass: 'For as Jonah was three days and three nights in the belly of the great fish, so will the Son of Man be three days and three nights in the heart of the earth' (Matthew 12:40). But we are told that the disciples did not understand what Christ was telling them (Luke 18:34).

Christ was on the outskirts of Jericho with the twelve when he performed another great miracle. Luke records that a blind man sat on the roadside begging. He couldn't work and depended upon good-hearted travellers to give him food or money. He had heard of Christ, and when he became aware that the Lord Jesus was coming along the road, he saw his opportunity to be made well. The crowds had gathered to welcome Jesus. Bartimaeus, the blind man, began to call out, 'Jesus, Son of David, have mercy on me!' (Luke 18:38).

But the crowds told Bartimaeus to be quiet. They wanted to hear anything that Jesus might say as he passed. Bartimaeus would not be quiet! He cried out even louder. Then we read some of the most comforting words in Scripture: 'So Jesus stood still' (Luke 18:40).

Jesus asked the man what he wanted, and when he told Jesus that he wanted to be able to see, the Lord said, 'Receive your sight; your faith has saved you' (Luke 18:42). Bartimaeus stood up and followed Jesus, shouting out praises of thanksgiving and glorifying God.

An even greater miracle occurs when spiritually blind people receive their spiritual sight so that they can faithfully follow Jesus. Are you one of these people?

If you are, you have every reason to give thanks to God for your salvation.

FIND OUT THE FACTS

1. Why was Christ crucified?
2. Has Christ performed any miracles for your family?
3. When did Jesus say the words found in Psalm 22:1?

Thank the Lord again today that he went to the cross to pay the price of sin for sinful men and women, boys and girls.

The cross is the only ladder high enough to touch the threshold of heaven. *George Boardman*

Matthew
20:20-28

'And whoever desires to be first among you, let him be your slave — just as the Son of Man did not come to be served, but to serve, and to give his life a ransom for many' (Matthew 20:27-28).

I have a brother named John, but I don't think we are the 'Sons of Thunder' (Mark 3:17). Most mothers want their children to do well and this was true too of Salome.

She came to Jesus with this request: 'Grant that these two sons of mine may sit, one on your right hand and the other on your left, in your kingdom' (Matthew 20:21). She had observed that they held a special place in the Lord's affections (Mark 5:37; Matthew 17:1; 26:37). Jesus had an inner group of the twelve; they were Peter, James and John. Of these three, it was John whom Jesus loved (John 13:23; 20:2;21:7,20).

The disciples believed that Jesus would sit upon David's throne as King of Israel. Salome bowed down before Jesus, just as people did to earthly kings and asked for what Christ did not have permission to give. Salome wanted her sons to be second and third rulers in Christ's kingdom.

Jesus rebuked her saying that 'to sit on my right hand and on my left is not mine to give, but it is for those for whom it is prepared' (Mark 10:40). When he asked if they were prepared to suffer as he was about to suffer, they indicated that they would. The death of James is in the Scriptures (Acts 12:2).

Salome had the wrong idea of Christ's kingdom and the authority to be exercised by the disciples. Our scripture verse lists the characteristics of those who want to rule in Christ's kingdom. The apostle Peter, later wrote, 'Shepherd the flock of God which is among you, serving as overseers, not by compulsion but willingly, not for dishonest gain but eagerly; nor as being lords over those entrusted to you, but being examples to the flock' (1 Peter 5:2-3).

Peter was taught this when Christ was about to wash his feet. 'You shall never wash my feet!' said Peter (John 13:8). But he surrendered to the Lord's words, and Christ washed his feet as he did the other disciples.

Then Jesus said, 'If I then, your Lord and Teacher, have washed your feet, you also ought to wash one another's feet. For I have given you an example, that you should do as I have done to you' (John 13:14-15). Followers of Christ are called to do many menial and unpleasant tasks.

Isaiah has left an example of God's humility: 'He will feed his flock like a shepherd; he will gather the lambs with his arm, and carry them in his bosom, and gently lead those who are with young' (Isaiah 40:11).

Do you follow this example?

FIND OUT THE FACTS

1. What is humility?
2. Why did Jesus wash his disciples' feet?
3. What works of humility can you do?

The Bible tells us more than once that pride and arrogance are the natural inclinations of the human heart. Humility does not come naturally. Ask the Lord to enable you to be genuinely humble.

The surest mark of true conversion is humility.   J. C. Ryle

Luke
19:1-10

'And Jesus said to him, "To-day salvation has come to this house, because he also is a son of Abraham; for the Son of Man has come to seek and to save that which was lost"' (Luke 19:9-10).

What wonderful words were spoken to Zacchaeus, the chief tax collector, for the Roman Empire in Jerusalem. Salvation had come to his family! Zacchaeus was a wealthy Jew who was hated by his fellow Jews because he collected taxes for the Empire that ruled God's people.

On his way to Jerusalem and the accursed cross, the Lord Jesus took the opportunity to preach the good news to the crowds who gathered to hear him. Poor Zacchaeus was a short man, unable to push his way through the watching crowd to see Christ. He quickly climbed a sycamore tree beside the roadway and probably had the best view of all in the crowd.

Unbeknown to him, Zacchaeus was one of God's chosen people. Paul wrote of all who would follow Christ: '[God] chose us in him [Christ] before the foundation of the world, that we should be holy and without blame before him in love' (Ephesians 1:4).

The Holy Spirit was to change his heart and give him a saving faith in Christ. Again Paul wrote, 'By grace you have been saved through faith, and that not of yourselves; it is the gift of God, not of works, lest anyone should boast' (Ephesians 2:8-9).

Who would have expected God to place his saving love on Zacchaeus, the tax collector? However, he was not the first tax collector to receive a saving faith in the Lord Jesus. A disciple named Matthew had been called to follow Christ, while he was at work collecting taxes on behalf of Rome (Matthew 9:9). Christ calls people from all groups to follow him. There's hope for everyone!

Christ said, 'All that the Father gives me will come to me, and the one who comes to me I will by no means cast out... No one can come to me unless the Father who sent me draws him; and I will raise him up at the last day' (John 6:37,44).

Christ called Zacchaeus down from the tree and indicated that he was going to stay at his home. While the surprised crowd was complaining that Christ was going to eat with a sinner, Zacchaeus, without being urged to do so, said that he would give half of his wealth to the poor. He also promised to give four times the amount to anyone from whom he had stolen money.

How wonderful! Zacchaeus the sinner was saved. His heart had been changed and no longer would he continue in his old ways. Now he would live a life of righteousness.

Do you love righteousness and hate evil?

FIND OUT THE FACTS

1. Why were the tax collectors hated by the Jews?
2. Why did Zacchaeus climb the tree?
3. What did Jesus mean when he said, 'Today salvation has come to this house'?

Thank the Lord that he saves people of all nations, backgrounds and classes of society.

I will take my repentance to the gates of heaven.   *Philip Henry*

John
11:45 - 12:1

'Nor do you consider that it is expedient for us that one man should die for the people, and not that the whole nation should perish' (John 11:50).

Every now and again we read of people being deliberately murdered by criminals who wish to protect themselves. The same was to happen concerning the Lord Jesus Christ.

The death of our Saviour was planned in eternity, before the world existed, as the only way to save sinners. It was God's plan, yet it involved the free actions of sinful men, who will be punished for what they did. Of this Luke wrote, 'Him, [that is, Jesus] being delivered by the determined purpose and foreknowledge of God, you have taken by lawless hands, have crucified, and put to death' (Acts 2:23).

The chief priests, Pharisees and other religious leaders wanted Christ dead. When Jesus spoke in such a way as to claim his divine nature, the Jews took up stones to kill him (John 8:58-59; 10:30-39).

When the Pharisees thought Christ had broken God's law, and their own man-made laws concerning the Sabbath, they started to make plans to have him killed (Matthew 12:14).

As we discussed in a previous devotion, Jesus had just performed one of his most majestic miracles: he raised the dead Lazarus to life. Because of this miracle, many people became his followers, which greatly infuriated the religious leaders. At once the Pharisees and chief priests met to discuss what they could do to rid themselves of this great miracle worker who claimed to be Messiah.

They argued, 'If we let him alone like this, everyone will believe in him, and the Romans will come and take away both our place and nation' (John 11:48). This was followed by the words of our verse, and was prophetic: Christ would die for the people, and not just the sinners of Israel, but sinners from every age and nation.

Christ and the disciples were on their way to Jerusalem to celebrate the Passover. There the Lord would lay down his life to save his people. The chief priests and Pharisees gave the order for Christ to be arrested. In the meantime they made their plans not only to kill Jesus, but also to murder Lazarus, whose resurrection was a constant reminder to the people that Jesus was the Messiah. Many people now followed Christ because of that great miracle. (John 12:9-11).

Very soon the Lord Jesus Christ would face his enemies and die for his people. Hallelujah! What a Saviour!

FIND OUT THE FACTS

1. Why did Jesus die on a cross?

2. Why did the religious leaders want to kill Lazarus?

3. Caiaphas was the High Priest who said the words in our verse. What did he mean?

4. How did the apostle John understand those words?

Thank the Lord Jesus
that he went to the cross
to die for sinners.

There is a fountain filled with blood
Drawn from Immanuel's veins;
And sinners plunged beneath that flood
Lose all their guilty stains.
William Cowper

Matthew	'Rejoice greatly, O daughter
21:1-11	of Zion! ... Behold, your King is
	coming to you; he is just and
	having salvation, lowly and rid-
	ing on a donkey, a colt, the foal
	of a donkey' (Zechariah 9:9).

The passage in Matthew records the last week of Christ's life, leading to his crucifixion. He was about to enter Jerusalem and was determined to enter in a manner befitting a king. Jesus would not be mounted on a horse as the horse was associated with war. No, he would enter Jerusalem riding on a lowly colt, the foal of an ass, which was a symbol of peace and humility. Christ was the 'Prince of Peace' (Isaiah 9:6).

Christ sent two of his disciples to bring the colt and its foal to him. Everything happened just as Jesus had said. Then, after the disciples put their outer clothing on the colt, Jesus mounted and began to make his way towards Jerusalem.

The crowds had gathered, and they also acknowledged Christ as king. They removed their coats, and with branches from palm trees, laid them down on the road before Christ.

This was not the first time this had been done to honour a king. Many years before, when Jehu was acknowledged as king, those with him removed their coats and 'put [them] under him on the top of the steps; and they blew trumpets, saying, "Jehu is king!"' (2 Kings 9:13).

The crowds accompanying Jesus as he made his way towards Jerusalem shouted:

'Hosanna to the Son of David!
Blessed is he who comes in the name of the LORD!
Hosanna in the highest!'
(Matthew 21:9).

The words 'Blessed is he who comes in the name of the LORD' are quoted from Psalm 118:26. When attached to the title 'Son of David', we understand that the people were singing the praises of Messiah. But they failed to look at Isaiah 53,

Psalm 22, Psalm 118 and Zechariah 9:9; 13:1. The word 'Hosanna' means save now or save, pray. Their words of praise were words of thanksgiving to God for providing the nation with such a great Prophet.

As the crowds began to enter the outskirts of Jerusalem, people came out of the city to find out why there was such a commotion. They were asking who the person was who was seated on the donkey, receiving the praise of the crowd. The reply came back, 'This is Jesus, the prophet from Nazareth of Galilee' (Matthew 21:11).

On this last Sunday before the crucifixion, the crowds proclaimed that Jesus was Messiah, but soon their mood would change and they would shout out, 'Crucify him, Crucify him!' (Luke 23:21).

Human beings are fickle. What would you have said if you had been in that crowd?

FIND OUT THE FACTS

1. What does 'Hosanna' mean?

2. Why did Jesus ride a donkey into Jerusalem?

3. Jesus was a king. Where is his kingdom?

The Lord Jesus is a great king. Spend time in prayer praising and worshipping him.

Where Christ does not rule, sin does. J. I. Packer

Matthew   'But be doers of the word, and
21:23-32   not hearers only, deceiving
           yourselves' (James 1:22).
           'You are my friends if you do
           whatever I command you'
           (John 15:14).

In the temple, Jesus was confronted by the chief priests, the elders and, no doubt, by others who were waiting to hear his reply to their questions. He had cursed the unfruitful fig tree, which died, and now the chief priests and elders asked by what authority he taught and performed miracles. Jesus replied by asking them a question, 'The baptism of John — where was it from? From heaven or from men?' (Matthew 21:25).

When the religious leaders said that they did not know the answer, the Lord refused to tell them by what authority he performed miracles and drove the money changers and those who sold sacrificial animals out of the temple.

He then told the parable you have read. In it the Father represented God, and the vineyard is the church. The sons represented two groups of people well known in that age. The second son who said he would work in the vineyard and then did not, pointed to the religious leaders: chief priests, priests, elders, Pharisees and scribes. They were well aware that Christ spoke of them.

The first son represented the great sinners of the day: the prostitutes, tax collectors and others who were hated by the religious leaders. They were like the son who refused to work in the vineyard, but later repented and went to work.

The Lord has set the example for all who profess to be Christians. He faithfully and perfectly obeyed his Father. He said, 'For I have come down from heaven, not to do my own will, but the will of him who sent me' (John 6:38). Today it is no different.

There are two groups in the church. First, there are those who profess to love Christ, but fail to obey God's Commandments from the heart.

The second group are sinners, who have a change of heart, brought about by the Holy Spirit, and who obey the Lord's commands out of love to Christ.

Our world is starving for bodily nourishment and so little is done. Our world is starving for spiritual food and again so little is done. Most professing Christians work quietly in their own vineyard, doing little more than quietly sitting in the pew. Spiritual work must be done now by all who love the Lord! Take note of the proverb: 'Tomorrow is the day on which idle men work and fools reform'. Is this you?

Are you like the first son? Then show your repentance by your works of obedience.

FIND OUT THE FACTS

1. Who in the church does the first son represent?
2. Who does the second son represent in today's church?
3. What is meant by your two scripture verses?

Pray and ask the Lord to give you the grace and the strength to obey his commands in all that you do today.

A saying to Remember

Sacrifice without obedience is sacrilege. *William Gurnall*

John
12:20-36

'Now is the judgement of this world; now the ruler of this world will be cast out. And I, if I am lifted up from the earth, will draw all peoples to myself' (John 12:31-32).

Many of our plans for the future fail miserably. The plans of God, however, never come unstuck because he has the power to bring them to pass.

It was almost the time of the Passover and this meant that Jerusalem would be crowded with Jews and proselytes from all over the world. They were 'going up' to the city in which the temple was built. Jerusalem was built on a rise some 2500 feet above sea level.

Some Greeks came to Philip with a request; they wanted to see Jesus. Possibly they wanted to learn of the salvation that Christ had been teaching. When his disciples told him this, Jesus responded by telling them of his forthcoming death: 'The hour has come that the Son of Man should be glorified. Most assuredly, I say to you, "Unless a grain of wheat falls into the ground and dies, it remains alone; but if it dies, it produces much grain. He who loves his life will lose it, and he who hates his life in this world will keep it for eternal life" ... Now my soul is troubled, and what shall I say? "Father, save me from this hour"? But for this purpose I came to this hour. "Father, glorify your name"' (John 12:23-25,27-28).

Jesus knew that soon he would be lifted up on a Roman cross as the substitute for his people. In this God, Father, Son and Holy Spirit would be glorified. Jesus would fulfil the purpose for which he had come into the world: to save sinners!

There came the voice of his heavenly Father which was heard by those who stood around Christ: 'I have both glorified [my name] and will glorify it again' (John 12:28).

Then Christ spoke the words of the scripture verse, and those words signified the way he would die, nailed to a

Roman cross. Jesus had indicated this to Nicodemus: 'And as Moses lifted up the serpent in the wilderness, even so must the Son of Man be lifted up, that whoever believes in him should not perish but have eternal life' (John 3:14-15).

The Prince of the world, Satan, was about to receive a death blow. The words spoken to the serpent in the Garden of Eden were soon to be fulfilled: 'And I will put enmity between you and the woman, and between your seed and her Seed; he shall bruise your head, and you shall bruise his heel' (Genesis 3:15).

Christ would certainly win this battle! Have you trusted your eternal security to the Saviour?

FIND OUT THE FACTS

1. On whose authority did Jesus speak? Refer to John 12:49.
2. Why did so many Jews disbelieve Christ's claim to be Messiah? See John 12:37-41.
3. What does your scripture verse mean?

In the reading mention was made of people who wanted to see Jesus. There are many people today who would be curious to see Jesus, but who would not necessarily be willing to believe in him. Pray that the Holy Spirit would convict sinners of their need to believe in Christ.

From Christ's death flow all our hopes.   J. C. Ryle

Matthew 22:15-22   'Render therefore to Caesar the things that are Caesar's, and to God the things that are God's' (Matthew 22:21).

Most people complain at the end of the tax year. They sit down and try to work out how much they must pay the government in tax. Of course, in most countries in the West, taxes are used to build hospitals, schools, pay the police, nurses, school teachers, build roads and other necessities. Taxes are used to make life easier for all the citizens of a country.

You have read a Scripture passage where the Pharisees again attempted to set a trap for Jesus. They asked him a question, the answer to which would upset many of the Jewish people. They made some pleasant comments about Jesus before the question came: 'Teacher, we know that you are true, and teach the way of God in truth; nor do you care about anyone, for you do not regard the person of men. Tell us, therefore, what do you think? Is it lawful to pay taxes to Caesar, or not?' (Matthew 22:16-17).

Jesus, the God-man, knew the reason behind the question. This was not a question to test his knowledge, but a question to trap him. To have answered, 'Yes' would invite the anger of his people. To have answered, 'No' would have infuriated the occupying Roman force. Christ rightly called those who questioned him 'hypocrites'. Many would have believed that the coins were unclean because they had Caesar's head stamped on them. These people were not sincerely seeking the truth, and for this reason Jesus called them 'hypocrites'.

He asked for the denarius which was the Poll-tax coin. Then, having asked, 'Whose image and inscription is this?' and receiving the answer, 'Caesar's,' he added, 'Render therefore to Caesar the things that are Caesar's, and to God the things that are God's' (Matthew 22:20,21). Jesus was also teaching that God alone is worthy of worship. The denarius had inscriptions on each side of the coin. One side read: 'Tiberius Caesar Augustus, Son of the divine Augustus'. The reverse read: 'Highest Priest'.

Jesus told the Jews that Caesar, or any ruler, had a right to raise taxes, but every day it was their duty too to show glory and gratitude to God.

Caesar claimed divine prerogatives, and no Jew could say 'Amen' to such claims. When faced with such a demand the Jews were to follow Peter's authoritative instruction: 'We ought to obey God rather than men' (Acts 5:29).

Christians are to give honour to those God has set over us, but when the claims of rulers conflict with the law of God, they are to obey God and, if necessary, accept the plundering of their goods, and even their lives. Regardless of what happens Christians should always remain loyal to God.

FIND OUT THE FACTS

1. Why do governments collect taxes?

2. Name a law of your government which is contrary to God's law?

3. Why should governments be obeyed? See Romans 13:3-7.

Pray for the leaders of your country that they will learn to fear God and to honour his laws in the way they rule the country.

Christ lovers prove their love by their obedience.   *John R. Stott*

A saying to Remember

Matthew   'You shall love the LORD your
22:34-38   God with all your heart, with
              all your soul, and with all your
              mind' (Matthew 22:37).

The Lord had silenced the hypocritical Sadducees who asked him a question concerning the resurrection; a truth which they denied (Matthew 22:23-33). Now the Pharisees decided to have one of their own, a man very well skilled in the Scriptures asked Christ which commandment he believed to be the most important.

The church leaders of that era spent many long hours discussing matters of little importance concerning God's law — which was the greatest commandment and which was the least important. It was generally believed that the least most important law of God was the requirement that one egg be left in a bird's nest when the nest was being raided.

The lawyer asked Christ a serious question: 'Teacher, which is the great commandment in the law?' (Matthew 22:36). To that honest question Christ gave a reply which is today's text.

But why should people love God? First, we love God because of all that he has done for us. He gives us life, our mental and physical abilities and a home in which to live. God gives us the people we live with, wives, husbands, fathers, mothers, brothers, sisters and grandparents.

We love God because of the salvation we have in his Son, the Lord Jesus. The Holy Spirit awakens the consciences of sinners to God's warning: 'It is appointed for men to die once, but after this the judgement' (Hebrews 9:27). When we see our sins, the Holy Spirit leads us to Jesus, where we find forgiveness and are given his righteousness. This is a love which comes from the knowledge of what God has done for us. It has the word 'because' in it: 'I love God because he saved me.'

The second reason for loving God is because of his attributes. Most people don't get married to someone until they discover something about the person's character. The same applies to our relationship with God.

We see God as a God of grace who pours blessings upon the greatest of sinners who deserve nothing but hell. He is a God of love and mercy, a God who is very patient with sinners, a God of power, wisdom and perfect justice.

The Holy Spirit opens people's eyes to behold the glory of Christ. Paul writes, 'For in [Christ] dwells all the fulness of the Godhead bodily' (Colossians 2:9). The very essence of the fulness of deity dwells in Christ, for he is God. Just as the apostle John wrote, 'In the beginning was the Word, and the Word was with God, and the Word was God' (John 1:1).

The glory of God is summarized well in the answer to question 4 of the *Westminster Shorter Catechism*: 'God is Spirit, infinite, eternal and unchangeable; in his being, wisdom, power, holiness, justice, goodness and truth.'

Do you love God?

FIND OUT THE FACTS

1. Why should we love God?
2. What has God done for you?
3. Make a list of God's attributes.

We can only love God as we should if he gives us the grace to do so. Pray for the grace to love God with all your being.

Even the heart of God thirsts after love. *Abraham Kuyper*

Mark
12:28-37

'You shall not take vengeance, nor bear any grudge against the children of your people, but you shall love your neighbour as yourself: I am the LORD' (Leviticus 19:18).

The lawyer was not given just one law but two that are bound together. First, sinners are to love God totally. But this law doesn't stand alone because Christ went on to say, 'And the second, like it, is this: "You shall love your neighbour as yourself"' (Mark 12:31).

This teaches us that our love for our fellow man is at the highest level. We must be ready to pick him up when he falls and help him whenever possible. Of course, we must know who our neighbour is. The Lord answered this question when he told the parable of the Good Samaritan (Luke 10:29-37).

When Christ heard the lawyer's accurate reply, he said to him, 'You are not far from the kingdom of God' (Mark 12:34). This man knew the truth, but he knew it intellectually and not in his heart.

He was apparently a righteous Pharisee, who had what he thought was a love for God. What was needed to gain entry into the kingdom of God was the new birth. He needed to become a new person with a saving faith in Christ and a repentant heart.

As a new person he would love his neighbour because the fruit of the Spirit would be formed in his heart. That fruit is 'love, joy, peace, longsuffering, kindness, goodness, faithfulness, gentleness, self control' (Galatians 5:22-23).

Love is the queen of the graces, and from love all others flow. Jesus gave the command, 'Love your enemies, bless those who curse you, do good to those who hate you, and pray for those who spitefully use you and persecute you' (Matthew 5:44).

The love spoken of here is not the love that exists between a husband and wife or between friends, but is a love that is controlled by the mind. Christian love is seen in the behaviour between people, a love that denies self in order to assist another. It is a love that involves a readiness to spend and be spent for others.

It is the love that Paul wrote about in 1 Corinthians 13:1-13. It is patient, kind, does not envy, does not boast, is not rude, does not demand its rights, is not resentful of others, does not think evil about other people, does not rejoice when others are hurt, endures the rebuffs of the world, and is not suspicious of the actions of another.

It is a love that reaches out in compassion to others without expecting anything in return. Christian love is the 'fulfilment of the law' (Romans 13:10). This love never fails.

FIND OUT THE FACTS

1. How many times are you to forgive others?
2. Why should you love other people?
3. Which is the greatest faith, hope or love? Why?
   Read 1 Corinthians 13.

Think of ways in which you can show the kind of love described in 1 Corinthians 13.

Brotherly love is the badge of Christ's disciples.   *Matthew Henry*

Matthew
22:1-14

'Then the king said to the servants, "Bind him hand and foot,
take him away, and cast him
into outer darkness; there will
be weeping and gnashing of
teeth"' (Matthew 22:13).

Here we have a parable about salvation. It tells us about those who believe the gospel and those who reject it.

I'm sure that most of my readers have been to a wedding where some guests have failed to appear. This parable is about a king (God) who is preparing a wedding for his Son (The Lord Jesus). The messengers are the prophets and preachers of the gospel.

The good news of salvation was initially given to the Jewish people. The apostle John wrote, 'He came to his own, and his own did not receive him. But as many as received him, to them he gave the right to become children of God, to those who believe in his name' (John 1:11-12). The people invited to this wedding feast refused to come, even killing some who presented the invitation (Acts 7:52-53).

As a nation, the Jews rejected the Lord Jesus as their Messiah. The rulers crucified him, believing that with his death his influence would end. However, the king sent out his armies to destroy those wicked people. In A.D. 70, the Roman armies overthrew Jerusalem and scattered the Jews across the world of that day.

Very few of God's covenant people looked to Christ as their Lord and Saviour. But the apostles, especially Paul, preached the good news concerning salvation in Christ. The gospel soon spread far and wide, into the highways, byways, streets and lanes. Many have been saved and invited to the great wedding feast in the eternal kingdom of heaven.

Again there is the warning: to have a place in this kingdom, people must come in the appropriate way. One of those who arrived at the wedding feast was not correctly dressed. The king had handed out the same suit of clothing to every guest who found salvation through faith in the Lord Jesus, a salvation all of grace.

God will bless his people as he sees fit. The last into the kingdom may well receive greater blessings than some who have been believers for a long time.

The interloper wore his own clothes, as did the Pharisees of the Lord's day. They wore a clothing of their own good works. The Scriptures clearly state: 'By the deeds of the law no flesh will be justified in [God's] sight' (Romans 3:20).

Jesus won salvation for his people, and they alone will wear the robe of Christ's righteousness. God will reject every person who does not live by faith in Christ. The destiny of such an individual is hell — the hopelessness of outer darkness.

FIND OUT THE FACTS

1. How is hell described in this parable?

2. Who is the bride of Christ? See Ephesians 5:22-33 and Revelation 21:9

3. Why is there a hell?

The Bible teaches that hell is a real place. If you know someone who is involved in the work of evangelism, pray that the Lord will make his work effective.

I have no right to work out my own salvation in the way I choose. *Helen Roseveare*

A saying to Remember

Matthew
23:24-36

'The scribes and the Pharisees sit in Moses' seat. Therefore whatever they tell you to observe, that observe and do, but do not do according to their works; for they say, and do not do' (Matthew 23:2-3).

How many times have you said of someone, 'That person doesn't practise what he preaches.' In other words he doesn't do what he tells others to do. That is what our scripture verse says about the Scribes and Pharisees. Jesus warned the people that they were to obey the religious leaders only in so far as they taught God's truth. But they needed to be especially wary of the Scribes and Pharisees, who didn't put into practice God's revealed will.

These people put heavy spiritual loads on the people: do this, do that, do what we tell you and you will be saved. The people stumbled along in an effort to gain salvation, obeying as far as possible not only the laws of God, but also all the laws and restrictions imposed on them by the Scribes and Pharisees. That is why Christ said to the people, 'Come to me, all you who labour and are heavy laden, and I will give you rest. Take my yoke upon you and learn from me, for I am gentle and lowly in heart, and you will find rest for your souls. For my yoke is easy and my burden is light' (Matthew 11:28-30). Salvation is not to be earned by keeping rules and regulations, but by a childlike faith in Christ.

The Pharisees and Scribes were proud men who acted the part of godly men before the people. They made sure they prayed where everyone could see them. When they put their gift into the temple treasury, they also made sure people saw and heard what they did.

Matthew 23:1-36 is an account of Christ exposing the Scribes and Pharisees. He spoke the truth about them, calling them fools and blind guides who were full of hypocrisy. They were serpents, a brood of vipers who gave the outward impression of being godly people, but inside were like the inside of a tomb filled with decomposing bodies.

Christians must be wary of acting like those people. Sometimes church leaders have special laws for church members, dictating to them what they should wear, where they should go and how they should conduct themselves in worship.

We should know the Bible in order to counter the arguments of those people who make rules they expect others to follow. Our Lord looks on the heart.

Christ plainly told the Scribes and Pharisees that unless they repented their destiny was eternal punishment!

You are called to obey God's law, not a host of man-made laws. There is a true liberty in serving Christ. Enjoy that liberty and faithfully serve your Lord and Saviour, Jesus Christ.

FIND OUT THE FACTS

1. How many 'woes' are there in the scripture passage?
2. What is a Pharisee?
3. What is Christ teaching us in Matthew 23:26-28?

Hypocrisy is a sin which tempts us all. Ask the Lord for the grace to resist this temptation.

Hypocrisy is nothing better than skin-deep holiness. *Anon*

Mark
12:41-44

'This poor widow has put in more than all those who have given to the treasury; for they all put in out of their abundance, but she out of her poverty put in all that she had, her whole livelihood' (Mark 12:43-44).

John Paton, the missionary to the New Hebrides in the nineteenth century, encouraged children to use money boxes to save for the purchase of a ship for mission work. Many small amounts, added together, made up a large sum of money. Christians have a God-given duty to support the work of the church.

Jesus was in the temple with his disciples. They could see people coming and giving to support the temple activities. What counted as far as the Lord was concerned, was not the amount that was given, but the state of the heart.

A poor widow came and dropped into the receptacle all she had, because she wanted to see the work of God progress. Any Pharisee, who witnessed the giving, would have mocked the widow. Yet in God's sight the offering was precious. She gave all she had.

Paul summed up the Christian's responsibility to give to the Lord's work in this way: 'So let each one give as he purposes in his heart, not grudgingly or of necessity; for God loves a cheerful giver' (2 Corinthians 9:7). Yes, Christians are to support the church, and this includes the wages of the pastor.

Again Paul wrote, 'For the Scripture says, "You shall not muzzle an ox while it treads out the grain," and "The labourer is worthy of his wages"' (1 Timothy 5:18; Deuteronomy 25:4). Just as the ox was allowed to take a mouthful of the grain that he was threshing, so the pastor is entitled to his pay.

Collections should be taken to assist people and congregations that are in need. Paul gave instructions concerning the collection being taken to help the saints in Jerusalem: 'On the first day of the week let each one of you lay something aside, storing up as he may prosper, that there be no collections when I come' (1 Corinthians 16:2).

When families make decisions about how much money will be given to the Lord's work, it is important that the Lord be given the best, the first fruits, and not the leftovers.

In making that decision, we should do so in the light of Paul's words: 'For you know the grace of our Lord Jesus Christ, that though he was rich, yet for your sakes he became poor, that you through his poverty might become rich' (2 Corinthians 8:9).

Our salvation cost God the death of his Son. Christians owe God everything!

FIND OUT THE FACTS

1. What did your salvation cost God?
2. How do you determine what family money is given to the Lord's work?
3. Make a list of areas of the Lord's work that should be supported financially.

Pray for missionaries who are supported by your local church. What can you give or what can you do to encourage them?

True liberality is the sponta-neous expression of love.
Geoffrey B. Wilson

Matthew   'O Jerusalem, Jerusalem, the
24:1-14   one who kills the prophets and
               stones those who are sent to
               her! How often I wanted to
               gather your children together,
               as a hen gathers her chicks
               under her wings, but you were
               not willing!' (Matthew 23:37).

The day of Christ's crucifixion had almost arrived. As he looked out over Jerusalem he saw the tragedy that would soon befall the nation. His words are filled with tenderness and love towards the covenant people who had been shepherded by God over many centuries.

Christ's efforts to gather the people under the shelter of his salvation had not drawn much response, and soon they would experience the anger of God, whose Son they were about to kill. There would be a remnant who, through the ages to come, would believe.

When Christ and the disciples reached the Mount of Olives, he sat down and was asked by the disciples to look in the direction of the temple. Jesus told them that the temple would be destroyed. So, they asked three questions. First, when would the temple be destroyed? Second, what would be the sign of Christ's return? And third, when would the age come to an end? Jesus sat down and answered their questions.

The first section of Christ's discourse (Matthew 24:4-35) concerned the destruction of the temple and the end of the age for the nation. Then came revelations concerning the return of the Lord (Matthew 24: 36-44).[1]

The passage you have read speaks about the situation that would arise following Christ's crucifixion. There would be warfare, earthquakes and Christians would be hated. They would also hear many people claiming to be the Christ.

Then came the statement: 'Therefore when you see the "abomination of desolation," spoken of by Daniel the prophet, standing in the holy place ... then let those who are in Judea flee to the mountains' (Matthew 24:15,16).

This made reference to the appearance of the Roman army in A.D. 70. The Christians escaped to the hills before Jerusalem was completely surrounded. There are also prophecies concerning the destruction of Jerusalem: 'Assuredly, I say to you, this generation will by no means pass away till all these things are fulfilled. Heaven and earth will pass away, but my words will by no means pass away' (Matthew 24:34-35).

Soon the temple, the pride of Israel, would be no more. No longer would there be sacrifices, because the one and only acceptable sacrifice for sin had been made. The Lord Jesus would have fulfilled his saving work and would be seated upon his heavenly throne. Soon he would send judgement upon the covenant people.

---

[1] There are a variety of interpretations of Matthew 24. See Hamilton,F., *The Basis of Millennial Faith*, Wm. Eerdmans Publishing Company, USA., 1955.

FIND OUT THE FACTS

1. Why was the temple so important to the Israelites?
2. Why can Christ be called a Priest?
3. What does Matthew 24:34-35 mean?

The end of our age will most surely come. Are you ready to meet the King of kings and Lord of lords?

In the history of the world no judgement can be compared with this that wiped out the Jews as a nation.   R. C. Lenski

A saying to Remember

Matthew   'But of that day and hour no
24:36-51   one knows, not even the angels
             of heaven, but my Father only'
             (Matthew 24:36).

Events are always taking place which cause people to predict the end of the world and the return of Christ. The passage of Scripture you have read teaches us that only the heavenly Father knows the time of Christ's return. Even Jesus Christ, the God-man, was unaware of the date.

From our reading we are taught that Christ's coming will be sudden and unannounced. The affairs of this world will be going on as usual, and suddenly the heavens will be opened, history will come to an end and the Lord Jesus Christ will descend from heaven with his mighty angels.

The purpose of Christ's return is to gather together his people, establish the judgement, and send all ungodly people into hell.

The Scriptures contain awe inspiring descriptions of this event. Paul wrote, 'When the Lord Jesus is revealed from heaven with his mighty angels, in flaming fire taking vengeance on those who do not know God, and on those who do not obey the gospel of our Lord Jesus Christ. These shall be punished with everlasting destruction from the presence of the Lord and from the glory of his power, when he comes, in that day, to be glorified in his saints and to be admired among all those who believe ...' (2 Thessalonians 1:7-10).

The Scripture passage tells us that some will be taken and others left behind. These passages should make us aware that not everyone will be saved and rise to meet the Lord in the air. No, only those who are born again are members of the kingdom. They alone will rise to be with Christ.

Every person who has ever lived, will stand before the Judge, Jesus Christ, to receive the verdict concerning his or her eternal destiny. All whose names are written in the Lamb's book of life will enter paradise and enjoy the presence of the Lamb of God for ever.

The Scriptures give some clues as to the time of Christ's return, but our reading tells us to be prepared to meet Christ every day.

We are encouraged to be busy in the Lord's work, which means that whatever work we do, we should do it as if it were being done for the Lord. Housewives should care for the house and family members as if they were doing this for Christ himself. Children at school will do the best work they can, again as if they are studying for the Lord himself; and men will do their work as if they are working for the Lord.

Are you prepared to meet the Lord Jesus Christ?

In the parable Christ warns professing Christians to live a holy life in anticipation of the Lord's return. He will come at the most unexpected moment!

FIND OUT THE FACTS

1. When will Christ return?
2. Who will rise to meet the Lord in the air?
3. How should Christians live each day?

Pray today that you will be prepared to meet the Lord at his return.

That day lies hidden that every day we be on the watch. *Augustine*

Matthew   '... having a form of godliness
25:1-13   but denying its power. And
             from such people turn away!'
             (2 Timothy 3:5).

When I look at the assembled church I wonder if every one is a servant of the Lord Jesus. The parable of the wise and foolish virgins describes a church where every member claims to be a Christian.

Ten young virgins went out to meet the bridegroom. They were all excited and kept watching and waiting for the groom. At first everyone was awake, but when the groom was delayed, they fell asleep. Suddenly all ten virgins were awakened by a cry at midnight, 'Behold, the bridegroom is coming; go out to meet him!' (Matthew 25:6).

While the five wise virgins trimmed their lamps, poured in the oil they had carried with them and prepared to meet the groom, the five foolish virgins found that they had no oil. When they asked for some from their well-prepared friends, the answer was, 'No.'

While the five foolish young women went to buy some oil, the five wise ones went into the wedding ceremony and the door was shut.

The foolish virgins returned and knocked on the closed door, asking for permission to enter. They were told, 'Assuredly, I say to you, I do not know you' (Matthew 25:12).

Then the Lord Jesus told his hearers, 'Watch, therefore, for you know neither the day nor the hour in which the Son of Man is coming' (Matthew 25:13).

This is a parable about our preparation for the second coming of Christ Jesus. The parable speaks about the visible church, all those who profess saving faith in the Lord Jesus. The wise virgins are those church members who love God and have a saving faith in the Lord Jesus. They are the people who, by God's grace, keep God's Commandments. They are people who hate sin and love righteousness. They have been justified in heaven's court, adopted into God's family, and are being sanctified. They are Christians who cope with the difficulties of life because of the grace of God.

The five foolish virgins are strangers to grace. They are strangers to the new birth, and enjoy their way of life in this world. They may be very moral people most of the time but they are proud of their good works. Of these people Christ said, 'I do not know you!' (Matthew 25:12).

The five foolish virgins often know in their hearts that they are hypocrites, but they expect to be able to believe in Christ when death approaches. In fact, they really sin and waste their life.

The grace of God is the oil in the lamps carried by the wise virgins. The grace of God helps Christians cope with whatever difficulties they face in life. In which group do you belong?

FIND OUT THE FACTS

1. In the church which people are represented by the wise virgins?

2. For what does the 'oil' stand?

3. In the church which people are represented by the foolish virgins?

Pray asking God to make you like the wise virgins who were prepared for the bridegroom's coming.

Grace will last when gold is past.
C. H. Spurgeon

Matthew 'And cast the unprofitable
25:14-30 servant into the outer darkness. There will be weeping and
gnashing of teeth' (Matthew
25:30).

Many people don't fear death, believing that the grave is the end of existence. Others believe that God will allow everyone to enter heaven. They have frequently heard ministers say this at the funerals of ungodly people.

This is not taught in Scripture! Very plainly we are told, 'It is appointed for men to die once, but after this the judgement' (Hebrews 9:27). Every person who has ever lived will one day face the judgement seat of the Lord Jesus.

This parable is of a wealthy man who, before leaving on a journey, gave his three servants some money. Upon his return he called them together to get a report on what they had done with the money. Two proved very successful business men, each doubling the money. The third man had simply hidden the money and could only return to the man the sum he had been given.

This parable was told to the disciples only a few days before the Lord's crucifixion. They were being taught several great truths that would apply to every person who claimed to be a Christian.

First, every Christian has been given abilities to be used in the service of the Lord. Not everyone will be a Luther or a Paul, but we all have God-given gifts.

Second, there will be a day of reckoning when Christ returns in majestic glory. Every Christian will face the Judge to give an account of the use made of his gifts. We are saved by faith alone, but that saving faith is never alone; it is united to works of righteousness (James 2:14-17; Ephesians 2:8-10).

The master rewarded his faithful servants. When he spoke to the third man, he was given a feeble excuse. This man said that he knew his master was hard and demanding. So, he did nothing except dig a hole and bury the money. Consequently, he was taken from the presence of his master, and with the words, 'You wicked and lazy servant' ringing in his ears, was thrown into hell (Matthew 25:26,30).

Christians are to confess Christ before men (Romans 10:9-10), and are to take up their cross daily to follow the Redeemer. The gospel has been entrusted to his people. It must be spread!

We all have different gifts and should not condemn others who are different from us. Each Christian is responsible to the Lord for what he does. For others to criticize another believer's service to the Lord is sin! Paul wrote, 'Who are you to judge another's servant? To his own master he stands or falls' (Romans 14:4; James 4:11-12).

Let us keep our eyes upon the Lord Jesus and serve him faithfully. And why? Because we love our Saviour!

FIND OUT THE FACTS

1. Who does the master in the parable represent?
2. When is the judgement day?
3. What are you taught in Matthew 25:30?

Think about what gifts you have which could be used in the Lord's work.

The judgement seat of Christ lends a seriousness to all life.   W. Robinson

Matthew
25:31-46

'Then the king will say to those on his right hand, "Come, you blessed of my Father, inherit the kingdom prepared for you from the foundation of the world"' (Matthew 25:34).

I'm sure that very few people think much about the Day of Judgement. They are involved with the things of this world, enjoying the comforts and benefits it has to offer.

The parable in today's reading tells us of the shepherd dividing the sheep from the goats. They are two different kinds of animal, just as the elect, God's people, are different from the ungodly of the world.

There is a day coming when history will end! The world will experience the very last moment of time, and the judgement will take place. The 'Son of Man' will return, but this time as a king, the only Son of God. In Daniel 7:13-14 it says, 'I was watching in the night visions, and behold, one like the Son of Man, coming with the clouds of heaven... Then to him was given dominion and glory and a kingdom... His dominion is an everlasting dominion, which shall not pass away, and his kingdom the one which shall not be destroyed.'

On that day there will be no unbelievers! Every knee will bow before the glorified, majestic Christ, the King. One by one each person will stand before him to receive his reward or punishment.

The great final division of humanity will take place on the basis of each individual's standing with the Redeemer. The 'sheep', the Redeemed, will stand on the right side of Christ, who is seated upon heaven's throne, and there hear the comforting words: 'Come, you blessed of my Father, inherit the kingdom prepared for you from the foundation of the world' (Matthew 25:34). The king will then declare that his people have done works of righteousness, often without being aware of doing them. They would have helped people in need, which

Christ says is just the same as if they were doing it to him: 'Assuredly, I say to you, inasmuch as you did it to one of the least of these my brethren, you did it to me' (Matthew 25:40).

Christ will identify himself with his people! It is the elect who will be declared righteous and will be welcomed into that eternal kingdom.

On the left side of the Lord stand the 'goats', those who are not his people. They are strangers to Christ, and will not have done works of righteousness in his name. Of these people Jesus says, 'And these will go away into everlasting punishment' (Matthew 25:46).

To the 'goats' the Lord will say, 'I never knew you; depart from me, you who practise lawlessness!' (Matthew 7:23).

In what group will you stand? Are you a 'sheep' or a 'goat'?

FIND OUT THE FACTS

1. When will the judgement of the sheep and the goats take place?
2. Who are the 'goats'?
3. In what group would you find Judas?

Think about the fact that Christ takes note of every kind deed that his people do. What encouragement is there for you to be more active in serving Christ and others from today's devotion?

The power of man can never reverse the sentence of God.
T. V. Moore

Matthew
26:6-16

'Assuredly, I say to you, wherever this gospel is preached in the whole world, what this woman has done will also be told as a memorial to her' (Matthew 26:13).

The religious leaders were making their plans to have Jesus executed, but not during the Passover feast, because they feared the crowds who admired him. Christ was well aware of what was to take place and told the disciples, 'You know that after two days is the Passover, and the Son of Man will be delivered up to be crucified' (Matthew 26:2).

Jesus and the disciples were in the home of Simon the leper in Bethany. A meal was being held in the Lord's honour. Mary and Martha were serving, and possibly Lazarus was reclining at the table. This meal took place the Saturday before Christ's words to his disciples concerning his crucifixion (John 12:2).

Mary approached the Lord and poured a pound of costly fragrant oil over his body. Soon a sweet smelling aroma filled the room. The disciples complained that this was waste; the oil could have been sold and the money given to the poor. Christ rebuked them saying that the poor would always be with them. Mary's action signified her great love for him which was done in preparation for his burial (Matthew 26:10-12).

The Lord promised Mary that her kindness would become known across the world, wherever the gospel was preached. How wonderful to be remembered for such a kindly act.

Judas, the treasurer, was most displeased about this waste of costly perfume. No doubt he needed money to replace the money he had stolen from the money bag. So, he secretly approached the chief priests and, for thirty pieces of silver, agreed to betray Christ.

The money was paid to him at once. This was a fulfilment of the prophecy of Zechariah 11:13 which states: 'And the Lord said to me, "Throw it to the potter — that princely price they set on me." So I took the thirty pieces of silver and threw them into the house of the LORD for the potter.'[1] To throw something to the potter was a proverb, dating back to days when the temple was built. It was the place where the Israelites once practised their idolatry, and which Josiah had defiled (2 Kings 23:10). In Matthew 27:9 we find this prophecy fulfilled.

What a miserable act by Judas! How true were the words of our Lord concerning Judas, 'The Son of Man indeed goes just as it is written of him, but woe to that man by whom the Son of Man is betrayed! It would have been good for that man if he had never been born' (Mark 14:21). What a wasted life!

You and I need to make sure that our faith in the Lord Jesus is a saving faith, and no one will be able to say of us, 'What a wasted life!'

---

[1] For a fuller commentary see Moore, T.V., *Zechariah*, Banner of Truth, Great Britain, 1968, pp. 180ff.

FIND OUT THE FACTS

1. Why did Mary pour the oil over the Lord?
2. What is meant by the word 'stewardship'?
3. What is a treasurer?

Mary loved the Lord and so nothing involved too much cost or effort when it came to serving him. Could the same be said of you?

A saying to Remember

Stewardship is what a man does after he says, 'I believe.' *W. Greaves*

John
13:1-15

'If I then, your Lord and Teacher, have washed your feet, you also ought to wash one another's feet. For I have given you an example, that you should do as I have done to you' (John 13:14-15).

It was the time of the Passover and Jesus sent John and Peter to make arrangements for the use of an upper room of a private home (Luke 22:8). They were told to go into the city where they would be met by a man carrying a pitcher of water. He was the man who would lead them to the house where the upper room was. Other arrangements were to be made too in order to celebrate the feast according to the Scriptures.

At last the twelve sat down with Jesus to eat the Passover. There was no servant to wash their feet. After the meal, Jesus stood up, removed his outer garments, and wrapping a towel about his waist, took a basin of water and commenced washing the disciples' feet.

When the Lord came to Peter, he refused to allow Christ to do so: 'You shall never wash my feet!' he said (John 13:8). Peter knew that Christ was doing the work of a lowly servant and he was not going to have him do such a menial task. However, Jesus replied, 'If I do not wash you, you have no part with me' (John 13:8). Jesus was referring to the spiritual realm.

To be united to Christ through the gracious work of the Holy Spirit means that sinners are justified: forgiven and clothed in his pure righteousness. Our sins, past, present and future are blotted out, and all that is now needed, is the daily confession of sins. This is why Christ referred only to the cleansing of the feet.

Christians sin daily. Martin Luther wrote, 'The devil allows no Christian to reach heaven with clean feet all the way.'[1]

Christ was teaching the disciples a very practical truth, in the words of our scripture verse. The disciples were not to be rulers, but servants of the church. They were to do willingly the most menial tasks. So also should all Christians be involved in works of service. This is the way of Christian love, the fruit of the Spirit.

Jesus then revealed to the disciples that one of them would be a traitor (John 13:18). He said that the disciple to whom he gave a piece of bread was the betrayer. When he gave it to Judas, Judas stood up and walked away to make final plans with the religious leaders. The other disciples were unaware of what was said.

The time for Christ's death was at hand. The hour had come!

---

[1] Ryle, J.C., *Expository Thoughts on the gospels*, John, Vol. 3, James Clarke and Co. Ltd, London, 1957, p.20.

FIND OUT THE FACTS

1. Discuss the character of Judas.
2. Why was the Passover meal celebrated?
3. Why did Jesus wash the disciples' feet?

To Think & to pray about

Jesus taught by example that we are to serve others. How willing are you to put yourself out for the sake of others?

A saying to Remember

I have a great need for Christ; I have a great Christ for my need.
C. H. Spurgeon

John
15:1-14

'But the Helper, the Holy
Spirit, whom the Father will
send in my name, he will teach
you all things, and bring to your
remembrance all things that I
said to you' (John 14:26).

Knowing that he was soon to die on a Roman cross, Jesus
taught the disciples some great truths. One important truth
was that Christianity is an exclusive faith. Christ, the only
Mediator between God and man (1 Timothy 2:5), said, 'I am
the way, the truth, and the life. No one comes to the Father
except through me' (John 14:6). Without Christ sinners have
no hope.

While he walked this earth he could be found in one place
only — that is, in his physical being. When he rose from the
dead and ascended into heaven, the Holy Spirit was sent by
the Father in his name. Now Christians everywhere have
direct access to the Father, through the Lord Jesus. This means
that the Father and Son take up residence in the converted
sinner's heart, in the power of the Holy Spirit.

Jesus also told a parable about the vine and its branches
(John 15:1-8). This is a covenant parable. Christ declared that
he was the vine and the heavenly Father the worker in the
vineyard.

The many branches attached to the vine are professing Christians. Those who are 'born again' people, involved in the works
of righteousness, are Christians. Of them the apostle Paul wrote,
'Work out your own salvation with fear and trembling; for it is
God who works in you both to will and to do for his good
pleasure' (Philippians 2:12-13). These are the branches that
bear fruit, because of the gracious work of the Holy Spirit in
their heart. These are the saints who bring glory to God.

Some branches bear no fruit. These are the people who are
found among God's worshipping people, yet are strangers to

the 'new birth'. On the Day of Judgement they are removed from the church and cast into the fire of eternal punishment. Christ could not be teaching that unrepentant sinners are united to him and then fall away. His sheep cannot be lost.

Christ teaches us that only those people who continually abide in him will bear fruit.

He went on to say that Christians ought to love one another and that he would set the perfect standard of that love: 'Greater love has no one than this, than to lay down one's life for his friends.' He also said, 'You are my friends if you do whatever I command you' (John 15:13,14).

Are you a close friend of the Lord Jesus Christ? I trust so!

FIND OUT THE FACTS

1. In the church, who are the unproductive branches?
2. In the church, who are the branches that bear fruit?
3. What is the teaching of John 15:6?

The challenge from today's devotion is this: do you bear fruit? Ask the Lord to enable you to do so.

A saying to Remember

Love is the root, obedience is the fruit. *Matthew Henry*

Luke
22:14-23

'For as often as you eat this bread and drink this cup, you proclaim the Lord's death till he comes' (1 Corinthians 11:26).

The disciples were still with the Lord, enjoying the Passover meal when Judas left to visit the chief priests and finalize his plans to deliver Christ to them.

Christ knew that soon his humiliation would come to an end and he would take his seat upon his heavenly throne, from where he would govern the earth to the glory of God and the good of the church. He looked forward to that day when he would sit down with his bride, the church, and enjoy the marriage feast.

But now he was to institute what has become known as the Lord's Supper, the sacrament by which the church remembers his sacrificial death. This feast of remembrance will continue until the day when the Lord returns to gather his people to himself.

The Lord took a piece of bread and after breaking it, distributed it among the disciples, saying, 'Take, eat; this is my body which is broken for you; do this in remembrance of me' (1 Corinthians 11:24). Then he took the cup of wine and passed it to his disciples saying, 'This cup is the new covenant in my blood. This do, as often as you drink it, in remembrance of me' (1 Corinthians 11:25).

Bread and wine are used as visible emblems to remind Christians of the Lord's sacrificial love for his people. At the Lord's table we look by faith to a risen Saviour to have our faith strengthened, and our love for God and man intensified.

At the same time we look forward to the day when the heavens will be rolled up like a scroll, and Christ, the King, surrounded by his great angels, will break into history. The judgement will take place and the saints will dwell in the new heavens and earth, wherein there is righteousness.

Sitting at the Lord's Table should also be a reminder that we have much in common with other Christians both within our own congregation and all groups of Christians. During the Lord's Supper we are reminded that Christians have so much in common, despite our social grouping, nationality, wealth, age and whether male or female.

We are all part of the Church, the Bride of Christ, forgiven, cleansed, justified, adopted into the Lord's family of believers and sanctified. We have a common Saviour; a common God-given faith in the Lord Jesus. We have a common baptism of the Holy Spirit; a common Mediator; a common joy; a common destiny and ... we could go on for pages!

Sitting at the Lord's Table is a time for reflection upon all that God has done for us through his Son and our Saviour, the Lord Jesus Christ.

FIND OUT THE FACTS

1. What do the bread and wine in the Lord's Supper represent?
2. What do the two church sacraments represent?
3. Of what does baptism remind you?

The Lord's Supper is a solemn occasion for the church but also one of rejoicing. Think about why this is so.

Tomorrow's history has already been written ... at the name of Jesus every knee must bow. *Paul E. Kauffman*

 John
17:6-19

'Father, the hour has come. Glorify your Son, that your Son also may glorify you ' (John 17:1).

Before leaving the upper room, Christ looked heavenward and prayed to his heavenly Father. This prayer has been called 'Christ's high-priestly prayer'. The only Mediator between God and his people was about to become both the High Priest and the sacrifice for his people's sins. This prayer can be divided into three sections.

First, verses 1-5 record Christ's prayer for himself. Second, verses 6-19 record Christ's prayer for the apostles; and third, verses 20-26 are Christ's prayer for the universal church of all ages.

In the first section of this prayer the Lord prayed that his Father would be glorified, as he would be, in his sacrificial death on the altar of the cross. He also prayed for a return to the glory and intimacy which he had with his heavenly Father.

Paul wrote of the glorification of the Lord Jesus: 'Therefore God also has highly exalted him and given him the name which is above every name, that at the name of Jesus every knee should bow, of those in heaven, and of those on earth, and of those under the earth, and that every tongue should confess that Jesus Christ is Lord, to the glory of God the Father' (Philippians 2:9-11). Jesus also prayed that eternal life would be given to all those who entrusted their eternal security to God.

In the section of the prayer that you read, Christ prayed for the disciples and for them alone. He asked that God would watch over them and grant them a close union with himself. He also spoke of the hatred of the world towards his disciples and prayed that God would not remove them from the world, but that he would 'keep them from the evil one' (John 17:15).

The apostles were the ones who would initially take the gospel to the Gentile nations. This happened within a short time following Pentecost, which is testified to by Paul. He wrote of the 'truth of the gospel, which has come to you, as it has also in all the world, and is bringing forth fruit' (Colossians 1:5,6).

The last section of Christ's prayer is for the church universal. He prayed that there might be true fellowship between believers, and a close unity between believers and God. He asked that the day would soon come when his bride, the church, would be with him, to behold his glory. He also prayed that believers might know the wonder of the Father's love for all of his church.

God's great love towards his people was made possible by Christ's sacrificial death on the cross. We owe everything to our Lord!

FIND OUT THE FACTS

1. What are the three sections of this prayer?
2. Why didn't Jesus ask his Father to take the disciples out of the world?
3. In what way did Jesus glorify God?

Christ prayed that his disciples would not be taken out of the world but would be kept from the evil one. Pray that you, too, would be kept from the evil one.

Christ is our hope of glory and the glory of our hope. *Anon*

Matthew
26:36-46

'O my Father, if this cup can-
not pass away from me unless
I drink it, your will be done'
(Matthew 26:42).

Accompanied by his disciples, Jesus walked to the Garden
of Gethsemane to pray to his Father. He knew what lay
before him and needed the comforting strength which only
God could impart.

At that time Judas was meeting with the religious leaders,
making the final arrangements for the Lord's arrest. He knew
that Jesus would be found in the Garden of Gethsemane, as he
often went there to pray.

When Jesus arrived at the garden, he told eight of his disciples to sit down and wait, while he, accompanied by Peter,
James and John, went further into the garden.

Wanting to be alone to pray, Jesus told the three disciples to
watch with him. He said, 'My soul is exceedingly sorrowful,
even to death. Stay here and watch with me' (Matthew 26:38).

You and I know that prayer is one of the most difficult
aspects of the Christian life. Left alone to pray, the three disciples, tired from a full day's activities, fell asleep.

Going a short distance into the garden, Jesus 'fell on his
face, and prayed, saying, "O my Father, if it is possible, let this
cup pass from me; nevertheless, not as I will, but as you will"'
(Matthew 26:39).

The Lord prayed to his heavenly Father concerning his crucifixion on the cross, and while he shrank from what lay before him, there was a perfect submission to the Father's will:
'Nevertheless not my will, but yours be done' (Luke 22:42).
The death of the Lord Jesus, the God-man, is a mystery we
cannot understand. But this we know, Jesus Christ submitted
entirely to the will of God. He would 'drink the cup' of death
for his people.

Several times Jesus returned to Peter, James and John, and finding the disciples asleep, rebuked them for their failure to pray.

There, alone in the Garden of Gethsemane, his heavenly Father sent an angel to strengthen him both physically and spiritually (Luke 22:43). No doubt the angel gave the God-man, Jesus Christ, the strength to face the future with resolve. The words of the writer to the Hebrews show us the mind of Christ at that time: '… who for the joy that was set before him endured the cross, despising the shame' (Hebrews 12:2).

Then, waking the disciples, Jesus said, 'Behold, the hour is at hand, and the Son of Man is being betrayed into the hands of sinners. Rise, let us be going. See, my betrayer is at hand' (Matthew 26:45-46).

FIND OUT THE FACTS

1. How would an angel strengthen Jesus?

2. Why did Jesus pray 'O My Father, if it is possible, let this cup pass from me'? (Matthew 26:39).

3. Who was about to betray Jesus?

Christ exhorted his disciples to pray so that they would not enter into temptation. Pray that you would be kept from temptation today.

Jesus was the most disturbing person in history.   *Vance Havner*

John
18:1-11

'Then Jesus said to Peter, "Put your sword into the sheath. Shall I not drink the cup which my Father has given me?"' (John 18:11).

Having spent three years with Christ, Judas led a band of soldiers to arrest the Lord he had betrayed. The chief priests and Pharisees had given him a detachment of troops to ensure that Christ could not escape. The Lord, knowing what was about to happen, asked the soldiers who they were looking for that night.

When they replied that they were searching for Jesus, he told them that he was the man. Judas had told the soldiers that the person he kissed was to be taken prisoner. After Jesus told them who he was, the soldiers stepped backwards and fell to the ground. Standing before them was King Jesus, who showed no fear.

Jesus asked a second time whom they were seeking and when they repeated their answer, he asked that the disciples be left alone. This was to fulfil the Scripture: 'Of those whom you gave me I have lost none' (John 18:9, compare John 6:39).

An over confident Peter, who was carrying a sword, unsheathed it and lashed out to protect Christ. In doing this he cut off the ear of Malchus, the high priest's servant. Jesus told him to return the sword to its sheath, saying, 'Shall I not drink the cup which my Father has given me?' (John 18:11).

Calling Malchus to him he healed him. The disciples, overcome by fear, turned and ran. A young man who was wearing only an outer robe also ran naked into the night when someone grabbed his clothing. Some say that this young man was John Mark, the author of the Gospel bearing his name.

Jesus was bound and taken to Annas. Peter and John followed the crowd to see what would take place. There near a fire, a young woman accused Peter of being one of Christ's disciples. This Peter denied with an oath!

Annas asked Jesus about his doctrine, and when he replied that he had openly taught, he was struck across the face by one of the officers, who accused him of being rude to Annas. To this Jesus replied, 'If I have spoken evil, bear witness of the evil; but if well, why do you strike me?' (John 18:23).

While Jesus stood before Annas, Peter was accused a second and a third time of being one of Christ's disciples. While the third denial was being uttered, the rooster crowed. Jesus turned and looked at Peter, who remembered what Christ had said. Heart broken, he went outside and wept bitterly, as he had openly denied his Lord and identified himself with the enemy!

Annas had played his part in the drama of that night, so he sent Jesus, securely tied, to his son-in-law, Caiaphas, the high priest.

FIND OUT THE FACTS

1. Why did Peter deny being a disciple of Christ?
2. Why did the soldiers fall to the ground?
3. What does Luke 22:53 teach you?

Thank the Lord Jesus that he willingly submitted to the shame of being arrested and tried as a common criminal.

Christ will either be a whole Saviour or none at all.   John Berridge

November

The fear of
the LORD
is a fountain
of life

Proverbs 14:27

Matthew
26:57-68

'Nevertheless, I say to you, hereafter you will see the Son of Man sitting at the right hand of the Power, and coming on the clouds of heaven' (Matthew 26:64).

Jesus was roughly dragged to Caiaphas, the high priest, where he was again questioned. False witnesses were called to testify against him, and eventually two came forward and said, 'This fellow said, "I am able to destroy the temple of God and to build it in three days"' (Matthew 26:61).

At first the Saviour refused to answer questions. But when the high priest asked, 'I put you under oath by the living God: Tell us if you are the Christ, the Son of God? 'Jesus said to him, "It is as you said"' (Matthew 26:63,64). Then come the words of our scripture verse.

The high priest and the Jewish council rejoiced because they thought that they had forced a confession out of Christ. He certainly wasn't the type of Messiah they expected. The high priest tore his clothing, declaring that Jesus had blasphemed by claiming to be the Christ. When he asked the council what should be done, the cry went up, 'He is deserving of death' (Matthew 26:66).

Now the Saviour began to experience the physical abuse of the Jews. Some spat on him, while other slapped his face and asked, 'Prophesy to us, Christ! Who is the one who struck you?' (Matthew 26:68). This was an attempt to humiliate Jesus, but really they were degrading themselves before the crowds.

Jesus Christ, the sinless Son of God, would soon die as Peter had written, 'For Christ also suffered once for sins, the just for the unjust, that he might bring us to God, being put to death in the flesh but made alive by the Spirit' (1 Peter 3:18). Peter had denied his Lord, and the other ten disciples had melted into the crowd of spectators. This left Jesus alone to face those who wanted him put to death.

Meanwhile Judas was ashamed with what he had done. Yet there was no spiritual repentance. He set out for the temple with the thirty pieces of silver, the price of a slave, and threw the coins down on the floor before the priests. He knew he'd betrayed an innocent man. Later the high priests used the thirty pieces of silver to purchase a field to be used as a burial place for strangers to the city.

Judas then went out and hanged himself. The rope must have broken, for we read, '... and falling headlong, he burst open in the middle and all his entrails gushed out' (Acts 1:18). What a gruesome end for the one who betrayed our Lord!

Of Judas, Christ had said, 'It would have been good for that man if he had never been born' (Mark 14:21).

FIND OUT THE FACTS

1. Why did Jesus say it would have been better if Judas had never been born?
2. Why do you think Judas betrayed the Lord?
3. What gave Christ the strength to stand firm at that time?

Those who reject Christ or betray him will surely pay the price for their sin. Pray for someone today who has no interest in the gospel.

All is loss that comes between us and Christ. *George Macdonald*

John
18:28-38

'Jesus answered, "My kingdom is not of this world. If my kingdom were of this world, my servants would fight, so that I should not be delivered to the Jews; ..."' (John 18:36).

The rulers of the Jews wanted Christ dead, but they did not have the right to impose capital punishment. The Romans alone had that right.

Christ was taken from the Jewish council to stand before Pilate, the Roman Governor. The Jews would not enter the Praetorium, because to do so would have made them spiritually unclean, and therefore unable to take part in the Passover feast.

They accused Christ of 'perverting the nation, and forbidding to pay taxes to Caesar, saying that he himself is Christ a king' (Luke 23:2). Pilate then asked Jesus, 'Are you the King of the Jews?' Christ answered, 'It is as you say' (v. 3).

The apostle John recorded more of Christ's reply: 'I have come into the world, that I should bear witness to the truth. Everyone who is of the truth hears my voice.' To this Pilate replied, 'What is truth?' (John 18:37-38). Pilate concluded that Jesus was an innocent person. When he heard that he came from Galilee he sent him to Herod, who hoped to see a miracle performed.

Herod began questioning Christ, but the Lord refused to answer that ungodly hypocrite. In this he fulfilled the prophecy of Isaiah 53:7, 'He was oppressed and he was afflicted, yet he opened not his mouth; he was led as a lamb to the slaughter, and as a sheep before its shearers is silent, so he opened not his mouth.'

Now the crowds began to treat Christ with contempt. They dressed him in kingly clothes and then mocked him. Even King Herod joined in the mocking. After a time he sent Christ back to Pilate where the trial recommenced. At that time Pilate's wife sent her husband a disturbing message: 'Have nothing to do with that just Man, for I have suffered many things today in a dream because of him' (Matthew 27:19).

Pilate knew that Christ was innocent, and as he was in the habit of releasing a prisoner to the Jews at the time of the Passover, he asked whom they wanted him to set free — Jesus or the murderer, Barabbas? The Jewish crowd shouted out for the release of Barabbas. Christ was then taken by the soldiers, who dressed him in purple, the colour of royalty, crowned him with a crown of thorns and assaulted and mocked him. Christ was whipped and abused by evil men.

When Pilate knew there was nothing he could do to obtain Christ's freedom, he washed his hands of the whole matter and handed Christ over to be crucified.

FIND OUT THE FACTS

1. Why did the Jews hate Jesus?
2. How did the soldiers abuse the Lord? See read Matthew 27:26-31.
3. Why did Pilate wash his hands?
4. What do you learn from Acts 4:27-28?

Thank the Lord Jesus that he endured such vile treatment from evil men and women for the sake of saving his people.

Death stung himself to death when he stung Christ. *William Romaine*

A Saying to Remember

Matthew   'And all the people answered
27:32-44   and said, "His blood be on us
            and on our children"' (Matthew
            27:25).

The mocking, spitting and whipping came to an end. The
rough Roman soldiers had had their fun abusing the 'King
of the Jews'. So having dressed the Lord in his own clothes,
they pushed him out onto the roadway where there lay an old
rugged cross. The Romans usually forced the victim to carry
his cross, but often their cruel handling left the person so
injured that he was unable to lift it to his shoulders.

As Christ was unable to carry the cross, the soldiers
ordered Simon from Cyrene, to carry it to a place called
Golgotha, the Place of a Skull, outside the city walls. (Simon
was the father of Alexander and Rufus. Paul in his Epistle to
the Romans (16:13) makes mention of a Rufus. William
Hendriksen in his commentary on Matthew suggests that Simon
became a Christian (p. 963). At least he witnessed a spectacle
that would have made a lasting impression on his mind.)
Executions always took place outside the city and Roman citizens were not expected to carry a cross. The law forbade a
Roman citizen from being crucified.

Arriving at the place of execution, someone gave Christ sour
wine and myrrh to drink. This mixture stupefied the one who
drank it, and was not intended to help the victim cope with
the pain. It was used to dope the person so that the crucifixion
could be carried out without too much struggling by the
victim. Realizing what the drink was, Jesus refused to drink
any more. He would die on a Roman cross, experiencing the
total anger of hell due to his people because of their sins.

Jesus was soon nailed to the cross, which was dropped into
the hole in the ground. More jarring followed as the soldiers
stood the cross perfectly upright. Two other Jews were crucified, one on each side of the Redeemer. Again this was to fulfil

the Scriptures, 'And they made his grave with the wicked' (Isaiah 53:9).

At the foot of the cross the soldiers threw lots for Christ's clothing, again fulfilling the words of the Scripture: 'They divided my garments among them, and for my clothing they cast lots' (Matthew 27:35, compare Psalm 22:18).

The cross was a particularly cruel way to die. Sometimes it took days before the victim died and for that reason the soldiers often broke the prisoner's leg bones in order to hasten death from a heart attack.

Christians have been commanded to take up their cross daily and to follow their Lord (Matthew 10:38).

The way of the cross meant suffering for the Lord, as it does for his people in all ages. But to carry our God-given cross is a great privilege and honour!

FIND OUT THE FACTS

1. What sign did Pilate have put above Christ on the cross?
2. What part of Christ's clothing was not torn apart?
3. Why is Jesus called 'the Lamb of God who takes away the sins of the world'?

Thank the Lord today that he endured the cruel death of the cross for sinners.

This precious Lamb of God gave up his precious fleece for us.
Christopher Nesse

Luke
23:26-43

'And they put up over his head the accusation written against him: This is Jesus the King of the Jews' Matthew 27:37.

Today we find signs everywhere: on streets, homes, buildings and even on clothing. A sign was prepared for Christ's cross, giving his title, 'King of the Jews'. This upset the Jewish leaders who wanted it changed to read, 'He said, "I am the King of the Jews"' (John 19:21). The title 'King of the Jews' was seen as an insult to the nation.

Jesus was crucified between two criminals, which was the fulfilment of Isaiah's prophecy: they 'made his grave with the wicked' (Isaiah 53:9). One of these men blasphemed the Lord, saying, 'If you are the Christ, save yourself and us' (Luke 23:39).

The other criminal spoke honestly. He said that he was getting his just deserts, but of Christ, he said, 'This man has done nothing wrong' (Luke 23:41). Turning to Christ, he asked, 'Lord, remember me when you come into your kingdom' (v. 42). To this Jesus replied, 'Assuredly, I say to you, today you will be with me in Paradise' (v. 43).

Nailed to a cross, naked, with blood pouring down his face and back, dust and perspiration on his body which was wracked with pain, that criminal recognized that Jesus was a king with a kingdom. He was assured that that very day he would be with Christ in paradise.

From the crowd standing near the cross came voices of mocking, 'He saved others; let him save himself if he is the Christ, the chosen of God… If you are the King of the Jews, save yourself' (Luke 23:35-37). 'You who destroy the temple and build it in three days, save yourself! If you are the Son of God, come down from the cross' (Matthew 27:40). 'Let the Christ, the King of Israel, descend now from the cross, that we may see and believe' (Mark 15:32).

There, suspended between earth and heaven, hung the only Mediator between God and man. There hung the Saviour, bearing the sins of his people and tasting the anger of God in their place. Christ experienced hell for all of his people, so that none of them might taste the flames of hell.

The death of the Lord Jesus Christ is beyond human understanding. God cannot die. It was Jesus, the Son of Man, who died upon the cross. Christ, the God-man experienced death for his people.

Christians owe their Saviour a debt they can never pay; but, by the grace of God, we shall glorify our Redeemer eternally in the new heavens and the new earth. Will you be there?

FIND OUT THE FACTS

1. Is it possible for God to die?

2. Christ experienced hell for his people. How could this be?

3. Why did Pilate put a sign on the cross over Christ's head?

Christ showed mercy to a dying criminal while on the cross. Thank the Lord for his great love for sinners.

Though God loved Christ as a Son he frowned upon him as a Surety. *Matthew Henry*

Luke
23:44-56

'Now it was about the sixth hour, and there was darkness over all the earth until the ninth hour' (Luke 23:44).

Our scripture verse tells us that a darkness settled over the earth for three hours — from midday until 3:00 p.m. It was as if the creation could not bear to gaze upon the dying Creator. The darkness was also a sign of the judgement that was taking place. Darkness and judgement go together (Joel 2:31; 3:14-15; Isaiah 5:30). The veiled suffering of our Redeemer showed his abandonment by God.

Upon the cross the Lord spoke seven times. His first words were: 'Father, forgive them, for they do not know what they do' (Luke 23:34). This prayer was soon answered, when on the day of Pentecost, Peter preached the gospel and some three thousand people were brought into the kingdom of heaven.

The Lord Jesus' second words were directed to a thief who hung on a cross beside him. The previous devotion mentioned this man who asked to be remembered by Christ when he entered his kingdom. To this Christ replied, 'Assuredly, I say to you, today you will be with me in paradise' (Luke 23:43).

Christ saved a thief! He came into this world to save sinners. Has he saved you?

From the cross, Jesus looked down upon his grieving, distressed mother, who was standing at the foot of the cross. Mary's husband Joseph had apparently died, and without someone to care for her, life would become very difficult.

Jesus could not use his hands, but to Mary he said, looking in the direction of John, 'Woman, behold your son!' (John 19:26). Looking then to John he said, 'Behold your mother!'(v. 27).

It was about 3:00 p.m. and the Lord Jesus had experienced the horror of hell for his people. He lost the sense of his Father's loving presence and cried out in anguish, 'My God, my God, why have you forsaken me?' (Matthew 27:46).

The perfect relationship that existed between Christ and his Father was broken. All Jesus could do was to cry out to his God. This was hell! Hell is the land of abandonment; the land where there is nothing good whatsoever. The apostle John wrote of hell under the name 'Babylon.' (Revelation 18:21-24). All that makes life pleasant is gone. That is hell! Hell is outer darkness, the bottomless pit, the lake of fire and brimstone.

Christ suffered the punishment due to his people. No Christian will suffer hell, because that would mean a double punishment for sin. No! Christ bore the penalty due to his people! The door of hell is closed as far as God's people are concerned.

What a sympathetic Saviour we have! Hallelujah!

FIND OUT THE FACTS

1. In what way did Jesus suffer the agony of hell?
2. 'Truth recognized too late' is written on the door into hell. What does this mean?
3. What is hell?

Jesus showed concern for his mother even when he was dying on the cross. How can you show such concern and appreciation for your mother?

If I'm afraid of sin I need not be afraid of hell. *Rowland Hill*

Matthew 27:45-54 · 'And when Jesus had cried out with a loud voice, he said, "Father, into your hands I commit my spirit." Having said this, he breathed his last' (Luke 23:46).

The time of Jesus' suffering was drawing to an end. His body was crushed by the weight of sin and God's anger. In order to fulfil the scripture, Jesus said, 'I thirst!' (John 19:28). When someone poured vinegar on a sponge and with some hyssop put it to Christ's lips, the words of Psalm 69:21 was fulfilled.

Christ needed that moisture so that he could shout out for everyone to hear, 'It is finished!' (John 19:30). These were not the words of a defeated man about to breathe his last, but were the cry of victory. Jesus knew that the salvation of his people had been accomplished. Nothing more was required! Now he could look upwards to God his Father: '"Father, into your hands I commit my spirit." And having said this, he breathed his last' (Luke 23:46). It was Jesus who dismissed his spirit! He knew that all that had to be done to ensure the salvation of his people had been completed.

In the temple, the curtain that shielded the Holy of Holies from public gaze was torn from the top to the bottom by the unseen hand of God.

This was at the time of the evening sacrifice and signified to the nation that the sacrificial work of the priests was finished. Christ had done what the sacrifice of animals could never do — save his people! At the same time the ground shook and the rocks were split apart. In a cemetery, many graves were opened and a resurrection of saints took place. They appeared to people in Jerusalem.

As night time was near, the command was given to break the leg bones of the victims on the cross, in order to hasten their deaths. However, when Christ was found to be dead, a soldier thrust his spear in his side, making blood and water gush forth. His legs were left unbroken. This fulfilled the prophecy of Psalm 34:20. Like the Passover lamb, no bone in his body was broken (Exodus 12:46).

One centurion who had seen the events of that day said, 'Truly this Man was the Son of God!' (Mark 15:39).

Joseph of Arimathea and Nicodemus approached the authorities and asked to be able to take Christ's body which they placed in Joseph's unused tomb. This was the first step towards Christ's exaltation. His body was wrapped in strips of linen which were coated in spices. The tomb was sealed and guards were stationed in the area to prevent anyone from stealing Christ's body and later claiming that he had not risen from the dead, as he said he would.

Broken-hearted disciples returned to their homes, believing Christ's plans had come to nothing.

FIND OUT THE FACTS

1. What did Jesus mean when he said, 'It is finished'?
2. What happened to Jesus' soul when he died?
3. Why were guards placed at Christ's tomb?

Even in this most appalling of events, God's power was present. Thank the Lord that no situation ever exists where he is not fully in control.

The blood of Christ is the seal of the testament. *Henry Smith*

Matthew 28:1-10 · 'So they went and made the tomb secure, sealing the stone and setting the guard' (Matthew 27:66).

As we read in the previous devotion, Jesus was buried in a stone cave, with his body placed on a shelf. Joseph and Nicodemus wrapped his body in linen saturated with spices. Several ladies, who had accompanied Christ and the disciples, came to see where the Lord was buried. In order to ensure his body was not stolen, Pilate placed guards near the tomb.

The women made preparations to visit the tomb on the first day of the week and to anoint Christ's body with precious oils. When the women approached the tomb, early on the first day of the week, they were unaware of the momentous events that had taken place.

The guards had felt the earthquake and had seen the angel move the huge stone from the tomb's entrance. They were unable to cope with that situation, and had become like dead men.

Mary Magdalene, Mary (the mother of James) and Salome arrived first. When they saw what appeared to them to be two men in dazzling white clothing, they bowed down in fear. One angel spoke to them, saying, 'Why do you seek the living among the dead? He is not here, but is risen! Remember how he spoke to you when he was still in Galilee, saying, "The Son of Man must be delivered into the hands of sinful men, and be crucified, and the third day rise again"' (Luke 24:5-7).

The women remembered the Lord's words. Mary Madgalene turned and ran to tell the disciples about the empty tomb. Upon hearing the news, the disciples hurried to the tomb, where Peter and John went inside. There they saw the linen strips neatly folded, but there was no corpse. However, soon the Lord was to appear to Peter.

When Mary returned to the tomb, she wept. Someone whom she thought was the gardener spoke to her, saying, 'Woman, why are you weeping? Whom are you seeking?'

To this Mary replied, 'Sir, if you have carried him away, tell me where you have laid him, and I will take him away.'

To this Jesus replied, 'Mary!'

Mary realized that she had been speaking to Jesus. She said, "Rabboni!' (which is to say, Teacher' (John 20:15,16).

At once she threw her arms about him, the one she loved as her Lord and Saviour. To this Christ said, 'Do not cling to me, for I have not yet ascended to my Father; but go to my brethren and say to them, "I am ascending to my Father and your Father, and to my God and your God"' (John 20:17).

At once Mary went to the disciples and told them she had met the Lord.

FIND OUT THE FACTS

1. What does the word 'resurrection' mean?
2. Why did the guards desert their post?
3. Why were dead bodies anointed with spices and ointment?

Thank the Lord today for the resurrection.

The best news the world ever had came from a graveyard. *Anon*

Luke
24:13-27

'And beginning at Moses and all the Prophets, he expounded to them in all the Scriptures the things concerning himself' (Luke 24:27).

When the guards reported to the chief priests all that they had seen take place, they were bribed and told to say that Christ's body had been stolen while they were asleep (Matthew 28:11-15).

The disciples did not understand what had happened in the tomb that day, and returned to their homes. Two people, Cleopas and a disciple, were walking to Emmaus, which was about seven miles from Jerusalem. While they were discussing the events of the past few days, another person caught up with them and joined in the discussion. By special divine intervention the two travellers did not recognize Jesus.

They said that they had heard the reports from the women who had seen the angels and heard them say that the Lord was alive. They also said that some of the disciples testified to the truth of the women's report.

Cleopas and his travelling companion weren't sure what to make of the reports, but the stranger travelling with them said, 'O foolish ones, and slow of heart to believe in all that the prophets have spoken! Ought not the Christ to have suffered these things and to enter into his glory' (Luke 24:25-26).

Then Jesus opened the understanding of the two travellers by giving them an explanation of the writings of Moses and the Prophets which spoke so clearly of him. This would have been a great sermon from the Master!

As night was falling the travellers invited Christ to eat with them, and when at the table, he took bread and broke it, their eyes were opened to see that he was the Christ. He then disappeared from their sight.

At once the two set out for Jerusalem to tell the others what had happened. As they were speaking to the other disciples, the Lord appeared and said, 'Peace to you.' (Luke 24:36). The disciples were terrified. They thought they had seen a ghost, but Jesus showed them his hands and invited them to touch him, arguing that spirits do not have bodies of flesh and blood.

When Christ asked for food, he was given some broiled fish and honeycomb. After eating the food in their presence, he explained those scriptures that spoke of him to the disciples.

He showed them that the Christ had to suffer, die and rise from the dead. He told them that the gospel was to be preached right across the world and that they were to be his witnesses of these events.

Then the Lord said, 'But tarry in the city of Jerusalem until you are endued with power from on high' (Luke 24:49).

FIND OUT THE FACTS

1. How did Jesus enter the room to see the disciples?
2. Which disciple was absent that night?
3. When did Cleopas and his companion recognize Jesus?

The Lord loves his people. He appeared to his disciples before ascending to his Father. Thank him that he delights to be with his people.

The Christian church has the resurrection written all over it.
E. G. Robinson

John
20:24-29
&
21:15-25

'And Thomas answered and said to him, "My Lord and my God!"' (John 20:28).

People today have a saying which goes like this: 'Seeing is believing.' The eleven had seen the risen Lord on the first day of the week, the day of the Lord's resurrection.

But one of the eleven was not present to witness what the others had seen. In fact, he said he would not believe their story, 'Unless I see in his hands the print of the nails, and put my finger into the print of the nails, and put my hand into his side, I will not believe' (John 20:25).

'The eleven' was the name given to the group of disciples after the defection of Judas. Before that they were known as 'the twelve'. They were still called 'the eleven' even though Thomas was absent initially.

On the first day of the second week, the eleven were in a closed room. Suddenly Jesus appeared before them and said, 'Peace to you!' (John 20:26).

Thomas was then invited to touch the nail marks in his hands and put his hand in the wound on the Lord's side. He was told by the Saviour, 'Do not be unbelieving, but believing' (John 20:27).

The disciples were to take the gospel to all the world; they were to be the living proof of the resurrection of the Lord Jesus. Later the apostle Paul would see the risen Christ so he too could bear witness to the resurrection of the Lord Jesus. Christ would next meet the disciples in Galilee, just as he had said (Matthew 28:10).

Upon his return to Galilee, Peter organized some fishing. Maybe the eleven were in need of finances and this was a sure way to earn a living. Possibly Peter thought he would have no part with the eleven, having denied the Lord three times.

That night the disciples caught nothing. But in the early light of a new day, they saw the Lord on the shore. When they told him that they had caught nothing, he commanded them to throw the net on the other side of the boat. When they did this, the net was so full of fish that they could not pull it in. With some help, the catch was landed, and soon the eleven sat down to eat with the Lord.

Christ then asked Peter, 'Simon, son of Jonah, do you love me more than these [those standing about]?' When Peter replied that he did, the Lord said, 'Feed my lambs' (John 21:15).

The second question asked was, 'Simon, son of Jonah, do you love me?'. When Peter answered in the affirmative, the Lord replied, 'Tend my sheep' (John 21:16).

Again Jesus asked the question, 'Simon, son of Jonah, do you love me?' Again Peter replied that he did, to which Christ said, 'Feed my sheep' (John 21:17).

FIND OUT THE FACTS

1. What did John 21:18 teach Peter?
2. Why did Jesus ask Peter *three* times if he loved him?
3. Of what would the apostles soon testify?

In response to seeing Christ's wounds himself, Thomas said, 'My Lord and my God!' Think about what it means to make that confession.

Christianity is essentially a religion of resurrection. *James Stewart*

Matthew   'But you shall receive power
28:16-20   when the Holy Spirit has come
            upon you; and you shall be
            witnesses to me in Jerusalem,
            and in all Judea and Samaria,
            and to the end of the earth'
            (Acts 1:8).

Jesus appeared to many people who could testify that they had seen him alive after the crucifixion. Our scripture passage states that the risen Christ appeared in Galilee to the eleven, but we read that some who were there doubted if it was the Christ. Possibly this meeting was not just with the eleven disciples, but also with the five hundred spoken of by the apostle Paul (1 Corinthians 15:6).

At that meeting Christ gave the disciples their marching orders, to 'go therefore and make disciples of all the nations, baptizing them in the name of the Father and of the Son and of the Holy Spirit, teaching them to observe all things that I have commanded you; and lo, I am with you always, even to the end of the age' (Matthew 28:19-20). Christ also appeared to James, his half brother (1 Corinthians 15:7).

The day arrived for the Lord to ascend into heaven. He opened the disciples' understanding to the biblical truth concerning his incarnation, life, death and resurrection. He also commanded the faithful group of followers to remain in Jerusalem until the coming of the Holy Spirit. They would be given power and courage to go out and preach the gospel fearlessly to an unbelieving world.

Having led the disciples out to Bethany, he blessed them with peace, power and strength to carry out his commands. He also spoke to the eleven the words of our scripture verse.

As the blessing concluded Christ 'was taken up, and a cloud received him out of their sight' (Acts 1:9). No doubt the disciples were amazed at what they had witnessed, but as they looked upwards two angels appeared saying, 'Men of Galilee, why do you stand gazing up into heaven? This same Jesus, who was taken up from you into heaven, will so come in like manner as you saw him go into heaven' (Acts 1:11).

Luke adds to the scene by saying that the disciples 'returned to Jerusalem with great joy, and were continually in the temple praising and blessing God' (Luke 24:52-53).

Mark then adds: 'So then, after the Lord had spoken to them, he was received up into heaven, and sat down at the right hand of God' (Mark 16:19). When the Lord ascended into heaven he took with him something he did not have before — a glorified human body. This would have been his coronation before the heavenly host. Psalm 2:6-7also speaks of Christ taking his heavenly throne.

FIND OUT THE FACTS

1. What did Jesus take back to heaven that he did not have before?
2. Where is the Lord Jesus now?
3. Why did Jesus meet with so many people before ascending to heaven?

To Think & to pray about

The great commission was not only given to the disciples. It is a commission which the church still has today. Pray for the evangelistic outreach in which your church is involved.

A saying to Remember

Christ is the meeting-point between the Trinity and the sinner's soul.
J. C. Ryle

Revelation '... And behold, one like the Son
5:1-14   of Man, coming with the clouds
            of heaven! ...Then to him was
            given dominion and glory and a
            kingdom, that all peoples,
            nations, and languages should
            serve him. His dominion is an
            everlasting dominion, which
            shall not pass away' (Daniel
            7:13-14).

The Lord Jesus Christ ascended into heaven and took his
rightful seat upon God's throne. Our Saviour, the Lord
Jesus Christ, was 'declared to be the Son of God with power,
according to the Spirit of holiness, by the resurrection from
the dead' (Romans 1:4). Through the resurrection, the Lord
Jesus was clearly to be the Son of God, 'the King of kings and
Lord of lords' (1 Timothy 6:15).

On the day of Christ's ascension, the words of Psalm 2:7-8
was fulfilled: 'I will declare the decree: the LORD has said to
me, "You are my Son, today I have begotten you. Ask of me,
and I will give you the nations for your inheritance, and the
ends of the earth for your possession."'

Christ had always been the Son of God, but now all people
and angels would bow before him, acknowledging that he is
indeed the King of kings. Now the Lord would rule the
nations, establishing his kingdom in the hearts of those given
to him by his heavenly Father.

In Revelation 5 a scene in heaven is described, where no
one is found worthy to open the scroll, outlining the history of
the church. We read, 'But one of the elders said to [John], "Do
not weep. Behold, the Lion of the tribe of Judah, the Root of
David, has prevailed to open the scroll and to loose its seven
seals." And I looked, and behold, in the midst of the throne
and of the four living creatures, and in the midst of the elders,
stood a Lamb as though it had been slain' (Revelation 5:5-6).

Christ sat down beside the Father on the heavenly throne. Then John saw and heard the heavenly choir sing:

Worthy is the Lamb who was slain
  to receive power and riches and wisdom,
and strength and honour and glory and blessing!
              (Revelation 5:12).

Paul wrote that God had exalted the Lord Jesus, giving him …'the name that is above every name' (Philippians 2:9) that 'at the name of Jesus every knee should bow … and … every tongue should confess that Jesus Christ is Lord, to the glory of God the Father' (Philippians 2:10,11).

The ungodly are warned: 'Kiss the Son, lest he be angry, and you perish in the way, when his wrath is kindled but a little' (Psalm 2:12).

Have you made peace with God through the Son?

FIND OUT THE FACTS

1. Who is the 'King of kings'?
2. What does it mean 'to kiss the Son'?
3. How long will Christ's kingdom last?

Spend time praising the King of kings and Lord of lords.

How divinely supreme is our Lord above all others!
Martyn Lloyd-Jones

Acts
2:1-13

'And they cast their lots, and
the lot fell on Matthias. And
he was numbered with the
eleven apostles' (Acts 1:26).

One hundred and twenty faithful followers of Christ, both
men and women, now met in an 'upper room' for prayer.
Some time before in an 'upper room' Christ had prayed for the
disciples. Now they would seek God's blessing upon themselves for the work they were commissioned to carry out.

The Scriptures had revealed that one close to Christ would
be his enemy (Psalm 41:9). Peter knew that another Scripture
had to be fulfilled: 'And let another take his office' (Psalm 109:8).
Joseph and Matthais were qualified for the position as both
had been witnesses to the Lord's resurrection. Lots were cast,
which left the choice entirely in the hands of God: 'The lot is
cast into the lap, but its every decision is from the LORD' (Proverbs 16:33). The traitor Judas was replaced with Matthais and
once again we can speak of 'the twelve'.

We should also note that one who was numbered with the
one hundred and twenty was Mary, the Lord's mother. This is
the last time that she is mentioned in the Scriptures.

Now the one hundred and twenty disciples would pray with
a common purpose. Before he had ascended to heaven the Lord
had promised the outpouring of the Holy Spirit. The one hundred and twenty returned to Jerusalem, where in the 'upper
room' prayer was made for the success in the propagation of
the gospel, particularly for the outpouring of the Holy Spirit
which would give the power and courage they needed to stand
firm and proclaim the way of salvation through the risen
Messiah.

The days passed and it was soon the Day of Pentecost, the
first day of the week. This feast day was determined according
to Scripture: 'Count fifty days to the day after the seventh
Sabbath; then you shall offer a new grain offering to the LORD'
(Leviticus 23:16).

Some have called this particular Pentecost, the 'birthday of the church'. This is not so, as the church consists of the elect from all ages. The Day of Pentecost was the day when the disciples were given courage and power to take the gospel across the world.

In the house there was suddenly what sounded like a mighty rushing wind. Then there appeared fire from heaven which divided and rested upon each of the disciples. They were then filled with the Holy Spirit and spoke in foreign languages.

Upon leaving the room they went about Jerusalem, telling the gospel message in the languages of everyone who was there for the feast of Pentecost. Some people said the disciples were drunk, but Peter rebuked them saying that what they heard was the fulfilment of the words of the prophet Joel (2:28-32).

FIND OUT THE FACTS

1. Why was it necessary to select another disciple?
2. What special qualification was needed by the apostles?
3. Why was the Day of Pentecost called 'The day of firstfruits'?

Thank the Lord that he always raises up men and women, boys and girls to do his work.

The Christian should learn two things about his tongue: how to hold it and how to use it. *Anon*

Acts
2:14-28

'Men of Israel, hear these words: Jesus of Nazareth, a Man attested by God to you by miracles, wonders, and signs which God did through him in your midst, as you yourselves also know' — (Acts 2:22)

The sermon of Peter continues: 'Him, being delivered by the determined counsel and foreknowledge of God, you have taken by lawless hands, have crucified, and put to death; whom God raised up, having loosed the pains of death, because it was not possible that he should be held by it' (Acts 2:23-24).

Having received the gift of the Holy Spirit and the ability to speak in foreign languages, the disciples set out to preach the gospel in Jerusalem. Peter, filled with courage, stood up and began preaching in the power of the Holy Spirit. This was a different Peter from the one who seven weeks earlier had denied any knowledge of the Lord Jesus. This day God also answered the prayer Christ prayed as he was being nailed to the cross: 'Father, forgive them, for they do not know what they do' (Luke 23:34).

Many Jews and Gentiles were in Jerusalem for the Passover, as it was one of the feast days when all male members of Israel were expected to visit Jerusalem. This also applied to the feast of Pentecost. Many would have remained in the city to avoid making two journeys.

No doubt many who had cried out, 'Crucify him, crucify him!' (Luke 23:21), had also shouted, 'His blood be on us and on our children' (Matthew 27:25). They were ready to accept the wrath of God if what they did was sinful.

We know from history that God has punished the Jewish people from A.D. 70. Not all Jews have hated Christ, but throughout the ages, a remnant of grace have also cried out, 'His blood be upon us and our children', because they have

known that without the sacrificial blood of Christ, they would
be lost sinners. Like the three thousand on the day of Pentecost who heard Peter preach and believed the gospel, they also
have come to Christ by faith and are numbered among his people.

Peter explained the prophecies concerning Christ in the Old
Testament, and when people saw their wickedness in crucify-
ing their Messiah, they cried out in despair. Peter told them,
'Repent, and let every one of you be baptized in the name of
Jesus Christ for the remission of sins; and you shall receive the
gift of the Holy Spirit.'

Peter went on to say, 'For the promise is to you and to your
children, and to all who are afar off, as many as the Lord our
God will call' (Acts 2:38,39). What a wonderful promise!

The prophet Joel had prophesied concerning the age when
the Spirit would be poured out. We live in that age! Hallelujah!

FIND OUT THE FACTS

1. Who cried out 'Crucify him, crucify him!'?

2. What promise is spoken about in Acts 2:39? Read
   Genesis 17:7.

3. How many people were baptized and admitted to
   church membership that first Pentecost?

What a different Peter we see in the
book of Acts. The Lord is able to change
anyone and to use that person mightily
in his work. Thank the Lord that
he sanctifies sinners and uses
them in his kingdom.

I would rather beg my bread
than preach without success.
Robert Murray M'Cheyne

A Saying to Remember

Acts
3:1-10

'Then Peter said, "Silver and gold I do not have, but what I do have I give to you: In the name of Jesus Christ of Nazareth, rise up and walk"' (Acts 3:6).

Having had some serious back surgery, I found life very difficult for a long time. At first, when I returned home from the hospital, I couldn't walk to the front gate. Over the months I was able to increase the distance covered.

Our Bible reading is about a man who was unable to stand. His friends carried him each day to a temple gate known as 'Beautiful'. There he would beg for alms — that is, money, so he could care for himself.

When he saw Peter and John about to enter the temple to speak to people about the Lord Jesus, he looked at them hopefully, expecting to be given some money. But Peter and John looked at the man and, as Peter took his hand and began lifting him to his feet, he said the words of our scripture verse.

At once the man's feet and ankles were strengthened and he found that he could stand up. We can only imagine his joy. He began jumping for joy as he went into the temple, praising God for what had happened to him. The people who saw the man healed knew the healing was indeed a great miracle.

Peter took the opportunity to announce that the healing was the work of Jesus Christ, whom they had crucified. He called Jesus, 'the Prince of life, whom God raised from the dead, of which we are witnesses.' He went on to tell them they had killed the Holy One (Acts 3:15).

Then he said, 'Repent therefore and be converted, that your sins may be blotted out, so that times of refreshing may come from the presence of the Lord' (Acts 3:19). Peter then referred to the words of Moses concerning the Prophet who was to come: 'The Lord your God will raise up for you a Prophet like me from your brethren. Him you shall hear in all things, whatever he says to you. And it shall be that every soul who will not hear that prophet shall be utterly destroyed from among the people' (Acts 3: 22-23).

Peter explained that the Old Testament prophets had prophesied concerning the coming of the Prince of Life; especially Abraham who was told that through his seed the nations of the world would be blessed. This 'Seed' of Abraham was his descendant, the Lord Jesus Christ.

Christ had been sent into the world to the Jews first, but they had refused his offer of salvation. Generally speaking, they wanted nothing to do with him.

Have you repented of your sins and do you live a life of obedience to Christ? You will, if you are born again.

FIND OUT THE FACTS

1. Who gave Peter the ability to perform the miracle?

2. What is a miracle?

3. What is meant by 'repentance'.

4. What was the purpose of the miracle?

To Think & to pray about

Thank the Lord once again that he changes people's lives and shows his power in their weakness.

A Saying to Remember

Those who need miracles are men of little faith. *John Huss*

Acts
4:1-12

'Nor is there salvation in any other, for there is no other name under heaven given among men by which we must be saved' (Acts 4:12).

The religious leaders in Jerusalem were angry that the disciples taught and performed miracles in the name of Jesus. The Christian church was growing and now had about five thousand men, as well as women and children.

Peter and John were arrested and kept prisoners until the following day when they appeared before a great number of officials who demanded to know by what authority and power the crippled man had been healed.

Peter spoke out with courage, 'Let it be known to you all, and to all the people of Israel, that by the name of Jesus Christ of Nazareth, whom you crucified, whom God raised from the dead, by him this man stands here before you whole' (Acts 4:10).

The leaders knew they could not harm Peter and John because the people had witnessed the great miracle. Both men were called before the leaders and warned not to go about preaching the name 'Jesus'. Then followed Peter and John's reply, 'Whether it is right in the sight of God to listen to you more than to God, you judge. For we cannot but speak the things which we have seen and heard' (Acts 4:19-20).

After Peter and John had been threatened with punishment if they continued to teach people about 'Jesus Christ', they were set free.

Those leaders, who were violently opposed to the Lord Jesus, could only look at the man who was once crippled, and now was perfectly well. The man was forty years old and everyone in Jerusalem knew he'd been crippled all his life. His healing was a momentous miracle and no trick.

At once the apostles began to preach Christ crucified, dead, buried, and risen from the grave. After further prayer, the Holy Spirit came upon them, giving them courage to speak the gospel with boldness.

They reminded all who listened to them of Jesus Christ who had been hated by both Jews and Gentiles. His death was the result of hatred by 'both Herod and Pontius Pilate, with the Gentiles and the people of Israel' (Acts 4:27). All were guilty!

Peter prayed that God would give them power to do great wonders in Christ's name, and so win sinners into God's kingdom. As the disciples were praying, suddenly the place began to shake and the Holy Spirit came upon them, giving the apostles courage to speak about the Lord Jesus with boldness.

FIND OUT THE FACTS

1. Who gave the apostles power and courage to speak about the Lord Jesus?

2. Why did the religious leaders not want the disciples to speak about Jesus?

3. Why were the apostles willing to risk their lives for Christ?

Think about the fact that the Holy Spirit works so powerfully in the preaching of the gospel. Pray for ministers that they may be enabled to preach with power.

When I preach, I regard neither doctors nor magistrates, of whom I have above forty in my congregation. My eyes are on the servant maids and the children.   *Martin Luther*

Acts
5:1-11

'So great fear came upon all the church and upon all who heard these things' (Acts 5:11).

Even though people are warned that they must not steal from God, many do. In Malachi, the last book of the Old Testament, the Jews were told that they were stealing from God: 'Will a man rob God? Yet you have robbed me! But you say, "In what way have we robbed you?" In tithes and offerings' (Malachi 3:8). The Lord promised great blessings only if his people gave their tithes and offerings to the church. Do you do this?

Today's reading tells us that the church was growing, and many members gave their property and money to the apostles to be used to pay those men who preached the gospel and to help people in need. One man, Joses, who was a Levite living in Cyprus, sold his property and gave all the money to the disciples.

When two other members of the church, Ananias and Sapphira, who were husband and wife, heard the praise that was heaped upon the godly Joses for his gift, they decided to be praised as well. They were a very proud couple, who loved their money. They sold their property and gave only a portion to the apostles, while pretending they had given all the money to the church. But the Holy Spirit had revealed to Peter that they were stealing from God and deceiving the people.

Peter told Ananias that he had both stolen from and lied to God and the church members. Instantly Ananias fell down dead, and his body was taken away to be buried.

When Sapphira arrived, she also said that she and her husband had given all the proceeds of the sale to the church. She too lied to Peter and to God. Peter said to her, 'How is it that you have agreed together to test the Spirit of the Lord? Look, the feet of those who have buried your husband are at the door, and they will carry you out' (Acts 5:9). Falling down dead, Sapphira was taken out and buried.

We next read that there was a great fear of Jehovah in the church. The saints realized that God would not tolerate wickedness. The church members knew that God expected obedience to his commands.

God still expects obedience today from all his people. Today God punishes those who fall into sin — he is a true Father who is concerned about his children. He will ensure that we are holy!

Following this, more miracles took place and great numbers of repentant sinners joined the church.

FIND OUT THE FACTS

1. What was Sapphira's and Ananias' sin?
2. Who did they sin against?
3. How do Christians support the work of the church?

People may be fooled by appearances for a time, but God is never. Think about the importance of being completely honest with God and with others.

A giving Saviour should have giving disciples.   J. C. Ryle

Acts
5:17-42

'But Peter and the other apostles answered and said, "We ought to obey God rather than men"' (Acts 5:29).

I have visited the jails used in the early days of the Australian colony, especially the cells used for solitary confinement. These were horrible and I could only feel pity for the poor convicts who spent days, and even months, all alone in the darkness. Many Christians have been imprisoned because of their love for the Lord.

The apostles performed many miracles in Jerusalem, but there were those who feared openly confessing their faith in Christ. The sick from the towns surrounding Jerusalem came to the city and were healed by the apostles, in the name of Christ. Some were healed even when Peter's passing shadow fell upon them.

The high priest, who was a Sadducee, wanted the name of Christ forgotten by the nation, so he had the apostles arrested and placed in prison. I'm sure the apostles would have prayed for God's help, as would the Christians in Jerusalem.

During the night, God sent one of his angels to the jail to open the doors and lead the apostles out. He told them, 'Go, stand in the temple and speak to the people all the words of this life' (Acts 5:20).

The apostles went to the temple and began to preach the gospel. Meanwhile the high priest and other leaders sent guards to the jail to bring the apostles to them. When it was reported that they were not in prison, but preaching Christ in the temple, the order was given to bring them to the high priest.

When the apostles were reminded that they had been told not to teach Christ, the apostles answered in the words of our scripture verse. They went on to say that God had raised Jesus from the dead and that they were witnesses of what had occurred.

The leaders were furious and wanted to put the apostles to death. But it was wise Gamaliel, a Pharisee, who said that if the apostles were, in fact, teaching God's truth, they could not be stopped. If they were just men teaching the doctrine of men, then they would come to nothing. In other words, the matter should be left in the hands of God.

The high priest had the apostles beaten, and told them not to speak of Christ. But they returned to the temple to continue preaching. They rejoiced that they had been counted worthy to suffer for the Lord Jesus.

FIND OUT THE FACTS

1. Why were the apostles locked up?

2. How did they escape from the jail?

3. Who was Gamaliel and what did he suggest to the leaders?

So devoted to the cause of Christ were these apostles that they were prepared to risk being imprisoned for failing to obey the authorities. How would you respond if you were in such a situation?

Mercy and punishment, they flow from God, as the honey and the sting from a bee. *Thomas Brooks*

A Saying to Remember

Acts
6:1-8
&
7:44-60

'And Stephen, full of faith and power, did great wonders and signs among the people' (Acts 6:8).

Congregations usually have two office bearers — the elders, who take care of the spiritual well-being of the church members, and deacons, who are largely responsible for the practical needs of the church: the payment of accounts, payment of the minister's salary, the upkeep of the church buildings and assisting people in need.

The church in Jerusalem was caring for widows. But the Greek widows complained that they were being neglected while the Jewish widows were being well cared for. The apostles made the decision to select seven men who would be responsible for this work, while they devoted themselves to prayer and gospel preaching.

The seven men selected were: Stephen, Phillip, Prochorus, Nicanor, Timon, Parmenas and Nicolas. These men were set apart for this special work and, after prayer, the apostles laid hands on them and they devoted their time to their particular duties.

Stephen, a most godly man, was able to defend the Christian faith with great ability. The religious leaders hated him and had him accused of teaching that Christ would destroy the temple and overthrow the laws of their great prophet, Moses.

The high priest had Stephen brought before the Sanhedrin to answer his accusers who wanted him put to death. As he was well versed in Jewish history and God's dealings with his covenant people, he commenced by speaking about God's relationship with Abraham.

He then traced the history of the nation: the slavery in Egypt, the invasion of the promised land of Canaan, and the humble leadership of God's people by Moses, the one whose teaching he had been accused of wanting to overthrow.

Stephen spoke of the greatness of Moses, and then accused the Jews of ill-treating the prophets God had sent to them. He told the leaders that the prophets had spoken of the coming Messiah, but also accused them of killing the 'Just One' who had come from God.

The leaders were furious and 'gnashed at him with their teeth' (Acts 7:54). As Stephen was dragged out of the city he said, 'Look! I see the heavens opened and the Son of Man standing at the right hand of God!' (Acts 7:56).

Then a shower of stones struck the godly Stephen and he died, saying, 'Lord Jesus, receive my spirit... Lord, do not charge them with this sin' (Acts 7:59,60). Those who threw their stones cast their clothes at Saul's feet.

FIND OUT THE FACTS

1. Why was Stephen hated so much?
2. Why was Stephen stoned and not crucified?
3. Who was the young man Saul?

Thank the Lord for godly elders and deacons. Thank him for the way that they serve the church.

If there be glory laid up for them that die *in* the Lord, much more shall they be glorified that die *for* the Lord. *Richard Baxter*

Acts
8:9-25

'Therefore those who were scattered went everywhere preaching the word' (Acts 8:4).

When the Holy Spirit changes a sinner's heart, they become a new person. Gone are the old sinful delights and in their place is a love of holiness.

In our last devotion we read of a young man, who held the clothing of those who stoned Stephen. This was Saul, the well-known Pharisee, who was involved in the persecution of Christians in and around Jerusalem. He was greatly feared by those who loved Christ. Paul was the agent who scattered many godly people throughout Judea and Samaria. As they went they spoke of the Lord Jesus, with the result that a scattered church grew in numbers.

Philip went down to Samaria where he preached the gospel and performed many miracles, even casting out demons in the name of Christ. There he met Simon, the well-known magician. When Simon heard the gospel preached by Stephen, he was baptized.

Upon hearing the news of the converts in Samaria, the apostles sent Peter and John down to see the events for themselves. The two apostles laid their hands on the converts and they received the gift of the Holy Spirit, just as had happened in Jerusalem on the Day of Pentecost.

When Simon saw this, he offered the apostles money for this gift so that he too could lay his hands on people and give them the Holy Spirit. Peter was angry with Simon and warned him that the gifts of God could not be bought with money. Simon was told to repent of his sins.

Meanwhile, Philip met an angel who told him to go to a desert place on the road from Jerusalem to Gaza. There he met an Ethiopian eunuch, who attended to the welfare of Queen

Candace of Ethiopia. He had visited Jerusalem for a time of worship, and was now in his chariot returning home. He was reading Isaiah 53:7-8, and wondered if the passage spoke of Isaiah or someone else.

Philip approached the man, asking if he understood what he was reading. The man replied that he needed someone to guide him. Philip explained the Scripture passage which spoke of the saving work of Jesus, the Son of God.

The man at once confessed his faith in Christ: 'I believe that Jesus Christ is the Son of God' (Acts 8:37). As they continued down the road, the eunuch saw some water. They stopped and Philip baptized him at once.

We should all be ready to speak to people about the Christ we love and serve. We need to know our Bibles well. Do you?

FIND OUT THE FACTS

1. Read Isaiah 53:7-8. What does the passage teach?
2. Who is the Holy Spirit?
3. What is the work of the Holy Spirit?

The conversion of the Ethopian eunuch is a beautiful story. Pray that people today would desire to understand the Scriptures as the Ethopian eunuch did.

A saying to Remember

The church is the fruit of the gospel. *Hywel R. Jones*

Acts
9:1-19

'But the Lord said to [Ananias],
"Go, for he is a chosen vessel
of mine to bear my name before Gentiles, kings, and the
children of Israel. For I will
show him how many things he
must suffer for my name's
sake"' (Acts 9:15-16).

Saul had received authority from the high priest in Jerusalem to visit Damascus and there take prisoners of any who
were followers of the Lord Jesus Christ. They would be
returned to Jerusalem to face trial and possibly death.

As he journeyed to Damascus with some friends, he found
himself surrounded by a bright light from heaven. He fell to
the ground in fear and heard a voice saying, 'Saul, Saul, why
are you persecuting me?' (Acts 9:4). 'And he said, "Who are
you, Lord?" And the Lord said, "I am Jesus, whom you are
persecuting. It is hard for you to kick against the goads"' (Acts
9:5). Fearfully Saul asked, 'Lord, what do you want me to do?'

Then the Lord said to him, 'Arise and go into the city, and
you will be told what you must do' (Acts 9:6).Saul's travelling
companions heard the voice but saw no one. When Saul struggled to his feet, he found that he was blind. His companions
had to lead him by the hand to Damascus, where he spent
three days without food.

The Lord spoke in a vision to a Christian named Ananias,
telling him to go to the address where Saul was staying. There
he was to place his hand upon Saul and restore his sight.But
Ananias knew of Saul's cruel reputation and expressed his
fear to the Lord. The Lord replied to him using the words of
our scripture verse. Ananias went to where Saul was and said
to him, 'Brother Saul, the Lord Jesus, who appeared to you on
the road as you came, has sent me that you may receive your
sight and be filled with the Holy Spirit' (Acts 9:17).At once
Saul could see, and having stood up, he was baptized.

The Christians were amazed that Saul, the one who had hated the church, was now an ardent follower of the Lord Jesus. He was a brilliant theologian, who knew the Old Testament. For a time in Damascus, he explained to the Jews that Jesus was the Christ, who fulfilled all the Old Testament prophecies concerning the Messiah.

As the Jews now planned to kill Saul, one night the Christians quietly lowered him down the city wall in a basket.

Upon arriving in Jerusalem, Saul found the Christians were fearful of him. They knew of his reputation as an enemy of the Christian church. However, he was welcomed into the church, where he spent much time boldly preaching Christ and disputing with the Jews. When there was danger from the 'Hellenists' — that is, the Greeks, the Christians helped him escape to Caesarea.

The church now had its greatest missionary!

FIND OUT THE FACTS

1. Who called Saul to serve him?
2. Why did the Jews hate Christians?
3. Why was Saul baptized?

The Lord has chosen to convert some of the most unlikely people. Ask the Lord to give you the grace to share the gospel of God's grace with all those you meet.

The martyrs shook the powers of darkness with the irresistible power of weakness.   *John Milton*

Acts
9:36-43

'But Peter put them all out, and knelt down and prayed. And turning to the body he said, "Tabitha, arise." And she opened her eyes, and when she saw Peter she sat up' (Acts 9:40).

The church was growing as the gospel was spread by persecuted Christians, who were forced to leave their homes and live in other towns and cities. Wherever they went they preached the Lord Jesus Christ. The apostle Peter also travelled about the countryside, preaching the gospel and performing miracles in the name of the Lord.

Another way of bearing witness to the salvation found in Christ was by the good works that flowed from saving faith. The apostle Paul (Saul) wrote, 'Therefore, as we have opportunity, let us do good to all, especially to those who are of the household of faith' (Galatians 6:10). You and I should always be looking out for ways we can help those in need.

You have read about a kind, godly Christian woman named Tabitha (Dorcas), who lived at Joppa. There can be no doubt that she loved the Lord Jesus because she showed this by her works of kindness. She was a good seamstress and she made clothes for people in need. Of Tabitha, we read: 'This woman was full of good works and charitable deeds which she did' (Acts 9:36).

Many people living in Joppa had received help from kindly Tabitha, but one day they were greatly upset because Tabitha died! The local women put her body in an upper room, where they washed it in preparation for her burial.

Some of the local Christians knew that Peter was only a short distance away from Joppa, and sent word to him. They told him about Tabitha's death and asked him to come at once and help them. Perhaps they expected Peter to conduct the funeral, and speak words of comfort to those who were mourning.

At once Peter set out for Joppa where he was shown many pieces of clothing that Tabitha had made for needy people.

After asking the mourners to leave the room in which Tabitha's body lay, Peter knelt down and prayed. Turning to the body, he said, 'Tabitha, arise' (Acts 9:40). I wonder what went through Tabitha's mind when she saw Peter standing beside her and heard the women outside mourning. Peter then took her hand, lifted her to her feet and presented her to the people waiting outside.

The news of this great miracle soon spread with the result that many people believed the gospel. Peter then stayed at Joppa with Simon, the tanner. Simon worked with dead animals which to the Jews made him ceremonially unclean. Peter knew that the church would be made up of people from all nations and cultures.

FIND OUT THE FACTS

1. What good works are mentioned in James 1:27?

2. What do good works prove? See James 2:26.

3. Make a list of the good works that your family could do.

Tabitha was known for her deeds of kindness. Think of ways in which you could follow her example.

Miracles are the swaddling-clothes of the infant church.
Thomas Fuller

Acts
10:1-16

'To [Christ] all the prophets witness that, through his name, whoever believes in him will receive remission of sins' (Acts 10:43).

In the days of the Old Testament there were Gentiles who believed the truth of God and became members of the covenant community. The males were circumcised, which meant that they carried the sign of the covenant in their flesh.

One such person was Cornelius, a centurion in the Italian Regiment. He loved God and did many good works in the name of Jehovah. However, he knew nothing of the Lord Jesus Christ.

An angel came from God telling him to send men to Peter, who would tell him what he should do.

Peter was in Joppa at the time, staying with Simon, the tanner. When he went to the housetop to pray he saw a big sheet, full of animals, descend from heaven. When he was told to kill and eat he refused, saying, "Not so, Lord! For I have never eaten anything common or unclean' ((Acts 10:14).

A voice came a second time, saying, 'What God has cleansed you must not call common' (Acts 10:15).

The sheet full of animals then rose in the air and was taken up into heaven. While Peter was thinking about the vision, some men arrived at Simon's house.

When Peter came down, they asked him to accompany them to their master, which Peter did. He was told that Cornelius was a good man who feared God and had helped the Jews in many ways. When Cornelius met Peter, he fell at his feet and worshipped him.

Peter lifted Cornelius to his feet, warning him that he must not worship a man. Then he told him that he would not ordinarily have come to the home of a Gentile, but that God had revealed to him that he should not call any man common or unclean. Peter knew that the Lord was teaching him that the

Gentiles were not spiritually unclean, but needed to hear the gospel just as the Jews did.

Cornelius then invited Peter to preach the salvation that Christ had won for his people, both Jew and Gentile. As he was speaking the Holy Spirit was poured out upon those who were listening and they began to speak in foreign languages. The Jews were surprised when they saw what happened, but they now knew that the gospel was not for them alone, but also for 'unclean' Gentiles.

At once, Peter baptized those who believed and spent several more days with the newly formed church, explaining the Scriptures to the new converts.

FIND OUT THE FACTS

1. In what way did God teach Peter that the Gentiles were not unclean?

2. Why did Peter baptize the new converts?

3 Why did the Jews treat the Gentiles as being 'unclean'?

Peter was willing to go to the home of a man whom he knew the Jews would not ordinarily approve of. Ask the Lord to help you to be willing to do things for the sake of the gospel that others may not approve of.

Every age is an age for evangelism. God has no grandchildren. *Eugene L. Smith*

Acts
12:1-11

'And the hand of the Lord was with them, and a great number believed and turned to the Lord' (Acts 11:21).

There is no doubt that times of persecution strengthen the church. Those who remain faithful are strengthened by the Holy Spirit, and those who are forced to leave home and possessions usually go about preaching the Lord of the gospel they love.

Following the death of Stephen, the persecuted Christians escaped to places of safety throughout the region and, as a result of their witness, many came to faith in Christ.

The church in Jerusalem sent Barnabas out on a preaching tour as far as Antioch. When he heard that Saul (Paul) was in Tarsus, he travelled there to meet him, and both men returned to Antioch where, for a year, they preached the gospel. The church grew and it was at Antioch that the saints were first called 'Christians' (Acts 11:26).

In Jerusalem, King Herod had James, the son of Zebedee, put to death, using a sword. When Herod saw that this pleased the ungodly Jews, he had Peter arrested and placed in prison under guard. He intended to deal with Peter during the feast of Unleavened Bread.

The night before Peter was to appear before Herod, he lay in a cold cell, chained between two soldiers. Outside, the Christians were praying.

In the prison, an angel, surrounded by light, suddenly appeared. The angel spoke to Peter, telling him to dress quickly and to follow him. The chains that held Peter fell off and he was led out of the prison, past the sleeping guards and through the gates. Peter was so surprised at what was happening that he thought he was dreaming.

When he was safely well away from the jail, the angel disappeared. Peter said to himself, 'Now I know for certain that the Lord has sent his angel, and has delivered me from the hand of Herod and from all the expectation of the Jewish people' (Acts 12:11).

Making his way to the house where the Christians were praying, he knocked on the door. When the servant girl, Rhoda, opened it and saw Peter, she turned and ran inside to tell the Christians that Peter was outside. They didn't believe her, even though they were praying for God to perform a miracle. Peter kept on knocking until he was admitted. Following a brief time with his friends, he left for Caesarea, where he hoped to find safety.

When Herod discovered that Peter had 'escaped' from prison, the guards were interrogated and sentenced to death. This great miracle would have strengthened the faith of the Christians in Jerusalem.

Christians have an all-powerful God!

FIND OUT THE FACTS

1. Name one Christian martyr you have read about.
2. Why did Herod have Peter arrested?
3. What sort of a person was Rhoda and her Christian friends who didn't believe God had answered their prayer for Peter?

With God nothing is impossible. Think about what that means for your life today.

Most joyfully will I confirm with my blood that truth which I have written and preached.   *Jan Huss*

Acts
12:20-25

'Then immediately an angel of the Lord struck him, because he did not give glory to God. And he was eaten by worms and died' (Acts 12:23).

Often the church has suffered persecution by those who rule nations. In Psalm 2:2-4 we read, 'The kings of the earth set themselves, and the rulers take counsel together, against the LORD and against his Anointed, saying, "Let us break their bonds in pieces and cast away their cords from us."' Then come the words that should terrify anyone who attempts to destroy the church: 'He who sits in the heavens shall laugh...'

The Lord Jesus promised the church that 'the gates of Hades [hell] shall not prevail against it' (Matthew 16:18). Let the world do its worst, but the church, Christ's bride, is safe and secure. The church will suffer times of persecution, but it will survive.

Our scripture passage tells us that King Herod Agrippa was angry with the citizens of Tyre and Sidon. They sent ambassadors to Herod, whose chamberlain, Blastus, was able to bring about a peaceful outcome. However, it was necessary for proud Herod Agrippa to make a public announcement.

He enjoyed the praise of his citizens, so he set aside a day during a special festival where the people vowed to ensure his safety. He promised to make a proclamation on that day.

On the second day of the festival, Herod dressed himself in his royal clothing. The sun shone brightly and this made his clothing sparkle. He gave an oration and people began to flatter him calling out, 'The voice of a god and not of a man!' (Acts 12:22). Those words were a deliberate breaking of the First Commandment: 'I am the LORD your God, who brought you out of the land of Egypt, out of the house of bondage. You shall have no other gods before me' (Exodus 20:2-3).

The Scriptures tell us that an angel from heaven struck him down, because he accepted the sinful praise of the people. Luke tells us that worms ate him as he was dying.

Josephus,[1] the Jewish historian, said that Herod looked up when the people called him a god and saw an owl sitting on a rope nearby. He took this as a messenger of bad times. Josephus says that suddenly he had severe stomach pains which persisted for five days. His body began to decay before his death. God is truly' angry with the wicked every day' (Psalm 7:11).

As a result of Herod's awful death, sinners were won to Christ, and the church grew.

Pride is a terrible sin!

---

[1] See Josephus, *The works of Flavius Josephus*, Vol. 4 , *Antiquities of the Jews*, Book XIX:VIII:2, Baker Book House, USA., 1979,pp.106-07.

FIND OUT THE FACTS

1. What Commandment did the people break by calling Herod a 'god'?
2. Why does God punish sinners?
3. How can we be sure that the church cannot be destroyed?

This incident clearly shows that God is not mocked. He will not share his glory with another. Pray for people in positions of authority in your community that they will not fall into this sin of arrogance.

Christ's followers cannot expect better treatment in the world than their Master had.   *Matthew Henry*

Acts
13:4-12

'Then Saul, who also is called Paul, filled with the Holy Spirit, looked intently at [Elymas] and said, "... you son of the devil, you enemy of all righteousness, will you not cease perverting the straight ways of the Lord?"' (Acts 13:9-10).

The Holy Spirit commanded Barnabas and Paul to commence a missionary work among the Gentiles. They travelled to Salamis, but at the island of Paphos they met a sorcerer named Elymas (Bar-Jesus) who opposed the missionaries.

Barnabas and Paul spoke to the Roman Proconsul, Sergius Paulus, about the risen Christ, but Elymas opposed their teaching. Paul, filled with the Holy Spirit, accused Elymas of being the 'son of the devil' (Acts 13:10). In the name of the Lord, Paul said that Elymas would become blind for a time. The Proconsul believed the truth spoken by Paul and Barnabas.

John Mark accompanied Paul and Barnabas when they set out for Cyprus, travelling as far as Paphos, a city on the west coast. He was the author of the Gospel of Mark and a cousin of Barnabas. He would have given the missionaries much assistance in their work.

The local synagogue ruler asked the missionaries to speak. Paul stood up and reminded those present of the history of Israel, and the way God had cared for them as they entered the Promised Land. He spoke of the failure of King Saul, their first king, but reminded them of King David, from whom their Messiah would descend.

Paul spoke to them of the treatment that the Lord Jesus had received; how he had been persecuted and finally nailed to a Roman cross which was the altar upon which Christ, the perfect sacrifice for sin, was nailed. Jesus Christ, the Son of God, carried the sins of his people to the cross, and there paid the debt owed to God. Paul said, 'But God raised him from the dead' (Acts 13:30). He continued explaining the ways in which the Lord Jesus Christ had fulfilled many Old Testament prophecies.

The Jews largely ignored what had been preached, but the Gentiles asked Paul and Barnabas to speak to them again. The following Sabbath a great crowd of people gathered to hear the gospel preached. When the Jews, who opposed the gospel, saw what was happening, they created a disturbance.

Paul and Barnabas said, 'It was necessary that the word of God should be spoken to you first; but since you reject it, and judge yourselves unworthy of everlasting life, behold, we turn to the Gentiles (Acts 13:46).

As the Gentiles listened, many were won into the kingdom of God. However, when persecution from the Jews followed, the two missionaries departed for Iconium.

FIND OUT THE FACTS

1. What causes people to believe the gospel?
2. In your atlas find the places mentioned in this devotion.
3. Why was Saul now called Paul?

The Lord will not always persevere with people who continually reject his Word. Pray for people today whom you know to be strongly opposed to the gospel message.

A saying to Remember

The gospel has the hallmark of heaven upon it. *William White*

Acts
14:8-25

'But the unbelieving Jews stirred up the Gentiles and poisoned their minds against the brethren' (Acts 14:2).

Paul found that in most places he visited, the Jews caused problems. They hated him because he had been a well-known Pharisee but was now a follower of Jesus, who claimed to be God's Messiah. In Iconium the unbelieving Jews stirred up the people against Paul and Barnabas. Nevertheless, for a time, they remained there preaching the gospel and performing miracles in Christ's name. When they heard they would soon face violence — abuse and stones — they moved on to the region of Lycaonia.

Our scripture passage tells the story of a man who, from his birth had been a cripple. Indeed we are told he 'had never walked' (Acts 14:8). When Paul saw that he was listening to him preaching, he gave the command: 'Stand up straight on your feet!' (Acts 14:10). This miracle caused such great excitement in Lystra that some of the people shouted out, 'The gods have come down to us in the likeness of men!' (Acts 14:11). They called Paul Hermes, because of his ability to speak, and Barnabas was given the name Zeus.

A priest from Zeus' temple came to sacrifice animals to Barnabas. The two distressed missionaries told the crowd that they were just ordinary men like themselves. Paul went on to say that they were servants of the God who created the heavens and the earth; the God who gave them the rain and food.

The Jews, from Antioch and Iconium, stirred up the crowd who began stoning Paul. When they thought he was dead, they dragged his body outside the city. The local Christians gathered about Paul's still body, and were overjoyed to discover he was still alive. He and Barnabas spent another night with the believers before leaving for Derbe, where many sinners were converted and became members of the Kingdom of God.

Paul and Barnabas returned to Antioch, passing through Lystra and Iconium, where they met the Christians and strengthened their faith in Christ.

The local churches were well organized before the missionaries departed. Elders were appointed to each congregation. After a time of fasting, they were commended to Christ in whom they had a saving faith.

When they reached Antioch they told the Christians about the good things the Lord had done. Everyone rejoiced that the Gentiles now worshipped the Jewish Messiah. The church was growing in numbers and in strength. Paul and Barnabas remained with the Christians in Antioch for a considerable time.

FIND OUT THE FACTS

1. How do you explain a miracle?

2. In what way is your congregation organized?

3. Fasting is mentioned in this devotion. What is fasting? What is the value of fasting?

In spite of the opposition of the Jews, the number of converts grew and the gospel continued to change people's lives. Pray for the Christians in a country where there is much opposition to the gospel.

A miracle is an event in the external world that is wrought by the immediate power of God. *J. Gresham Machen*

Acts
15:22-41

'Known to God from eternity are all his works' (Acts 15:18).

Imagine what your friends and relatives would say to you if you decided to change your religion. It could well be that you suddenly found yourself the object of persecution. In the days of the apostle Paul, the Christians found themselves the object of Jewish hatred.

Some Jews who came down from Judea taught the following: 'Unless you are circumcised according to the custom of Moses, you cannot be saved' (Acts 15:1). They were not denying that salvation was through faith in Christ, but that faith in Christ had to be accompanied by obedience to the law of Moses, which included circumcision and keeping the feast days. This was adding to the gospel message and meant a return to the Pharisees' yoke of bondage (Acts 15:10)

The apostle Paul had faced this problem in Galatia and written an epistle in which he explained the place of the law in the salvation of sinners. He always argued that sinners are saved by faith in Christ alone. Of any other doctrine he wrote, 'But even if we, or an angel from heaven, preach any other gospel to you than what we have preached to you, let him be accursed' (Galatians 1:8).

When this issue surfaced, the apostles, including Paul and Barnabas, went to Jerusalem to discuss the place of the law. There the church representatives discussed the problem and made the following decisions, which became a portion of a circular letter sent to the Christian churches:

First, 'Abstain from things offered to idols'; second, abstain 'from blood, from things strangled'; third, abstain 'from sexual immorality.'

The letter concluded with: 'If you keep yourselves from these, you will do well' (Acts 15:29).

Paul and Barnabas were given the responsibility of carrying the letter to the churches. When they arrived at Antioch and read the letter to the Christians, there was great rejoicing. Judas and Silas, both prophets, were in Antioch with Paul and Barnabas. Judas returned to Jerusalem with news of Antioch, leaving the three missionaries to preach the gospel and strengthen God's people in the city.

When Paul decided to set out on a second missionary journey, visiting all the churches they had established, he had a falling out with Barnabas who wanted to take Mark with him. In the end, Barnabas and Mark sailed for Cyprus and Paul and Silas set out to visit the churches he had founded.

Today, most churches meet, usually annually, to discuss church policy. In doing so the Bible is used to determine truth.

Do you read your Bible?

FIND OUT THE FACTS

1. Why did Paul and Barnabas have a disagreement?
2. In Acts 15 whose speech was recorded?
3. Who required Christians to keep the law of Moses in order to be saved?

Thank the Lord Jesus Christ that salvation is complete in him; it does not need any additional deeds or rituals.

The conduct of our lives is the true mirror of our doctrine.
Michel de Montaigne

Acts
16:1-15

'The Lord opened [Lydia's] heart to heed the things spoken by Paul' (Acts 16:14).

When Paul and Silas passed through Derbe and Lystra they met a disciple called Timothy. He had probably been converted sometime during Paul's first preaching tour. He was the son of Eunice and grandson of Lois, both of them Christian women. They had taken very seriously their God-given responsibility to teach their son the things of God.

Writing to Timothy, Paul mentioned 'that from childhood you have known the Holy Scriptures, which are able to make you wise for salvation through faith which is in Christ Jesus' (2 Timothy 3:15). Timothy's father was a Greek.

Meeting Timothy, whom Paul often called his spiritual 'son,' gave him great joy (1 Corinthians 4:17). Paul had him circumcised so that he could mix freely with the Jews who kept the law of Moses. This circumcision was a matter of convenience, but had the Jews demanded his circumcision, Paul would have refused. He had fought that battle with the Jews in Galatia (Galatians 5:1ff).

As Paul continued on his way, he was met by a heavenly messenger who said, 'Come over to Macedonia and help us' (Acts 16:9). Immediately Paul and his companions left Troas by ship for Neapolis. Soon they moved on to Philippi, where the missionaries met with the Jewish women who gathered at the riverside each Sabbath for prayer. There he came into contact with Lydia, a seller of purple dye and purple dyed material. She came from Thyatira and was in Philippi to sell what was a very costly dye, made from a shell-fish. This shell-fish was the 'purpura murex'.

The Holy Spirit had prepared her heart to receive the gospel. Having confessed her faith in Christ, she and her household were baptized. Consequently the missionaries were invited to her home.

It wasn't long before Paul faced difficulties. A slave girl, who told 'fortunes,' and who made a lot of money for her owners, followed Paul, crying out, 'These men are the servants of the Most High God, who proclaim to us the way of salvation' (Acts 16:17). When this continued for many days Paul commanded the demon to leave her.

Her owners, furious that they had lost a valuable source of income, dragged Paul and Silas to the city magistrates, saying, 'These men, being Jews, exceedingly trouble our city; and they teach customs which are not lawful for us, being Romans, to receive or observe'. Soon Paul and Silas would suffer the abuse of the ungodly Jews and Gentiles (Acts 16:20-21).

FIND OUT THE FACTS

1. Why was purple dye so expensive?
2. Why did Paul call Timothy his 'son'?
3. Why was Timothy circumcised?
4. In what way is Lydia an example to all believers?

Thank the Lord for his providence in bringing people to salvation.

We are not saved *for* believing, but *by* believing. *Thomas Taylor*

Acts
16:25-40

'So they said, "Believe on the Lord Jesus Christ, and you will be saved, you and your household"' (Acts 16:31).

When my brother John and I were young, we often pretended to be cowboys using a whip. One would hit the other with it, but in such a way that it didn't hurt. From a distance it looked very painful. Occasionally we would hit in the wrong spot and the tears would flow.

Paul and Silas were arrested, stripped of their clothing and severely whipped. In pain and with blood dripping from their wounds, they were thrown into prison. At midnight they were singing psalms and praying, when there was a severe earthquake, which threw open all the prison doors.

The jailor, awakened by the trembling earth, thought all the prisoners had escaped. If this had occurred he would have been put to death by his superior officers. He took out his sword and was about to commit suicide, when Paul called out, telling him that they were still there and that he should not hurt himself.

The jailer then ran in to where Paul and Silas were and fell at their feet. After bringing them out, he asked, 'Sirs, what must I do to be saved?' (Acts 16:30). Paul and Silas quickly answered with the words he needed to hear, 'Believe on the Lord Jesus Christ, and you will be saved, you and your household' (Acts 16:31).

Paul and Silas were taken to the jailer's home where they preached about the risen Saviour to the jailer and all his household. As a consequence, he believed in the gospel, with all his household and they were baptized. There was much rejoicing that night. The jailer had Paul and Silas bathed, their wounds cleansed and then he gave them a much needed meal.

The next day when the magistrates declared that the missionaries should be given their freedom so they could leave the city, Paul refused, as he was a Roman citizen and should not have been so badly treated. He sent word back to the magistrates that they were 'uncondemned Romans', who should not have been thrown in prison or whipped (Acts 16:37). They had been locked up while everyone watched; now they would wait for the magistrates to come and personally release them. This reply terrified the magistrates who went to the prison, released the missionaries and begged them to leave their city.

Paul and Silas visited Lydia, where they spoke to the Christians, encouraging them to be faithful to their Lord. Then they left the city.

FIND OUT THE FACTS

1. Why were Paul and Silas locked away in jail?
2. Is suicide sinful? Read Exodus 20:13. Adults might consider: Is suicide the unforgivable sin? Discuss this in the light of the doctrine of justification by faith alone.
3. Why wouldn't Paul and Silas leave the prison?

To Think & to pray about

This incident assures us that even in difficult situations, like being thrown into prison, the Lord is working. Thank him for this.

A saying to Remember

Scars are the price which every believer pays for his loyalty to Christ.
William Hendriksen

Psalm
37:1-11

'Nor is there salvation in any other, for there is no other name under heaven given among men by which we must be saved' (Acts 4:12).

Sinners are commanded to trust their eternal security to the Lord Jesus. All who have a saving faith in the Lord know that their sins have been forgiven and Christ's righteousness has been imputed to them.

One day our cat was stuck up a tree. I nailed a dustbin to a long pole, held it up under the cat and called him, hoping he would jump in — and he did! I was the cat's saviour! He committed his well-being to me. As I lowered the dustbin to the ground, it fell off. I don't know if the cat would trust me a second time. But Jesus never lets us down. He will escort each of his people into paradise.

Many years ago I tried digging potatoes. When the large bag was full, I had to pick it up and carry it to a trailer. Those bags were very heavy and when another man saw me struggling, he came, lifted the bag from my shoulders and carried it for me. Sinners carry a heavy burden of sins, and the only way to get rid of them is to place them on the crucified Saviour.

In Psalm 55:22 we read: 'Cast your burden on the LORD, and he shall sustain you…' Faith involves trusting in Christ who removed our sins and carried them to the cross. There, as the sinners' substitute, he was punished by God.

Here is another story which illustrates faith. We had ten or twenty fowls on the farm, and usually they had some chickens. One day, when the chicken hawk appeared, the fowls knew there was danger, so they called their chickens. The small chickens ran to their mother and hid under her outstretched wings. That was the place of protection.

Our place of protection is found in Jesus. Psalm 57:1 says, 'Be merciful to me, O God, be merciful to me! For my soul trusts in you; and in the shadow of your wings I will make my refuge, until these calamities have passed by.'

Christ is our protection against God's anger. Christ, our sin-bearer, carried our sins to the cross, and there carried the punishment due for them. Our protection is found at the foot of the cross. In Isaiah 50:10 we read that sinners must 'trust in the name of the LORD and rely [lean] upon ... God'.

Faith is leaning upon Jesus Christ who has all power in heaven and earth. Alone I would never reach heaven, but I can lean upon him. He is the sinners' guide on that narrow way which leads to paradise.

Have you a saving faith in the Lord Jesus?

FIND OUT THE FACTS

1. What is meant by 'faith in Jesus'?
2. How do you show you have faith in Christ? See James 2:26.
3. Why do sinners trust in the Lord Jesus?
4. Discuss: 'Faith is a bird that can sing in winter.'

Thank the Lord Jesus that he forgives sinners and makes them members of his family.

Faith is the marriage of the soul to Christ. Richard Sibbes

December

How much better to get wisdom than gold!

Proverbs 16:16

Revelation 12:13-17 'Do not love the world or the things in the world. If anyone loves the world, the love of the Father is not in him' (1 John 2:15).

One of the first parables that the Lord told was that of 'the sower'. The gospel is the 'seed' which falls on the various soils. The good soil is a heart which has been prepared by the Holy Spirit to receive the gospel. These people become citizens of the kingdom of God.

The seed that falls among the thorns is the person who 'hears the word, and the cares of this world and the deceitfulness of riches choke the word, and he becomes unfruitful' (Matthew 13:22).

As you look about you, I'm sure you will find the world to be attractive. There is so much in the world which glitters and is desirable. The music, the cars, the easy life, the colourful clothes, the TV and films, the clubs, the drugs and alcohol and everything else that has appeal is there for the taking.

The apostle John wrote, warning men and women about the love of the world, 'For all that is in the world — the lust of the flesh, the lust of the eyes, and the pride of life — is not of the Father but is of the world. And the world is passing away, and the lust of it; but he who does the will of God abides for ever' (1 John 2:16,17).

Christians should keep their eyes upon their Redeemer, the Lord Jesus Christ. They are to use the world wisely. A man I know walks on the opposite side of the street when he sees a hardware shop. He finds it difficult to resist buying more tools! The world can creep into the life of a Christian and damage his faith. If this happens to you, repent and return to the Lord who loves you.

Just as the world must be kept out of the Christian's life, so it must be kept out of the church.

The scripture passage refers to the church escaping from the devil into the wilderness. Away from the devil and his schemes there is safety. However, Satan tries to 'wash' the church back into his reach where he can cause trouble. Worldliness can destroy the spiritual zeal of individuals and congregations. We should all be on guard against the temptations of the world, or our life will be shown to be that of the seed which fell among the thorns.

Spend time with your Christian friends, attend worship, read your Bible, learn as much Scripture as you can, read good books and show your love for God by doing good deeds. This will keep the love of the world out of your heart.

FIND OUT THE FACTS

1. What is meant by 'the world'?
2. How can Christians make use of the world?
3. Name some ways in which the world can harm the church.

Thank the Lord that he does keep his people. Ask the Lord to help you to turn from the temptations of the world.

A man caught up with this world is not ready for the next. *Anon*

Acts
17:10-15

'They received the word with all readiness, and searched the Scriptures daily to find out whether these things were so' (Acts 17:11).

Paul, Silas and Timothy travelled through Amphipolis and Apollonia, arriving at Thessalonica, where a small congregation was founded. They met with the Jews for three Sabbaths, proving that Jesus was the Christ, promised by God many generations before.

The Jews could not accept that their Messiah had to die. But the missionaries opened the Scriptures to prove that not only was Messiah to die, but he was also to rise again. No doubt they expounded Isaiah 53 which taught that the Lord's Servant would die as a substitute for his people.

All the disciples, including Paul, were witnesses to Christ's resurrection. Luke records that some of the Jews believed, as well as 'a great multitude of the devout Greeks, and not a few of the leading women' (Acts 17:4).

Again the Jews set about raising opposition to Paul and Silas. The angry crowd went to Jason's home where the missionaries were staying. Finding them absent, they dragged Jason out and took him to the city rulers, where they complained, 'These who have turned the world upside down have come here too. Jason has harboured them, and these are all acting contrary to the decrees of Caesar, saying there is another king — Jesus' (Acts 17:6-7).

When Jason was released, the saints suggested that Paul and his companions leave during the night. This they did making their way to Berea, where once again they visited the synagogue and preached the gospel. The Berean Jews were 'more fair-minded than those in Thessalonica, in that they received the word with all readiness, and searched the Scriptures daily to find out whether these things were so' (Acts 17:11). Consequently, many believed what Paul taught.

This is how you should approach any doctrine preached by your pastor. Go back to your Bible and check what has been taught, against the infallible Word of God. The better you know your Bible, the smaller the chance of being led astray.

Do you know the reasons behind the administration of the Lord's Supper in your congregation, or why baptism is administered as it is? Just because someone has given you an answer to these questions is no guarantee that what has been said is correct. You have your Bibles and you should be like those noble, fair-minded Bereans. Make sure that what you are told is confirmed by the Scriptures — your eternal security may depend upon it!

When the troublesome Jews in Thessalonica heard of the events in Berea, they arrived and stirred up trouble for the missionaries. Consequently, Paul left for Athens, leaving Silas and Timothy behind.

FIND OUT THE FACTS

1. List three reasons why you should read your Bible.
2. Why did the Jews oppose the teaching that Jesus was the Messiah?
3. Who is Jesus to you?

Ask the Lord to help you to develop and maintain the discipline of reading his Word.

The Old Testament Scriptures are intelligible only when understood as predicting and prefiguring Christ. *Charles Hodge*

A saying to Remember

 1 Thessalonians 'Then we who are alive and
4:13 - 5:4   remain shall be caught up
together with them in the
clouds to meet the Lord in the
air. And thus we shall always
be   with   the   Lord'
(1 Thessalonians 4:17).

Paul, Silas and Timothy rejoiced when they heard the news
that the Thessalonian church was continuing to be faithful, despite the persecution it was suffering. Thus Paul wrote
two letters of encouragement to them. It also appears that Paul
received some questions, which he answered in those epistles.

Paul had preached about the coming of the Lord Jesus, but
since he had not come quickly, and some of the people in the
congregation had died, the others had wanted to know what
would happen to those who had passed away. Would they take
part in the resurrection?

Paul wrote extensively about the second coming of Christ
whom he declared would return, accompanied by his mighty
angels. Those who were strangers to God's grace would 'be
punished with everlasting destruction from the presence of
the Lord and from the glory of his power' (2 Thessalonians 1:9).

In the scripture passage you have read, Paul explained that
the living will have no advantage over the dead when the Lord
returns from heaven. Apparently, there was a great deal of
sorrow because the Thessalonians saw no hope for their dead
Christian friends and relatives.

The first great truth is an encouragement to all Christians;
the souls of dead believers pass into the presence of Christ in
heaven. We read in Revelation 6:9, 'I saw under the altar the
souls of those who had been slain for the word of God and for
the testimony which they held.' (See Philippians 1:21-23.)
Everyone who had 'fallen asleep' would accompany Christ and
his holy angels when the Lord broke into history the second
time (1 Thessalonians 4:13,14).

At the voice of the archangel and the sound of the trumpet, the dead in Christ would be united to their Christ-like, resurrection bodies. Those who were alive, would then find their bodies and souls changed 'in the twinkling of an eye' (1 Corinthians 15:52). All believers would rise in the air to meet their Lord in the clouds. This meeting would be the beginning of life in the new heavens and earth with Christ.

Paul concludes this section of his letter with, 'Therefore comfort one another with these words' (1 Thessalonians 4:18). Paul's words in the reading today should be a comfort. In life and death the saints cannot be separated from the Lord.

FIND OUT THE FACTS

1. Our salvation will be complete after our resurrection. Why?
2. Where are our dead Christian friends and relatives?
3. Do the living have any advantage over the dead when Christ returns? Give a reason for your answer.

Thank the Lord that he takes complete care of the lives and the death of his people.

We are more sure to arise out of our graves than out of our beds.
Thomas Watson

Acts
17:22-34

'But now [God] commands all men everywhere to repent, because he has appointed a day on which he will judge the world in righteousness by the Man whom he has ordained. He has given assurance of this to all by raising him from the dead' (Acts 17:30-31).

In the days of the apostle Paul, Athens was a major city in Greece where its citizens had plenty of time to discuss issues while their slaves worked hard. Paul journeyed there and went to the synagogue to speak to the Jews and the God-fearing Gentiles. Realizing that he would need help, he sent word, asking for Silas and Timothy to join him as soon as possible.

In the market place, he soon found himself reasoning with the philosophers concerning Christ and the resurrection. The Athenians were interested in Paul's new teaching, so they took him to the Areopagus (Mars Hill) so they could hear all he had to say. Paul had noticed that the Athenians were very religious. He saw many idols, and one in particular caught his attention: 'To the unknown God' (Acts 17:23).

Paul begun his address by telling them about their unknown God, who created the world and was not confined to man-made temples. This God created life and caused people to live in various parts of the world. Paul's God was spirit and close to everyone, so it was possible for men and women to find him. He was totally unlike any of their idols.

In the generations before the days of Christ, God had endured the sins of the Gentile nations, but now he commanded men and women everywhere to repent of their sins, because a judgement day was coming. The Judge he had appointed was Jesus Christ, who had died and been raised from the dead.

The resurrection of the Lord Jesus was the proof that his death as a substitute had made him the divine Saviour of his people. The gospel stands or falls on the resurrection of the Lord Jesus. Paul said, 'For if the dead do not rise, then Christ is not risen. And if Christ is not risen, your faith is futile; you are still in your sins' (1 Corinthians 15:16-17).

The resurrection was something new to the Athenians, especially as they believed the body to be the cause of man's problems and a hindrance to enjoying a perfect existence. The Greeks looked forward to their death when they believed they would be freed from their bodies and so live a perfect life.

Other Athenians were sure that death meant the end. To talk about some future life in the body was against all they ever believed.

Some who were present mocked Paul, while others were more courteous saying, 'We will hear you again on this matter' (Acts 17:32). But some believed, and a small church was formed.

FIND OUT THE FACTS

1. Find Athens in your atlas.

2. List some 'gods' that people have today.

3. What was the 'Areopagus'?

God's Word always has an effect. Some reject it, others mock it, and still others are converted. Thank the Lord that the preaching of his gospel is never in vain.

The resurrection and the judgement will demonstrate before all worlds who won and who lost. We can wait! A.W. Tozer

A saying to Remember

Acts
18:1-18

'Now the Lord spoke to Paul in the night by a vision, "Do not be afraid, but speak, and do not keep silent; for I am with you, and no one will attack you to hurt you; for I have many people in this city"' (Acts 18:9-10).

The gospel was being preached far and wide by the apostle Paul. Having left Athens he made his way to Corinth, a city situated on the Greek Isthmus, with a port on either side. It was famous for commerce, the easy life and immorality.

In Corinth Paul met a Jew named Aquila and his wife, Priscilla. As they were tent makers, Paul, also being a tent maker, lived and worked with them. Every Sabbath he preached the gospel in the synagogue to the Jews and Gentiles who had been converted.

While in Corinth, Silas and Timothy arrived from Macedonia and assisted him, witnessing to the Jews. When persecution began, Paul 'shook his garments and said to them, "Your blood be upon your own heads; I am clean. From now on I will go to the Gentiles"' (Acts 18:6).

Paul then moved to the home of godly Justus, who lived next door to the synagogue. There he preached the gospel. Crispus, the ruler of the synagogue, 'believed on the Lord with all his household' (v. 8), and they, along with many other Corinthians who believed, were baptized. The work of the missionaries produced fruit; even Crispus believed in the Lord.

Following the vision Paul had from the Lord, the gospel was preached with much success to the Gentiles for more than eighteen months. Soon, however, the Jews stirred up trouble and had Paul brought before the Proconsul. They claimed that 'this fellow persuades men to worship God contrary to the law' (Acts 18:13). Gallio refused to listen to their complaints and had them all sent away from the judgement seat. He apparently knew the troublesome nature of the Jews, and refused to become involved in their squabbles.

The Jews decided to persecute the Christians and began by assaulting Sosthenes, the synagogue ruler. Sosthenes could have been the ruler who succeeded Crispus. It is more likely that he was the second leader of the synagogue as synagogue leadership was usually in the hands of two men (or more). Again the Proconsul refused to become involved in what he thought to be a religious squabble between different Jewish sects. This fulfilled God's promise in the scripture verse.

The time had arrived for Paul to leave Corinth for Jerusalem, which he wanted to visit at the time of the Passover or Pentecost.

Paul's second missionary journey concluded with his return to Jerusalem, where he reported to the Christians the good things the Lord had done among the Gentiles.

FIND OUT THE FACTS

1. Find Corinth on a map of Greece.
2. Who was the Roman Proconsul in Corinth?
3. Find out all you can about Corinth.

To Think & to pray about

The apostle Paul was given grace to persevere in difficult circumstances. Ask the Lord to give you that grace too.

A saying to Remember

The law gives menaces, the gospel gives promises.
Thomas Adams

1 Corinthians 'And now abide faith, hope,
13:4-8a   love, these three; but the
             greatest of these is love'
             (1 Corinthians 13:13).

Sometimes at weddings you will hear today's Bible reading used to describe the love that exists between a husband and wife. However, this is not that very special love that exists between married couples. 1 Corinthians 13 speaks of the Christian love that should be found in every relationship, including husbands and wives! The world would be a much better place in which to live if Christian love was found everywhere.

Speaking in 'tongues' became very important in Corinth, but, according to Paul, if they were exercised without love, they meant nothing. The gift of prophecy and knowledge, without love, added nothing to the speaker.

Even giving everything a person owned to feed the poor, or becoming a martyr meant nothing, if it was not done in love. It is easy to love nice people — our friends and relatives — but this is not the love that Paul is speaking about here. He lists the characteristics of Christian love which should be seen in every person who claims to be a lover of the Lord Jesus.

This love doesn't require you to throw your arms around another and give him or her a big hug. Rather, it is a love that wants the very best for others. It is the love that puts others before yourself. It is a love that can rejoice when another is preferred before you.

Often, when another person gets the promotion one was expecting, the complaints start. The love that Paul has written about is seen when the person who missed out on the promotion congratulates the successful person, and truly means what he says!

Christian love helps a drunk person to his feet and makes sure he gets home safely. It is patient in difficulties and endures the hardships another may be inflicting. Christian love prays for others, even the enemy. It does not ask for anything in return.

The Lord is always watching what happens on this earth. Every kindness shown to another is written in God's book of remembrance which will be opened on the Day of Judgement (Revelation 20:12-13).

Paul writes that this love 'never fails' (1 Corinthians 13:8) because in the end it will win the respect of other people.

The chapter ends with: 'And now abide faith, hope, love, these three; but the greatest of these is love' (1 Corinthians 13:13).

When you reach heaven your hopes will be realized: 'Hope that is seen is not hope; for why does one still hope for what he sees?' (Romans 8:24). Faith is our grasp on an eternal future. When we walk the streets of heaven, faith will not be necessary. But love is everlasting!

FIND OUT THE FACTS

1. Why is love the greatest of faith, hope and love?

2. How can you show Christian love at home?

3. Read Romans 12:20. What do these words mean?

The kind of love described in 1 Corinthians 13 is not one that comes naturally to sinful human beings. Ask the Lord to give you the grace to love others in this way.

A saying to Remember

Love is the master key to a happy home. *Anon*

Acts
19:21-41

'So the word of the Lord grew
mightily and prevailed' (Acts
19:20).

Paul commenced his third missionary journey, accompanied by Priscilla and Aquila. They made their way to Ephesus, the busiest commercial city in Asia Minor.

When Paul met some Christian disciples with a very limited knowledge of the faith, he asked them if they had received the Holy Spirit when they believed. (Every Christian is born again of the Holy Spirit. But these people were ignorant of many Christian truths and had not experienced any miraculous effects following conversion as had happened in Jerusalem on the day of Pentecost. These disciples had known only the baptism of John the Baptist.) Paul then baptized them in the name of the triune God, and 'they spoke with tongues and prophesied' (Acts 19:6).

For two years Paul remained in Ephesus, preaching Christ, and many Greeks and Jews were converted. A loving local congregation was formed there. Paul performed many miracles, confirming the truth of the gospel to those who came to a saving faith in the Lord Jesus. Converted magicians made piles of their expensive books and burnt them all.

Timothy and Erastus were sent to Macedonia, while Paul continued his evangelistic work in Ephesus.

Demetrius, a silversmith, who made shrines for the worship of Diana, found his trade falling away as people turned to Christ. He gathered together those who made such shrines and idols and, after he had addressed them, they commenced shouting 'Great is Diana of the Ephesians!' (Acts 19:28).

Crowds gathered and in the confusion Paul's companions, Gaius and Aristarchus, were dragged into a very large amphitheatre which seated twenty thousand people. Paul wanted to join his friends, but the disciples said, 'No!'

When a disciple, Alexander, stood up to defend the Christian faith, he was shouted down, because the people found out that he was a Jew. For two hours the crowd shouted, 'Great is Diana of the Ephesians!' (Acts 19:34).

When a city official stood up the crowd became quiet. He warned the people that what was happening was against Roman law. He urged those who had a case against the Christians to make use of the law courts. He warned them that if they continued to act as they were, they would be called before the city magistrates.

The crowd dispersed and the city became calm for a time. Soon Paul was to leave by ship for Troas where again the gospel would be preached. The number of Christians was growing quickly, as men and women believed in the salvation that is found in Christ.

FIND OUT THE FACTS

1. What is a missionary?
2. What is an amphitheatre? Draw one.
3. Why should you only worship Jehovah?

To Think & to pray about

The silversmiths were losing trade because people were being converted. The gospel changes people and this results in changes in the community. Pray that your church would make an impact on the community where you live.

A saying to Remember

The occupational hazard of the Christian ministry and evangelism is discouragement. *John Stott*

Ephesians   'Therefore I also, after I
5:22 - 6:9   heard of your faith in the Lord
             Jesus and your love for all the
             saints, do not cease to give
             thanks for you, making mention
             of you in my prayers'
             (Ephesians 1:15-16).

We write letters to our friends and to people we love. It is always good to receive a reply. The apostle Paul was a good letter writer. The New Testament contains twelve of his letters, and possibly thirteen. We cannot be certain who wrote the Epistle to the Hebrews. If it was Paul, then he wrote thirteen of the epistles in the New Testament. What we do know is that he wrote more than those which form part of the New Testament, and these additional ones have been lost.

It was five years since he had left the saints at Ephesus, and during that time he had heard very encouraging news about the congregation. As we read his letter to the Ephesians, we cannot find any rebukes. It seems that all was well in the congregation. We know this from the words of our scripture verse.

Paul had heard stories of both their faith in the Lord Jesus and their love for their Christian brethren. This was the outworking of faith in Christ: 'For we are his workmanship, created in Christ Jesus for good works, which God prepared beforehand that we should walk in them' (Ephesians 2:10).

Their Christian love for one another was the fulfilment of Christ's words: 'A new commandment I give you, that you love one another; as I have loved you, that you also love one another. By this all will know that you are my disciples, if you have love for one another' (John 13:34-35).

His letter was one of encouragement as well as Christian teaching. During the two years he had spent with them, Paul had not avoided preaching all the great Christian truths (Acts 20:27).

His letter taught the great doctrines of grace. God had blessed the people greatly, because of Christ's saving work. He strengthened their faith by reminding them that they were chosen by God for salvation, 'before the foundation of the world' (Ephesians 1:4).

He had not avoided teaching them doctrines that today are unacceptable to many professing Christians: election and predestination. These doctrines provide great comfort for believers because they know that those who are chosen by God to salvation, will never be lost (John 10:27-29).

In the passage you have read, Paul instructs all members of the church — husbands, wives, parents and children. Paul even gives teaching concerning the workplace — servants and masters.

The world would be a more joyful place if these commands were obeyed by everyone.

FIND OUT THE FACTS

1. Why are Christians greatly blessed by God?
2. What does the doctrine of election teach?
3. What is the evidence of saving faith?

The letter to the Ephesians has some great truths for Christians to learn today. Take one of these truths, think about what it is teaching you and pray, asking the Lord to help you to put it into practice.

Faith and love are a wonderful pair of twins. *Chrysostom*

Acts
20:17-38

'Therefore take heed to yourselves and to all the flock ...
For I know this, that after my
departure savage wolves will
come in among you, not sparing the flock' (Acts 20:28-29).

Paul was preparing to leave for Jerusalem with his companions, aiming to arrive there for the feast of Pentecost. They
were carrying with them the gifts of money from the Gentile
churches to the church at Jerusalem which was suffering greatly
from the famine.

Paul travelled to Macedonia (part of present day Turkey),
encouraging the churches. In Philippi he sent his travelling
companions on before him and arranged to meet them again at
Troas where he stayed for seven days.

On the first day of the week the congregation met in an
upper room to enjoy the 'love feast' (Jude 12), the Lord's
Supper, and a worship service where Paul preached. During
the sermon, a young man, Eutychus, who was sitting on the
window sill, fell asleep. He fell from the window and died.
But Paul, who knew that the young man's life was still in him,
went down, fell on him and embraced him. The young man
lived.

This is the first record of a Christian worship service being
held on the first day of the week, which became known as
'The Lord's Day' (Revelation 1:10).

The ship sailed from Troas with a stopover at Miletus. This
was probably for the unloading or loading of cargo, so Paul
took the opportunity to invite the Ephesian elders to come to
him.

When they met, he outlined all he had done while in
Ephesus. As a humble evangelist he had preached the gospel,
despite the opposition from both Jews and Gentiles. He taught
the whole counsel of God and kept nothing back from the
congregation. He had even gone door-to-door with the good news.

He said, too, that the Holy Spirit had testified 'that chains and tribulations' were waiting for him (Acts 20:23). However, he would continue to preach, calling men and women to faith in Christ.

He warned the elders, in the words of our scripture verse, of dangerous times ahead for the congregation at Ephesus. Wicked men would rise up from their midst, teaching lies, and leading people astray. They were to be always on their guard! The elders were told that strong congregations should support the weak saying, 'It is more blessed to give than to receive' (Acts 20:35).

Paul then knelt down and prayed for the elders and the church in Ephesus. Following this he stood up as the elders wept, because 'they would see his face no more' (Acts 20:38).

Parting was an unpleasant business for those present. Paul was truly their spiritual father and to him they owed so much.

FIND OUT THE FACTS

1. Why were the elders so upset?
2. What was to happen to Paul when he returned to Jerusalem?
3. In the Christian church, what are elders?

Paul was a godly father to the Christians in Ephesus. Think of one godly man whom you know and thank the Lord for his life, witness and service to Christ.

Who is more innocent than Christ? And who are more persecuted? The world is the world still. *John Flavel*

Revelation 2:1-7

'Therefore I also, after I heard of your faith in the Lord Jesus and your love for all the saints, do not cease to give thanks for you' (Ephesians 1:15-16).

It is surprising how quickly things can change. Just look at your photographs and you will easily notice the way you have changed. Congregations can also change. Over the years people come and go. We know that God has no grandchildren; every generation must be converted.

In our previous devotions we saw that the Ephesian Church was marked by faith in the Lord Jesus and love between Christian brothers and sisters. But now we have read a letter written by the Lord Jesus to the head of the Ephesian church, rebuking the members for their lack of Christian love. The church at Ephesus had changed!

Within a generation, the church, known for its love, became a church known for its lack of Christians love. In fact, we are told that if the congregation did not repent of this sin, it would die (Revelation 2:5).

The King of the churches didn't rebuke the Ephesian church for incorrect doctrine. In fact, they took action against those who did not teach the truth. They 'tested those who [said]they [were] apostles and [were] not, and have found them liars... You hate the deeds of the Nicolaitans, which I [Jesus Christ] also hate' (Revelation 2:2,6).

The Ephesian Church exercised discipline with the people who made out they were apostles. It also taught sound doctrine, and the members were known for their good works. The Lord knew their works were carried out in his name, and they did 'not become weary' (Revelation 2:3).

The Ephesian Church seemed to be a godly church, but things had changed! The Lord said: 'Nevertheless I have this against you, that you have left your first love. Remember therefore from where you have fallen; repent and do the first works, or else I will come to you quickly and remove your lampstand from its place — unless you repent' (Revelation 2:4-5).

Faith and works without love grieve the Holy Spirit. Jesus said, 'This is my commandment, that you love one another as I have loved you' (John 15:12).

We have looked at 1 Corinthians 13 which explains what Christian love is. There we find Paul writing: 'Though I bestow all my goods to feed the poor, and though I give my body to be burned, but have not love, it profits me nothing' (1 Corinthians 13:3). Love is the fundamental grace which every Christian must have. What about you?

All sinners who are born again, exhibit love in their new character, but the character of churches can and do change. May all God's people exercise their influence in the church for good.

FIND OUT THE FACTS

1. What do you think of the Ephesian church?
2. What was missing in the church?
3. What did the Lord tell the church to do?

Ask the Lord to give you a heart that loves him and all other Christian believers sincerely.

True doctrine without love is dead orthodoxy and will be buried. *Anon*

A saying to Remember

Acts
21:26-40

'But Paul said, 'I am a Jew from Tarsus, in Cilicia, a citizen of no mean city; and I implore you, permit me to speak to the people' (Acts 21:39).

Paul's third missionary journey was drawing to a close. Leaving the meeting with the Ephesian elders, Paul boarded the ship which was to sail to Tyre where the cargo was to be unloaded. There he met the saints, who told him not to go to Jerusalem. This had been revealed to them by the Holy Spirit.

After seven days the ship sailed for Caesarea where Paul and his companions stayed with Philip, the evangelist. This Philip was one of the deacons elected in Jerusalem (Acts 6:5). He was forced to leave Jerusalem when persecution became severe. A prophet visited them, and taking Paul's belt, he wrapped it about his own feet and hands, saying, 'Thus says the Holy Spirit, 'So shall the Jews at Jerusalem bind the man who owns this belt, and deliver him into the hands of the Gentiles''' (Acts 21:11).

A courageous Paul was soon on his way to Jerusalem where the Christians met him with joy. He told them of the good things the Lord was doing among the Gentiles. James and the elders of the Jerusalem church glorified God when they heard Paul's news, but were concerned that some Jews reported that Paul opposed obedience to the 'Law of Moses'.

To refute those reports, Paul told them of the four men who accompanied him to the temple, where a vow they had made could be concluded. There he paid their expenses so their heads could be shaved. All who heard of this should have realized that Paul was not opposed to the law of Moses.

Just before the conclusion of the seven day purification period, some Jews from Asia arrived, and seeing Paul, had the crowd take him by force. They announced for all to hear: 'Men of Israel, help! This is the man who teaches all men everywhere against the people, the law, and this place; and furthermore he also brought Greeks into the temple and has defiled this holy place' (Acts 21:28).

In the riot that followed, Paul was dragged out of the temple. The crowd of Jews then decided to kill him. When the commander of the Roman garrison heard the noise, soldiers were sent to investigate the shouting. Those who were assaulting Paul, saw the soldiers coming and stopped what they were doing.

The commander had Paul placed in chains and then asked the reason for the noise. The officer couldn't find out the truth with everyone shouting, so he took Paul back to the barracks, where, in the words of our scripture verse, Paul was given permission to speak.

FIND OUT THE FACTS

1. Why was Paul arrested by the soldiers?
2. What did being a citizen of Tarsus mean to Paul?
3. Was Paul foolish to return to Jerusalem, knowing he was going to be bound hands and legs? Why?

Paul's love for Christ and his concern to see the gospel preached led him to suffer great hardship. Think about what it means to suffer for the sake of Christ.

The fire of God can't be damped out by the waters of man's persecution.
A.W. Tozer

Acts
22:1-21

'Then the commander came and said to him, "Tell me, are you a Roman?" He said, "Yes." The commander answered, "With a large sum I obtained this citizenship." And Paul said, "But I was born a citizen"' (Acts 22:27-28).

The Roman commander thought that Paul was an Egyptian who had revolted against the Romans, but now he was ready to hear him defend himself. This gave Paul the opportunity to speak about Jesus Christ, the Messiah, who had been killed by the Jews.

He stood on the stairs, and speaking in Hebrew began to explain why he became a follower of Christ, the Son of God. He explained that once he had been a Pharisee who persecuted the Christian church.

He told the people how the Lord had met him on the road to Damascus, striking him blind for a time. When he was taken to Damascus, his sight was restored to him by Ananias. Then he was baptized after being told, 'The God of our fathers has chosen you that you should know his will, and see the Just One, and hear the voice of his mouth. For you will be his witness to all men of what you have seen and heard' (Acts 22:14-15).

Paul also confessed that he had played a part in the death of godly Stephen. When he quoted the Lord's words, commanding him to take the gospel to the Gentiles, the Jews had heard enough. The shouting recommenced: 'Away with such a fellow from the earth, for he is not fit to live!' (Acts 22:22).

The Roman commander ordered that Paul be brought into the barracks for further questioning, after he had been whipped. As Paul was being tied up, he asked, 'Is it lawful for you to scourge a man who is a Roman, and uncondemned?' (Acts 22:25). Paul knew his rights as a Roman citizen, and this he used to spread the good news concerning Christ further.

The centurion, hearing that Paul was a Roman citizen, warned the commander, 'Take care what you do, for this man is a Roman' (Acts 22:26). At once Paul was treated with much more respect. No more questions were asked until the next day, when the bonds were released. He then commanded the chief priests and the members of the Sanhedrin to assemble at once. Paul was also brought into the room.

God's plan to spread the gospel was perfect. In that age, Greek was the common language spoken by most people, while the time of the Roman empire meant that there were well guarded, good roads to travel. Roman law gave protection to the citizens of the Empire, which gave Paul the right to move about with considerable ease.

FIND OUT THE FACTS

1. What is a centurion?
2. What part did Paul play in Stephen's death?
3. Why was Paul baptized?
4. Why should you praise God for the gospel being taken across the world?

Paul was a Roman citizen. God had ordered all the circumstances of his life perfectly. Thank the Lord that he does this for all of his children.

Jesus promised his disciples three things: that they would be completely fearless, absurdly happy and in constant trouble. F. R. Maltby

Acts
23:1-11

'But the following night the Lord stood by him and said, "Be of good cheer, Paul; for as you have testified for me in Jerusalem, so you must also bear witness at Rome"' (Acts 23:11).

Paul showed great wisdom when he was confronted by the Pharisees and the Sadducees. He knew that the Pharisees believed in an afterlife, while the Sadducees taught that there would be no resurrection. When he said that he believed in the resurrection, he was supported by the Pharisees who found him innocent of the charges brought against him.

The Roman commander, Claudius Lysias, removed Paul from the scene to prevent him from being torn limb from limb by the unruly crowd. The following night the Lord appeared to Paul and spoke the words of our scripture verse. Paul now knew that he would reach Rome alive!

Later, Paul's nephew overheard that some Jews were plotting to kill him. More than forty had taken an oath not to eat or drink until Paul was dead. Their plan was to have him brought before the Sanhedrin, saying that they needed to examine him further. At an opportune moment the forty assailants would grab him and kill him. When his nephew gave him this information, Paul sent to the commander to inform him also.

The commander gave the order for 'two hundred soldiers, seventy horsemen, and two hundred spearmen' to guard Paul as he was taken to Caesarea (Acts 23:23). The commander was not going to lose a Roman citizen to the Jewish rabble. What a wonderful God we have! He was taking great care of his apostle!

A letter was written to the governor, Felix, which explained the situation concerning Paul and suggested that Felix examine the matter further.

With such a large group of guards, the Jews found it impossible to carry out their wicked plan. At this point we should look again at our scripture verse. God promised that Paul would preach the gospel in Rome, just as he had done in Jerusalem. If the Jews had sent a million men in an attempt to kill him, their plans would have been frustrated. God had ordained that Paul would bear witness to the Lord Jesus in the capital city of the Roman Empire.

God's promises always come to pass. He has the right to make his promises and he also has the power to carry them out.

Governor Felix decided to invite Paul's accusers to Caesarea where he would adjudicate after hearing the evidence. Paul was then sent to Herod's headquarters where his safety was assured.

FIND OUT THE FACTS

1. Why was Paul supported by the Pharisees?
2. What did the Sadducees believe about the after-life and angels?
3. Why did Paul find it easy to move about?
4. Why do God's plans always come to pass?

The Lord saved Paul from the hands of his enemies. Thank the Lord that he protects his people.

'Testimony' is not a synonym for 'autobiography'! When we are truly witnessing, we are not talking about ourselves but about Christ. John Stott

Acts
24:10-27

'Now as he reasoned about righteousness, self-control, and the judgement to come, Felix was afraid and answered, "Go away for now; when I have a convenient time I will call for you"' (Acts 24:25).

When the members of the Sanhedrin arrived at Caesarea, they were accompanied by an orator called Tertullus. There they were required to give evidence before Governor Felix. Paul was accused of being a troublemaker, not just in Israel, but wherever he went. He was also accused of profaning the temple and being a leader of a religious sect known as the 'Nazarenes' (Acts 24:5). When Tertullus had finished his address, the elders of Israel who had accompanied him, agreed with all he had said.

Governor Felix called upon Paul to reply to the charges which he did with great clarity. He rejected the accusation that he had profaned the temple in any way. Then he confirmed that he worshipped the 'God of my fathers, believing all things which are written in the Law and in the Prophets' (Acts 24:14). He went on to speak of his belief in the resurrection of the dead, and the Christian faith, which he called 'the Way' (Acts 24:14,22).

After Paul had enlightened Felix concerning 'the Way', the case was adjourned until the Roman commander from Jerusalem arrived to speak. Felix indicated that he would make his decision after hearing all the evidence. Again Paul was confined, but in such a way that he could receive relatives and friends. Felix was hoping that he would receive a bribe for making a decision to grant Paul his freedom.

Drusilla, Felix's Jewish wife, arrived at Caesarea. Now and again over a period of two years, she and her husband heard Paul speak of Christ and the gospel. This is the account of Paul's witness to them: 'Now as he reasoned about righteousness, self-control, and the judgement to come, Felix was afraid and answered, "Go away for now; when I have a convenient time I will call for you"' (Acts 24:25).

After two years, Felix was replaced by Porcius Festus who decided to visit Jerusalem and meet the leaders of Israel. They asked him to have Paul brought to the city at once in order to face his accusers. Still the officers, with their 'righteous living' and the law of God, proved themselves to be common criminals. They would not forget the past and still longed to kill Paul!

They expected that Festus, not knowing the situation, would have Paul escorted by a small squad of soldiers, who would be easily overthrown by some well-armed Jews. In this way Paul would be swiftly eliminated.

FIND OUT THE FACTS

1. Why do you think the Christians were called the 'Nazarenes' and 'the Way'?

2. Why did Felix leave Paul in prison for two years without adjudicating his case?

3. Who in Acts 24 delayed coming to salvation in Christ?

Persecution has been part of the Christian's witness throughout the history of the church. Pray for Christians who are being persecuted for their faith today.

The martyrs are bound, imprisoned, scourged, racked, burnt, rent, butchered — and they multiplied. *Augustine*

Acts
25:13-27

'And if I ... have committed anything worthy of death, I do not object to dying; but if there is nothing in these things of which these men accuse me, no one can deliver me to them. I appeal to Caesar' (Acts 25:11).

The Jews had planned Paul's death, but this was not in accordance with God's plan. So, Festus refused the Jews' request to have a judgement made against Paul, saying that he would soon be in Caesarea and would judge the case there.

Arriving in Caesarea he gave the order for Paul to appear before him. His Jewish opponents made serious accusations against Paul, whose reply was, 'Neither against the law of the Jews, nor against the temple, nor against Caesar have I offended in anything at all' (Acts 25:8).

When Festus asked Paul if he would appear in Jerusalem to face trial, Paul argued that he should be judged at 'Caesar's judgement seat' (Acts 25:10). Then he spoke the words recorded in our scripture verse. Paul, a Roman citizen, appealed to the highest earthly authority of his day: the emperor at Rome.

In reading our scripture verse, we should note that Paul stated that he was willing to suffer the death penalty if his crime deserved it. The death penalty was accepted as the most severe penalty to be used by the civil authority (Romans 13:4).

When King Agrippa came to visit Festus and bade him welcome to his new office, Festus told him all he could about Paul and his accusers who had made charges which were not deserving of the death penalty. Festus said the quarrel was one of a religious nature, not really worthy of any great attention.

When Agrippa asked to hear Paul, 'I also would like to hear the man myself,' Festus replied, 'Tomorrow, ... you shall hear him' (Acts 25:22). Here again we see the fulfilment of God's command to Paul: 'Go, for [you are] a chosen vessel of mine to bear my name before Gentiles, kings, and the children of Israel' (Acts 9:15). King Agrippa would hear the gospel!

The following day, Festus, King Agrippa and his wife, Bernice, many soldiers and important citizens of the city came to hear Paul speak. Festus told King Agrippa that Paul had done nothing worthy of the death penalty, but as he had appealed to Caesar, to Caesar Augustus he should go. Festus also said that he had no specific charges to make against Paul. Perhaps he hoped that, at this hearing, Paul would incriminate himself in some way.

King Agrippa then said to Paul, 'You are permitted to speak for yourself' (Acts 26:1).

FIND OUT THE FACTS

1. What charges had the Jews made against Paul?
2. What did Paul's appeal to Caesar mean?
3. Why did the Jews want Paul's case to be heard in Jerusalem?

Proverbs 21:1 tells us that even the king's heart is in the hand of the Lord. Thank him that he rules sovereignly over the leaders of nations. Pray for your country's leaders today.

The real problem for Christianity is not atheism or scepticism, but the non-witnessing Christian trying to smuggle his own soul into heaven.
James Stewart

Acts
26:19-32

'Then Agrippa said to Paul, "You almost persuade me to become a Christian"' (Acts 26:28).

Paul was God's spokesman to King Agrippa and the multitude who had gathered to hear him speak. Later he would have the opportunity to tell the citizens of Rome about Christ, possibly even the Emperor himself.

Paul spoke plainly to King Agrippa who was a Jew and understood the Jewish religion. He had had control of the temple for a time and was responsible for the appointment of the high priests. Paul was pleased to speak to such a man. In fact, Paul could truthfully say that Agrippa was an expert in Jewish laws and customs.

He described his past, explaining how he had become a Christian after persecuting the church of the Lord Jesus. Christ's words to Paul were repeated for everyone to hear. This was followed by his statement that he then preached a risen Christ to the Jews and the Gentiles, urging them to repent of their sins and turn to the Saviour in faith.

When Paul spoke about the resurrection of the Lord Jesus, Festus called out, 'Paul, you are beside yourself! Much learning is driving you mad!' (Acts 26:24).

Paul insisted that he was not insane, but spoke truthfully. Then turning his attention to King Agrippa, he said that the king knew the facts of which he was speaking, since the life and death of Christ were well known to most citizens in Israel. Looking at the King, Paul said, 'King Agrippa, do you believe the prophets? I know that you do believe' (Acts 26:27). To this Agrippa replied, 'You almost persuade me to become a Christian' (Acts 26:28).

Paul then said, 'I would to God that not only you, but also all who hear me today, might become both almost and altogether such as I am, except for these chains' (Acts 26:29).

Rising from his chair the king gathered his officials about him and said, 'This man is doing nothing worthy of death or chains... This man might have been set free if he had not appealed to Caesar' (Acts 26:31,32). However, this could never be, as God had planned the situation so that Paul would eventually make his way to Rome.

How sad it was for the king to turn away from the truth spoken by the apostle Paul. Today, when most people hear of Christ, they close their ears, shut their eyes and turn away.

FIND OUT THE FACTS

1. How was it that King Agrippa understood the ways of the Jews?

2. What is meant by today's 'Saying to remember'?

3. Find out something about Francis Schaeffer.

The gospel is foolishness to those who do not believe. Pray for an unconverted friend or relative today.

Love — and the unity it attests to — is the mark Christ gave Christians to wear before the world. Only with this mark may the world know that Christians are indeed Christians and that Jesus was sent by the Father.   *Francis Schaeffer*

Acts
27:29-44

'For there stood by me this night an angel of the God to whom I belong and whom I serve, saying, "Do not be afraid, Paul; you must be brought before Caesar; and indeed God has granted you all those who sail with you"' (Acts 27:23-24).

As the time had come for Paul to travel to Rome, he and other prisoners were placed under the guard of Julius, a centurion of the Augustan Regiment. Passage was found on a ship leaving for Rome. The ship had many ports of call along the coast, and Paul was given permission to visit Christians in those ports.

Reaching Myra, the prisoners were herded on board another ship, leaving for Italy. Paul was concerned about going on the journey at that time of the year and spoke out, saying: 'Men, I perceive that this voyage will end with disaster and much loss, not only of the cargo and ship, but also our lives' (Acts 27:10). This was not a revelation to Paul, but his considered opinion about setting sail at that time of the year.

Confident of success, the ship's owner ordered the helmsman and sailors to prepare for their journey. The plan was to reach Crete where they would shelter for a time. Upon arriving there, they sailed along the coast, not far out from the shore, expecting to reach Phoenix quickly . Before they arrived there a typhoon, named 'Euroclydon', broke upon the ship, driving it along.

To save the boat in the gale force winds it was decided to lighten the load by throwing overboard the ship's tackle and cargo. The storm raged for many days during which there was no sign of the sun, and the crew was unable to prepare food.

All on board were fearful of what might happen, but Paul spoke saying that there would be no loss of life. The reason for this is found in our scripture verse. God would protect Paul's life and this meant that those with him on the ship would all live. Paul said that the ship would run aground without loss of life. He urged everyone on board to have something to eat, as they would need all their strength to reach the shore when the ship grounded.

When the stern began breaking up, the soldiers decided to kill the prisoners, making sure none escaped. However, the centurion who wanted to save Paul's life instructed all who could swim to abandon the ship first.

The rest followed, clinging to whatever was floating about them. When the time came to count everyone, all were found to be safe and well. Again God had fulfilled his promise to Paul!

FIND OUT THE FACTS

1. Why did the soldiers want to kill the prisoners? (See Acts 27:42).

2. Why was Paul going to Rome?

3. How did Paul know that no life would be lost when the ship broke up?

God was powerfully in control of all things in this event. Thank him that this was so.

I believe the promises of God enough to venture an eternity on them. *Isaac Watts*

Acts
28:1-13

'And these signs will follow those who believe: in my name they will cast out demons; ... speak with new tongues; ... take up serpents; and if they drink anything deadly, it will by no means hurt them; they will lay hands on the sick, and they will recover' (Mark 16:17-18).

Two hundred and seventy six people made their way through wind and waves to the shore. They were on the island of Malta and were welcomed by the native people who lit a fire to warm the survivors. The wind and rain made it very cold, so the locals cared for their unexpected visitors.

While Paul was helping to gather sticks for the fire, a snake bit into his hand. At once the locals misjudged him, saying, 'No doubt this man is a murderer, whom, though he has escaped the sea, yet justice does not allow to live' (Acts 28:4).

When an unharmed Paul shook the snake from his hand, the natives waited to see if it would swell up and, when it didn't, they made another incorrect assumption and concluded that he must be a god. The miracle that occurred had been prophesied by the Lord Jesus while he was upon the earth. Our scripture verse lists some of the powers that would accompany the apostles, and was proof that Paul was indeed an apostle of Christ.

Paul was also involved in miraculous healings, which resulted in honours being bestowed upon him and those rescued from the ship. When the time came for the ship's party to move on, they were amply supplied with all that was necessary for their survival. They boarded the Alexandrian ship which had a figurehead named 'The Twin Brothers' (Acts 28:11). These two painted carvings were of the gods of the sailors, the twin boys of Zeus, Castor and Pollux. In all probability this ship was a grain ship owned by the Roman government.

When the ship reached Syracuse, it remained there for three days, during which time it is believed that Paul preached the gospel, and founded a Christian congregation.

The ship again set sail, reaching Rhegium, a settlement on the southern most tip of Italy. Finally the ship reached Puteoli, the harbour on the northern side of the city of Naples. Paul would soon be in Rome, bearing witness to his Lord and Saviour, Jesus Christ. This would be a great encouragement to the Christians in Rome, who were suffering persecution from both the Jews and the Gentiles.

What God had said about Paul bearing witness to the Gentiles across the known world would soon be fulfilled. The good news concerning Christ would spread throughout the Roman Empire.

FIND OUT THE FACTS

1. Why did the Maltese people think Paul was a god?
2. In what way did the incident with the snake fulfil Christ's words?
3. Find Naples in your atlas.

Paul had great confidence in God to carry him through each trial and to provide for him in every circumstance. Ask God to give you that kind of trust and confidence today.

If you were arrested for being a Christian would there be enough evidence to convict you? David Otis Fuller

Acts
28:21-31

'Therefore let it be known to you that the salvation of God has been sent to the Gentiles, and they will hear it!' (Acts 28:28).

Paul had reached the vicinity of Rome, the capital of one of the world's great empires. Along the way he was met by some Christians who had walked the forty miles from Rome to Appii Forum, and then by another group who had walked thirty miles from Rome to Three Inns.

The news of Paul's arrival in Italy had quickly circulated, and Christians everywhere were thrilled to be given the opportunity of meeting the church's greatest missionary.

Paul was very encouraged by the welcome he received from the Christians. In Rome he was permitted to live in a house with a soldier as a guard. Because of this, he could receive visitors.

Paul invited the leaders of the Jews to meet with him. Upon their arrival, he explained why he was in Rome as a prisoner. Those present said that they had not heard anything to Paul's discredit, but they wanted to hear from him everything 'concerning this sect, [for] we know that it is spoken against everywhere' (Acts 28:22).

Everyone present agreed that upon a set day, Paul would speak about Christ and the Christian church. When the day came, Paul, using the law of Moses and the writings of the prophets, preached the truth concerning Christ and the king-dom of God. No doubt he was pleased that some of those present believed what was said and became followers of Messiah.

Many left the meeting unconvinced. However, Paul saw that this was the fulfilment of prophecy. He said, 'The Holy Spirit spoke rightly through Isaiah the prophet to our fathers, say-ing, "Go to this people and say: hearing you will hear and shall not understand; and seeing you will see, and not perceive"' (Acts 28:25-26).

Paul continued, saying, 'Therefore let it be known to you that the salvation of God has been sent to the Gentiles, and they will hear it!' (Acts 28:28). As the Jews left Paul's house, they began to argue with one another concerning Christ.

Paul spent two years in his private house, where he was given total freedom to preach the gospel to anyone who visited him.

No doubt his Roman guards heard of salvation in the Lord Jesus Christ, and possibly many believed. The Day of Judgement will reveal to us all, the number of people who came to faith in Jesus during those two years of confinement.

The Lord's words to Paul had come to pass: 'Be of good cheer, Paul; for as you have testified for me in Jerusalem, so you must also bear witness at Rome' (Acts 23:11).

FIND OUT THE FACTS

1. Discuss the words found in Acts 28:26-27.

2. When Paul reached Rome, what prophecy was fulfilled?

3. In Rome, what did Paul preach?

In Rome Paul was again given an opportunity for ministry. Thank the Lord that he always provides his people with opportunities for service.

Wherever we go, let us not fail to take our religion along with us. *Matthew Henry*

Revelation
2:8-11

'He who has an ear, let him hear what the Spirit says to the churches. He who overcomes shall not be hurt by the second death' (Revelation 2:11).

Some time ago we read about the church at Ephesus which had departed from its love of Christ. The church was called to repent or it would no longer exist. We now read of the church at Smyrna. The messages to the churches came from Jesus Christ, the Head of the church, and his words have application to the churches of today.

The original city of Smyrna had been destroyed and later rebuilt by Alexander the Great. It was one of Rome's oldest allies. The city was well known for its library, huge stadium and the temples of Roma, Cybele and Zeus. In the first century it had a population of about two hundred thousand citizens.

The letter to this church came from 'the First and the Last, who was dead, and came to life' (Revelation 2:8). These words point to Christ being Jehovah, for we read elsewhere in the Scriptures: 'Thus says the LORD, the King of Israel, and his Redeemer, the LORD of Hosts: "I am the First and I am the Last; besides me there is no God"' (Isaiah 44:6).

This church was a poor church in the eyes of the world, but it was rich towards God. Maybe this was the church written about in Hebrews 10:34. They 'joyfully accepted the plundering of [their] goods, knowing that [they had] a better and an enduring possession for [themselves] in heaven.'

It was also being slandered by the Jews of whom the Lord said belonged to 'a synagogue of Satan' (Revelation 2:9). Soon the members of the church would be facing more persecution, but faithfulness would receive its reward: eternal life.

The best known martyr of this church was the elderly Polycarp. He had known the apostle John, and had been a Christian for over sixty years. The Christians were hated. At one Roman festival the cry went up that Christians should be put to death. The crowd then began to call for Polycarp. Soon he was found, brought before the Roman proconsul and sentenced to death. When he was asked to deny Christ as Lord, he replied, 'Eighty and six years have I served him, and he has done me no wrong; how then can I blaspheme my king who saved me.'

The fire was brought and the old Christian died a martyr's death, passing into the presence of his Lord and Saviour. The message to this church, which doesn't include any rebuke, finishes with the words of our scripture verse. The second death — that is, hell, has no claim upon any who are born into the kingdom of heaven. Praise the Lord!

FIND OUT THE FACTS

1. Find out all you can about Polycarp.

2. Using your atlas find Smyrna.

3. What is the martyrs' reward? Read Matthew 5:8-12 and Revelation 6:9-11.

To Think & to pray about

Satan has always had his agents who seek to destroy the work of God. Thank the Lord that his word and his work stand firm.

A saying to Remember

The blood of the martyrs is the seed of the church. *Jerome*

Revelation 2:12-17   'And to the angel of the church in Pergamos write, "These things says he who has the sharp two-edged sword"' (Revelation 2:12).

Do you see something of your church in these letters from Christ to the seven churches? If you do, you might work and pray to bring about a godly change.

The writer of this letter is Christ, who has the sharp two-edged sword of judgement in his hand, ready to strike down all who oppose him. He knows all that is happening in Pergamos, as his eyes are 'like a flame of fire' (Revelation 1:14).

Pergamos was a great city of commerce and industry. It had a huge library of over two hundred thousand scrolls and was well known for emperor worship. Everyone was expected to worship the Emperor as god, saying, 'Caesar is Lord.' This Christians could never do, and, as a result the persecution of the Christians increased in the city.

One of their gods was Aesculapius, who, represented by a snake, was supposed to have great healing powers. People flocked there, hoping to be healed. Temples to Zeus, the king of the gods, and Athena were built as was one to Emperor Augustus. Despite these sins, there were faithful church members in the city who courageously followed Christ. Some became martyrs for their Lord!

Pergamos was known as the place 'where Satan dwells' (Revelation 2:13). This meant that false teaching crept into the church, especially the teachings of Balaam and the Nicolatians. It seems that the church tolerated these sinful doctrines and did little to drive out those who taught them. The Nicolatians believed that after a person had confessed his faith in Christ, all his sins would be forgiven and he could live as he pleased.

The sin of Balaam taught Balak to place a stumbling block before Israel: the eating of food sacrificed to idols, and sexual immorality (Numbers 25:1-2; 31:16).

Because these sins were found in the church at Pergamos, Christ called the members to repent, or face the sword of judgement. Christ will have his people holy!

The faithful discipline of evil people would be rewarded by Christ, the Head of the church. Those who listened to the promptings of the Holy Spirit, would eat 'the hidden manna' (Revelation 2:17). They would feast on heavenly, spiritual food: the love and truth of Christ.

Repentance would bring forgiveness, which was the teaching of the white stone. In many courts the judge placed a black stone down if the decision was 'guilty'. A white stone meant 'innocent.'

Good things were in store for faithful Christians who would carry the name of their Lord.

FIND OUT THE FACTS

1. Was the church at Pergamos a perfect church? Why?
2. Where is Pergamos?
3. What sins are sometimes found in the church today?

Faithfulness in our walk and witness for Christ is not always the easiest thing to do. Thank the Lord that he takes note of faithful believers and will reward such a life in his heavenly kingdom.

A saying to Remember

Sin puts hell into the soul and the soul into hell. *Anon*

Revelation 2:18-29	'These things says the Son of God, who has eyes like a flame of fire, and his feet like fine brass' (Revelation 2:18).

Thyatira was a great commercial city, well known for woollen goods, linen cloth, bronze workers, tanners and potters. One lady we have mentioned before migrated from Thyatira to Philippi; her name was Lydia and she was known for her purple dye.

The one who wrote this letter was 'the Son of God, who has eyes like a flame of fire, and ... feet like fine brass' (Revelation 2:18). Christ could see all that was happening in Thyatira because he said of himself that he was the one 'who searches the minds and hearts' (Revelation 2:23).

The city worshipped many gods, the most important being Tyrimnos, the son of Zeus. It was believed that the Roman emperor was Tyrimnos, in human form. Membership of the guilds (unions) involved the eating of food sacrificed to idols and sexual immorality. No Christian could remain a member of a guild.

However, the church tolerated Jezebel, a prophetess, who taught that Christians could eat food sacrificed to idols and become involved in the sexual impurities of the guilds. This Jezebel was like her namesake who had married the wicked King Ahab.

Today there are churches which are no better. They do not condemn forms of sexual expression which the Bible clearly teaches are sinful in God's sight. Christianity forbids immoral sexual behaviour. Christ teaches us that Christians must 'pursue ... holiness, without which no one will see the Lord' (Hebrews 12:14). Paul also wrote, 'He chose us in him before the foundation of the world, that we should be holy and without blame before him in love' (Ephesians 1:4). God will have his people holy!

Christ warned the church that failure to repent of the sins of Jezebel would bring judgement.

There were some faithful people in the church at Thyatira. Christ told them to hold fast until he returned. They had patiently done works of love, and for this they were praised (Revelation 2:19).

These faithful saints would sit with Christ judging the nations and would be given the morning star. This can be taken to mean that Christ would reveal more of himself to his people. Christ's words are: 'I am the Root and Offspring of David, the Bright and Morning Star' (Revelation 22:16).

Is your church like the church at Thyatira? I trust not. We should be willing to suffer for holiness, and should always use the Bible as our guide for holy living. The Jezebels about today lead people to hell!

FIND OUT THE FACTS

1. How did Ahab's wife, Jezebel die? See 2 Kings 9:30-37.
2. Who in the church would hear and repent?
3. What was a 'guild'?

Pray for the churches in your area. Ask the Lord to keep them faithful to his Word.

Sleep with clean hands, either kept clean all day by integrity or washed clean at night by repentance. *John Donne*

Revelation
3:1-6

'He who overcomes shall be
clothed in white garments, and
I will not blot out his name
from the book of life; but I
will confess his name before
my Father and before his
angels' (Revelation 3:5).

We are now looking at one of the letters written by Christ, who sends the Holy Spirit to the churches. This is a letter of rebuke to a church that was almost spiritually dead.

Sardis was a city built on the mountain Tmolus, at the entrance to the Hermus Valley. The citizens believed that their city was impregnable, but on several occasions foreign forces climbed the mountain and took the city, much to the surprise of the inhabitants. In A.D. 19 an earthquake did much damage to it and in A.D. 1402 the city was destroyed by an earthquake.

The church at Sardis had a good reputation. The members were frequently seen doing good works, but they had no value in the sight of God. This was an almost dead church! Their motivation for these works was not love for God. In 1 Corinthians 13 Paul teaches us the truth about Christian love. He even wrote that if a person gave away everything he owned to feed the poor and gave his body to be burnt, but had no love, it was all worth nothing.

On the Day of Judgement unbelievers will cry out to the Lord saying that they have done many works in his name. The Saviour will reply, 'I never knew you; depart from me, you who practise lawlessness!' (Matthew 7:23). This church was called upon to repent or the Lord would come in judgment like a thief who broke into a house without warning.

There were several members of the congregation who were godly people. They had maintained their righteous living, despite the influence of the others. The Lord wrote most encouraging words to these people: 'They shall walk with me in white, for they are worthy' (Revelation 3:4).

Everyone assembled before the throne of God and the Lamb of God is dressed in 'white robes' (Revelation 7:9). This clothing is the righteous acts of the saints' (Revelation 19:8). The works have been purified by Christ, so God's people are clothed in his perfect righteousness.

Those godly church members would never have their name removed from the 'book of life'. The Lord's people always persevere to the end, and on the Day of Judgement, Christ will find before him every person whose name is in that book.

Is yours found there?

FIND OUT THE FACTS

1. Find Sardis in your atlas.

2. What is Christian love?

3. Why do Christians do good works?

This church did good works out of a sense of duty. But Christ desires his people to serve him out of a heart of love. Ask the Lord to give a heart to love and to serve him as you serve others.

All men's secret sins are printed in heaven, and God will at last read them aloud in the ears of all the world. *Thomas Brooks*

Revelation
3:7-13

'These things says he who is holy, he who is true, "He who has the key of David, he who opens and no one shuts, and shuts and no one opens"' (Revelation 3:7).

The church at Philadelphia, the city of 'brotherly love,' had a small group of Christians who were about to experience revival. The preaching of the gospel had produced small results, but now Christ had set before them 'an open door,' which no one could shut (Revelation 3:8). The Holy Spirit had been preparing sinners' hearts and soon they would be converted. Some would be Jews! Christ, by his Spirit, was the one who opened the door and led sinners to salvation.

The words of our scripture verse point back to events in the days of King Hezekiah, who had a servant, Shebna. Shebna was unfaithful and was replaced by Eliakim, who had the authority to decide who could visit the king. He opened and closed doors.

God's people in Philadelphia had suffered persecution from the local Jews who wanted nothing to do with Christians. But it would not be long before some Jews, who attended 'the synagogue of Satan' (Revelation 3:9), would acknowledge that Jesus was their Messiah. A Jew without Christ was apostate.

The saints had persevered, but now they had the Lord's promise that they would be spared the 'hour of trial' that was coming upon the world (Revelation 3:10). In every age Christians have been persecuted by ungodly people. This is to be expected. God's people in all ages are urged to stand firm. This would mean their crown of life was safe and secure.

The reward of faithfulness is membership in God's eternal kingdom. Each believer will wear his crown of life and is promised that he will be 'a pillar in the temple of ... God' (Revelation 3:12). When the last of God's people is safe in the kingdom, God's temple will be complete. God's people in all ages, Jews and Gentiles, are the building blocks of the temple. The prophets and apostles 'being fitted together, [grow] into a holy temple in the Lord ... Jesus Christ himself being the Chief Cornerstone.' This temple is 'being built together for a dwelling place of God in the Spirit' (Ephesians 2:20-22).

Believers can say with David, 'And I will dwell in the house of the LORD for ever' (Psalm 23:6). These people will have a threefold name. First, 'the name of God' which indicates that we shall be like Christ. Second, we shall bear the name of God's city. This means we shall have our part in the New Jerusalem.

Finally, Christ will write on the saint, his 'new name'. This indicates that we shall share Christ's glory. Do you have an ear to hear the message to the church at Philadelphia?

FIND OUT THE FACTS

1. What is 'the New Jerusalem'? Refer to Revelation 21:2.
2. Why is the Jewish synagogue called 'the synagogue of Satan'?
3. Christians persevere. What does this mean?

You have read today of the blessings which God gives to his people. Thank the Lord that he blesses his people abundantly.

If a church does not evangelize it will fossilize.   A.W. Pink

A saying to Remember

Revelation   'Behold, I stand at the door
3:14-22   and knock. If anyone hears my
                voice and opens the door, I will
                come in to him and dine with
                him, and he with me' (Revela-
                tion 3:20).

This church at Laodicea thought it was the apple of the
Lord's eye when in reality Christ had no kind words for it.
Christ, the author of this letter, describes himself as the 'Amen,
the Faithful and True Witness, the Beginning of the creation of
God' (Revelation 3:14). Jesus is the 'Amen' of the Scriptures.
He bore a faithful witness to his heavenly Father and is truth
incarnate.

Jesus is also the origin, the beginning of everything, with
the obvious exception of God. Paul wrote that 'all things were
created through him and for him' (Colossians 1:16).

This church went through the motions of doing good works,
but without any zeal or love for God. Because they were lukewarm, the Lord said he would vomit them out of his mouth.
He wanted them to be either hot or cold. He was referring to
water which is pleasant to drink and useful to treat medical
problems. Some argue that what Christ is really saying is that
he wanted people to be either for him, i.e., hot or against him,
i.e., cold but not lukewarm. The hot and cold water springs in
the area were used for medical treatment. The lukewarm
springs were good for nothing. The same applies to drinking
water. Hot or cold water is pleasant to drink. But lukewarm
water is only good for spitting out of the mouth!

Laodicea was a city at the junction of three important trade
routes. It was well known for its banking facilities, commerce
and woollen goods, especially black wool. The city also had a
popular medical centre which was renowned for its eye salve.
The church believed it was rich in the things of God, but in
reality it was a stranger to spiritual blessings; it was 'wretched,
miserable, poor, blind, and naked' (Revelation 3:17).

The Lord told this congregation to come to him in repentance and to receive the precious clothing of Christ's righteousness to cover its shame, and eye salve so it could see the truth.

Something happened to the church at Laodicea that cannot happen to a believer: Christ had been pushed outside! God's people cannot be lost, but will persevere to the end. He was knocking on the church door, seeking admission. If it were opened, he would come in and revive the congregation.

This church is so much like churches today where life is easy. Who speaks out against the great evils of our age?

The Laodicean church was urged to find salvation, the pearl of great price. For all who repented, there was a place with Christ on his throne of glory. There is no doubt that there are wonderful things in store for God's people!

FIND OUT THE FACTS

1. Discuss the Saying to remember.
2. Read John 1:1. What does it teach you?
3. What was wrong with the church at Laodicea?

The church at Laodicea had deceived itself. Pray for churches today that they would not be deceived into seeing themselves in ways that Christ does not see them.

A saying to Remember

Let us beware of repentance without evidence. J. C. Ryle

Philippians   'For the wages of sin is death'
1:19-26   (Romans 6:23).

Unless the Lord returns we shall all die. Our heart will stop beating and our body will return to the dust. When our representative, Adam, sinned, a portion of the punishment mankind received was physical death: 'In the sweat of your face you shall eat bread till you return to the ground, for out of it you were taken; for dust you are, and to dust you shall return' (Genesis 3:19). Death is the punishment for sin!

Reading through the Scriptures we find that only two men passed into heaven without experiencing death — Enoch and Elijah. In Eden, before Adam sinned, death was not known. For human beings, death is unnatural.

Death is the separation of the soul from the body as Ecclesiastes 12:7 states: 'Then the dust will return to the earth as it was, and the spirit will return to God who gave it.' This means that death is not the end of existence.

For the Christian, death is the doorway to paradise. It can be likened to a child who falls asleep on the floor and awakens in his own bed. It is the final step in the sanctification of the believer's soul. Immediately they become 'the spirits of just men made perfect' (Hebrews 12:23).

God is not the God of the dead, but of the living. Thus Paul could say, 'For me, to live is Christ, and to die is gain' (Philippians 1:21). Jesus could say, 'I am the resurrection and the life. He who believes in me, though he may die, he shall live. And whoever lives and believes in me shall never die' (John 11:25-26).

The Psalmist says, 'Precious in the sight of the LORD is the death of his saints' (Psalm 116:15). In the parable of the rich man and Lazarus we are told 'that the beggar died, and was carried by the angels to Abraham's bosom' (Luke 16:22). When

Stephen was dying, he 'gazed into heaven and saw the glory of God, and Jesus standing at the right hand of God, and said, "Look! I see the heavens opened and the Son of Man standing at the right hand of God!"' (Acts 7:55-56).

Some Christians wonder how they will face death. God promises to give us the grace to die courageously when the time comes. We don't need grace to die today.

Paul tell us that Christ will reign until all of his enemies are defeated. 'The last enemy that will be destroyed is death' (1 Corinthians 15:26).

Can you say this with Paul: 'I have fought the good fight, I have finished the race, I have kept the faith. Finally, there is laid up for me the crown of righteousness, which the Lord, the righteous Judge, will give to me on that day?' (2 Timothy 4:7-8).

FIND OUT THE FACTS

1. What is death?

2. What happens to Christians when they die?

3. Why should Christians not be afraid of how they will die?

Ask the Lord to help you to see life in the same way as Paul did. For him life in this world was lived with eternity in mind.

Death is but a passage out of a prison into a palace. *John Bunyan*

Revelation 'And Jesus said to him,
6:9-11   "Assuredly, I say to you,
           today you will be with me in
           paradise"' (Luke 23:43).

It is important that we know what happens to us after death because this knowledge helps us face our departure courageously.

Two thieves were nailed to a cross and were dying beside the Lord Jesus. One thief cursed him, while the other rebuked his companion. Turning to Jesus he asked, 'Lord, remember me when you come into your kingdom' (Luke 23:42). The Lord replied with the words we find in our scripture verse.

After death, and before the resurrection, that redeemed thief was in paradise with Christ. The apostle Paul said that he was 'well pleased rather to be absent from the body and to be present with the Lord' (2 Corinthians 5:8). The halfway house between this earth and the new heavens is a place of perfection in the presence of Christ.

Elsewhere he wrote, 'For to me, to live is Christ, and to die is gain ... I have a desire to depart and be with Christ, which is far better' (Philippians 1:21,23). We also have a picture of God's people in heaven, before the resurrection: 'I saw under the altar the souls of those who had been slain for the word of God... And they cried with a loud voice, saying, "How long, O Lord, holy and true, until you judge and avenge our blood on those who dwell on the earth?"' (Revelation 6:9,10).

This is not heaven, for we are told that when Christ returns this world will be destroyed and there will be a new heavens and a new earth (2 Peter 3:10).

When unrepentant sinners die, they will pass into a place of punishment. In the parable of the rich man and Lazarus, when the rich man found himself 'in torments in Hades, he lifted up his eyes and saw Abraham afar off and Lazarus in his bosom. Then, he cried and said, 'Father Abraham, have mercy on me, and send Lazarus that he may did the tip of his finger in water and cool my tongue; for I am tormented in this flame' (Luke 16:23-24).

The souls of the wicked are in torment during the intermediate state.[1] Following the Day of Judgement, 'death and Hades [are] cast into the lake of fire. This is the second death' (Revelation 20:14). This place of eternal punishment is the end for all unrepentant sinners. It is the place of 'no hope!'

When you die, where will you go — to paradise or to Hades? Now is the time to make preparations.

---

[1] See Morey, R.A., *Death and the Afterlife*, Bethany House Publishers, USA, 1984, pp. 72-99.

FIND OUT THE FACTS

1. Read 2 Peter 2:9. What are you taught?

2. When a Christian friend dies, Christians do not grieve as those who have no hope, Why?

3. What happens when ungodly people die?

Death is not a popular subject. But we need to think seriously about eternity and to make sure that we are prepared for it.

Death may be the king of terrors but Jesus is the King of kings.
Anon

2 Peter
3:1-13

'When the Son of Man comes in his glory, and all the holy angels with him, then he will sit on the throne of his glory' (Matthew 25:31).

Christians are divided concerning the end times, but we all agree on two great truths: first, the Scriptures are infallible; and second, at some time in the future the Lord will return in majesty and power. Perhaps you will not agree with what I write here but this is how I see the end times.

The Lord Jesus will return one day to gather his people together and sit upon the throne of judgement to judge every person who has ever lived. We are told that no one knows the day of Christ's return. Jesus said, 'But of that day and hour no one knows, no, not even the angels of heaven, but my Father only' (Matthew 24:36).

From my reading of the Scriptures I believe that two events must still happen before the Lord returns. First, there will be a future conversion of many of the people of Israel (Romans 11:1-29). Second, the antichrist will be revealed, the church will suffer a great tribulation and many will desert the Christian faith for the world and pleasure (2 Thessalonians 2:3;).

We are told that the coming of our Lord will be as a thief in the night. The ungodly will be taunting Christians with these words: 'Where is the promise of his coming? For since the fathers fell asleep, all things continue as they were from the beginning of creation' (2 Peter 3:4).

These people may laugh, but when the last sinner becomes a citizen of the kingdom of God, history will conclude and Christ will appear in power, majesty and glory. There will be frightening signs in the heavens above, a great earthquake, and the blue heavens above will be rolled up like a scroll (Revelation 6:12-17).

The Lord will be accompanied by his mighty angels who will watch over the resurrection of the dead saints and the reunion of their body and soul. Then, with believers who have been changed, all will rise to meet the Lord in the air.

The ungodly will also be given a resurrection body, and they will awake 'to shame and everlasting contempt' (Daniel 12:2). These people will try and hide from the Lord Jesus, but the mighty angels will gather them and bring them to face Jesus Christ, the Judge.

Are you ready for that day?

FIND OUT THE FACTS

1. When will Christ return?
2. How are we to prepare for that day? Read 2 Peter 3:11.
3. Describe some of the events that will take place when Christ appears.

Thank the Lord for the resurrection when all his people will be given perfect and eternal bodies.

He who came in humility and shame will return in spectacular magnificence. *John Stott*

Revelation   'For we must all appear before
20:11-15   the judgement seat of Christ,
               that each one may receive the
               things done in the body,
               according to what he has done,
               whether good or bad'
               (2 Corinthians 5:10).

The final judgement is an event that follows the return of Christ and the resurrection of all mankind. It is Christ, the Mediator, who will sit upon the judgement throne. We shall each stand before the judgement seat and the books will be opened; nothing will be hidden on that day!

Solomon wrote, 'God will bring every work into judgement, including every secret thing, whether good or evil' (Ecclesiastes 12:14). Of course, God's people will be confident on that day because Paul wrote, 'There is therefore now no condemnation to those who are in Christ Jesus' (Romans 8:1). There is peace between God and his people through the redemption found in the Saviour.

We shall each give an account for what we have spoken. Jesus said, 'But I say to you that for every idle word men may speak, they will give account of it in the Day of Judgement' (Matthew 12:36). Our tongue is the most difficult part of our body to control, but control it Christians must!

James wrote, 'Out of the same mouth proceed blessing and cursing. My brethren, these things ought not to be so!' (James 3:10). So often we find ourselves speaking unkind words about others. On the Day of Judgement we shall be called to give an account for those words we have spoken even without thinking.

Paul wrote of 'the day when God will judge the secrets of men by Jesus Christ' (Romans 2:16). We would not like others to discover our secret sins, sins that are done when we are all alone; but God is watching. On that day they will be revealed. What will we say if they are not covered by the redeeming blood of Christ? Even our thoughts will be revealed and be the subject of judgement.

We shall all be judged in the light of God's revealed will. Those who were brought up in Christian homes, with Bibles, prayer, worship and Christian teaching, should be prepared for that day.

Jesus said, 'And that servant who knew his master's will, and did not ... do according to his will, shall be beaten with many stripes. But he who did not know, yet committed things deserving of stripes, shall be beaten with few. For everyone to whom much is given, from him much will be required; and to whom much has been committed, of him they will ask the more' (Luke 12:47-48).

The Day of Judgement for Christians holds no fear. Everyone else trembles, for 'it is a fearful thing to fall into the hands of the living God' (Hebrews 10:31).

FIND OUT THE FACTS

1. Who will sit upon the judgement seat?
2. How will you feel on that day?
3. Are there degrees of punishment and reward? How do you know?

Think about the judgement seat of Christ. How should this influence the way you live today?

Sin is the weight on the clock which makes the hammer to strike.
George Swinnock

A saying to Remember

Revelation 'And the smoke of their
18:21-24 torment ascends for ever and
          ever; and they have no rest
          day or night, who worship the
          beast and his image, and who-
          ever receives the mark of his
          name' (Revelation 14:11).

I have heard people say, 'You can go to hell!' These are foolish words because no person has the power to send anyone
to hell. Hell is the place of the damned. It is the bottomless pit
of no hope for all who are there. Over the mouth of hell are the
words, 'No Hope', and from the mouth of the pit can be heard
the cries of the damned, 'If only! '

All the descriptions of hell should strike fear into sinners'
hearts, yet many will say, 'If I go to hell, I'll have a lot of friends
there.' There is no joy in hell. Our scripture passage speaks of
Babylon, this world's system, being brought to an end and
being thrown into the depths of the ocean. There, all the things
that made life enjoyable on earth are missing.

Hell is that place where God is not. There will be no opportunity to repent and be saved!

Hell is also called 'outer darkness' (Matthew 22:13). The
Jews feared darkness, as many believed that the evil spirits
were to be found there. Many Israelites kept a lamp burning
all night just in case! The man in this parable, who attended
the wedding, wearing the wrong clothes, found himself in outer
darkness. This parable would have filled the hearts of many
hearers with horror.

Another description of hell was 'fire and brimstone'. John
wrote, 'But the cowardly, unbelieving, abominable, murderers, sexually immoral, sorcerers, idolaters, and all liars shall
have their part in the lake which burns with fire and brimstone, which is the second death' (Revelation 21:8).

One day Jesus warned his listeners that if their hand, eye
or foot should caused them to sin, they should be wise and

remove the cause of their sin. He said, 'It is better for you to enter into life with one eye, rather than having two eyes, to be cast into hell [Gehenna] fire' (Matthew 18:9).

Gehenna was Jerusalem's rubbish tip where the fires would seemingly smoulder for ever. It was here that Ahaz and Manasseh sacrificed their children to Moloch (2 Kings 16:3; 21:6). It was an unclean place with no redeeming feature.

Hell is God's place of eternal punishment for all unrepentant sinners. Will hell be your eternal destiny?

Following the final judgement we read that 'Death and Hades were cast into the lake of fire. This is the second death. And anyone not found written in the book of life was cast into the lake of fire' (Revelation 20:14-15).

FIND OUT THE FACTS

1. How did Jesus describe hell?
2. Who will be sentenced to everlasting hell?
3. What is the meaning of the Saying to remember?
4. What makes heaven so enjoyable?

The issues of life and death are serious. Pray again today for unconverted family and friends.

A saying to Remember

Exit is not a word found in the vocabulary of hell. *Robert G. Lee*

Revelation   'And there shall be no more
21:1-8   curse, but the throne of God
                and of the Lamb shall be in it,
                and his servants shall serve
                him' (Revelation 22:3).

This world is not heaven for God's people, but the ungodly will one day recall it as their heaven. It is the training ground for life in the presence of the Lord Jesus Christ. Sin has destroyed this pleasant relationship. In the Garden of Eden, Christ walked with Adam and Eve before they sinned. A covenant was made with Abraham where God promised 'to be God to you and your descendants after you' (Genesis 17:7).

God met with his covenant people, Israel, between the cherubim above the mercy seat of the ark. Christ then came into the world as a baby. He would live and die to save sinners. His name would be 'Immanuel,' which is translated, 'God with us' (Matthew 1:23).

In the New Jerusalem the covenant promise given to Abraham will be fulfilled: 'Behold, the tabernacle of God is with men, and he will dwell with them, and they shall be his people. God himself will be with them and be their God' (Revelation 21:3).

Heaven is the place of perfection, won by Christ for his people (John 14:2-3). Our scripture passage tells us that in heaven God will wipe the tears away, even before they form in our eyes. There will be nothing to cause us pain, sorrow or troubles. There cannot be death in paradise, because in that place there is no more sin. It is sin which causes us distress and death in this world.

In that new creation, Christ's bride, the New Jerusalem, descends out of heaven to its place on the newly formed earth. Some long to be in heaven, because there they will be reunited with loved ones who went before them. This should not be the main reason for going to heaven, but rather, it should be to gaze upon the Saviour, the Lord Jesus. There God's people will serve their God. Eternal life stretches before the saints, but this does not just mean that life will go on for ever, but that the quality of endless life is perfect. In heaven we shall meet God's people from all ages and have the opportunity of speaking to them all. What stories we shall hear!

In heaven we shall be with God's holy angels and there experience perfect love, joy and beauty. The saints will sing the praises of God and the Lamb, and in our glorious resurrected bodies we shall serve Jesus Christ, our Saviour:

THE KING OF KINGS
AND LORD OF LORDS
(Revelation 19:16).

Will you?

FIND OUT THE FACTS

1. What is best about heaven?

2. What is the covenant promise?

3. 'Heaven is a prepared place for a prepared people.' What does that mean?

Praise the Lord today for the fact that he is preparing a place in heaven for his people.

We must be saints on earth if we ever mean to be saints in heaven.
J. C. Ryle

A saying to Remember

'Champions of the faith' series

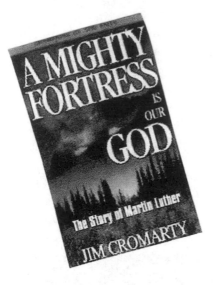

A Mighty Fortress is our God
The story of Martin Luther
ISBN 0 85234 411 2

'Fresh and fast-moving, Jim Cromarty's account of the life and influence of the great Reformer brings Martin Luther out of the pages of the history books, portraying his warm, vibrant personality and unwavering faith. Packed with detail. *A Mighty Fortress is our God* lays an excellent foundation for further study of the Reformation period and Luther's own testimony, which remains as relevant now as it ever was. Not only is this book valuable as an introduction to Martin Luther's life, but it also serves as a reminder to those cardinal doctrines of the faith which can alone transform the lives of men and women today.'

Faith Cook

'Jim Cromarty's rendition of Luther sings sweetly. Though clearly aware of critical scholarship, Cromarty has written a narrative to entice and delight. The story is ever fresh, written in a lively, engaging and, at times, enchanting style. Luther never fails to fascinate, encourage and bring prayers of thanks for God's deliverance from the soul tyranny of medieval Rome. Cromarty's story unleashes Luther in all his strength and sweetness and keeps the reader absorbed in the drama with its tensions and celebrations.'

Tom Nettles

A Mighty Fortress in our God is also available as 5 Audio Cassettes read by his brother John Cromarty.
ISBN 05234 496 1

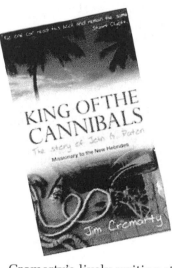

King of the Cannibals
The story of John G. Paton
Missionary to the New Hebrides
ISBN – 0 85234 401 5

'John Paton is one of those nearly-forgotten pioneer missionary saints who are too little remembered these days. This engrossing account of his life and ministry will make Paton live again for a whole new generation. Parents and teachers alike will love the book's practical format, with its careful, clear application of the spiritual truths in each chapter. And Jim Cromarty's lively writing style makes this a book that is hard to put down.

John MacArthur

In *Food for Cannibals* Jim Cromarty has revisited *King of the Cannibals* and rewritten it in a straight-forward style that is especially suitable for young people. The author takes the reader through John Paton's life, from his birth in a humble cottage in rural Scotland through to his death in Melbourne, Australia, eighty-three years later.

The Pigtail and Chopstick man
The story of J. Hudson Taylor and the
China Inland Mission
ISBN 0 85234 519 4

This popular biography will
appeal to all Christians wanting
to know more about this famous
missionary to China and the
times in which he lived.

It is a good story for young and
old alike, and the chapter lengths
are just right for devotional reading with children.

The title of this book originated from the cries that went up from
the children when they saw Hudson Taylor approaching (dressed
in his Chinese clothing) – 'Here comes the pigtail and chopstick
man.'

Books for family reading

A book for Family Worship
ISBN – 0 85234 388 4
'A book which parents and children can enjoy and benefit
from together. From the world
of Wags the dog and Truffles
the cat, the presence of koala
bears, the taste of Oysters, the
sight of an explosion and the
meaning of "morphing", Jim
Cromarty skilfully leads us to
the teaching of Scripture and
provides vital guidelines for
Christian living.'

Sinclair B. Ferguson

A book for Family Reading series

The cat's birthday and other stories that teach biblical truth
ISBN – 0 85234 352 3

One that didn't get away and other stories that teach biblical truths
ISBN – 0 85234 391 4

A sad little dog - 52 stories that teach biblical truths
ISBN – 0 85234 463 5

Take care in the bath - 52 stories that teach biblical truths
ISBN – 0 85234 417 1

You sank my boat - 52 stories that teach biblical truths
ISBN – 0 85234 432 5

A review of the series

'Reliable books which parents and children can enjoy together'
Sinclair B. Ferguson

'...a welcome find for parents on the look-out for suitable reading material for use in family prayers'
Faith Cook

'Simple, biblical and practical, these notes will surely prove of immense help to many in establishing and maintaining family worship...'
John Blanchard

'Jim Cromarty has a gift for telling stories'
Banner of Truth

A wide range of excellent books on spiritual subject is available from Evangelical Press. Please write to us for your free catalogue or contact us by e-mail.

Evangelical Press
Faverdale North Industrial Estate, Darlington, DL3 OPH, England

Evangelical Press USA
PO Box 825, Webster, New York 14580, USA

e-mail sales: sales@evangelicalpress.org

web: http://www.evangelicalpress.org